THE STONE READER

THE STONE READER

MODERN PHILOSOPHY
IN 133 ARGUMENTS

*Edited and
introduced by*

PETER CATAPANO
AND **SIMON CRITCHLEY**

LIVERIGHT PUBLISHING CORPORATION
A Division of W. W. NORTON & COMPANY
Independent Publishers Since 1923
NEW YORK   LONDON

Copyright © 2016 by The New York Times Company

Introduction by Peter Catapano
Prefatory chapter introductions by Simon Critchley

For information about permission to reproduce selections from
this book, write to Permissions, Liveright Publishing
Corporation, a division of W. W. Norton & Company, Inc.,
500 Fifth Avenue, New York, NY 10110

For information about special discounts for bulk purchases,
please contact W. W. Norton Special Sales at specialsales@
wwnorton.com or 800-233-4830

Manufacturing by RR Donnelley, Harrisonburg, VA
Book design by Barbara M. Bachman
Production manager: Anna Oler

Library of Congress Cataloging-in-Publication Data

The stone reader : modern philosophy in 133 arguments / edited and
introduced by Peter Catapano and Simon Critchley.—First Edition.
    pages cm
ISBN 978-1-63149-071-2 (hardcover)
1. Philosophy, Modern—21st century. 2. New York times.
3. Newspapers—Sections, columns, etc.—Philosophy. I. Catapano,
Peter, editor.
B805.S76 2015
190—dc23

                    2015033307

Liveright Publishing Corporation
500 Fifth Avenue, New York, N.Y. 10110
www.wwnorton.com

W. W. Norton & Company Ltd.
Castle House, 75/76 Wells Street, London W1T 3QT

1 2 3 4 5 6 7 8 9 0

CONTENTS

THE GEOGRAPHY OF PHILOSOPHY

RETHINKING THINKERS

OLD PROBLEMS, NEW SPINS

Section II: Science

Section III: Religion and Morals

SOME HARD MORAL CASES

Section IV: Society

ECONOMICS AND POLITICS

THE MODERN FAMILY

INTRODUCTION

I.

What is a philosopher? And more important, who cares?

These two questions, and our attempt to answer them, are central to explaining this book, a collection of more than 130 essays and arguments from *The New York Times'* philosophy series, The Stone.

The questions are not arbitrary; they arose as we began this project in 2010, guided us as we developed it over the next five years, and like all the best questions, presented themselves again and again, and forced us to rethink our answers as we went along.

As might be expected, the answer to the first—What is a philosopher?—is somewhat elusive. At least one of the contributors to this book has taken a stab at it—Simon Critchley, my coeditor and coconspirator in this project, devotes the opening essay to it. Many others over the last few centuries have, too, and their conclusions vary: Truth seeker. Rationalist. Logician. Metaphysician. Troublemaker. Tenured professor. Scholar. Visionary. Madperson. Gadfly. Seer.

Underlying at least some of these definitions is a common perception—that a philosopher is a marginal, perhaps useless, creature, typically unemployable, poorly wired for worldly pursuits and ill suited for normal life. In other words, a philosopher is a person whose habitual introspection renders him or her of little practical use to those in the "real world." Remarkably, that perception hasn't changed much over time. When was the last time you heard a proud parent mention "my son, the philosopher," or "my daughter, the metaphysician"? Philosopher—as opposed to, say, firefighter, web developer or regional risk-assessment manager—isn't quite a *job*, is it? In polite or expensively educated company, wherever that might be found, identifying oneself as a philosopher might only raise a few eyebrows; in certain other precincts, that is to say practically every-where, the admission would more likely be met with laughter, puzzlement, scorn or worse.

Implicit here is the view that philosophy itself is somehow deficient, an impractical, even indulgent intellectual pursuit. This strain of anti-intellectualism is thought to be especially virulent in the United States, with its can-do, colonialist DNA and a bloodthirsty manifest destiny at its historical core—a view Richard Hofstadter laid out famously in his book *Anti-Intellectualism in American Life* (1963). We may even go as far as to say that in America, where the evangelical overlords of material productivity still hover, "navel-gazing" of the sort philosophers engage in might be considered a punishable offense, or worst yet, a sin. It might follow, then, that the United States is a nation in which any sort of intense thoughtfulness has no real place.

All this leads us to the second question—Who cares?—because if the answer is "no one," why waste any time answering the first or even thinking about any of this?

Let's be guileless for a moment, put aside the question's implied dismissal, and take it literally. The answer in that case is actually simple and surprising: A lot of people care. Despite a robust global appetite for cat videos, pop music and porn, and the alleged collapse of "the humanities" in American life, millions care deeply about, study, consume and practice philosophy. It is not confined to its traditional place in the university system. In fact, more people than ever have access to philosophical works and schools of thought, and they use them. As you no doubt know, the works of any philosopher under the sun—from Plato to Avicenna to Heidegger to the seventeen-year-old Spinoza devotee with a blog—are available electronically in most of the developed world. That was not the case a few decades ago.

Given all this, we find the often heard argument that philosophy, along with the rest of the humanities, is rapidly becoming obsolete to be a tired one. With all due respect, we reject that claim. We maintain that the reports of the death of American intellectual life (and such life elsewhere) have been greatly exaggerated, and that philosophy both inside and out of the academy is more vital than ever. And we offer this collection, as well as the popular success of The Stone, as a small bit of evidence.

II.

To those new to this particular philosophical project, here are a few basic facts: The Stone is an ongoing series, launched in 2010 as a part of the online Opinion report of *The New York Times*. Each week we publish at least one philosophic essay, often dealing with a current social, political or cultural issue. As the short description on the *Times* website says, the series "features the writing of contemporary philosophers and other thinkers on issues both timely and timeless." In other words, we aim to examine the world we find ourselves in by putting forward new ideas without discarding—or forgetting—the established wisdom of the past.

As series moderator, Simon often serves as a liaison between the world of professional or academic philosophers and our journalistic work at The Stone. He is part ambassador and part talent scout, inviting philosophers and other original thinkers to write pieces for us, and writing them himself at least a few times a year. Back in the Times Building on Eighth Avenue, I do some of the same; I assign and solicit pieces based on current events or the attractiveness of certain topics and review submissions from writers. Since this is ultimately a product of *The New York Times*, we conduct the fact-checking, editing and publishing of each essay in-house and take full editorial responsibility for the final product.

The book, as you find it here, is a selection from The Stone's first four years of essays, organized into four sections, not chronologically but by way of broad subject areas: Philosophy, Science, Religion and Morals, and Society, each beginning with a short preface written by Simon. Within each of these sections are subsections that offer a sharper focus on the essays. The aim of this structure is to make it easy for readers to navigate the large body of work here. As with any anthology, readers may either work through the material from beginning to end or move back and forth between sections at will. It is neither a "text book" designed to provide some form of tutelage nor a mere collection of "newspaper columns" but an anthology of contemporary essays and arguments that we hope will engage readers and reward many readings, and make clear the continued relevance of philosophy.

The seed for The Stone was planted in a much larger initiative at the *Times*. In late 2005 I was hired as an editor in Opinion by the editorial page editor at the time, Gail Collins, to help with the effort to develop material that would take full advantage of the possibilities in the digital space. What could we do here that we could not do on the printed page? While I can't speak for the intent or vision of my superiors or the great institution for which I work, I can say that as an editor with deep interests in not just world events, as a job like mine normally requires, but in artistic, intellectual and cultural life as well, I was excited by the possibilities. There was the sense, rare at a big newspaper—or an organization of any kind, really—of being given space to create new forms, to pursue themes, ideas and writers both within and outside the typical realm of opinion journalism, and venture into areas that were socially or culturally relevant, whether they responded directly to the news, danced around it or just shed a broader light on it. New ideas and approaches were encouraged, green-lighted and supported. The field was open.

One of the approaches we hit upon to broaden the scope of our report was the online opinion series. This involved curating a series of pieces based on a larger single theme over the course of one month or more. The idea was not primarily to stake out positions on particular issues—the traditional role of the op-ed—but to offer readers a greater variety of voices, perspectives and insights into a topic that mattered.

Over the next few years, I was given opportunities to develop and edit a number of these series, most featuring the writing of nonjour-nalists. Early on we published a collection of real-time dispatches written by Iraqi citizens during the war (Day to Day in Iraq), then one by soldiers serving in Iraq and Afghanistan (Frontlines), and later, by veterans as they returned home (Home Fires). As the form proved successful, we broadened our scope. We heard from insomniacs (All-Nighters), migraine sufferers (Migraine), American composers (The Score), songwriters (Measure for Measure), school teachers (Lesson Plans), drinkers and teetotalers (Proof), and soon after the economic crash of 2008, ordinary people in search of contentment in hard times.

That last series, called Happy Days, is where we got an inkling of what eventually became The Stone. We didn't follow the news as reported. We let people tell their own stories and share their thoughts about their place in the economically transformed world around them, even as it continued to shift under their feet. We didn't ask very much except that the writing be true, sound, compelling and that it give some sense of an actual human experience.

One of the Happy Days writers was a philosopher I'd recently read, Simon Critchley, who wrote two pieces for the series—one on the relationship between water, contemplation and happiness, and one on money. These were, in journalistic terms, "think pieces" or even meditations that, in the tradition of Montaigne or Rousseau, combined present-day commentary within a historical framework of philosophy. I found this mix of elements to be both immediately engaging and meaningful, not only in Simon's work but in the others' as well. Still, I had no idea whether *Times* readers—a famously well-informed, opinionated and exacting group—would agree.

On the whole, they did, and appeared, judging by their comments, not to find the writing "too intellectual" or abstract. Some were surprised to discover something in *The New York Times* that addressed not just external events like politics or health-care policy but aspects of their inner lives—their ethics, faith or lack thereof, their desires, anxieties and imaginations. It seemed that these issues were just as important to them as what had happened in the West Bank, Iraq or Washington and could often inform their views of these events.

At the end of that project, Simon and I began discussing a series that would focus more distinctly on philosophy—why not? We met one day in 2010 at Ceol, a now defunct Irish bar on Smith Street in Brooklyn, to see if we could hatch a plan. He pointed out how many great writers and thinkers in the field were not being read in mainstream publications, and I quickly saw how right he was. Over a number of pints we talked it through. It seemed viable. We made a list of philosophers we wanted to work with and subjects we hoped to cover. Then we bandied about series titles for a while, none very good, until The Stone—a clipped reference to that legendarily transformative *prima materia*, the philosopher's stone—dropped into our laps.

Within a few weeks, I proposed the project, got a go-ahead from our editorial page editor, Andy Rosenthal, and our Op-Ed editor at the time, David Shipley, and we went to work.

Simon wrote the first piece: "What Is a Philosopher?"

And when it appeared online on May 16, 2010, we received a shock. By our humble expectations, it was wildly popular. It became the most e-mailed article on the *Times* site within a day—840 people replied, an almost staggering amount. Also notably, everyone had a different answer to the question posed in the title.

The intense reader engagement was a revelation to us: we saw that essays like this could offer more than just an unquestioned voice of authority; it could be a public platform for large numbers of people to argue and discuss questions of political, social, cultural and humanistic importance—a massive, bustling, sprawling electronic version of the ancient Agora.

Perhaps most exciting, we saw that by reaching readers in all walks of life (we had the foundation of the *Times*' enviably large readership to thank for that, of course), most of them outside the academic and professional precincts of philosophy, we had the opportunity to engage the person "on the street"—or what I like to call "the naturally occurring philosopher"—in an activity typically confined to universities.

Here is one reader's response to "What Is a Philosopher?" that illustrates this point beautifully:

Before we talk about philosophy and its role in the advancement of human understanding, we first have to know what a philosopher is. Try this on for size, folks: a philosopher is anyone who thinks about existence and takes a whack at trying to explain it. Just ask the guy seated next to you on the subway what he thinks—then duck, just in case he's had it up to here with those who think one has to turn philosophy into sticky treacle with Socratic anecdotes before a spark of interest can be coaxed from the masses.

Next question. Why are we here?

That's an excellent philosophical point of departure, considering where this column left us! Having myself sat in a subway car at the crack of dawn, I have asked that very same question many a time. Indeed, had Socrates sat next to me, we would have had a grand time: he questioning me, me responding until, all of a sudden, my answers revealed even to me the foolishness of my assumptions about existence, not to mention the intelligence of my seat-mate.

Seriously, tho', now there was a philosopher! Someone who refused to accept even the sacred judgment of the Delphic Oracle when it pronounced him the wisest man on earth! And then it hit him like a knuckle sandwich: maybe true wisdom was knowing that you know nothing at all about anything.

Sounds like he coulda written one helluva column. But then, he knew better than to try.

In some ways, engagement like this from many thousands of *Times* readers are the foundation on which The Stone was built.

III.

In publishing The Stone, we try to abide by a few basic principles. We do not presume editorial authority and, as much as possible, let the writers say what they want the way they want, provided their facts are clear and reasoning sound. We ask the readers and philosophers to meet halfway—at the intersection of a traditional newspaper op-ed and true philosophical inquiry. We avoid dumbed-down philosophy—"watered-down versions of arid technical discussions and inspirational/self-help pieces with no philosophical spine," as our frequent contributor and adviser Gary Gutting once put it—and strive for sound, well-wrought and jargon-free philosophical essays and arguments that speak in some way to the present moment, each adhering to the long-established editorial standards of the *Times*.

The strong positive response to this entire range of essays is a confirmation that readers are not looking only for "big name" philosophers. They want thoughtful, penetrating essays, no matter the author's resumé or professional rank. This was a lesson we learned quickly, and one which also taught us that behind the best of these essays is the conviction that philosophy can in some cases function as "literature"—meaning an essay on moral relativism or logic or free will can be a "good read" and potentially give aesthetic pleasure comparable to that given by a short story or a poem. Rigorous philosophical writing, we found, could put forth a provable or persuasive argument and provide a sense of exploration and delight at the same time.

Philosophers are more than just exceptional thinkers. They tend to be—whether in the mold of rationalist, poet, gadfly or seeker—fascinating people. As a result, readers of this book will hopefully gain a deeper appreciation of the insightful (sometimes even wise) writers and doers living among them, and a sense of where they fit in the scheme of things, in both public and private life.

IV.

Readers who come upon The Stone for the first time are often puzzled by the mixing of philosophy and old-fashioned media commentary. They can't be blamed, of course. A typical newspaper reader generally won't flinch at an article by a doctor, economist, politician or policy expert of some sort, but they might be surprised to see one by a philosopher. How often do we find any brand of philosophical thinking in newspaper and magazines, or in mainstream media of any kind?

But in a broad sense, philosophy and journalism are a natural fit. Both possess a license to tackle any subject. If it occurs in the course of human experience, it is fair game. And in many cases, their methods are similar. A reporter will gather facts objectively, analyze them, break them down and present what he or she sees as the truth of a situation. With some variations, that's essentially how a philosopher works.

Philosophy and journalism also complement each other. Each gives the other a quality it may be missing. Journalism has an urgency driven by events that philosophy tends to lack, while philosophy relies on analysis or contemplation that journalists often don't have time for because of the demands of the profession.

Finally, there is the idea of philosopher as a "gadfly," as Socrates described himself, an agitator of conventional wisdom, an annoyance to state power and the status quo, which is very much in keeping with the role of the media as a watchdog—the fourth estate. In this volume you'll find that philosophy did indeed respond to crucial events as they occurred: an urgent series of pieces on guns and violence in the wake of the Newtown school massacre, and essays coming to terms with the Occupy Wall Street movement, radical Islam, the crisis of privacy, hacker culture and the racial anger simmering and sometimes exploding in the United States.

Despite all this, philosophy seems to retain that bad rap out in the "real world." People like Stephen Hawking and Neil deGrasse Tyson have called it essentially useless when compared to science and other more "practical" subjects. Those who persist in this folly will tell you that the problem with philosophy is that it is too insular, that it does not "solve" real problems and makes no effort to be useful or even understood to the majority of the human race it is supposed to inform. But that is a too simple assessment of the situation. The intense interest in The Stone, and these writers' deep engagement with the world in which we live, belies that narrow-minded take.

This, like all truly interesting questions, will be debated for as long as we have the capacity to argue with each other. But I'd like to close with a few passages from an assessment Simon wrote after the series' first year, one that offers a more generous and expansive definition of the meaning and use of philosophy. The Stone, he wrote, offered some proof "that philosophy still matters. That it is not some otherworldly activity conducted by a handful of remote individuals safely incarcerated away in institutions of higher learning." He continued:

> *Philosophy assesses and presses public opinion by asking essential questions: "What is knowledge?" "What is justice?" "What is love?"*
>
> *The hope that drives this activity is that the considerations to which such universal questions give rise can, through inquiry and argumentation, have an educative or even emancipatory effect. Philosophy, as the great American philosopher Stanley Cavell puts it, is the education of grown-ups.*
>
> *It is my view that philosophy must form part of the life of a culture. It must engage the public and influence how a culture converses with itself, understands itself, talks to other cultures and seeks to understand them.*

That's what we try to do each week in The Stone. And that's how, and why, this book was born.

So, who cares?

—Peter Catapano,
New York,
2015

PHILOSOPHY

PHILOSOPHY IS A NOTORIOUSLY SELF-REFLEXIVE DISCIPLINE. OFTEN, a lifetime devoted to it begins and ends with the question, what is philosophy? This leads to the common accusation of navel-gazing or armchair-pondering. But such accusations are shortsighted.

Philosophy in its recognizable form begins in ancient Greece with the person of Socrates. Before his eventual trial and execution by the city of Athens on the charges of impiety toward the gods and the corruption of the young, he spent his days talking to people and engaging them in dialogue. Often these dialogues would be with people sometimes called "Sophists" because they claimed to provide wisdom (sophia). Socrates would simply ask them questions that revealed that they didn't really know what they were talking about and that the wisdom they sought to retail was bogus in its claims.

Philosophy begins by asking difficult questions of a very general form (What is knowledge? What is truth?) and by using critical techniques of argumentation in order to show that those who "know" are often advancing questionable claims. But this doesn't imply that the philosopher him- or herself possesses knowledge or wisdom. Socrates was pronounced by the Oracle at Delphi to be the wisest man in Greece, but he constantly professed to know nothing. Philosophy, then, commences as a movement into perplexity about the most general and fundamental issues that concern human affairs.

This perplexity is directed most fiercely toward philosophy itself. It is therefore appropriate that *The Stone Reader* opens with a series of questions about the nature, scope, history and identity of the discipline. Good philosophy should never be hidebound by tradition or stuck in its past.

In the first two parts of Section 1, "New Impressions of an Old Profession" and "The Geography of Philosophy," the reader will find various attempts to define and redefine the nature of the philosophical task. Does the fact that philosophy began in ancient Greece with Socrates entail a bias toward men over women? Does the entire history and study of philosophy betray a geographical prejudice toward the West, particularly Europe over the rest of the world? Such questions are engaged pressingly here, and this is in line with the mission of The Stone, which is not only to show what philosophy can do, but also to try and expand the domain of its inclusiveness. It is our modest contention, very simply, that philosophy is for everyone.

The study of philosophy will often be focused on the reading of canonical texts, such as those of Plato, Spinoza and Hume. But once again, this activity is not pursued out of some antiquarian interest. It is a question of constantly rereading those texts in order to both question the way in which they had previously been interpreted and offer new interpretations that speak to our contemporary condition. In "Rethinking Thinkers," a number of our authors take on this task.

Philosophy at its best is simultaneously old and new, both showing the persistence and the difficulty of basic themes and questions and the need to adapt those questions to the pressing demands of the surrounding world. In the fourth part of this section, "Old Problems, New Spins," the reader will find investigations of absolutely classical philosophical themes, such as the nature of time, free will, truth and logic. But there are also reflections on life in the digital world and how philosophy might adapt to the experimental techniques of cognitive psychology.

Often people speak, sometimes with good reason, of philosophy as an activity that is distinct from literature and fiction. On this view, philosophy is seen as a good example of bad writing. Some of the essays in the final part of this section, "Philosophy, Literature and Life," show the inadequacy of that view. Philosophy has many of the same virtues as literature and can even be a form of literature itself.

And if literature does indeed tell us something profound about our existence, then this is also true of philosophy, which is not simply a professional or narrowly buttoned-down academic pursuit, but a way of life that can permit us to raise again the question of our significance and the possible pursuits of happiness.

—Simon Critchley

NEW IMPRESSIONS OF AN OLD PROFESSION

What Is a Philosopher?

—Simon Critchley

THERE ARE AS MANY DEFINITIONS OF PHILOSOPHY AS THERE ARE philosophers—perhaps there are even more. After three millennia of philosophical activity and disagreement, it is unlikely that we'll reach a consensus, and I certainly don't want to add more hot air to the volcanic cloud of unknowing. What I'd like to do in the opening column in this new venture—The Stone—is to kick things off by asking a slightly different question: What is a philosopher?

As Alfred North Whitehead said, philosophy is a series of footnotes to Plato. Let me risk adding a footnote by looking at Plato's provocative definition of the philosopher that appears in the middle of his dialogue, *Theaetetus*, in a passage that some scholars consider a "digression." But far from being a footnote to a digression, I think this moment in Plato tells us something hugely important about what a philosopher is and what philosophy does.

Socrates tells the story of Thales, who was by some accounts the first philosopher. He was looking so intently at the stars that he fell into a well. Some witty Thracian servant girl is said to have made a joke at Thales's expense—that in his eagerness to know what went on in the sky he was unaware of the things in front of him and at his feet. Socrates adds, in Seth Benardete's translation, "The same jest suffices for all those who engage in philosophy."

What is a philosopher, then? The answer is clear: a laughing stock, an absentminded buffoon, the butt of countless jokes from

Aristophanes's *The Clouds* to Mel Brooks's *History of the World, Part I.* Whenever the philosopher is compelled to talk about the things at his feet, he gives not only the Thracian girl but the rest of the crowd a belly laugh. The philosopher's clumsiness in worldly affairs makes him appear stupid or "gives the impression of plain silliness." We are left with a rather Monty Pythonesque definition of the philosopher: the one who is silly.

But as always with Plato, things are not necessarily as they first appear, and Socrates is the greatest of ironists. First, we should recall that Thales believed that water was the universal substance out of which all things were composed. Water was Thales's philosopher's stone, as it were. Therefore, by falling into a well, he inadvertently pressed his basic philosophical claim.

But there is a deeper and more troubling layer of irony here that I would like to peel off more slowly. Socrates introduces the "digression" by making a distinction between the philosopher and the lawyer, or what Benardete nicely renders as the "pettifogger." The lawyer is compelled to present a case in court and time is of the essence. In Greek legal proceedings, a strictly limited amount of time was allotted for the presentation of cases. Time was measured with a water clock, or *clepsydra*, which literally steals time, as in the Greek *kleptes*, a thief or embezzler. The pettifogger, the jury, and by implication the whole society live with the constant pressure of time. The water of time's flow is constantly threatening to drown them.

By contrast, we might say, the philosopher is the person who has time or who takes time. Theodorus, Socrates's interlocutor, introduces the "digression" with the words, "Aren't we at leisure, Socrates?" The latter's response is interesting. He says, "It appears we are." As we know, in philosophy appearances can be deceptive. But the basic contrast here is between the lawyer, who has no time, or for whom time is money, and the philosopher, who takes time. The freedom of the philosopher consists in either moving freely from topic to topic or simply spending years returning to the same topic out of perplexity, fascination and curiosity.

Pushing this a little further, we might say that to philosophize is to take your time, even when you have no time, when time is constantly pressing at your back. The busy readers of *The New York Times* will doubtless understand this sentiment. It is our hope that some of them will make the time to read The Stone. As Wittgenstein says, "This is how philosophers should salute each other: 'Take your time.'" Indeed, it might tell you something about the nature of philosophical dialogue to confess that my attention was recently drawn to this passage from *Theaetetus* in leisurely discussions with a doctoral student at the New School, Charles Snyder.

Socrates says that those in the constant press of business, like lawyers, policy makers, mortgage brokers and hedge fund managers, become "bent and stunted" and they are compelled "to do crooked things." The pettifogger is undoubtedly successful, wealthy and extraordinarily honey tongued but, Socrates adds, "small in his soul and shrewd and a shyster." The philosopher, by contrast, is *free* by virtue of his or her otherworldliness, by their capacity to fall into wells and appear silly.

Socrates adds that the philosopher neither sees nor hears the so-called unwritten laws of the city—that is, the mores and conventions that govern public life. The philosopher shows no respect for rank and inherited privilege and is unaware of anyone's high or low birth. It also does not occur to the philosopher to join a political club or a private party. As Socrates concludes, the philosopher's body alone dwells within the city's walls. In thought, they are elsewhere.

This all sounds dreamy, but it isn't. Philosophy should come with the kind of health warning one finds on packs of European cigarettes: PHILOSOPHY KILLS. Here we approach the deep irony of Plato's words. Plato's dialogues were written after Socrates's death. Socrates was charged with impiety toward the gods of the city and with corrupting the youth of Athens. He was obliged to speak in court in defense of these charges, to speak against the water clock, that thief of time. He ran out of time and suffered the consequences: he was condemned to death and forced to take his own life.

A couple of generations later, during the uprisings against Macedonian rule that followed the death of Alexander the Great in 323

BCE, Alexander's former tutor, Aristotle, escaped Athens saying, "I will not allow the Athenians to sin twice against philosophy." From the ancient Greeks to Giordano Bruno, Spinoza, Hume and right up to the shameful lawsuit that prevented Bertrand Russell from teaching at the City College of New York in 1940 on the charge of sexual immorality and atheism, philosophy has repeatedly and persistently been identified with blasphemy against the gods, whichever gods they might be. Nothing is more common in the history of philosophy than the accusation of impiety. Because of their laughable otherworldliness and lack of respect for social convention, rank and privilege, philosophers refuse to honor the old gods, and this makes them politically suspicious, even dangerous. Might such dismal things still happen in our happily enlightened age? That depends where one casts one's eyes and how closely one looks.

Perhaps the last laugh is with the philosopher. Although the philosopher will always look ridiculous in the eyes of pettifoggers and those obsessed with maintaining the status quo, the opposite happens when the nonphilosopher is obliged to give an account of justice in itself or happiness and misery in general. Far from eloquent, Socrates insists, the pettifogger is "perplexed and stutters."

Of course, one might object that ridiculing someone's stammer isn't a very nice thing to do. Benardete rightly points out that Socrates assigns every kind of virtue to the philosopher apart from moderation. Nurtured in freedom and taking their time, there is something dreadfully uncanny about philosophers, something either monstrous or godlike or indeed both at once. This is why many sensible people continue to think the Athenians had a point in condemning Socrates to death. I leave it for you to decide. I couldn't possibly judge.

MAY 16, 2010

The Flight of Curiosity

—Justin E. H. Smith

Must one be endowed with curiosity in order to become a philosopher?

Today, in the academic realm at least, the answer is surely and regrettably no. When a newly minted philosopher goes on the job market, her primary task is to show her prospective colleagues how perfectly focused she has been in graduate school, and to conceal her knowledge of any topic (Shakespeare's sonnets, classical Chinese astronomy, the history of pigeon breeding) that does not fall within the current boundaries of the discipline.

But how were these boundaries formed in the first place? Did they spring from the very essence of philosophy, a set of core attributes present at inception, forever fixed and eternal? The answer to that latter question is also no. What appears to us today to be a core is only what is leftover after a centuries-long process by which the virtue of curiosity—once nearly synonymous with philosophy—migrated into other disciplines, both scientific and humanistic. As this migration was occurring, many curiosity-driven activities—such as insect collecting and stargazing, long considered at least tributaries of philosophy—were downgraded to the status of mere hobbies. This loss of curiosity has played an important but little-noticed role in the widespread perception that professional philosophy has become out of touch with the interests of the broader society.

Let me rush to qualify what no doubt sounds like a harsh assessment of the state of my own discipline. I am certainly not saying that, as individuals, philosophers will not often be "curious people," in the very best sense of that phrase, but only that they are habituated by their discipline to make a sharp distinction between their sundry interests and what they do professionally, as philosophers. The distinction is as clear as that between Richard Feynman's contribution to theoretical physics and his enjoyment of Tuvan throat singing.

Today's natural scientist easily distinguishes his own work not only from his hobbies, but also from the activity of his pseudoscientific counterpart. When we look back in history, however, it becomes difficult to keep this distinction in view, for it has often happened that false beliefs have produced significant experimental results and have led to real discoveries. It is no less difficult to separate the history either of science or of pseudoscience from what I will dare to call the "real" history of philosophy, for until very recently, what we now call science was not merely of interest to philosophers, but was in fact constitutive of philosophy. In fact, it was not called science at all, but rather natural philosophy.

Thus, tellingly, among the articles in the *Philosophical Transactions* of 1666, the second year of the journal's publication, we find titles such as "Of a Considerable Load-Stone Digged Out of the Ground in Devonshire" and "Observations Concerning Emmets or Ants, Their Eggs, Production, Progress, Coming to Maturity, Use, &c." Throughout the seventeenth and eighteenth centuries, researchers studying the properties of magnetism continued to refer to their area of interest as "the magnetical philosophy," and as late as 1808, John Dalton published *A New System of Chemical Philosophy*. A year later Jean-Baptiste Lamarck brought out his *Philosophie zoologique*. Yet by the early twentieth century, this usage of the word *philosophy* had entirely vanished. What happened?

One of the charges brought against Socrates in Plato's great dialogue, *The Apology*, is that he "speculated about the heavens above, and searched into the earth beneath." Today philosophers are more likely to pick out the other charges—sophism, corrupting the youth, atheism—as most relevant to our understanding of the Socratic-

Platonic revolution in the history of Western thought. But what are we to make of this charge of curiosity? It may be that in restyling themselves as "scientists," natural philosophers, or *curiosi*, have succeeded in the past few hundred years in overcoming their bad reputation. Little awareness lingers at this point (excepting, say, the occasional nuclear meltdown, when we start to feel we've gone too far too fast) of what might have made the activity of looking into the earth and the heavens a crime.

This restyling occurred over the course of the early modern period, at just the same time as questions that were once purely speculative—concerning, for instance, the nature of life, or the causes of planetary orbits—came to be much more tractable than before, thanks to the increasing mathematization of the sciences, and to newly emerging standards for scientific observation and experimentation. Their new tractability by scientists left the philosophers to establish themselves on their own. But what exactly is left over for philosophy to do once the earth, the heavens, the animals and plants are turned over to this new breed of scientists to explain?

There will certainly always be a place for epistemology, or the theory of knowledge. But in order for a theory of knowledge to tell us much, it needs to draw on examples of knowledge of something or other. And so philosophy agrees to a partial reconciliation with the "sciences" some years after its divorce from "natural philosophy." Philosophy comes back to physics with the philosophy of physics, and to biology with the philosophy of biology, even though physics and biology are no longer part of philosophy itself.

Now surely it is a good thing that today there are, say, helminthologists, who can devote all their time to the study of worms without having to worry about how these creatures fit into the cosmic order, or into God's design, as you wish. But if helminthology has cleared away the cosmological dross that weighed it down back when it was part of natural philosophy, philosophy meanwhile may have lost something that once helped to fuel it: a curiosity about the world in all its detail, a desire to know everything encyclopedically, rather than to bound its pure activity off from the impure world of worms and so on, a world philosophy might approach through that succinct preposition, *of*—as in "philosophy of physics," "philosophy of law"—which permits philosophy to stand apart, and implicitly above, the mundane objects of its attention.

So long as contemporary philosophy conceives itself in this way, it is rather a difficult task to pursue the sort of research on the history of philosophy that is adequate to the material it studies, that respects actors' categories, and that takes seriously theories and entities that have long since been rejected by reasonable people. Consider Kenelm Digby's 1658 account of the weapon salve, or the treatment of wounds at a distance by manipulation of the weapon that caused them. Digby, in fact, offered a fascinating, sophisticated application of early modern corpuscularianism, yet many philosophers today suppose that to take an interest in a false theory from the past such as this one, to research it and to write about it, implies a rejection of the idea of truth itself. I myself was once dismissed as a "postmodernist" by a referee for a journal to which I submitted an article on the weapon salve.

There is no basis for such an accusation. For among the great many truths in the world is this one: a man named Digby once believed something false. To take an interest in that false belief is not to reject the truth, but only to wish to fill out our picture of the truth with as much detail as possible, and not because of some aesthetic inclination to the baroque, but rather because false theories are an important part of the puzzle that we as philosophers should be trying to complete: that of determining the range of ways people conceptualize the world around them.

This is a project, I believe, that philosophers ought to recognize themselves as having in common with the other human sciences, and most of all with anthropology, as well as with newer disciplines such as cognitive science, which takes the substantial interconnection between philosophy and the study of the natural world as seriously as it was taken in the seventeenth century. The new "experimental philosophy" movement is also returning to an earlier conception of the inseparability of philosophical reflection and scientific inquiry, though curiously "x-phi" advocates describe themselves as breaking with "traditional" philosophy, rather than as returning to it, which is what in fact they are doing.

But for the most part philosophers prefer to keep their distance from the world, to do philosophy of this or that, and to disavow any interest in reckoning up the actual range of ways in which people, past or present, have explained the world. For some historians of philosophy, this makes things difficult, since we find we cannot live up to the expectation of our colleagues to show the immediate "philosophical" payoff of our research, by which of course is meant the relevance to the set of issues that happen to interest them.

I BELIEVE IT IS IMPERATIVE, indeed that it amounts to nothing short of respect paid to the dead, that historians of philosophy resist this demand for relevance. Scholarship in the history of philosophy must not aim to contribute to the resolution of problems on the current philosophical agenda. What it must do instead is reveal the variety of problems that have in different times and places been deemed philosophical, thereby providing a broader context within which current philosophers can understand the contingency, and future transformability, of their own problems. In this way, historians of philosophy contribute to the vitality of current philosophy, but on their own terms, and not on the terms dictated by their nonhistorian colleagues.

Recently I have noticed, when holding forth on, say, G. W. Leibniz's interest in the pharmaceutical properties of the Brazilian ipecacuanha root, the way in which the term *erudite* now serves in some philosophical circles as a sort of backhanded compliment. What it really says is that the compliment's recipient cannot quite cut it as a real philosopher, which is to say as a producer of rigorous arguments, and so instead compensates by filling her head with so much historical trivia. Rigor has decidedly won out over erudition as the reigning philosophical virtue, yet it is with a curious lack of rigor that philosophers assume, without argument, that there is a zero-sum competition for space in our heads between rigor and erudition.

As Laurence Sterne said in a related context, this is like assuming that you cannot hiccup and flatulate at the same time.

It is noteworthy in this connection that in 1682 a journal was founded in Leipzig, as the German response to the *Philosophical Transactions*, with the title *Acta eruditorum* (Acts of the erudite). This journal, too, contained much on the generation of maggots and other such matters. Now the figure of the eruditus was in the seventeenth century very close to the curiosus, and it is around the same time that we also witness the foundation of societies of natural philosophers with names such as the Societas Leopoldina naturae curiosorum (the Leopoldine Society for Those Who Are Curious about Nature).

It was before the members of this very society that Leibniz, in 1695, at the very peak of his innovation as a metaphysical thinker of the first order, presented what he described as his most important contribution to learning so far: a treatise entitled "On the New American Antidysenteric"—namely, ipecacuanha, better known today through its derivative product, "syrup of ipecac." It had already been known that this root, first described in Willem Piso's *Natural History of Brazil* of 1648, could be used to stop diarrhea, and indeed its usefulness in saving Louis XIV from a bad case of dysentery was legendary around Paris when Leibniz lived there in the 1670s. But in front of the audience of German curiosi twenty years later, Leibniz could claim for himself the credit for discovering the emetic properties of the root, and again, he would, evidently without hyperbole, compare this discovery favorably to everything else he had yet accomplished, and for which he remains so widely know today.

This is, to put it mildly, very curious. It shows at the very least that Leibniz conceived of his life's work, as a learned man, as a curiosus, and as a philosopher, very differently than we conceive of it today, and very differently than philosophers today conceive of their own work. And this different conception matters to the historian of philosophy, since to take an interest in Leibniz's pharmaceutical endeavors (or his mine-engineering endeavors, or his paleontological endeavors . . .) might, just might, reveal to us something we would not have noticed about what matters to us had we limited ourselves to the canonical "philosophical" treatises. And it might, finally, force us to reconsider the adequacy of our current list of philosophical problems. And even if it doesn't, something else from philosophy's past that has fallen off the list eventually surely will.

As a historian of philosophy, I believe it is a terrible thing to attempt to fit figures from the history of philosophy into the narrow confines of a conception of philosophy that has really only emerged over the most recent centuries. Such confinement fails to do justice to the scope and richness of their thought. Perhaps more importantly, it deprives us of the possibility of rediscovering that spirit of curiosity that fueled the development of philosophy during its first few millennia.

MAY 22, 2011

Philosophy as an Art of Dying

—*Costica Bradatan*

IT HAPPENS RARELY, BUT WHEN IT DOES, IT CAUSES A COMMOTION of great proportions; it attracts the attention of all, becomes a popular topic for discussion and debate in marketplaces and taverns. It drives people to take sides, quarrel and fight, which for things philosophical is quite remarkable. It happened to Socrates, Hypatia, Thomas More, Giordano Bruno, Jan Patočka, and a few others. Due to an irrevocable death sentence, imminent mob execution or torture to death, these philosophers found themselves in the most paradoxical of situations: lovers of logic and rational argumentation, silenced by brute force; professional makers of discourses, banned from using the word; masters of debate and contradiction, able to argue no more. What was left of these philosophers then? Just their silence, their sheer physical presence. The only means of expression left to them, their own bodies—and dying bodies at that.

The situation has its irony. It is an old custom among philosophers of various stripes and persuasions to display a certain contempt toward the body. Traditionally, in Western philosophy at least, the body has been with few exceptions seen as inferior to the mind, spirit or soul—the realm of "the flesh," the domain of the incomprehensible, of blind instincts and unclean impulses. And so here are the condemned philosophers: speechless, with only their dying bodies to express themselves. One may quip that the body has finally got its chance to take its revenge on the philosophers.

But how have they arrived there in the first place? It so happens that some philosophers entertain and profess certain ideas that compel them to lead a certain way of life. Sometimes, however, their way of life leads them to a situation where they have to choose between remaining faithful to their ideas or renouncing them altogether. The former translates into "dying for idea," whereas the latter usually involves not only a denunciation of that philosopher's lifestyle, but also, implicitly, an invalidation of the philosophical views that inspired that way of life. This seems to be the toughest of choices. In simpler terms, it boils down to the following dilemma: if you decide to remain faithful to your views, you will be no more. Your own death will be your last opportunity to put your ideas into practice. On the other hand, if you choose to "betray" your ideas (and perhaps yourself as well), you remain alive, but with no beliefs to live by.

The situation of the philosopher facing such a choice is what is commonly called a "limit situation." Yet this limit does not concern only the philosopher involved; in an important sense, this is the limit of philosophy itself, a threshold where philosophy encounters its other (whatever philosophy *is not*) and, in the process, is put to the test.

Long before he was faced with such a choice through the good offices of the Czechoslovakian political police in 1977, Jan Patočka may have intuited this limit when he said that "philosophy reaches a point where it no longer suffices to pose questions and answer them, both with extreme energy; where the philosopher will progress no further unless he manages to make a decision." Whatever that decision may mean in other contexts, the implication of Patočka's notion for this discussion is unambiguous. There is a point beyond which philosophy, if it is not to lose face, must turn into something else: *performance*. It has to pass a test in a foreign land, a territory that's not its own. For the ultimate testing of our philosophy takes place not in the sphere of strictly rational procedures (writing, teaching, lecturing) but elsewhere: in the fierce confrontation with death of the animal that we are. The worthiness of one's philosophy reveals itself, if anywhere, in the live performance of one's encounter with one's own death; that's how we find out whether it is of some substance or it is all futility. Tell me how you deal with your fear of annihilation, and I will tell you about your philosophy.

Furthermore, death is such a terrifying event, and the fear of it so universal, that *to invite* it by way of faithfulness to one's ideas is something that fascinates and disturbs at the same time. Those who do so take on an aura of uncanny election, of almost unhuman distinction; all stand in awe before them. With it also comes a certain form of power. This is why, for example, one's self-immolation (meant as political protest) can have devastating social and political effects, as we saw recently in Tunisia, when twenty-six-year-old Mohammed Bouazizi set himself on fire. This is also why the death of those philosophers who choose to die for an idea comes soon to be seen as an essential part of their work. In fact their deaths often become far more important than their lives. Why is Socrates such an important and influential figure? Mostly because of the manner and circumstances of his death. He may have never written a book, but he crafted one of the most famous endings of all time: his own. Any philosophical text would pale in comparison. Nor have Hypatia's writings survived; yet, the exquisite, if passive, performance of her death in the early fifth century has not ceased to fascinate us. A modern scholar, Maria Dzielska, recounts how, at the instigation of the patriarch Cyril (later sanctified by the Church), some of the zealous Christians of Alexandria helped her to join the Socratic tradition of dying:

> [A] mob executed the deed on a day in March 415, in the tenth consulship of Honorius and the sixth consulship of Theodosius II, during Lent. Hypatia was returning home . . . from her customary ride in the city. She was pulled out of the chariot and dragged to the church Caesarion . . . There they tore off her clothes and killed her with "broken pits of pottery" . . . Then they hauled her body outside the city to a place called Kinaron, to burn it on a pyre of sticks.

One of the accounts of Giordano Bruno's death is particularly eloquent. A chronicle of the time (*Avviso di Roma*, February 19, 1600) reads, "On Friday they burned alive in Campo de' Fiore that Domini-can brother of Nola, a persistent heretic; his tongue was immobilized [con la lingua in giova] because of the terrible things he was saying, unwilling to listen either to his comforters or to anybody else."

Con la lingua in giova! There is hardly a better illustration of what "silencing an opponent" can mean. I don't really have anything against the Holy Office, except maybe that sometimes they have a tendency to take things a bit too literally.

"Dying for an idea" in this fashion is, admittedly, a rare occur-rence. Thank goodness philosophers are not put to death on a regu-lar basis. I hasten to add, however, as rare as it may be, the situation is *not* hypothetical. These things have happened and will happen again. In a certain sense, the possibility of one's dying *in relation to* one's thinking lies at the heart of the Western definition of philos-ophy. When Plato's Socrates states in the *Phaedo* that philosophy is *meletē thanatou*—that is to say, an intense practice of death—he may mean not just that the object of philosophy should be to help us bet-ter cope with our mortality, but also that the one who practices phi-losophy should understand the risks that come with the job. After all, this definition of philosophy comes from someone condemned to death for the ideas he expressed, only a few hours away from his execution. The lesson? Perhaps that to be a philosopher means more than just being ready to "suffer" death, to accept it passively at some indefinite point in time; it may also require one to *provoke his own death*, to meet it somehow midway. That's mastering death. Philoso-phy has sometimes been understood as "an art of living," and rightly so. But there are good reasons to believe that philosophy can be an "art of dying" as well.

"DYING FOR AN IDEA" is the stuff of martyrdom—"philosophic martyrdom." For martyrdom to be possible, however, one's death, spectacular as it may be, is not enough. Dying is just half of the job; the other half is weaving a good narrative of martyrdom and find-ing an audience for it. A philosopher's death would be in vain without the right narrator, as well as the guilty conscience of a receptive audience. A sense of collective guilt can do wonders for a narrative of martyrdom about to emerge. I have written elsewhere about the importance of storytelling and collective memory for the construction of political martyrdom. Much of the same goes for philosopher-martyrs. In a certain sense, they cease to be people in flesh and blood and are recast into literary characters of sorts; their stories, if they are to be effective, have to follow certain rules, fit into a certain genre, respond to certain needs. Certainly, there are the historians who always seek to establish "the facts." Yet—leaving aside that history writing, as Hayden White showed a long time ago, is itself a form of literature—inconvenient "facts" rarely manage to challenge the narratives that dominate popular consciousness.

Enlightenment writers, and then the feminist scholarship of the twentieth century, have played a major role in the "making" of Hypatia the philosopher-martyr. Countless anticlerical writers and public intellectuals have done the same for Bruno, as has Václav Havel for Patočka. Yet the most influential martyr maker is by far Plato. Not only did he make Socrates into the archetypal philosopher-martyr, he practically invented the genre. In Plato's rendering of Socrates's case, we have almost all the ingredients of any good narrative of martyrdom: a protagonist who, because of his commitment to a life of virtue and wisdom seeking, antagonizes his community; his readiness to die for his philosophy rather than accept the dictates of a misguided crowd; a hostile political environment marked by intolerance and narrow-mindedness; a situation of crisis escalating into a chain of dramatic events; the climax in the form of a public trial and the confrontation with the frenzied crowd; and finally the heroic, if unjust, death of the hero, followed by his apotheosis.

Beyond this, Plato's writings have apparently shaped the actual behavior of people facing a choice similar to Socrates's. When Thomas More, for example, shortly before losing his head, said, "I die the King's good servant, but God's first," he was making an obvious reference to Socrates's words during his trial, as rendered in this passage from the *Apology*: "Gentlemen, I am your very grateful and devoted servant, but I owe a greater obedience to God than to you."

These philosophers—they cannot even die without giving proper scholarly references! Just as he was saying this, More must have had a sudden glimpse that what he was about to do was not as real as he would have liked it to be, as though something "unreal"—the world of fiction, the books he had read—had now crept into his own act of dying. Certainly, dying itself is a brutally real experience, maybe the most brutal of all. And yet, I am afraid More was right: dying for an idea never comes in pure form. It is always part reality, part fiction (in an undisclosed proportion). Like most things in life.

JUNE 12, 2011

Philosophy—What's the Use?

—Gary Gutting

THERE IS AN IMPORTANT CONCEPTION OF PHILOSOPHY THAT FALLS to this criticism. Associated especially with earlier modern philosophers, particularly René Descartes, this conception sees philosophy as the essential *foundation* of the beliefs that guide our everyday life. For example, I act as though there is a material world and other people who experience it as I do. But how do I know that any of this is true? Couldn't I just be dreaming of a world outside my thoughts? And since (at best) I see only other human bodies, what reason do I have to think that there are any minds connected to those bodies? To answer these questions, it would seem that I need rigorous philosophical arguments for my existence and the existence of other thinking humans.

Of course, I don't actually need any such arguments, if only because I have no practical alternative to believing that I and other people exist. As soon as we stop thinking weird philosophical thoughts, we immediately go back to believing what skeptical arguments seem to call into question. And rightly so, since, as David Hume pointed out, we are human beings before we are philosophers.

But what Hume and, by our day, virtually all philosophers are rejecting is only what I'm calling the *foundationalist* conception of philosophy. Rejecting foundationalism means accepting that we have every right to hold basic beliefs that are not legitimated by philosophical reflection. More recently, philosophers as different as

Richard Rorty and Alvin Plantinga have cogently argued that such basic beliefs include not only the "Humean" beliefs that no one can do without, but also substantive beliefs on controversial questions of ethics, politics and religion. Rorty, for example, maintained that the basic principles of liberal democracy require no philosophical grounding ("the priority of democracy over philosophy").

If you think that the only possible "use" of philosophy would be to provide a foundation for beliefs that need no foundation, then the conclusion that philosophy is of little importance for everyday life follows immediately. But there are other ways that philosophy can be of practical significance.

Even though basic beliefs on ethics, politics and religion do not require prior philosophical justification, they do need what we might call "intellectual maintenance," which itself typically involves philosophical thinking. Religious believers, for example, are frequently troubled by the existence of horrendous evils in a world they hold was created by an all-good God. Some of their trouble may be emotional, requiring pastoral guidance. But religious commitment need not exclude a commitment to coherent thought. For instance, often enough believers want to know if their belief in God makes sense given the reality of evil. The philosophy of religion is full of discussions relevant to this question. Similarly, you may be an atheist because you think all arguments for God's existence are obviously fallacious. But if you encounter, say, a sophisticated version of the cosmological argument, or the design argument from fine-tuning, you may well need a clever philosopher to see if there's anything wrong with it.

In addition to defending our basic beliefs against objections, we frequently need to clarify what our basic beliefs mean or logically entail. So, if I say I would never kill an innocent person, does that mean that I wouldn't order the bombing of an enemy position if it might kill some civilians? Does a commitment to democratic elections require one to accept a fair election that puts an antidemocratic party into power? Answering such questions requires careful conceptual distinctions, for example, between direct and indirect results of actions, or between a morality of intrinsically wrong actions and a morality of consequences. Such distinctions are major philosophical topics, of course, and most nonphilosophers won't be in a position to enter into high-level philosophical discussions. But there are both nonphilosophers who are quite capable of following such discussions and philosophers who enter public debates about relevant topics.

The perennial objection to any appeal to philosophy is that philosophers disagree among themselves about everything, so that there is no body of philosophical knowledge on which nonphilosophers can rely. It's true that philosophers do not agree on answers to the "big questions" like God's existence, free will, the nature of moral obligation, and so on. But they do agree about many logical interconnections and conceptual distinctions that are essential for thinking clearly about the big questions. Some examples: thinking about God and evil requires the key distinction between evil that is gratuitous (not necessary for some greater good) and evil that is not gratuitous; thinking about free will requires the distinction between a choice's being caused and its being compelled; and thinking about morality requires the distinction between an action that is intrinsically wrong (regardless of its consequences) and one that is wrong simply because of its consequences. Such distinctions arise from philosophical thinking, and philosophers know a great deal about how to understand and employ them. In this important sense, there is a body of philosophical knowledge on which nonphilosophers can and should rely.

JANUARY 25, 2012

In the Cave: Philosophy and Addiction

—Peg O'Connor

I INTRODUCE THE NOTION OF ADDICTION AS A SUBJECT OF PHILO-sophical inquiry here for a reason. I am a philosopher, yes, but I am also an alcoholic who has been sober for more than twenty-four years—only the last four of them as part of a recovery program. I am often asked how I got and stayed sober for those first nineteen years; it was because of philosophy, which engendered in me a commitment to living an examined life and gave me the tools and concepts to do so. My training in moral philosophy made it natural for me to wrestle with issues of character, responsibility, freedom, care and compassion in both work and life.

Philosophy has always been about the pursuit of knowledge, but one that included the higher aim of living a good and just life. This pursuit has involved examining the nature of just about everything. Socrates's guiding question was, "What is it?" The "it" in question could be justice, piety, beauty, courage, temperance, or knowledge. For Socrates, these are the crucial virtues around which life should turn. Socrates's agenda was to draw the line between what appears to be just or pious and what justice or piety really is. In the person of Socrates, Plato provides the powerful tools of conceptual analysis and allegory that can be fruitfully applied to the questions about addiction.

In his pursuit of knowledge about the nature of virtues, Socrates first had to debunk popular opinions about them. The debunking took the form of a dialogue but in reality more closely resembled a cross examination. Socrates looked for the essence, necessary property or ineliminable trait that made particular acts pious or just. Socrates interrogated every definition offered to him by asking for examples, pushing and pulling against those definitions, turning them inside out and upside down, stretching that definition to see if weird things followed, exploring what follows when a particular definition is put into practice and excavating hidden assumptions behind those definitions.

This isn't exactly glamorous work, but it is vital in the pursuit of knowledge of any sort. This kind of work prompted the seventeenth-century philosopher John Locke to describe himself as an under-laborer, clearing away the rubbish that gets in the way of acquiring knowledge. We now call this work conceptual analysis, one of the most powerful tools a philosopher has to wield.

How might philosophy approach or provide us with a better understanding of addiction? Socrates would ask, "What is it?" He would not be alone. Psychiatrists, psychologists, chemical dependency counselors and people in recovery programs the world over are constantly asking this question. Neuroscientists have now entered the fray, searching for both the cause and effective management of addiction. Yet there is no consensus. Defining addiction remains an area of heated debate.

Yet despite differences of opinion, most of us can recognize—and through recognition, perhaps better understand—certain behaviors and situations in which "normal" use of alcohol or other drugs turns to destructive dependency.

A sort of recognition may be found in examining allegory—in this case, a very familiar one from Plato. Allegory—a story that functions as an extended metaphor and has both literal and figurative meanings—is clearly not science. But it does offer the potential for a sort of insight that conceptual analysis cannot. An allegory allows us to unpack many of those dimensions that escape more scientific description. With the cave allegory that Plato offers in *The Republic* to draw the line between appearance and reality, we have a potentially powerful tool for understanding the crisis of the addicted person. Briefly, Plato's allegory is this:

There is a cave in which prisoners are chained facing a wall. They cannot move their heads and therefore cannot look sideways or behind; they only can look forward. Behind them are a burning fire and a half wall where puppeteers hold up puppets that cast shadows. To the chained men, the shadows are real; they have no conception of the objects that cause shadows. Appearance is mistaken for reality, and thus there is no real knowledge.

Now imagine that the prisoners are released from their chains. They look behind them and see the objects that caused the shadows. Most likely they will be confused and horrified and unwilling to accept that these objects caused the shadows. Imagine now that the prisoners start to leave the cave. They will be painfully blinded as soon as they encounter light. Once their eyes begin to adjust, they will be confronted by a harsh bright world with a whole host of horrifying objects. Some of the men will flee back to the safety of the darkness and shadows, valuing the familiar more highly than the unfamiliar. Anyone who returns and tells his friends who are still enchained what he has seen will be regarded as a nut lacking any credibility. Other men, once their eyes have more fully adjusted to the light, will want to stay above ground. Such people come to realize that world of light is the real one where genuine knowledge is possible. One further point to consider: some of the people who have seen the light of truth and reality need to go into the cave to help those who are still enchained to leave the cave. This is the philosopher's burden, according to Plato.

This allegory is richly wonderful for understanding addiction, relapse and recovery. Most people who become addicted become enchained to their drug of choice. The word *addiction* comes from the Latin verb *addicere*, which means to give over, dedicate, or surrender. In the case of many alcoholics, for instance, including my own, this is just what happens. What had perhaps started as fun and harmless use begins to grow troubling, painful and difficult to stop. The alcoholic becomes chained to alcohol in a way different from others who "drink normally."

In various scenarios of addiction, the addicted person's fixation on a shadow reality—one that does not conform to the world outside his or her use—is apparent to others. When the personal cost of drinking or drug use becomes noticeable, it can still be written off or excused as merely atypical. Addicts tend to orient their activities around their addictive behavior; they may forego friends and activities where drinking or drug use is not featured. Some may isolate themselves; others may change their circle of friends in order to be with people who drink or use in the same way they do. They engage in faulty yet persuasive alcoholic reasoning, willing to take anything as evidence that they do not have a problem; no amount of reasoning will persuade them otherwise. Each time the addict makes a promise to cut down or stop but does not, the chains get more constricting.

Yet for many reasons, some people begin to wriggle against the chains of addiction. Whether it is because they have experiences that scare them to death (not uncommon) or lose something that really matters (also not uncommon), some people begin to work themselves out of the chains. People whose descent into addiction came later in life have more memories of what life can be like sober. Some will be able to turn and see the fire and the half wall and recognize the puppets causing the shadows. Those whose use started so young that it is all they really know will often experience the fear and confusion that Plato described. But as sometimes happens in recovery, they can start to come out of the cave, too.

The brightness of the light can be painful, as many alcoholic- or drug-dependent people realize once their use stops. Those who drank or used drugs to numb feelings or avoid painful memories may feel defenseless. This is why they will retreat back to the familiar darkness of the cave. Back with their drinking friends, they will find comfort. This is one way to understand relapse.

Others will make it farther out of the cave and have their eyes adjust. They will struggle to stay sober and balanced. So many of their old coping behaviors will not work, and they are faced with a seemingly endless task of learning how to rebuild their emotional lives. Some will stay clean and sober for a good while and later relapse. People relapse for all sorts of reasons, and often these have to do with old patterned ways of thinking and behaving that make a roaring comeback. When people who have had some sobriety relapse and go back to the darkness of the cave, they may be met with derision—an "I told you so" attitude.

Those who do make it out of the cave and manage never to relapse again are few and far between. They know just how precarious their sobriety is and what they need to do to maintain it. People with long-term sobriety are often the ones who need to go back down into the cave, not as saviors, but for their own survival. People with years of sobriety often say that newcomers help them to stay sober because their pain, loss, and confusion are so fresh. Their stories remind old timers of enchained life in the cave. Old-timers can share their stories, too, and in the process show them different ways to be in the world.

Of course, our stories are real and deeply personal, but like allegories they can wield a transformative power. Transformation can come from many sources, including some of the earliest and most profound investigations in philosophy. Plato's cave, Montaigne's cat, Kierkegaard's leap of faith, Nietzsche's myth of eternal recurrence, Wittgenstein's fly in the fly bottle, and feminist conceptions of self-identity—to name but a few—are ready companions in the pursuit to understand the complexities of addiction, relapse and recovery.

JANUARY 8, 2012

Women in Philosophy? Do the Math

—Sally Haslanger

MANY OF US HAVE HAD THE EXPERIENCE OF SITTING ON AN AIRplane and being asked by the person in the next seat, "What do you do?"

It is a moment of uncertainty: What to say? There are risks if you reply, "I'm a philosopher," for you may then have the neighbor expounding "their philosophy" at length, or recounting how awful their experience was when taking Philosophy 101. ("We read some crazy article about being kidnapped and hooked up to a famous violinist to keep him alive!") One time, a male friend of mine got the enthusiastic response, "Oh, you're a philosopher? Tell me some of your sayings!" However, when I've tried the "I'm a philosopher" reply, it has prompted laughter. Once when I queried why the laughter, the response was, "I think of philosophers as old men with beards, and you're definitely not that! You're too young and attractive to be a philosopher." I'm sure he intended this as a compliment. But I stopped giving the answer "I'm a philosopher."

Although most philosophers these days are not old men with beards, most professional philosophers are men; in fact, white men. It is a surprise to almost everyone that the percentage of women earning philosophy doctorates is less than in most of the physical sciences. As recently as 2010, philosophy had a lower percentage of women doctorates than math, chemistry, and economics. Note, however, that of these fields, philosophy has made the most progress on this count in the past five years.

The percentage of women philosophers in the faculty ranks is much more difficult to determine. Although for decades the American Philosophical Association's Committee on the Status of Women lobbied the association to collect demographic data, it failed to do so. We have mostly relied on the efforts of individuals to do head counts. The best data we have suggests that in 2011, the tenured/tenure-track faculty in the fifty-one graduate programs ranked by the Leiter Report—the most widely used status ranking of Anglophone philosophy departments—included only 21.9 percent women.

This is potentially quite misleading, however, for the Digest of Education Statistics reports that in 2003 (the most recent data compiled for philosophy), the percentage of women in full-time instructional postsecondary positions was a mere 16.6 percent of the total thirteen thousand philosophers, a year when 27.1 percent of the doctorates went to women. Soon we will know more, however, for the APA has thankfully started to collect demographic data.

The numbers of philosophers of color, especially women of color, is even more appalling. The 2003 number of 16.6 percent full-time women philosophy instructors includes *zero* women of color. Apparently there was insufficient data for any racial group of women other than white women to report. The APA Committee on the Status of Black Philosophers and the Society of Young Black Philosophers report that currently in the United States there are 156 blacks in philosophy, including doctoral students and philosophy PhDs in academic positions; this includes a total of 55 black women, 31 of whom hold tenured or tenure-track positions. Assuming that there are still 13,000 full-time philosophy instructors in the United States, the representation of scholars of color is plausibly worse than in *any other field in the academy*, including not only physics, but also engineering. Inexcusable.

With these numbers, you don't need sexual harassment or racial harassment to prevent women and minorities from succeeding, for alienation, loneliness, implicit bias, stereotype threat, microaggression, and outright discrimination will do the job. But in a world of such small numbers, harassment and bullying is easy.

"Bad actors" are a problem, but the deeper problem is the context that gives "bad actors" power. Change needs to happen on multiple fronts for us to make progress. Philosophy lacks the infrastructure that other disciplines have to bring about systematic change. We don't have the funding or the clout of anything like the National Science Foundation.

We do have a small community of feminist and antiracist activists and some important recent changes in the governance of the APA—like the appointment of a new executive director, Amy Ferrer, who not only has a strong background in nonprofit administration, but also a degree in women's studies. The McGinn case is a tipping point, not because it has taken down someone with great power and influence, but because his case and the response to it demonstrates that the persistent activism of the past twenty years is becoming institutionalized. We are the winning side now. We will not relent, so it is only a matter of time.

SEPTEMBER 2, 2013

What's Wrong With Philosophy?

—Linda Martín Alcoff

Wнат is wrong with philosophy?

This is the question posed to me by journalists last year while I served as president of the American Philosophical Association, Eastern Division. Why is philosophy so far behind every other humanities department in the diversity of its faculty? Why are its percentages of women and people of color (an intersecting set) so out of tune with the country, even with higher education? What *is* wrong with philosophy?

And now our field has another newsworthy event: the claims of sexual harassment against the influential philosopher Colin McGinn and his subsequent resignation, a story that made the front page of *The New York Times*. Here is a leading philosopher of language unable to discern how sexual banter becomes sexual pressure when it is repetitively parlayed from a powerful professor to his young female assistant. It might lead one to wonder, what is wrong with the field of philosophy of language?

McGinn defended himself by deflecting blame. The student, he argued, simply did not understand enough philosophy of language to get the harmlessness of his jokes. He did not intend harm, nor did his statements logically entail harm; therefore, her sense of harm is on her.

Alas, McGinn's self-defense echoes a common narrative in the discipline concerning its demographic challenges. As the *Times* article reports, and the philosophy blogosphere will confirm, the paucity in philosophy of women and people of color is often blamed on us. Some suggest it is philosophy's "rough and tumble" style of debate that has turned us women and nonwhite males away. Logical implication: we may just not be cut out for such a demanding field.

ONCE IN GRADUATE SCHOOL, I ventured to raise a series of skeptical questions to one of the most world-renowned philosophers, Roderick Chisholm, in his seminar on the theory of knowledge. I leaned toward American pragmatism and Wittgenstein—he was a famous foundationalist. He wiped the floor with me, turning my questions to mush and getting a good laugh from the class. This did not surprise me, but what did was that, the next day, Chisholm approached me in the student lounge and asked me gently if I was OK. I answered, "Yes, of course," which was the truth.

I had observed Chisholm's pedagogical style for two years, and I knew his capacity to turn a student's dissenting opinion into a Jell-O mold of quivering meaninglessness, to the class's mirth. I admired his abilities. But I still wanted to see how he would respond to my specific questions. Despite his jokes, one could garner from his response to my questions a substantive philosophical rejoinder. It was a perfectly legitimate philosophical exchange, livened up a bit to keep his students awake.

Chisholm was typical of the best philosophers of his day and ours in his combination of philosophical acumen and rhetorical skill. Yet he was atypical at that time in his sensitivity to the practical contexts of the argumentative arena. He had enough respect for me to treat me like all other disputants, but also to want me to stay in the game. As one of two women in the class, he was aware I might be experiencing an alienation-induced anxiety about my public performance.

The issue is not debate, simpliciter, but how it is done. Too many philosophers accept the idea that truth is best achieved by a marketplace of ideas conducted in the fashion of ultimate fighting. But aggressive styles that seek easy victories by harping on arcane counterexamples do not maximize truth. Nor does making use of the social advantages one might have by virtue of one's gender, ethnicity or seniority. Nor does stubbornly refusing to acknowledge the real world contexts, rife with implicit bias and power distortions, in which even philosophical debates always occur.

Sometimes, interestingly, the aim of truth is enhanced less by adversarial argument than by a receptivity that holds back on disagreement long enough to try out the new ideas on offer, push them further, see where they might go. Sometimes pedagogy works best not by challenging but by getting on board a student's own agenda. Sometimes understanding is best reached when we expend our skeptical faculties, as Montaigne did, on our own beliefs, our own opinions. If debate is meant to be a means to truth—an idea we philosophers like to believe—the best forms turn out to be a variegated rather than uniform set.

The demographic challenges of philosophy cannot be blamed on the supposed deficiencies of the minority. Unlike Professor Chisholm, McGinn did not check in with his student but continued to lace his e-mails with sexual innuendo, if not propositions. Women who have had this experience in the discipline (me and nearly everyone I know) can be discomfited by the thought that their professor's intellectual praise is strategically motivated, designed with an intent other than the truth. It can throw their confidence and certainly disable debate. Which may, of course, be quite intentional.

SEPTEMBER 3, 2013

The Disappearing Women

—Rae Langton

"HOW MANY PHILOSOPHERS DOES IT TAKE TO CHANGE A LIGHT bulb?"

"It depends what you mean by 'change' . . ."

That joke pokes gentle fun at a popular caricature: the chin-stroking graybeard, with his fetish for word meanings, his practical irrelevance and his philosophy that "leaves everything as it is," as Wittgenstein said. The caricature is misleading, for philosophy also prides itself on its capacity to ask hard questions and challenge prejudice. Socrates was executed for stirring up trouble. Descartes began his *Meditations* with a rousing call to "demolish completely" a long-standing edifice of falsehoods—to uproot our "habit of holding on to old opinions" and look at the world with fresh, unbiased eyes.

That radical power has inspired many women in philosophy, and much political work. The English philosopher Mary Astell wrote irreverently, in 1700, that an opinion's age is no guide to its truth, that "a rational mind" is not made for servitude, and that a woman's obligation to a man "is only a Business by the Bye"—"just as it may be any Man's Business and Duty to keep Hogs." From Descartes's idea that we are *essentially thinking beings* she deduced a conclusion too daring for her peers: *colleges for women.* Husband-keeping is like hog-keeping: a contingent duty, not what a woman is made for.

Many women have, like Astell, found in philosophy a source of joyful challenge and liberation, fascinating in its own terms, with illuminating consequences for life and the social world. Given philosophy's ambitions, we might fondly expect a profession especially free from bias and welcoming to those targeted by prejudice. That hope is somewhat hard to square with its dearth of women.

There are many possible explanations. Bias is harder to notice than Descartes expected, being unconscious, near-universal and more readily revealed in the psychologist's lab than by the "natural light of reason."

There is the effort of juggling work and family life (but why philosophy, more than other disciplines?) There are startling reports of sexual harassment, at the website What Is It Like to Be a Woman in Philosophy (Worse than other fields? Who knows, but it should be *better*!). Some have looked to gender norms for an explanation, supposing that if "men are from Mars," they thrive better in our martial debating culture (but why philosophy, more than economics?). Some have, more plausibly, invoked a "perfect storm" of diverse factors (see Louise Antony's article) "Different Voices or Perfect Storm: Why Are There So Few Women in Philosophy?").

That caricature of Philosophy must be partly to blame: the "man of reason" pictured as a serious, high-minded Dumbledore (for some nice correctives, see the site Looks Philosophical). When a field is group stereotyped, outsiders often feel less welcome. They often perform less well when something triggers group awareness. Stereotype threat can make anyone, from white athletes to black students, underperform, when appropriately primed. Philosophy itself may be a source of priming influence, with its mostly male lineup for reading lists, conferences and teachers (see Jennifer Saul's work on the psychological biases affecting philosophy).

Philosophy is often introduced through its history, beginning with Socrates, who banished the weeping women, as prelude to the real business of philosophizing. Other banishments followed, so it can be tempting to see an unbroken all-male succession, as course lists (including my own) still testify. That part, too, is misleading. Princess Elisabeth of Bohemia, in her notable correspondence with Descartes, offered the most enduring objection to Descartes's dualism: How can immaterial mind and material body interact? She is puzzlingly absent from standard editions that include his contemporary critics. Maria von Herbert provoked a deep question for Kant: Is moral perfection compatible with utter apathy? She is puzzlingly absent from the latest Kant biography, and her letters survive elsewhere for their gossip value (sex! suicide!). With omissions like these we let down philosophers of past, present and future. We feed the stereotype and the biases Descartes despised.

One more joke, then: "How many feminists does it take to change a light bulb?"

"It's not the light bulb that needs changing."

SEPTEMBER 4, 2013

The Difficulty of Philosophy

—Alexander George

ONE OFTEN HEARS THE LAMENT, WHY HAS PHILOSOPHY BECOME so remote? Why has it lost contact with people?

The complaint must be as old as philosophy itself. In Aristophanes's *Clouds*, we meet Socrates as he is being lowered to the stage in a basket. His first words are impatient and distant: "Why do you summon me, O creature of a day?" He goes on to explain pompously what he was doing before he was interrupted: "I tread the air and scrutinize the sun." Already in ancient Greece, philosophy had a reputation for being troublesomely distant from the concerns that launch it.

Is the complaint justified, however? On the face of it, it would seem not to be. I run AskPhilosophers.org, a website that features questions from the general public and responses by a panel of professional philosophers. The questions are sent by people at all stages of life: from the elderly wondering when to forgo medical intervention to successful professionals asking why they should care about life at all, from teenagers inquiring whether it is irrational to fear aging to ten-year-olds wanting to know what the opposite of a lion is. The responses from philosophers have been humorous, kind, clear, and at the same time sophisticated, penetrating, and informed by the riches of the philosophical traditions in which they were trained. The site has evidently struck a chord as we have by now posted thousands of entries, and the questions continue to arrive daily from around the world. Clearly, philosophers can—and do—respond to philosophical questions in intelligible and helpful ways.

But admittedly, this is casual stuff. And at the source of the lament is the perception that philosophers, when left to their own devices, produce writings and teach classes that are either unhappily narrow or impenetrably abstruse. Full-throttle philosophical thought often appears far removed from, and so much more difficult than, the questions that provoke it.

It certainly doesn't help that philosophy is rarely taught or read in schools. Despite the fact that children have an intense interest in philosophical issues, and that a training in philosophy sharpens one's analytical abilities, with few exceptions our schools are de-philosophized zones. This has as a knock-on effect that students entering college shy away from philosophy courses. Bookstores—those that remain—boast philosophy sections cluttered with self-help guides. It is no wonder that the educated public shows no interest in, or perhaps even finds alien, the fully ripened fruits of philosophy.

While all this surely contributes to the felt remoteness of philosophy, it is also a product of it: for one reason why philosophy is not taught in schools is that it is judged irrelevant. And so we return to the questions of why philosophy appears so removed and whether this is something to lament.

This situation seems particular to philosophy. We do not find physicists reproached in the same fashion. People are not typically frustrated when their questions about the trajectory of soccer balls get answered by appeal to Newton's laws and differential calculus.

The difference persists in part because to wonder about philosophical issues is an occupational hazard of being human in a way in which wondering about falling balls is not. Philosophical questions can present themselves to us with an immediacy, even an urgency, that can seem to demand a correspondingly accessible answer. High philosophy usually fails to deliver such accessibility—and so the dismay that borders on a sense of betrayal.

Must it be so? To some degree, yes. Philosophy may begin in wonder, as Plato suggested in the *Theaetetus*, but it doesn't end there. Philosophers will never be content merely to catalog wonders, but will want to illuminate them—and whatever kind of work that involves will surely strike some as air treading.

But how high into the air must one travel? How theoretical, or difficult, need philosophy be? Philosophers disagree about this, and the history of philosophy has thrown up many competing conceptions of what philosophy should be. The dominant conception today, at least in the United States, looks to the sciences for a model of rigor and explanation. Many philosophers now conceive of themselves as more like discovery-seeking scientists than anything else, and they view the great figures in the history of philosophy as likewise "scientists in search of an organized conception of reality," as W. V. Quine, the leading American philosopher of the twentieth century, once put it. For many, science not only provides us with information that might be pertinent to answering philosophical questions, but also with exemplars of what successful answers look like.

Because philosophers today are often trained to think of philosophy as continuous with science, they are inclined to be impatient with expectations of greater accessibility. Yes, philosophy does begin in wonder, such philosophers will agree. But if one is not content to be a wonder-monger, if one seeks illumination, then one must uncover abstract, general principles through the development of a theoretical framework.

This search for underlying, unifying principles may lead into unfamiliar, even alien, landscapes. But such philosophers will be undaunted, convinced that the correct philosophical account will often depend on an unobvious discovery visible only from a certain level of abstraction. This view is actually akin to the conception advanced by Aristophanes's Socrates when he defends his airborne inquiries: "If I had been on the ground and from down there contemplated what's up here, I would have made no discoveries at all." The resounding success of modern science has strengthened the attraction of an approach to explanation that has always had a deep hold on philosophers.

But the history of philosophy offers other conceptions of illumination. Some philosophers will not accept that insight demands the discovery of unsuspected general principles. They are instead sympathetic to David Hume's dismissal, over 250 years ago, of remote speculations in ethics: "New discoveries are not to be expected in these matters," he said. Ludwig Wittgenstein took this approach across the board when he urged that "the problems [in philosophy] are solved, not by giving new information, but by arranging what we have always known." He was interested in philosophy as an inquiry into "what is possible *before* all new discoveries and inventions," and insisted that "if one tried to advance *theses* in philosophy, it would never be possible to debate them, because everyone would agree to them." Insight is to be achieved not by digging below the surface, but rather by organizing what is before us in an illuminatingly perspicuous manner.

The approach that involves the search for "new discoveries" of a theoretical nature is now ascendant. Since the fruits of this kind of work, even when conveyed in the clearest of terms, can well be remote and difficult, we have here another ingredient of the sense that philosophy spends too much time scrutinizing the sun.

Which is the correct conception of philosophical inquiry? Philosophy is the only activity such that to pursue questions about the nature of that activity is to engage in it. We can certainly ask what we are about when doing mathematics or biology or history—but to ask those questions is no longer to do mathematics or biology or history. One cannot, however, reflect on the nature of philosophy without doing philosophy. Indeed, the question of what we ought to be doing when engaged in this strange activity is one that has been wrestled with by many great philosophers throughout philosophy's long history.

Questions, therefore, about philosophy's remove cannot really be addressed without doing philosophy. In particular, the question of how difficult philosophy ought to be, or the kind of difficulty it ought to have, is itself a philosophical question. In order to answer it, we need to philosophize—even though the nature of that activity is precisely what puzzles us.

And that, of course, is another way in which philosophy can be difficult.

The Philosophical Dinner Party

—Frieda Klotz

WHAT IS THE MEANING OF LIFE? IS THERE A GOD? DOES THE human race have a future? The standard perception of philosophy is that it poses questions that are often esoteric and almost always daunting. So another pertinent question, and one implicitly raised by Alexander George's essay "The Difficulty of Philosophy," is, Can philosophy ever be fun?

Philosophy was a way of life for ancient philosophers, as much as a theoretical study—from Diogenes the Cynic masturbating in public ("I wish I could cure my hunger as easily" he replied, when challenged) to Marcus Aurelius obsessively transcribing and annotating his thoughts—and its practitioners didn't mind amusing people or causing public outrage to bring attention to their message. Divisions between academic and practical philosophy have long existed, for sure, but even Plato, who was prolific on theoretical matters, may have tried to translate philosophy into action: ancient rumor has it that he traveled to Sicily to tutor first Dionysios I, king of Syracuse, and later his son (each ruler fell out with Plato and unceremoniously sent him home).

For at least one ancient philosopher, the love of wisdom was not only meant to be practical, but also to combine "fun with serious effort." This is the definition of Plutarch, a Greek who lived in the post-Classical age of the second century AD, a time when philosophy tended to focus on ethics and morals. Plutarch is better known as a biographer than a philosopher. A priest, politician, and Middle Platonist who lived in Greece under Roman rule, he wrote parallel lives of Greeks and Romans, from which Shakespeare borrowed liberally and Emerson rapturously described as "a bible for heroes." At the start and end of each "life" he composed a brief moral essay, comparing the faults and virtues of his subjects. Although artfully written, the *Lives* is really little more than brilliant realizations of Plutarch's own very practical take on philosophy, aimed at teaching readers how to live.

Plutarch thought philosophy should be taught at dinner parties. It should be taught through literature, or written in letters giving advice to friends. Good philosophy does not occur in isolation; it is about friendship, inherently social and shared. The philosopher should engage in politics, and he should be busy, for he knows, as Plutarch sternly puts it, that idleness is no remedy for distress.

Many of Plutarch's works are concerned with showing readers how to deal better with their day-to-day circumstances. In Plutarch's eyes, the philosopher is a man who sprinkles seriousness into a silly conversation; he gives advice and offers counsel but prefers a discussion to a conversation-hogging monologue. He likes to exchange ideas but does not enjoy aggressive arguments. And if someone at his dinner table seems timid or reserved, he's more than happy to add some extra wine to the shy guest's cup.

He outlined this benign doctrine over the course of more than eighty moral essays (far less often read than the *Lives*). Several of his texts offer two interpretive tiers—advice on philosophical behavior for less educated readers, and a call to further learning for those who would want more. It's intriguing to see that the guidance he came up with has much in common with what we now call cognitive behavioral therapy. Writing on the subject of contentment, he tells his public: Change your attitudes! Think positive nongloomy thoughts! If you don't get a raise or a promotion, remember that means you'll have less work to do. He points out that "there are storm winds that vex both the rich and the poor, both married and single."

In one treatise, aptly called "Table Talks," Plutarch gives an account of the dinner parties he attended with his friends during his lifetime. Over innumerable jugs of wine they grapple with ninety-five topics, covering science, medicine, social etiquette, women, alcohol, food and literature: When is the best time to have sex? Did Alexander the Great really drink too much? Should a host seat his guests or allow them to seat themselves? Why are old men very fond of strong wine? And, rather obscurely, why do women not eat the heart of lettuce? (This last, sadly, is fragmentary and thus unanswered.) Some of the questions point to broader issues, but there is plenty of gossip and philosophical loose talk.

Plutarch begins "Table Talks" by asking his own philosophical question: Is philosophy a suitable topic of conversation at a dinner party? The answer is yes, not just because Plato's "Symposium" is a central philosophic text (*symposium* being Greek for "drinking party"); it's because philosophy is about conducting oneself in a certain way—the philosopher knows that men "practice philosophy when they are silent, when they jest, even, by Zeus! when they are the butt of jokes and when they make fun of others."

Precisely because of its eclecticism and the practical nature of his treatises, Plutarch's work is often looked down on in the academic world, and even Emerson said he was "without any supreme intellectual gifts," adding, "He is not a profound mind . . . not a metaphysician like Parmenides, Plato or Aristotle." When we think of the lives of ancient philosophers, we're far more likely to think of Socrates, condemned to death by the Athenians and drinking hemlock, than of Plutarch, a Greek living happily with Roman rule, quaffing wine with his friends.

Yet in our own time-poor age, with anxieties shifting from economic meltdowns to oil spills to daily stress, it's now more than ever that we need philosophy of the everyday sort. In the Plutarchan sense, friendship, parties and even wine are not trivial; and while philosophy may indeed be difficult, we shouldn't forget that it should be fun.

When Socrates Met Phaedrus: Eros in Philosophy

—Simon Critchley

CRAZY HOT

LET ME SET THE SCENE. IT'S HOT. IT'S REALLY HOT. IT'S THE middle of the Greek summer. Socrates is in Athens where he bumps into an acquaintance called Phaedrus. They say hi. They begin to talk.

Phaedrus is a little excited. He has just heard what he thinks is an amazing speech on love—eros—by the orator Lysias. For the ancient Greeks, eros denoted both sexual pleasure and the name of a god— that is, love has both physical and metaphysical aspects.

Socrates persuades Phaedrus to read him the speech (he has a copy hidden under his cloak). After a long morning listening to speeches, Phaedrus is eager to stretch his legs, and Socrates agrees to accompany him on a stroll out of the city. What is remarkable is that this is the only time in all the Platonic dialogues that Socrates leaves the city of Athens. He is no nature boy. Trees have nothing to teach him.

Indeed, the climate influences this dialogue more than any other text by Plato that I know. Such is the heat of eros described by Sappho,

> *Sweat pours down me, I shake*
> *all over, I go pale as green*
> *grass. I'm that close to being dead.*

Like I said, it's hot.

The two men walk some distance along the Ilissos River. They are both barefoot and walk in the water. Sweat pours down their faces. They decide to sit down by the banks of the river in the shade of a broad-leaved plane tree—in Greek, a *platanos*. A Plato-tree. It is hardly mere accident that the shade that provides the shelter for the dialogue is broad-shouldered Plato—from *platus*, meaning broad— the tree in which cicadas sing.

Socrates tells a story about the cicadas. Because they were so enthused by the Muses, cicadas sing constantly, stopping for neither food nor drink until they die. If cicadas are inspired by the Muses, Socrates suggests, then philosophers should be inspired by cicadas. The difference between philosophers and cicadas is that the former don't sing so beautifully or so constantly . . . although they do get to live a little longer.

Lounging under a tree by the river, Phaedrus remarks that Socrates appears "to be totally out of place." In leaving the city, Socrates seems to leave himself behind, to become beside himself, to become ecstatic, indeed a little manic. Love, or what the Greeks call *eros*, as Socrates insists, is "manike," a madness. It's crazy hot.

EROS IS A FORCE

What is eros? More specifically, what is the eros of philosophy and the philosopher? We commonly understand it to be a force that compels physical love, but we might also speculate as to whether eros is a force that compels philosophy, a force that is somehow outside the self, but toward which the soul can incline itself, what Socrates calls a god, a force that perhaps even compels the philosopher to leave the cave in Plato's *Republic*. Of course, it is not at all clear how the first prisoner in the cave emancipates himself. He frees the others, but who frees him? It is unexplained in the text. Perhaps eros is the animating and primal force that shapes philosophy and moves the philosopher to break free from the cave and move toward the light.

It is peculiar indeed that the enabling condition for freedom is a force that compels: a compulsion, a necessity. Unconditional freedom appears to be conditioned by what contradicts it. Eros, in making philosophy possible, somehow turns the freedom of the philosopher inside out, back to front. It is a nice, if totally incidental, peculiarity that the numerals of this year, 2013, looked at backwards and with a slight squint spell *eros*. Perhaps we can only see eros back to front, in the form of indirect communication, like a dialogue.

PHILOSOPHY'S PRIMAL SCENE

But how are we to understand the nature of eros as it appears in Plato's *Phaedrus*? And here we approach the central enigma of the dialogue. For it appears to deal with two distinct topics: eros and rhetoric. My thought is very simple: I will try and show that these twin themes of eros and rhetoric are really one and they help explain that peculiar form of discourse that Socrates calls philosophy.

For the ancient Greeks, there was obviously a close connection between the passions or emotions, like eros, and rhetoric. We need only recall that Aristotle's discussion of the emotions is in the *Rhetoric*. Emotion was linked to rhetoric, for Aristotle, because it could influence judgment, in the legal, moral or political senses of the word.

Of course, in the Athens of Socrates's time, the two groups of people capable of stirring up powerful emotions were the tragic poets and the Sophists. Let's just say that Socrates had issues with both groups. Tragedy, again in Aristotle's sense, stirs up the emotions of pity and fear in a way that leads to their katharsis, understood as purgation or, better, purification. The Sophists exploited the link between emotion and rhetoric in order to teach the art of persuasive speech that was central to the practice of law and litigation. Classical Athens was a very litigious place but mercifully did not have lawyers. Therefore, men (and it was just men) had to defend themselves, and Sophists taught those who could pay a fee how to do it.

Socrates's inability to defend himself in the law court and how such an inability is the defining criterion of the philosopher recurs in dialogue after dialogue in the *Apology*, obviously, but with particular power in the *Theatetus*, as I tried to suggest in the very first column of The Stone in 2010. The philosopher is presented as a kind of madman or fool, like Thales, who falls into ditches because he is contemplating the stars. This is why the Thracian maid laughs. The philosopher is continually contrasted with the pettifogging citizen who speaks in the law court. Where the latter is skilled in speaking in court against the clock—the clepsydra, or water clock, that quite literally steals time—the philosopher has no sense of time and consequently takes his time, but uses it badly. The philosopher's inability to defend himself persuasively in the law court leads directly to being found guilty and sentenced to execution. Socrates's inability to defend himself leads to his death.

Such is the primal scene of philosophy. Socrates is the tragic hero whose death moves the drama off the stage of the Theater of Dionysus on the south slope of the Acropolis into the heart of the city of Athens. To understate matters somewhat, there is no obvious historical alliance between philosophy and democracy. In killing Socrates (and it is highly arguable that this was justified), Athenian democracy stands indicted.

WHO IS PHAEDRUS?

Philosophy's main question, then and now, is how might there be a true speech that refuses the corrosive effects of bad rhetoric and sophistry? This brings us back to the *Phaedrus*. The purpose of the dialogue is to arouse an emotion, specifically a philosophical eros, in the rather unphilosophical Phaedrus.

We have to be honest about Phaedrus. Who is this guy? He is not the kind of feisty, angry, and highly intelligent opponent that Socrates finds in Callicles from the *Gorgias* or even Thrasymachus from the *Republic*, let alone the superior intellect of the Stranger from the *Sophist* whose stunning dialectical ability reduces Socrates to silence.

Phaedrus is a more simple soul. We might define him as a being who lives in order to receive pleasure from listening to speeches. He is like someone nowadays who compulsively watches TED talks. So Socrates gives him that pleasure in order both to please and persuade him. Not just once, but twice. Indeed, the sheer length of Socrates's second speech on eros might arouse our suspicion, for we know from elsewhere that Socrates hates long speeches, even delivered by the most eloquent of speakers. Why is Socrates doing what he hates?

Now, I am not suggesting that Phaedrus is stupid, but he's perhaps not the brightest spark in Athens (admittedly a city with many bright sparks). There appear to be many facts of which he is unaware, and he also keeps forgetting Socrates's argument and needs constant reminders. "So it seemed," he says at one point, "but remind me again how we did it." And this occurs during a discussion of recollection versus reminding. Phaedrus forgets the argument during a discussion of memory. You get the point.

Much of Socrates's rather obvious and extended passages of irony in the dialogue also seem to pass him by completely. Occasionally, Phaedrus will burst out with something like, "Socrates, you're very good at making up stories from Egypt or wherever else you want." Phaedrus is very nice but a little bit dim.

DIRECTING THE SOUL: BAD RHETORIC AND GOOD

Rhetoric is defined by the Sophist Gorgias as inducing persuasion in the soul of the listener. But Socrates goes further and defines rhetoric as what he calls a techne psychagogia, an art of leading or directing the soul, a kind of bewitchment that holds the listener's soul spellbound. Of course, the irony here is that it is precisely in these terms that Socrates criticizes the effects of tragic poetry in the *Republic*, which is why the poets cannot be admitted into a philosophically well-ordered city.

However, Socrates's speeches in the *Phaedrus* are precisely this kind of bewitching psychagogy. Phaedrus, who loves speeches, is completely entranced. His soul is conjured by Socrates with complete success. The dialogue brings Phaedrus to love philosophy by loving philosophically.

Now, it might appear on a superficial reading that the question of eros disappears in the second half of the *Phaedrus*. But this is deceptive, for the forensic discussion of Lysias's speech on eros leads to a definition of artful or true speech. The dialogue culminates in a definition of the philosopher as the true lover or lover of truth, by which point Phaedrus is completely persuaded by Socrates.

The intention of the *Phaedrus* is thus to persuade Phaedrus. Nothing more. The purpose of the dialogue, as Alexander Nehamas has convincingly suggested, is to inflame philosophical eros in Phaedrus that gives him the ability to distinguish bad rhetoric, of the kinds found in Lysias's speech and in Socrates's first speech, from true rhetoric, of the kind found in the second speech and then analyzed in the second half of the dialogue.

What does this suggest about philosophical dialogue? I think it leads us to the view that each dialogue is radically singular, as singular as a proper name of its title. This is why the dialogue is called in Greek *Phaidros*. The dialogue is addressed to a specific and named interlocutor. It meets Phaedrus on his ground (it even walks out with him barefoot into the countryside) and brings him to philosophical eros. It meets him in his own terms—namely, in terms of his questionable estimation of the high importance of speeches. It meets him by accepting his preferences, his prejudices, his sense of what matters and then slowly turning his sophistical delight in speeches into a commitment to philosophy.

THE PURPOSE OF PHILOSOPHICAL DIALOGUE

Philosophy is addressed to a particular and existent other, not the empty personification of some particular virtue or vice (which is arguably the error of the dialogues of later philosophers like Berkeley and Hume, which can appear oddly contrived and wooden). Dialogue is the attempt to persuade that other in terms that they will understand and accept, whatever it is that they believe. Otherwise, philosophy is building castles in the air with its concepts, its systems, and its bizarre jargon, which go right over the head of someone as unphilosophical as Phaedrus.

In philosophy, we have to meet the other on their ground and in their own terms and try and bring them around, slowly, cautiously and with good humor. Socrates does not say how awful he finds Lysias's speech, and he shouldn't. It would mean that the dialogue had failed, and we should note that Platonic dialogues do sometimes fail. For example, Callicles simply refuses to play Socrates's question-and-answer game and the *Gorgias* ends up as a crazed monologue of Socrates talking to himself. Socrates doesn't always get his way.

But the *Phaedrus* is a success in that Socrates completely persuades his interlocutor. We might want to say that a philosophical dialogue is more like a case study in psychotherapy, which also sometimes fails. Such case studies might be exemplary and thereby exert a general claim, as the *Phaedrus* unquestionably does, but each dialogue is a singular and highly specific case.

PHILOSOPHY AS PERFORMANCE

Socrates specifies the conditions that any rhetoric must meet in order to be a philosophical rhetoric capable of engendering eros. If rhetoric is a kind of psychagogia, or soul leading, then a philosophical rhetoric must be based on knowledge of the nature of various kinds of soul and which sorts of speeches would appeal to which sorts of souls.

Socrates then goes on, and listen closely to his words:

> *On meeting someone he will be able to discern what he is like and make clear to himself that the person actually standing in front of him is of just this particular sort of character . . . that he must now apply speeches of such-and-such a kind in this particular way in order to secure conviction about such-and-such an issue. When he has learned all this . . . then, and only then, will he have finally mastered the art well and completely.*

Of course, this is an exquisite commentary on the very situation in which Socrates finds himself during the *Phaedrus*. He has to make his speech address "the person actually standing in front of him"—

namely, Socrates has to speak to Phaedrus in terms that he will accept "in order to secure conviction." He will have to say the right thing in the right way at the right time to the person right in front of him.

The sheer reflexivity of the *Phaedrus* is astonishing. It is not only a piece of the most beautiful writing that, in its final scene, denounces writing. It is also an enactment of the very conditions of true philosophical rhetoric theorized in the dialogue. It is the enactment of philosophical theory as a practice of dialogue. The opposite of a self-contradiction, the *Phaedrus* is a performative self-enactment of philosophy.

If eros is a force that shapes the philosopher, then rhetoric is the art by which the philosopher persuades the nonphilosopher to assume philosophical eros, to incline his or her soul toward truth. But to do this does not entail abandoning the art of rhetoric or indeed sophistry, which teaches that art, although it does so falsely. Philosophy uses true rhetoric against false rhetoric.

The subject matter of the *Phaedrus* is rhetoric, true rhetoric. Its intention is to show that veritable eros, as opposed to the kind of vulgar pederasty that Socrates criticizes and which was the Athenian specialty of the time, is both subject *to* true rhetoric and the subject *of* true rhetoric. Philosophical eros is the effect of rhetoric, of language used persuasively. To state the obvious, sometimes it succeeds, and sometimes it fails.

NOVEMBER 3, 2013

THE GEOGRAPHY OF PHILOSOPHY

The Enlightenment's "Race" Problem, and Ours

—Justin E. H. Smith

IN 1734, ANTON WILHELM AMO, A WEST AFRICAN STUDENT AND former chamber slave of Duke Anton Ulrich of Braunschweig-Wolfenbüttel, defended a philosophy dissertation at the University of Halle in Saxony, written in Latin and entitled "On the Impassivity of the Human Mind." A dedicatory letter was appended from the rector of the University of Wittenberg, Johannes Gottfried Kraus, who praised "the natural genius" of Africa, its "appreciation for learning," and its "inestimable contribution to the knowledge of human affairs" and of "divine things." Kraus placed Amo in a lineage that includes many North African Latin authors of antiquity, such as Terence, Tertullian and St. Augustine.

In the following decade, the Scottish philosopher David Hume would write, "I am apt to suspect the Negroes, and in general all other species of men to be naturally inferior to the whites. There never was any civilized nation of any other complection than white, nor even any individual eminent in action or speculation."

Hume had not heard of Amo—that much is clear. But we can also detect a tremendous difference between Hume's understanding of human capacities and that of Kraus: the author of Amo's dedicatory letter doesn't even consider the possibility of anchoring what individual human beings are capable of doing to something as arbitrary as "complection." For Kraus, Amo represents a continent and its long and distinguished history; he does not represent a "race."

Another two decades on, Immanuel Kant, considered by many to be the greatest philosopher of the modern period, would manage to let slip what is surely the greatest nonsequitur in the history of philosophy: describing a report of something seemingly intelligent that had once been said by an African, Kant dismisses it on the grounds that "this fellow was quite black from head to toe, a clear proof that what he said was stupid."

Kraus, the rector of Wittenberg, had been expressing an understanding of the nature of human diversity that was, in 1734, already in decline, soon to be thoroughly drowned out by the fundamentally racist view of human populations as dividing into a fixed set of supposedly natural, species-like kinds. This is the view lazily echoed by Hume, Kant, and so many of their contemporaries.

In his lifetime, Amo was principally known as a legal theorist. His first publication, in 1729, which has since been lost (or, one might suspect, intentionally purged), was a jurisprudential treatise, *On the Right of Moors in Europe*. Here he argues, on the basis of a reading of Roman history and law, that in antiquity "the kings of the Moors were enfeoffed by the Roman Emperor" Justinian, and that "every one of them had to obtain a royal patent from him." This meant, in Amo's view, that African kingdoms were all recognized under Roman law, and therefore all Africans in Europe have the status of visiting royal subjects with a legal protection that precludes their enslavement.

Historically, this is highly implausible, since much of the continent of Africa was unknown to Europeans at the time of Justinian. Still, Amo's understanding is remarkably different from, say, Kant's account of global history, on which black Africans stood, from the very beginning and as if by definition, beyond the pale of history and therefore led lives of no intrinsic value, lives that could only be given value through absorption into a global system dominated by Europe.

Scholars have been aware for a long time of the curious paradox of Enlightenment thought, that the supposedly universal aspiration to liberty, equality and fraternity in fact only operated within a very circumscribed universe. Equality was only ever conceived as equality among people presumed in advance to be equal, and if some person or group fell by definition outside of the circle of equality, then it was no failure to live up to this political ideal to treat them as unequal.

It would take explicitly counter-Enlightenment thinkers in the eighteenth century, such as Johann Gottfried Herder, to formulate antiracist views of human diversity. In response to Kant and other contemporaries who were positively obsessed with finding a scientific explanation for the causes of black skin, Herder pointed out that there is nothing inherently more in need of explanation here than in the case of white skin: it is an analytic mistake to presume that whiteness amounts to the default setting, so to speak, of the human species.

The question for us today is why we have chosen to stick with categories inherited from the eighteenth century, the century of the so-called Enlightenment, which witnessed the development of the slave trade into the very foundation of the global economy, and at the same time saw racial classifications congeal into pseudobiological kinds, piggybacking on the division folk science had always made across the natural world of plants and animals. Why, that is, have we chosen to go with Hume and Kant, rather than with the preracial conception of humanity espoused by Kraus, or the antiracial picture that Herder offered in opposition to his contemporaries?

Many who are fully prepared to acknowledge that there are no significant natural differences between races nonetheless argue that there are certain respects in which it is worth retaining the concept of race: for instance, in talking about issues like social inequality or access to health care. There is, they argue, a certain pragmatic utility in retaining it, even if they acknowledge that racial categories result from social and historical legacies, rather than being dictated by nature. In this respect "race" has turned out to be a very different sort of social construction than, say, "witch" or "lunatic." While generally there is a presumption that to catch out some entity or category as socially constructed is at the same time to condemn it, many thinkers are prepared to simultaneously acknowledge both the nonnaturalness of race as well as a certain pragmatic utility in retaining it.

Since the mid-twentieth century, no mainstream scientist has considered race a biologically significant category; no scientist believes any longer that "Negroid," "Caucasoid," and so on represent real natural kinds or categories.* For several decades it has been well established that there is as much genetic variation between two members of any supposed race as between two members of supposedly distinct races. This is not to say that there are no real differences, some of which are externally observable, between different human populations. It is only to say, as Lawrence Hirschfeld wrote in his 1996 book, *Race in the Making: Cognition, Culture, and the Child's Construction of Human Kinds*, that "races as socially defined do not (even loosely) capture interesting clusters of these differences."

Yet the category of race continues to be deployed in a vast number of contexts, and certainly not just by racists, but by ardent antiracists as well, and by everyone in between. The history of race, then, is not like the history of, say, witches: a group that is shown not to exist and that accordingly proceeds to go away. Why is this?

Philosophers disagree. Kwame Anthony Appiah identifies himself as a racial skeptic to the extent that the biological categories to which racial terms refer have been shown not to exist. Yet at the same time he acknowledges that the adoption of "racial identities" may often be socially expedient, and even unavoidable, for members of perceived racial minorities. Ron Mallon has in turn distinguished between metaphysical views of race on the one hand, which make it out to describe really existent kinds, and normative views on the other, which take race to be useful in some way or other, but not real. Mallon divides the latter into "eliminativist" and "conservationist" camps, supposing, variously, that the concept can only be put to bad uses and must be got rid of, or that some of its uses are worth holding onto. On his scheme, one

---

*This is not to deny that there are limited contexts in which self-reporting of "racial" identity may be informative in a local or regional context. It is indeed helpful for a doctor to know, within the context of the American health-care system, the "race" of a patient. What it does mean to say that race is no longer a legitimate scientific category is that this limited, contextual helpfulness tells us *nothing* about a natural kind or real subdivision of the human species. The category of "race" can be useful in a local, medical context to the extent that it often correlates with other, useful information about tendencies within a given population. But this population need not be conceptualized in terms of race. Race is a dummy variable here, but not of interest as such.

may very well coherently remain metaphysically antirealist about race but still defend the conservation of the concept on normative grounds.

But given that we now know that the identity groups in modern multicultural states are plainly constituted on ethno-linguistic and cultural grounds, rather than on biological-essential grounds, it remains unclear why we should not allow a concept such as "culture" or "ethnie" to do the semantic work for us that until now we have allowed the historically tainted and misleading concept of "race" to do. We have alternative ways of speaking of human diversity available to us, some of which are on vivid display in Amo's early life and work, and which focus on rather more interesting features of different human groups than their superficial phenotypic traits.

It is American culture that is principally responsible for the perpetuation of the concept of race well after its loss of scientific respectability by the mid-twentieth century. Even the most well-meaning attempts to grapple with the persistence of inequality between "blacks" and "whites" in American society take it for granted at the outset that racial categories adequately capture the relevant differences under investigation (see, for example, Thomas B. Edsall's recent column, "The Persistence of Racial Resentment"). This may have something to do with the fact that the two broad cultural-historical groupings of people in this country, which we call "white" and "black" and which have been constituted through the complicated histories of slavery, immigration, assimilation, and exclusion, tend at their extremes to correlate with noticeably different phenotypic traits.

An African-American is likely to look more different from an American of exclusively European descent than, say, an Orthodox Serb is likely to look from a Bosnian Muslim. This creates the illusion that it is the phenotypic difference that is causing the perception of cultural-historical distinctness, along with the injustice and inequality that has gone along with this distinctness. This also creates the illusion of American uniqueness: that our history of ethnic conflict cannot be understood comparatively or in a global context, because it, unlike conflict between Serbs and Bosnian Muslims or between Tutsi and Hutu, is supposedly based on "race" rather than history, politics, and culture. But where people are living with a different historical legacy, as in much of European history prior to the high modern period hailed in by Hume and Kant, the supposedly manifest phenotypic differences between "blacks" and "whites" can easily recede into the background as irrelevant.

Amo did not meet a happy end in Germany. His original manumission and education appear to have been a strategy on the part of Duke Anton Ulrich to impress Tsar Peter the Great of Russia, who had recently adopted his own chamber slave, Abram Petrovich Gannibal, as his own son. Gannibal would go on to a career as a brilliant engineer, military strategist, and politician; Amo, for his part, would be largely abandoned by his sponsors when the geopolitical winds shifted, and Russia fell off the duke's list of priorities.

For a while the African philosopher eked out a living as a tutor in Jena and Wittenberg, and in 1747, after being made the butt of a libelous broadside accusing him of falling in love with a woman beyond his station, he returned to West Africa in disgrace. A French seafarer, David-Henri Gallandat, finds him there a few years later, and writes of meeting a man who "was very learned in astrology and astronomy, and was a great philosopher. At that time he was around 50 years old . . . He had a brother who was a slave in the colony of Suriname."

The hopefulness of the 1734 dissertation was now long behind him. It is not known when Amo died, or under what circumstances. What we can say for certain is that he would not spend his final years as a successor to Augustine and Terence, but rather in the degraded position where someone like Kant supposed he belonged: outside of history, philosophically disenfranchised and entirely defined by something as trivial as skin color.

As long as we go on speaking as if racial categories captured something real about human diversity, we are allowing the eighteenth-century legacy of Kant and Hume, which was never really anything more than an ad hoc rationalization of slavery, to define our terms for us. We are turning our backs on the legacy of Anton Wilhelm Amo, and of his European contemporaries who were prepared to judge him on his merits.

Kung Fu for Philosophers

—Peimin Ni

In a 2005 news report about the Shaolin Temple, the Buddhist monastery in China well-known for its martial arts, a monk addressed a common misunderstanding: "Many people have a misconception that martial arts is about fighting and killing," the monk was quoted as saying. "It is actually about improving your wisdom and intelligence."

Indeed, the concept of kung fu (or gongfu) is known to many in the West only through martial arts fighting films like *Enter the Dragon*, *Drunken Master*, or more recently, *Crouching Tiger, Hidden Dragon*. In the cinematic realm, skilled, acrobatic fighters like Bruce Lee, Jackie Chan and Jet Li are seen as "kung fu masters."

But as the Shaolin monk pointed out, kung fu embodies much more than fighting. In fact any ability resulting from practice and cultivation could accurately be said to embody kung fu. There is a kung fu of dancing, painting, cooking, writing, acting, making good judgments, dealing with people, even governing. During the Song and Ming dynasties in China, the term *kung fu* was widely used by the neo-Confucians, the Daoists and Buddhists alike for the art of living one's life in general, and they all unequivocally spoke of their teachings as different schools of kung fu.

This broad understanding of kung fu is a key (though by no means the only key) through which we can begin to understand traditional Chinese philosophy and the places in which it meets and departs from philosophical traditions of the West. As many scholars have pointed out, the predominant orientation of traditional Chinese philosophy is the concern about *how* to live one's life, rather than finding out the truth about reality.

The well-known question posed by Zhuangzi in the fourth century BC—was he, Zhuangzi, who had dreamt of being a butterfly or was he a butterfly dreaming he was Zhuangzi?—which pre-dated virtual reality and *The Matrix* by a couple of thousand years, was as much a kung fu inspiration as it was an epistemological query. Instead of leading to a search for certainty, as Descartes's dream did, Zhuangzi came to the realization that he had perceived "the transformation of things," indicating that one should go along with this transformation rather than trying in vain to search for what is real.

Confucius's call for "rectification of names"—one must use words appropriately—is more a kung fu method for securing sociopolitical order than for capturing the essence of things, as "names," or words, are placeholders for expectations of how the bearer of the names should behave and be treated. This points to a realization of what J. L. Austin calls the "performative" function of language. Similarly, the views of Mencius and his later opponent Xunzi's views about human nature are more recommendations of how one should view oneself in order to become a better person than metaphysical assertions about whether humans are by nature good or bad. Though each man's assertions about human nature are incompatible with each other, they may still function inside the Confucian tradition as alternative ways of cultivation.

The Buddhist doctrine of no-self surely looks metaphysical, but its real aim is to free one from suffering, since according to Buddhism suffering comes ultimately from attachment to the self. Buddhist meditations are kung fu practices to shake off one's attachment, and not just intellectual inquiries for getting propositional truth.

Mistaking the language of Chinese philosophy for, in Richard Rorty's phrase, a "mirror of nature" is like mistaking the menu for the food. The essence of kung fu—various arts and instructions about how to cultivate the person and conduct one's life—is often hard to digest for those who are used to the flavor and texture of mainstream Western philosophy. It is understandable that, even after sincere willingness to try, one is often still turned away by the lack of clear definitions of key terms and the absence of linear arguments in classic Chinese texts. This, however, is not a weakness, but rather a requirement of the kung fu orientation—not unlike the way that learning how to swim requires one to focus on practice and not on conceptual understanding. Only by going beyond conceptual descriptions of reality can one open up to the intelligence that is best exemplified through arts like dancing and performing.

This sensitivity to the style, subtle tendencies and holistic vision requires an insight similar to that needed to overcome what Jacques Derrida identified as the problem of Western logocentrism. It even expands epistemology into the nonconceptual realm in which the accessibility of knowledge is dependent on the cultivation of cognitive abilities, and not simply on whatever is "publicly observable" to everyone. It also shows that cultivation of the person is not confined to "knowing how." An exemplary person may well have the great charisma to affect others but does not necessarily know how to affect others. In the art of kung fu, there is what Herbert Fingarette calls "the magical" but "distinctively human" dimension of our practicality, a dimension that "always involves great effects produced effortlessly, marvelously, with an irresistible power that is itself intangible, invisible, unmanifest."

Pierre Hadot and Martha Nussbaum, partially as a result of the world-historical dialogue of philosophy in our time, have both tried to "rectify the name" of "philosophy" by showing that ancient Western philosophers such as Socrates, the Stoics, and the Epicureans were mainly concerned with virtue, with spiritual exercises and practices for the sake of living a good life rather than with pure theoretical endeavors. In this regard, Western philosophy at its origin is similar to classic Chinese philosophy. The significance of this point is not merely in revealing historical facts. It calls our attention to a dimension that has been eclipsed by the obsession with the search for eternal, universal truth and the way it is practiced—namely, through rational arguments. Even when philosophers take their ideas as pure theoretical discourse aimed at finding the Truth, their ideas have never stopped functioning as guides to human life. The power of modern enlightenment ideas has been demonstrated fully both in the form of great achievements we have witnessed since the modern era and in the form of profound problems we are facing today. Our modes of behavior are very much shaped by philosophical ideas that looked innocent enough to be taken for granted. It is both ironic and alarming that when Richard Rorty launched full-scale attacks on modern rationalistic philosophy, he took for granted that philosophy can only take the form of seeking for objective Truth. His rejection of philosophy falls into the same trap that he cautions people about—taking philosophical ideas merely as "mirrors" and not as "levers."

One might well consider the Chinese kung fu perspective a form of pragmatism. The proximity between the two is probably why the latter was well received in China early last century when John Dewey toured the country. What the kung fu perspective adds to the pragmatic approach, however, is its clear emphasis on the cultivation and transformation of the person, a dimension that is already in Dewey and William James but that often gets neglected. A kung fu master does not simply make good choices and use effective instruments to satisfy whatever preferences a person happens to have. In fact the subject is never simply accepted as a given. While an efficacious action may be the result of a sound rational decision, a good action that demonstrates kung fu has to be rooted in the entire person, including one's bodily dispositions and sentiments, and its goodness is displayed not only through its consequences but also in the artistic style one does it. It also brings forward what Charles Taylor calls the "background"—elements such as tradition and community—in our understanding of the formation of a person's beliefs and attitudes. Through the kung fu approach, classic Chinese philosophy displays a holistic vision that brings together these marginalized dimensions and thereby forces one to pay close attention to the ways they affect each other.

This kung fu approach shares a lot of insights with the Aristotelian virtue ethics, which focuses on the cultivation of the agent instead of on the formulation of rules of conduct. Yet unlike Aristotelian ethics, the kung fu approach to ethics does not rely on any metaphysics for justification. One does not have to believe in a predetermined *telos* for humans in order to appreciate the excellence that kung fu brings. This approach does lead to recognition of the important guiding function of metaphysical outlooks, though. For instance, a person who follows the Aristotelian metaphysics will clearly place more effort in cultivating her intelligence, whereas a person who follows the Confucian relational metaphysics will pay more attention to learning rituals that would harmonize interpersonal relations. This approach opens up the possibility of allowing multiple competing visions of excellence, including the metaphysics or religious beliefs by which they are understood and guided, and justification of these beliefs is then left to the concrete human experiences.

The kung fu approach does not entail that might is right. This is one reason why it is more appropriate to consider kung fu as a form of art. Art is not ultimately measured by its dominance of the market. In addition, the function of art is not accurate reflection of the real world; its expression is not constrained to the form of universal principles and logical reasoning, and it requires cultivation of the artist, embodiment of virtues/virtuosities, and imagination and creativity. If philosophy is "a way of life," as Pierre Hadot puts it, the kung fu approach suggests that we take philosophy as the pursuit of the art of living well, and not just as a narrowly defined rational way of life.

DECEMBER 8, 2010

Bridging the Analytic-Continental Divide

—Gary Gutting

MANY PHILOSOPHERS AT LEADING AMERICAN DEPARTMENTS ARE specialists in metaphysics: the study of the most general aspects of reality such as being and time. The major work of one of the most prominent philosophers of the twentieth century, Martin Heidegger, is *Being and Time*, a profound study of these two topics. Nonetheless, hardly any of these American metaphysicians have paid serious attention to Heidegger's book.

The standard explanation for this oddity is that the metaphysicians are *analytic* philosophers, whereas Heidegger is a *continental* philosopher. Although the two sorts of philosophers seldom read one another's work, when they do, the results can be ugly. A famous debate between Jacques Derrida (continental) and John Searle (analytic) ended with Searle denouncing Derrida's "obscurantism" and Derrida mocking Searle's "superficiality."

The distinction between analytic and continental philosophers seems odd, first of all, because it contrasts a geographical characterization (philosophy done on the European continent, particularly Germany and France) with a methodological one (philosophy done by analyzing concepts). It's like, as Bernard Williams pointed out, dividing cars into four-wheel-drive and made-in-Japan. It becomes even odder when we realize that some of the founders of analytic philosophy (like Frege and Carnap) were Europeans, that many of the leading centers of "continental" philosophy are at American universities, and that many "analytic" philosophers have no interest in analyzing concepts.

Some attention to history helps make sense of the distinction. In the early twentieth century, philosophers in England (Russell, Moore, Wittgenstein) and in Germany and Austria (Carnap, Reichenbach, Hempel—all of whom, with the rise of the Nazis, emigrated to the United States) developed what they saw as a radically new approach to philosophy, based on the new techniques of symbolic logic developed by Frege and Russell.

The basic idea was that philosophical problems could be solved (or dissolved) by logically analyzing key terms, concepts or propositions. (Russell's analysis of definite descriptions of what does not exist—e.g., "The present king of France"—remains a model of such an approach.) Over the years, there were various forms of logical, linguistic and conceptual analysis, all directed toward resolving confusions in previous philosophical thought and presented as examples of analytic philosophy. Eventually, some philosophers, especially Quine, questioned the very idea of "analysis" as a distinctive philosophical method. But the goals of clarity, precision, and logical rigor remained and continue to define the standards for a type of philosophy that calls itself analytic and is dominant in English-speaking countries.

At roughly the same time that analytic philosophy was emerging, Edmund Husserl was developing his "phenomenological" approach to philosophy. He, too, emphasized high standards of clarity and precision, and had some fruitful engagements with analytic philosophers such as Frege. Husserl, however, sought clarity and precision more in the rigorous *description* of our immediate experience (the phenomena) than in the logical analysis of concepts or language. He saw his phenomenology as operating at the fundamental level of knowledge on which any truths of conceptual or linguistic analysis would have to be based. In *Being and Time* Husserl's student Heidegger turned phenomenology toward "existential" questions about freedom, anguish and death. Later, French thinkers influenced by Husserl and Heidegger, especially Sartre and Merleau-Ponty, developed their own versions of phenomenologically based existentialism.

The term *continental philosophy* was, as Simon Critchley and Simon Glendinning have emphasized, to an important extent the invention of analytic philosophers of the mid-twentieth century who wanted to distinguish themselves from the phenomenologists and existentialists of continental Europe. These analytic philosophers (Gilbert Ryle was a leading figure) regarded the continental appeal to immediate experience as a source of subjectivity and obscurity that was counter to their own ideals of logical objectivity and clarity. The analytic-continental division was institutionalized in 1962 when American proponents of continental philosophy set up their own professional organization, the Society for Phenomenology and Existential Philosophy (SPEP), as an alternative to the predominantly (but by no means exclusively) analytic American Philosophical Association (APA).

Over the last fifty years, the term *continental philosophy* has been extended to many other European movements, such as Hegelian idealism, Marxism, hermeneutics and especially poststructuralism and deconstruction. These are often in opposition to phenomenology and existentialism, but analytic philosophers still see them as falling far short of standards or clarity and rigor. As a result, as Brian Leiter has emphasized, "continental philosophy" today designates "a series of partly overlapping traditions in philosophy, some of whose figures have almost nothing in common with [each] other."

The scope of "analytic philosophy" has likewise broadened over the years. In the 1950s, it typically took the form of either logical positivism or ordinary-language philosophy, each of which involved commitment to a specific mode of analysis (roughly, following either Carnap or Wittgenstein) as well as substantive philosophical views. These views involved a rejection of much traditional philosophy (especially metaphysics and ethics) as essentially meaningless. There was, in particular, no room for religious belief or objective ethical norms. Today, analytic philosophers use a much wider range of methods (including quasi-scientific inference to the best explanation and their own versions of phenomenological description). Also, there are analytic cases being made for the full range of traditional philosophical positions, including the existence of God, mind-body dualism, and objective ethical norms.

Various forms of empiricism and naturalism are still majority views, but any philosophical position can be profitably developed using the tools of analytic philosophy. There are Thomists and Hegelians who are analytic philosophers, and there is even a significant literature devoted to expositions of major continental philosophers in analytic terms. The claim that working in the analytic mode restricts the range of our philosophical inquiry no longer has any basis.

This development refutes the claim that analytic philosophers, as Santiago Zabala recently put it, do not discuss "the fundamental questions that have troubled philosophers for millennia." This was true in the days of positivism, but no more. Zabala's claim that analytic philosophers have not produced "deep historical research" is similarly outdated. It was true back when the popularity of Russell's *A History of Western Philosophy* signaled the analytic disdain for serious history. Now, however, even though many analytic philosophers still have little interest in history, many of the best current historians of philosophy employ the conceptual and argumentative methods of analytic philosophy.

Because of such developments, Leiter has argued that there are no longer substantive philosophical differences between analytic and continental philosophy, although there are sometimes important differences of "style." He has also suggested that the only gap in principle between the two camps is sociological, that (these are my examples) philosophers in one camp discount the work of those in the other simply because of their personal distaste for symbolic logic or for elaborate literary and historical discussions.

I agree with much of what Leiter says, but I think there are still important general philosophical differences between analytic philosophy and continental philosophy, in all their current varieties. These differences concern their conceptions of *experience* and of *reason* as standards of evaluation. Typically, analytic philosophy appeals to experience understood as common-sense intuitions (as well as their developments and transformations by science) and to reason understood as the standard rules of logical inference. A number of continental approaches claim to access a privileged domain of *experience* that penetrates beneath the veneer of common sense and science experience. For example, phenomenologists, such as Husserl, the early Heidegger, Sartre and Merleau-Ponty, try to describe the concretely lived experience from which common-sense/scientific experience is a pale and distorted abstraction, like the mathematical frequencies that optics substitutes for the colors we perceive in the world. Similarly, various versions of neo-Kantianism and idealism point to a "transcendental" or "absolute" consciousness that provides the fuller significance of our ordinary experiences.

Other versions of continental thought regard the essential activity of reason not as the logical regimentation of thought but as the creative exercise of intellectual *imagination*. This view is characteristic of most important French philosophers since the 1960s, beginning with Foucault, Derrida and Deleuze. They maintain that the standard logic analytic philosophers use can merely explicate what is implicit in the concepts with which we happen to begin; such logic is useless for the essential philosophical task, which they maintain is learning to think beyond these concepts.

Continental philosophies of experience try to probe *beneath* the concepts of everyday experience to discover the meanings that underlie them, to think the conditions for the possibility of our concepts. By contrast, continental philosophies of imagination try to think *beyond* those concepts, to, in some sense, think what is impossible.

Philosophies of experience and philosophies of imagination are in tension, since the intuitive certainties of experience work as limits to creative intellectual imagination, which in turn challenges those alleged limits. Michel Foucault nicely expressed the tension when he spoke of the competing philosophical projects of critique in the sense of "knowing what limits knowledge has to renounce transgressing" and of "a practical critique that takes the form of a possible transgression." However, a number of recent French philosophers (e.g., Levinas, Ricoeur, Badiou and Marion) can be understood as developing philosophies that try to reconcile phenomenological experience and deconstructive creativity.

In view of their substantive philosophical differences, it's obvious that analytic and continental philosophers would profit by greater familiarity with one another's work, and discussions across the divide would make for a better philosophical world. Here, however, there is a serious lack of symmetry between analytic and continental thought. This is due to the relative clarity of most analytic writing in contrast to the obscurity of much continental work.

Because of its commitment to clarity, analytic philosophy functions as an effective lingua franca for any philosophical ideas. (Even the most difficult writers, such as Sellars and Davidson, find disciples who write clarifying commentaries.) There is, moreover, a continuing demand for analytic expositions of major continental figures. It's obvious why there is no corresponding market for, say, expositions of Quine, Rawls or Kripke in the idioms of Heidegger, Derrida or Deleuze. With all due appreciation for the limits of what cannot be said with full clarity, training in analytic philosophy would greatly improve the writing of most continental philosophers.

Of course, analytic philosophers could often profit from exposure to continental ideas. Epistemologists, for example, could learn a great deal from the phenomenological analyses of Husserl and Merleau-Ponty, and metaphysicians could profit from the historical reflections of Heidegger and Derrida. But in view of the unnecessary difficulty of much continental writing, most analytic philosophers will do better to rely on a secondhand acquaintance through reliable and much more accessible secondary sources.

It may be that the most strikingly obscure continental writing (e.g., of the later Heidegger and of most major French philosophers since the 1960s) is a form of literary expression, producing a kind of abstract poetry from its creative transformations of philosophical concepts. This would explain the move of academic interest in such work toward English and other language departments. But it is hard to see that there is much of serious philosophical value lost in the clarity of analytic commentaries on Heidegger, Derrida and others.

There are some encouraging recent signs of philosophers following philosophical problems wherever they are interestingly discussed, regardless of the author's methodology, orientation or style. But the primary texts of leading continental philosophers are still unnecessary challenges to anyone trying to come to terms with them. The continental-analytic gap will begin to be bridged only when seminal thinkers of the Continent begin to write more clearly.

FEBRUARY 19, 2012

Of Cannibals, Kings and Culture:
The Problem of Ethnocentricity

—Adam Etinson

IN AUGUST OF 1563, MICHEL DE MONTAIGNE, THE FAMOUS FRENCH
essayist, was introduced to three Brazilian cannibals who were visiting Rouen, France, at the invitation of King Charles the Ninth. The
three men had never before left Brazil, had just been subjected to
a long interrogation by the king (who was thirteen years old at the
time), and if they had not already contracted some dangerous European illness, they were surely undergoing a rather severe case of
culture shock. Despite this, they still had enough poise to lucidly
respond to Montaigne's questions about what they thought of their
new surroundings.

The observations shared by the native Brazilians have a certain
comical quality. Because they looked on French society with such fresh
eyes, their observations make the familiar seem absurd. But they are
also morally revealing. First, the Brazilians expressed surprise that
"so many tall, bearded men, all strong and well armed" (i.e., the king's
guards) were willing to take orders from a small child: something that
would have been unthinkable in their own society. And second, the
Brazilians were shocked by the severe inequality of French citizens,
commenting on how some men "were gorged to the full with things
of every sort" while others "were beggars at their doors, emaciated
with hunger and poverty." Since the Brazilians saw all human beings
"as halves of one another . . . they found it strange that these poverty-

stricken halves should suffer such injustice, and that they did not take the others by the throat or set fire to their houses."

Montaigne records these observations in an essay entitled, "Des cannibals." Well ahead of its time, the essay challenges the haughty denigration of cannibals that was so common among Montaigne's contemporaries, but not by arguing that cannibalism itself is a morally acceptable practice. Instead, Montaigne makes the more provocative claim that, as barbaric as these Brazilian cannibals may be, they are not nearly as barbaric as sixteenth-century Europeans themselves. To make his case, Montaigne cites various evidence: the wholesome simplicity and basic nobility of native Brazilian life; the fact that some European forms of punishment—which involved feeding people to dogs and pigs while they were still alive—were decidedly more horrendous than the native Brazilian practice of eating one's enemies after they are dead; and the humane, egalitarian character of the Brazilians' moral sensibility, which was on display in their recorded observations.

The fact that, despite all this, sixteenth-century Western Europeans remained so deeply convinced of their own moral and intellectual superiority was, to Montaigne, evidence of a more general phenomenon. He writes,

> We all call barbarous anything that is contrary to our own habits. Indeed we seem to have no other criterion of truth and reason than the type and kind of opinions and customs current in the land where we live. There we always see the perfect religion, the perfect political system, the perfect and most accomplished way of doing everything.

Montaigne most certainly wasn't the first to make note of our tendency to automatically assume the superiority of local beliefs and practices; Herodotus, the Greek historian of the fifth century BC, made very similar observations in his *Histories*, noting how all peoples are "accustomed to regard their own customs as by far the best." And in his famous Letter 93, which presents an early argument against religious toleration, the medieval Catholic theologian

Saint Augustine laments the way in which old customs produce a closed-minded resistance to alternative beliefs and practices that, he argues, is best broken by the threat of punishment. When the nineteenth-century sociologist William Graham Sumner later named this tendency "ethnocentrism," the term, and the allegation, became a mantra of twentieth-century cultural anthropology.

Ethnocentrism—our culture's tendency to twist our judgment in favor of homegrown beliefs and practices and against foreign alternatives—is not, I take it, a phenomenon in need of further empirical confirmation. It is quite obvious that we are all ethnocentric to at least some extent. I am a Canadian and grew up with free, government-provided health care—a system that seems both fair and feasible to most Canadians, including myself. As such, I have a hard time comprehending the ferocity with which so many have opposed health-care reform in the United States. But equally, someone raised in a conservative swath of Texas is just as likely to find my sense of what is "fair" highly dubious.

Philosophers have long been aware of the role of culture and upbringing in facilitating moral disagreements of this sort. And more recently, moral psychologists have begun to offer insightful accounts of the psychological forces that make such disagreements so impervious to resolution through reasoned debate. For instance, in his recent book, *The Righteous Mind: Why Good People Are Divided by Politics and Religion*, Jonathan Haidt argues that, far from being a way of holding our moral beliefs up to critical scrutiny, moral reasoning is generally something we use merely to convince others of long-held beliefs that we are unwilling to abandon. If we reflect on what it's actually like to argue with others who fundamentally disagree with us on moral or political matters, Haidt seems to get something right; often, no amount of persuasive reasoning, clear argument or exposed contradiction can shake us from what we already believe.

In light of the recent escalation of partisanship in the United States, not to mention other widening global ideological fissures, I think it's important that we reflect, however briefly, on what we should make of this fact, with regard to our own ethnocentrism. Is ethnocentrism something we're doomed to? Can we avoid it? If so, should we avoid it? Is it even a bad thing?

Philosophers have responded to the pervasive influence of culture on our moral beliefs in various ways. Many have embraced some form of skepticism. To take a contemporary example, John L. Mackie (1917–81) famously cited ethnocentrism as evidence that there are no objective moral facts, or at least none that we can access. If our moral beliefs are dictated by our culture or way of life, he argued, then it is senseless to think of ourselves as capable of discerning objective moral truths; what room is left for such facts to make an impact on our consciousness? Mackie thought of himself as an "error theorist"—because, in his view, anytime we make a moral judgment that purports to be objectively true we are inevitably wrong—but there are other skeptical ways of responding to the fact of ethnocentrism. Many have argued, for instance, that the influence of culture on our moral beliefs is evidence not of error theory but of moral relativism: the idea that the moral truth, for any given people, is determined by their culture—the set of shared practices and beliefs that they ascribe to. We know from various sources, including Plato's dialogues, that some ancient Greeks defended such a view. And contemporary philosophers like David Wong and Gilbert Harman are among its serious proponents.

Tempting as these skeptical reactions to ethnocentrism may seem at first glance, there are important reasons to be hesitant. For one, however obvious it may be that culture plays an important role in our moral education, it is nevertheless very hard to prove that our moral beliefs are entirely determined by our culture, or to rule out the possibility that cultures themselves take some direction from objective moral facts. Since it is these hard-to-prove claims that Mackie and other error theorists need to make their argument work, we should hesitate before jumping on board. Second, moral relativism, for its part, seems like an odd and unwarranted response to ethnocentrism. For it's not at all clear why the influence of culture on our moral beliefs should be taken as evidence that cultures influence the moral truth itself—so that, for instance, child sacrifice would be morally permissible in any community with enough members that believe it to be so. Not only does that conclusion seem unmotivated by the phenomenon under discussion, it would also paradoxically convert ethnocentrism into a kind of virtue (since assimilating the views of one's culture would be a way of tapping into the moral truth), which is at odds with the generally pejorative understanding of the term.

Most important of all is the fact that there are other, more straightforward and less overtly skeptical ways of responding to ethnocentrism. Chief among these, in my view, is the simple but humbling acknowledgment that ethnocentrism is a danger that confronts us all, but not one that should disillusion us from the pursuit of truth altogether. This is the sort of response to ethnocentrism one finds, for instance, in the work of the nineteenth-century English philosopher John Stuart Mill. Mill is quick to acknowledge the "magical influence of custom" on our thought, and the way in which local beliefs and practices inevitably appear to us to be "self-evident and self-justifying," but he does not see this as a reason to lapse into skepticism. Instead, and quite reasonably, he takes it to be evidence of both our intellectual laziness and our fallibility—the ever-present possibility that our beliefs might be wrong. The fact that our deepest-held beliefs would be different had we been born elsewhere on the planet (or even, sometimes, to different parents farther down the street) should disconcert us, make us more open to the likelihood of our own error, and spur us to rigorously evaluate our beliefs and practices against alternatives, but it need not disillusion.

In a more candid moment of "Des cannibales," of which there are many across Montaigne's writings, the author unabashedly admits to having forgotten a third observation that the native Brazilians shared with him in response to his question. His forgetfulness is a pity not just because it deprives us of a window onto a 500-year-old cultural confrontation that is fascinating in its own right, but also because it deprives us of a potential opportunity to do just what Mill recommends: reexamine our beliefs and practices, become alert to weaknesses and inconsistencies in our own thinking, discover something plausible in a culturally unfamiliar point of view and in so doing, become better than the ethnocentric creatures that we are.

Found in Translation

—*Hamid Dabashi*

Though it is common to lament the shortcomings of reading an important work in any language other than the original and of the "impossibility" of translation, I am convinced that works of philosophy (or literature, for that matter—are they different?) in fact gain far more than they lose in translation.

Consider Heidegger. Had it not been for his French translators and commentators, German philosophy of his time would have remained an obscure metaphysical thicket. And it was not until Derrida's own take on Heidegger found an English readership in the United States and Britain that the whole Heidegger-Derridian undermining of metaphysics began to shake the foundations of the Greek philosophical heritage. One can in fact argue that much of contemporary continental philosophy originates in German with significant French and Italian glosses before it is globalized in the dominant American English and assumes a whole new global readership and reality. This has nothing to do with the philosophical wherewithal of German, French or English. It is entirely a function of the imperial power and reach of one language as opposed to others.

I. THE MOTHER TONGUE

At various points in history, one language or another—Latin, Persian, Arabic—was the lingua franca of philosophical thinking. Now it is English. And for all we know it might again turn around and become Chinese.

In eleventh-century Iran, the influential philosopher Avicenna wrote most of his work in Arabic. One day his patron prince, who did not read Arabic, asked whether Avicenna would mind writing his works in Persian instead, so that he could understand them. Avicenna obliged and wrote an entire encyclopedia on philosophy for the prince and named it after him: *Danesh-nameh Ala'i.*

Avicenna was of course not the only one who had opted to write his philosophical work in Arabic. So did al-Ghazali (circa 1058–1111) and Shihab al-Din Yahya al-Suhrawardi (circa 1155–1208)—who were both perfectly capable of writing in their mother tongue of Persian and had in fact occasionally done so, notably al-Ghazali in his *Kimiya-ye Sa'adat* (a book on moral philosophy) and al-Suhrawardi in his magnificent short allegorical treatises. But in Avicenna's time, Arabic was so solidly established in its rich and triumphant philosophical vocabulary that no serious philosopher would opt to write his major works in any other language. Persian philosophical prose had to wait for a couple of generations after Avicenna. With the magnificent work of Afdal al-din Kashani (died circa 1214) and that of Avicenna's follower Khwajah Muhammad ibn Muhammad ibn Hasan al-Tusi (1201–1274)—particularly *Asas al-Iqtibas*—Persian philosophical prose achieved its zenith.

Today the term *Persian philosophy* is not so easy to separate from *Islamic philosophy*, much of which is indeed in Arabic. This was the case even in the sixteenth century, when Mulla Sadra wrote nearly his entire major opus in Arabic. Although some major philosophers in the nineteenth and twentieth centuries did write occasionally in Persian, it was not until Allameh Muhammad Iqbal (1877–1938) opted to write his major philosophical works in Persian that Persian philosophical prose resumed a serious significance in the larger Muslim context. (Iqbal also wrote major treatises on Persian philosophy in English.)

It is Amir Hossein Aryanpour's magnificent Persian translation of Muhammad Iqbal's *The Development of Metaphysics in Persia*

(1908), which he rendered as *Seyr-e falsafeh dar Iran* (The course of philosophy in Iran, 1968), that stands now in my mind as the paramount example of excellence in Persian philosophical prose and a testimony to how philosophical translation is a key component of our contemporary intellectual history. If there were a world for philosophy, or if philosophy were to be worldly, these two men, philosopher and translator, having graced two adjacent philosophical worlds, would be among its most honored citizens.

II. TWO TEACHERS

It is impossible to exaggerate the enduring debt of gratitude that my generation of Iranians have to Aryanpour (1925–2001), one of the most influential social theorists, literary critics, philosophers and translators of his time and for us a wide and inviting window to the rich and emancipatory world of critical thinking in my homeland. He is today remembered for generations of students he taught at Tehran University and beyond and for a rich array of his pathbreaking books he wrote or translated and that enabled and paved the way for us to wider philosophical imagination.

Having been exposed to both scholastic and modern educational systems, and widely and deeply educated in Iran (Tehran University), Lebanon (American University of Beirut), England (Cambridge) and the United States (Princeton), Aryanpour was a cosmopolitan thinker and a pioneering figure who promoted a dialectical (jadali) disposition between the material world and the world of ideas. Today, more than forty years after I arrived in Tehran from my hometown of Ahvaz in late summer 1970 to attend college, I still feel under my skin the excitement and joy of finding out how much there was to learn from a man whose name was synonymous with critical thinking, theorizing social movements and above all with the discipline of sociology.

Aryanpour was the product of many factors: Reza Shah's heavy-handed, state-sponsored "modernization"; the brief post–World War II intellectual flowering; travels and higher education in Iran, the Arab world, Europe and the United States; the McCarthy witch hunts of the 1950s; and finally the CIA-sponsored coup of 1953, after which university campuses in his homeland became the primary site of his intellectual leadership of a whole new generation. He was a pain in the neck to both the Pahlavi monarchy and the Islamic Republic that succeeded it, making him at times dogmatic in his own positions, but always pathbreaking in a mode of dialectical thinking that became the staple of his students, both those who were fortunate enough to have known and worked with him directly and the millions of others (like me) who benefited from his work from a distance.

Aryanpour was sacked from his teaching position with the theology faculty in 1976, retired in 1980, and just before his death on July 30, 2001, one of his last public acts was to sign a letter denouncing censorship in the Islamic Republic.

His legendary translation of and expanded critical commentary on Iqbal's *Development of Metaphysics in Persia* became the first and foremost text of my generation's encounter not only with a learned history of philosophy in our homeland, but also with a far wider and more expansive awareness of the world of philosophy. It is impossible to exaggerate the beautiful, overwhelming, exciting and liberating first reading of that magnificent text by a wide-eyed provincial boy having come to the capital of his moral and intellectual imagination.

Iqbal was born and raised in Punjab, British India (Pakistan today), to a devout Muslim family, and was educated by both Muslim teachers and at the Scotch Mission College in Sialkot, growing up multilingual and polycultural. After an unhappy marriage and subsequent divorce, Iqbal studied philosophy, English, Arabic and Persian literatures at the Government College in Lahore, where he was deeply influenced by Thomas Arnold, who became a conduit for his exposure to European thought, an exposure that ultimately resulted in his traveling to Europe for further studies.

While in England, Iqbal received a bachelor's degree from Trinity College, Cambridge, in 1907, around when his first Persian poems began to surface. As he became increasingly attracted to politics, he also managed to write his doctoral dissertation, "The Development of Metaphysics in Persia," with Friedrich Hommel. Reading *Seyr-e falsafeh dar Iran*, Aryanpour's Persian translation of Iqbal's seminal work, became a rite of passage for my generation of college students eager to discover our philosophical heritage.

We grew up and matured into a much wider circle of learning about Islamic philosophy and the place of Iranians in that tradition. There were greener pastures, more learned philosophers who beckoned to our minds and souls. We learned of the majestic writings of Seyyed Jalal Ashtiani, chief among many other philosophical sages of our time, who began to guide our ways into the thicket of Persian and Arabic philosophical thinking. But the decidedly different disposition of Allameh Iqbal in Aryanpour's translation was summoned precisely in the fact that it had not reached us through conventional scholastic routes and was deeply informed by the worldly disposition of our own defiant time. In this text we were reading a superlative Persian prose from a Pakistani philosopher who had come to fruition in both a colonial subcontinent and the postcolonial cosmopolis. There was a palpable worldliness in that philosophical prose that became definitive to my generation.

III. BEYOND EAST AND WEST

When today I read a vacuous phrase like "the Western mind"—or "the Iranian mind," "the Arab mind," or "the Muslim mind," for that matter—I cringe. I wonder what "the Western mind" can mean when reading the Persian version of a Pakistani philosopher's English prose composed in Germany on an aspect of Islamic philosophy that was particular to Iran. Look at the itinerary of a philosopher like Allameh Iqbal; think about a vastly learned and deeply caring intellect like Amir Hossein Aryanpour. Where is "the Western mind" in those variegated geographies of learning, and where is "the Eastern mind"? What could they possibly mean?

The case of *Seyr-e falsafeh dar Iran* was prototypical of my generation's philosophical education—we read left, right and center, then north and south from the Indian subcontinent to Western Europe and North America, Latin America and postcolonial Africa with a voracious worldliness that had no patience for the East or West of any colonial geography. We were philosophically "in the world," and our world was made philosophical by an imaginative geography that knew neither East nor West.

Works of philosophy—and their readers—gain in translation not just because their authors begin to breathe in a new language but because the text signals a world alien to its initial composition. Above all they gain because these authors and their texts have to face a new audience. Plato and Aristotle have had a life in Arabic and Persian entirely alien to the colonial codification of "Western philosophy"—and the only effective way to make the foreign echoes of that idea familiar is to make the familiar tropes of "Western philosophy" foreign.

JULY 28, 2013

Born Again in a Second Language

—Costica Bradatan

I<small>N HER EXPLORATION OF THE</small> C<small>ATHOLIC RELIGION,</small> "L<small>ETTER TO A</small> Priest," written the year before her death in 1943, Simone Weil noticed at some point that "for any man a change *of religion is as dangerous a thing as a change of language is for a writer.* It may turn out a success, but it can also have disastrous consequences." The Romanian philosopher Emil Cioran, who was one such writer, talks of the change of language as a catastrophic event in any author's biography. And rightly so.

When you become a writer, you don't do so in abstract, but in relation to a certain language. To practice writing is to grow roots into that language; the better writer you become, the deeper the roots. Literary virtuosity almost always betrays a sense of deep, comfortable immersion into a familiar soil. As such, if for any reason the writer has to change languages, the experience is nothing short of life threatening. Not only do you have to start everything again from scratch, but you also have to undo what you have been doing for almost as long as you have been around. Changing languages is not for the fainthearted, nor for the impatient.

Painful as it can be at a strictly human level, the experience can also be philosophically fascinating. Rarely do we get the chance to observe a more dramatic remaking of oneself. For a writer's language, far from being a mere means of expression, is above all a mode of subjective existence and a way of experiencing the world.

She needs the language not just to describe things, but to *see* them. The world reveals itself in a certain manner to the Japanese writer, and in quite another to the one who writes in Finnish. A writer's language is not just something she uses, but a constitutive part of what she is. This is why to abandon your native tongue and to adopt another is to dismantle yourself, piece by piece, and then to put yourself together again, in a different form.

To begin with, when changing languages you descend to a zero-point of your existence. There must be even a moment, however brief, when you cease to be. You've just quit the old language and the new one hasn't received you yet; you are now in limbo, between worlds, hanging over the abyss. A change of language usually happens when the writer is exiled or self-exiled. Yet the physical exile is doubled in such cases by an ontological one—an exile on the margins of being. It is as though, for a moment, as she passes through the void—the narrow crack between languages, where there are no words to hold onto and nothing can be named—the self of the writer is not anymore. Weil's comparison to the religious conversion is indeed apt because, just like in the case of the convert, the writer who changes languages undergoes a death-and-rebirth experience. In an important way, that person dies and then comes back as another. "When I changed my language, I annihilated my past. I changed my entire life," says Cioran.

When she starts writing in the new language, the world is born anew to the writer. Yet the most spectacular rebirth is her own. For this is a project of total reconstruction of the self, where no stone is left unturned and nothing will look the same again. Your native language—what you were before—appears as less and less familiar to you. But that doesn't bother you at all; in fact, you look forward to a moment when you will use it as just another foreign language. Not long after adopting French, Samuel Beckett, an Irishman, complained of his native English, "Horrible language, which I still know too well." The ontological promise of complete renewal that comes with the new language is nothing short of intoxicating.

When you are reborn in this manner, it is as if all the possibilities are open; you are given a chance to refashion yourself into whatever shape you choose. You are your own demiurge: out of nothing, as it were, you can become everything. Asked in 1954 why he chose to change languages, Beckett answered: out of a "need to be ill equipped." His response is exceedingly sly because, if you listen more attentively, its boastful tone is deafening. For in French, the need "to be ill equipped" (d'être mal armé) doesn't sound very different from the need to be (another) Mallarmé (d'être Mallarmé). Anything less than a Mallarmé status would not have been enough for Beckett on his quest for the new self. Eventually, he didn't become Mallarmé, but Samuel Beckett, the French author of *Molloy*, *Malone Dies* and *Waiting for Godot*, which is probably just as good. And as if there was not enough alienation in his adoption of a new language, he alienated himself one more time by translating his French work into English. Elsewhere Beckett claimed that he preferred French because it allowed him to write "without style." Yet writing "without style" is one of the writing styles most difficult to accomplish; you really need to be well equipped to do it.

There is something "natural" in one's becoming a writer in one's native language. Having reached self-consciousness into that language, having assimilated it along with the mother's milk, so to speak, such a writer finds himself in a somewhat privileged position: he only has to bring to perfection whatever he has received. Granted, rigorous training, self-discipline and constant practice are necessary; after all, art is the opposite of nature. Yet no matter how you look at it, there is a distinct sense of continuity and organic growing in this writer's trajectory.

Becoming a writer in a language that is not yours by birth, though, goes against nature; there is nothing organic in this process, only artifice. There are no linguistic "instincts" to guide you on the path, and the language's guardian angels rarely whisper into your ear; you are truly on your own. Says Cioran, "When I wrote in Romanian, words were not *independent* of me. As soon as I began to write in French I consciously chose each word. I had them before me, outside of me, each in its place. And I chose them: now I'll take you, then you."

Many who shift to writing in a second language develop an unusually acute linguistic awareness. In an interview he gave in 1979, some seven years after he moved to the United States from his native Russia, Joseph Brodsky speaks of his ongoing "love affair with the English language." Language is such an overwhelming presence for these people that it comes to structure their new biographies. "English is the only interesting thing that's left in my life," says Brodsky. The need to find le mot juste starts out as a concern, turns into an obsession, and ends up as a way of life. These writers excel at the art of making virtue of necessity: out of a need to understand how the new language works, they turn into linguistic maniacs; out of a concern for correctness, they become compulsive grammarians.

When he moved to France at the age of twenty-six, Cioran's command of French was barely decent, yet he ended up as one of the greatest stylists of that language. Similarly, Joseph Conrad learned English relatively late in life—which did not prevent him from coming to be one of its most sophisticated representatives. Vladimir Nabokov is doubtlessly another such representative, even though he started learning English at an early age. The same pattern again and again: everything out of nothing, from halting ignorance to a mode of expression of the first order.

Toward the end of Ray Bradbury's novel *Fahrenheit 451*, the reader comes across something whose significance exceeds the confines of the story. It is the scene where Montag meets the "book people." In a world where printed texts are banned, they have dedicated their lives to preserving the "great books" of humankind; each commits a book to memory and spends his or her whole life reciting it. They are living texts, these people, language incarnated. Apart from the masterpieces that inhabit them, they don't mean much. Their bodies matter as little as the paper on which a book is printed. In a way, a writer who has changed languages is not very different from these people. In the long run, because of their compulsive preoccupation with linguistic precision and stylistic perfection, a colonization of sorts takes place: language penetrates all the details of that writer's life, it informs and reshapes it, it proclaims its dominion over her—it takes over. The writer's self is now under the occupation of an invading power: her own writing in the new language.

In a certain sense, then, it could be said that in the end you don't really change languages; the language changes you. At a deeper, more personal level, writing literature in another language has a distinctly performative dimension: as you do it, something happens *to* you, the language acts *upon* you. The book you are writing ends up writing you in turn. The result is a "ghostification" of sorts. For to change languages as a writer is to undergo a process of dematerialization: before you know it, you are language more than anything else. One day, suddenly, a certain intuition starts visiting you— namely, that you are not made primarily out of flesh anymore, but out of lines and rhymes, of rhetorical strategies and narrative patterns. Just like the "book people," you don't mean much apart from the texts that inhabit you. More than a man or a woman of flesh and blood, you are now rather a fleshing out of the language itself, a literary project, very much like the books you write. The writer who has changed languages is truly a ghostwriter—the only one worthy of the name.

Having done all this, having gone through the pain of changing languages and undergone the death-and-rebirth initiation, you are sometimes given—as a reward, as it were—access to a metaphysical insight of an odd, savage beauty. It is the notion that the world may be nothing other than a story in the making and that we, who inhabit it, may be nothing more than characters. Characters in search of an author, that is.

AUGUST 4, 2013

Philosophy's Western Bias

—Justin E. H. Smith

THERE IS MUCH TALK IN ACADEMIC PHILOSOPHY ABOUT THE NEED to open up the discipline to so-called non-Western traditions and perspectives, both through changes to the curriculum and also within the demographics of philosophy departments themselves. These two aspects are seen as connected: it is thought that greater representation of non-Western philosophy will help to bring about greater diversity among the women and men who make up the philosophical community.

When I teach classical Indian philosophy, or advocate teaching it, for example, I often hear in response that doing so provides a service to the university community, and to the student body, insofar as it enhances the diversity of the philosophy curriculum and makes the curriculum representative of a wider portion of the student body. But what I'm teaching are topics such as fifth-century Indian theories of logical inference, or the concept of qualitative atomism in classical Buddhism: material that is sufficiently obscure that no student, of any background, should be expected at the outset to recognize him- or herself in it.

The goal of reflecting the diversity of our own society by expanding the curriculum to include non-European traditions has so far been a tremendous failure. And it has failed for at least two reasons. One is that non-Western philosophy is typically represented in philosophy curricula in a merely token way. Western philosophy is always the unmarked category, the standard in relation to which non-Western philosophy provides a useful contrast.

Non-Western philosophy is not approached on its own terms, and thus philosophy remains, implicitly and by default, Western. Second, non-Western philosophy, when it does appear in curricula, is treated in a methodologically and philosophically unsound way: it is crudely supposed to be wholly indigenous to the cultures that produce it and to be fundamentally different than Western philosophy in areas like its valuation of reason or its dependence on myth and religion. In this way, non-Western philosophy remains fundamentally "other."

One good way to begin to correct this problem would be to stop describing it as "non-Western," but instead to be explicit about which geographical region, or which tradition, we are discussing: Kashmir Shaivism, for example, or Chinese Mohist logic, just as we would speak of German Aristotelian Scholasticism or American Pragmatism, without, ordinarily, bothering to specify that these are both "Western."' Imagine, for comparison, the righteous vigor with which we would condemn the academic subfield of agricultural history if 95 percent of all the research in this field were devoted to irrigation techniques in Southeast Asia, while the remaining 5 percent was required to package itself as the study of "non-Southeast Asian irrigation techniques." This sounds absurd, and it is, but it really is no more so than when the small minority of scholars who work on, say, Indian or Chinese philosophy are obligated to present their research as having something to do with "non-Western philosophy" for the simple reason that it does not come from Northwest Eurasia.

An alternative approach to the history of philosophy—one that takes the aim of opening up the discipline seriously—would treat both Western and non-Western philosophy as the regional inflections of a global phenomenon.

When we say "West," we mean, ordinarily, Europe, along with its recent extension into North America. Europe is, literally, a peninsula of Eurasia, comparable roughly in size, cultural diversity and civilizational antiquity to the Indian subcontinent. Certain significant things happened first in Europe rather than elsewhere, such as industrialization; other important things first appeared outside of Europe, such as movable type. Now it is, of course, very difficult to define "philosophy," but if we think of it broadly as systematic reflection on the nature of reality and on humanity's place in that reality, then it is clear that Europe can make no special claim to be the home of philosophy.

What Europe does claim is a certain tradition reaching back to Greek antiquity. But even that claim is in question. The "Greek miracle" is in the end only a historiographical artifact, a result of our habit of beginning our histories when and where we do, for there was always influence from neighboring civilizations. But whatever the complexities of the world in which Plato wrote, it is at least true that the subsequent tradition that would come to be called "Western" or "European"—with, of course, a long detour through Islamic Spain, North Africa, Persia and Central Asia, without which the Greek tradition would surely have died out—really does constitute, as Alfred North Whitehead put it, a "series of footnotes to Plato." Seen from this perspective, the only reason to take European philosophy as the default tradition for our curricula is that it just happens to be, for contingent historical reasons, *our* tradition.

But nearly every subject taught in Western universities developed in large part out of the Western intellectual tradition, yet this legacy has not prevented any discipline other than philosophy from aspiring to an objective, global and, I dare say, scientific perspective on its object of study, free of the idea that the European instance of it is something special in the history of humanity.

Now, a large part of the difficulty of thinking of Western philosophy as one tradition among others has to do with the fact that many if not most of its practitioners reject the idea that what they do is essentially bound to the discipline's past. Philosophy is conceived on the model of the sciences, which are indeed free to ignore disproven theories from long ago, and thus to ignore not just, say, ancient China but early modern Europe as well. In this respect the history of ancient Chinese philosophy is doubly peripheral, not just because of Eurocentrism, but also because of presentism, a lack of interest in history in general. This stems from the fact that philosophy, modeling itself after the sciences, believes it is closer to the truth than it was in the past, and that if a theory is not true, there is little reason to spend much time on it.

I will not argue against this view of philosophy here. But I will point out that it does make the current situation of philosophy, when considered from a global perspective, fairly difficult to comprehend. Chinese and American polymer researchers speak exactly the same language when they are doing their job, and there was never any danger that A. Q. Khan's development of Pakistan's nuclear program would be slowed down by cultural differences in the understanding of uranium enrichment. With philosophy, however, it is plainly a different story.

In the developing world in particular, the version of philosophy put forward—be it French or Anglo-American in character, or entirely homegrown—has very much to do with the country's broader project of national identity construction. In Iran, Islamic philosophy is given priority; in Turkey, at least until recently, there was scarcely any mention of local or regional traditions in the university philosophy curriculum, but only a fervent devotion to a vision of philosophy principally concerned with analysis of the language and methodology of science. Now one can't say—or at least I'm not prepared to say— that Iran is doing things wrong, as one might if they were to teach medieval Islamic alchemy in their chemistry departments. The difference is that philosophy is simply not like science; it is much more intricately wrapped up in cultural legacies (some have argued that science is just another cultural practice, too, but I'm not prepared to say that either). Much of the difficulty of taking a rigorous and serious approach to the teaching and study of non-Western philosophy in Western philosophy departments is that many philosophers remain attached to the article of faith that philosophy is something independent of culture.

G. W. Leibniz, writing in the early eighteenth century on the future course of Sino-European relations, suggested evocatively that "the commerce of light," which is to say of illumination, or knowledge, always piggybacks on the commerce of goods. Indeed, the past two thousand years reveal a fairly close correspondence between the global centers of economic activity and the centers of intellectual production. Most tellingly, Europe becomes the principal locus of philosophical and scientific activity only when it comes to dominate the global economy through the conquest of the New World and the consequent shifting of the economic center of the world from Asia to Europe.

It is no secret that the center is shifting once again, this time toward the Pacific. A bit of historical perspective makes it easy to see that this shift will have consequences for our understanding of what philosophy is, and of who gets to define the set of questions with which it is concerned.

The West has an extremely rich philosophical tradition—one of the two or three richest, in fact—and it is eminently worthy of preservation and transmission to future generations. But its richness has always been a result of its place as a node in a global network through which ideas and things are always flowing. This was true in 500 BC and is no less true today. Increasingly, moreover, this interconnectedness is something that is not only of interest to the antiquarian trivia collector who can't wait to tell you where the printing press really comes from. It is fast becoming the defining fact about our geopolitical reality. In this reality, Western academic philosophy will likely come to appear utterly parochial in the coming years if it does not find a way to approach non-Western traditions that is much more rigorous and respectful than the tokenism that reigns at present.

JUNE 3, 2012

RETHINKING THINKERS

Spinoza's Vision of Freedom, and Ours

—*Steven Nadler*

BARUCH SPINOZA, THE SEVENTEENTH-CENTURY DUTCH THINKER, may be among the more enigmatic (and mythologized) philosophers in Western thought, but he also remains one of the most relevant, to his time and to ours. He was an eloquent proponent of a secular, democratic society, and was the strongest advocate for freedom and tolerance in the early modern period. The ultimate goal of his *Theological-Political Treatise*—published anonymously to great alarm in 1670, when it was called by one of its many critics "a book forged in hell by the devil himself"—is enshrined both in the book's subtitle and in the argument of its final chapter: to show that the "freedom of philosophizing" not only *can* be granted "without detriment to public peace, to piety, and to the right of the sovereign, but also that it must be granted if these are to be preserved."

Spinoza was incited to write the *Treatise* when he recognized that the Dutch Republic, and his own province of Holland in particular, was wavering from its uncommonly liberal and relatively tolerant traditions. He feared that with the rising political influence in the 1660s of the more orthodox and narrow-minded elements in the Dutch Reformed Church, and the willingness of civil authorities to placate the preachers by acting against works they deemed "irreligious," "licentious" and "subversive," the nearly two decades—long period of the "True Freedom" was coming to an end. The *Treatise* is both a personally angry book—a friend of Spinoza's, the author of a radical treatise, had recently been thrown in prison, where he soon died—and a very public plea to the Dutch Republic not to betray the political, legal and religious principles that made its flourishing possible.

In this work, Spinoza approaches the issue of individual liberty from several perspectives. To begin with, there is the question of belief, and especially the state's tolerance of the beliefs of its citizens. Spinoza argues that all individuals are to be absolutely free and unimpeded in their beliefs, by right and in fact. "It is impossible for the mind to be completely under another's control; for no one is able to transfer to another his natural right or faculty to reason freely and to form his own judgment on any matters whatsoever, nor can he be compelled to do so."

For this reason, any effort on the government's part to rule over the beliefs and opinions of citizens is bound to fail, and will ultimately serve to undermine its own authority. A sovereign is certainly free to try and limit what people think, but the result of such a policy, Spinoza predicts, would be only to create resentment and opposition to its rule.

It can be argued that the state's tolerance of individual belief is not a difficult issue. As Spinoza points out, it is "impossible" for a person's mind to be under another's control, and this is a necessary reality that any government must accept. The more difficult case, the true test of a regime's commitment to toleration, concerns the liberty of citizens to express those beliefs, either in speech or in writing. And here Spinoza goes further than anyone else of his time: "Utter failure," he says, "will attend any attempt in a commonwealth to force men to speak only as prescribed by the sovereign despite their different and opposing opinions . . . The most tyrannical government will be one where the individual is denied the freedom to express and to communicate to others what he thinks, and a moderate government is one where this freedom is granted to every man."

Spinoza has a number of compelling arguments for the freedom of expression. One is based both on the natural right (or natural power) of citizens to speak as they desire, as well as on the apparent fact that (as in the case of belief per se) it would be self-defeating for a government to try to restrain that freedom. No matter what laws are enacted against speech and other means of expression, citizens will continue to say what they believe (because they can), only now they will do so in secret. The result of the suppression of freedom is, once again, resentment and a weakening of the bonds that unite subjects to their government. In Spinoza's view, intolerant laws lead ultimately to anger, revenge and sedition. The attempt to enforce them is a "great danger to the state." (This would certainly have been the lesson gleaned from recent history, as the Dutch revolt originated in the repressive measures that the Spanish crown imposed on its northern territories in the sixteenth century.)

Spinoza also argues for freedom of expression on utilitarian grounds—that it is necessary for the discovery of truth, economic progress, and the growth of creativity. Without an open marketplace of ideas, science, philosophy and other disciplines are stifled in their development, to the technological, fiscal and even aesthetic detriment of society. As Spinoza puts it, "This freedom [of expressing one's ideas] is of the first importance in fostering the sciences and the arts, for it is only those whose judgment is free and unbiased who can attain success in these fields."

Spinoza's extraordinary views on freedom have never been more relevant. In 2010, for example, the United States Supreme Court declared constitutional a law that, among other things, criminalized certain kinds of speech. The speech in question need not be extremely and imminently threatening to anyone or pose "a clear and present danger" (to use Justice Oliver Wendell Holmes's phrase). It may involve no incitement to action or violence whatsoever; indeed, it can be an exhortation to *nonviolence*. In a troubling 6-3 decision, *Holder v. Humanitarian Law Project*, the Court, acceding to most of the arguments presented by President Obama's attorney general, Eric Holder, upheld a federal law which makes it a crime to provide support for a foreign group designated by the State Department as a "terrorist organization," even if the "help" one provides involves only peaceful and legal advice, including speech encouraging that organization to adopt nonviolent means for resolving conflicts and educating it in the means to do so. (The United States, of course, is not alone among Western nations in restricting freedom of expression. Just this week, France—fresh from outlawing the wearing of veils by Muslim women, and in a mirror image of Turkey's criminalizing the public affirmation of the Armenian genocide—made it illegal to deny, in print or public speech, officially recognized genocides.)

For Spinoza, by contrast, there is to be no criminalization of ideas in the well-ordered state. *Libertas philosophandi*, the freedom of philosophizing, must be upheld for the sake of a healthy, secure and peaceful commonwealth and material and intellectual progress.

Now Spinoza does not support *absolute* freedom of speech. He explicitly states that the expression of "seditious" ideas is *not* to be tolerated by the sovereign. There is to be no protection for speech that advocates the overthrow of the government, disobedience to its laws or harm to fellow citizens. The people are free to argue for the repeal of laws that they find unreasonable and oppressive, but they must do so peacefully and through rational argument; and if their argument fails to persuade the sovereign to change the law, then that must be the end of the matter. What they may not do is "stir up popular hatred against [the sovereign or his representatives]."

Absolutists about the freedom of speech will be troubled by these caveats on Spinoza's part, and rightly so. After all, who is to decide what kind of speech counts as seditious? May not the government declare to be seditious simply those views with which it disagrees or that it finds contrary to its policies? Spinoza, presumably to allay such concerns, does offer a definition of "seditious political beliefs" as those that "*immediately* have the effect of annulling the covenant whereby everyone has surrendered his right to act just as he thinks fit" (my emphasis). The salient feature of such opinions is "the action that is implicit therein"—that is, they are more or less verbal incitements to act against the government and thus they are directly contrary to the tacit social contract of citizenship.

What is important is that Spinoza draws the line, albeit a somewhat hazy one, between ideas and action. The government, he insists, has every right to outlaw certain kinds of actions. As the party responsible for the public welfare, the sovereign must have absolute and exclusive power to monitor and legislatively control what people may or may not do. But Spinoza explicitly does not include ideas, even the *expression* of ideas, under the category of "action." As individuals emerged from a state of nature to become citizens through the social contract, "it was only the right to act as he thought fit that each man surrendered, and not his right to reason and judge."

In the penultimate paragraph of the *Treatise*, Spinoza insists that "the state can pursue no safer course than to regard piety and religion as consisting solely in the exercise of charity and just dealing, and that the right of the sovereign, both in religious and secular spheres, should be restricted to men's actions, with everyone being allowed to think what he will and to say what he thinks." There is no reason to think that Spinoza believed that this remarkable and unprecedented principle of toleration and liberty was to be qualified according to who was speaking, the ideas being expressed (with the noted exception of explicit calls for sedition), or the audience being addressed.

I cited the case of *Holder v. Humanitarian Law Project* not to make a constitutional point—I leave it to legal scholars to determine whether or not the Supreme Court's decision represents a betrayal of our country's highest ideals—but rather to underscore the continuing value of Spinoza's philosophical one.

Well before John Stuart Mill, Spinoza had the acuity to recognize that the unfettered freedom of expression is in the state's own best interest. In this post-9/11 world, there is a temptation to believe that "homeland security" is better secured by the suppression of certain liberties than their free exercise. This includes a tendency by justices to interpret existing laws in restrictive ways and efforts by lawmakers to create new limitations, as well as a willingness among the populace, "for the sake of peace and security," to acquiesce in this. We seem ready not only to engage in a higher degree of self-censorship, but also to accept a loosening of legal protections against prior restraint (whether in print publications or the dissemination of information via the Internet), unwarranted surveillance, unreasonable search and seizure, and other intrusive measures. Spinoza, long ago, recognized the danger in such thinking, both for individuals and for the polity at large. He saw that there was no need to make a trade-off between political and social well-being and the freedom of expression; on the contrary, the former depends on the latter.

FEBRUARY 5, 2012

Of Hume and Bondage

—Simon Blackburn

ANYONE ADMIRING DAVID HUME AS I DO FINDS MUCH TO CHEER, but much to lament in the state of academic philosophy, as this year, the three hundredth anniversary of his birth, comes to a close. Hume was an anatomist of the mind, charting the ways we think and feel—a psychologist or cognitive scientist before his time. The cheering feature of the contemporary scene is that plenty of people are following in those footsteps. The nature versus nurture battle has declared an uneasy draw, but the human nature industry is in fine fettle, fed by many disciplines and eagerly consumed by the public.

Yet among philosophers it is not uncommon to find Hume patronized as a slightly dim, inaccurate or naive analytical philosopher who gamely tried to elucidate the meanings of terms but generally failed hopelessly to do so. In fact, Immanuel Kant, a German near-contemporary of Hume, who is often billed as his opponent, had cause to defend him against a similar complaint more than two centuries ago. "One cannot without feeling a certain pain," Kant wrote in 1783, "behold how utterly and completely his opponents, Reid, Oswald, Beattie and finally Priestley missed the point of his problem and constantly misjudged his hints for improvement—constantly taking for granted just what he doubted, and conversely, proving with vehemence and, more often than not, with great insolence exactly what it had never entered his mind to doubt." Plus ça change.

The most visible example of this is the rumpus surrounding the famous passage in which Hume declares that reason by itself is inert and has no other office than to serve and obey the passions. The mountains of commentary this has excited include accusations that Hume is a skeptic about practical reasoning (whatever that might mean); that he is a nihilist who cannot have any values; that in his eyes nothing matters; that he is too stupid to realize that learning that a glass contains benzene instead of gin might extinguish your desire to drink from it; that he constantly forgets his own theory; and indeed, in the words of one contemporary writer—the frothing and foaming and insolence here reach a crescendo—that philosophers like Hume only avoid being "radically defective specimens of humanity" by constantly forgetting and then contradicting their own views. It is melancholy to see one's colleagues going so far astray, for it is surely sensible enough to say that practical reasoning works by mobilizing considerations that engage our desires and wishes, passions and concerns. Those facts that do not concern us indeed remain inert; but far from implying that nothing matters, Hume crafts a straightforward and entirely plausible account of what it is for things to matter to us as they do.

So why the panic? Plato taught philosophers to regard themselves as the special guardians of reason: mandarins whose cozy acquaintance with the forms, or with logic, or with rationality entitles them to special authority in the deliberations of mankind. Take away the role and you destroy a whole professorial raison dêtre. And reasons have become the Holy Grail of contemporary philosophy. They beam down at us, or at least beam down at the illuminati among us. They are the highest court of appeal, what William James called the giver of "moral holidays," inescapable, inexorable, and independent of us, free from the trail of the human serpent. Worldly pains are one thing, but the pain of irrationality—well, even the threat of that is a fearful thing, a Medusa or gorgon's head to turn your opponents to stone.

I think there is something in the water that makes this self-image so seductive at present—a cultural need prompting philosophers to separate themselves as far as possible from the unwashed skeptics, nihilists, relativists or ironists of postmodernism, of which the best known American spokesman was the late Richard Rorty. These are the people who have infiltrated many humanities departments for a generation and who, curiously enough given their usual political colors, anticipated today's politicians in being unable to talk of facts or data—let alone reasons—without sneering quote marks. To be fair, however, while the postmodernists used the quotes because they obsessed over the idea that reality is capable of many different interpretations, the politicians and pundits tend to use them because they cannot bear the thought that reality might get in the way of their God-given right to simple certainties, simple visions and simple nostrums. It's a different motivation, and Fox News may be relieved to hear that it is not really the heir of Jacques Derrida.

Perhaps the cultural situation of the West is sufficiently insecure, like that of Athens after the war with Sparta, for us to need the same defenses against the skeptical quote marks that were provided by Socrates and Plato. They taught us that we can respond to an eternal independent beacon, the heavenly structures of reason itself. The idea that down in our foundations there lie grubby creatures like desires, or passions, or needs, or culture is like some nightmarish madwoman in the attic, and induces the same kind of reaction that met Darwin when he, too, drew attention to our proximity to animals rather than to angels. Surely we, the creatures of reason, are not in bondage to the horrible contingencies that go with being an animal. From their *professorial* aeries the mandarins fight back, reassuring each other that the Holy Grail is there to be seen, spilling into tomes and journals and conferences, e-mails, blogs and tweets, the torrents of what Wittgenstein nicely called the "slightly hysterical style of university talk."

So does Hume actually give comfort to the postmodernists? Are Foucault and Derrida his true heirs? Certainly not, although he is well seen as a pragmatist: an ancestor of James, Dewey, Wittgenstein or even the less apocalyptic parts of Nietzsche or Richard Rorty. But it never occurred to Hume to doubt that there are standards of both reasoning and conduct. He has no inhibitions about condemning aspects of our minds that he regards as useless or pernicious:

gullibility, enthusiasm, stupidity, and the "whole train of monkish virtues." And in doing so, he thinks he can stand foursquare with uncorrupted human nature, the party of mankind. This is where the authority of our moral standards rests, and the base is firm enough. Nor is it anything esoteric or surprising, since we all know when life is going well or badly, and when we hear the words people use about us, we all know whether they express admiration or aversion, praise or blame.

The pragmatist slogan that "meaning is use" directs us to look at the actual functioning of language. We then come at the nature of our thinking by understanding the ways we express ourselves. Meaning is important, as analytical philosophy always held. But it is a house with many mansions. It is not monolithically and myopically concerned with recording the passing show, as if all we can do is make public whichever aspect of reality has just beamed upon us. We are agents in our world, constantly doing things—so much so that perception, like reason, is itself an adaptation whose function is not to pick out the truth, the whole truth, and nothing but the truth, but only to foreground what is salient in the service of our goals and needs. Meaning, therefore, needs to look two ways: back to the environment within which our mental lives are situated, but also forward to the changes in that environment that our desires and goals determine. Fortunately these ideas have percolated widely into areas outside philosophy: it is widely understood, for instance, that animal signals are more like injunctions telling other animals what to do than simple registrations of elements in the environment.

Hume was able to use his pragmatism and his pluralism about the many functions of the mind to avoid metaphysics. About that he was famously a pyromaniac, advocating that we commit to the flames most of what has passed as philosophy from Parmenides to Berkeley. But people need philosophy: we need defenses against the corrosive drips of skepticism. This need surely motivates the apostles of reason to persevere at metaphysics, exploring the world of being and becoming, delineating the true and ultimate nature of reality, finding what is truly there behind the superficial appearances of things. And combined with this image of what we should be doing there comes the inability to read or appreciate anyone who is doing something entirely different. So the stark $64,000 question in much contemporary interpretation of Hume is whether he was a "realist" or not about values and causes, or even persons and ordinary things—questions that should actually be nowhere on the agenda, since it imports precisely the way of looking at things that Hume commits to the flames.

Hume's road is subtle, and too few philosophers dare take it. Yet the whirligig of time may bring in its revenges, as a new generation of pragmatists look at much contemporary writing with the same horror as Hume directed at Spinoza, Nietzsche at Kant, or Russell at Hegel. Meanwhile one soldiers on, hoping, as Hume himself did, for the downfall of some of the prevailing systems of superstition.

DECEMBER 11, 2011

A Feminist Kant

—Carol Hay

I<small>N ONE OF HIS MORE MEMORABLE ESSAYS,</small> "G<small>ETTING</small> A<small>WAY FROM</small> Already Being Pretty Much Away from It All," David Foster Wallace describes a visit to the Illinois State Fair. The friend who accompanies him, whom he calls Native Companion because she's a local, gets on one of the fair's rides. While she's hanging upside down, the men operating the ride stop it so that her dress falls over her head and they can ogle her. After she gets off the ride, Wallace and Native Companion have a heated discussion about the incident. He thinks she's been sexually harassed and thinks something should be done about it.

Wallace asks, "Did you sense something kind of sexual-harass-mentish going on through that whole little sick exercise? . . . this doesn't bother you? As a Midwesterner, you're unbothered?" to which Native Companion replies, "So if I noticed or I didn't, why does it have to be *my* deal? What, because there's [harassers] in the world I don't get to ride on The Zipper? I don't get to ever spin? . . . What's getting hot and bothered going to do about it except keep me from getting to have fun?" Then, Wallace: "This is potentially key. . . . The core value informing a kind of willed politico-sexual stoicism on your part is your prototypically Midwestern appreciation of fun . . . whereas on the East Coast, politico-sexual indignation *is* the fun. . . . I'm telling you. Personal and political fun merge somewhere just east of Cleveland, for women." Native Companion: "They might ought to try just climbing on and spinning and ignoring [them]. That's pretty much all you can do with [expletive]."

Situations like this are ubiquitous, and hardly the worst thing women have to put up with in a sexist society such as ours. But I've grown tired of discussing what's wrong with the carnies' behavior. (It's a textbook case of sexual harassment, and more than enough feminist ink has been spilled explaining why and how this sort of thing is morally unacceptable.) Instead, I want to ask a different set of questions: What is Native Companion obligated to do here? In general, are victims of oppression obligated to resist their oppression?

In short, yes. And the philosophical resources for this claim can be found in a somewhat surprising place: in the moral philosophy of the eighteenth-century German philosopher Immanuel Kant.

I wasn't always so optimistic about Kant's prospects. I first started thinking about these questions while I was in grad school, a feminist who was training to be an analytic philosopher. Analytic philosophers are generally friendly toward Kant (friendlier than many of them tend to be toward feminism, in any case). But most feminist philosophers make no secret of their dislike of him. They rightly decry the horrifically misogynistic things Kant actually said about women (there are some real doozies), and they argue that, among other things, he is committed to a conception of personhood that unfairly and inaccurately privileges our rationality and autonomy over the social, interdependent, embodied, and emotional aspects of our lives. This misrepresentation of human nature encourages us to think about people as fundamentally independent, and this, they argue, leads to the exploitation of those people (usually women) who are responsible for caring for those people who are not independent (children, the elderly, the disabled and infirm—all of us at some point in our lives, really).

Consulting yet another dead white male about the problems of oppression didn't initially strike me as the best idea. But I've now come to think that Kant's account of what our rational nature is, why it's valuable, how it can be compromised and deformed, and why it must be fostered and protected, should be of interest not only to feminists, but to anyone who cares about the victims of oppression, harassment, bullying, or abuse.

Kant argues throughout his moral philosophy that what's distinctive about us as human beings is our rational nature—our ability to set and pursue ends according to reason (or, more colloquially, our ability to figure out what we want, to figure out how to get it, and to ask ourselves whether we should want it). This rational nature, he argues, is what makes us morally valuable and what makes us deserve an important sort of respect.

This respect requires that we always be treated as an end and never merely as a means. As Kant puts it, "So act that you use humanity, whether in your own person or in the person of any other, always at the same time as an end, never merely as a means." We treat people as means whenever we ignore the ends they've set for themselves and instead use them for our own purposes. Kantian philosophers typically focus on how this morally impermissible use of another person involves deception and coercion. But Kant's moral framework can also be used to show what's wrong with other frustrations of rational nature, including those that pop up under oppression.

Feminists have been discussing the devastating psychological effects of sexist oppression for quite some time. Mary Wollstonecraft and J. S. Mill argued, in the eighteenth and nineteenth centuries respectively, that sexist social norms of genteel society and motherhood, combined with sexist legal institutions such as marriage and property, damaged women's rational capacities by depriving them of equal opportunities with men to develop their talents. Contemporary feminists have continued this discussion in a number of ways. Many focus on what happens when women internalize sexist oppression, when women come to believe in, are weakened by, and are motivated to fulfill the stereotypes that represent them as inferior. One way to think about these various harms is that they're instances where oppression has harmed women's rational nature in some way.

Of course, Kantianism is hardly the only philosophical framework with the resources to explain what's wrong with these harms.

What sets Kant apart from almost every other thinker in the Western philosophical canon is his ability to make sense of duties to the self, particularly the duty of self-respect. (Most non-Kantian philosophers think of duties as the sorts of things that you can only have to other people, not the sort of thing you can have to yourself.) Kant's duty of self-respect, first introduced in his 1785 *Groundwork of the Metaphysics of Morals*, is a duty each of us has to recognize the value of the rational nature within us and to respond accordingly. Just as we have a duty to respect others in virtue of their rational nature, we have a duty to respect ourselves.

Without this duty of self-respect, we could explain why someone like Native Companion has a duty to respond to the oppression of other women, simply by appealing a general duty to resist injustice. But we can't explain why she has a particular duty to resist her own oppression. Given that self-sacrifice is routinely expected of oppressed people in ways it's not expected of others (think, for example, of the ideal of the self-abnegating mother who unfailingly puts her family's interests before her own), establishing the duty of self-respect is especially important in these contexts.

What the marriage of Kantianism and feminism gets us, then, is this. Because we have an obligation to prevent harms to our rational nature, and because oppression can harm our capacity to act rationally, we have an obligation to resist our own oppression. Despite what Kant himself might've thought, we know that women's rational capacities are no different from men's. Thus, we can use Kantianism to explain why women are just as deserving of respect as men and why this respect is incompatible with sexist oppression.

So it looks like Native Companion is wrong. The duty of self-respect demands that she stand up for herself by resisting her oppression. Of course, this isn't the only duty that's operative here. The carnies have a duty to stop their immoral behavior; Wallace probably has a duty to stand up for his friend, and certainly has a more general duty to protest injustice; and Native Companion has a duty to other women to do what she can to undermine the manifestations of sexist oppression that all women face. But the duty of self-respect under oppression has received considerably less philosophical attention than these other duties.

The most obvious objection to this line of argument is that holding Native Companion responsible for resisting her oppression shifts the moral burden in this situation onto the party who hasn't done anything wrong—in effect, it blames the victim. But here, too, is a place where the resources of Kantianism are uniquely well-suited to help. In a later work, his 1797 *The Metaphysics of Morals*, Kant expands upon a distinction first introduced in his earlier *Groundwork*: a distinction between perfect and imperfect duties. Unlike perfect duties, imperfect duties aren't duties to perform specific actions. Instead, imperfect duties are duties to adopt certain general maxims, or principles of action, that can be satisfied by more than one action.

The obligation to resist oppression is this sort of duty: there are lots of things one can do to fulfill it. Native Companion could confront the carnies directly. She could lodge a formal complaint with the fair's management. We might even think that she actually is resisting her oppression internally by refusing to feel humiliated, refusing to let the carnies dictate when and how she can have fun, and refusing to believe that their sexually objectifying her demeans her moral status in any way. In some cases, there might be nothing an oppressed person can do to resist her oppression other than simply recognizing that there's something wrong with her situation. This is, in a profound sense, better than nothing. It means she hasn't acquiesced to the innumerable forces that are conspiring to convince her that she's the sort of person who has no right to expect better. It means she recognizes that her lot in life is neither justified nor inevitable.

DECEMBER 8, 2013

Sartre and Camus in New York

—Andy Martin

IN DECEMBER 1944, ALBERT CAMUS, THEN EDITOR OF *COMBAT*, the main newspaper of the French Resistance, made Jean-Paul Sartre an offer he couldn't refuse: the job of American correspondent. Perhaps, in light of the perpetual tension and subsequent acrimonious split between the two men, he was glad to get him out of Paris. What is certain is that Sartre was delighted to go. He'd had enough of the austerities and hypocrisies of postliberation France and had long fantasized about the United States. Camus himself would make the trip soon after, only to return with a characteristically different set of political, philosophical and personal impressions.

In some sense, existentialism was going home. The "roots" of twentieth-century French philosophy are canonically located on mainland Europe, in the fertile terrain of Hegel, Kierkegaard, Nietzsche, Husserl and Heidegger. But it was not entirely immune to the metaphysical turmoil of the United States at the end of the nineteenth century. French philosophy retained elements of the pragmatism of C. S. Peirce and the psychologism of William James (each receives an honorable mention in Sartre's *Being and Nothingness*). More significantly, both Camus and Sartre had learned and borrowed from twentieth-century writers like Faulkner, Hemingway and Dos Passos—and, of course, from the films of Humphrey Bogart. Camus, in particular, cultivated the trench coat with the upturned collar and described himself as a mix of Bogart, Fernandel and a samurai.

When Sartre stepped off the plane in New York in January 1945, only months after the liberation of Paris, his head full of American movies, architecture and jazz, he might have expected to feel in his natural habitat— the preeminent philosopher of *liberté* setting foot in the land of freedom, a nation temperamentally and constitutionally addicted to liberty. Was there not already something of the existential cowboy and intellectual gunslinger in Sartre's take-no-hostages attitude? Camus must have thought so in dispatching him to the United States.

Sartre wrote dozens of articles for *Combat* while in the States, often phoning them back to Camus in Paris, and eventually went on to talk philosophy at Harvard, Princeton, Yale and elsewhere. In the process, he acquired an American girlfriend (about whom he wrote abundantly and explicitly to Simone de Beauvoir: "I am killed by passion and lectures"). But the very personal article he wrote for *Town & Country*, "Manhattan: The Great American Desert," records that he suffered on arrival from "le mal de New York." He never really recovered.

Sartre, leaving the confines of the Plaza Hotel, walked up Fifth Avenue beneath a frozen sky, looking for New York but not finding it. There was nothing on which to focus his gaze; it was a city for "the far-sighted," he wrote, since the natural focal point was somewhere around infinity, over the horizon. He missed the intimate quartiers of Paris, finding in their place only "filmy atmospheres, longitudinally stretched masses with nothing to mark a beginning or end." Just the kind of place, one might think, where an expatriate existentialist ought to fit right in. And yet he suffered stubbornly from a sense of disorientation. "In the numerical anonymity of roads and avenues," he wrote, "I am just anybody, anywhere." New York put him in mind of the steppes or the pampas.

But soon enough he started to realize what his fundamental objection really was. The whole point of the city was to fortify itself against nature. But Manhattan failed to do that: an "open" city with a limitless sky above, it let nature in on every side. It was, of course, an island, and thus too exposed to the elements: to storm, hurricane, snow, heat, wind, floods. It had no real protection against anything. "I feel as though I were camping in the heart of a jungle crawling with insects." Therefore he learned to appreciate it only while crossing it in a car, as if he were "driving across the great plains of Andalusia."

And just as he inverts the perception of the American city, so too Sartre turns the notion of American freedom inside out. By February, having been shuttled to and fro across the States, wined, dined and given propaganda tours to industrial installations, he comes to the conclusion in another article, written for *Le Figaro*, that America is the land of conformism. He finds that beneath its notional attachment to "individualism," America does not actually trust the solitary individual. Despite the "liberal economy," America is an embodiment of a Rousseauist "social contract" in which the general will of the "collectivity" dominates: "Each American is educated by other Americans and he educates others in turn. Everywhere in New York, in colleges and beyond, there are courses in Americanization." Existentialist anomie is prohibited: America is hypernormative, producing citizen clones.

It is Sartre's most powerful and recurrent complaint: that people are being treated as things. The "nausea" of the 1930s, elicited by pebbles and trees and ocean depths (and thus, as in New York, nature in general) morphed, in the 1940s and '50s, into a specific aversion to the nonorganic products of economic forces. In America he understood that things (the "in-itself"), in all their massiveness, were threatening to reify the amorphous human (or "for-itself") and produce what he called in a later formulation the "practico-inert."

Still, Sartre holds out the hope that New York is moving in a generally Sartrean and semiapocalyptic direction. All those skyscrapers? Obviously, they are doomed. "They are already a bit run-down; tomorrow, perhaps, they will be torn down. In any case, their construction required a faith that we no longer have." The Chrysler and the Empire State buildings already appear to Sartre like ancient ruins.

Camus—officially a cultural emissary of the French government—followed in Sartre's footsteps in 1946, providing an ironic commentary on his predecessor. Where Sartre was obsessed with architecture, Camus was indifferent, oblivious. "I notice that I have not noticed the skyscrapers, they seemed to me perfectly natural." He had no issues with commodity capitalism. He admired colors, foodstuffs, smells, taxis, tie shops, ice cream, the "orgy of violent lights" that was Broadway, a jazz bar in Harlem and the giant Camel advertising icon of "an American soldier, his mouth open, puffing out clouds of real smoke."

He fell in love several times over, notably with Patricia Blake, a nineteen-year-old student and *Vogue* apprentice. He read her pages from *The Plague*, and she, in return, noting his fascination with the American way of death, found him issues of undertakers' trade magazines—*Sunnyside*, *Casket* and *Embalmer's Monthly*. He particularly admired a funeral parlor ad: "You die. We do the rest."

At Vassar he gave a lecture on "The Crisis of Mankind" and was dazzled by the spectacle of "an army of long-legged young starlets, lazing on the lawn." But he was preoccupied by what he thought of as the "American tragedy." The tragedy of the students was that they lacked a sense of the tragic. For Sartre, the tragic was the mechanization and objectification of the human. For Camus, the tragic was something more elusive: whatever it was, it was missing in America.

There was an obvious difference of context between Camus and the students he was addressing. He'd come from Europe, which had just spent several years tearing itself apart, whereas they remained more or less physically untouched by the war. Camus was welcomed both as literary luminary (the translation of *The Outsider* came out during his stay) and Resistance hero. But his tragic perception of life was not reducible to the question of the Second World War. Sailing back from New York to France, at night in the middle of the Atlantic, staring down from the deck into the ocean, mesmerized by the wake of the ship, Camus spoke of his love for "these seas of forgetfulness, these unlimited silences that are like the enchantment of death."

Camus, the Resistance philosopher of solidarity, discovered (or perhaps rediscovered) the problem of other minds in New York. Unlike Sartre, he had no difficulty with things, trees, the Empire

State Building, the impersonal ocean. It was only on looking into the face of another human being that he fully experienced a sense of the tragic. While hell-is-other-people Sartre came to invoke a notion of the "group-in-fusion," Camus—who had to keep explaining to the students that he was not and never had been an "existentialist"— increasingly redefined the "absurd" in terms of an inevitable failure of language to bridge the gap between individuals. And it was not just the problem of inadequate English in speaking to Americans. He had the same feeling in Quebec.

The clash between Sartre and Camus would come to be defined by their political divergence in the 1950s, crystallized by the publication of *The Rebel* by Camus. But already, in their different reactions to the United States—and particularly New York—we have the ingredients of a philosophical schism. Sartre, on his return to Europe, recalls above all America's racism and practice of segregation, the inevitable counterpart to its drive to conformity. He writes a play, *The Respectful Prostitute*, that dramatizes the episode of the Scottsboro Boys in the 1930s. The split between contending forces—East and West, black and white, bourgeoisie and proletariat, humans and things—becomes the defining concern of his philosophy, summarized in the (admittedly rebarbative) phrase he comes up with in his *Critique of Dialectical Reason* to define boxing, but which also applies to his relationship with Camus: "a binary praxis of antagonistic reciprocity." Existentialism in this form, inflected with Marxism, infiltrates the American intelligentsia, is absorbed into black power philosophy ("black existentialism") and finds an echo in writers as disparate as Richard Wright and Norman Mailer.

Camus, on the other hand, begins to sound more like Samuel Beckett. While Sartre after the war was more than ever a self-professed "writing machine," Camus was increasingly graphophobic, haunted by a "disgust for all forms of public expression." Sartre's philosophy becomes sociological and structuralist in its binary emphasis. Camus, all alone, in the night, between continents, far away from everything, is already less the solemn "moralist" of legend ("the Saint," Sartre called him), more a (pre-) poststructuralist in his greater concern and anxiety about language, his emphasis on difference and refusal to articulate a clear-cut theory: "I am too young to have a system," he told one audience. And it is this antisystematic aspect of America that he retains and refuses to clarify: "After so many months I know nothing about New York."

Paradoxically, it is clear that Sartre took his notion of collective action from what he witnessed in the United States rather than in the Soviet Union. It is typical that he should choose to frame his notion of freedom and the fate of individual identity in essentially literary (or textual) terms. Beware the editor! He didn't like the way his articles were butchered when they appeared in American journals and admits to being apprehensive of something similar—"le rewriting"—happening to his plays, should they ever be put on in the United States. The FBI, while accusing Camus of writing "inaccurate reports," also misidentified him as "Canus" and "Corus."

Sartre and Camus's love-hate relationship was played out and reflected in their on-off romance with America. As Camus put it, "It is necessary to fall in love . . . if only to provide an alibi for all the random despair you are going to feel anyway." Above all the two thinkers emphasize that America is always balanced precariously, like a tightrope walker, on the thread of a philosophical dialectic.

JULY 14, 2012

Kierkegaard's *Antigone*

—Ulrika Carlsson

ERHAPS THE MOST CENTRAL THEME IN SØREN KIERKEGAARD'S religious thought is the doctrine of original sin: the idea that we share in some essential human guilt simply by being born. But guilt is an important concept also in Kierkegaard's secular writings. He thought that the modern era was defined by its concept of guilt. Kierkegaard's two hundredth birthday gives us an occasion to assess the modern relevance of his legacy and the viability of his own view of modernity.

Kierkegaard thought of Socrates as the person who first discovered human autonomy—the fact that we are free to determine our own actions and therefore responsible for those actions. This insight undermined the ancient worldview, which found its perfect representation in tragic drama, where characters bring about their own ruin because they are fated to do so. In his 1843 essay, "Ancient Tragedy's Reflection in the Modern," Kierkegaard grappled with this question partly through an analysis of the work of Sophocles. In the play *Oedipus the King*, the gods have cursed the tragic hero with a fate to commit two terrible crimes.

The curse is visited upon his children, too, including his daughter who in the follow-up play *Antigone* commits a crime of her own. Sophocles thus invites us to think of this curse as something like a hereditary disease, passed on from parents to children. In Antigone's crime and punishment, we see the reverberation of her father's misfortune, and if original sin is sometimes called "hereditary sin," Antigone's is a "hereditary guilt." Such a concept is nonsensical to the Socratic mindset. We are responsible only for what we do—not for what happens to us, or for the actions of others.

Oedipus's crimes are to kill his father and marry his mother; Antigone's is to defy the state. She is sentenced to live burial for burying her brother, a traitor, against a state prohibition. But in the midst of this horrible destiny is a relief. Sophocles allows both the fictional character Antigone and the spectators to take comfort in the fact that her transgression against the state is done out of obedience to a divine mandate to honor one's family and, moreover, that her own terrible fate is ultimately the work of the gods. She is then only partly responsible for the deed and for bringing the subsequent punishment upon herself. Fate and divine mandate are the heroine's ruination, but they also absolve her of guilt and, by precluding any real choice, redeem her from anxiety and regret.

Socrates, ever defiant of authority, would have found no such excuses for Antigone. Whether or not she was right to bury her brother, she was personally responsible for doing so. She should bear her punishment stoically, as Socrates bore his. When modernity severs the individual from his ties to kin, state, tradition and divine authority, "it must turn the individual over to himself," Kierkegaard writes, so that, in effect, he "becomes his own creator."

But our faith in freedom is excessive. It would be naive to think that happiness requires nothing more than the freedom to choose. Modernity cannot evade tragedy, and in fact Kierkegaard proceeds to outline a modern version of Sophocles's play—a post-Socratic *Antigone*. The Danish term he uses for hereditary guilt literally means "inheritance guilt," which unlike the English term calls to mind the wealth and property left to children upon their parents' death. The term is especially appropriate for his modern Antigone, who considers the curse on her father not so much a disease as a birthright. In Kierkegaard's modern play, the drama does not revolve around her brother's treason, death and burial but concerns Antigone's relation to her father and his crimes.

Whereas the kinship between the ancient Antigone and Oedipus is an objective relation, so that his curse is passed down to her through blood and name, their kinship in the modern version is ultimately a subjective one. The modern Antigone is not fated to share her father's curse, not obliged to share his guilt. But she is compelled to share his grief out of compassion, and so strong is this compassion that she wants to share also his guilt—wants to make of herself, retroactively, an accomplice to his crimes. She loves her father with all her soul, Kierkegaard writes, and it is this love that "pulls her away from herself, into her father's guilt."

But love is not merely a feeling that overcomes her—it is a feeling she happily affirms, actively reinforces. Oedipus gives Antigone's life a center of gravity, something that binds her freedom. She welcomes the suffering that manifests her love of her father and to a certain degree she inflicts it upon herself. Love is indeed ambiguous between passivity and activity, necessity and freedom. On the one hand, a lover regards the beloved as the cause of her love. Love appears to strike us from the outside and we cannot love at will. In this sense, loving is passive. Yet when I say that I speak "from the bottom of my heart" or that I do something "wholeheartedly," I use a metaphor for love to express full and voluntary investment in what I say and do. In these idioms, love represents responsibility, activity.

Life is partly a task and partly a gift, Kierkegaard wrote. Unlike a curse, a right or a genetic disease, a gift cannot be bestowed upon a person against her will. She can choose to accept or decline it. A child does not choose her parents but is offered them as gifts upon her birth, and to love them and grieve with them is to appropriate them as her kin. Love is this project of accepting a gift, cultivating a heritage, assuming another's fate as one's own. If freedom is the ailment, it is willful surrender to her emotions and her ties to others that is the modern Antigone's redemption.

MAY 5, 2013

Freud's Radical Talking

—Benjamin Y. Fong

D EATH IS SUPPOSED TO BE AN EVENT PROCLAIMED BUT ONCE, and yet some deaths, curiously enough, need to be affirmed again and again, as if there were a risk that the interred will crawl back up into the world of the living if fresh handfuls of dirt are not tossed on their graves. One such member of the living dead, accompanying the likes of God and Karl Marx, is Sigmund Freud. How often one hears, thanks recently to the fetishization of neuroscience, that psychoanalysis is now bunk, irrelevant, its method decadent and "dangerous," as the recent David Cronenberg film *A Dangerous Method*, informs us.

Over the years, the "talking cure"—so dubbed by Bertha Pappenheim, aka "Anna O.," who became Freud's first psychoanalytic case study—has received quite a bit of ridicule and reworking. With countless children and adults taking behavior-altering drugs, many are again tolling the bell for psychoanalysis. Who wouldn't choose fast-acting pills over many years on the couch, health insurance companies most of all? Perhaps, after surviving scandal, revision and pop characterization, drugs and money will definitively put old Sigmund to rest.

If psychoanalysis were simply a way of "curing" certain individuals of socially unwanted behavior, then I would have no problem with its disappearance. Similarly, if psychoanalysis were just a way for wealthy individuals to talk to one another about their lackluster existences, it might as well continue on its way to the dustbin of history. And if, God forbid, psychoanalysis has devolved into just another addition to the theory toolkit of academics in the humanities, someone ought to put it out of its misery now.

That said, I think there is something of great worth in the "talking cure" that would be troubling to see succumb to a cultural death. That something has to do with the relation between two realms of psychic activity that Freud called the "primary" and "secondary" processes. The former domain is instinctual and relentless, a deep reservoir of irrational drives that lie just beneath the apparently calm façade of our civilized selves. The latter is the façade itself, the measured and calculating exterior we unconsciously create to negotiate everyday life. Although these two terms are somewhat obscure, the basic divide between them is familiar to the point of obviousness.

We know all too well, for instance, that the secondary process often fails to contain the depths below, which sends envoys to the surface in the form of anxiety, depression, prejudice and hypocrisy. The more we devote ourselves to the dominant cultural norms, the more those drives begin to fester within us, until eventually they seep through the cracks in most unexpected ways. It is, therefore, necessary to confront the "problem" of the primary process, which has in recent times received two "answers."

The first stresses the need for the secondary process to conquer the primary by means of an "education to reality." From a very early age, we are asked to recall facts, to support our statements, to string together arguments, to anticipate counterarguments, to make decisions, and, if our teachers and parents are sufficiently sensitive to the ways of our pluralistic society, to remain respectful toward those who disagree with us. Some social critics would have us believe that the only thing wrong with this picture is its disjunction with reality: if only our schools and our families were better training our youth in the public use of reason, our democracy would not be in the decrepit state it is in.

No doubt there is some truth here, but this general attitude blinds us to how crippling the exercise of our reasoning faculties can often be. In professional settings, of course, this kind of objective problem solving and collective decision making is needed and rewarded in turn. When problems have a clear and precise answer, the gears of production can keep spinning. Nothing, however, could be more detrimental to the sort of understanding required by our social existence than the widespread belief that all problems have answers (or, for that matter, that all problems are problems).

The second "answer" calls for the liberation rather than the repression of the primary process. We all need, so the logic goes, to appease our inner selves. So we may take vacations, pop pills, go to the movies, drink, smoke, or shop. And when we are done caring for our "self," that uniquely American preoccupation of the twentieth century, we may resume our rational behavior all the better, unencumbered temporarily by that pesky inner turmoil that makes us human.

Freud himself suggested neither of these alternatives. Rather, he proposed that we engage in a particular kind of conversation that runs something like this: one person talks without worrying about whether his words are "right," in the sense of their being both correct and appropriate, and the other listens without judging any disclosure to be more important than another. In contrast to most conversations, which have certain culturally defined limits and rhythms of propriety, this exchange has no such rigid rules. It ventures to awkward places. It becomes too intense. And more often than not, it is utterly boring, reducing both partners to long bouts of silence.

From an outside perspective, the conversation is pointless. And indeed, most of the time it appears to be a waste. But in its disjunction with routine human interaction, it opens a space for our knotted interiors, so used to "having a point," to slowly unravel. As each piece flakes off, it is examined and seen in relation to other pieces. After a long while, we gain what might be called, to borrow a term from Martin Heidegger, a "free relation" to these parts of ourselves and our world, such that the unmovable density they once comprised becomes pliable and navigable. Some key pieces appear and others vanish, but the puzzle is never complete. The aim of the conversation, however, is not completion, which short of death itself is an illusion, but the ability to change. This change involves neither the victory of the secondary process nor the liberation of the primary process but rather the opening of lines of communication between them.

We have become accustomed to temporarily putting aside our knotted interiors only to return to them as they were. "Reality will always be what it is; we can only hope for breaks every once in awhile." This is a dogma both psychological and political. What Freud proposed, and what remains revolutionary in his thought today, is that human beings have the capacity for real change, the kind that would undo the malicious effects of our upbringings and educations so as to obviate the need for "breaks from real life," both voluntary and involuntary.

What is paradoxical in his proposal is that this revolution requires less "work," not more. There is a premium today on "doing," as if we are now suffering, amid astounding productivity, from an essential passivity. Freud's conversation is, of course, a kind of work that is often very taxing. Yet it is always and inevitably what the classical economists called "unproductive labor."

Against our culture of productivity and its attendant subculture of "letting off steam," Freud hypothesized that the best way to refashion our world for the better is to adopt a new way of speaking to one another. Above all, this radical way of talking is defined by what appears to be extended pointlessness, something we are increasingly incapable of tolerating as the world around us moves ever faster. There are books to read, mouths to feed, meetings to attend, corporations to fight or defend, new places to visit, starving children to save . . . who has the time? And yet it is precisely in not allowing ourselves the time to be "unproductive" that reality is insured to remain rigid and unchanging.

According to Hannah Arendt, the world, as opposed to the earth, is something man-made. It is planned out with the ideas from our heads and composed of the work of our hands. But without deep human relatedness, it is but a static "heap of things," a hardened reality that we run around while remaining in the same place. What lends pliability to reality, she claims, as Freud did decades earlier, is taking the time to talk with one another without any predetermined purpose, without hurrying from one topic to another, without seeking solutions, and without skirting the real difficulty of actually communicating with one another. It is here that the continuing value of Freud's discovery asserts itself. If psychoanalysis is dead—that is, if we no longer care about Freud's problems—then so, too, is the human capacity to enact change.

MARCH 18, 2012

Was Wittgenstein Right?

—Paul Horwich

THE SINGULAR ACHIEVEMENT OF THE CONTROVERSIAL EARLY twentieth-century philosopher Ludwig Wittgenstein was to have discerned the true nature of Western philosophy—what is special about its problems, where they come from, how they should and should not be addressed, and what can and cannot be accomplished by grappling with them. The uniquely insightful answers provided to these metaquestions are what give his treatments of specific issues within the subject—concerning language, experience, knowledge, mathematics, art and religion among them—a power of illumination that cannot be found in the work of others.

Admittedly, few would agree with this rosy assessment—certainly not many professional philosophers. Apart from a small and ignored clique of hard-core supporters, the usual view these days is that his writing is self-indulgently obscure and that behind the catchy slogans there is little of intellectual value. But this dismissal disguises what is pretty clearly the real cause of Wittgenstein's unpopularity within departments of philosophy: namely, his thoroughgoing rejection of the subject as traditionally and currently practiced, and his insistence that it can't give us the kind of knowledge generally regarded as its raison d'être.

Wittgenstein claims that there are no realms of phenomena whose study is the special business of a philosopher, and about which he or she should devise profound a priori theories and sophisticated supporting arguments. There are no startling discoveries to be made of facts, not open to the methods of science, yet accessible "from the armchair" through some blend of intuition, pure reason and conceptual analysis. Indeed the whole idea of a subject that could yield such results is based on confusion and wishful thinking.

This attitude is in stark opposition to the traditional view, which continues to prevail. Philosophy is respected, even exalted, for its promise to provide fundamental insights into the human condition and the ultimate character of the universe, leading to vital conclusions about how we are to arrange our lives. It's taken for granted that there is deep understanding to be obtained of the nature of consciousness, of how knowledge of the external world is possible, of whether our decisions can be truly free, of the structure of any just society, and so on—and that philosophy's job is to provide such understanding. Isn't that why we are so fascinated by it?

If so, then we are duped and bound to be disappointed, says Wittgenstein. For these are mere pseudoproblems, the misbegotten products of linguistic illusion and muddled thinking. So it should be entirely unsurprising that the "philosophy" aiming to solve them has been marked by perennial controversy and lack of decisive progress—by an embarrassing failure, after over 2,000 years, to settle any of its central issues. Therefore, traditional philosophical theorizing must give way to a painstaking identification of its tempting but misguided presuppositions and an understanding of how we ever came to regard them as legitimate. But in that case, he asks, "where does [our] investigation get its importance from, since it seems only to destroy everything interesting, that is, all that is great and important? (As it were all the buildings, leaving behind only bits of stone and rubble)," and answers that "what we are destroying is nothing but houses of cards and we are clearing up the ground of language on which they stand."

Given this extreme pessimism about the potential of philosophy—perhaps tantamount to a denial that there is such a subject—it is hardly surprising that "Wittgenstein" is uttered with a curl of the lip in most philosophical circles. For who likes to be told that his or her life's work is confused and pointless? Thus, even Bertrand Russell, his early teacher and enthusiastic supporter, was eventually led to complain peevishly that Wittgenstein seems to have "grown tired of serious thinking and invented a doctrine which would make such an activity unnecessary."

But what is that notorious doctrine, and can it be defended? We might boil it down to four related claims.

- *The first is that traditional philosophy is scientistic: its primary goals, which are to arrive at simple, general principles, to uncover profound explanations, and to correct naive opinions, are taken from the sciences. And this is undoubtedly the case.*

- *The second is that the nonempirical ("armchair") character of philosophical investigation—its focus on conceptual truth—is in tension with those goals. That's because our concepts exhibit a highly theory-resistant complexity and variability. They evolved, not for the sake of science and its objectives, but rather in order to cater to the interacting contingencies of our nature, our culture, our environment, our communicative needs and our other purposes. As a consequence, the commitments defining individual concepts are rarely simple or determinate and differ dramatically from one concept to another. Moreover, it is not possible (as it is within empirical domains) to accommodate superficial complexity by means of simple principles at a more basic (e.g., microscopic) level.*

- *The third main claim of Wittgenstein's metaphilosophy—an immediate consequence of the first two—is that traditional philosophy is necessarily pervaded with oversimplification; analogies are unreasonably inflated; exceptions to simple regularities are wrongly dismissed.*

- *Therefore—the fourth claim—a decent approach to the subject must avoid theory construction and instead be merely "therapeu-*

tic," *confined to exposing the irrational assumptions on which theory-oriented investigations are based and the irrational conclusions to which they lead.*

Consider, for instance, the paradigmatically philosophical question, "What is truth?" This provokes perplexity because, on the one hand, it demands an answer of the form, "Truth is such-and-such," but on the other hand, despite hundreds of years of looking, no acceptable answer of that kind has ever been found. We've tried truth as "correspondence with the facts," as "provability," as "practical utility," and as "stable consensus," but all turned out to be defective in one way or another—either circular or subject to counterexamples. Reactions to this impasse have included a variety of theoretical proposals. Some philosophers have been led to deny that there is such a thing as absolute truth. Some have maintained (insisting on one of the aforementioned definitions) that although truth exists, it lacks certain features that are ordinarily attributed to it—for example, that the truth may sometimes be impossible to discover. Some have inferred that truth is intrinsically paradoxical and essentially incomprehensible. And others persist in the attempt to devise a definition that will fit all the intuitive data.

But from Wittgenstein's perspective, each of the first three of these strategies rides roughshod over our fundamental convictions about truth, and the fourth is highly unlikely to succeed. Instead we should begin, he thinks, by recognizing (as mentioned) that our various concepts play very different roles in our cognitive economy and (correspondingly) are governed by defining principles of very different kinds. Therefore, it was always a mistake to extrapolate from the fact that empirical concepts, such as *red* or *magnetic* or *alive*, stand for properties with specifiable underlying natures to the presumption that the notion of *truth* must stand for some such property as well.

Wittgenstein's conceptual pluralism positions us to recognize that notion's idiosyncratic function and to infer that truth itself will not be reducible to anything more basic. More specifically, we can see that the concept's function in our cognitive economy is merely to serve as a device of generalization. It enables us to say such things as "Einstein's last words were true," and not be stuck with "If Einstein's last words were that E = mc², then E = mc²: and if his last words were that nuclear weapons should be banned, then nuclear weapons should be banned; . . . and so on," which has the disadvantage of being infinitely long! Similarly we can use it to say, "We should want our beliefs to be true" (instead of struggling with "We should want that if we believe that E = mc² then E = mc²; and that if we believe . . . etc."). We can see, also, that this sort of utility depends upon nothing more than the fact that the attribution of truth to a statement is obviously equivalent to the statement itself—for example, "It's true that E = mc²" is equivalent to "E = mc²." Thus, possession of the concept of truth appears to consist in an appreciation of that triviality, rather than a mastery of any explicit definition. The traditional search for such an account (or for some other form of reductive analysis) was a wild-goose chase, a pseudoproblem. Truth emerges as exceptionally unprofound and as exceptionally unmysterious.

This example illustrates the key components of Wittgenstein's metaphilosophy, and suggests how to flesh them out a little further. Philosophical problems typically arise from the clash between the inevitably idiosyncratic features of special-purpose concepts—*true, good, object, person, now, necessary*—and the scientistically driven insistence upon uniformity. Moreover, the various kinds of theoretical moves designed to resolve such conflicts (forms of skepticism, revisionism, mysterianism, and conservative systematization) are not only irrational, but unmotivated. The paradoxes to which they respond should instead be resolved merely by coming to appreciate the mistakes of perverse overgeneralization from which they arose. And the fundamental source of this irrationality is scientism.

As Wittgenstein put it in the *Blue Book*:

> *Our craving for generality has [as one] source . . . our preoccupation with the method of science. I mean the method of reducing the explanation of natural phenomena to the smallest possible number of primitive natural laws; and, in mathematics, of uni-*

fying the treatment of different topics by using a generalization. Philosophers constantly see the method of science before their eyes, and are irresistibly tempted to ask and answer in the way science does. This tendency is the real source of metaphysics, and leads the philosopher into complete darkness. I want to say here that it can never be our job to reduce anything to anything, or to explain anything. Philosophy really is "purely descriptive."

These radical ideas are not obviously correct, and may on close scrutiny turn out to be wrong. But they deserve to receive that scrutiny—to be taken much more seriously than they are. Yes, most of us have been interested in philosophy only because of its promise to deliver precisely the sort of theoretical insights that Wittgenstein argues are illusory. But such hopes are no defense against his critique. Besides, if he turns out to be right, satisfaction enough may surely be found in what we still can get—clarity, demystification, and truth.

MARCH 3, 2013

OLD PROBLEMS, NEW SPINS

Experiments in Philosophy

—*Joshua Knobe*

ARISTOTLE ONCE WROTE THAT PHILOSOPHY BEGINS IN WONDER, but one might equally well say that philosophy begins with inner conflict. The cases in which we are most drawn to philosophy are precisely the cases in which we feel as though there is something pulling us toward one side of a question but also something pulling us, perhaps equally powerfully, toward the other.

But how exactly can philosophy help us in cases like these? If we feel something within ourselves drawing us in one direction but also something drawing us the other way, what exactly can philosophy do to offer us illumination?

One traditional answer is that philosophy can help us out by offering us some insight into human nature. Suppose we feel a sense of puzzlement about whether God exists, or whether there are objective moral truths, or whether human beings have free will.

The traditional view was that philosophers could help us get to the bottom of this puzzlement by exploring the sources of the conflict within our own minds. If you look back to the work of some of the greatest thinkers of the nineteenth century—Mill, Marx, Nietzsche—you can find extraordinary intellectual achievements along these basic lines.

This traditional approach is back with a vengeance. Philosophers today are once again looking for the roots of philosophical conflicts in our human nature, and they are once again suggesting that we can make progress on philosophical questions by reaching a better understanding of our own minds. But these days, philosophers are going after these issues using a new set of methodologies. They are pursuing the traditional questions using all the tools of modern cognitive science. They are teaming up with researchers in other disciplines, conducting experimental studies, publishing in some of the top journals of psychology. Work in this new vein has come to be known as experimental philosophy.

Discussions of this movement often bring up an important question that is worth pursuing further. The study of human nature, whether in Nietzsche or in a contemporary psychology journal, is obviously relevant to certain purely scientific questions, but how could this sort of work ever help us to answer the distinctive questions of *philosophy*? It may be of some interest just to figure out how people ordinarily think, but how could facts about how people ordinarily think ever tell us which views were actually right or wrong?

Instead of just considering this question in the abstract, let's focus in on one particular example. Take the age-old problem of free will—a topic discussed at length here at The Stone by various contributors. If all of our actions are determined by prior events—just one thing causing the next, which causes the next—then is it ever possible for human beings to be morally responsible for the things we do? Faced with this question, many people feel themselves pulled in competing directions—it is as though there is something compelling them to say yes, but also something that makes them want to say no.

What is it that draws us in these two conflicting directions? The philosopher Shaun Nichols and I thought that people might be drawn toward one view by their capacity for abstract, theoretical reasoning, while simultaneously being drawn in the opposite direction by their more immediate emotional reactions. It is as though their capacity for abstract reasoning tells them, "This person was completely determined and therefore cannot be held responsible," while their capacity for immediate emotional reaction keeps screaming, "But he did such a horrible thing! Surely, he is responsible for it."

To put this idea to the test, we conducted a simple experiment. All participants in the study were told about a deterministic universe (which we called "Universe A"), and all participants received exactly the same information about how this universe worked. The question then was whether people would think that it was possible in such a universe to be fully morally responsible.

But now comes the trick. Some participants were asked in a way designed to trigger abstract, theoretical reasoning, while others were asked in a way designed to trigger a more immediate emotional response. Specifically, participants in one condition were given this abstract question:

In Universe A, is it possible for a person to be fully morally responsible for their actions?

Meanwhile, participants in the other condition were given a more concrete and emotionally fraught example:

In Universe A, a man named Bill has become attracted to his secretary, and he decides that the only way to be with her is to kill his wife and three children. He knows that it is impossible to escape from his house in the event of a fire. Before he leaves on a business trip, he sets up a device in his basement that burns down the house and kills his family.

Is Bill fully morally responsible for killing his wife and children?

The results showed a striking difference between conditions. Of the participants who received the abstract question, the vast majority (86 percent) said that it was not possible for anyone to be morally responsible in the deterministic universe. But then, in the more concrete case, we found exactly the opposite results. There, most participants (72 percent) said that Bill actually *was* responsible for what he had done.

What we have in this example is just one very simple initial experiment. Needless to say, the actual body of research on this topic involves numerous different studies, and the scientific issues arising here can be quite complex. But let us put all those issues to the side for the moment. Instead, we can just return to our original question. How can experiments like these possibly help us to answer the more traditional questions of philosophy?

The simple study I have been discussing here can offer at least a rough sense of how such an inquiry works. The idea is not that we subject philosophical questions to some kind of Gallup poll. ("Well, the vote came out 65 percent to 35 percent, so I guess the answer is . . . human beings do have free will!") Rather, the aim is to get a better understanding of the psychological mechanisms at the root of our sense of conflict and then to begin thinking about which of these mechanisms are worthy of our trust and which might simply be leading us astray.

So, what is the answer in the specific case of the conflict we feel about free will? Should we be putting our faith in our capacity for abstract theoretical reasoning, or should we be relying on our more immediate emotional responses? At the moment, there is no consensus on this question within the experimental philosophy community. What all experimental philosophers do agree on, however, is that we will be able to do a better job of addressing these fundamental philosophical questions if we can arrive at a better understanding of the way our own minds work.

SEPTEMBER 7, 2010

Your Move: The Maze of Free Will

—Galen Strawson

YOU ARRIVE AT A BAKERY. IT'S THE EVENING OF A NATIONAL HOLiday. You want to buy a cake with your last ten dollars to round off the preparations you've already made. There's only one thing left in the store—a ten-dollar cake.

On the steps of the store, someone is shaking an Oxfam tin. You stop, and it seems quite clear to you—it surely is quite clear to you—that it is entirely up to you what you do next. You are—it seems—truly, radically, ultimately free to choose what to do, in such a way that you will be ultimately morally responsible for whatever you do choose. Fact: you can put the money in the tin, or you can go in and buy the cake. You're not only completely, radically free to choose in this situation. You're not free not to choose (that's how it feels). You're "condemned to freedom," in Jean-Paul Sartre's phrase. You're fully and explicitly conscious of what the options are and you can't escape that consciousness. You can't somehow slip out of it.

You may have heard of determinism, the theory that absolutely everything that happens is causally determined to happen exactly as it does by what has already gone before—right back to the beginning of the universe. You may also believe that determinism is true. (You may also know, contrary to popular opinion, that current science gives us no more reason to think that determinism is false than that determinism is true.) In that case, standing on the steps of the store, it may cross your mind that in five minutes' time you'll be able to look back on the situation you're in now and say truly, of what you will by then have done, "Well, it was determined that I should do that." But even if you do fervently believe this, it doesn't seem to be able to touch your sense that you're absolutely morally responsible for what you do next.

The case of the Oxfam tin, which I have used before to illustrate this problem, is relatively dramatic, but choices of this type are common. They occur frequently in our everyday lives, and they seem to prove beyond a doubt that we are free and ultimately morally responsible for what we do. There is, however, an argument, which I call the Basic Argument, which appears to show that we can never be ultimately morally responsible for our actions. According to the Basic Argument, it makes no difference whether determinism is true or false. We can't be ultimately morally responsible either way.

The argument goes like this.

1. *You do what you do—in the circumstances in which you find yourself—because of the way you then are.*

2. *So if you're going to be ultimately responsible for what you do, you're going to have to be ultimately responsible for the way you are—at least in certain mental respects.*

3. *But you can't be ultimately responsible for the way you are in any respect at all.*

4. *So you can't be ultimately responsible for what you do.*

The key move is 3. Why can't you be ultimately responsible for the way you are in any respect at all? In answer, consider an expanded version of the argument.

a. *It's undeniable that the way you are initially is a result of your genetic inheritance and early experience.*

b. *It's undeniable that these are things for which you can't be held to be in any way responsible (morally or otherwise).*

c. *But you can't at any later stage of life hope to acquire true or ultimate moral responsibility for the way you are by trying to*

> change the way you already are as a result of genetic inheri-
> tance and previous experience.
>
> d. Why not? Because both the particular ways in which you try
> to change yourself and the amount of success you have when
> trying to change yourself will be determined by how you
> already are as a result of your genetic inheritance and previous
> experience.
>
> e. And any further changes that you may become able to bring
> about after you have brought about certain initial changes will
> in turn be determined, via the initial changes, by your genetic
> inheritance and previous experience.

There may be all sorts of other factors affecting and changing you. Determinism may be false: some changes in the way you are may come about as a result of the influence of indeterministic or random factors. But you obviously can't be responsible for the effects of any random factors, so they can't help you to become ultimately morally responsible for how you are.

Some people think that quantum mechanics shows that determinism is false, and so holds out a hope that we can be ultimately responsible for what we do. But even if quantum mechanics had shown that determinism is false (it hasn't), the question would remain: How can indeterminism, objective randomness, help in any way whatever to make you responsible for your actions? The answer to this question is easy. It can't.

And yet we still feel that we are free to act in such a way that we are absolutely responsible for what we do. So I'll finish with a third, richer version of the Basic Argument that this is impossible.

> i.   Interested in free action, we're particularly interested in
> actions performed for reasons (as opposed to reflex actions or
> mindlessly habitual actions).
>
> ii. When one acts for a reason, what one does is a function of how
> one is, mentally speaking. (It's also a function of one's height,
> one's strength, one's place and time, and so on, but it's the

mental factors that are crucial when moral responsibility is in question.)

iii. *So if one is going to be truly or ultimately responsible for how one acts, one must be ultimately responsible for how one is, mentally speaking—at least in certain respects.*

iv. *But to be ultimately responsible for how one is, in any mental respect, one must have brought it about that one is the way one is, in that respect. And it's not merely that one must have caused oneself to be the way one is, in that respect. One must also have consciously and explicitly chosen to be the way one is, in that respect, and one must also have succeeded in bringing it about that one is that way.*

v. *But one can't really be said to choose, in a conscious, reasoned, fashion, to be the way one is in any respect at all, unless one already exists, mentally speaking, already equipped with some principles of choice, "P1"—preferences, values, ideals—in the light of which one chooses how to be.*

vi. *But then to be ultimately responsible, on account of having chosen to be the way one is, in certain mental respects, one must be ultimately responsible for one's having the principles of choice, P1, in the light of which one chose how to be.*

vii. *But for this to be so one must have chosen P1 in a reasoned, conscious, intentional fashion.*

viii. *But for this to be so one must already have had some principles of choice, P2, in the light of which one chose P1.*

ix. *And so on. Here we are setting out on a regress that we cannot stop. Ultimate responsibility for how one is is impossible, because it requires the actual completion of an infinite series of choices of principles of choice.*

x. *So ultimate, buck-stopping moral responsibility is impossible, because it requires ultimate responsibility for how one is, as noted in iii.*

Does this argument stop me feeling entirely morally responsible for what I do? It does not. Does it stop you feeling entirely morally responsible? I very much doubt it. Should it stop us? Well, it might not be a good thing if it did. But the logic seems irresistible. . . . And yet we continue to feel we are absolutely morally responsible for what we do, responsible in a way that we could be only if we had somehow created ourselves, only if we were "causa sui," the cause of ourselves. It may be that we stand condemned by Nietzsche:

> The causa sui is the best self-contradiction that has been con- ceived so far. It is a sort of rape and perversion of logic. But the extravagant pride of man has managed to entangle itself pro- foundly and frightfully with just this nonsense. The desire for "freedom of the will" in the superlative metaphysical sense, which still holds sway, unfortunately, in the minds of the half- educated; the desire to bear the entire and ultimate responsibility for one's actions oneself, and to absolve God, the world, ancestors, chance, and society involves nothing less than to be precisely this causa sui and, with more than Baron Münchhausen's audacity, to pull oneself up into existence by the hair, out of the swamps of nothingness . . . (Beyond Good and Evil, 1886)

Is there any reply? I can't do better than the novelist Ian McEwan, who wrote to me, "I see no necessary disjunction between having no free will (those arguments seem watertight) and assuming moral responsibility for myself. The point is ownership. I own my past, my beginnings, my perceptions. And just as I will make myself respon- sible if my dog or child bites someone, or my car rolls backwards down a hill and causes damage, so I take on full accountability for the little ship of my being, even if I do not have control of its course. It is this sense of being the possessor of a consciousness that makes us feel responsible for it."

The Limits of the Coded World

—*William Egginton*

IN AN INFLUENTIAL ARTICLE IN THE *ANNUAL REVIEW OF NEURO-science*, Joshua Gold of the University of Pennsylvania and Michael Shadlen of the University of Washington sum up experiments aimed at discovering the neural basis of decision making. In one set of experiments, researchers attached sensors to the parts of monkeys' brains responsible for visual pattern recognition. The monkeys were then taught to respond to a cue by choosing to look at one of two patterns. Computers reading the sensors were able to register the decision a fraction of a second before the monkeys' eyes turned to the pattern. As the monkeys were not deliberating, but rather reacting to visual stimuli, researchers were able to plausibly claim that the computer could successfully predict the monkeys' reaction. In other words, the computer was reading the monkeys' minds and knew before they did what their decision would be.

The implications are immediate. If researchers can in theory predict what human beings will decide before they themselves know it, what is left of the notion of human freedom? How can we say that humans are free in any meaningful way if others can know what their decisions will be before they themselves make them?

Research of this sort can seem frightening. An experiment that demonstrated the illusory nature of human freedom would, in many people's mind, rob the test subjects of something essential to their humanity.

If a machine can tell me what I am about to decide before I decide it, this means that, in some sense, the decision was already made before I became consciously involved. But if that is the case, how am I, as a moral agent, to be held accountable for my actions? If, on the cusp of an important moral decision, I now know that my decision was already taken at the moment I thought myself to be deciding, does this not undermine my responsibility for that choice?

Some might conclude that resistance to such findings reveals a religious bias. After all, the ability to consciously decide is essential in many religions to the idea of humans as spiritual beings. Without freedom of choice, a person becomes a cog in the machine of nature; with action and choice predetermined, morality and ultimately the very meaning of that person's existence is left in tatters.

Theologians have spent a great deal of time ruminating on the problem of determination. The Catholic response to the theological problem of theodicy—that is, of how to explain the existence of evil in a world ruled by a benevolent and omnipotent God—was to teach that God created humans with free will. It is only because evil does exist that humans are free to choose between good and evil; hence, the choice for good has meaning. As the theologians at the Council of Trent in the sixteenth century put it, freedom of will is essential for Christian faith, and it is anathema to believe otherwise. Protestant theologians such as Luther and Calvin, to whom the Trent statement was responding, had disputed this notion on the basis of God's omniscience. If God's ability to know were truly limitless, they argued, then his knowledge of the future would be as clear and perfect as his knowledge of the present and of the past. If that were the case, though, then God would already know what each and every one of us has done, is doing, and will do at every moment in our lives. And how, then, could we be truly free?

Even though this particular resistance to a deterministic model of human behavior is religious, one can easily come to the same sorts of conclusions from a scientific perspective. In fact, when religion and science square off around human freedom, they often end up on remarkably similar ground because both science and religion base their assumptions on an identical understanding of the world as something intrinsically knowable, either by God or ourselves.

Let me explain what I mean by way of an example. Imagine we suspend a steel ball from a magnet directly above a vertical steel plate, such that when I turn off the magnet, the ball hits the edge of the plate and falls to either one side or the other.

Very few people, having accepted the premises of this experiment, would conclude from its outcome that the ball in question was exhibiting free will. Whether the ball falls on one side or the other of the steel plate, we can all comfortably agree, is completely determined by the physical forces acting on the ball, which are simply too complex and minute for us to monitor. And yet we have no problem assuming the opposite to be true of the application of the monkey experiment to theoretical humans: namely, that because their actions are predictable they can be assumed to lack free will. In other words, we have no reason to assume that either predictability or lack of predictability has anything to say about free will. The fact that we do make this association has more to do with the model of the world that we subtly import into such thought experiments than with the experiments themselves.

The model in question holds that the universe exists in space and time as a kind of ultimate code that can be deciphered. This image of the universe has a philosophical and religious provenance, and has made its way into secular beliefs and practices as well. In the case of human freedom, this presumption of a "code of codes" works by convincing us that a prediction somehow decodes or deciphers a future that already exists in a coded form. So, for example, when the computers read the signals coming from the monkeys' brains and make a prediction, belief in the code of codes influences how we interpret that event. Instead of interpreting the prediction as what it is—a statement about the neural process leading to the monkeys' actions—we extrapolate about a supposed future as if it were already written down, and all we were doing was reading it.

To my mind the philosopher who gave the most complete answer to this question was Immanuel Kant. In Kant's view, the main mistake philosophers before him had made when considering how humans could have accurate knowledge of the world was to forget the necessary difference between our knowledge and the actual subject of that knowledge. At first glance, this may not seem like a very easy thing to forget; for example, what our eyes tell us about a rainbow and what that rainbow actually is are quite different things. Kant argued that our failure to grasp this difference was further reaching and had greater consequences than anyone could have thought.

Taking again the example of the rainbow, Kant would argue that while most people would grant the difference between the range of colors our eyes perceive and the refraction of light that causes this optical phenomenon, they would still maintain that more careful observation could indeed bring one to know the rainbow as it is in itself, apart from its sensible manifestation. This commonplace understanding, he argued, was at the root of our tendency to fall profoundly into error, not only about the nature of the world, but about what we were justified in believing about ourselves, God, and our duty to others.

The problem was that while our senses can only ever bring us verifiable knowledge about how the world appears in time and space, our reason always strives to know more than appearances can show it. This tendency of reason to always know more is and was a good thing. It is why human kind is always curious, always progressing to greater and greater knowledge and accomplishments. But if not tempered by a respect for its limits and an understanding of its innate tendencies to overreach, reason can lead us into error and fanaticism.

Let's return to the example of the experiment predicting the monkeys' decisions. What the experiment tells us is nothing other than that the monkeys' decision-making process moves through the brain, and that our technology allows us to get a reading of that activity faster than the monkeys' brain can put it into action. From that relatively simple outcome, we can now see what an unjustified series of rather major conundrums we had drawn. And the reason we drew them was because we unquestioningly translated something unknowable—the stretch of time including the future of the monkeys' as of yet undecided and unperformed actions—into a neat scene that just needed to be decoded in order to be experienced. We treated the future as if it had already happened and hence as a series of events that could be read and narrated.

From a Kantian perspective, with this simple act we allowed reason to override its boundaries, and as a result we fell into error. The error we fell into was, specifically, to believe that our empirical exploration of the world and of the human brain could ever eradicate human freedom.

This, then, is why, as "irresistible" as their logic might appear, none of the versions of Galen Strawson's "Basic Argument" for determinism, which he outlined in The Stone, have any relevance for human freedom or responsibility. According to this logic, responsibility must be illusory, because in order to be responsible at any given time an agent must also be responsible for how he or she became how he or she is at that time, which initiates an infinite regress, because at no point can an individual be responsible for all the genetic and cultural forces that have produced him or her as he or she is. But this logic is nothing other than a philosophical version of the code of codes; it assumes that the sum history of forces determining an individual exists as a kind of potentially legible catalog.

The point to stress, however, is that this catalog is not even legible in theory, for to be known it assumes a kind of knower unconstrained by time and space, a knower who could be present from every possible perspective at every possible deciding moment in an agent's history and prehistory. Such a knower, of course, could only be something along the lines of what the monotheistic traditions call God. But as Kant made clear, it makes no sense to think in terms of ethics, or responsibility, or freedom when talking about God; to make ethical choices, to be responsible for them, to be free to choose poorly—all of these require precisely the kind of being who is constrained by the minimal opacity that defines our kind of knowing.

As much as we owe the nature of our current existence to the evolutionary forces Darwin first discovered, or to the cultures we grow up in, or to the chemical states affecting our brain processes at any given moment, none of this impacts on our freedom. I am free because neither science nor religion can ever tell me, with certainty, what my future will be and what I should do about it. The dictum from Sartre that Strawson quoted thus gets it exactly right: I am condemned to freedom. I am not free because I *can* make choices, but because I *must* make them, all the time, even when I think I have no choice to make.

JULY 25, 2010

On Modern Time

—Espen Hammer

W E LIVE IN TIME. ON DAYS LIKE THIS ONE, WHEN WE FIND OUR-
selves carried without any effort or intent from the end of one calendar year to the next, this observation is perhaps especially clear.

Our lives are temporal. Time passes, and with that our lives.
Dissolving into things, processes and events as the mode of their
becoming, time is a medium within which every being is able to exist
and develop. Time is, however, also destructive. Its power means that
everything, including ourselves, is transient, provisional and bound
to come to an irreversible end.

Many philosophers have tried to articulate what it means to be
not only temporal but aware of oneself as such. How should we interpret the fact of our own temporality? One response would be that
the question is uninteresting or even banal. It simply involves living with clock time, the kind of time that scientists take for granted
when they study nature and that we continuously keep track of via
our watches and calendars.

So time has passed? You are getting older? It just means that a
certain number of homogenous moments (seconds, minutes, hours,
and so on) have succeeded one another in a linear fashion: tick, tack,
tick, tack . . . Now look in the mirror!

At least since the introduction of the pocket watch in the sixteenth
century brought exact time measurement into everyday life, modern
agents have found themselves increasingly encased in a calculable

and measurable temporal environment. We measure and organize time as never before, and we worry about not "losing" or "wasting" time, as though time was a finite substance or a container into which we should try to stuff as many good experiences as possible.

Clock time is the time of our modern, busy and highly coordinated and interconnected lives. It is the time of planning and control, of setting goals and achieving them in the most efficient manner. We move through such time in the same way we drive a car: calculating the distance passed while coordinating our movement with that of other drivers, passing through an environment that can never be particularly significant and which will soon be observable in the mirror.

Modern society is unimaginable without clock time. With the rise of the chronometer came a vast increase in discipline, efficiency and social speed, transforming every institution and human endeavor. The factory, the office, transportation, business, the flow of information, indeed almost everything we do and relate to is to a greater or lesser extent controlled by the clock.

It was not always like this. In a medieval village, the day started not with the beep of the alarm clock but with birds gradually beginning to twitter, the light slowly starting to shine through the windows. When the observation of natural cycles played a greater role in people's awareness of temporality, change was "softer," less precisely calculable, and intimately tied to a more fluid and large-scale sense of rhythm. In all likelihood, the inhabitant of a medieval village could also contrast sublunar time with some vision of eternity or "higher time" in which the soul was allowed to participate in a higher order of being.

So what of all this? This yoking of our lives to clock time? Despite our increasing reliance on the mechanical measurement of time to structure our lives, many of us find some part of us resisting it. We find it confining, too rigid perhaps to suit our natural states, and long for that looser structure of the medieval village (while retaining our modern comforts and medical advances, of course).

What is behind this resistance? The modern time frame brings about two fundamental forms of dissatisfaction. For one thing, it exacerbates and intensifies our sense of *transience*. If time is under-stood as a succession of discrete moments, then, strictly speaking, our experience will be one of perpetual loss: every instant, every unit of time, is a mere passing from that which has not yet been to that which will never again be, and the passing itself will not endure but simply be a boundary between future and present. "In time," the philosopher Schopenhauer put it, "each moment is, only in so far as it has effaced its father the preceding moment, to be again effaced just as quickly itself. Past and future . . . are as empty and unreal as any dream; but present is only the boundary between the two, having neither extension nor duration."

Responding to this sense of transience, Schopenhauer rather des-perately throws in a salvific conception of beauty as being capable of suspending our normal temporal awareness. Aesthetic experience, he claims, pulls us beyond our normal subjection to temporal sequenti-ality. The sunset or the Beethoven string quartet can be so ravishing that we find ourselves lost in the unchanging essentiality they pres-ent to us. Whatever merits this view has, it only promises temporary respite. When, from an observer's standpoint, the act of transcen-dence comes to an end, we necessarily have to return to everyday life.

The modern time frame also generates a problem of *existential meaning*. The "now" of clock time is contingent. It is neutral with regard to the kind of established, historical meaning that historians and social theorists think was important in premodern societies. *Why me now?* What am I to do with myself in a world apparently bereft of deep, collective meaning? From the idea that what was done was right by some sacred authorization, a divine order perhaps, the mod-ern agent turns to the future, cut loose from tradition. The moment is there to be seized upon. We are entrepreneurs and consumers in a liquid, fast-moving society. We look forward rather than backward, to the new rather than the old, and while a huge space of innova-tion and possible change is then opened up, we seem to have lost a sense of the unquestionable meaning that those who came before us seemed to have had in abundance.

Modern philosophy, especially in the European tradition, contains plenty of attempts both to diagnose and remedy this situation. Some thinkers—Schopenhauer among them—have hoped that philosophy could identify ways in which we may *escape* the modern time frame altogether. Others, like Heidegger, have tried to show that clock time is *not as fundamental as we often think it is*. In addition to the objective time of the clock, they argue, there are temporalities of human experience and engagement that, while often ignored, deserve to be explored and analyzed. Perhaps clock time is one mode of temporality among others. If so, then it is not obvious that clock time should always be our preferred mode of temporal self-interpretation. Perhaps we have to recognize a tension in human life between the demands of clock time and those other temporalities, between the clock or the calendar and life as it is truly experienced.

For several reasons the notion of escape seems the least promising. How could we ever escape clock time? Where would we go? If the answer is to a pre- or nonmodern society where people live happily without clocks, then surely we could not envision this as a plan for society as a whole. Few or any such societies still exist, and the changes necessary would not be acceptable in light of the interests we have in enjoying the benefits of a well-organized, industrial civilization. If the answer hinges on some sort of individual escape—perhaps, as in Schopenhauer, to the timeless realm of pure essence—then one needs to show that something like this is actually possible. Does it make sense to conceive of a perfectly timeless experience? Probably not. Experience is necessarily temporal. Can there be false sanctuaries from clock time? Perhaps. Heroin and video game addiction spring to mind.

We thus fall back on the first alternative—the one involving a rethinking of temporality. Yes, there is clock time, but in addition to that there are other and more unruly temporalities. There are, no doubt, temporalities of the human body, of nature and of the psyche. At least they follow certain biological, cosmological, and psychological rhythms, often involving perceived patterns of birth or creation, growth, decay and regeneration. Equally significant, however, the way we interpret ourselves and our relations to other human beings is deeply shaped by its own forms of temporality. We don't simply live in Schopenhauer's fluctuating "now." Rather, human life is a continuous and highly complex negotiation of existing commitments and remembrances with future demands and expectations.

My friend returns the car he borrowed yesterday. I understand and interpret his action by viewing it as the fulfillment of a promise. The sense I make of it will be based on the memory I have of the promise as well as on knowledge of the manner in which promises both create commitments and constrain people's future plans and actions. There is an interplay between recollections and anticipations, and between beliefs and inferences—all of which both opens up and presupposes a temporal space.

Even direct forms of awareness involve such an interplay. We see the blooming flowers as manifestations of spring and situate them temporally by invoking the sequences associated by the annual changes in nature from winter to spring and summer, and all of this while viewing the whole process in terms of concepts like regeneration, life, or perhaps the fleetingness of beauty. We bring certain inferences to bear on what we experience such as to transform mere succession into meaning and form.

In these ways, human beings structure their lives around narratives. Some narratives will tend to remain in the foreground of one's engagements and orientations. These will include things like our self-conception and our relationships with others. Others, such as how we organize our day, will be more rarely reflected upon. I could give an account of how I organize my day, but that would typically be to a child or someone with scant knowledge of my own culture. By contrast, stories about our relationships almost always tend to be matters of reflection, rethinking and revision.

Most of our narratives are socially constituted. Becoming an investment banker is possible because such occupations exist in our society, and because there are socially constituted routes to obtaining that status. The investment banker is in possession of and identifies with the banker narrative: it largely determines this person's identity.

Some narratives, however, are intimate and personal, based on experiences and commitments made by individuals independently of social expectation. These are the kinds of narratives that novelists often use. These are the ones that not only point beyond the deadening sequentiality of mere clock time but have the capacity to open new territories and vistas for human growth and authenticity. Discontinuity is the key here: the pregnant moment outside the regular flow of time when some unexpected yet promising or individually challenging event occurs.

We need these moments, and we need to be attentive to them. They are the moments when new possibilities emerge. The narratives that frame such forms of exposure to the sudden and unexpected will tend to deviate from the standard, causal "this because of that" structure. They will have cracks and breaks, intimating how we genuinely come to experience something as opposed to merely "moving through" it. Falling in love is one such narrative context. While we can tell when it happens to us, the involvement it demands is open, promissory, risky, possibly life changing, and sometimes deeply disappointing.

Experiences like this, which explode the empty repetition of standard clock time, offer glimpses of a different and deeply intriguing type of temporality that has the power to invest our lives with greater meaning, possibility and excitement than a life merely measured on a grid could ever provide.

JANUARY 1, 2012

Logic and Neutrality

—Timothy Williamson

Here's an idea many philosophers and logicians have about the function of logic in our cognitive life, our inquiries and debates. It isn't a player. Rather, it's an umpire, a neutral arbitrator between opposing theories, imposing some basic rules on all sides in a dispute. The picture is that logic has no substantive content, for otherwise the correctness of that content could itself be debated, which would impugn the neutrality of logic. One way to develop this idea is by saying that logic supplies no information of its own, because the point of information is to rule out possibilities, whereas logic only rules out inconsistencies, which are not genuine possibilities. On this view, logic in itself is totally uninformative, although it may help us extract and handle nonlogical information from other sources.

The idea that logic is uninformative strikes me as deeply mistaken, and I'm going to explain why. But it may not seem crazy when one looks at elementary examples of the cognitive value of logic, such as when we extend our knowledge by deducing logical consequences of what we already know. If you know that either Mary or Mark did the murder (only they had access to the crime scene at the right time), and then Mary produces a rock-solid alibi, so you know she didn't do it, you can deduce that Mark did it. Logic also helps us recognize our mistakes, when our beliefs turn out to contain inconsistencies. If I believe that no politicians are honest, and that John is a politician, and that he is honest, at least one of those three beliefs must be false, although logic doesn't tell me which one.

The power of logic becomes increasingly clear when we chain together such elementary steps into longer and longer chains of reasoning, and the idea of logic as uninformative becomes correspondingly less and less plausible. Mathematics provides the most striking examples, since all its theorems are ultimately derived from a few simple axioms by chains of logical reasoning, some of them hundreds of pages long, even though mathematicians usually don't bother to analyze their proofs into the most elementary steps.

For instance, Fermat's Last Theorem was finally proved by Andrew Wiles and others after it had tortured mathematicians as an unsolved problem for more than three centuries. Exactly which mathematical axioms are indispensable for the proof is only gradually becoming clear, but for present purposes what matters is that together the accepted axioms suffice. One thing the proof showed is that it is a truth of pure logic that those axioms imply Fermat's Last Theorem. If logic is uninformative, shouldn't it be uninformative to be told that the accepted axioms of mathematics imply Fermat's Last Theorem? But it wasn't uninformative; it was one of the most exciting discoveries in decades. If the idea of information as ruling out possibilities can't handle the informativeness of logic, that is a problem for that idea of information, not for the informativeness of logic.

The conception of logic as a neutral umpire of debate also fails to withstand scrutiny, for similar reasons. Principles of logic can themselves be debated, and often are, just like principles of any other science. For example, one principle of standard logic is the law of excluded middle, which says that something either is the case, or it isn't. Either it's raining, or it's not. Many philosophers and others have rejected the law of excluded middle, on various grounds. Some think it fails in borderline cases, for instance, when very few drops of rain are falling, and avoid it by adopting fuzzy logic. Others think the law fails when applied to future contingencies, such as whether you will be in the same job this time next year. On the other side, many philosophers—including me—argue that the law withstands these challenges. Whichever side is right, logical theories are players in these debates, not neutral umpires.

Another debate in which logical theories are players concerns the ban on contradictions. Most logicians accept the ban but some, known as dialetheists, reject it. They treat some paradoxes as black holes in logical space, where even contradictions are true (and false).

A different dispute in logic concerns "quantum logic." Standard logic includes the "distributive" law, by which a statement of the form "x and either y or z" is equivalent to the corresponding statement of the form "Either x and y or x and z." On one highly controversial view of the phenomenon of complementarity in quantum mechanics, it involves counterexamples to the distributive law: for example, since we can't simultaneously observe both which way a particle is moving and where it is, the particle may be moving left and either in a given region or not, without either moving left and being in that region or moving left and not being in that region. Although that idea hasn't done what its advocates originally hoped to solve the puzzles of quantum mechanics, it is yet another case where logical theories were players, not neutral umpires.

As it happens, I think that standard logic can resist all these challenges. The point is that each of them has been seriously proposed by (a minority of) expert logicians, and rationally debated. Although attempts were made to reinterpret the debates as misunderstandings in which the two sides spoke different languages, those attempts underestimated the capacity of our language to function as a forum for debate in which profound theoretical disagreements can be expressed. Logic is just not a controversy-free zone. If we restricted it to uncontroversial principles, nothing would be left. As in the rest of science, no principle is above challenge. That does not imply that nothing is known. The fact that you know something does not mean that nobody else is allowed to challenge it.

Of course, we'd be in trouble if we could never agree on anything in logic. Fortunately, we can secure enough agreement in logic for most purposes, but nothing in the nature of logic guarantees those agreements. Perhaps the methodological privilege of logic is not that its principles are so weak, but that they are so strong. They are formulated at such a high level of generality that, typically, if they crash, they crash so badly that we easily notice, because the counter-examples to them are simple. If we want to identify what is genuinely distinctive of logic, we should stop overlooking its close similarities to the rest of science.

MAY 13, 2012

Paradoxical Truth

—*Graham Priest*

Professor Greene is lecturing. Down the hall, her archrival, Professor Browne, is also lecturing. Professor Greene is holding forth at length about how absurd Professor Browne's ideas are. She believes Professor Browne to be lecturing in Room 33. So to emphasize her point, she writes on the blackboard this single sentence:

EVERYTHING WRITTEN ON THE BOARD IN ROOM 33
IS FALSE.

But Professor Greene has made a mistake. She, herself, is in Room 33. So is what she has written on the board true or false? If it's true, then since it itself is written on the board, it's false. If it's false, then since it is the only thing written on the board, it's true. Either way, it's both true and false.

Philosophers and logicians love paradoxes, and this is one—one of the many versions of what is usually called the Liar Paradox, discovered by the ancient Greek philosopher Eubulides (fourth century BC).

Paradoxes are apparently good arguments that lead to conclusions that are beyond belief (Greek: *para* = beyond, *doxa* = belief). And when you meet a paradox, you've got only two choices. One is to accept that the conclusion, implausible as it may seem, is actually true; the other is to reject the conclusion, and explain what has gone wrong in the argument.

Both responses are possible. To illustrate the first, here's another paradox. The whole numbers and the even whole numbers can be paired off, one against the other, as follows:

```
1       2       3       4      .    .    .

↑       ↑       ↑       ↑      .    .    .
↓       ↓       ↓       ↓

2       4       6       8      .    .    .
```

This appears to show that there are exactly the same number of even numbers as whole numbers. That seems false, since obviously the even numbers leave some numbers out.

This paradox was known to the medievals, and to Galileo. So let's call it Galileo's Paradox. Until the nineteenth century, the paradox was taken to show that the whole notion of infinity was incoherent. But toward the end of that century, the work of the German mathematician George Cantor on the infinite led to one of the most major revolutions in the history of mathematics. Fundamental to it was accepting that there are indeed exactly as many even numbers as whole numbers. It is the very *nature* of infinite totalities that you can throw away some of their members, and have as many as you started with.

The other possibility (saying what is wrong with the argument) is illustrated by another paradox. Another ancient Greek philosopher, Zeno, who flourished about a century before Eubulides, produced a number of paradoxes concerning motion. Here's one of them, often called the Dichotomy. Suppose a car is moving from to A to B. Let's measure the distance between A and B by a scale according to which A is at point 0 and B is at point 1. Then before the car gets to point 1, it has to get halfway there, point 1/2; and once it has got there, it has to get to a point halfway between 1/2 and 1, 3/4; and so on . . . In other words, it has to get to every one of the infinite number of points 1/2, 3/4, 7/8, . . . But you can't do an infinite number of things in a finite time. So the car will never get to point B.

Here we can't just accept the conclusion: we know that the car can get to point *B*. So something must be wrong with the argument. In fact, there is now a general consensus about what is wrong with it (based on other developments in nineteenth-century mathematics concerning infinite series). You *can* do an infinite number of things in a finite time—at least provided that these things can be done faster and faster.

So let's come back to the Liar Paradox. Which of the two kinds of paradoxes is this? Can we accept the conclusion, or must there be something wrong with the argument? Well, notice that the conclusion of the argument is a bald contradiction: the claim on the blackboard is both true and false. Now, the principle of noncontradiction says that you can never accept a contradiction. And the principle of noncontradiction has been high orthodoxy in Western philosophy since Aristotle mounted a spirited defense of it in his *Metaphysics*—so orthodox that no one seems to have felt the need to mount a sustained defense of it ever since. So the paradox must be of the second kind: there must be something wrong with the argument. Or must there?

Not according to a contentious new theory that's currently doing the rounds. According to this theory, some contradictions are actually true, and the conclusion of the Liar Paradox is a paradigm example of one such contradiction. The theory calls a true contradiction a *dialetheia* (Greek: *di* = two (way); *aletheia* = truth), and the view itself is called dialetheism. One thing that drives the view is that cogent diagnoses of what is wrong with the Liar argument are seemingly impossible to find. Suppose you say, for example, that paradoxical sentences of this kind are simply meaningless (or neither true nor false, or some such). Then what if Professor Greene had written on the board,

EVERYTHING WRITTEN ON THE BOARD IN ROOM 33
IS EITHER FALSE OR MEANINGLESS.

If this were true or false, we would be in the same bind as before. And if it's meaningless, then it's *either* false *or* meaningless, so it's true. We are back with a contradiction. This sort of situation (often called a *strengthened paradox*) affects virtually all suggested attempts to explain what has gone wrong with the reasoning in the Liar Paradox.

At any rate, even after two and a half thousand years of trying to come up with an explanation of what is wrong with the argument in the Liar Paradox, there is still no consensus on the matter. Contrast this with Zeno's paradoxes, where there is virtually complete consensus. Maybe, then, we have just been trying to find a fault where there is none.

Of course, this means junking the principle of noncontradiction. But why should we accept that anyway? You might think that since Aristotle's defense established the principle in Western philosophy, his arguments must have been pretty good. Were they? No. The main argument is so tortured that experts can't even agree on *how* it is meant to work, let alone *that* it works. There's a bunch of smaller arguments as well, but most of these are little more than throwaway comments, many of which are clearly beside the point. Interestingly, virtually everything else that Aristotle ever defended has been overthrown—or at least seriously challenged. The principle of noncontradiction is, it would seem, the last bastion!

Naturally, there is more to be said about the matter—as there always is in philosophy. If you ask most modern logicians why there can be no true contradictions, they will probably tell you that everything follows logically from a contradiction, so if even one contradiction were true, everything would be true. Clearly, everything is too much!

This principle of inference that everything follows from a contradiction sometimes goes by its medieval name, *ex falso quodlibet*, but it is often now called by a more colorful name: explosion. There is, in fact, a connection between explosion and the principle of noncontradiction. A common suggestion of what it is for B to follow logically from A is that you can't have A without having B. Given the principle of noncontradiction, if A is a contradiction, you can't have it. And if you can't have A, you certainly can't have A *and* B. That is, everything follows from a contradiction.

Evidently, if this argument is invoked against dialetheism, it is entirely question begging, since it takes for granted the principle of noncontradiction, which is the very point at issue.

Moreover, for all its current orthodoxy, explosion seems a pretty implausible principle of inference. It tells us, after all, that if, for example, Melbourne were and were not the capital of Australia, Caesar would have invaded England in 1066. There really doesn't seem to be much connection between these things. Explosion would itself seem to be a pretty paradoxical consequence of whatever it is supposed to follow from.

Unsurprisingly, then, the last forty years or so have seen fairly intensive investigations of logics according to which explosion is not correct. These are called paraconsistent logics, and there is now a very robust theory of such logics. In fact, the mathematical details of these logics are absolutely essential in articulating dialetheism in any but a relatively superficial way. But the details are, perhaps, best left for consenting logicians behind closed doors.

You might think that there is another problem for dialetheism: if we could accept some contradictions, then we could never criticize someone whose views were inconsistent, since they might just be true. Suppose that I am charged with a crime. In court, I produce a cast-iron alibi, showing that I was somewhere else. The prosecutor accepts that I was not at the crime scene, but claims that I was there anyway. We certainly want to be able to say that this is not very sensible!

But the fact that it is rational to accept *some* contradictions does not mean that it is rational to accept *any* contradiction. If the principle of noncontradiction fails, then contradictions cannot be ruled out by logic alone. But many things cannot be ruled out by logic alone, though it would be quite irrational to believe them. The claim that the earth is flat is entirely consistent with the laws of logic. It's crazy for all that.

And no one has yet mastered the trick of being in two places at the same time, as both we and the prosecutor know.

Indeed, if you consider all the statements you have met in the last twenty-four hours (including the ones in this article), the number that might plausibly be thought to be dialetheias is pretty small. So it seems safe to assume that the probability of any given contradiction being true is pretty low. We have, then, quite good *general* grounds for rejecting a contradiction we come across. But of course, those general grounds may be trumped on the occasions where we do have good reason to believe that the contradiction is true—as with the Liar Paradox.

If dialetheias are pretty rare, and if they appear to be fairly esoteric things like the Liar sentence, you might wonder why we should bother about them at all. Why not just ignore them? One ignores them at great risk. Scientific advances are often triggered by taking oddities seriously. For example, at the end of the nineteenth century, most physicists thought that their subject was pretty much sewn up, except for a few oddities that no one could account for, such as the phenomenon of black-body radiation. Consideration of this eventually generated quantum theory. Had it been ignored, we would not have had the revolution in physics produced by the theory. Similarly, if Cantor had not taken Galileo's paradox seriously, one of the most important revolutions in mathematics would never have happened either.

Revolutions in logic (of various kinds) have certainly occurred in the past. Arguably, the greatest of these was around the turn of the twentieth century, when traditional Aristotelian logic was overthrown, and the mathematical techniques of contemporary logic were ushered in. Perhaps we are on the brink of another.

NOVEMBER 28, 2010

The Drama of Existentialism

—Gary Gutting

L AST YEAR I PUBLISHED A BOOK ON FRENCH PHILOSOPHY SINCE 1960 with a chapter entitled "Whatever Happened to Existentialism?" The title referred to the fast and apparently complete fall of existentialism from favor among leading French intellectuals, beginning at least as early as the 1960s. My chapter analyzed the fall, asked whether it was as decisive as it seemed, and ended with suggestions that the movement may have had more long-term influence than it seemed to.

Adam Gopnik's recent *New Yorker* essay on Albert Camus and his relation to Jean-Paul Sartre reminded me how irrelevant my title's question appears from a broader cultural standpoint. Whatever the ups and downs of Camus's or Sartre's stock on the high cultural exchange, their existentialism (not to mention that of their nineteenth-century predecessors, Kierkegaard and Nietzsche) has continued to spark interest among the larger population of educated people. The point is also illustrated by the strong reactions, both for and against Sartre and Camus, in the comments on Andy Martin's recent piece in The Stone. And, of course, the enduring sign of interest has been the perennial popularity of undergraduate college courses on existentialist philosophy and literature.

Gopnik shows the reason for this continuing attraction. I would not recommend his essay as an accurate technical presentation of existentialist thought. For example, Sartre's magnum opus, *Being and Nothingness*, is not an effort to "reconcile Marxism and existentialism"; that comes much later in his *Critique of Dialectical Reason*. Nor did Sartre reason to his support of Marxist revolution through an atheistic version of Pascal's wager. But Gopnik has a ready response to such philosophical quibbles. The popular appeal of existentialism lies more in its sense of drama than in careful analysis and argument. As Gopnik exclaims, "Philosophers? They [Sartre and Camus] were performers with vision, who played on the stage of history."

This is not to say that existentialists—particularly Sartre and Simone de Beauvoir—are not intellectually serious thinkers. But in contrast to most other philosophers, they work out of a continuing sense of human existence as a compelling drama. In part this derives from the heightened stakes of the war and occupation from which their mature work emerged. Recall Sartre's example of his student who was trying to decide whether to abandon his mother and join the Free French Army. On the conventional view, the student's decision would depend on whether he loved his mother or his country more. But Sartre insisted that the decision itself would create the greater love the student might later evoke to justify it.

The war even intrudes into the thorny ontological analyses of *Being and Nothingness*. Arguing for the absoluteness of our freedom even in the face of severe constraints, Sartre—no doubt thinking of members of the Resistance captured by the Gestapo—insists that, even under torture, we are free. Those who yield and betray their comrades afterwards live in guilt because they know that, at the moment of betrayal, they could have held out for at least another minute.

But existentialism also ties into the drama of everyday life. Sartre's study of "bad faith" (self-deception) is driven by striking vignettes like that of the woman torn between her psychological desire for a man's attention and her lack of sexual interest in him, who allows him to caress her while thinking of herself as a pure consciousness, with no essential tie to the body he is touching. Similarly, Sartre describes an overly zealous waiter, so self-consciously intent on doing everything just right that he winds up as much pretending to be a waiter as being one.

Drama can always distort, and Sartre's examples are open to criticism for ignoring ambiguities and complexities for the sake of a vivid impact. When an interviewer much later confronted him with a passage expressing his stark early view of freedom under torture, Sartre replied that what was remarkable was that, when he wrote such things, he actually believed them. In another vein, feminist critics have noted the relentlessly masculine standpoint of Sartre's descriptions of what is supposed to be "human reality."

An emphasis on drama also has the advantages and the disadvantages of inevitably connecting the philosophy with the personal life of the philosopher. Gopnik rightly emphasizes how Sartre and Camus's theoretical disagreements over political philosophy are reflected in the sad history of their lost friendship. This personal drama illuminates their philosophical differences and vice versa. Similarly, it is fair to look at Sartre's and Beauvoir's philosophy of freedom in the light of their famous pact to maintain an "essential love" for one another, while allowing for any number of "contingent lovers." Still, too much concern with the messy and ultimately impenetrable details of a life can lure us across the line between philosophical insight and titillating gossip.

Despite its dangers, the drama of existentialism has kept some of the deepest philosophical questions alive in popular intellectual culture and provides students with remarkably direct access to such questions. I am always impressed by the frisson in my class when students realize that there's a sense in which Sartre is right: they could, right now, get up, leave the classroom, drop out of school, and go live as beach bums in a perpetually warm climate. But it's equally impressive to see them—still stimulated by what they've read in Sartre and other existentialists like Camus and Merleau-Ponty—reflect on why this sense of radical freedom is far from the whole story of their lives as moral agents. This combination of drama and reflection is the reason existentialism will always be with us.

Reasons for Reason

—Michael P. Lynch

T HE VOCAL DISMISSALS OF EVOLUTION FROM RICK PERRY, THE Republican governor of Texas, during his 2012 presidential campaign and his confident assertion that "God is how we got here" reflect an obvious divide in our culture. In one sense, that divide is just over the facts: some of us believe God created human beings just as they are now; others of us don't. But underneath this divide is a deeper one. Really divisive disagreements are typically not just over the facts. They are also about the best way to support our views of the facts. Call this a disagreement in epistemic principle. Our epistemic principles tell us what is rational to believe, what sources of information to trust. Thus, while a few people may agree with Perry because they really think that the scientific evidence supports creationism, I suspect that for most people, scientific evidence (or its lack) has nothing to do with it. Their belief in creationism is instead a reflection of a deeply held epistemic principle: that, at least on some topics, scripture is a more reliable source of information than science. For others, including myself, this is never the case.

Disagreements like this give rise to an unnerving question: How do we rationally defend our most fundamental epistemic principles? Like many of the best philosophical mysteries, this is a problem that can seem both unanswerable and yet extremely important to solve.

The ancient Greek skeptics were the first to show why the problem is so difficult to solve. Every one of our beliefs is produced by some method or source, be it humble (like memory) or complex (like technologically assisted science). But why think our methods, whatever they are, are trustworthy or reliable for getting at the truth? If I challenge one of your methods, you can't just appeal to the same method to show that it is reliable. That would be circular. And appealing to another method won't help either—for unless *that* method can be shown to be reliable, using it to determine the reliability of the first method answers nothing. So you end up either continuing on in the same vein—pointlessly citing reasons for methods and methods for reasons forever—or arguing in circles, or granting that your method is groundless. Any way you go, it seems you must admit you can give no reason for trusting your methods, and hence can give no reason to defend your most fundamental epistemic principles.

This skeptical argument is disturbing because it seems to suggest that in the end, all "rational" explanations end up grounding out on something arbitrary. It all just comes down to what you happen to believe, what you feel in your gut, your faith. Human beings have historically found this to be a very seductive idea, in part because it is liberating. It levels the playing field, intellectually speaking. After all, if all reasons are grounded on something arbitrary, then no one's principles rest on any firmer foundation than anyone else's. It seems to give us the freedom to go with any epistemic principle we choose.

Many people who are committed to the core epistemic principles of science—say, that observation and experiment should be trusted over appeals to scripture—are inclined to shrug this worry off. Why, they ask, should I care about convincing people who don't understand the obvious fact that science is always the better method for knowing about matters like the origin of life on this planet? Again, epistemic principles tell us what is rational. So anyone who doubts my basic epistemic principles is going to appear to *me* as someone who doubts the rules of rationality. So, why should I care about what they think? It's not as if they'll be able to recognize my (good) reasons anyway, and to me, *their* "reasons" will not be legitimate.

But what counts as "legitimate"? There's the rub. A legitimate challenge is presumably a rational challenge. Disagreements over epistemic principles are disagreements over which methods and sources to trust. And there we have the problem. We can't decide on what counts as a legitimate reason to doubt my epistemic principles unless we've already settled on our principles—and that is the very issue in question. The problem that skepticism about reason raises is not about whether I have good evidence by my principles for my principles. Presumably I do. The problem is whether I can give a more objective defense of them—that is, whether I can give reasons for them that can be appreciated from what Hume called a "common point of view"—reasons that can "move some universal principle of the human frame, and touch a string, to which all mankind have an accord and symphony."

I think that we ignore this problem—the problem of defending our epistemic principles from a common point of view—at our peril. It is not that I think we should come up with a list of bullet points to convince people to employ scientific reason in public discourse. That would be a waste of time. Nor is my point that it is *politically* stupid to dismiss other people's viewpoints in a democratic society. (Although it is. You don't help your message by displaying a haughty indifference to others' challenges.) My point is that defending some of our epistemic principles, our faith in reason, is required by some of our other principles. Hume's point, in alluding to what he also sometimes called "the principle of humanity," was that the ideal of civility requires us to find common currency with those with whom we must discuss practical matters. More recent political philosophers like Rawls and Habermas have seen this ideal as a key component of a functioning liberal democracy. In this view, democracies aren't simply organizing a struggle for power between competing interests; democratic politics isn't war by other means. Democracies are, or should be, spaces of reason.

So one reason we should take the project of defending our epistemic principles seriously is that the ideal of civility demands it. But there is also another even deeper reason. We need to justify our epistemic principles from a common point of view because we need shared epistemic principles in order to even have a common point of view. Without a common background of standards against which we measure what counts as a reliable source of information, or a reliable method of inquiry, and what doesn't, we won't be able *to agree on the facts*, let alone values. Indeed, this is precisely the situation we seem to be headed toward in the United States. We live isolated in our separate bubbles of information culled from sources that only reinforce our prejudices and never challenge our basic assumptions. No wonder that—as in the debates over evolution or what to include in textbooks illustrate—we so often fail to reach agreement over the history and physical structure of the world itself. No wonder joint action grinds to a halt. When you can't agree on your principles of evidence and rationality, you can't agree on the facts. And if you can't agree on the facts, you can hardly agree on what to do in the face of the facts.

Put simply, we need an epistemic common currency because we often have to decide, jointly, what to do in the face of disagreement. Sometimes we can accomplish this, in a democratic society, by voting. But we can't decide every issue that way, and we certainly can't decide on our epistemic principles—which methods and sources are *actually* rationally worthy of trust—by voting. We need some forms of common currency before we get to the voting booth. And that is one reason we need to resist skepticism about reason: we need to be able to give reasons for why some standards of reason—some epistemic principles—should be part of that currency and some not.

Yet this very fact—the fact that a civil democratic society requires a common currency of shared epistemic principles—should give us hope that we can answer the skeptical challenge. Even if, as the skeptic says, we can't defend the truth of our principles without circularity, we might still be able to show that some are better than others. Observation and experiment, for example, aren't just good because they are reliable means to the truth. They are valuable because almost everyone can appeal to them. They have roots in our natural instincts, as Hume might have said. If so, then perhaps we can hope to give reasons for our epistemic principles. Such reasons will be "merely" practical, but reasons—reasons for reason, as it were—all the same.

Reclaiming the Imagination

—Timothy Williamson

IMAGINE BEING A SLAVE IN ANCIENT ROME. NOW REMEMBER BEING one. The second task, unlike the first, is crazy. If, as I'm guessing, you never were a slave in ancient Rome, it follows that you can't remember being one—but you can still let your imagination rip. With a bit of effort one can even imagine the impossible, such as discovering that Dick Cheney and Madonna are really the same person. It sounds like a platitude that fiction is the realm of imagination, fact the realm of knowledge.

Why did humans evolve the capacity to imagine alternatives to reality? Was storytelling in prehistoric times like the peacock's tail, of no direct practical use but a good way of attracting a mate? It kept Scheherazade alive through those one thousand and one nights—in the story.

On further reflection, imagining turns out to be much more reality directed than the stereotype implies. If a child imagines the life of a slave in ancient Rome as mainly spent watching sports on TV, with occasional household chores, they are imagining it wrong. That is not what it was like to be a slave. The imagination is not just a random idea generator. The test is how close you can come to imagining the life of a slave as it really was, not how far you can deviate from reality.

A reality–directed faculty of imagination has clear survival value. By enabling you to imagine all sorts of scenarios, it alerts you to dangers and opportunities. You come across a cave. You imagine wintering there with a warm fire—opportunity. You imagine a bear waking up inside—danger. Having imagined possibilities, you can take account of them in contingency planning. If a bear is in the cave, how do you deal with it? If you winter there, what do you do for food and drink? Answering those questions involves more imagining, which must be reality directed. Of course, you can imagine kissing the angry bear as it emerges from the cave so that it becomes your lifelong friend and brings you all the food and drink you need. Better not to rely on such fantasies. Instead, let your imaginings develop in ways more informed by your knowledge of how things really happen.

Constraining imagination by knowledge does not make it redundant. We rarely know an explicit formula that tells us what to do in a complex situation. We have to work out what to do by thinking through the possibilities in ways that are simultaneously imaginative and realistic, and not less imaginative when more realistic. Knowledge, far from limiting imagination, enables it to serve its central function.

To go further, we can borrow a distinction from the philosophy of science, between contexts of discovery and contexts of justification. In the context of discovery, we get ideas, no matter how—dreams or drugs will do. Then, in the context of justification, we assemble objective evidence to determine whether the ideas are correct. On this picture, standards of rationality apply only to the context of justification, not to the context of discovery. Those who downplay the cognitive role of the imagination restrict it to the context of discovery, excluding it from the context of justification. But they are wrong. Imagination plays a vital role in justifying ideas as well as generating them in the first place.

Your belief that you will not be visible from inside the cave if you crouch behind that rock may be justified because you can imagine how things would look from inside. To change the example, what would happen if all NATO forces left Afghanistan by 2011? What will happen if they don't? Justifying answers to those questions requires imaginatively working through various scenarios in ways deeply informed by knowledge of Afghanistan and its neighbors. Without imagination, one couldn't get from knowledge of the past and present to justified expectations about the complex future. We also need it to answer questions about the past. Were the Rosenbergs innocent? Why did Neanderthals become extinct? We must develop the consequences of competing hypotheses with disciplined imagination in order to compare them with the available evidence. In drawing out a scenario's implications, we apply much of the same cognitive apparatus whether we are working online, with input from sense perception, or off-line, with input from imagination.

Even imagining things contrary to our knowledge contributes to the growth of knowledge: for example, in learning from our mistakes. Surprised at the bad outcomes of our actions, we may learn how to do better by imagining what would have happened if we had acted differently from how we know only too well we did act.

In science, the obvious role of imagination is in the context of discovery. Unimaginative scientists don't produce radically new ideas. But even in science imagination plays a role in justification, too. Experiment and calculation cannot do all its work. When mathematical models are used to test a conjecture, choosing an appropriate model may itself involve imagining how things would go if the conjecture were true. Mathematicians typically justify their fundamental axioms, in particular those of set theory, by informal appeals to the imagination.

Sometimes the only honest response to a question is "I don't know." In recognizing that, one may rely just as much on imagination, because one needs it to determine that several competing hypotheses are equally compatible with one's evidence.

The lesson is not that all intellectual inquiry deals in fictions. That is just to fall back on the crude stereotype of the imagination, from which it needs reclaiming. A better lesson is that imagination is not only about fiction: it is integral to our painful progress in separating fiction from fact. Although fiction is a playful use of imagination, not all uses of imagination are playful. Like a cat's play with a mouse, fiction may both emerge as a by-product of un-playful uses and hone one's skills for them.

Critics of contemporary philosophy sometimes complain that in using thought experiments, it loses touch with reality. They complain less about Galileo and Einstein's thought experiments, and those of earlier philosophers. Plato explored the nature of morality by asking how you would behave if you possessed the ring of Gyges, which makes the wearer invisible. Today, if someone claims that science is by nature a human activity, we can refute them by imaginatively appreciating the possibility of extraterrestrial scientists. Once imagining is recognized as a normal means of learning, contemporary philosophers' use of such techniques can be seen as just extraordinarily systematic and persistent applications of our ordinary cognitive apparatus. Much remains to be understood about how imagination works as a means to knowledge—but if it didn't work, we wouldn't be around now to ask the question.

AUGUST 15, 2010

Are There Natural Human Rights?

—*Michael Boylan*

THIS HAS BEEN A YEAR OF UPRISINGS. THE SERIES OF POPULAR revolts, struggles and crackdowns by governments, which continue to this day, began in Tunisia when protesters demanded the removal of president Zine al-Abidine Ben Ali. The claims of the protesters were about the right to eat (the cost of food), political corruption, freedom of speech and basic political rights. Then came Egypt, as thousands flocked to Tahrir Square in Cairo and elsewhere. Their demands were similar to those in Tunisia. Both sets of protesters were successful: the leaders of both countries fled. This was the first wave. It was largely peaceful.

Then the citizens of other countries became involved: Bahrain, Yemen, Syria and Libya. The leaders in these countries were not content to ride away into the sunset. They ordered their soldiers to fire live ammunition into the crowds and imprison the ring leaders. Many were killed. Colonel Muammar el-Qaddafi set out a bloody counterattack so brutal that it prompted a United Nations and NATO military response. The second wave has been violent.

Third-wave countries such as Jordan, Oman and Kuwait also felt the pressure of these events and have made a few changes in response to mostly peaceful demonstrations (reminiscent of the Prague Spring in 1968).

———

REVOLUTIONS ARE BASED UPON complaints. These complaints can arise from practical concerns, like having food at an affordable price, or from more theoretical or social concerns, such as being able to publicly speak one's mind. Both are grounded in an understanding of what people ought to be able to enjoy as citizens of a country. This expectation of fundamental entitlements is what we talk about when we talk about human rights. But whether or not every person on earth has certain rights just by virtue of being a person alive on the planet—a concept I will refer to here as *natural human rights*—is a question of some controversy. In these times, when new questions of rights, complaints and subsequent conflicts seem to arise anew each week, it's worth knowing where we stand on the matter.

Philosophers and legal scholars have intensely debated this issue over the past few decades. One important starting point for this discussion is H. L. A. Hart's controversial 1955 article, "Are There Any Natural Rights?" The article argued that natural rights (what we typically call human rights) were an invention of the European Enlightenment, mere social constructions. This followed in the footsteps of another legal positivist from the nineteenth century, John Austin, in his very influential work, *Lectures on Jurisprudence*. For Hart and Austin an examination of ancient European texts does not uncover an actual word for either "rights" or "duties." The absence of these words means there is no operational concept of a right or a duty (if all concepts require words to express them). If there is no operational concept of right or duty, then such ideas did not exist before the European Enlightenment.

If this argument is correct, then human rights were invented by Locke, Hobbes, Rousseau, Kant and Hume and are not "natural" or "true" as such, but rather an arbitrary social construction that applies only to societies that choose to adopt it—as they might choose to adopt high-speed Internet access or a particular agricultural irrigation strategy. Under this scenario, the concept of natural human rights is not a legitimate universal category by which to judge societal or individual conduct.

Obviously, this is a very important question. International policy would cease to be able to advocate universally for certain fundamental rights—such as those set out in the United Nations' Declaration of Human Rights or the United States' Bill of Rights and Declaration of Independence or Liu Xiaobo's Charter 08. And of course, the idea that NATO, France, the United States or any other country should intervene in Libya would have never arisen. Instead, each nation would be free to treat its citizens as it chooses, subject only to the rule of power. Hitler would not have been wrong in carrying out the Holocaust, but only weak because he lost the war. The logical result of such a position is a radical moral relativism vis-à-vis various cultural anthropologies.

There are two avenues by which to address the truth of the natural basis of human rights: (a) whether authors argued for human rights before the European Enlightenment, and (b) whether there is a logical basis for human rights that would demonstrate its applicability to all people regardless of when it was recognized to be correct.

The first tack is too long to encompass here. I have argued for a moral basis of human rights in the Stoics; Henrik Syse has made a similar attempt by citing ancient Roman writers; and Alan Gewirth has suggested that the concept can be extracted from Aristotle. At the very least, there is at least a vibrant philological argument here.

The second case, it seems, is much more interesting. If it is true that there is a logical, objective, concrete basis for human rights that is not tied to time or place, then such an argument would be sufficient to show that there are natural human rights. Now the candidates for such a presentation can be put into two camps: the interest-based approach and the agency-based approach. In the interest-based approach (championed by Joseph Raz and James Griffin) the critical question to ask is what conditions are necessary to ensure minimal well-being among people in a society. The force of the argument is that all people everywhere are entitled to at least a minimum level of well-being and the liberties and goods necessary to get them there.

The agency approach is rather different. It comes in two varieties. The first variety is capability theory (championed by Amartya Sen and Martha Nussbaum). In its simplest form this approach seeks to promote human agency—roughly, the capacity for people to act—via public policy strategies that promote individual liberty and opportunity to seek after those goods that each person feels will promote his or her own human flourishing. Agency is thus enhanced through social initiatives.

The second variety seeks to uncover the origins of agency itself—what are the essential features that permit the execution of human action? Under this account (championed by me and Alan Gewirth, among others) particular goods are set out as necessary for action. In my account they are put into a hierarchical order, analogous to Maslow's hierarchy of needs: the most basic needs should be satisfied first for everyone before addressing other needs (the claim for food and water by person X trumps the claim for a new car by person Y). Policy decisions are made by comparing rights claims made by various individuals and groups, and then ascertaining where each falls in the hierarchy: primary claims trump lower-ranked claims. (This also gives a strong defense for progressive taxation policy contra those who think that taxes are a governmental larceny scheme.) Both the interest approach and the agency approach operate under the assumption that there are natural human rights that apply to every person on earth from the beginning of *Homo sapiens*'s existence on the planet (defended by separate arguments).

There are, of course, other justifications of human rights that are *not* universalist but rather based upon conventional criteria such as general agreement (the social contract approach). These depend either upon real people signing treaties in the world as we know it (often multilateral agreements via internationally recognized institutions such as the United Nations) or they are hypothetical contract situations set in a fictional context (such as John Rawls's original position or John Locke's social contract, et al.). These foundations for human rights may be conceptually appealing, but they are subject to variation according to the real people involved or the particular philosopher or practitioner playing out the scenario according to his or her vision of the good. The end result will not be the universalism that is needed to fend off moral relativism.

A second sort of objector to natural human rights claims comes from the People's Republic of China and from one popular interpretation of Islam. The basis of these claims derives from a historical (conventional) view of the grounding of ethics in China and Islam.

In the case of China, the theorist is Confucius. In his very influential work, *Analects*, Confucius established two grounding points:

1. *The essential unit of analysis is the community (aka communitarianism).*

2. *The key values to be observed are ren (a virtue of care) and li (a virtue of balance presented through the metaphor of dance).*

Both of these personal and civic virtues are relational. The relation works this way: (a) there is a community and its existence is a given historical fact that is not up for discussion; (b) there is an individual and he or she is free to decide just how he or she might fit into that community in a caring and balanced way (much of the modern analysis of this comes from the work by Angle and Svensson). Individual interpretations of the community standards are only welcomed if they are supportive. Our care and personal balance are determined via an understanding of community values. Each person's individual liberty consists of finding a way to fit his or her own life's desires within the confines of the community. Thus, the Chinese government says against objections of the West, let us alone. We are working within the confines of our own community-based standards that have existed since Confucius wrote almost 2,500 years ago. We allow free expression within the confines of this ethical construct.

In the second case we have the role of "umma" in Islam. Umma means community in Arabic. The prophet Muhammad personally set out one description of a community in his Constitution of Medina. In Medina there were contentions among various religious groups over rights and privileges. This was a severe problem because each group—Jews, Muslims and indigenous religions—wanted to domi-nate and set the agenda. What Muhammad set out was a way to satisfy the claims of the disparate religious groups that lived there within a contractarian framework so that all might enjoy basic rights as citi-zens. Many in the Middle East feel that the Constitution of Medina creates a blueprint of how to address human rights concerns: create a political or social contract that satisfies everyone's negotiated needs and human rights claims. Once this process has occurred, human rights emerge. They are negotiated rights and not natural rights.

These are both challenging objections to natural human rights, and they are both essentially the same. On the one hand, the social history is setting the standard (one sort of convention), and on the other, a political compromise among contending factions is based upon a compromise of self-interests (another sort of convention). If these two responses are correct, then there are no universal natural human rights.

In contrast to these objections, I would contend that if all commu-nities or nations on earth enjoy the same sort of autonomy that legit-imates any action that they deem acceptable and can be sustained for a period of time, then the moral relativists win. There are no natu-ral human rights, and the whole enterprise should be thrown into the gutter. However, if communities are not self-justifying actors (meaning that they must act within a higher moral structure), then the conventional communitarian gambit fails and natural human rights exist and demand that we recognize and implement them.

The way we think about the turmoil in the Middle East and North Africa is also conditioned by the way we understand human rights. If natural human rights exist, then the autocrats in charge that sup-press them are wrong and they should create either a constitutional monarchy or a democratic republic. If natural human rights do not exist, then the whole process is one of political negotiation that on the one hand involves peaceful protests and on the other involves bloody civil war. Our entire understanding of these events requires us to take sides. But how can we do this?

I have a thought experiment that might help the reader decide what he or she thinks is the correct position: Imagine living in a society in which the majority hurts some minority group (here called "the other"). The reason for this oppression is that "the other" are thought to be bothersome and irritating or that they can be used for social profit. Are you fine with that? Now imagine that *you* are the bothersome irritant and the society wants to squash you for speaking your mind in trying to improve the community. Are you fine with that? These are really the same case. Write down your reasons. If your reasons are situational and rooted in a particular cultural context (such as adhering to socially accepted conventions, like female foot binding or denying women the right to drive), then you may cast your vote with Hart, Austin and Confucius. In this case there are no natural human rights. If your reasons refer to higher principles (such as the Golden Rule), then you cast your vote with the universalists: natural human rights exist. This is an important exercise. Perform this exercise with everyone you are close to—today—and tell me what you think.

MAY 29, 2011

PHILOSOPHY, LITERATURE AND LIFE

Is Philosophy Literature?

—*Jim Holt*

IS PHILOSOPHY LITERATURE? DO PEOPLE READ PHILOSOPHY FOR pleasure? Of course it is, and of course they do.

People savor the aphorisms of Nietzsche, the essays of Schopenhauer, the philosophical novels of Sartre. They read the dialogues of Plato (and they would doubtless read the dialogues of Aristotle, too, had Western civilization not been so careless as to mislay them). Some even claim to enjoy the more daunting treatises in the philosophical canon. "When I have a leisure moment, you will generally find me curled up with Spinoza's latest," Bertie Wooster swankily announces in one of P. G. Wodehouse's Jeeves novels.

Now let me narrow my query: Does anybody read *analytic* philosophy for pleasure? Is *this* kind of philosophy literature? Here you might say, "Certainly not!" Or you might say, "What the heck is analytic philosophy?"

Allow me to address the latter reply first. "Analytic" philosophy is the kind that is practiced these days by the vast majority of professors in philosophy departments throughout the English-speaking world. It's reputed to be rather dry and technical—long on logical rigor, short on lyrical profundity. Analytic philosophy got its start in Cambridge in the first decade of the twentieth century, when Bertrand Russell and G. E. Moore revolted against the rather foggy continental idealism prevailing among English philosophers at the time. Under their influence, and that of Ludwig Wittgenstein (who arrived in Cambridge in 1912 to study with Russell), philosophers came to see their task as consisting not in grand metaphysical system building, but in the painstaking analysis of language. This, they thought, would enable them to lay bare the logical structure of reality and to put all the old philosophical perplexities to rest.

Today, analytic philosophy has a broader scope than it used to. (Many of its qualities were examined in a previous post in this series by Gary Gutting, "Bridging the Analytic-Continental Divide.") It's less obsessed with dissecting language; it's more continuous with the sciences. (This is partly due to the American philosopher Willard Quine, who argued that language really has no fixed system of meanings for philosophers to analyze.) Yet whether they are concerned with the nature of consciousness, of space-time, or of the good life, analytic philosophers continue to lay heavy stress on logical rigor in their writings. The result, according to Martha Nussbaum (herself a sometime member of the tribe), is a prevailing style that is "correct, scientific, abstract, hygienically pallid"—a style meant to serve as "a kind of all-purpose solvent." Timothy Williamson, the current occupant of the illustrious Wykeham Chair of Logic at Oxford, makes a virtue of the "long haul of technical reflection" that is analytic philosophy today. Does it bore you? Well, he says, too bad. "Serious philosophy is always likely to bore those with short attention-spans."

This kind of philosophy, whatever its intellectual merits, doesn't sound like a whole lot of fun. And it doesn't sound like literature.

But what is literature? That in itself might appear to be a philosophical question. Yet the most persuasive answer, to my mind, was supplied by a novelist, Evelyn Waugh. (Well, not just a novelist—also the most versatile master of English prose in the last one hundred years.) "Literature," Waugh declared, "is the right use of language irrespective of the subject or reason of utterance." Something doesn't have to rhyme or tell a story to be considered literature. Even a VCR instruction manual might qualify, or a work of analytic philosophy. (Waugh, as it happens, was not a fan of analytic philosophy, dismissing it as "a parlor game of logical quibbles.")

And what is "the right use of language"? What distinguishes literature from mere communication, or sheer trash? Waugh had an answer to this, too. "Lucidity, elegance, individuality": these are the three essential traits that make a work of prose "memorable and unmistakable," that make it *literature*.

So how does the writing of professional philosophers of the past one hundred years or so fare in the light of these three criteria? Well, it gets high marks for lucidity—which, by the way, is not the same thing as simplicity, or easy intelligibility. (Think of Henry James.) Some prominent analytic philosophers can be turbid in their writing, even preposterously so—the recently deceased Michael Dummett, an admirable thinker in so many other ways, comes to mind. Yet precision of expression is, among their ranks, far more honored in the observance than in the breach. Indeed, it's something of a professional fetish (and not a bad guide to truth).

Individuality? Here, too, analytic philosophers, the greatest of them anyway, shine. Stylistically speaking, there is no mistaking Willard Quine (spare, polished, elaborately lucid) for, say, Elizabeth Anscombe (painstaking, imperious). Or David K. Lewis (colloquially natural, effortlessly clever) for John Searle (formidable, patient, sardonic). Or Thomas Nagel (intricately nuanced, rich in negative capability) for Philippa Foot (dry, ironically homely, droll).

Finally, we come to elegance. This honorific has been overused to the point of meaninglessness, but Waugh had something definite in mind by it: "Elegance is the quality in a work of art which imparts direct pleasure." And pleasure, though by no means an infallible guide to literary value, is (as W. H. Auden observed) the least fallible guide. What does it mean to take pleasure in a piece of prose? Is there a sort of tingle you feel as you read it? That can't very well be, since then it would be the tingle you were enjoying, not the prose. (And wouldn't such a tingle distract you from your reading?) Oddly, one of the most pleasurable pieces of analytic philosophy I've come across is itself an article entitled "Pleasure," where, in a mere nine pages, all the reigning understandings of pleasure are gently deflated. Its author, the Oxford philosopher Gilbert Ryle (1900–76), was among the dominant figures in midcentury analytic philosophy. He was also a supremely graceful prose stylist, the coiner of phrases like "the ghost in the machine," and, not incidentally, a votary of Jane Austen. (Asked if he ever read novels, Ryle was reputed to have replied, "Oh yes—all six, every year.")

Ryle may head the hedonic honor roll of analytic philosophy, but the roll is a long one. It includes all the philosophers I mentioned—especially Quine, whose classic article "On What There Is" can be read over and over again, like a poem. It also includes the Harvard philosopher Hilary Putnam, whose logical lump is leavened by a relaxed command of language and a gift for imaginative thought experiments. It includes younger philosophers (well, younger than sixty-five) like Kwame Anthony Appiah and Colin McGinn—both of whom, in addition to their technical and not-so-technical philosophical work, have written novels. (One of Appiah's is a philosophical murder mystery bearing the title *Another Death in Venice*.) And it certainly includes Bertrand Russell, who was actually awarded a Nobel Prize in Literature—although not, I hasten to add, for his work on *Principia Mathematica*.

Literary pleasures can turn up even in the most seemingly abstruse reaches of analytic philosophy. Take the case of Saul Kripke—widely (though not unanimously) considered the one true genius in the profession today. Kripke's work can be dauntingly technical. The first volume of his collected papers, recently published by Oxford University Press under the arresting title *Philosophical Troubles*, will be a treasure trove to his fellow philosophers of logic and language, but it is not for the casual reader. However, an earlier work of his, the revolutionary *Naming and Necessity*, is so lucidly, inventively and even playfully argued that even a newcomer to analytic philosophy will find it hard to put down. The book is actually a transcription of three lectures Kripke gave, extemporaneously and without notes, at Princeton in January 1970—hence its lovely conversational tone.

Ranging over deep matters like metaphysical necessity, the a priori and the mind-body problem, Kripke proceeds by way of a dazzling series of examples involving Salvador Dalí and Sir Walter Scott, the standard meter stick in Paris, Richard Nixon (plus David Frye's impersonation of him), and an identity-like logical relation Kripke calls "schmidentity." There is not a dogmatic or pompous word in the lectures—and not a dull one either. Kripke the analytic philosopher reveals himself to be a literary stylist of the first water (just as, say, Richard Feynman the physicist did). The reader more than forgives Kripke when he remarks at one point, apropos of his unwillingness to give a thoroughly worked-out theory of reference, "I'm sort of too lazy at the moment."

I hope I have clinched my case for analytic philosophy as belles lettres. But perhaps I should give the last word to a real literary man, John Milton, who prophetically wrote of Kripke, Russell and their kind:

> How charming is divine philosophy!
> Not harsh and crabbèd as dull fools suppose,
> But musical as is Apollo's lute
> And a perpetual feast of nectared sweets . . .

JUNE 30, 2012

Does Great Literature Make Us Better?

—Gregory Currie

Y OU AGREE WITH ME, I EXPECT, THAT EXPOSURE TO CHALLENG-
ing works of literary fiction is good for us. That's one reason we
deplore the dumbing down of the school curriculum and the rise of
the Internet and its hyperlink culture. Perhaps we don't all read very
much that we would count as great literature, but we're apt to feel
guilty about not doing so, seeing it as one of the ways we fall short of
excellence. Wouldn't reading about Anna Karenina, the good folk of
Middlemarch and Marcel and his friends expand our imaginations
and refine our moral and social sensibilities?

If someone now asks you for evidence for this view, I expect you
will have one or both of the following reactions. First, why would
anyone need evidence for something so obviously right? Second,
what kind of evidence would he want? Answering the first question is
easy: if there's no evidence—even indirect evidence—for the civilizing value of literary fiction, we ought not to assume that it does civi-
lize. Perhaps you think there are questions we can sensibly settle in
ways other than by appeal to evidence: by faith, for instance. But even
if there are such questions, surely no one thinks this is one of them.

What sort of evidence could we present? Well, we can point to
specific examples of our fellows who have become more caring, wiser
people through encounters with literature. Indeed, we are such people ourselves, aren't we?

I hope no one is going to push this line very hard. Everything we know about our understanding of ourselves suggests that we are not very good at knowing how we got to be the kind of people we are. In fact we don't really know, very often, what sorts of people we are. We regularly attribute our own failures to circumstance and the failures of others to bad character. But we can't all be exceptions to the rule (supposing it is a rule) that people do bad things because they are bad people.

We are poor at knowing why we make the choices we do, and we fail to recognize the tiny changes in circumstances that can shift us from one choice to another. When it comes to other people, can you be confident that your intelligent, socially attuned and generous friend who reads Proust got that way partly because of the reading? Might it not be the other way around: that bright, socially competent and empathic people are more likely than others to find pleasure in the complex representations of human interaction we find in literature?

There's an argument we often hear on the other side, illustrated earlier this year by a piece on *The New Yorker*'s website. Reminding us of all those cultured Nazis, Teju Cole notes the willingness of a president who reads novels and poetry to sign weekly drone-strike permissions. What, he asks, became of "literature's vaunted power to inspire empathy?" I find this a hard argument to like, and not merely because I am not yet persuaded by the moral case against drones. No one should be claiming that exposure to literature protects one against moral temptation absolutely, or that it can reform the truly evil among us. We measure the effectiveness of drugs and other medical interventions by thin margins of success that would not be visible without sophisticated statistical techniques; why assume literature's effectiveness should be any different?

We need to go beyond the appeal to common experience and into the territory of psychological research, which is sophisticated enough these days to make a start in testing our proposition.

Psychologists have started to do some work in this area, and we have learned a few things so far. We know that if you get people to read a short, lowering story about a child murder, they will afterward report feeling worse about the world than they otherwise would. Such changes, which are likely to be very short-term, show that fictions press our buttons; they don't show that they refine us emotionally or in any other way.

We have learned that people are apt to pick up (purportedly) factual information stated or implied as part of a fictional story's background. Oddly, people are more prone to do that when the story is set away from home: in a study conducted by Deborah Prentice and colleagues and published in 1997, Princeton undergraduates retained more from a story when it was set at Yale than when it was set on their own campus (don't worry Princetonians—Yalies are just as bad when you do the test the other way around). Television, with its serial programming, is good for certain kinds of learning; according to a study from 2001 undertaken for the Kaiser Foundation, people who regularly watched the show *ER* picked up a good bit of medical information on which they sometimes acted. What we don't have is compelling evidence that suggests that people are morally or socially better for reading Tolstoy.

Not nearly enough research has been conducted; nor, I think, is the relevant psychological evidence just around the corner. Most of the studies undertaken so far don't draw on serious literature but on short snatches of fiction devised especially for experimental purposes. Very few of them address questions about the effects of literature on moral and social development, far too few for us to conclude that literature either does or doesn't have positive moral effects.

There is a puzzling mismatch between the strength of opinion on this topic and the state of the evidence. In fact I suspect it is worse than that; advocates of the view that literature educates and civilizes don't overrate the evidence—they don't even think that evidence comes into it. While the value of literature ought not to be a matter of faith, it looks as if, for many of us, that is exactly what it is.

Now, philosophers are careful folk, trained in the ways of argument and, you would hope, above these failings. It's odd, then, that some of them write so confidently and passionately about the kinds of learning we get from literature, and about the features of literature that make it a particularly apt teacher of moral psychology. In her influential book *Love's Knowledge*, Martha Nussbaum argues that the narrative form gives literary fiction a peculiar power to generate moral insight; in the hands of a literary master like Henry James, fiction is able to give us scenarios that make vivid the details of a moral issue, while allowing us to think them through without the distortions wrought by personal interest.

I'm not inclined to write off such speculations; it is always good to have in mind a stock of ideas about ways literature might enhance our thought and action. But it would be refreshing to have some acknowledgment that suggestions about how literature might aid our learning don't show us that it does in fact aid it. (Suppose a schools inspector reported on the efficacy of our education system by listing ways that teachers might be helping students to learn; the inspector would be out of a job pretty soon.)

I'm confident we can look forward to better evidence. I'm less optimistic about what the evidence will show. Here, quickly, is a reason we already have for thinking the idea of moral and social learning from literature may be misguided.

One reason people like Martha Nussbaum have argued for the benefits of literature is that literature, or fictional narrative of real quality, deals in complexity. Literature turns us away from the simple moral rules that so often prove unhelpful when we are confronted with messy real-life decision making, and gets us ready for the stormy voyage through the social world that sensitive, discriminating moral agents are supposed to undertake. Literature helps us, in other words, to be, or to come closer to being, moral "experts."

The problem with this argument is that there's long been evidence that much of what we take for expertise in complex and unpredictable domains—of which morality is surely one—is bogus. Beginning fifty years ago with work by the psychologist Paul Meehl, study after study has shown that following simple rules—rules that take account of many fewer factors than an expert would bother to consider—does at least as well and generally better than relying on an expert's judgment. (Not that rules do particularly well either; but they do better than expert judgment.)

Some of the evidence for this view is convincingly presented in Daniel Kahneman's recent book, *Thinking, Fast and Slow*: spectacular failures of expertise include predictions of the future value of wine, the performance of baseball players, the health of newborn babies and a couple's prospects for marital stability.

But why, I hear you say, do you complain about people's neglect of evidence when you yourself have no direct evidence that moral expertise fails? After all, no one has done tests in this area.

Well, yes, I grant that in the end the evidence could go in favor of the idea that literature can make moral experts of us. I also grant that moral thinking is probably not a single domain, but something that goes on in bewilderingly different ways in different circumstances. Perhaps we can find kinds of moral reasoning where experts trained partly by exposure to the fictional literature of complex moral choice do better than those who rely on simple moral rules of thumb.

I haven't, then, in any way refuted the claim that moral expertise is a quality we should aspire to. But I do think we have identified a challenge that needs to be met by anyone who seriously wants to press the case for moral expertise.

Everything depends in the end on whether we can find direct, causal evidence: we need to show that exposure to literature itself makes some sort of positive difference to the people we end up being. That will take a lot of careful and insightful psychological research (try designing an experiment to test the effects of reading *War and Peace*, for example). Meanwhile, most of us will probably soldier on with a positive view of the improving effects of literature, supported by nothing more than an airy bed of sentiment.

I have never been persuaded by arguments purporting to show that literature is an arbitrary category that functions merely as a badge of membership in an elite. There is such a thing as aesthetic merit, or more likely, aesthetic merits, complicated as they may be to articulate or impute to any given work.

But it's hard to avoid the thought that there is something in the anti-elitist's worry. Many who enjoy the hard-won pleasures of literature are not content to reap aesthetic rewards from their reading; they want to insist that the effort makes them more morally enlightened as well. And that's just what we don't know yet.

Stormy Weather: Blues in Winter

—*Avital Ronell*

I HAVE BEEN TRYING TO GET A GRIP ON MY WINTER BLUES. PHI-losophy has a long history of handling the experience of distressed states. The ancients were concerned with stand-out types of psychic debilitation; Descartes, Kant, and Nietzsche probed, each in his own way, into the dark side of mood and temperament; Kierkeg-aard passed the mic to fear and trembling; Heidegger based his existential analyses on anxiety; and Sartre drilled down on sheer nothingness. Philosophers wondered whether it was possible to feel at-home in the world, given our basic homelessness—a predicament that many of them saw as the uprooted nature of our dwelling on this earth. I count on these abyss gazers to land me safely, without much illusion, and somehow to keep me going, even if the trek is bound to be mournful.

From childhood on, I have been trained to clear really scary and voided chasms, dense existential passageways. My education does not come with an E-ZPass. Like nearly everyone else who isn't entirely sociopathic, I continue to falter and know defeat. Ever on the alert, philosophy offers some emergency supplies of meaning when I feel especially exposed and vulnerable, when I lie fallow on wintered grounds.

Very often, when the chips are down, philosophers can be a wel-coming crew—well, not all of them. One has to sift and sort, find the byways, pass the arrogant know-it-all types, overtake the misogynists and leave in the dust those who claim to have a firm hold on truth. Not many are left standing, but they are the worthy ones. They stay close to poetry and music and let themselves be instructed by literature's astonishing comfortableness off the cognitive grid. There are things that we simply cannot know or understand. Literature lives with that sublime stall, and fires off extravagant hypotheses, basking in transgression and feats of rhetorical frontier crossing. When philosophy becomes accomplice to such stretches of imagination and frees itself up from a certain number of constraints, it can turn in exhilarating and life-affirming performances. It can deliver even when you are seriously in the dumps, ready to call it a wrap.

Of course, people used to say to me that it was the study itself of philosophy that brought me down, a charge that cannot be altogether denied. Yet, upon reflection, I have to think it's the other way round. I consider philosophy my survival kit. In any case philosophy does the groundwork and comes face-to-face with my basic repertory of distress: forlornness, the shakes, and other signs of world-weary discomfort. Thud, thud. Today's blues seem very specific, however. Maybe I can summon the master thinkers to help me get a handle on my internal downturn, my current sense of loss.

Nearly every philosophy I have known has built a sanctuary, however remote and uncharted, for the experience of mourning. Sometimes a philosopher accidentally or furtively mentions the pull of loss, even when trying, like Nietzsche, to affirm all of life's tragic edges and the necessity of mourning lost friendship or the destructive operations (and operas) of love.

My teacher, Jacques Derrida, considered various forms of mourning disorder—the difficulty we have in letting go of a beloved object or libidinal position. Freud says that we go into mourning over lost ideals or figures, which include persons or even your country when it lets you down. Loss that cannot be assimilated or dealt with creates pockets of resistance in the psyche. One may incorporate a phantom other, keeping the other both alive and dead, or one may fall into states of melancholy, unable to move on, trapped in the energies of an ever-shrinking world.

Many of the themes in films give expression to failed mourning, a relation to death that invents the population of the undead—vampires, zombies, trolls, real housewives of Beverly Hills. In America, we are often encouraged to "let go," "move on," "get over it," even to "get a life," locutions that indicate a national intolerance for prolonged states of mourning. Yet the quickened pace of letting go may well mean that we have not let go, that we are haunted and hounded by unmetabolized aspects of loss. In Freud's work, the timer is set for two years of appropriate mourning. When Hamlet tries to extend that deadline, the whole house threatens to fall apart, and he is admonished by Claudius to get over himself, man up. The inability to mourn or let go is sometimes called melancholy. Many of us have slipped into states of melancholic depression for one reason or another, for one unreason or another—one cannot always nail the object that has been lost or causes pain.

For Derrida, melancholy implies an ethical stance, a relation to loss in the mode of vigilance and constant re-attunement. You do not have to know or understand the meaning of a loss and the full range of its disruptive consequences, but you somehow stand by it, leaning into a depleting emptiness. It takes courage to resist the temptation to bail or distract oneself. Entire industries stand ready to distract the inconsolable mourner.

Let's see if I can try to stay focused. Maybe it is possible to get an aerial view of my own cluster of blues.

I actually think that I, like many New Yorkers, am having a delayed response to Hurricane Sandy. Or that, continually flooding my psyche, it keeps on returning. I see no off switch to the effects of Sandy, some of which remain very real to neighboring areas.

So. I AM SLOWLY climbing out of the inundation of 2012 like the Swamp Thing. In order to dry off and reflect on what happened this past autumn in New York, I had to remove myself from the premises, surrender to a stance of meditation from another urban site. Off-center and beat, I decided to go to Paris to watch the year turn. My intention was to see my friends and colleagues and reboot myself, preparing the newest year's anticipated yield of projects, looking forward and backward in a mood of self-gathering.

And so I arrived in Paris to welcome our newest baby year. Drip, drip.

Coming in to Charles de Gaulle a few days before Christmas, I had a rocky landing—emotionally speaking. It wasn't due merely to the weather—though weather, the disjunctive edge of climate, seemed implacably poised to compromise this grrrl. But it wasn't the dismal weather, the droplets of rain, that depressed me, but an accumulation of all sorts of internalized weather systems and pressure zones that I would need to understand. Yes, maybe I could install my own weather prophet to read off the mists of mind's droopiness.

I used to study weather and the scandalous beginnings of weather forecasting. Do you know who set up the first meteorological prediction center? My main man, Goethe. At the time, in the eighteenth century, the very idea of grasping weather competed with the prerogatives of the gods. Mortals should not have access to such clusters of immateriality, it was thought. Only gods and poets should try to divine weather conditions.

Like much of the weather, my mood proved unpredictable. Exhausted and shaken following a semester of overload, I crawled around Paris for days, waiting for some sign of surviving the holidays. It was long in coming. My pangs were suspended when I would meet my friends and alternative families. But the minute they unleashed me, after a lunch or afternoon stroll, I spun on my own, in considerable agony, my stomach falling out: "Merry, merry, merry Christmas." I'm not the only one, I know, for who does not come with a crash cushion for family holidays, and so I sputter. This year was different in terms of seasonal despair, which makes me wonder why.

It seems far away. But Sandy continues to return, to rage in my stomach—site of anxiety, where events show up as severe and unyielding. I know that greater parts of our world regularly live on the subthreshhold of calamity, awaiting the next trial, the next move commissioned by an unfathomable enmity—I think of friends in Haiti and Malaysia, those who try to keep it together in areas that are rarely disaster-free or earthquake-proof: I will never forget the day in the fall of 1989 at Berkeley when Philippe Lacoue-Labarthe and Jean-Luc Nancy taught their first seminar together and the building rattled, the earth shook, our complexions showed different shades of green. I was strangely steady as things and people started crumbling around me. I prided myself on being a strong warrior, able to hold still as things fall apart, leaning into anguish, whether externally pitched or internally churning. I was earthquake proof, I told myself.

In the Bay Area a building is earthquake proof when it has built-in fissures and intentional crevices. Normed solidity or, rather, *rigidity* is a sure killer, because if you're too rigid, you will be cut down, toppled. Like the World Trade Center—too massive, *too strong*, architecturally speaking.

When weakness is part of the concept of the building's stance, it can sway and shift around as part of its very own survival mechanism. This "architecture of pain," as psychoanalyst Jacques Lacan says in another context altogether, was my model for a long while, a model that I am trying to reconstruct today, with ample allowance for punctuated lacerations and weak points meant to bolster part of my psychic suppleness.

One of the aspects of the earthquake in Berkeley was that you could not tell if it was happening inside or outside. The staccato outbreak started out as if it had originated in one's body. Only when one looked out the window and saw the sway of buildings did the sense of collapse spread to the outside. The fitful spurts and earth lunges functioned like Freud's endopsychic perception: Was this merely a projection of inner turmoil or suppressed rage? Or had we regressed to biblical law, under penalty for a collective wrongdoing?

Since one of my personalities is that of teacher, I usually want to prepare something to say to students when a so-called natural disaster breaks. At the time of the earthquake I turned to Kant and traced what happened to and in philosophy, from the outposts of literature, as a consequence of the earthquake of Lisbon in 1755. Everyone was shaken, and in many ways we never stopped quaking. In Goethe, Nature became irreversibly maimed: demonic and glacialized with indifference to the human manifestation of being, Nature became an unbeatable adversary.

For the inundation of New York, I went to Freud and primitive attitudes toward violent weather events, trying to make sense of that which seizes you and throws you against a new wall of experience.

First, I needed to critically dismantle any idea of a "natural" disaster in our day, in our way of trampling on the planet, carbon footprint by carbon footprint. I do not believe in "natural" disasters, but only in the effects of man's failed custodianship, primed by the incessant prod of pollution, planetary exploitation and spoilage: the usual menu of historical recklessness.

On a more local and personal plane, I needed to reflect on my own sorry failures: I was shaken by my fearfulness and the collapse I observed of my warrior self when during the worst of the storm I lost any sense of social responsibility and just caved, became isolated, felt unsheltered. I stayed at the level of acute worry about electronic disconnection. All I could do was spread around my own sense of unprotectedness.

From now on, I said to myself, I will follow Gandhi's directive: *be what you want the world to be.* Rather than crumbling and trembling, isolating, waiting for Someone to rescue me, I will be the one to arrive on the scene, a "first responder," prepared to take charge, stage street theater, check in on my isolated neighbors, make and deliver creative meals. Sometimes you have to turn yourself into an animal in order to be brave and reassuring, to leap with cheer or still yourself. Thus, lately, golden retrievers and Labradors have been called upon to visit trauma sites and bring soothing steadiness, messages from another realm.

Many people continue to be affected by the storm and its invisible after-tremors. They were and remain stuck, and I was psychically not flowing, unable either to surrender or act, energy-trapped. For seven days or so Lower Manhattan earned the designation, according to our resident philosopher Jon Stewart, of "Little North Korea."

We were stunned to have lost our sense of "New York, New York," to witness the powering down of its habitual trajectories and hard-edged rhythms.

When Freud reviews the attitude of so-called primitive peoples to calamities missile-guided by Nature or gods, he points to these peoples' felt failure. Natural disruption, which puts into play and unleashes something like the *supernatural*, appears to be sent our way as a message from above. Most often, it represents a form of reactivity, an accusation. The supernatural (Sandy was so often called a *super*storm) is something that humankind has called upon itself in response to stinging acts of frivolity. Freud's examples involve failed mourning—of the enemy. The so-called primitives believed that storms mark down those who have neglected to honor or properly bury their enemies.

I try to review our recent wars, whether mapped on Afghanistan or in ghetto streets and surrounding precarious clinics. I try to gauge the implication, however remote, of every citizen, in the waging of these and other aggressions. This seems far-fetched—perhaps closer to science fiction than to science. Is there a way in which radically disrupted weather systems tell us, maybe merely on an unconscious register, that we are involved in world-class wrongdoing? In a Shakespearean way, I keep on punctuating such observations by the refrain, "No, such a reproach cannot be addressed to us." I am also of the scientific epoch and understand the repercussions of global warming.

Still, could the superstorm have been a call from elsewhere? A reminder of the stripped-down disposal of enemy troops or tropes, our graceless menu of aggressions brought home to us, the world-class homeless? I may or may not have my finger on the pulse of Hegel's Weltgeist, the guiding world spirit, but something about my very private and idiomatic blues comes from the pressure of a sustained injustice, a dishonoring that occurs in my name and that may affect all Americans on one level of consciousness or another.

FEBRUARY 2, 2013

Poetry, Medium and Message

—*Ernie Lepore*

HERE IS A QUESTION THAT HAS BEEN CONFOUNDING OR EVEN infuriating poets for eons:

So what is your poem *about*?

(If you happen to personally know any poets, you may even have empirical evidence of this.)

That frustration has little, if anything, to do with the supposed stormy temperaments of poets. It rather derives, at least partly, from the fact that the question, simple as it may appear, is one that in fact has no satisfactory answer.

Why?

In *The Well Wrought Urn*—that well-known and well-wrought book of literary criticism—Cleanth Brooks described what he called "the heresy of paraphrase." The main idea—that efforts at paraphrasing poetry into prose fail in ways that parallel attempts for prose do not—was not new. It has been generally agreed upon since Aristotle. This skeptical thesis was championed in the first half of the twentieth century by the New Critics as well as by their guiding spirit, T. S. Eliot, who, when asked to interpret the lines "Lady, three white leopards sat under a juniper tree / In the cool of the day . . ." from his poem "Ash Wednesday," responded, "It means 'Lady, three white leopards sat under a juniper tree / In the cool of the day.'"

Eliot's implication was that repetition is the best we can hope to achieve in interpreting poetry. Translators of Rimbaud likewise lament that because French is soft, melodious and fluid in cadence, English and other non-Romance languages are unsuitable for translation. The poet E. E. Cummings went further, claiming that even the visual impact of the typography of his poems renders them unparaphraseable.

Contemporary philosophers and linguists have either ignored such skepticism or dismissed it out of hand. The idea that an unambiguous word might mean one thing in a news article or shopping list and something altogether different in a poem is not so easy to embrace. How do we figure out what a poem means if its words do not carry familiar learned meanings? And further, isn't this skepticism vulnerable to the following simple refutation: Take any expression in any poem and introduce by fiat a new expression to mean exactly what the first one does; how could this practice fail to succeed at paraphrase or translation? Though such substitutions can change the aesthetic, emotive or imagistic quality of a poem, how could any of them change meaning?

Despite the simple refutation, the heresy of paraphrase remains compelling. Anyone familiar with Roman Jakobson's or Vladimir Nabokov's lamentations over translating Pushkin into English will feel its force. But can their irresistible skepticism concerning poetry translation and paraphrase be reconciled with the obvious logic of the simple refutation?

There is a way out, but to find it one must first attend to a crucial but universally ignored distinction between linguistic expressions and their vehicles of articulation: to this end, consider two individuals, both of whom know English, but one only speaks while the other only writes. For them, communication is impossible even though they share a common language.

Since each expression requires articulation for its presentation, it is easy to conflate words and their articulations. (Many philosophers and linguists have!) And, of course, more often than not, the linguistic sounds or marks with which we articulate our language make little difference to our intended message. It usually matters little if at all to our grasp of what someone says whether he speaks or writes. But if you reflect upon the distinct possibilities for presenting language, it's easy to see how what normally goes unnoticed can take center stage.

For instance, typing the word "brick" in italics (as in *brick*) obviously draws attention to a particular presentation of the word, not to the word itself. But it is one of many. The word might have been spoken, rendered in Braille or even signed. Surprisingly, in this instance, a moment's reflection ought to convince you that no *other* articulation could have been used to make this point in this way. In short, that *brick* is italicized cannot be said out loud or signed or rendered in Braille. In effect, the practice of italicization allows the presentation of a language to become a part of the language itself.

If poems too can be (partly) about their own articulations, this would explain why they can resist paraphrase or translation into another idiom, why, for example, substituting "luster" for "sheen" in Coleridge's "Rime of the Ancient Mariner" breaks the bind between its lines and thereby alters the poem itself.

> *And through the drifts the snowy clifts*
> *Did send a dismal sheen:*
> *Nor shapes of men nor beasts we ken—*
> *The ice was all between.*

Since synonym substitution in a poem can change meter or rhyme, etc., to the extent that poems are about their own articulation they prohibit paraphrase and translation. Accordingly, as with other forms of mentioning, any effort at re-articulation inevitably changes the topic. Here's another illustration of the point. Although Giorgione—Big George—was so-called because of his size, Giorgio Barbarelli da Castelfranco was not, even though he *is* Giorgine. This is possible because the "so-called" construction is partly about its own articulation. Change the articulation and you change the claim even if substitutions are synonymous. These sorts of considerations expose what's misguided about the simple refutation.

Of course, we can introduce a new expression to mean exactly whatever an old expression means but since poems can be about their own articulations, substituting synonyms will not result in an exact paraphrase or translation. To do so requires not *only* synonymies but also identical articulations, and only repetition ensures this end.

This explanation of the heresy of paraphrase differs from the New Critics' quasi-mystical invocation of *form shaping content*. Linguistic expressions mean whatever they mean wherever they occur, but in poetry (as in other forms of mentioning) the medium really becomes the message. From this, however, it does *not* follow that the language of poetry is magical or even distinct from the languages of other discourses; they are identical. The words in a Cummings poem mean exactly what they do in prose. But because a poem can be a device for presenting its own articulation, re-articulating Cummings while ignoring his versification fails.

Is this what Sartre might have meant when he said the poet "considers words as things and not as signs"? Likewise, Dylan Thomas writes of his first experiences with poetry that "before I could read them for myself I had come to love just the words of them, the words alone. What the words stood for, symbolized, or meant, was of very secondary importance; what mattered was the *sound* of them as I heard them for the first time on the lips of the remote and incomprehensible grown-ups who seemed, for some reason, to be living in my world." Thomas might have simply said that his first concern was with *articulation*, especially sounds—a perceptible property.

Pause and examine these letters as you read them—their shapes are not unappealing. The poet concurs. But, unlike ordinary folk, the poet wants to draw the audience's attention to these articulations as much as to the ideas the words so articulated express. The poet achieves this end through the devices, for example, of rhyme, alliteration and sundry others. Unintended, rhyme or alliteration and other mishaps and distractions are often rectified by re-articulation, perhaps with different pronunciations of the same words or with different words or linguistic structures that convey the same content. In such circumstances, the discourse is decidedly not *about* its own articulation. With poetry it is different.

As W. M. Urban noted, the poet does not first intuit her object and then find an appropriate medium in which to articulate it. It is rather in and through a chosen medium that the poet intuits the object in the first place. The philosopher Suzanne Langer once wrote, "though the *material* of poetry is verbal, its import is not the literal assertion made in the words, but *the way the assertion is made,* and this involves the sound, the tempo . . . and the unifying, all-embracing artifice of rhythm."

Given this, what might poetic effects achieve? Poe's "The Raven" is an over-the-top case, but a clear one. The poem is partly about sound and its effects on thought, and words and meter are chosen to evoke the sounds themselves, as well as the words: "*the silken, sad, uncertain rustling of each purple curtain* . . ." The repeated rhyme is also important; by the time the raven first says "nevermore," the pattern is established so that the raven's pronouncement arrives with a sense of finality and inevitability which echoes or mirrors or just helps the reader appreciate the way thoughts of death and loss have taken over the narrator's mind—the bleak obsession that is the theme of the poem.

Brooks and the New Critics would have us believe that what is at work is somehow magical. But there is no mystery here.

JULY 31, 2011

Boxing Lessons

—Gordon Marino

I OFFER TRAINING IN BOTH PHILOSOPHY AND BOXING. OVER THE years, some of my colleagues have groused that my work is a contradiction, building minds and cultivating rational discourse while teaching violence and helping to remove brain cells. Truth be told, I think philosophers with this gripe should give some thought to what really counts as violence. I would rather take a punch in the nose any day than be subjected to some of the attacks that I have witnessed in philosophy colloquia. However, I have a more positive case for including boxing in my curriculum for sentimental education.

Western philosophy, even before Descartes's influential case for a mind-body dualism, has been dismissive of the body. Plato—even though he competed as a wrestler—and most of the sages who followed him, taught us to think of our arms and legs as nothing but a poor carriage for the mind. In *Phaedo*, Plato presents his teacher Socrates on his deathbed as a sort of Mr. Spock yearning to be free from the shackles of the flesh so he can really begin thinking seriously. In this account, the body gives rise to desires that will not listen to reason and that becloud our ability to think clearly.

In much of Eastern philosophy, in contrast, the search for wisdom is more holistic. The body is considered inseparable from the mind, and is regarded as a vehicle, rather than an impediment, to enlightenment. The unmindful attitude toward the body so prevalent in the West blinkers us to profound truths that the skin, muscles and breath can deliver like a punch.

While different physical practices may open us to different truths, there is a lot of wisdom to be gained in the ring. Socrates, of course, maintained that the unexamined life was not worth living, that self-knowledge is of supreme importance. One thing is certain: boxing can compel a person to take a quick self-inventory and gut check about what he or she is willing to endure and risk. As Joyce Carol Oates observes in her minor classic, *On Boxing*,

> *Boxers are there to establish an absolute experience, a public accounting of the outermost limits of their beings; they will know, as few of us can know of ourselves, what physical and psychic power they possess—of how much, or how little, they are capable.*

Though the German idealist philosopher G. W. F. Hegel (1770–1831) never slipped on the gloves, I think he would have at least supported the study of the sweet science. In his famous lord and bondsman allegory, Hegel suggests that it is in mortal combat with the other, and ultimately in our willingness to give up our lives, that we rise to a higher level of freedom and consciousness. If Hegel is correct, the lofty image that the warrior holds in our society has something to do with the fact that in her willingness to sacrifice her own life, she has escaped the otherwise universal choke hold of death anxiety. Boxing can be seen as a stylized version of Hegel's proverbial trial by battle and as such affords new possibilities of freedom and selfhood.

Viewed purely psychologically, practice in what used to be termed the "manly art" makes people feel more at home in themselves, and so less defensive and perhaps less aggressive. The way we cope with the elemental feelings of anger and fear determines to no small extent what kind of person we will become. Enlisting Aristotle, I shall have more to say about fear in a moment, but I don't think it takes a Freud to recognize that many people are mired in their own bottled-up anger. In our society, expressions of anger are more taboo

than libidinal impulses. Yet, as our entertainment industry so powerfully bears out, there is plenty of fury to go around. I have trained
boxers, often women, who find it extremely liberating to learn that
they can strike out, throw a punch, express some rage, and that no
one is going to die as a result.

And let's be clear: life is filled with blows. It requires toughness
and resiliency. There are few better places than the squared circle
to receive concentrated lessons in the dire need to be able to absorb
punishment and carry on, "to get off the canvas" and "roll with the
punches." It is little wonder that boxing, more than any other sport,
has functioned as a metaphor for life. Aside from the possibilities for
self-fulfillment, boxing can also contribute to our moral lives.

In his *Nicomachean Ethics*, Aristotle argues that the final end for
human beings is *eudaimonia*—the good life, or as it is most often
translated, happiness. In an immortal sentence Aristotle announces,
"The Good of man (*eudaimonia*) is the active exercise of his soul's
faculties in conformity with excellence or virtue, or if there be several human excellences or virtues, in conformity with the best and
most perfect among them."

A few pages later, Aristotle acknowledges that there are in fact two
kinds of virtue or excellence—namely, intellectual and moral. Intellectual excellence is simple book learning, or theoretical smarts.
Unlike his teacher, Plato, and his teacher's teacher, Socrates, Aristotle recognized that a person could know a great deal about the Good
and not lead a good life. "With regard to excellence," says Aristotle,
"it is not enough to know, but we must try to have and use it."

Aristotle offers a table of the moral virtues that includes, among
other qualities, temperance, justice, pride, friendliness and truth-
fulness. Each semester when I teach ethics, I press my students to
generate their own list of the moral virtues. "What," I ask, "are the
traits that you connect with having character?" Tolerance, kindness,
self-respect, creativity always make it onto the board, but it is usually
only with prodding that courage gets a nod. And yet, courage seems
absolutely essential to leading a moral life. After all, if you do not
have mettle, you will not be able to abide by your moral judgments.

Doing the right thing often demands going down the wrong side of the road of our immediate and long-range self-interests. It frequently involves sacrifices that we do not much care for, sometimes of friendships, or jobs—sometimes, as in the case with Socrates, even of our lives. Making these sacrifices is impossible without courage.

According to Aristotle, courage is a mean between rashness and cowardliness; that is, between having too little trepidation and too much. Aristotle reckoned that in order to be able to hit the mean, we need practice in dealing with the emotions and choices corresponding to that virtue. So far as developing grit is concerned, it helps to get some swings at dealing with manageable doses of fear. And yet, even in our approach to education, many of us tend to think of anything that causes a shiver as traumatic. Consider, for example, the demise of dodgeball in public schools. It was banned because of the terror that the flying red balls caused in some children and of the damage to self-esteem that might come with always being the first one knocked out of the game. But how are we supposed to learn to stand up to our fears if we never have any supervised practice in dealing with the jitters? Of course, our young people are very familiar with aggressive and often gruesome video games that simulate physical harm and self-defense, but without, of course, any of the consequences and risks that might come with putting on the gloves.

Boxing provides practice with fear and, with the right, attentive supervision, in quite manageable increments. In their first sparring session, boxers usually erupt in "fight or flight" mode. When the bell rings, novices forget everything they have learned and simply flail away. If they stick with it for a few months, their fears diminish; they can begin to see things in the ring that their emotions blinded them to before. More importantly, they become more at home with feeling afraid. Fear is painful, but it can be faced, and in time a boxer learns not to panic about the blows that will be coming his way.

While Aristotle is able to define courage, the study and practice of boxing can enable us not only to comprehend courage, but "to have and use" it. By getting into the ring with our fears, we will be less likely to succumb to trepidation when doing the right thing demands taking a hit. To be sure, there is an important difference between physical and moral courage. After all, the world has seen many a brave monster. The willingness to endure physical risks is not enough to guarantee uprightness; nevertheless, it can, I think, contribute in powerful ways to the development of moral virtue.

SEPTEMBER 15, 2010

The Practical and the Theoretical

—Jason Stanley

OUR SOCIETY IS DIVIDED INTO CASTES BASED UPON A SUPPOSED division between theoretical knowledge and practical skill. The college professor holds forth on television, as the plumber fumes about detached ivory-tower intellectuals. The felt distinction between the college professor and the plumber is reflected in how we think about our own minds. Humans are thinkers, and humans are doers. There is a natural temptation to view these activities as requiring distinct capacities. When we *reflect*, we are guided by our knowledge of truths about the world. By contrast, when we *act*, we are guided by our knowledge of how to perform various actions. If these are distinct cognitive capacities, then knowing how to do something is not knowledge of a fact—that is, there is a distinction between practical and theoretical knowledge. The world of the college professor is supposedly so different than the world of the plumber because they are viewed as employing fundamentally different mental capacities in their daily lives. The college professor doesn't "get it," because her knowledge is purely theoretical, knowledge of truths. The plumber isn't qualified to reason about a political system or the economy because skill in complex action is not an exercise of such knowledge.

Most of us are inclined immediately to classify activities like repairing a car, riding a bicycle, hitting a jump shot, taking care of a baby, or cooking a risotto as exercises of practical knowledge. And we are inclined to classify proving a theorem in algebra, testing a hypothesis in physics and constructing an argument in philosophy as exercises of the capacity to operate with knowledge of truths. The cliché of the learned professor, as inept in practical tasks as he is skilled in theoretical reasoning, is just as much a leitmotif of popular culture as that of the dumb jock. The folk idea that skill at action is not a manifestation of intellectual knowledge is also entrenched in contemporary philosophy, though it has antecedents dating back to the ancients.

According to the model suggested by this supposed dichotomy, exercises of theoretical knowledge involve active reflection, engagement with the propositions or rules of the theory in question that guides the subsequent exercise of the knowledge. Think of the chess player following an instruction she has learned for an opening move in chess. In contrast, practical knowledge is exercised automatically and without reflection. The skilled tennis player does not reflect on instructions before returning a volley—she exercises her knowledge of how to return a volley *automatically*. Additionally, the fact that exercises of theoretical knowledge are guided by propositions or rules seems to entail that they involve instructions that are universally applicable—the person acting on theoretical knowledge has an instruction booklet, which she reflects upon before acting. In contrast, part of the skill that constitutes skill at tennis involves reacting to situations for which no instruction manual can prepare you. The skilled tennis player is skilled in part because she knows how to adjust her game to a novel serve, behavior that does not seem consistent with following a rule book.

The thought that aptitude at acquiring skills at practical activities is different from aptitude at acquiring knowledge of truths affects our most fundamental interactions with others. When our child exhibits skill at a physical activity, and an initial lack of interest in mathematics, we might suppose that the child has aptitude for practical activities but not intellectual pursuits (and vice versa).

But once one begins to bear down upon the supposed distinction between the practical and the theoretical, cracks appear. When one acquires a practical skill, one *learns* how to do something. But when one acquires knowledge of a scientific proposition, that, too, is an instance of learning. In many (though not all) of the world's languages, the same verb is used for practical as well as theoretical knowledge (for example, *know* in English *savior* in French). More important, when one reflects upon *any* exercise of knowledge, whether practical or theoretical, it appears to have the characteristics that would naively be ascribed to the exercise of both practical and intellectual capacities. A mathematician's proof of a theorem is the ideal example of the exercise of theoretical knowledge. Yet in order to count as skilled at math, the mathematician's training—like that of the tennis player—must render her adept in reacting to novel difficulties she may encounter in navigating mathematical reality. Nor does exercising one's knowledge of truths require active reflection. I routinely exercise my knowledge that one operates an elevator by depressing a button, without giving the slightest thought to the matter. From the other direction, stock examples of supposedly merely practical knowledge are acquired in apparently theoretical ways. People can and often do learn how to cook a risotto by reading recipes in cookbooks.

Perhaps one way to distinguish practical knowledge and theoretical knowledge is by *talking*. When we acquire knowledge of how to do something, we may not be able to express our knowledge in words. But when we acquire knowledge of a truth, we are able to express this knowledge in words. Somebody may know how to make a baby laugh but not be able to express how they do it. But if someone knows that Washington, DC, is the capital of the United States, they are presumably able to express this knowledge in words.

However, the distinction between what we are able to express in words and what we are unable to so express does not track any supposed distinction between practical and theoretical knowledge. I may know that the secret password is 415XH, but I may not be able to express this knowledge in words—I may only be able to press the keys when given a keypad (the knowledge resides, so to speak, in my fingers). One might then think that being able to express something in words is not necessary for theoretical knowledge. Conversely, one may think that anyone who knows how to do something is able to express that knowledge in words. After all, someone who knows how to make a baby laugh can, when asked how to do it, say, "This is the way to make a baby laugh," while he makes a baby laugh.

I have argued here (and at length elsewhere) that once one bears down on the supposed distinction between practical knowledge and knowledge of truths, it breaks down. The plumber's or electrician's activities are a manifestation of the same kind of intelligence as the scientist's or historian's latest articles—knowledge of truths. It is true that someone might be adept at car mechanics and hopeless at philosophy. But it is also true that someone might be adept at theoretical physics and hopeless at philosophy. Distinctions between what one is adept at and what one is not adept at do not correlate with the folk distinction between practical and theoretical pursuits. If only to appropriate student loans rationally, we must also recognize distinctions between professions whose mastery requires learning many and perhaps more complex truths and professions that one can master more easily. But these are distinctions along a continuum, rather than distinctions in *kind*, as the folk distinction between practical and theoretical pursuits is intended to be.

These are barriers in our society erected by a false dichotomy between practical work and theoretical reflection. If someone develops early on a skill at repairing cars, she may falsely assume that she will not be adept at literary analysis or theorem proving. This robs not only her of opportunities but also society of a potentially important contributor to literary analysis or mathematics. The reward structure of society also assumes it, reflected in both the pay and the cost of pursuing what are thought of as the theoretical pursuits. The supposed distinction also operates on an everyday level. If one spends one's time repairing cars, one may think that one does not have the appropriate capacities to evaluate the arguments of economic "experts" on television. One might then feel alienated from such discussions and find one's sense of alienation reflected in the angry rhetoric of propagandists.

The distinction between the practical and theoretical is used to warehouse society into groups. It alienates and divides. It is fortunate, then, that it is nothing more than a fiction.

MAY 6, 2012

The Meaningfulness of Lives

—Todd May

W HO AMONG US HAS NOT ASKED WHETHER HIS OR HER LIFE IS A meaningful one? Who has not wondered—on a sleepless night, during a long stretch of dull or taxing work, or when a troubled child seems a greater burden than one can bear—whether in the end it all adds up to anything? On this day, too, ten years after the September 11 attacks, when many are steeped in painful reminders of personal loss, it is natural to wonder about the answers.

The philosopher Jean-Paul Sartre thought that without God, our lives are bereft of meaning. He tells us in his essay "Existentialism," "If God does not exist, we find no values or commands to turn to which legitimize our conduct. So, in the bright realm of values, we have no excuse behind us, nor justification before us." On this view, God gives our lives the values upon which meaning rests. And if God does not exist, as Sartre claims, our lives can have only the meaning we confer upon them.

This seems wrong on two counts. First, why would the existence of God guarantee the meaningfulness of each of our lives? Is a life of unremitting drudgery or unrequited struggle really redeemed if there's a larger plan, one to which we have no access, into which it fits? That would be small compensation for a life that would otherwise feel like a waste—a point not lost on thinkers like Karl Marx, who called religion the "opium of the people." Moreover, does God actually ground the values by which we live? Do we not, as Plato recognized 2,500 years ago, already have to think of those values as good in order to ascribe them to God?

Second, and more pointedly, must the meaningfulness of our lives depend on the existence of God? Must meaning rely upon articles of faith? Basing life's meaningfulness on the existence of a deity not only leaves all atheists out of the picture but also leaves different believers out of one another's picture. What seems called for is an approach to thinking about meaning that can draw us together, one that exists alongside or instead of religious views.

A promising and more inclusive approach is offered by Susan Wolf in her recent and compelling book, *Meaning in Life and Why It Matters*. A meaningful life, she claims, is distinct from a happy life or a morally good one. In her view, "meaning arises when subjective attraction meets objective attractiveness." A meaningful life must, in some sense then, *feel* worthwhile. The person living the life must be engaged by it. A life of commitment to causes that are generally defined as worthy—like feeding and clothing the poor or ministering to the ill—but that do not move the person participating in them will lack meaningfulness in this sense. However, for a life to be meaningful, it must also *be* worthwhile. Engagement in a life of tiddlywinks does not rise to the level of a meaningful life, no matter how gripped one might be by the game.

Often one defends an idea by giving reasons for it. However, sometimes the best defense is not to give reasons at the outset but instead to pursue the idea in order to see where it leads. Does it capture something important if we utilize it to understand ourselves? It's this latter tack that I would like to try here. The pursuit of this core idea—that a meaningful life is both valued and valuable—allows us to understand several important aspects of our attitudes toward ourselves and others.

In this pursuit, the first step we might take beyond what Wolf tells us is to recognize that lives unfold over time. A life is not an unrelated series of actions or projects or states of being. A life has, we might say, a trajectory. It is lived in a temporal thickness. Even if my life's trajectory seems disjointed or to lack continuity, it is *my* life that is disconnected in its unfolding, not elements of several different lives.

If a life has a trajectory, then it can be conceived narratively. A human life can be seen as a story, or as a series of stories that are more or less related. This does not mean that the person whose life it is must conceive it or live it narratively. I needn't say to myself, "Here's the story I want to construct," or, "This is the story so far." What it means, rather, is that, if one reflected on one's life, one could reasonably see it in terms of various story lines, whether parallel or intersecting or distinct. This idea can be traced back to Aristotle's *Ethics* but has made a reappearance with some recent narrative conceptions of what a self is.

What makes a trajectory a meaningful one? If Wolf is right, it has to feel worthwhile and, beyond that, has to be engaged in projects that are objectively worthwhile. There is not much difficulty in knowing what feels worthwhile. Most of us are good at sensing when we're onto something and when we're not. Objective worthiness is more elusive. We don't want to reduce it simply to a morally good life, as though a meaningful life were simply an unalienated moral life. Meaningful lives are not so limited and, as we shall see, are sometimes more vexed. So we must ask what lends objective worthiness to a life outside the moral realm. Here is where the narrative character of a life comes into play.

There are values we associate with a good narrative and its characters that are distinct from those we associate with good morals. A fictional character can be intense, adventurous, steadfast, or subtle. Think here of the adventurousness of Ishmael in *Moby-Dick*, the quiet intensity of Kip in *The English Patient*, the steadfastness of Dilsey in *The Sound and the Fury* or the subtlety of Marco Polo in *Invisible Cities*. As with these fictional characters, so with our lives. When a life embodies one or more of these values (or others) and feels engaging to the one who lives it, it is to that extent meaningful. There are narrative values expressed by human lives that are not reducible to moral values. Nor are they reducible to happiness; they are not simply matters of subjective feeling. Narrative values are not felt; they are lived. And they constitute their own arena of value, one that has not been generally recognized by philosophers who reflect on life's meaningfulness.

An intense life, for instance, can be lived with abandon. One might move from engagement to engagement, or stick with a single engagement, but always (well, often) by diving into it, holding nothing back. One throws oneself into swimming or poetry or community organizing or fundraising, or perhaps all of them at one time or another. Such a life is likely a meaningful one. And this is true even where it might not be an entirely moral one.

We know of people like this, people whose intensity leads them to behavior that we might call morally compromised. Intense lovers can leave bodies in their wake when the embers of love begin to cool. Intense athletes may not be the best of teammates. Our attitudes toward people like this are conflicted. There is a sense in which we might admire them and another sense in which we don't. This is because meaningful lives don't always coincide with good ones. Meaningful lives can be morally compromised, just as morally good lives can feel meaningless to those who live them.

We should not take this to imply that there is no relationship between meaningfulness and morality. They meet at certain moral limits. An evil life, no matter how intense or steadfast, is not one we would want to call meaningful. But within the parameters of those moral limits, the relationship between a meaningful life and a moral one is complicated. They do not map directly onto each other.

Why might all this matter? What is the point of understanding what makes lives meaningful? Why not just live them? On one level, the answer is obvious. If we want to live meaningful lives, we might want to know something about what makes a life so. Otherwise, we're just taking stabs in the dark. And in any event, for most of us it's just part of who we are. It's one of the causes of our lying awake at night.

There is another reason as well. This one is more bound to the time in which we live. In an earlier column for The Stone, I wrote that we are currently encouraged to think of ourselves either as consumers or as entrepreneurs. We are told to be shoppers for goods or investors for return. Neither of these types of lives, if they are the dominant character of those lives, strike me as particularly meaningful. This is because their narrative themes—buying, investing—are rarely the stuff of which a compelling life narrative is made. (I say "rarely" because there may be, for example, cases of intensely lived but morally compromised lives of investment that do not cross any moral limit to meaningfulness.) They usually lack what Wolf calls "objective attractiveness." To be sure, we must buy things and may even enjoy shopping. And we should not be entirely unconcerned with where we place our limited energies or monies. But are these the themes of a meaningful life? Are we likely to say of someone that he or she was a great networker or shopper and so really knew how to live?

In what I have called an age of economics, it is even more urgent to ask the question of a meaningful life: what it consists in, how we might live one. Philosophy cannot prescribe the particular character of meaning that each of us should embrace. It cannot tell each of us individually how we might trace the trajectory that is allotted to us. But it can, and ought to, reflect upon the framework within which we consider these questions, and in doing so perhaps offer a lucidity we might otherwise lack. This is as it should be. Philosophy can assist us in understanding how we might think about our lives, while remaining modest enough to leave the living of them to us.

SEPTEMBER 11, 2011

The Spoils of Happiness

—David Sosa

IN 1974, ROBERT NOZICK, A PRECOCIOUS YOUNG PHILOSOPHER AT Harvard, scooped *The Matrix*:

> *Suppose there were an experience machine that would give you any experience you desired. Super-duper neuropsychologists could stimulate your brain so that you would think and feel you were writing a great novel, or making a friend, or reading an interesting book. All the time you would be floating in a tank, with electrodes attached to your brain. Should you plug into this machine for life, preprogramming your life experiences? . . . Of course, while in the tank you won't know that you're there; you'll think that it's all actually happening . . . Would you plug in?* (Anarchy, State, and Utopia, *p. 3*)

Nozick's thought experiment—or the movie, for that matter—points to an interesting hypothesis: happiness is not a state of mind.

"What is happiness?" is one of those strange questions philosophers ask, and it's hard to answer. Philosophy, as a discipline, doesn't agree about it. Philosophers are a contentious, disagreeable lot by nature and training. But the question's hard because of a problematic prejudice about what *kind* of thing happiness might be. I'd like to diagnose the mistake and prescribe a corrective.

Nozick's thought experiment asks us to make a decision about a possible circumstance. If things were thus-and-so, what would you do? Would you plug in? Some people dismiss the example because they think the very idea of that sort of decision, with respect to a hypothetical situation, is somehow bogus and can't show anything. "These are all just hypothetical! Who cares? Get real!"

But the fact that a scenario is hypothetical doesn't make it imponderable or worthless. Compare a simpler case: Suppose there were a fire in your building and you could either save your neighbors, who'd otherwise be trapped, by dragging them outside, or you could save your pencil by holding on tight to that as you escaped, but not both. What would you do? I hope the answer's easy. And that's the point: we can, sometimes at least, answer this sort of question very easily. You are given a supposition and asked whether you would do this or that; you consider the hypothetical situation and give an answer. That's what Nozick's example is like.

So, would you plug in?

I think that for very many of us the answer is no. it's Morpheus and Neo and their merry band of rebels who are the heroes of *The Matrix*. Cypher, who cuts the deal with the Agents, is a villain. And just as considering what we would grab in case of an emergency can help us learn about what we *value*, considering whether to plug into the experience machine can help us learn about the sort of happiness we aspire to.

In refusing to plug in to Nozick's machine, we express our deep-seated belief that the sort of thing we can get from a machine isn't the most valuable thing we can get; it isn't what we most deeply want, whatever we might think if we were plugged in. life on the machine wouldn't constitute achieving what we're after when we're pursuing a happy life. There's an important difference between having a friend and *having the experience of* having a friend. There's an important difference between writing a great novel and *having the experience of* writing a great novel. On the machine, we would not parent children, share our love with a partner, laugh with friends (or even smile at a stranger), dance, dunk, run a marathon, quit smoking, or lose ten pounds in time for summer. Plugged in, we would have the sorts of experience that people who actually achieve or accomplish those things have, but they would all be, in a way, *false*—an intellectual mirage.

Now, of course, the difference would be lost on you if you were plugged into the machine—*you wouldn't know* you weren't really anyone's friend. But what's striking is that even that fact is not adequately reassuring. On the contrary, it adds to the horror of the prospect. We'd be ignorant, too—duped, to boot! We wouldn't suffer the pain of loneliness and that's a good thing. But it would be better if we weren't so benighted, if our experiences of friendship were the genuine article.

To put the point in a nutshell, watching your child play soccer for the first time is a great thing not *because* it produces a really enjoyable experience; on the contrary, what normally makes the experience so special is that it's an experience of watching *your child, playing soccer, for the first time.* Sure it feels good—paralyzingly good. It matters, though, that the feeling is there *as a response to the reality*: the feeling *by itself* is the wrong sort of thing to make for a happy life.

Happiness is more like knowledge than like belief. There are lots of things we believe but don't know. Knowledge is not just up to you; it requires the cooperation of the world beyond you—you might be mistaken. Still, even if you're mistaken, you believe what you believe. Pleasure is like belief that way. But happiness isn't just up to you. It also requires the cooperation of the world beyond you. Happiness, like knowledge, and unlike belief and pleasure, is *not* a state of mind.

Here's one provocative consequence of this perspective on happiness. If happiness is not a state of mind, if happiness is a kind of tango between your feelings on one hand and events and things in the world around you on the other, then there's the possibility of *error* about whether you're happy. If you believe you're experiencing pleasure or, perhaps especially, pain, then, presumably, you are. But the view of happiness here allows that "you may think you're happy, but you're not."

One especially apt way of thinking about happiness—a way that's found already in the thought of Aristotle—is in terms of "flourishing." Take someone really flourishing in their new career, or really flourishing now that they're off in college. The sense of the expression is not just that they *feel* good, but that they're, for example, accomplishing some things and taking appropriate pleasure in those accomplishments. If they were simply sitting at home playing video games all day, even if this seemed to give them a great deal of pleasure, and even if they were not frustrated, we wouldn't say they were flourishing. Such a life could not in the long term constitute a happy life. To live a happy life is to flourish.

A stark contrast is the life of the drug addict. He is often experiencing intense pleasure. But his is not a life we admire; it is often quite a pitiful existence. Well, one might think, it has its displeasures, being a user. There are withdrawal symptoms and that kind of thing—maybe he's frustrated that he can't kick the habit. But suppose that weren't the case. Suppose the user never had to suffer any displeasure at all—had no interest in any other sort of life. How much better would that make it?

Better perhaps, but it would not be a *happy* life. It might be better than some others—lives filled with interminable and equally insignificant pain, for example. Better simple pleasure than pain, of course. But what's wrong with the drug addict's life is not just the despair he feels when he's coming down. It's that even when he's feeling pleasure, that's not a very significant fact about him. It's just a feeling, the kind of pleasure we can imagine an animal's having. Happiness is harder to get. It's enjoyed after you've worked for something, or in the presence of people you love, or upon experiencing a magnificent work of art or performance—the kind of state that requires us to engage in real activities of certain sorts, to confront real objects and respond to them. And then, too, we shouldn't ignore the modest happiness that can accompany pride in a clear-eyed engagement with even very painful circumstances.

We do hate to give up control over the most important things in our lives. And viewing happiness as subject to external influence limits our control—not just in the sense that whether you get to live happily might depend on how things go, but also in the sense that what happiness *is* is partly a matter of how things beyond you are. We might do everything we can to live happily—and have everything it takes on our part to be happy, all the right thoughts and feelings— and yet fall short, even unbeknownst to us. That's a threatening idea. But we should be brave. Intellectual courage is as important as the other sort.

OCTOBER 6, 2010

SCIENCE

PHILOSOPHY IS NOT A SCIENCE IN THE USUALLY ACCEPTED SENSE OF the word. Namely, it is not an inquiry into the natural world whose validity can be assessed with reference to empirical evidence and data. However, throughout its three-millennia history, from Aristotle onward, and even in the Pre-Socratic thinkers that preceded him, philosophy has been obsessively concerned with the nature of science and its discoveries and methods of inquiry. Aristotle thought that in addition to science there was a special area of philosophical activity that was concerned with what was beyond science. This area was called by a later tradition "metaphysics," which literally means that which comes "after" (*meta*) the physical world (*ta physika*).

In many ways, the question that animates this second section of *The Stone Reader* is whether it makes any sense to talk about that which comes after or beyond nature. Is everything explicable through science? There is a prevalent—indeed, often dominant—view in philosophy called "naturalism," which claims that the only things that can be said to exist are the components of the natural world. Therefore, in order to be consistent with science, philosophy should have as its realm of activity nothing beyond what can be understood or explained by science. Nothing, that is, beyond the precincts of the natural world.

In many ways, all of the essays in the following pages move around this topic. In "Can Science Explain Everything?" two crystal-clear debates on naturalism and its limits are staged, where the arguments move back and forth between proponents and opponents of naturalism. In recent decades, the debate around science has focused in particular on the psychological realm—namely, what takes places between our ears. The question is whether science explains the experience of consciousness or not. The dominant expression of naturalism in the domain of psychology is provided by neuroscience, and many of the arguments in "Where Is my Mind?" and "Blinded by Neuroscience?" take up that challenge and launch strong critiques against it. Should philosophy become "neurophilosophy" in order to remain scientifically relevant and legitimate? Or is there something about the experience of consciousness that is simply irreducible to neuroscience or empirical psychology?

The debate rages here back and forth in a very engaging manner. Does neuroscience close down the space for free will? Do machines, especially highly developed forms of artificial intelligence, eliminate the domain of morality? Is there a legitimate place for philosophy and the humanities in a neuroscientific worldview? Or might we not require a richer, broader conception of the mind that is offered by contemporary brain-based and brain-obsessed approaches?

What is particularly compelling in these pages of *The Stone Reader* is that it is not just a question of philosophers arguing back and forth about science. One can also find important and influential scientists raising questions of the most general philosophical import on the basis of their scientific background. For example, in two important pieces, the preeminent biologist Edward O. Wilson uses the evidence of evolutionary biology in order to criticize the concept of intelligent design or the idea that the universe has a supernatural cause. But science here is not employed in any reductive manner. It is an essential part of the story that explains what Wilson calls "the riddle of the human species," but it is not the whole picture.

A set of reflections on "The Social Impact of Science" raises questions of how we are to assess science in the light of the technological transformation of the planet into what is now called the Anthropocene—an age in which human impact is the dominant force of change on nature. Is science the villain in this narrative or does it have the power to save us from ecological devastation? Or is it both?

A recurring theme in this section is the problem of pseudoscience. There is a debate around the status of Chinese medicine, and a critique of the fetishization of the uncertainty principle found in many New Age so-called philosophies.

The reader is free to derive whatever lesson he or she chooses from the various arguments presented, but a leitmotif is that the proper understanding of science does not eliminate the need for free moral reflection; it requires such reflection. Indeed, given the ecological crisis that we face, the need for morality has arguably never been stronger.

—Simon Critchley

CAN SCIENCE EXPLAIN EVERYTHING?

What Is Naturalism?

—Timothy Williamson

M ANY CONTEMPORARY PHILOSOPHERS DESCRIBE THEMSELVES as naturalists. They mean that they believe something like this: there is only the natural world, and the best way to find out about it is by the scientific method. I am sometimes described as a naturalist. Why do I resist the description? Not for any religious scruple: I am an atheist of the most straightforward kind. But accepting the naturalist slogan without looking beneath the slick packaging is an unscientific way to form one's beliefs about the world, not something naturalists should recommend.

What, for a start, is the natural world? If we say it is the world of matter, or the world of atoms, we are left behind by modern physics, which characterizes the world in far more abstract terms. Anyway, the best current scientific theories will probably be superseded by future scientific developments. We might therefore define the natural world as whatever the scientific method eventually discovers. Thus naturalism becomes the belief that there is only whatever the scientific method eventually discovers, and (not surprisingly) the best way to find out about it is by the scientific method. That is no tautology. Why can't there be things only discoverable by nonscientific means, or not discoverable at all?

Still, naturalism is not as restrictive as it sounds. For example, some of its hard-nosed advocates undertake to postulate a soul or a god, if doing so turns out to be part of the best explanation of our experience, for that would be an application of scientific method. Naturalism is not incompatible in principle with all forms of religion. In practice, however, most naturalists doubt that belief in souls or gods withstands scientific scrutiny.

What is meant by "the scientific method"? Why assume that science only has one method? For naturalists, although natural sciences like physics and biology differ from each other in specific ways, at a sufficiently abstract level they all count as using a single general method. It involves formulating theoretical hypotheses and testing their predictions against systematic observation and controlled experiment. This is called the hypothetico-deductive method.

One challenge to naturalism is to find a place for mathematics. Natural sciences rely on it, but should we count it a science in its own right? If we do, then the description of scientific method just given is wrong, for it does not fit the science of mathematics, which proves its results by pure reasoning, rather than the hypothetico-deductive method. Although a few naturalists, such as W. V. Quine, argued that the real evidence in favor of mathematics comes from its applications in the natural sciences, so indirectly from observation and experiment, that view does not fit the way the subject actually develops. When mathematicians assess a proposed new axiom, they look at its consequences within mathematics, not outside. On the other hand, if we do not count pure mathematics a science, we thereby exclude mathematical proof by itself from the scientific method, and so discredit naturalism. For naturalism privileges the scientific method over all others, and mathematics is one of the most spectacular success stories in the history of human knowledge.

Which other disciplines count as science? Logic? Linguistics? History? Literary theory? How should we decide? The dilemma for naturalists is this. If they are too inclusive in what they count as science, naturalism loses its bite. Naturalists typically criticize some traditional forms of philosophy as insufficiently scientific, because they ignore experimental tests. How can they maintain such objections unless they restrict scientific method to hypothetico-deductivism? But if they are too exclusive in what they count as science, naturalism loses its credibility, by imposing a method appropriate to natural science on areas where it is inappropriate. Unfortunately, rather than clarify the issue, many naturalists oscillate. When on the attack, they assume an exclusive understanding of science as hypothetico-deductive. When under attack themselves, they fall back on a more inclusive understanding of science that drastically waters down naturalism. Such maneuvering makes naturalism an obscure article of faith. I don't call myself a naturalist because I don't want to be implicated in equivocal dogma. Dismissing an idea as "inconsistent with naturalism" is little better than dismissing it as "inconsistent with Christianity."

Still, I sympathize with one motive behind naturalism—the aspiration to think in a scientific spirit. It's a vague phrase, but one might start to explain it by emphasizing values like curiosity, honesty, accuracy, precision, and rigor. What matters isn't paying lip service to those qualities (that's easy) but actually exemplifying them in practice (the hard part). We needn't pretend that scientists' motives are pure. They are human. Science doesn't depend on indifference to fame, professional advancement, money, or comparisons with rivals. Rather, truth is best pursued in social environments, intellectual communities, that minimize conflict between such baser motives and the scientific spirit by rewarding work that embodies the scientific virtues. Such traditions exist, and not just in natural science.

The scientific spirit is as relevant in mathematics, history, philosophy, and elsewhere as in natural science. Where experimentation is the likeliest way to answer a question correctly, the scientific spirit calls for the experiments to be done; where other methods— mathematical proof, archival research, philosophical reasoning— are more relevant, it calls for them instead. Although the methods of natural science could beneficially be applied more widely than they have been so far, the default assumption must be that the practitioners of a well-established discipline know what they are doing and use the available methods most appropriate for answering its questions. Exceptions may result from a conservative tradition, or one that does not value the scientific spirit. Still, impatience with all methods except those of natural science is a poor basis on which to identify those exceptions.

Naturalism tries to condense the scientific spirit into a philosophical theory. But no theory can replace that spirit, for any theory can be applied in an unscientific spirit, as a polemical device to reinforce prejudice. Naturalism as dogma is one more enemy of the scientific spirit.

SEPTEMBER 4, 2011

Why I Am a Naturalist

—Alex Rosenberg

NATURALISM IS THE PHILOSOPHICAL THEORY THAT TREATS SCIence as our most reliable source of knowledge and scientific method as the most effective route to knowledge. In a recent essay for The Stone, Timothy Williamson correctly reports that naturalism is popular in philosophy. In fact it is now a dominant approach in several areas of philosophy—ethics, epistemology, the philosophy of mind, philosophy of science and, most of all, metaphysics, the study of the basic constituents of reality. Metaphysics is important: if it turns out that reality contains only the kinds of things that hard science recognizes, the implications will be grave for what we value in human experience.

Naturalism is itself a theory with a research agenda of unsolved problems. But naturalists' confidence that it can solve them shouldn't be mistaken for dogmatism, nor can its successes be written off as "slick packaging," two terms Professor Williamson used in his essay to describe why he rejects naturalism.

Before taking up Professor Williamson's challenges to naturalism, it's worth identifying some of this success in applying science to the solution of philosophical problems, some of which even have payoffs for science. Perhaps the most notable thing about naturalism is the way its philosophers have employed Darwin's theory of natural selection to tame purpose. In 1784 Kant wrote, "There will never be a Newton for the blade of grass." What he meant was that physical science could never explain anything with a purpose, whether it be human thought or a flower's bending toward the sun. That would have made everything special about living things—and especially us—safe from a purely scientific understanding. It would have kept questions about humanity the preserve of religion, mythmaking and the humanities.

Only twenty-five years or so later, the Newton of the blade of grass was born to the Darwin family in Shropshire, England. *On the Origin of Species* revealed how physical processes alone produce the illusion of design. Random variation and natural selection are the purely physical source of the beautiful means/ends economy of nature that fools us into seeking its designer. Naturalists have applied this insight to reveal the biological nature of human emotion, perception and cognition, language, moral value, social bonds, and political institutions. Naturalistic philosophy has returned the favor, helping psychology, evolutionary anthropology and biology solve their problems by greater conceptual clarity about function, adaptation, Darwinian fitness and individual-versus-group selection.

While dealing with puzzles that vexed philosophy as far back as Plato, naturalism has also come to grips with the very challenges Professor Williamson lays out: physics may be our best take on the nature of reality, but important parts of physics are not just "abstract," as he says. Quantum mechanics is more than abstract. It's weird. Since naturalistic philosophers take science seriously as the best description of reality, they accept the responsibility of making sense of quantum physics. Until we succeed, naturalists won't be any more satisfied than Professor Williamson that we know what the natural world is. But four hundred years of scientific success in prediction, control and technology shows that physics has made a good start. We should be confident that it will do better than any other approach at getting things right.

Naturalists recognize that science is fallible. Its self-correction, its continual increase in breadth and accuracy, give naturalists confidence in the resources they borrow from physics, chemistry and biology. The second law of thermodynamics, the periodic table, and the principles of natural selection are unlikely to be threatened by future science. Philosophy can therefore rely on them to answer many of its questions without fear of being overtaken by events.

"Why can't there be things only discoverable by nonscientific means, or not discoverable at all?" Professor Williamson asked in his essay. His question may be rhetorical, but the naturalist has an answer to it: nothing that revelation, inspiration or other nonscientific means ever claimed to discover has yet to withstand the test of knowledge that scientific findings attain. What are those tests of knowledge? They are the experimental/observational methods all the natural sciences share, the social sciences increasingly adopt, and that naturalists devote themselves to making explicit. You can reject naturalists' epistemology, or treat it as question begging, but you can't accuse them of not having one.

As Professor Williamson notes, naturalism's greatest challenge "is to find a place for mathematics." The way it faces the challenge reveals just how undogmatic naturalism really is. It would be easy to turn one's back on the problems mathematics presents (What are numbers? How can we have the certainty about them that math reveals?). One excuse to turn our backs is that mathematicians and scientists don't care much about these problems; another is that no one has ever provided a satisfactory answer to these questions, so no other philosophy can be preferred to naturalism on this basis. But naturalism has invested a huge amount of ingenuity, even genius, seeking scientifically responsible answers to these hardest of questions. Not with much success as yet by our own standards, one must admit. But that is the nature of science.

Naturalism takes the problem of mathematics seriously since science cannot do without it. So naturalism can't either. But what about other items on Professor Williamson's list of disciplines that would be hard to count as science: history, literary theory? Can science and naturalistic philosophy do without them? This is a different question from whether people, as consumers of human narratives and enjoyers of literature, can do without them. The question naturalism faces is whether disciplines like literary theory provide real understanding.

Naturalism faces these questions because it won't uncritically buy into Professor Williamson's "default assumption . . . that the practitioners of a well-established discipline know what they are doing and use the . . . methods most appropriate for answering its questions." If semiotics, existentialism, hermeneutics, formalism, structuralism, post-structuralism, deconstruction and postmodernism transparently flout science's standards of objectivity, or if they seek arbitrarily to limit the reach of scientific methods, then naturalism can't take them seriously as knowledge.

That doesn't mean anyone should stop doing literary criticism any more than forgoing fiction. Naturalism treats both as fun, but neither as knowledge.

What naturalists really fear is not becoming dogmatic or giving up the scientific spirit. It's the threat that the science will end up showing that much of what we cherish as meaningful in human life is illusory.

SEPTEMBER 17, 2011

On Ducking Challenges to Naturalism

—*Timothy Williamson*

IN RESPONSE TO THE QUESTION POSED IN MY PREVIOUS ESSAY IN The Stone—"What is Naturalism?"—Alex Rosenberg defines it as "the philosophical theory that treats science as our most reliable source of knowledge and scientific method as the most effective route to knowledge." His post, "Why I Am a Naturalist," nicely exemplifies one of my main complaints, by leaving it unclear what he means by "science" or "scientific method," even though it is crucial for what he is committing himself to as a "naturalist." Still, there are clues. He describes "the test of knowledge that scientific findings attain" as "experimental/observational methods," which suggests that theorems of mathematics would not count as scientific findings. The impression is confirmed by Professor Rosenberg's phrase "mathematicians and scientists," as though he doesn't see mathematicians as scientists. That's bad news for his naturalism, for mathematical proof is just as effective a route to knowledge as experimental/observational methods. Of course, since the natural sciences depend on mathematics, Rosenberg desires to find a place for it—but admits that he doesn't know how.

In just the way noted in my post, Professor Rosenberg's defense of naturalism trades on ambiguities. Interpreted one way, some naturalist claims are boring truths; interpreted another way, they are obvious falsehoods. Rightly noting the successes of physics, he says, "We should be confident that it will do better than any other approach at getting things right." What things? If he means questions of physics, what reasonable person denies that physics will do better than any other approach at answering those questions? But if he means all questions, why should we be confident that physics will do better than history at getting right what happened at Gettysburg?

I raised history and literary theory as test cases. According to Professor Rosenberg, naturalism treats literary criticism as fun, but not as knowledge. Does he really not know whether Mr. Collins is the hero of *Pride and Prejudice*? Every normal reader has that sort of elementary literary critical knowledge. Those who know far more about the historical context in which literary works were produced, read them many times with unusual attention, carefully analyze their structure, and so on, naturally have far more knowledge of those works than casual readers do, whatever the excesses of postmodernism.

As for history, Rosenberg conveniently avoids discussing it. He seems not to regard it as a science but does not come out and say that there is no historical knowledge, or none worth having. It might suit some politicians for there to be no historical knowledge; the rest of us must hope that they don't attain or retain power. It isn't even clear how natural science could manage without historical knowledge, as R G. Collingwood long ago pointed out, since knowledge of the results of past experiments and observations is itself historical.

For Professor Rosenberg, it may turn out that "reality contains only the kinds of things that hard science recognizes." By "hard science" he seems to mean something like physics. He doesn't explain how that could turn out. How could physics show that reality contains only the kinds of things that physics recognizes? It sounds embarrassingly like physics acting as judge and jury in its own case. That physics does not show that there is such a thing as a debt crisis does not mean that physics shows that there is no such thing as a debt crisis: physics simply does not address the question. That is no criticism of physics; it has other work to do. For it to turn out that reality contains only the kinds of things that hard science recognizes, where they exclude things like debt crises, it would have to turn out that a radically reductionist metaphysical theory is true. That in turn would require industrial-scale argument at a characteristically philosophical level of reasoning. But I doubt that Professor Rosenberg counts philosophy as hard science.

We can formulate the underlying worry as a sharp argument against the extreme naturalist claim that all truths are discoverable by hard science. If it is true that all truths are discoverable by hard science, then it is discoverable by hard science that all truths are discoverable by hard science. But it is not discoverable by hard science that all truths are discoverable by hard science. "Are all truths discoverable by hard science?" is not a question of hard science. Therefore the extreme naturalist claim is not true.

Such problems pose far less threat to more moderate forms of naturalism, based on a broader conception of science that includes mathematics, history, much of philosophy, and the sensible parts of literary criticism, as well as the natural and social sciences. But we should not take for granted that reality contains only the kinds of things that science even in the broad sense recognizes. My caution comes not from any sympathy for mysterious kinds of cognition alien to science in the broad sense, but simply from the difficulty of establishing in any remotely scientific way that reality contains only the kinds of things that we are capable of recognizing at all. In any case, Professor Rosenberg does not rest content with some moderate form of naturalism. He goes for something far more extreme, in the process lapsing into hard scientism.

Professor Rosenberg concludes, "What naturalists really fear is not becoming dogmatic or giving up the scientific spirit. It's the threat that the science will end up showing that much of what we cherish as meaningful in human life is illusory." But what people really fear is not always what most endangers them. Those most confident of being undogmatic and possessing the scientific spirit may thereby become all the less able to detect dogmatism and failures of the scientific spirit in themselves. If one tries to assess naturalism in a scientific spirit, one will want to get more precise than most self-labeled naturalists (and antinaturalists) do about what hypothesis is under test. Nor will one dogmatically assume that, once a clear hypothesis is on the table, testing it will be just a matter for hard science. The evidence so far suggests otherwise.

SEPTEMBER 28, 2011

The Core of *Mind and Cosmos*

—Thomas Nagel

This is a brief statement of positions defended more fully in my book Mind and Cosmos: Why the Materialist Neo-Darwinian Conception of Nature Is Almost Certainly False, *which was published by Oxford University Press last year. Since then the book has attracted a good deal of critical attention, which is not surprising, given the entrenchment of the worldview that it attacks. It seemed useful to offer a short summary of the central argument.*

———

THE SCIENTIFIC REVOLUTION OF THE SEVENTEENTH CENTURY, which has given rise to such extraordinary progress in the understanding of nature, depended on a crucial limiting step at the start: it depended on subtracting from the physical world as an object of study everything mental—consciousness, meaning, intention or purpose. The physical sciences as they have developed since then describe, with the aid of mathematics, the elements of which the material universe is composed and the laws governing their behavior in space and time.

We ourselves, as physical organisms, are part of that universe, composed of the same basic elements as everything else, and recent advances in molecular biology have greatly increased our understanding of the physical and chemical basis of life. Since our mental lives evidently depend on our existence as physical organisms, especially on the functioning of our central nervous systems, it seems natural to think that the physical sciences can in principle provide the basis for an explanation of the mental aspects of reality as well—that physics can aspire finally to be a theory of everything.

However, I believe this possibility is ruled out by the conditions that have defined the physical sciences from the beginning. The physical sciences can describe organisms like ourselves as parts of the objective spatiotemporal order—our structure and behavior in space and time—but they cannot describe the subjective experiences of such organisms or how the world appears to their different particular points of view. There can be a purely physical description of the neurophysiological processes that give rise to an experience, and also of the physical behavior that is typically associated with it, but such a description, however complete, will leave out the subjective essence of the experience—how it is from the point of view of its subject—without which it would not be a conscious experience at all.

So the physical sciences, in spite of their extraordinary success in their own domain, necessarily leave an important aspect of nature unexplained. Further, since the mental arises through the development of animal organisms, the nature of those organisms cannot be fully understood through the physical sciences alone. Finally, since the long process of biological evolution is responsible for the existence of conscious organisms, and since a purely physical process cannot explain their existence, it follows that biological evolution must be more than just a physical process, and the theory of evolution, if it is to explain the existence of conscious life, must become more than just a physical theory.

This means that the scientific outlook, if it aspires to a more complete understanding of nature, must expand to include theories capable of explaining the appearance in the universe of mental phenomena and the subjective points of view in which they occur—theories of a different type from any we have seen so far.

There are two ways of resisting this conclusion, each of which has two versions. The first way is to deny that the mental is an irreducible aspect of reality, either (a) by holding that the mental can be identified with some aspect of the physical, such as patterns of behavior or patterns of neural activity, or (b) by denying that the mental is part of reality at all, being some kind of illusion (but then, illusion to whom?). The second way is to deny that the mental requires a scientific explanation through some new conception of the natural order, because either (c) we can regard it as a mere fluke or accident, an unexplained extra property of certain physical organisms, or else (d) we can believe that it has an explanation, but one that belongs not to science but to theology, in other words that mind has been added to the physical world in the course of evolution by divine intervention.

All four of these positions have their adherents. I believe the wide popularity among philosophers and scientists of (a), the outlook of psychophysical reductionism, is due not only to the great prestige of the physical sciences but to the feeling that this is the best defense against the dreaded (d), the theistic interventionist outlook. But someone who finds (a) and (b) self-evidently false and (c) completely implausible need not accept (d), because a scientific understanding of nature need not be limited to a physical theory of the objective spatiotemporal order. It makes sense to seek an expanded form of understanding that includes the mental but that is still scientific— that is, still a theory of the immanent order of nature.

That seems to me the most likely solution. Even though the theistic outlook, in some versions, is consistent with the available scientific evidence, I don't believe it, and am drawn instead to a naturalistic, though nonmaterialist, alternative. Mind, I suspect, is not an inexplicable accident or a divine and anomalous gift but a basic aspect of nature that we will not understand until we transcend the built-in limits of contemporary scientific orthodoxy. I would add that even some theists might find this acceptable, since they could maintain that God is ultimately responsible for such an expanded natural order, as they believe he is for the laws of physics.

AUGUST 18, 2013

Things Fall Apart

—Philip Kitcher

THOMAS NAGEL, ONE OF THE WORLD'S MOST EMINENT PHILOSO-
phers, is especially noted for his ability to write about the most difficult questions with subtlety and clarity. His recent book, *Mind
and Cosmos*, has sparked lively discussion, as he observed recently
in his précis of the book's main argument in The Stone. He has
found new—not always welcome—allies ("Nagel has paved the way
for a religious world-view!"), and some long-time admirers have
denounced his claims and arguments ("Nagel has paved the way
for religious mumbo-jumbo!"). But the link with religion is a side-
show. Nagel's main concern lies with the requirements of a complete metaphysical view.

J. L. Austin is reputed to have remarked that, when philosophy is
done well, all the action is over by the bottom of the first page. Nagel
does philosophy very well. Once he has set up the framework within
which the possible positions will be placed, his arguments are not
easy to resist. In my view, though, the framework itself is faulty.

In his Queries to the *Opticks*, Newton looked forward to a vision of
the cosmos in which everything would be explained on the basis of a
small number of physical principles. That Newtonian vision remains
highly popular with many scientists who turn philosophical in their
later years and announce their dreams of a final theory. Yet, since the
nineteenth century—since Darwin, in fact—that has not been a convincing picture of how the sciences make their advances. Darwin did

not supply a major set of new principles that could be used to derive general conclusions about life and its history: he crafted a framework within which his successors construct models of quite specific evolutionary phenomena. Model building lies at the heart of large parts of the sciences, including parts of physics. There are no grand theories, but lots of bits and pieces, generating local insights about phenomena of special interest. In the revealing terms that Nancy Cartwright has borrowed from Gerard Manley Hopkins, we live in a "dappled world."

Nagel wants to know how mind and values will fit into a Newtonian physical picture. The right way to address his concerns is to recognize how biology has become richly illuminated through contributions from physics and chemistry, without fitting into any such picture. Molecular genetics is one of the great glories of recent science, but there is no molecular account of all and only those things that are genes. The lives of those who analyze DNA sequence data would be so much simpler if there were. Instead, the notion of a gene is partly functional: (provided we ignore retroviruses) genes are those segments of DNA that code for proteins or for RNAs.

Similarly, molecular biology provides an immensely powerful account of how genes are transcribed into messenger RNA: particular molecules enter into association with the chromosomes, the DNA is reconfigured so the sequence can be "read," and an RNA molecule with the right sequence is (usually) produced. What exactly are the conditions of the association or the reconfiguration? Biochemistry supplies no general account. In specific instances, it's possible to probe and identify just how close the molecules must be—but the instances are extraordinarily diverse.

Thinkers in the grip of the Newtonian picture of science want a general basis for general phenomena. Life isn't like that. Unity fails at both ends. To understand the fundamental processes that go on in living things—mitosis, meiosis, inheritance, development, respiration, digestion and many, many more—you need a vast ensemble of models, differing on a large number of details. Spelling out the explanations requires using metaphors ("reading" DNA) or notions that cannot be specified generally and precisely in the austere languages of physics and chemistry ("close association"). But the phenomena to be explained also decompose into a number of different clusters.

The molecular biologist doesn't account for *life*, but for a particular function of life (usually in a particular strain of a particular species). Nagel's nineteenth-century predecessors wondered how life could be characterized in physico-chemical terms. That particular wonder hasn't been directly addressed by the extraordinary biological accomplishments of past decades. Rather, it's been shown that they were posing the wrong question: don't ask what life is (in your deepest Newtonian voice); consider the various activities in which living organisms engage and try to give a piecemeal understanding of those.

Dewey, a thinker who understood the philosophical significance of Darwin better than anyone else in the first century after *The Origin of Species*, appreciated two things that are crucial to the controversy in which Nagel is engaged.

First, philosophy and science don't always answer the questions they pose—sometimes they get over them. Second, instead of asking what life and mind and value *are*, think about what living things and minds *do* and what is going on in the human practices of valuing. This shift of perspective has already occurred in the case of life. A Nagel analog who worried about the fact that we lack a physico-chemical account of life would probably be rudely dismissed; a kinder approach would be to talk about the ways in which various aspects of living things have been illuminated.

Minds do lots of different things. Neuroscience and psychology have been able to explore a few of them in promising ways. Allegedly, however, there are "hard problems" they will never overcome. The allegations are encouraged by an incautious tendency for scientists to write as if the most complex functions of mental life—consciousness, for example—will be explained tomorrow.

The route to the molecular account of organic functions began in a relatively humble place, with eye color in fruit flies. A useful moral for neuroscience today would be to emulate the efforts of the great geneticists in the wake of the rediscovery of Mendel's ideas. Start with more tractable questions—for example, how do minds direct the movement of our muscles?—and see how far you can get. With luck, in a century or so, the issue of how mind fits into the physical world will seem as quaint as the corresponding concern about life.

Many people, Nagel included, believe that problems about values are especially hard. In my judgment, the same strategy should be pursued in this case, too. There are human practices of valuing. They are complex and they have a long and intricate history. By decomposing them into a set of more basic functions, we might hope to understand how to integrate some of them into a naturalistic perspective. In my work on ethics and evolution, I have tried to make a beginning on this venture.

Nagel is in the grip of a philosophical perspective on science, once very popular, that the work of the last four decades has shown to be inadequate to cope with large parts of the most successful contemporary sciences. Because of that perspective, a crucial option disappears from his menu: the phenomena that concern him, mind and value, are not illusory, but it might nevertheless be an illusion that they constitute single topics for which unified explanations can be given. The probable future of science in these domains is one of decomposition and the provision of an enormous and heterogeneous family of models. Much later in the day, it may fall to some neuroscientist to explain the illusion of unity, a last twist on successful accounts of many subspecies of mental processes and functions. Or, perhaps, it will be clear by then that the supposed unity of mind and of value were outgrowths of a philosophical mistake, understandable in the context of a particular stage of scientific development, but an error nonetheless.

SEPTEMBER 8, 2013

THE EVOLUTION OF RIGHT AND WRONG

Moral Camouflage or Moral Monkeys?

—*Peter Railton*

After being shown proudly around the campus of a prestigious American university built in gothic style, Bertrand Russell is said to have exclaimed, "Remarkable. As near Oxford as monkeys can make." Much earlier, Immanuel Kant had expressed a less ironic amazement: "Two things fill the mind with ever new and increasing admiration and awe . . . the starry heavens above and the moral law within." Today many who look at morality through a Darwinian lens can't help but find a charming naïveté in Kant's thought. "Yes, remarkable. As near morality as monkeys can make."

So the question is, just how near is that? Optimistic Darwinians believe, near enough to be morality. But skeptical Darwinians won't buy it. The great show we humans make of respect for moral principle they see as a civilized camouflage for an underlying, evolved psychology of a quite different kind.

This skepticism is not, however, your great-grandfather's Social Darwinism, which saw all creatures great and small as pitted against one another in a life-or-death struggle to survive and reproduce—"survival of the fittest." We now know that such a picture seriously misrepresents both Darwin and the actual process of natural selection. Individuals come and go, but genes can persist for a thousand generations or more. Individual plants and animals are the perishable vehicles that genetic material uses to make its way into the next generation ("A chicken is an egg's way of making another egg"). From this perspective, relatives, who share genes, are to that extent not really in *evolutionary* competition; no matter which one survives, the shared genes triumph. Such "inclusive fitness" predicts the survival not of selfish individuals but of "selfish" genes, which tend in the normal range of environments to give rise to individuals whose behavior tends to propel those genes into the future.

A place is thus made within Darwinian thought for such familiar phenomena as family members sacrificing for one another—helping when there is no prospect of payback, or being willing to risk life and limb to protect one's people or avenge harms done to them.

But what about unrelated individuals? "Sexual selection" occurs whenever one must attract a mate in order to reproduce. Well, what sorts of individuals are attractive partners? Henry Kissinger claimed that power is the ultimate aphrodisiac, but for animals who bear a small number of young over a lifetime, each requiring a long gestation and demanding a great deal of nurturance to thrive into maturity, potential mates who behave selfishly, uncaringly, and unreliably can lose their chance. And beyond mating, many social animals depend upon the cooperation of others for protection, foraging and hunting, or rearing the young. Here, too, power can attract partners, but so can a demonstrable tendency to behave cooperatively and share benefits and burdens fairly, even when this involves some personal sacrifice—what is sometimes called "reciprocal altruism." Baboons are notoriously hierarchical, but Joan Silk, a professor of anthropology at UCLA, and her colleagues recently reported a long-term study of baboons in which they found that among females, maintaining strong, equal, enduring social bonds—even when the individuals were not related—can promote individual longevity more effectively than gaining dominance rank, and can enhance the survival of progeny.

A picture thus emerges of selection for "proximal psychological mechanisms"—for example, individual dispositions like parental devotion, loyalty to family, trust and commitment among partners, generosity and gratitude among friends, courage in the face of enemies, intolerance of cheaters—that make individuals into good vehicles, from the gene's standpoint, for promoting the "distal goal" of enhanced inclusive fitness.

Why would human evolution have selected for such messy, emotionally entangling proximal psychological mechanisms, rather than produce yet more ideally opportunistic vehicles for the transmission of genes—individuals wearing a perfect camouflage of loyalty and reciprocity, but fine-tuned underneath to turn self-sacrifice or cooperation on or off exactly as needed? Because the same evolutionary processes would also be selecting for improved capacities to detect, preempt, and defend against such opportunistic tendencies in other individuals—just as evolution cannot produce a perfect immune system, since it is equally busily at work improving the effectiveness of viral invaders. Devotion, loyalty, honesty, empathy, gratitude, and a sense of fairness are credible signs of value as a partner or friend precisely *because* they are messy and emotionally entangling, and so cannot simply be turned on and off by the individual to capture each marginal advantage. And keep in mind the small scale of early human societies, and Abraham Lincoln's point about our power to deceive.

Why, then, aren't we *better*—more honest, more committed, more loyal? There will always be circumstances in which fooling some of the people some of the time is enough—for example, when society is unstable or individuals mobile. So we should expect a capacity for opportunism and betrayal to remain an important part of the mix that makes humans into monkeys worth writing novels about.

How close does all this take us to morality? Not all the way, certainly. An individual psychology primarily disposed to consider the interests of all equally, without fear or favor, even in the teeth of social ostracism, might be morally admirable but simply wouldn't cut it as a vehicle for reliable replication. Such *pure* altruism would not be favored in natural selection over an impure altruism that conferred benefits and took on burdens and risks more selectively—for "my kind" or "our kind." This puts us well beyond pure selfishness, but only as far as an impure *us*-ishness. Worse, us-ish individuals can be a greater threat than purely selfish ones, since they can gang up so effectively against those outside their group. Certainly greater atrocities have been committed in the name of "us vs. them" than "me vs. the world."

So, are the optimistic Darwinians wrong, and impartial morality beyond the reach of those monkeys we call humans? Does thoroughly logical evolutionary thinking force us to the conclusion that our love, loyalty, commitment, empathy, and concern for justice and fairness are always at bottom a mixture of selfish opportunism and us-ish clannishness? Indeed, is it only a sign of the effectiveness of the moral camouflage that we ourselves are so often taken in by it?

Speaking of what "thoroughly logical evolutionary thinking" might "force" us to conclude provides a clue to the answer. Think for a moment about science and logic themselves. Natural selection operates on a need-to-know basis. Between two individuals—one disposed to use scarce resources and finite capacities to seek out the most urgent and useful information and the other, heedless of immediate and personal concerns and disposed instead toward pure, disinterested inquiry, following logic wherever it might lead—it is clear which natural selection would tend to favor.

And yet, Darwinian skeptics about morality believe, humans somehow have managed to redeploy and leverage their limited, partial, human-scale psychologies to develop shared inquiry, experimental procedures, technologies and norms of logic and evidence that have resulted in genuine scientific knowledge and responsiveness to the force of logic. This distinctively human "cultural evolution" was centuries in the making, and overcoming partiality and bias remains a constant struggle, but the point is that these possibilities were not foreclosed by the imperfections and partiality of the faculties we inherited. As Wittgenstein observed, crude tools can be used to make refined tools. Monkeys, it turns out, can come surprisingly near to objective science.

We can see a similar cultural evolution in human law and morality—a centuries-long process of overcoming arbitrary distinctions, developing wider communities, and seeking more inclusive shared standards, such as the Geneva Conventions and the Universal Declaration of Humans Rights. Empathy might induce sympathy more readily when it is directed toward kith and kin, but we rely upon it to understand the thoughts and feelings of enemies and outsiders as well. And the human capacity for learning and following rules might have evolved to enable us to speak a native language or find our place in the social hierarchy, but it can be put into service understanding different languages and cultures, and developing more cosmopolitan or egalitarian norms that can be shared across our differences.

Within my own lifetime, I have seen dramatic changes in civil rights, women's rights, and gay rights. That's just one generation in evolutionary terms. Or consider the way that empathy and the pressure of consistency have led to widespread recognition that our fellow animals should receive humane treatment. Human culture, not natural selection, accomplished these changes, and yet it was natural selection that gave us the capacities that helped make them possible. We still must struggle continuously to see to it that our widened empathy is not lost, our sympathies engaged, our understandings enlarged, and our moral principles followed. But the point is that we have done this with our imperfect, partial, us-ish native endowment. Kant was right to be impressed. In our best moments, we can come surprisingly close to being moral monkeys.

JULY 18, 2010

Evolution and Our Inner Conflict

—Edward O. Wilson

ARE HUMAN BEINGS INTRINSICALLY GOOD BUT CORRUPTIBLE BY the forces of evil, or the reverse, innately sinful yet redeemable by the forces of good? Are we built to pledge our lives to a group, even to the risk of death, or the opposite, built to place ourselves and our families above all else? Scientific evidence, a good part of it accumulated during the past twenty years, suggests that we are all of these things simultaneously. Each of us is inherently complicated. We are all genetic chimeras, at once saints and sinners—not because humanity has failed to reach some foreordained religious or ideological ideal but because of the way our species originated across millions of years of biological evolution.

Don't get me wrong. I am not implying that we are driven by instinct in the manner of animals. Yet in order to understand the human condition, it is necessary to accept that we do have instincts and will be wise to take into account our very distant ancestors, as far back and in as fine a detail as possible. History is not enough to reach this level of understanding. It stops at the dawn of literacy, where it turns the rest of the story over to the detective work of archaeology; in still deeper time the quest becomes paleontology. For the real human story, history makes no sense without prehistory, and prehistory makes no sense without biology.

Within biology itself, the key to the mystery is the force that lifted prehuman social behavior to the human level. The leading candidate in my judgment is multilevel selection by which hereditary social behavior improves the competitive ability not of just individuals within groups but among groups as a whole. Its consequences can be plainly seen in the caste systems of ants, termites and other social insects. Between-group selection as a force operating in addition to between-individual selection simultaneously is not a new idea in biology. Charles Darwin correctly deduced its role, first in the insects and then in human beings—respectively in *On the Origin of Species* and *The Descent of Man*.

Even so, the reader should be warned that the revival of multilevel selection as the principal force of social evolution remains a hotly contested idea. Its opponents believe the principal force to be kin selection: when individuals favor kin (other than offspring), the evolution of altruistic behavior is favored. The loss suffered by the genes of the altruist are compensated by genes in the recipient made identical by common descent of the altruist and recipient. If the altruism thus created is strong enough, it can lead to advanced social behavior. This seems plausible, but in 2010 two mathematical biologists, Martin Nowak and Corina Tarnita, and I demonstrated that the mathematical foundations of the kin-selection theory are unsound, and that examples from nature thought to support kin-selection theory are better explained as products of multilevel selection.

A strong reaction from supporters of kin selection not surprisingly ensued, and soon afterward more than 130 of them famously signed on to protest our replacement of kin selection by multilevel selection, and most emphatically the key role given to group selection. But at no time have our mathematical and empirical arguments been refuted or even seriously challenged. Since that protest, the number of supporters of the multilevel-selection approach has grown, to the extent that a similarly long list of signatories could be obtained. But such exercises are futile: science is not advanced by polling. If it were, we would still be releasing phlogiston to burn logs and navigating the sky with geocentric maps.

I am convinced after years of research on the subject that multilevel selection, with a powerful role of group-to-group competition, has forged advanced social behavior—including that of humans, as I documented in my recent book *The Social Conquest of Earth*. In fact, it seems clear that so deeply ingrained are the evolutionary products of group-selected behaviors, so completely a part of the human condition, that we are prone to regard them as fixtures of nature, like air and water. They are instead idiosyncratic traits of our species. Among them is the intense, obsessive interest of people in other people, which begins in the first days of life as infants learn particular scents and sounds of the adults around them. Research psychologists have found that all normal humans are geniuses at reading the intentions of others, whereby they evaluate, gossip, proselytize, bond, cooperate and control. Each person, working his way back and forth through his social network, almost continuously reviews past experiences while imagining the consequences of future scenarios.

A second diagnostic hereditary peculiarity of human behavior is the overpowering instinctual urge to belong to groups in the first place. To be kept in solitude is to be kept in pain and put on the road to madness. A person's membership in his group—his tribe—is a large part of his identity. It also confers upon him to some degree or other a sense of superiority. When psychologists selected teams at random from a population of volunteers to compete in simple games, members of each team soon came to think of members of other teams as less able and trustworthy, even when the participants knew they had been selected at random.

All things being equal (fortunately things are seldom equal, not exactly), people prefer to be with others who look like them, speak the same dialect, and hold the same beliefs. An amplification of this evidently inborn predisposition leads with frightening ease to racism and religious bigotry.

It might be supposed that the human condition is so distinctive and came so late in the history of life on Earth as to suggest the hand of a divine creator. Yet in a critical sense the human achievement was not unique at all. Biologists have identified about two dozen evolutionary lines in the modern world fauna that attained advanced social life based on some degree of altruistic division of labor. Most arose in the insects. Several were independent origins, in marine shrimp, and three appeared among the mammals—that is, in two African mole rats, and us. All reached this level through the same narrow gateway: solitary individuals, or mated pairs, or small groups of individuals built nests and foraged from the nest for food with which they progressively raised their offspring to maturity.

Until about three million years ago, the ancestors of *Homo sapiens* were mostly vegetarians, and they most likely wandered in groups from site to site where fruit, tubers, and other vegetable food could be harvested. Their brains were only slightly larger than those of modern chimpanzees. By no later than half a million years ago, however, groups of the ancestral species *Homo erectus* were maintaining campsites with controlled fire—the equivalent of nests—from which they foraged and returned with food, including a substantial portion of meat. Their brain size had increased to midsize, between that of chimpanzees and modern *Homo sapiens*. The trend appears to have begun one to two million years previously, when the earlier prehuman ancestor *Homo habilis* turned increasingly to meat in its diet. With groups crowded together at a single site, and an advantage added by cooperative nest building and hunting, social intelligence grew, along with the centers of memory and reasoning in the prefrontal cortex.

Probably at this point, during the habiline period, a conflict ensued between individual-level selection, with individuals competing with other individuals in the same group, versus group-level selection, with competition among groups. The latter force promoted altruism and cooperation among all the group members. It led to group-wide morality and a sense of conscience and honor. The competitor between the two forces can be succinctly expressed as follows: within groups selfish individuals beat altruistic individuals, but groups of altruists beat groups of selfish individuals. Or, risking oversimplification, individual selection promoted sin, while group selection promoted virtue.

So it appeared that humans are forever conflicted by their prehistory of multilevel selection. They are suspended in unstable and constantly changing locations between the two extreme forces that created us. We are unlikely to yield completely to either force as an ideal solution to our social and political turmoil. To yield completely to the instinctual urgings born from individual selection would dissolve society. To surrender to the urgings from group selection would turn us into angelic robots—students of insects call them ants.

The eternal conflict is not God's test of humanity. It is not a machination of Satan. It is just the way things worked out. It might be the only way in the entire universe that human-level intelligence and social organization can evolve. We will find a way eventually to live with our inborn turmoil, and perhaps find pleasure in viewing it as a primary source of our creativity.

JUNE 24, 2012

If Peas Can Talk, Should We Eat Them?

—*Michael Marder*

IMAGINE A BEING CAPABLE OF PROCESSING, REMEMBERING, AND sharing information—a being with potentialities proper to it and inhabiting a world of its own. Given this brief description, most of us will think of a human person, some will associate it with an animal, and virtually no one's imagination will conjure up a plant.

Since November 2, however, one possible answer to the riddle is *Pisum sativum*, a species colloquially known as the common pea. On that day, a team of scientists from the Blaustein Institutes for Desert Research at Ben-Gurion University in Israel published the results of its peer-reviewed research, revealing that a pea plant subjected to drought conditions communicated its stress to other such plants with which it shared its soil. In other words, through the roots, it relayed to its neighbors the biochemical message about the onset of drought, prompting them to react as though they, too, were in a similar predicament.

Curiously, having received the signal, plants not directly affected by this particular environmental stress factor were better able to withstand adverse conditions when they actually occurred. This means that the recipients of biochemical communication could draw on their "memories"—information stored at the cellular level—to activate appropriate defenses and adaptive responses when the need arose.

In 1973, the publication of *The Secret Life of Plants*, by Peter Tompkins and Christopher Bird, which portrayed vegetal life as exquisitely sensitive, responsive and in some respects comparable to human life, was generally regarded as pseudoscience. The authors were not scientists, and clearly the results reported in that book, many of them outlandish, could not be reproduced. But today, new, hard scientific data appears to be buttressing the book's fundamental idea that plants are more complex organisms than previously thought.

The research findings of the team at the Blaustein Institutes form yet another building block in the growing fields of plant intelligence studies and neurobotany that, at the very least, ought to prompt us to rethink our relation to plants. Is it morally permissible to submit to total instrumentalization living beings that, though they do not have a central nervous system, are capable of basic learning and communication? Should their swift response to stress leave us coldly indifferent, while animal suffering provokes intense feelings of pity and compassion?

Evidently, empathy might not be the most appropriate ground for an ethics of vegetal life. But the novel indications concerning the responsiveness of plants, their interactions with the environment and with one another, are sufficient to undermine all simple, axiomatic solutions to eating in good conscience. When it comes to a plant, it turns out to be not only a what but also a who—an agent in its milieu, with its own intrinsic value or version of the good. Inquiring into justifications for consuming vegetal beings thus reconceived, we reach one of the final frontiers of dietary ethics.

Recent findings in cellular and molecular botany mean that eating preferences, too, must practically differentiate between vegetal what-ness and who-ness, while striving to keep the latter intact. The work of such differentiation is incredibly difficult because the subjectivity of plants is not centered in a single organ or function but is dispersed throughout their bodies, from the roots to the leaves and shoots. Nevertheless, this dispersion of vitality holds out a promise of its own: the plasticity of plants and their wondrous capacity for regeneration, their growth by increments, quantitative additions or reiterations of already-existing parts do little to change the form of living beings that are neither parts nor wholes because they are not hierarchically structured organisms. The "renewable" aspects of perennial plants may be accepted by humans as a gift of vegetal being and integrated into their diets.

But it would be harder to justify the cultivation of peas and other annual plants, the entire being of which humans devote to externally imposed ends. In other words, ethically inspired decisions cannot postulate the abstract conceptual unity of all plants; they must, rather, take into account the singularity of each species.

The emphasis on the unique qualities of each species means that ethical worries will not go away after normative philosophers and bioethicists have delineated their sets of definitive guidelines for human conduct. More specifically, concerns regarding the treatment of plants will come up again and again, every time we deal with a distinct species or communities of plants.

In Hans Christian Andersen's fairy tale *The Princess and the Pea*, the true identity of a princess is discovered after she spends a torturous night on top of twenty mattresses and twenty feather beds, with a single pea lodged underneath this pile. The desire to eat ethically is, perhaps, akin to this royal sensitivity, as some would argue that it is a luxury of those who do have enough food to select, in a conscious manner, their dietary patterns. But there is a more charitable way to interpret the analogy.

Ethical concerns are never problems to be resolved once and for all; they make us uncomfortable and sometimes, when the sting of conscience is too strong, prevent us from sleeping. Being disconcerted by a single pea to the point of unrest is analogous to the ethical obsession, untranslatable into the language of moral axioms and principles of righteousness. Such ethics do not dictate how to treat the specimen of *Pisum sativum*, or any other plant, but they do urge us to respond, each time anew, to the question of how, in thinking and eating, to say "yes" to plants.

APRIL 28, 2012

The Future of Moral Machines

—Colin Allen

A ROBOT WALKS INTO A BAR AND SAYS, "I'LL HAVE A SCREW-driver." A bad joke, indeed, but even less funny if the robot says, "Give me what's in your cash register."

The fictional theme of robots turning against humans is older than the word itself, which first appeared in the title of Karel Čapek's 1920 play about artificial factory workers rising against their human overlords. Just twenty-two years later, Isaac Asimov invented the "Three Laws of Robotics" to serve as a hierarchical ethical code for the robots in his stories: first, never harm a human being through action or inaction; second, obey human orders; last, protect oneself. From the first story in which the laws appeared, Asimov explored their inherent contradictions. Great fiction, but unworkable theory.

The prospect of machines capable of following moral principles, let alone understanding them, seems as remote today as the word *robot* is old. Some technologists enthusiastically extrapolate from the observation that computing power doubles every eighteen months to predict an imminent "technological singularity" in which a threshold for machines of superhuman intelligence will be suddenly surpassed. Many Singularitarians assume a lot, not the least of which is that intelligence is fundamentally a computational process. The techno-optimists among them also believe that such machines will be essentially friendly to human beings. I am skeptical about the Singularity, and even if "artificial intelligence" is not an oxymoron, "friendly AI" will require considerable scientific progress on a number of fronts.

The neuro- and cognitive sciences are presently in a state of rapid development in which alternatives to the metaphor of mind as computer have gained ground. Dynamical systems theory, network science, statistical learning theory, developmental psychobiology, and molecular neuroscience all challenge some foundational assumptions of AI and the last fifty years of cognitive science more generally. These new approaches analyze and exploit the complex causal structure of physically embodied and environmentally embedded systems, at every level, from molecular to social. They demonstrate the inadequacy of highly abstract algorithms operating on discrete symbols with fixed meanings to capture the adaptive flexibility of intelligent behavior. But despite undermining the idea that the mind is fundamentally a digital computer, these approaches have improved our ability to use computers for more and more robust simulations of intelligent agents—simulations that will increasingly control machines occupying our cognitive niche. If you don't believe me, ask Siri.

This is why, in my view, we need to think long and hard about machine morality. Many of my colleagues take the very idea of moral machines to be a kind of joke. Machines, they insist, do only what they are told to do. A bar-robbing robot would have to be instructed or constructed to do exactly that. On this view, morality is an issue only for creatures like us who can choose to do wrong. People are morally good only insofar as they must overcome the urge to do what is bad. We can be moral, they say, because we are free to choose our own paths.

There are big themes here: freedom of will, human spontaneity and creativity, and the role of reason in making good choices—not to mention the nature of morality itself. Fully human-level moral agency, and all the responsibilities that come with it, requires developments in artificial intelligence or artificial life that remain, for now, in the domain of science fiction. And yet . . .

Machines are increasingly operating with minimal human

oversight in the same physical spaces as we do. Entrepreneurs are actively developing robots for home care of the elderly. Robotic vacuum cleaners and lawn mowers are already mass-market items. Self-driving cars are not far behind. Mercedes is equipping its 2013 model S-Class cars with a system that can drive autonomously through city traffic at speeds up to 25 mph. Google's fleet of autonomous cars has logged about 200,000 miles without incident in California and Nevada, in conditions ranging from surface streets to freeways. By Google's estimate, the cars have required intervention by a human copilot only about once every 1,000 miles, and the goal is to reduce this rate to once in 1,000,000 miles. How long until the next bank robber will have an autonomous getaway vehicle?

This is autonomy in the engineer's sense, not the philosopher's. The cars won't have a sense of free will, not even an illusory one. They may select their own routes through the city, but for the foreseeable future, they won't choose their own paths in the grand journey from dealership to junkyard. We don't want our cars leaving us to join the Peace Corps, nor will they anytime soon. But as the layers of software pile up between us and our machines, they are becoming increasingly independent of our direct control. In military circles, the phrase "man on the loop" has come to replace "man in the loop," indicating the diminishing role of human overseers in controlling drones and ground-based robots that operate hundreds or thousands of miles from base. These machines need to adjust to local conditions faster than can be signaled and processed by human tele-operators. And while no one is yet recommending that decisions to use lethal force should be handed over to software, the Department of Defense is sufficiently committed to the use of autonomous systems that it has sponsored engineers and philosophers to outline prospects for ethical governance of battlefield machines.

Joke or not, the topic of machine morality is here to stay. Even modest amounts of engineered autonomy make it necessary to outline some modest goals for the design of artificial moral agents. Modest because we are not talking about guidance systems for the Terminator or other technology that does not yet exist. Necessary, because as machines with limited autonomy operate more often than before in open environments, it becomes increasingly important to design a kind of functional morality that is sensitive to ethically relevant features of those situations. Modest, again, because this functional morality is not about self-reflective moral agency—what one might call "full" moral agency—but simply about trying to make autonomous agents better at adjusting their actions to human norms. This can be done with technology that is already available or can be anticipated within the next five to ten years.

The project of designing artificial moral agents provokes a wide variety of negative reactions, including that it is preposterous, horrendous, or trivial. My coauthor Wendell Wallach and I have been accused of being, in our book *Moral Machines*, unimaginatively human centered in our views about morality, of being excessively optimistic about technological solutions, and of putting too much emphasis on engineering the machines themselves rather than looking at the whole context in which machines operate.

In response to the charge of preposterousness, I am willing to double down. Far from being an exercise in science fiction, serious engagement with the project of designing artificial moral agents has the potential to revolutionize moral philosophy in the same way that philosophers' engagement with science continuously revolutionizes human self-understanding. New insights can be gained from confronting the question of whether and how a control architecture for robots might utilize (or ignore) general principles recommended by major ethical theories. Perhaps ethical theory is to moral agents as physics is to outfielders—theoretical knowledge that isn't necessary to play a good game. Such theoretical knowledge may still be useful after the fact to analyze and adjust future performance.

Even if success in building artificial moral agents will be hard to gauge, the effort may help to forestall inflexible, ethically blind technologies from propagating. More concretely, if cars are smart enough to navigate through city traffic, they are certainly smart enough to detect how long they have been parked outside a bar (easily accessible through the marriage of GPS and the Internet) and to ask you, the driver, to prove you're not drunk before starting the engine so you can get home. For the near term (say, five to ten years), a responsible human will still be needed to supervise these "intelligent" cars, so you had better be sober. Does this really require artificial morality, when one could simply put a Breathalyzer between key and ignition? Such a dumb, inflexible system would have a kind of operational morality in which the engineer has decided that no car should be started by a person with a certain blood alcohol level. But it would be ethically blind—incapable, for instance, of recognizing the difference between, on the one hand, a driver who needs the car simply to get home and, on the other hand, a driver who had a couple of drinks with dinner but needs the car because a four-year-old requiring urgent medical attention is in the back seat.

It is within our current capacities to build machines that are able to determine, based on real-time information about current traffic conditions and access to actuarial tables, how likely it is that this situation might lead to an accident. Of course, this only defers the ethical question of how to weigh the potential for harm that either option presents, but a well-designed system of human-machine interaction could allow for a manual override to be temporarily logged in a "black box" similar to those used on airplanes. In case of an accident, this would provide evidence that the person had taken responsibility. Just as we can envisage machines with increasing degrees of autonomy from human oversight, we can envisage machines whose controls involve increasing degrees of sensitivity to things that matter ethically. Not perfect machines, to be sure, but better.

DOES THIS TALK OF artificial moral agents overreach, contributing to our own dehumanization, to the reduction of human autonomy, and to lowered barriers to warfare? If so, does it grease the slope to a horrendous, dystopian future? I am sensitive to the worries but optimistic enough to think that this kind of techno-pessimism has, over the centuries, been oversold. Luddites have always come to seem quaint, except when they were dangerous. The challenge for philosophers and engineers alike is to figure out what should and can reasonably be done in the middle space that contains somewhat autonomous, partly ethically sensitive machines. Some may think the exploration of this space is too dangerous to allow. Prohibitionists may succeed in some areas—robot arms control, anyone?—but they will not, I believe, be able to contain the spread of increasingly autonomous robots into homes, eldercare, and public spaces, not to mention the virtual spaces in which much software already operates without a human in the loop. We want machines that do chores and errands without our having to monitor them continuously. Retailers and banks depend on software controlling all manner of operations, from credit card purchases to inventory control, freeing humans to do other things that we don't yet know how to construct machines to do.

Where's the challenge, a software engineer might ask? Isn't ethical governance for machines just problem solving within constraints? If there's fuzziness about the nature of those constraints, isn't that a philosophical problem, not an engineering one? Besides, why look to human ethics to provide a gold standard for machines? My response is that if engineers leave it to philosophers to come up with theories that they can implement, they will have a long wait, but if philosophers leave it to engineers to implement something workable, they will likely be disappointed by the outcome. The challenge is to reconcile these two rather different ways of approaching the world, to yield better understanding of how interactions among people and contexts enable us, sometimes, to steer a reasonable course through the competing demands of our moral niche. The different kinds of rigor provided by philosophers and engineers are both needed to inform the construction of machines that, when embedded in well-designed systems of human-machine interaction, produce morally reasonable decisions even in situations where Asimov's laws would produce deadlock.

DECEMBER 25, 2011

Cambridge, Cabs and Copenhagen:
My Route to Existential Risk

—Huw Price

IN COPENHAGEN THE SUMMER BEFORE LAST, I SHARED A TAXI WITH a man who thought his chance of dying in an artificial intelligence–related accident was as high as that of heart disease or cancer. No surprise if he'd been the driver, perhaps (never tell a taxi driver that you're a philosopher!), but this was a man who has spent his career with computers.

Indeed, he's so talented in that field that he is one of the team who made this century so, well, twenty-first—who got us talking to one another on video screens, the way we knew we'd be doing in the twenty-first century, back when I was a boy, half a century ago. For this was Jaan Tallinn, one of the team who gave us Skype. (Since then, taking him to dinner in Trinity College here in Cambridge, I've had colleagues queuing up to shake his hand, thanking him for keeping them in touch with distant grandchildren.)

I knew of the suggestion that AI might be dangerous, of course. I had heard of the "singularity," or "intelligence explosion"—roughly, the idea, originally due to the statistician I. J. Good (a Cambridge-trained former colleague of Alan Turing's), that once machine intelligence reaches a certain point, it could take over its own process of improvement, perhaps exponentially, so that we humans would soon be left far behind. But I'd never met anyone who regarded it as such a pressing cause for concern—let alone anyone with their feet so firmly on the ground in the software business.

I was intrigued, and also impressed, by Tallinn's commitment to doing something about it. The topic came up because I'd asked what he worked on these days. The answer, in part, is that he spends a lot of his time trying to improve the odds, in one way or another (talking to philosophers in Danish taxis, for example).

I was heading for Cambridge at the time, to take up my new job as Bertrand Russell professor of philosophy—a chair named after a man who spent the last years of his life trying to protect humanity from another kind of technological risk, that of nuclear war. And one of the people I already knew in Cambridge was the distinguished cosmologist Martin Rees—then master of Trinity College and former president of the Royal Society. Lord Rees is another outspoken proponent of the view that we humans should pay more attention to the ways in which our own technology might threaten our survival. (Biotechnology gets most attention, in his work.)

So it occurred to me that there might be a useful, interesting and appropriate role for me, as a kind of catalyst between these two activists, and their respective circles. And that, to fast-forward a little, is how I came to be taking Jaan Tallinn to dinner in Trinity College, and how he, Martin Rees and I now come to be working together, to establish here in Cambridge the Centre for the Study of Existential Risk (CSER).

By "existential risks" (ER) we mean, roughly, catastrophic risks to our species that are "our fault," in the sense that they arise from human technologies. These are not the only catastrophic risks we humans face, of course: asteroid impacts and extreme volcanic events could wipe us out, for example. But in comparison with possible technological risks, these natural risks are comparatively well studied and, arguably, comparatively minor (the major source of uncertainty being on the technological side). So the greatest need, in our view, is to pay a lot more attention to these technological risks. That's why we chose to make them the explicit focus of our center.

I have now met many fascinating scholars—scientists, philosophers and others—who think that these issues are profoundly important and seriously understudied. Strikingly, though, they differ about where they think the most pressing risks lie. A Cambridge zoologist I met recently is most worried about deadly designer bacteria, produced—whether by error or by terror, as Rees puts it—in a nearby future in which there's almost an app for such things. To him, AI risk seemed comparatively far-fetched—though he confessed that he was no expert (and added that the evidence is that even experts do little better than chance, in many areas).

Where do I stand on the AI case, the one that got me into this business? I don't claim any great expertise on the matter (perhaps wisely, in the light of the evidence just mentioned). For what it's worth, however, my view goes like this. On the one hand, I haven't yet seen a strong case for being quite as pessimistic as Jaan Tallinn was in the taxi that day. (To be fair, he himself says that he's not always that pessimistic.) On the other hand, I do think that there are strong reasons to think that we humans are nearing one of the most significant moments in our entire history: the point at which intelligence escapes the constraints of biology. And I see no compelling grounds for confidence that if that does happen, we will survive the transition in reasonable shape. Without such grounds, I think we have cause for concern.

My case for these conclusions relies on three main observations. The first is that our own intelligence is an evolved biological solution to a kind of optimization problem, operating under very tight constraints of time, energy, raw materials, historical starting point and no doubt many other factors. The hardware needs to fit through a mammalian birth canal, to be reasonably protected for a mobile life in a hazardous environment, to consume something like one thousand calories per day, and so on—not to mention being achievable by mutation and selection over a timescale of some tens of millions of years, starting from what existed back then!

Second, this biological endowment, such as it is, has been essentially constant for many thousands of years. It is a kind of fixed point in the landscape, a mountain peak on which we have all lived for hundreds of generations. Think of it as Mount Fuji, for example. We are creatures of this volcano. The fact that it towers above the surrounding landscape enables us to dominate our environment and accounts for our extraordinary success, compared with most other species on the planet. (Some species benefit from our success, of course: cockroaches and rats, perhaps, and the many distinctive bacteria that inhabit our guts.) And the distinctive shape of the peak—also constant, or nearly so, for all these generations—is very deeply entangled with our sense of what it is to be us. We are not just creatures of any volcano; we are creatures of this one.

Both the height and the shape of the mountain are products of our biological history, in the main. (The qualification is needed because cultural inheritance may well play a role, too.) Our great success in the biological landscape, in turn, is mainly because of the fact that the distinctive intelligence that the height and shape represent has enabled us to control and modify the surrounding environment. We've been exercising such control for a very long time, of course, but we've recently gotten much better at it. Modern science and technology give us new and extraordinarily powerful ways to modify the natural world, and the creatures of the ancient volcano are more dominant than ever before.

This is all old news, of course, as is the observation that this success may ultimately be our undoing. (Remember Malthus.) But the new concern, linked to speculation about the future of AI, is that we may soon be in a position to do something entirely new: to unleash a kind of artificial volcanism that may change the shape and height of our own mountain, or build new ones, perhaps even higher, and perhaps of shapes we cannot presently imagine. In other words—and this is my third observation—we face the prospect that designed nonbiological technologies, operating under entirely different constraints in many respects, may soon do the kinds of things that our brain does, but very much faster, and very much better, in whatever dimensions of improvement may turn out to be available.

The claim that we face this prospect may seem contestable. Is it really plausible that technology will reach this stage (ever, let alone soon)? I'll come back to this. For the moment, the point I want to make is simply that if we do suppose that we are going to reach such a stage—a point at which technology reshapes our human Mount Fuji, or builds other peaks elsewhere—then it's not going to be business as usual, as far as we are concerned. Technology will have modified the one thing, more than anything else, that has made it "business as usual" so long as we have been human.

Indeed, it's not really clear who "we" would be, in those circumstances. Would we be humans surviving (or not) in an environment in which superior machine intelligences had taken the reins, so to speak? Would we be human intelligences somehow extended by nonbiological means? Would we be in some sense entirely posthuman (though thinking of ourselves perhaps as descendants of humans)? I don't claim that these are the only options, or even that these options are particularly well formulated—they're not! My point is simply that if technology does get to this stage, the most important fixed point in our landscape is no longer fixed—on the contrary, it might be moving, rapidly, in directions we creatures of the volcano are not well equipped to understand, let alone predict. That seems to me a cause for concern.

These are my reasons for thinking that at some point over the horizon, there's a major tipping point awaiting us, when intelligence escapes its biological constraints, and that it is far from clear that that's good news, from our point of view. To sum it up briefly, the argument rests on three propositions: (i) the level and general shape of human intelligence is highly contingent, a product of biological constraints and accidents; (ii) despite its contingency in the big scheme of things, it is essential to us—it is who we are, more or less, and it accounts for our success; (iii) technology is likely to give us the means to bypass the biological constraints, either altering our own minds or constructing machines with comparable capabilities, and thereby reforming the landscape.

But how far away might this tipping point be, and will it ever happen at all? This brings me back to the most contested claim of these three—the assertion that nonbiological machines are likely, at some point, to be as intelligent or more intelligent than the "biological machines" we have in our skulls.

Objections to this claim come from several directions. Some contest it based on the (claimed) poor record of AI so far; others on the basis of some claimed fundamental difference between human minds and computers; yet others, perhaps, on the grounds that the claim is simply unclear—it isn't clear what intelligence is, for example.

To arguments of the last kind, I'm inclined to give a pragmatist's answer: don't think about what intelligence is; think about what it does. Putting it rather crudely, the distinctive thing about our peak in the present biological landscape is that we tend to be much better at controlling our environment than any other species. In these terms, the question is then whether machines might at some point do an even better job (perhaps a vastly better job). If so, then all the aforementioned concerns seem to be back on the table, even though we haven't mentioned the word *intelligence*, let alone tried to say what it means. (You might try to resurrect the objection by focusing on the word *control*, but here I think you'd be on thin ice: it's clear that machines already control things, in some sense—they drive cars, for example.)

Much the same point can be made against attempts to take comfort in the idea that there is something fundamentally different between human minds and computers. Suppose there is, and that that means that computers will never do some of the things that we do—write philosophy, appreciate the sublime, or whatever. What's the case for thinking that without these gifts, the machines cannot control the terrestrial environment a lot more effectively than we do?

People who worry about these things often say that the main threat may come from accidents involving "dumb optimizers"—machines with rather simple goals (producing IKEA furniture, say) that figure out that they can improve their output astronomically by taking control of various resources on which we depend for our survival. Nobody expects an automated furniture factory to do philosophy. Does that make it less dangerous? (Would you bet your grandchildren's lives on the matter?)

But there's a more direct answer, too, to this attempt to take comfort in any supposed difference between human minds and computers. It also cuts against attempts to take refuge in the failure of AI to live up to some of its own hype. It's an answer in two parts. The first part—let me call it, a little aggressively, the blow to the head—points out that however biology got us onto this exalted peak in the landscape, the tricks are all there for our inspection: most of it is done with the glop inside our skulls. Understand that, and you understand how to do it artificially, at least in principle. Sure, it could turn out that there's then no way to improve things—that biology, despite all the constraints, really has hit some sort of fundamental maximum. Or it could turn out that the task of figuring out how biology did it is just beyond us, at least for the foreseeable future (even the remotely foreseeable future). But again, are you going to bet your grandchildren on that possibility?

The second part of the argument—the blow from below—asks these opponents just how far up the intelligence mountain they think that AI could get us. To the level of our fishy ancestors? Our early mammalian ancestors? (Keep in mind that the important question is the pragmatic one: Could a machine do what these creatures do?) Wherever they claim to draw the line, the objection challenges them to say what biology does next that no nonbiological machine could possibly do. Perhaps someone has a plausible answer to this question, but for my part, I have no idea what it could be.

At present, then, I see no good reason to believe that intelligence is never going to escape from the head, or that it won't do so in timescales we could reasonably care about. Hence it seems to me eminently sensible to think about what happens if and when it does so, and whether there's something we can do to favor good outcomes over bad, in that case. That's how I see what Rees, Tallinn and I want to do in Cambridge (about this kind of technological risk, as about others): we're trying to assemble an organization that will use the combined intellectual power of a lot of gifted people to shift some probability from the bad side to the good.

Tallinn compares this to wearing a seat belt. Most of us agree that that makes sense, even if the risk of an accident is low, and even though we can't be certain that it would be beneficial if we were to have an accident. (Occasionally, seat belts make things worse.) The analogy is apt in another way, too. It is easy to turn a blind eye to the case for wearing a seat belt. Many of us don't wear them in taxis, for example. Something—perhaps optimism, a sense that caution isn't cool, or (if you're sufficiently English!) a misplaced concern about hurting the driver's feelings—just gets in the way of the simple choice to put the thing on. Usually it makes no difference, of course, but sometimes people get needlessly hurt.

Worrying about catastrophic risk may have similar image problems. We tend to be optimists, and it might be easier, and perhaps in some sense cooler, not to bother. So I finish with two recommendations. First, keep in mind that in this case our fate is in the hands, if that's the word, of what might charitably be called a very large and poorly organized committee—collectively shortsighted, if not actually reckless, but responsible for guiding our fast-moving vehicle through some hazardous and yet completely unfamiliar terrain. Second, remember that all the children—all of them—are in the back. We thrill-seeking grandparents may have little to lose, but shouldn't we be encouraging the kids to buckle up?

JANUARY 27, 2013

WHERE IS MY MIND?

Mary and the Zombies:
Can Science Explain Consciousness?

—Gary Gutting

W<small>E TRUST SCIENCE BECAUSE ITS CLAIMS ARE BASED ON EXPERI-</small>
ence. But experience itself is a subjective reality that seems to
elude the objectivity of scientific understanding. We know that
our experiences—of seeing red, feeling pain, falling in love and so
forth—depend on physical systems like the brain that science can,
in principle, exhaustively explain. But it's hard to make sense of the
idea that experiences themselves could be physical. No doubt experiences correlate with objective physical facts, but, as subjective
phenomena, how could they be such facts? When I feel intense pain,
scientists may be able to observe brain events that cause my pain,
but they cannot observe the very pain that I feel. What science can
observe is public and objective; what I feel is private and subjective.

Perhaps, though, it's hard to understand how experiences could be
physical only because we lack the relevant concepts. After all, before
scientists developed the concepts of biochemistry, many found it
impossible to imagine how organisms could be entirely physical.
Now the idea is far more plausible. What's to say that future scientific
developments won't allow us to understand how experiences can be
entirely physical?

Nevertheless, some of the most interesting recent philosophical
discussions have centered around two thought experiments suggesting that experiences cannot be physical. These thought experiments
have by no means settled the issue, but they have convinced quite

a few philosophers and have posed a serious challenge to the claim that experience is entirely physical.

First, consider Mary, a leading neuroscientist who specializes in color perception. Mary lives at a time in the future when the neuroscience of color is essentially complete, and so she knows all the physical facts about colors and their perception. Mary, however, has been totally color-blind from birth. (Here I deviate from the story's standard form, in which—for obscure reasons—she's been living in an entirely black-and-white environment.)

Fortunately, due to research Mary herself has done, there is an operation that gives her normal vision. When the bandages are removed, Mary looks around the room and sees a bouquet of red roses sent by her husband. At that moment, Mary for the first time experiences the color red and now knows what red looks like. Her experience, it seems clear, has taught her a fact about color that she did not know before. But before this she knew all the physical facts about color. Therefore, there is a fact about color that is not physical. Physical science cannot express all the facts about color.

Second, consider a zombie. Not the brain-eating undead of movies, but a philosophical zombie, defined as physically identical to you or me but utterly lacking in internal subjective experience. Imagine, for example, that in some alternative universe you have a twin, not just genetically identical but identical in every physical detail, made of all the same sorts of elementary particles arranged in exactly the same way. Isn't it logically possible that this twin has no experiences?

It may, of course, be true that in our world the laws of nature require that certain objective physical structures be correlated with corresponding subjective experiences. But laws of nature are not logically necessary (if they were, we could discover them as we do laws of logic or mathematics, by pure thought, independent of empirical facts). So in an alternative universe, there could (logically) be a being physically identical to me but with no experiences: my zombie-twin.

But if a zombie-twin is logically possible, it follows that my experiences involve something beyond my physical makeup. For my zombie-twin shares my entire physical makeup but does not share my experiences. This, however, means that physical science cannot express all the facts about my experiences.

It's worth noting that that philosophers who find these thought experiments convincing do not conclude that there is no sense in which an experience is physical. Seeing red, for example, involves photons striking the retina, followed by a whole string of physical events that process the retinal information before we actually have a subjective sense of color. There's a purely physical sense in which this is "seeing." This is why we can say that a surveillance camera "sees" someone entering a room. But the "seeing" camera has no subjective experience; it has no phenomenal awareness of what it's like to see something. That happens only when we look at what the camera recorded. The claim that experience is not physical applies only to this sense of experience. But, of course, it is experience in this sense that makes up the rich inner experience that matters so much to us.

Also, few philosophers think these thought experiments show that there are souls or some other sort of supernatural entities. Frank Jackson, who first proposed the Mary scenario, and David Chalmers, who gave the most influential formulation of the zombie example, remain philosophical naturalists. They maintain that there is no world beyond the natural one in which we live. Their claim is rather that this world contains a natural reality (consciousness) that escapes the scope of physical explanation. Chalmers, in particular, supports a "naturalistic dualism" that proposes to supplement physical science by postulating entities with irreducibly subjective (phenomenal) properties that would allow us to give a natural explanation of consciousness. Not surprisingly, however, some philosophers have seen Jackson's and Chalmer's arguments as supporting a traditional dualism of a natural body and a supernatural soul.

I myself have come to no firm conclusions about the questions raised by these thought experiments, but the arguments for dualism they suggest are not obviously unsound. They at least show a possible path for reviving a form of mind-body dualism that does not deny established scientific facts.

A Real Science of Mind

—Tyler Burge

Ⅰ N RECENT YEARS POPULAR SCIENCE WRITING HAS BOMBARDED US
with titillating reports of discoveries of the brain's psychological
prowess. Such reports invade even introductory patter in biology
and psychology. We are told that the brain—or some area of it—sees,
decides, reasons, knows, emotes, is altruistic/egotistical, or wants to
make love. For example, a recent article reports a researcher's "looking at love, quite literally, with the aid of an MRI machine." One wonders whether lovemaking is to occur between two brains, or between
a brain and a human being.

There are three things wrong with this talk.

First, it provides little insight into psychological phenomena. Often the discoveries amount to finding stronger activation in some area of the brain when a psychological phenomenon
occurs—as if it is news that the brain is not dormant during psychological activity! The reported neuroscience is often descriptive
rather than explanatory. Experiments have shown that neurobabble produces the illusion of understanding. But little of it
is sufficiently detailed to aid, much less provide, psychological
explanation.

Second, brains-in-love talk conflates levels of explanation. Neurobabble piques interest in science but obscures how science works.
Individuals see, know, and want to make love. Brains don't. Those
things are psychological—not, in any evident way, neural. Brain

activity is necessary for psychological phenomena, but its relation to them is complex.

Imagine that reports of the mid-twentieth-century break-throughs in biology had focused entirely on quantum mechanical interactions among elementary particles. Imagine that the reports neglected to discuss the structure or functions of DNA. Inheritance would not have been understood. The level of explanation would have been wrong. Quantum mechanics lacks a notion of function, and its relation to biology is too complex to replace biological understanding. To understand biology, one must think in biological terms.

Discussing psychology in neural terms makes a similar mistake. Explanations of neural phenomena are not *themselves* explanations of psychological phenomena. Some expect the neural level to replace the psychological level. This expectation is as naive as expecting a single cure for cancer. Science is almost never so simple. See John Cleese's apt spoof of such reductionism.

The third thing wrong with neurobabble is that it has pernicious feedback effects on science itself. Too much immature science has received massive funding, on the assumption that it illuminates psychology. The idea that the neural can replace the psychological is the same idea that led to thinking that all psychological ills can be cured with drugs.

Correlations between localized neural activity and specific psychological phenomena are important facts. But they merely set the stage for explanation. Being purely descriptive, they explain nothing. Some correlations do *aid* psychological explanation. For example, identifying neural events underlying vision constrains explanations of timing in psychological processes and has helped predict psychological effects. We will understand both the correlations and the psychology, however, only through *psychological* explanation.

Scientific explanation is our best guide to understanding the world. By reflecting on it, we learn better what we understand about the world.

Neurobabble's popularity stems partly from the view that psychology's explanations are immature compared to neuroscience.

Some psychology is indeed still far from rigorous. But neurobabble misses an important fact.

A powerful, distinctively psychological science has matured over the last four decades. Perceptual psychology, preeminently vision science, should be grabbing headlines. This science is more advanced than many biological sciences, including much neuroscience. It is the first science to explain psychological processes with mathematical rigor in distinctively psychological terms. (Generative linguistics—another relatively mature psychological science—explains psychological structures better than psychological processes.)

What are distinctively psychological terms? Psychology is distinctive in being a science of representation. The term *representation* has a generic use and a more specific use that is distinctively psychological. I start with the generic use and will return to the distinctively psychological use. States of an organism *generically* represent features of the environment if they *function to correlate with* them. A plant or bacterium generically represents the direction of light. States involved in growth or movement functionally correlate with light's direction.

Task-focused explanations in biology and psychology often use *represent* generically, and proceed as follows. They identify a natural task for an organism. They then measure environmental properties relevant to the task, and constraints imposed by the organism's biophysical makeup. Next, they determine the mathematically optimal performance of the task, given the environmental properties and the organism's constraints. Finally, they develop hypotheses and test the organism's fulfillment of the task against optimal performance.

This approach identifies systematic correlations between organisms' states and environmental properties. Such correlations constitute generic representation. However, task-focused explanations that use *representation* generically are not distinctively psychological. For they apply to states of plants, bacteria, and water pumps, as well as to perception and thought.

Explanation in perceptual psychology is a subtype of task-focused explanation. What makes it *distinctively psychological* is that it uses notions like representational accuracy, a specific type of correlation.

The difference between functional correlation and representational accuracy is signaled by the fact that scientific explanations of light sensitivity in plants or bacteria invoke functional correlation, but not states capable of accuracy. Talk of accuracy would be a rhetorical afterthought. States capable of accuracy are what vision science is fundamentally about.

Why are explanations in terms of representational accuracy needed? They explain *perceptual constancies*. Perceptual constancies are capacities to perceive a given environmental property under many types of stimulation. You and a bird can see a stone as the same size from six inches or sixty yards away, even though the size of the stone's effect on the retina differs. You and a bee can see a surface as yellow bathed in white or red light, even though the distribution of wavelengths hitting the eye differ.

Plants and bacteria (and water pumps) lack perceptual constancies. Responses to light by plants and bacteria are explained by reference to states determined by properties of the light stimulus—frequency, intensity, polarization—and by how and where light stimulates their surfaces.

Visual perception is getting the environment right—seeing it, representing it accurately. Standard explanations of neural patterns cannot explain vision because such explanations do not relate vision, or even neural patterns, to the environment. Task-focused explanations in terms of functional correlation do relate organisms' states to the environment. But they remain too generic to explain visual perception.

Perceptual psychology explains how perceptual states that represent environmental properties are formed. It identifies psychological patterns that are learned, or coded into the perceptual system through eons of interaction with the environment. And it explains how stimulations cause individuals' perceptual states via those patterns. Perceptions and illusions of depth, movement, size, shape, color, sound localization, and so on, are explained with mathematical rigor.

Perceptual psychology uses two powerful types of explanation—one, geometrical and traditional; the other, statistical and cutting-edge.

Here is a geometrical explanation of distance perception. Two angles and the length of one side determine a triangle. A point in the environment forms a triangle with the two eyes. The distance between the eyes in many animals is constant. Suppose that distance to be innately coded in the visual system. Suppose that the system has information about the angles at which the two eyes are pointing, relative to the line between the eyes. Then the distance to the point in the environment is computable. Descartes postulated this explanation in 1637. There is now rich empirical evidence to indicate that this procedure, called "convergence," figures in perception of distance. Convergence is one of over fifteen ways human vision is known to represent distance or depth.

Here is a statistical explanation of contour grouping. Contour grouping is representing which contours (including boundary contours) "go together"—for example, as belonging to the same object. Contour grouping is a step toward perception of object shape. Grouping boundary contours that belong to the same object is complicated by this fact: objects commonly occlude other objects, obscuring boundary contours of partially occluded objects. Grouping boundaries on opposite sides of an occluder is a step toward perceiving object shape.

To determine how boundary contours should ideally be grouped, numerous digital photographs of natural scenes are collected. Hundreds of thousands of contours are extracted from the photographic images. Each pair is classified as to whether or not it corresponds to boundaries of the same object. The distances and relative orientations between paired image contours are recorded. Given enough samples, the probability that two photographic image contours correspond to contours on the same object can be calculated. Probabilities vary depending on distance—and orientation relations among the image contours. So whether two image contours correspond to boundaries of the same object depends statistically on properties of image contours.

Human visual systems are known to record contour information. In experiments, humans are shown only image contours in photographs, not full photographs. Their performance in judging which contours belong to the same object, given only the image contours, closely matches the objective probabilities established from the photographs. Such tests support hypotheses about how perceptions of object shape are formed from cues regarding contour groupings.

Representation, in the specific sense, and consciousness are the two primary properties that are distinctive of psychological phenomena. Consciousness is the what-it-is-like of experience. Representation is the being-about-something in perception and thought. Consciousness is introspectively more salient. Representation is scientifically better understood.

Where does mind begin? One beginning is the emergence of representational accuracy—in arthropods. (We do not know where consciousness begins.) Rigorous *science* of mind begins with *perception*, the first distinctively psychological representation. Maturation of a science of mind is one of the most important intellectual developments in the last half century. Its momentousness should not be obscured by neurobabble that baits with psychology but switches to brain science. Brain and psychological sciences are working toward one another. Understanding their relation depends on understanding psychology. We have a rigorous perceptual psychology. It may provide a model for further psychological explanation that will do more than display an MRI and say, "Behold, love."

DECEMBER 19, 2010

Out of Our Brains

—Andy Clark

*W*HERE IS MY MIND?

The question—memorably posed by rock band the Pixies in their 1988 song—is one that, perhaps surprisingly, divides many of us working in the areas of philosophy of mind and cognitive science. Look at the science columns of your daily newspapers and you could be forgiven for thinking that there is no case to answer. We are all familiar with the colorful "brain blob" pictures that show just where activity (indirectly measured by blood oxygenation level) is concentrated as we attempt to solve different kinds of puzzles: blobs here for thinking of nouns, there for thinking of verbs, over there for solving ethical puzzles of a certain class, and so on, ad blobum. (In fact, the brain-blob picture has seemingly been raised to the status of visual art form of late with the publication of a book of high-octane brain images.)

There is no limit, it seems, to the different tasks that elicit subtly, and sometimes not so subtly, different patterns of neural activation. Surely then, all the thinking must be going on in the brain. That, after all, is where the lights are.

But then again, maybe not. We've all heard the story of the drunk searching for his dropped keys under the lone streetlamp at night. When asked why he is looking there, when they could surely be anywhere on the street, he replies, "Because that's where the light is." Could it be the same with the blobs?

Is it possible that, sometimes at least, some of the activity that enables us to be the thinking, knowing, agents that we are occurs outside the brain?

The idea sounds outlandish at first. So let's take a familiar kind of case as a first illustration. Most of us gesture (some of us more wildly than others) when we talk. For many years, it was assumed that this bodily action served at best some expressive purpose, perhaps one of emphasis or illustration. Psychologists and linguists such as Susan Goldin-Meadow and David McNeill have lately questioned this assumption, suspecting that the bodily motions may themselves be playing some kind of active role in our thought process. In experiments where the active use of gesture is inhibited, subjects show decreased performance on various kinds of mental tasks. Now whatever is going on in these cases, the brain is obviously deeply implicated! No one thinks that the physical hand wavings are all by themselves the repositories of thoughts or reasoning. But it may be that they are contributing to the thinking and reasoning, perhaps by lessening or otherwise altering the tasks that the brain must perform, and thus helping us to move our own thinking along.

It is noteworthy, for example, that the use of spontaneous gesture increases when we are actively thinking a problem through, rather than simply rehearsing a known solution. There may be more to so-called hand waving than meets the eye.

This kind of idea is currently being explored by a wave of scientists and philosophers working in the areas known as "embodied cognition" and "the extended mind." Uniting these fields is the thought that evolution and learning don't give a jot what resources are used to solve a problem. There is no more reason, from the perspective of evolution or learning, to favor the use of a brain-only cognitive strategy than there is to favor the use of canny (but messy, complex, hard-to-understand) combinations of brain, body and world. Brains play a major role, of course. They are the locus of great plasticity and processing power, and will be the key to almost any form of cognitive success. But spare a thought for the many resources whose task-related burst of activity take place elsewhere, not just in the physical motions of our hands and arms while reasoning, or in the muscles of the dancer or the sports star, but even outside the biological body—in the iPhones, BlackBerrys, laptops and organizers that transform and extend the reach of bare biological processing in so many ways. These blobs of less-celebrated activity may sometimes be best seen, myself and others have argued, as bio-external elements in an extended cognitive process: one that now crisscrosses the conventional boundaries of skin and skull.

One way to see this is to ask yourself how you would categorize the same work were it found to occur "in the head" as part of the neural processing of, say, an alien species. If you'd then have no hesitation in counting the activity as genuine (though nonconscious) cognitive activity, then perhaps it is only some kind of bioenvelope prejudice that stops you counting the same work, when reliably performed outside the head, as a genuine element in your own mental processing.

Another way to approach the idea is by comparison with the use of prosthetic limbs. After a while, a good prosthetic limb functions not as a mere tool but as a nonbiological bodily part. Increasingly, the form and structure of such limbs is geared to specific functions (consider the carbon-fiber running blades of the Olympic and Paralympic athlete Oscar Pistorius) and does not replicate the full form and structure of the original biological template. As our information-processing technologies improve and become better and better adapted to fit the niche provided by the biological brain, they become more like cognitive prosthetics: nonbiological circuits that come to function as parts of the material underpinnings of minds like ours.

Many people I speak to are perfectly happy with the idea that an implanted piece of nonbiological equipment, interfaced to the brain by some kind of directly wired connection, would count (assuming all went well) as providing material support for some of their own cognitive processing. Just as we embrace cochlear implants as genuine but nonbiological elements in a sensory circuit, so we might embrace "silicon neurons" performing complex operations as elements in some future form of cognitive repair. But when the emphasis shifts from repair to extension, and from implants with wired interfacing to "explants" with wire-free communication, intuitions sometimes shift. That shift, I want to argue, is unjustified. If we can repair a cognitive function by the use of nonbiological circuitry, then we can extend and alter cognitive functions that way, too. And if a wired interface is acceptable, then, at least in principle, a wire-free interface (such as links your brain to your notepad, BlackBerry or iPhone) must be acceptable, too. What counts is the flow and alteration of information, not the medium through which it moves.

Perhaps we are moved simply by the thought that these devices (like prosthetic limbs) are detachable from the rest of the person. Ibn Sina Avicenna, a Persian philosopher-scientist who lived between AD 980 and 1037, wrote in the seventh volume of his epic *Liber de anima seu sextus de naturalibus* that "these bodily members are, as it were, no more than garments; which, because they have been attached to us for a long time, we think are us, or parts of us [and] the cause of this is the long period of adherence: we are accustomed to remove clothes and to throw them down, which we are entirely unaccustomed to do with our bodily members" (translation by R. Martin). Much the same is true, I want to say, of our own cognitive circuitry.

The fact that there is a stable biological core that we do not "remove and throw down" blinds us to the fact that minds, like bodies, are collections of parts whose deepest unity consists not in contingent matters of undetachability but in the way they (the parts) function together as effective wholes. When information flows, some of the most important unities may emerge in integrated processing regimes that weave together activity in brain, body, and world.

Such an idea is not new. Versions can be found in the work of James, Heidegger, Bateson, Merleau-Ponty, Dennett and many others. But we seem to be entering an age in which cognitive prosthetics (which have always been around in one form or another) are displaying a kind of Cambrian explosion of new and potent forms. As the forms proliferate, and some become more entrenched, we might do well to pause and reflect on their nature and status. At the very least, minds like ours are the products not of neural processing alone but of the complex and iterated interplay between brains, bodies, and the many designer environments in which we increasingly live and work.

Please don't get me wrong. Some of my best friends are neuroscientists and neuroimagers (as it happens, my partner is a neuroimager, so brain blobs are part of our daily diet). The brain is a fantastic beast, more than worthy of the massive investments we make to study it. But we—the human beings with versatile bodies living in a complex, increasingly technologized, and heavily self-structured world—are more fantastic still. Really understanding the mind, if the theorists of embodied and extended cognition are right, will require a lot more than just understanding the brain. We may just, as the Pixies did, find our minds "way out in the water. . . . See it swimming."

DECEMBER 12, 2010

Do Thrifty Brains Make Better Minds?

—*Andy Clark*

Might the miserly use of neural resources be one of the essential keys to understanding how brains make sense of the world? Some recent work in computational and cognitive neuroscience suggests that it is indeed the frugal use of our native neural capacity (the inventive use of restricted "neural bandwidth," if you will) that explains how brains like ours so elegantly make sense of noisy and ambiguous sensory input. That same story suggests, intriguingly, that perception, understanding and imagination, which we might intuitively consider to be three distinct chunks of our mental machinery, are inextricably tied together as simultaneous results of a single underlying strategy known as "predictive coding." This strategy saves on bandwidth using (who would have guessed it?) one of the many technical wheezes that enable us to economically store and transmit pictures, sounds and videos using formats such as JPEG and MP3.

In the case of a picture (a black-and-white photo of Laurence Olivier playing Hamlet, to activate a concrete image in your mind) predictive coding works by assuming that the value of each pixel is well predicted by the value of its various neighbors. When that's true—which is rather often, as gray-scale gradients are pretty smooth for large parts of most images—there is simply no need to transmit the value of that pixel. All that the photo-frugal need transmit are the deviations from what was thus predicted. The simplest prediction would be that neighboring pixels all share the same value (the same gray-scale value, for example), but much more complex predictions are also possible. As long as there is detectable regularity, prediction (and hence, this particular form of data compression) is possible.

Such compression by informed prediction (as Bell Telephone Labs first discovered back in the 1950s) can save enormously on bandwidth, allowing quite modest encodings to be reconstructed, by in effect "adding back in" the successfully predicted elements, into rich and florid renditions of the original sights and sounds. The basic trick is one we can use in daily life, too. Suppose you make a plan with your friend Duke by saying that if you *don't* call him, then all is "as expected" and that he should therefore meet your plane at the Miami airport next Wednesday at 9:00 a.m. local time. Your *failure* to call is then (technically speaking) a tiny little one-bit signal that conveys a large amount of neatly compressed information! The trick is trading intelligence and foreknowledge (expectations, informed predictions) on the part of the receiver against the costs of encoding and transmission on the day.

A version of this same trick may be helping animals like us to sense and understand the world by allowing us to use what we already know to predict as much of the current sensory data as possible. When you think you see or hear your beloved cat or dog when the door or wind makes just the right jiggle or rustle, you are probably using well-trained prediction to fill in the gaps, saving on bandwidth and (usually) knowing your world better as a result.

Neural versions of this predictive coding trick benefit, however, from an important added dimension: the use of a stacked hierarchy of processing stages. In biological brains, the prediction-based strategy unfolds within multiple layers, each of which deploys its own specialized knowledge and resources to try to predict the states of the level below it.

This is not easy to imagine, but it rewards the effort. A familiar, but still useful, analogy is with the way problems and issues are passed up the chain of command in rather traditional management hierarchies. Each person in the chain must learn to distil important (hence, usually surprising or unpredicted) information from those lower down the chain. And they must do so in a way that is sufficiently sensitive to the needs (hence, expectations) of those immediately above them.

In this kind of multilevel chain, all that flows upward is *news*. What flows forward, in true bandwidth-miser style, are the deviations (be they for good or for ill) from each level's predicted events and unfoldings. This is efficient. Valuable bandwidth is not used for sending well-predicted stuff forward. Why bother? We were expecting all that stuff anyway. Who in corporate headquarters wants to know that the work of Jill/Jack proceeded exactly as expected? Instead, that expensive bandwidth is used only to flag what may more plausibly demand attention: outcomes that gloriously exceeded or sadly fell short of expectations. Things work similarly—if the predictive coding account is correct—in the neural incarnation. What is marked and passed forward in the brain's flow of processing are the divergences from predicted states: divergences that may be used to demand more information at those very specific points, or to guide remedial action.

All this, if true, has much more than merely engineering significance. For it suggests that perception may best be seen as what has sometimes been described as a process of "controlled hallucination" (Ramesh Jain) in which we (or rather, various parts of our brains) try to predict what is out there, using the incoming signal more as a means of tuning and nuancing the predictions rather than as a rich (and bandwidth-costly) encoding of the state of the world. This in turn underlines the surprising extent to which the structure of our expectations (both conscious and nonconscious) may quite literally be determining much of what we see, hear and feel.

The basic effect hereabouts is neatly illustrated by a simple but striking demonstration (used by the neuroscientist Richard Gregory back in the 1970s to make this very point) known as "the hollow-face illusion." This is a well-known illusion in which an ordinary face mask viewed from the back can appear strikingly convex. That is, it looks (from the back) to be shaped like a real face, with the nose sticking outward rather than having a concave nose cavity. Just about any hollow face mask will produce some version of this powerful illusion.

The hollow-face illusion illustrates the power of what cognitive psychologists call "top-down" (essentially, knowledge-driven) influences on perception. Our statistically salient experience with endless hordes of convex faces in daily life installs a deep expectation of convexness: an expectation that here trumps the many other visual cues that ought to be telling us that what we are seeing is a concave mask.

You might reasonably suspect that the hollow-face illusion, though striking, is really just some kind of psychological oddity. And to be sure, our expectations concerning the convexity of faces seem especially strong and potent. But if the predictive-coding approaches I mentioned earlier are on track, this strategy might actually pervade human perception. Brains like ours may be constantly trying to use what they already know so as to predict the current sensory signal, using the incoming signal to constrain those predictions, and sometimes using the expectations to "trump" certain aspects of the incoming sensory signal itself. (Such trumping makes adaptive sense, as the capacity to use what you know to outweigh some of what the incoming signal seems to be saying can be hugely beneficial when the sensory data is noisy, ambiguous, or incomplete—situations that are, in fact, pretty much the norm in daily life.)

This image of the brain (or more accurately, of the sensory and motor cortex) as an engine of prediction is a simple and quite elegant one that can be found in various forms in contemporary neuroscience. It has also been shown, at least in restricted domains, to be computationally sound and practically viable. Just suppose (if only for the sake of argument) that it is on track, and that perception is indeed a process in which incoming sensory data is constantly matched with "top-down" predictions based on unconscious expectations of how that sensory data should be. This would have important implications for how we should think about minds like ours.

First, consider the unconscious expectations themselves. They derive mostly from the statistical shape of the world as we have experienced it in the past. We see the world by applying the expectations generated by the statistical lens of our own past experience, and not (mostly) by applying the more delicately rose-nuanced lenses of our political and social aspirations. So if the world that tunes those expectations is sexist or racist, future perceptions will also be similarly sculpted—a royal recipe for tainted evidence and self-fulfilling negative prophecies. That means we should probably be very careful about the shape of the worlds to which we expose ourselves, and our children.

Second, consider that perception (at least of this stripe) now looks to be deeply linked to something not unlike imagination. For insofar as a creature can indeed predict its own sensory inputs from the "top down," such a creature is well positioned to engage in familiar (though perhaps otherwise deeply puzzling) activities like dreaming and some kind of free-floating imagining. These would occur when the constraining sensory input is switched off, by closing down the sensors, leaving the system free to be driven purely from the top down. We should not suppose that all creatures deploying this strategy can engage in the kinds of self-conscious deliberate imagining that we do. Self-conscious deliberate imagining may well require substantial additional innovations, like the use of language as a means of self-cuing. But where we find perception working in this way, we may expect an interior mental life of a fairly rich stripe, replete with dreams and free-floating episodes of mental imagery.

Finally, perception and understanding would also be revealed as close cousins. For to perceive the world in this way is to deploy knowledge not just about how the sensory signal should be right now, but about how it will probably change and evolve over time. For it is only by means of such longer-term and larger-scale knowledge that we can robustly match the incoming signal, moment to moment, with apt expectations (predictions). To know that (to know how the present sensory signal is likely to change and evolve over time) just *is* to understand a lot about how the world is, and the kinds of entity and event that populate it. Creatures deploying this strategy, when they see the grass twitch in just that certain way, are already expecting to see the tasty prey emerge, and already expecting to feel the sensations of their own muscles tensing to pounce. But an animal, or machine, that has *that kind of grip* on its world is already deep into the business of understanding that world.

I find the unity here intriguing. Perhaps we humans, and a great many other organisms, too, are deploying a fundamental, thrifty, prediction-based strategy that husbands neural resources and (as a direct result) delivers perceiving, understanding and imagining in a single package.

Now there's a deal!

JANUARY 15, 2012

BLINDED BY NEUROSCIENCE?

Bursting the Neuro-utopian Bubble

—*Benjamin Y. Fong*

URING MY GRADUATE STUDIES IN THE DEPARTMENT OF RELI-
gion at Columbia, I spent countless hours in the Burke Library of
Union Theological Seminary where I had a spectacular, catercor-
ner view of the construction and unveiling of the Northwest Corner Building, Columbia's new interdisciplinary science building.
Although the fourteen-story steel and aluminum tower was designed
to complement the brick and limestone gothic tower of Union, its
dominating presence on the corner of Broadway and 120th serves as
a heavy-handed reminder of where we are heading. Walking from
Union toward Columbia's main campus through its doors, I often
felt, passing through the overwhelmingly aseptic marble lobby, as if
the building was meant to cleanse northwesterly intruders who have
not been intimidated by the facade.

The ninth floor of this building houses a laboratory of Rafael
Yuste, lead author of an ambitious brief that appeared in the prominent neuroscience journal *Neuron* in 2012. The paper proposed the
need for the "Brain Activity Map Project, aimed at reconstructing the
full record of neural activity across complete neural circuits." This
April, the Obama administration endorsed the project, setting aside
$100 million for it in 2014 alone and renaming it the Brain Research
through Advancing Innovative Neurotechnologies Initiative, or the
BRAIN Initiative for short.

The project has been compared by the administration to the

Human Genome Project, which focused on a problem—the sequencing of the human genome—as daunting as the recording and map-
ping of brain circuits in action. The success of the Human Genome
Project was both scientific and financial: the $3.8 billion invested in
it by the federal government has reportedly returned $796 billion, a
fact that advocates of the BRAIN Initiative have been quick to cite as
justification for their own undertaking.

Critics of the Human Genome Project have voiced many concerns
about genomic sequencing, most of which can also be leveled at the
BRAIN Initiative: What happens when health insurance companies
get hold of this information? Could it lead to invasions of our privacy? And, perhaps most fundamentally, aren't these scientists once
again trying to play God?

The rebuttal from the scientific community has generally gone
something like this: The living organism is a complex machine. To
understand it, one must take it apart and put it back together again, as
one would the engine of a car. Opposing this research but encouraging
medical advance is like asking your mechanic to fix your car. Opposing this research but encouraging medical advance is like asking your
mechanic to fix your car without popping open the hood. We're not
playing God. We simply want the allowance, both financial and legal,
to advance down the road to a true knowledge, a true mastery, of life.
As this mastery grows, both physiological and psychological diseases
will slowly be rooted out, and the moral and political questions will
become more tractable, where they do not disappear entirely.

What precisely is objectionable about this vision? Why should
we be worried about the advances of neuroscience, and in particular those of the BRAIN Initiative? On one level, its proponents are
simply naive about the corporate wolves with whom they run. George
Church, a genetics professor at Harvard and one of the faces of the
initiative, describes his sponsors, including Chevron, Procter &
Gamble and Merck, as institutions that are "very pragmatic and
practical about helping our world get better." This willful ignorance
regarding corporate influence is even more disturbing in the case
of the BRAIN Initiative, which promises a very fine control over

the seat of consciousness. With the help of this research, today's neuromarketing—marketing researched not with focus groups but MRIs—may soon look quite primitive.

It is not enough, however, to point to the indissoluble marriage of science and industry, to follow the money and lament corrupted applications of this research. It is necessary, rather, to confront the pristine fantasy that guides it, so that the troubles the embodied vision faces cannot be parried as mere problems of implementation.

So what, then, is worrying about this scientific plan for human betterment, sans corruption, about the technician's dream of total control over the human body, and in particular the human brain? First off, I believe the time has passed for saving that ethereal entity called "mind" from its biological reduction. We should accept the real possibility that one day, having monitored the active brain from birth to adulthood and uncovered both the constitutional and environmental factors of various disorders, we will be able to tell the developmental story in which selves emerge in neurological terms.

The real trouble with the BRAIN Initiative is not philosophical but practical. In short, the instrumental approach to the treatment of physiological and psychological diseases tends to be at odds with the traditional ways in which human beings have addressed their problems: that is, by talking and working with one another to the end of greater personal self-realization and social harmony.

In *Biology as Ideology*, Richard Lewontin points to the profound difference between the fact that one cannot get tuberculosis without a tubercle bacillus and the claim that the tubercle bacillus is the "cause" of tuberculosis. Registering that tuberculosis was a disease common in sweatshops in the nineteenth century, Lewontin contends, "We might be justified in claiming that the cause of tuberculosis is unregulated industrial capitalism, and if we did away with that system of social organization, we would not need to worry about the tubercle bacillus." Having narrowed their view of "cause" to the biological realm, neuroscientists today are effectively chasing tubercle bacilli, drawing our focus away from the social practices and institutions that contribute to problems of mental health.

We know, for instance, that low socioeconomic status at birth is associated with a greater risk of developing schizophrenia, but the lion's share of research into schizophrenia today is carried out by neurobiologists and geneticists, who are intent on uncovering the organic "cause" of the disease rather than looking into psychosocial factors. Though this research may very well bear fruit, its dominance over other forms of research, in the face of the known connection between poverty and schizophrenia, attests to a curious assumption that has settled into a comfortable obviousness: that socioeconomic status, unlike human biology, is something we cannot change "scientifically." That it is somehow more realistic, "scientifically," to find a way to change the human being itself than it is to work together to change the kind of environment that lends itself to the emergence of a disorder like schizophrenia.

Psychology has traditionally concerned itself with the ways in which we engage with the world and grow into social beings with the hope of improving our personal relationships and communal well-being. Neuroscience could complement this project by offering better information about the material substrate of consciousness, but it is rather, and often self-consciously, a usurper, a harbinger of a new psychological paradigm that replaces the socially formed self with the active brain. It neglects the forms of private and public conversation that hold out the possibility of self-transformation for instrumental dissections of the brain that promise only self-manipulation. Its future is not one that is worked toward in concert with other human beings, but one that is physiologically shaped by a vanguard of synthetic biologists.

I do not doubt that my body will be the beneficiary of the many new technologies that the Human Genome Project, the BRAIN Initiative, and other such cutting-edge ventures produce. My point is simply that the attempt to gain control over life itself has severely detracted from the work of figuring out how we talk to and work with one another in order to better ourselves and our world. To be clear, I do not believe that this communicative project is easier or more efficient than the instrumental approach—how we go about changing socioeconomic conditions is a problem we have not even begun to solve—but only that it is an important part of what it means to be a human being. And no matter how precisely we can manipulate the brain with drugs, electrodes, and other such contrivances, the emerging insights of neuroscience will never provide sufficient help with this work.

This is not to question the intentions of neuroscientists. Doubtless they are driven, at least in part, by a desire to better human life. But as Freud argued back in 1930, the forces of civilization have a strange tendency to work at cross-purposes with themselves, imperiling the very projects they also make possible. By humbly claiming ignorance about the "causes" of mental problems, and thus the need for a project like the BRAIN Initiative, neuroscientists unconsciously repress all that we know about the alienating, unequal, and dissatisfying world in which we live and the harmful effects it has on the psyche, thus unwittingly foreclosing the kind of communicative work that could alleviate mental disorder.

Like many others, I worry that the work of neuroscience will fall, almost of necessity, into the wrong hands—say, corporations interested in controlling consumers at a neurobiological level; but its development in the "right" hands is, perhaps, even more disconcerting.

AUGUST II, 2013

Bodies in Motion: An Exchange

—Alex Rosenberg and William Egginton

I N THE FOLLOWING EXCHANGE, ALEX ROSENBERG AND WILLIAM Egginton stake out their opposing positions on the relationship between the humanities and the sciences.

Galileo's Gambit

By *Alex Rosenberg*

Can neurophilosophy save the humanities from hard science?

Hard science—first physics, then chemistry and biology—got going in the 1600s. Philosophers like Descartes and Leibniz almost immediately noticed its threat to human self-knowledge. But no one really had to choose between scientific explanations of human affairs and those provided in history and the humanities until the last decades of the twentieth century. Now, every week newspapers, magazines and scientific journals report on how neuroscience is trespassing into domains previously the sole preserve of the interpretive humanities. Neuroscience's explanations and the traditional ones compete; they cannot both be right. Eventually we will have to choose between human narrative self-understanding and science's explanations of human affairs. Neuroeconomics, neuroethics, neuro–art history and neuro–lit crit are just tips of an iceberg on a collision course with the ocean liner of human self-knowledge.

Let's see why we will soon have to face a choice we've been able to postpone for four hundred years.

It is hard to challenge the hard science's basic picture of reality. That is because it began by recursively reconstructing and replacing the common beliefs that turned out to be wrong by standards of everyday experience. The result, rendered unrecognizable to everyday belief after four hundred years or so, is contemporary physics, chemistry and biology. Why date science only to the 1600s? After all, mathematics dates back to Euclid, and Archimedes made empirical discoveries in the third century BC. But 1638 was when Galileo first showed that a little thought is all we need to undermine the mistaken belief that neither Archimedes nor Aristotle had seen through but that stood in the way of science.

Galileo offered a thought experiment that showed, contrary to common beliefs, that objects can move without any forces pushing them along at all. It sounds trivial and yet this was the breakthrough that made physics and the rest of modern science possible. Galileo's reasoning was undeniable: roll a ball down an incline, it speeds up; roll it up an incline, it slows down. So, if you roll it onto a frictionless horizontal surface, it will have to go forever. Stands to reason, by common sense. But that simple bit of reasoning destroyed the Aristotelian world picture and ushered in science. Starting there, four hundred years of continually remodeling everyday experience has produced a description of reality incompatible with common sense; that reality includes quantum mechanics, general relativity, natural selection and neuroscience.

Descartes and Leibniz made important contributions to science's seventeenth-century "takeoff." But they saw exactly why science would be hard to reconcile with historical explanation, the human "sciences," the humanities, theology and in our own interior psychological monologs. These undertakings trade on a universal, culturally inherited "understanding" that interprets human affairs via narratives that "make sense" of what we do. Interpretation is supposed to explain events, usually in motivations that participants themselves recognize, sometimes by uncovering meanings the participants don't themselves appreciate.

Natural science deals only in momentum and force, elements and compounds, genes and fitness, neurotransmitters and synapses. These things are not enough to give us what introspection tells us we have: meaningful thoughts about ourselves and the world that bring about our actions. Philosophers since Descartes have agreed with introspection, and they have provided fiendishly clever arguments for the same conclusion. These arguments ruled science out of the business of explaining our actions because it cannot take thoughts seriously as causes of anything.

Descartes and Leibniz showed that thinking about one's self, or for that matter anything else, is something no purely physical thing, no matter how big or how complicated, can do. What is most obvious to introspection is that thoughts are about something. When I think of Paris, there is a place three-thousand miles away from my brain, and my thoughts are *about* it. The trouble is, as Leibniz specifically showed, no chunk of physical matter could be "about" anything. The size, shape, composition or any other physical fact about neural circuits is not enough to make them be about anything. Therefore, thought can't be physical, and that goes for emotions and sensations, too. Some influential philosophers still argue that way.

Neuroscientists and neurophilosophers have to figure out what is wrong with this and similar arguments. Or they have to conclude that interpretation, the stock in trade of the humanities, does not after all really explain much of anything at all. What science can't accept is some "off-limits" sign at the boundary of the interpretative disciplines.

Ever since Galileo, science has been strongly committed to the unification of theories from different disciplines. It cannot accept that the right explanations of human activities must be logically incompatible with the rest of science, or even just independent of it. If science were prepared to settle for less than unification, the difficulty of reconciling quantum mechanics and general relativity wouldn't be the biggest problem in physics. Biology would not accept the gene as real until it was shown to have a physical structure—

DNA—that could do the work geneticists assigned to the gene. For exactly the same reason science can't accept interpretation as providing knowledge of human affairs if it can't at least in principle be absorbed into, perhaps even reduced to, neuroscience.

That's the job of neurophilosophy.

This problem, that thoughts about ourselves or anything else for that matter couldn't be physical, was for a long time purely academic. Scientists had enough on their plates for four hundred years just showing how physical processes bring about chemical processes, and through them biological ones. But now neuroscientists are learning how chemical and biological events bring about the brain processes that actually produce everything the body does, including speech and all other actions.

Research—including Nobel Prize—winning neurogenomics and fMRI (functional magnetic resonance imaging)—has revealed how bad interpretation's explanations of our actions are. And there are clever psychophysical experiences that show us that introspection's insistence that interpretation really does explain our actions is not to be trusted.

These findings cannot be reconciled with explanation by interpretation. The problem they raise for the humanities can no longer be postponed. Must science write off interpretation the way it wrote off phlogiston theory—a nice try but wrong? Increasingly, the answer that neuroscience gives to this question is, "Afraid so."

Few people are prepared to treat history, (auto)biography and the human sciences like folklore. The reason is obvious. The narratives of history, the humanities and literature provide us with the *feeling* that we understand what they seek to explain. At their best they also trigger emotions we prize as marks of great art.

But that feeling of understanding, that psychological relief from the itch of curiosity, is not the same thing as knowledge. It is not even a mark of it, as children's bedtime stories reveal. If the humanities and history provide only feelings (ones explained by neuroscience), that will not be enough to defend their claims to knowledge.

The only solution to the problem faced by the humanities, history and (autobiography) is to show that interpretation can somehow be grounded in neuroscience. That is job no. 1 for neurophilosophy. And the odds are against it. If this project doesn't work out, science will have to face plan B: treating the humanities the way we treat the arts, indispensable parts of human experience but not to be mistaken for contributions to knowledge.

The Cosmic Imagination

By William Egginton

Do the humanities need to be defended from hard science?

They might, if Alex Rosenberg is right when he claims that "neuroscience is trespassing into domains previously the sole preserve of the interpretive disciplines," and that "neuroscience's explanations and the traditional ones compete; they cannot both be right."

While neuroscience may well have very interesting things to say about how brains go about making decisions and producing different interpretations, though, it does not follow that the knowledge thus produced replaces humanistic knowledge. In fact, the only way we can understand this debate is by using humanist methodology—from reading historical and literary texts to interpreting them to using them in the form of an argument—to support a very different notion of knowledge than the one Professor Rosenberg presents.

In citing Galileo, Professor Rosenberg seeks to show us how a "little thought is all we need to undermine the mistaken belief that neither Archimedes nor Aristotle had seen through but that stood in the way of science." A lone, brave man, Galileo Galilei, defies centuries of tradition and a brutal, repressive Church armed just with his reason, and "that simple bit of reasoning destroyed the Aristotelian world picture and ushered in science."

The only problem is that this interpretation is largely incomplete; the fuller story is far more complex and interesting.

Galileo was both a lover of art and literature, and a deeply religious man. As the mathematician and physicist Mark A. Peterson has shown in his new book, *Galileo's Muse: Renaissance Mathematics and the Arts*, Galileo's love for the arts profoundly shaped his thinking and in many ways helped pave the way for his scientific discoveries. An early biography of Galileo by his contemporary Niccolò Gherardini points out that "he was most expert in all the sciences and arts, as if he were professor of them. He took extraordinary delights in music, painting, and poetry." For its part, Peterson takes great delight in demonstrating how his immersion in these arts informed his scientific discoveries, and how art and literature prior to Galileo often planted the seeds of scientific progress to come.

Professor Rosenberg believes that Galileo was guided solely by everyday experience and reason in debunking the false idea that for an object to keep moving it must be subjected to a continuous force. But one could just as well argue that everyday experience would, and did, dictate some version of that theory. As humans have no access to a frictionless realm and can only speculate as to whether unimpeded motion would continue indefinitely, the repeated observations that objects in motion do come to a rest if left on their own certainly supported the standard theory. So if it was not mere everyday experience that led to Galileo's discovery, what did?

Clearly Galileo was an extraordinary man, and a crucial aspect of what made him that man was the intellectual world he was immersed in. This world included mathematics, of course, but it was also full of arts and literature, of philosophy and theology. Peterson argues forcefully, for instance, that Galileo's mastery of the techniques involved in creating and thinking about perspective in painting could well have influenced his thinking about the relativity of motion, since both require comprehending the importance of multiple points of view.

The idea that the perception of movement depends on one's point of view also has forebears in proto-scientific thinkers who are far less suitable candidates for the appealing story of how common sense suddenly toppled a two-thousand-year-old tradition to usher modern science into the world. Take the poet, philosopher and theologian Giordano Bruno, who seldom engaged in experimentation and who, thirty years before Galileo's own trial, refused to recant the beliefs that led him to be burned at the stake, beliefs that included the infinity of the universe and the multiplicity of worlds.

The theory of the infinity of the world was not itself new, having been formulated in various forms before Bruno, notably by Lucretius, whom Bruno read avidly, and more recently by Nicholas of Cusa. Bruno was probably the first, though, to identify the stars as solar systems, infinite in number, possibly orbited by worlds like our own.

Such a view had enormous consequences for the theory of motion. For the scholastics, the universe was finite and spherical. The circular motion of the heavens was imparted by the outermost sphere, which they called the *primum mobile*, or first mover, and associated with God. The cosmos was hence conceived of as being divided into an outer realm of perfect and eternal circular motion, and an inner realm of corruptibility, where objects moved in straight lines. As the scholastics denied the existence of space outside the *primum mobile*, citing Aristotle's dictum that nature abhors a vacuum, the motion of the outer cosmos could only be conceived of as occurring in relation to a motionless center.

When Bruno disputed that the cosmos had boundaries, however, he undermined the justification for assuming that the earth (or anywhere else, for that matter) was its center. From there it was but a short step to realizing that everything can equally be considered at rest or in motion, depending on your point of view. Indeed, this very reasoning animated Galileo's thought, which he expressed in the literary form of the dialog, very much like Bruno did.

In Galileo's magisterial *Dialogue Concerning the Two Chief World Systems*, his key argument for the diurnal rotation of the earth relies on proving that bodies in motion together will be indistinguishable from bodies at rest.

> *It is obvious, then, that motion which is common to many moving things is idle and inconsequential to the relation of these movables among themselves, nothing being changed among them, and that it is operative only in the relation that they have with other bodies lacking that motion, among which their location is changed. Now, having divided the universe into two parts, one of*

which is necessarily movable and the other motionless, it is the
same thing to make the earth alone move, and to move all the rest
of the universe, so far as concerns any result which may depend
upon such movement.

Galileo's insight into the nature of motion was not merely the epiphany of everyday experience that brushed away the fog of scholastic dogma; it was a logical consequence of a long history of engagements with an intellectual tradition that encompassed a multitude of forms of knowledge. That force is not required for an object to stay in motion goes hand in hand with the realization that motion and rest are not absolute terms, but can only be defined relative to what would later be called inertial frames. And this realization owes as much to a literary, philosophical and theological inquiry as it does to pure observation.

Professor Rosenberg uses his brief history of science to ground the argument that neuroscience threatens the humanities, and the only thing that can save them is a neurophilosophy that reconciles brain processes and interpretation. "If this project doesn't work out," he writes, "science will have to face plan B: treating the humanities the way we treat the arts, indispensable parts of human experience but not to be mistaken for contributions to knowledge."

But if this is true, should we not then ask what neuroscience could possibly contribute to the very debate we are engaged in at this moment? What would we learn about the truth-value of Professor Rosenberg's claims or mine if we had even the very best neurological data at our disposal? That our respective pleasure centers light up as we each strike blows for our preferred position? That might well be of interest, but it hardly bears on the issue at hand: namely, the evaluation of evidence—historical or experimental—underlying a claim about knowledge. That evaluation must be interpretative. The only way to dispense with interpretation is to dispense with evidence, and with it knowledge altogether.

If I am right, then Professor Rosenberg's view is wrong, and all the neuroscience in the world won't change that.

Is Neuroscience the Death of Free Will?

—Eddy Nahmias

Is FREE WILL AN ILLUSION? SOME LEADING SCIENTISTS THINK SO. For instance, in 2002 the psychologist Daniel Wegner wrote, "It seems we are agents. It seems we cause what we do. . . . It is sobering and ultimately accurate to call all this an illusion." More recently, the neuroscientist Patrick Haggard declared, "We certainly don't have free will. Not in the sense we think." And in June, the neuroscientist Sam Harris claimed, "You seem to be an agent acting of your own free will. The problem, however, is that this point of view cannot be reconciled with what we know about the human brain."

Such proclamations make the news; after all, if free will is dead, then moral and legal responsibility may be close behind. As the legal analyst Jeffrey Rosen wrote in *The New York Times Magazine*, "Since all behavior is caused by our brains, wouldn't this mean all behavior could potentially be excused? . . . The death of free will, or its exposure as a convenient illusion, some worry, could wreak havoc on our sense of moral and legal responsibility."

Indeed, free will matters in part because it is a precondition for deserving blame for bad acts and deserving credit for achievements. It also turns out that simply exposing people to scientific claims that free will is an illusion can lead them to misbehave—for instance, cheating more or helping other less. So, it matters whether these scientists are justified in concluding that free will is an illusion.

Here, I'll explain why neuroscience is not the death of free will and does not "wreak havoc on our sense of moral and legal responsibility," extending a discussion begun in Gary Gutting's recent Stone column. I'll argue that the neuroscientific evidence does not undermine free will. But first, I'll explain the central problem: these scientists are employing a flawed notion of free will. Once a better notion of free will is in place, the argument can be turned on its head. Instead of showing that free will is an illusion, neuroscience and psychology can actually help us understand how it works.

When Haggard concludes that we do not have free will "in the sense we think," he reveals how this conclusion depends on a particular definition of free will. Scientists' arguments that free will is an illusion typically begin by assuming that free will, by definition, requires an immaterial soul or nonphysical mind, and they take neuroscience to provide evidence that our minds are physical. Haggard mentions free will "in the spiritual sense . . . a ghost in the machine." The neuroscientist Read Montague defines free will as "the idea that we make choices and have thoughts independent of anything remotely resembling a physical process, Free will is the close cousin to the idea of the soul." They use a definition of free will that they take to be demanded by ordinary thinking and philosophical theory. But they are mistaken on both counts.

We should be wary of defining things out of existence. Define Earth as the planet at the center of the universe and it turns out there is no Earth. Define what's moral as whatever your God mandates and suddenly most people become immoral. Define marriage as a union only for procreation, and you thereby annul many marriages.

The sciences of the mind do give us good reasons to think that our minds are made of matter. But to conclude that consciousness or free will is thereby an illusion is too quick. It is like inferring from discoveries in organic chemistry that life is an illusion just because living organisms are made up of nonliving stuff. Much of the progress in science comes precisely from understanding wholes in terms of their parts, without this suggesting the disappearance of the wholes. There's no reason to define the mind or free will in a way that begins by cutting off this possibility for progress.

Our brains are the most complexly organized things in the known universe, just the sort of thing that could eventually make sense of why each of us is unique, why we are conscious creatures, and why humans have abilities to comprehend, converse and create that go well beyond the precursors of these abilities in other animals. Neuroscientific discoveries over the next century will uncover how consciousness and thinking work the way they do *because* our complex brains work the way they do.

These discoveries about how our brains work can also explain how free will works rather than explaining it *away*. But first, we need to define free will in a more reasonable and useful way. Many philosophers, including me, understand free will as a set of capacities for imagining future courses of action, deliberating about one's reasons for choosing them, planning one's actions in light of this deliberation and controlling actions in the face of competing desires. We act of our own free will to the extent that we have the opportunity to exercise these capacities, without unreasonable external or internal pressure. We are responsible for our actions roughly to the extent that we possess these capacities and we have opportunities to exercise them.

These capacities for conscious deliberation, rational thinking and self-control are not magical abilities. They need not belong to immaterial souls outside the realm of scientific understanding (indeed, since we don't know how souls are supposed to work, souls would not help to explain these capacities). Rather, these are the sorts of cognitive capacities that psychologists and neuroscientists are well positioned to study.

This conception of free will represents a long-standing and dominant view in philosophy, though it is typically ignored by scientists who conclude that free will is an illusion. It also turns out that most nonphilosophers have intuitions about free and responsible action that track this conception of free will. Researchers in the new field of experimental philosophy study what "the folk" think about philosophical issues and why. For instance, my collaborators and I have found that most people think that free will and responsibility are compatible with *determinism*, the thesis that all events are part of a lawlike chain of events such that earlier events necessitate later events. That is, most people judge that you can have free will and be responsible for your actions even if all of your decisions and actions are entirely caused by earlier events in accord with natural laws.

Our studies suggest that people sometimes *misunderstand* determinism to mean that we are somehow cut out of this causal chain leading to our actions. People are threatened by a possibility I call "bypassing"—the idea that our actions are caused in ways that bypass our conscious deliberations and decisions. So, if people mistakenly take causal determinism to mean that everything that happens is inevitable *no matter what* you think or try to do, then they conclude that we have no free will. Or if determinism is presented in a way that suggests all our decisions are just chemical reactions, they take that to mean that our conscious thinking is bypassed in such a way that we lack free will.

Even if neuroscience and psychology were in a position to establish the truth of determinism—a job better left for physics—this would not establish bypassing. As long as people understand that discoveries about how our brains work do not mean that what we think or try to do makes no difference to what happens, then their belief in free will is preserved. What matters to people is that we have the capacities for conscious deliberation and self-control that I've suggested we identify with free will.

But what about neuroscientific evidence that seems to suggest that these capacities *are* cut out of the causal chains leading to our decisions and actions? For instance, doesn't neuroscience show that our brains make decisions before we are conscious of them such that our conscious decisions are bypassed? With these questions, we can move past the debates about whether free will requires souls or indeterminism—debates that neuroscience does not settle—and examine actual neuroscientific evidence. Consider, for instance, research by neuroscientists suggesting that nonconscious processes in our brain cause our actions, while conscious awareness of what we are doing occurs later, too late to influence our behavior. Some interpret this research as showing that consciousness is merely an observer of the output of nonconscious mechanisms. Extending the paradigm developed by Benjamin Libet, John-Dylan Haynes and his collaborators used fMRI research to find patterns of neural activity in people's brains that correlated with their decision to press either a right or left button up to seven seconds before they were aware of deciding which button to press. Haynes concludes, "How can I call a will 'mine' if I don't even know when it occurred and what it has decided to do?"

However, the existing evidence does not support the conclusion that free will is an illusion. First of all, it does not show that a *decision* has been made before people are aware of having made it. It simply finds discernible patterns of neural activity that precede decisions. If we assume that conscious decisions have neural correlates, then we should expect to find early signs of those correlates "ramping up" to the moment of consciousness. It would be miraculous if the brain did nothing at all until the moment when people became aware of a decision to move. These experiments all involve quick, repetitive decisions, and people are told not to plan their decisions but just to wait for an urge to come upon them. The early neural activity measured in the experiments likely represents these urges or other preparations for movement that precede conscious awareness.

This is what we should expect with simple decisions. Indeed, we are lucky that conscious thinking plays little or no role in quick or habitual decisions and actions. If we had to consciously consider our every move, we'd be bumbling fools. We'd be like perpetual beginners at tennis, overthinking every stroke. We'd be unable to speak fluently, much less dance or drive. Often we initially attend consciously to what we are doing precisely to reach the point where we act without consciously attending to the component decisions and actions in our complex endeavors. When we type, tango, or talk, we don't want conscious thinking to precede every move we make, though we do want to be aware of what we're doing and correct any mistakes we're making. Conscious attention is relatively slow and effortful. We must use it wisely.

We need conscious deliberation to make a difference when it matters—when we have important decisions and plans to make. The evidence from neuroscience and psychology has not shown that consciousness doesn't matter in those sorts of decisions—in fact, some evidence suggests the opposite. We should not begin by assuming that free will requires a conscious self that exists beyond the brain (where?), and then conclude that *any* evidence that shows brain processes precede action thereby demonstrates that consciousness is bypassed. Rather, we should consider the role of consciousness in action on the assumption that our conscious deliberation and rational thinking are carried out by complex brain processes, and then we can examine whether those very brain processes play a causal role in action.

For example, suppose I am trying to decide whether to give $1,000 to charity or buy a new TV. I consciously consider the reasons for each choice (e.g., how it fits with my goals and values). I gather information about each option. Perhaps I struggle to overcome my more selfish motivations. I decide based on this conscious reasoning (it certainly would not help if I could magically decide on *no* basis at all), and I act accordingly. Now, let's suppose each part of this process is carried out by processes in my brain. If so, then to show that consciousness is bypassed would require evidence showing that those very brain processes underlying my conscious reasoning are dead ends. It would have to show that those brain processes do not connect up with the processes that lead to my typing my credit card number into the Best Buy website (I may then regret my selfish decision and reevaluate my reasons for my future decisions).

None of the evidence marshaled by neuroscientists and psychologists suggests that those neural processes involved in the conscious aspects of such complex, temporally extended decision making are in fact causal dead ends. It would be almost unbelievable if such evidence turned up. It would mean that whatever processes in the brain are involved in conscious deliberation and self-control—and the substantial energy these processes use—were as useless as our appendix, that they evolved only to observe what we do after the fact, rather than to improve our decision making and behavior. No doubt these conscious brain processes move too slowly to be involved in each finger flex as I type, but as long as they play their part in what I do down the road—such as considering what ideas to type up—then my conscious self is not a dead end, and it is a mistake to say my free will is bypassed by what my brain does.

So, does neuroscience mean the death of free will? Well, it could if it somehow demonstrated that conscious deliberation and rational self-control did not really exist or that they worked in a sheltered corner of the brain that has no influence on our actions. But neither of these possibilities is likely. True, the mind sciences will continue to show that consciousness does not work in just the ways we thought, and they already suggest significant limitations on the extent of our rationality, self-knowledge, and self-control. Such discoveries suggest that most of us possess *less* free will than we tend to think, and they may inform debates about our degrees of responsibility. But they do not show that free will is an illusion.

If we put aside the misleading idea that free will depends on supernatural souls rather than our quite miraculous brains, and if we put aside the mistaken idea that our conscious thinking matters most in the milliseconds before movement, then neuroscience does not kill free will. Rather, it can help to explain our capacities to control our actions in such a way that we are responsible for them. It can help us rediscover free will.

NOVEMBER 13, 2011

Is the "Dumb Jock" Really a Nerd?

—Jason Stanley and John W. Krakauer

IN THE FREQUENT DEBATES OVER THE MERITS OF SCIENCE AND philosophy, or the humanities in general, it is often assumed that the factual grounding and systematic methodology of the sciences serve as a corrective to the less rigorous wanderings of the humanities. And while many take the position that the humanities can provide their own important path to enlightenment, few argue that considerations from philosophy can or should correct the considered judgment of scientists. Even most defenders of the humanities hold that the sciences are directed at truth, whereas the humanities have an alternate goal, perhaps the molding of ideal citizens.

We believe that in the enterprise of uncovering truth, the paths of the scientist and the humanist must often intersect. Rather than argue in generalities, we will develop a specific example, though we assume that there are many others like it.

The example concerns the seminal case study of Henry Molaison—known to the public as H. M.—a patient with severe epilepsy. H. M. was treated with a bilateral temporal lobectomy. Afterward, he was left unable to form lasting memories from short-term memories. He would generally forget events within thirty seconds after they occurred.

In a groundbreaking experiment published in 1962, the psychologist Brenda Milner had H. M. perform a mirror-drawing task. The task required H. M. to trace the outline of a star with a pencil, using a mirror to guide him, with vision of his arm obscured. Over the course of three days, H. M. improved his performance of this task, even though he had no explicit memory of having encountered it on previous days. This is an admittedly fascinating and important result. But what exactly is its significance?

The standard interpretation is that H. M. was able to *acquire and improve motor skills*, even though he could not retain *knowledge of facts*. As a recent newspaper article explains in the context of an interview with the distinguished neuroscientist Suzanne Corkin,

> *Henry was not capable of learning new information, though his knowledge of past events—the Wall Street Crash, Pearl Harbor and so on—was clear. Only a very few tiny details of TV programmes he watched repetitively ever stuck. He could, however, learn and retain new motor skills, which led to important understanding of the difference between conscious memory and unconscious. The latter category would include learning how to play tennis or ride a bicycle, or even play the piano—things that the brain encodes and transmits to the muscles through conditioning, memories which we come to think of as intuitive.*

According to this article, H. M. was able to "learn and retain new motor skills" (and even improve). Examples of such learning are "how to play tennis or ride a bicycle." H. M. is therefore taken to show that motor skills, a paradigm example of which is *tennis*, are not the employment of knowledge.

In a recent paper, we argue that the case of H. M. has been misinterpreted. First, there are mistaken assumptions about the nature of knowledge and the nature of skill. Secondly, the importation of a merely cultural dichotomy between practical and theoretical pursuits has distorted the interpretation of experiments about motor skill. Neuroscience has not vindicated the cultural distinction between practical and theoretical activities. Rather, fueled by misconceptions about knowledge and skill, a merely cultural distinction has skewed the interpretation of scientific results.

A clue to the misinterpretation of the significance of H. M. lies in a 2010 paper by Shumita Roy and N. W. Park, in the journal *Neuropsychologia*. Roy and Park introduced several patients with the same amnestic condition as H. M. to novel tools. They discovered that the patients could not learn how to use the tools over days. The patients could not remember how the tool worked. They were able to exhibit improvements in execution similar to the improvement H. M. showed in mirror learning, but only after they were instructed what to do each day. Roy and Park conclude that tool use is not a motor skill, since it requires remembering facts.

What is of interest is that they favor this conclusion over the obvious alternative—that motor skill, like any other cognitive task, requires knowledge. Perhaps patients with H. M.'s condition can acquire one part of what is required for skill, but not other parts. If so, then neuroscientists have made an overly hasty identification of a noncognitive component of motor skill with the category of motor skill itself. This identification overlooks the knowledge component of anything that common sense classifies as a motor skill, like tennis. Indeed, we would predict that just as with the tools of Roy and Park, H. M. would never have been able to learn how to play a tennis match (assuming he had never encountered the game before his surgery).

Roy and Park's conclusion that even tool use is not a motor skill should ring alarm bells about whether the concept of a skill is what is at issue in these discussions. Martin Heidegger uses the example of hammering with a hammer as a paradigm example of a motor skill. Philosophers from Aristotle to Gilbert Ryle have held that whether or not to employ a skill is under a person's rational control. But this seems to require knowledge—knowing how, when and with what means to do it. A skilled archer knows what to do to initiate the activity; this is in part why she *can* decide to do that activity. Still, we are not supposed to call LeBron James a "genius" because cultural biases have infected science without the moderating input of the humanities.

Neuroscientists and psychologists have other views that argue that motor skill does not involve knowledge. But these arguments involve false assumptions about knowledge.

We discuss and reject one such assumption, that a person must be capable of *verbally explaining* her knowledge. A second false assumption is that anyone who acts on knowledge must be *considering* that knowledge while acting upon it; for example, that the center fielder must be actively thinking about how to field the ball if he is acting on knowledge. A third false assumption is that anyone who knows something must *be aware* of knowing it (the following tempting argument appeals to this third assumption: it is possible to forget that one knows how to ride a bicycle, yet still retain the skill of riding a bicycle. Therefore, skill at bicycle riding does not involve knowledge). All of these assumptions have been widely rejected by philosophers who have recently considered them.

It turns out that H. M., too, had to be reinstructed in certain details—how to hold his hand, the correct placement of the mirror and other aspects of the task. He was not able to acquire a skill. One *facet* of skill improved, but this does not mean that he acquired the skill. One way to improve motor skill is by acquiring knowledge. For any given skill, it's an open question as to how much knowledge is needed to acquire it and improve significantly. Skilled football players and cabinetmakers possess a large amount of complex knowledge about these activities, which accumulates over time and contributes to success. That someone can master such a complex knowledge base for these "practical" skills suggests that they could also be successful at activities that are considered more intellectual.

The significance of many scientific results is conveyed in the vocabulary of the humanities. In the case of H. M., these terms are *skill* and *knowledge*. Gary Gutting has argued in The Stone that scientific significance should be assessed in tandem with those who are familiar with the history and role of the relevant concepts—often humanists. We have argued that he is right. It is not possible to separate humanists and nonhumanists in the successful pursuit of truth, even if they employ different methodologies.

Constructing an argument in mathematics or history is one kind of human activity. Football and cabinetmaking are others. We argue that skilled human activity generally requires the acquisition and manipulation of knowledge, as well as implicit processes that do not depend on propositional knowledge (for example, increased dexterity). It is hard, and perhaps not possible, to forge a theoretically significant distinction between working with one's hands and working with one's mind.

OCTOBER 27, 2013

THE SOCIAL IMPACT OF SCIENCE

Learning How to Die in the Anthropocene

—Roy Scranton

I.

Driving into Iraq just after the 2003 invasion felt like driving into the future. We convoyed all day, all night, past army checkpoints and burned-out tanks, till in the blue dawn Baghdad rose from the desert like a vision of hell: flames licked the bruised sky from the tops of refinery towers, cyclopean monuments bulged and leaned against the horizon, broken overpasses swooped and fell over ruined suburbs, bombed factories, and narrow ancient streets.

With "shock and awe," our military had unleashed the end of the world on a city of six million—a city about the same size as Houston or Washington. The infrastructure was totaled: water, power, traffic, markets and security fell to anarchy and local rule. The city's secular middle class was disappearing, squeezed out between gangsters, profiteers, fundamentalists and soldiers. The government was going down, walls were going up, tribal lines were being drawn, and brutal hierarchies were being savagely established.

I was a private in the United States Army. This strange, precarious world was my new home. If I survived.

Two and a half years later, safe and lazy back in Fort Sill, OK, I thought I had made it out. Then I watched on television as Hurricane

Katrina hit New Orleans. This time it was the weather that brought shock and awe, but I saw the same chaos and urban collapse I'd seen in Baghdad, the same failure of planning and the same tide of anarchy. The 82nd Airborne hit the ground, took over strategic points and patrolled streets now under de facto martial law. My unit was put on alert to prepare for riot-control operations. The grim future I'd seen in Baghdad was coming home: not terrorism, not even WMDs, but a civilization in collapse, with a crippled infrastructure, unable to recuperate from shocks to its system.

And today, with recovery still going on more than a year after Sandy and many critics arguing that the Eastern Seaboard is no more prepared for a huge weather event than we were last November, it's clear that future's not going away.

This March, Admiral Samuel J. Locklear III, the commander of the United States Pacific Command, told security and foreign policy specialists in Cambridge, MA, that global climate change was the greatest threat the United States faced—more dangerous than terrorism, Chinese hackers, and North Korean nuclear missiles. Upheaval from increased temperatures, rising seas and radical destabilization "is probably the most likely thing that is going to happen," he said, ". . . that will cripple the security environment, probably more likely than the other scenarios we all often talk about."

Locklear's not alone. Tom Donilon, the national security adviser, said much the same thing in April, speaking to an audience at Columbia's new Center on Global Energy Policy. James Clapper, director of national intelligence, told the Senate in March that "extreme weather events (floods, droughts, heat waves) will increasingly disrupt food and energy markets, exacerbating state weakness, forcing human migrations, and triggering riots, civil disobedience, and vandalism."

On the civilian side, the World Bank's recent report, "Turn Down the Heat: Climate Extremes, Regional Impacts, and the Case for Resilience," offers a dire prognosis for the effects of global warming, which climatologists now predict will raise global temperatures by 3.6 degrees Fahrenheit within a generation and 7.2 degrees Fahrenheit within ninety years. Projections from researchers at the University of Hawaii find us dealing with "historically unprecedented" climates as soon as 2047. The climate scientist James Hansen, formerly with NASA, has argued that we face an "apocalyptic" future. This grim view is seconded by researchers worldwide, including Anders Levermann, Paul and Anne Ehrlich, Lonnie Thompson and many, many, many others.

This chorus of Jeremiahs predicts a radically transformed global climate forcing widespread upheaval—not possibly, not potentially, but *inevitably*. We have passed the point of no return. From the point of view of policy experts, climate scientists and national security officials, the question is no longer whether global warming exists or how we might stop it, but how we are going to deal with it.

II.

There's a word for this new era we live in: the Anthropocene. This term, taken up by geologists, pondered by intellectuals and discussed in the pages of publications such as the *Economist* and *The New York Times*, represents the idea that we have entered a new epoch in Earth's geological history, one characterized by the arrival of the human species as a geological force. The biologist Eugene F. Stoermer and the Nobel-Prize—winning chemist Paul Crutzen advanced the term in 2000, and it has steadily gained acceptance as evidence has increasingly mounted that the changes wrought by global warming will affect not just the world's climate and biological diversity, but its very geology—and not just for a few centuries, but for millenniums. The geophysicist David Archer's 2009 book, *The Long Thaw: How Humans Are Changing the Next 100,000 Years of Earth's Climate*, lays out a clear and concise argument for how huge concentrations of carbon dioxide in the atmosphere and melting ice will radically transform the planet, beyond freak storms and warmer summers, beyond any foreseeable future.

The Stratigraphy Commission of the Geological Society of London—the scientists responsible for pinning the "golden spikes" that demarcate geological epochs such as the Pliocene, Pleistocene, and Holocene—has adopted the Anthropocene as a term deserving further consideration, "significant on the scale of Earth history." Working groups are discussing what level of geological timescale it might be (an "epoch" like the Holocene, or merely an "age" like the Calabrian), and at what date we might say it began. The beginning of the Great Acceleration, in the middle of the twentieth century? The beginning of the Industrial Revolution, around 1800? The advent of agriculture?

The challenge the Anthropocene poses is a challenge not just to national security, to food and energy markets, or to our "way of life"—though these challenges are all real, profound, and inescapable. The greatest challenge the Anthropocene poses may be to our sense of what it means to be human. Within one hundred years— within three to five generations—we will face average temperatures seven degrees Fahrenheit higher than today, rising seas at least three to ten feet higher, and worldwide shifts in crop belts, growing seasons and population centers. Within a thousand years, unless we stop emitting greenhouse gases wholesale right now, humans will be living in a climate the Earth hasn't seen since the Pliocene, three million years ago, when oceans were seventy-five *feet* higher than they are today. We face the imminent collapse of the agricultural, shipping and energy networks upon which the global economy depends, a large-scale die-off in the biosphere that's already well on its way, and our own possible extinction. If *Homo sapiens* (or some genetically modified variant) survive the next millenniums, it will be survival in a world unrecognizably different from the one we have inhabited.

Geological timescales, civilization collapse and species extinction give rise to profound problems that humanities scholars and academic philosophers, with their taste for fine-grained analysis, esoteric debates and archival marginalia, might seem remarkably ill suited to address. After all, how will thinking about Kant help us trap carbon dioxide? Can arguments between object-oriented ontology and historical materialism protect honeybees from colony collapse disorder? Are ancient Greek philosophers, medieval theologians, and contemporary metaphysicians going to keep Bangladesh from being inundated by rising oceans?

Of course not. But the biggest problems the Anthropocene poses are precisely those that have always been at the root of humanistic and philosophical questioning: What does it mean to be human? and What does it mean to live? In the epoch of the Anthropocene, the question of individual mortality—What does *my life* mean in the face of death?—is universalized and framed in scales that boggle the imagination. What does human existence mean against 100,000 years of climate change? What does one life mean in the face of species death or the collapse of global civilization? How do we make meaningful choices in the shadow of our inevitable end?

These questions have no logical or empirical answers. They are philosophical problems *par excellence*. Many thinkers, including Cicero, Montaigne, Karl Jaspers, and The Stone's own Simon Critchley, have argued that studying philosophy is learning how to die. If that's true, then we have entered humanity's most philosophical age—for this is precisely the problem of the Anthropocene. The rub is that now we have to learn how to die not as individuals, but as a civilization.

III.

Learning how to die isn't easy. In Iraq, at the beginning, I was terrified by the idea. Baghdad seemed incredibly dangerous, even though statistically I was pretty safe. We got shot at and mortared, and IEDs laced every highway, but I had good armor, we had a great medic, and we were part of the most powerful military the world had ever seen. The odds were good I would come home. Maybe wounded, but probably alive. Every day I went out on mission, though, I looked down the barrel of the future and saw a dark, empty hole.

"For the soldier death is the future, the future his profession assigns him," wrote Simone Weil in her remarkable meditation on war, *The* Iliad *or the Poem of Force*. "Yet the idea of man's having death for a future is abhorrent to nature. Once the experience of war makes visible the possibility of death that lies locked up in each moment, our thoughts cannot travel from one day to the next without meeting death's face." That was the face I saw in the mirror, and its gaze nearly paralyzed me.

I found my way forward through an eighteenth-century samurai manual, Yamamoto Tsunetomo's *Hagakure*, which commanded, "Meditation on inevitable death should be performed daily." Instead of fearing my end, I owned it. Every morning, after doing maintenance on my Humvee, I'd imagine getting blown up by an IED, shot by a sniper, burned to death, run over by a tank, torn apart by dogs, captured and beheaded, and succumbing to dysentery. Then, before we rolled out through the gate, I'd tell myself that I didn't need to worry, because I was already dead. The only thing that mattered was that I did my best to make sure everyone else came back alive. "If by setting one's heart right every morning and evening, one is able to live as though his body were already dead," wrote Tsunetomo, "he gains freedom in the Way."

I got through my tour in Iraq one day at a time, meditating each morning on my inevitable end. When I left Iraq and came back Stateside, I thought I'd left that future behind. Then I saw it come home in the chaos that was unleashed after Katrina hit New Orleans. And then I saw it again when Sandy battered New York and New Jersey: government agencies failed to move quickly enough, and volunteer groups like Team Rubicon had to step in to manage disaster relief.

Now, when I look into our future—into the Anthropocene—I see water rising up to wash out Lower Manhattan. I see food riots, hurricanes, and climate refugees. I see 82nd Airborne soldiers shooting looters. I see grid failure, wrecked harbors, Fukushima waste, and plagues. I see Baghdad. I see the Rockaways. I see a strange, precarious world.

Our new home.

The human psyche naturally rebels against the idea of its end. Likewise, civilizations have throughout history marched blindly toward disaster, because humans are wired to believe that tomorrow will be much like today—it is unnatural for us to think that this way of life, this present moment, this order of things is not stable and permanent. Across the world today, our actions testify to our belief that we can go on like this forever, burning oil, poisoning the seas, killing off other species, pumping carbon into the air, ignoring the ominous silence of our coal mine canaries in favor of the unending robotic tweets of our new digital imaginarium. Yet the reality of global climate change is going to keep intruding on our fantasies of perpetual growth, permanent innovation and endless energy, just as the reality of mortality shocks our casual faith in permanence.

The biggest problem climate change poses isn't how the Department of Defense should plan for resource wars, or how we should put up seawalls to protect Alphabet City, or when we should evacuate Hoboken. It won't be addressed by buying a Prius, signing a treaty, or turning off the air-conditioning. The biggest problem we face is a philosophical one: understanding that this civilization is *already dead*. The sooner we confront this problem, and the sooner we realize there's nothing we can do to save ourselves, the sooner we can get down to the hard work of adapting, with mortal humility, to our new reality.

The choice is a clear one. We can continue acting as if tomorrow will be just like yesterday, growing less and less prepared for each new disaster as it comes, and more and more desperately invested in a life we can't sustain. Or we can learn to see each day as the death of what came before, freeing ourselves to deal with whatever problems the present offers without attachment or fear.

If we want to learn to live in the Anthropocene, we must first learn how to die.

NOVEMBER 10, 2013

Can Neuroscience Challenge *Roe v. Wade?*

—William Egginton

W̶HEN I WAS ASKED THIS SUMMER TO SERVE AS AN EXPERT WIT-
ness in an appellate case that some think could lead to the next
Supreme Court test of Roe v. Wade, I was surprised.

Rick Hearn is the attorney representing Jennie McCormack, an
Idaho woman who was arrested for allegedly inducing her own abortion using mifepristone and misoprostol—two FDA-approved drugs,
also known as RU-486—and for obtaining the drugs from another
state over the Internet. While the case against Ms. McCormack has
been dropped for lack of evidence, Mr. Hearn, who is also a doctor,
is pursuing a related suit against an Idaho statute, the Pain-Capable
Unborn Child Protection Act (*Idaho Code*, section 18–501 through
18–510), and others like it that cite neuroscientific findings of pain
sentience on the part of fetuses as a basis for prohibiting abortions
even prior to viability.

The authors of a 2005 review of clinical research in the *Journal of
the American Medical Association* have written, "Evidence regarding
the capacity for fetal pain is limited but indicates that fetal perception of pain is unlikely before the third trimester." Still, not surprisingly, opinions on whether and when fetal sensitivity to pain may
develop vary widely.

So why not call an actual neuroscientist as an expert witness
instead of a scholar of the humanities?

As Mr. Hearn explained, his suit challenges the government's use of results from the natural sciences, including neuroscience, as a basis for expanding or contracting the rights of its citizens. In this case, neuroscience is being used to expand the rights of fetuses by contracting the rights of women to choose whether to continue or terminate their pregnancies. In other words, a biological fact about women is being used by the state to force women to accept one societal role rather than another. Mr. Hearn approached me because of arguments I have made, including here in The Stone, that criticize the hubris of scientific claims to knowledge that exceeds the boundaries of what the sciences in fact demonstrate.

The turn to legislation based on alleged neuroscientific findings in search of an end run around the protections provided by *Roe v. Wade* is popular among Republicans. Mitt Romney voiced his strong support for such legislation in 2011, when he wrote in a piece in *National Review*, "I will advocate for and support a Pain-Capable Unborn Child Protection Act to protect unborn children who are capable of feeling pain from abortion." Since viability is, according to *Roe v. Wade*, the point at which the state's interest in protecting "the potentiality of human life" becomes compelling enough to override its interest in protecting the right of a woman to make decisions regarding her body and its reproductive organs, Idaho's statute and others like it would either be found unconstitutional or, if upheld, entail overturning a fundamental aspect of *Roe v. Wade.*

For neuroscientific findings of fetal pain to serve as basis for permitting states to prohibit abortion prior to viability, they must tell us something about the nature of a fetus that makes the state's interest in protecting it more compelling than its interest in protecting a woman's right to make basic decisions about her own body. As pain sentience does not serve as a basis for legal prohibitions in general (or else mousetraps and deer hunting would be prohibited), the statutes' real purpose is to use potential evidence of pain sentience in fetuses to indicate the presence of something far more compelling—namely, personhood.

Those wishing to abolish abortion believe that "the fetus is a 'person' within the language and meaning of the Fourteenth Amendment." If, as Justice Harry A. Blackmun continues in his opinion in 1973, "this suggestion of personhood is established, the appellant's case, of course, collapses, for the fetus' right to life would then be guaranteed specifically by the Amendment." If a fetus is a person, in other words, then it is not a potential human life at all, but is a fully human life deserving of full legal protection, and abortion must be murder and punishable as such. The intent of current fetal pain statutes is, clearly, to infer from the ability to feel pain on the part of a human fetus—if it can be established by neuroscience—a claim for actual human life or full personhood.

The implicit vehicle for this inference is the concept of consciousness. Nebraska's Pain-Capable Unborn Child Protection Act, passed in 2010, for instance, not only refers to "ability to feel pain," it also characterizes the unborn child as "having the physical structures necessary to experience pain," and claims that the evidence shows that "unborn children seek to evade certain stimuli." It is obvious from the terms *experience* and *seek* that the statute's implicit understanding of the ability to feel pain is that "feeling" refers not merely to what neuroscientists call the nociceptive capacity of an organism—the ability of its nervous system to detect and respond to potentially noxious stimuli—but to conscious awareness of the presence of such stimuli.

Current neuroscience distinguishes a spectrum of degrees of "consciousness" among organisms, ranging from basic perception of external stimuli to fully developed self-consciousness. Even the idea of self is subject to further differentiation. The neuroscientist Antonio Damasio, for instance, distinguishes degrees of consciousness in terms of the kind of "self" wielding it: while nonhuman animals may exhibit the levels he calls proto-self and core self, both necessary for conscious experience, he considers the autobiographical self, which provides the foundations of personal identity, to be an attribute largely limited to humans.

This more robust concept of consciousness that distinguishes human personhood from more basic forms of perception has a very specific history, which dates to the early seventeenth century and is most associated with the French philosopher René Descartes and the school of thinkers that followed him. While Descartes considered whether a neonate or even young children might have consciousness of this kind, in the end he rejected this hypothesis, insisting on the "reflective" nature of consciousness. As he writes in a letter responding to some objections voiced by Antoine Aranauld, "I call the first and simple thoughts of children, that come to them as, for example, they feel the pain caused when some gas enclosed in their intestines distends them, or the pleasure caused by the sweetness of the food that nourishes them. . . . I call these direct and not reflexive thoughts; but when the young man feels something new and at the same time perceives that he has not felt the same thing before, I call this second perception a reflection, and I relate it only to the understanding, insofar as it is so attached to sensation that the two cannot be distinguished."

Consciousness, in other words, presents a much higher, and much harder-to-establish, standard than mere potentiality of life. Therefore, implicit recourse to the concept fails as a basis for replacing viability as the line dividing the permissibility of abortion from its prohibition. For a fetus to be conscious in a sense that would establish it as a fully actualized human life, according both to current neuroscientific standards and to the philosophical tradition from which the concept stems, it would have to be capable of self-perception as well as simple perception of stimuli. And as philosophers of many stripes since Descartes have argued, self-perception is a reflexive state involving a concept of self in contrast with that of others—concepts it would be hard to imagine being meaningful for a fetus, even if fetuses could be shown to have access to concepts in the first place. By turning to consciousness in an attempt to push Roe's line in the sand back toward conception, in other words, abortion opponents would in effect be pushing it forward, toward the sort of self-differentiation that only occurs well after birth and the emergence of what the phenomenological tradition has called "world."

More than two hundred years ago the German philosopher Immanuel Kant argued in his *Critique of Pure Reason* that, while science can tell us much about the world we live in, it can tell us nothing about the existence of God, the immortality of the soul, or the origin of human freedom; moreover, he demonstrated with exquisite precision that should it try to come to conclusions about these questions, it would necessarily fall into error.

This is the same sort of error committed by the polemicist Sam Harris in his recent argument against the existence of free will. In his book he cites advances in the neurosciences showing, for example, that computers attached to sensors can "read" test subjects' decisions some three hundred milliseconds before the subjects report being aware of them. While he draws grand conclusions from such experiments regarding the nonexistence of free will and how we should organize and think about law and ethics, most reasonable people's response will inevitably be similar to that of Diogenes the cynic who, when faced with Zeno of Elea's watertight proof of the impossibility of motion, simply got up and walked.

Likewise, while neuroscience may or may not be able to tell us something about the development of fetal nociceptive capacity, it has nothing to say about the fundamental question of what counts as a full-fledged person deserving of the rights afforded by a society. Science can no more decide that question than it can determine the existence or nonexistence of God. Indeed, I doubt that members of the Idaho State Legislature would approve of using scientific evidence of the nonexistence of God to write a law depriving citizens of the right to worship as they choose; in the same way, they should avoid turning to neuroscience for evidence concerning the limits of personhood.

The brain sciences, like all branches of the natural sciences, are immeasurably useful tools for individuals and communities to deploy (one hopes) for the improvement of our understanding of the natural world and the betterment of society. The basic rights guaranteed by the Constitution, however, have nothing at all to do with the truths of science. They are, to use Karl Popper's terminology, nonfalsifiable, like religious beliefs or statements about the immortality of the soul; to use Thomas Jefferson's word, they are inalienable. Like the equality of its citizens, in other words, the basic liberties of Americans should not be dependent on the changing opinions of science.

When science becomes the sole or even primary arbiter of such basic notions as personhood, it ceases to be mankind's most useful servant and threatens, instead, to become its dictator. Science does not and should not have the power to absolve individuals and communities of the responsibility to choose. This emphatically does not mean that science should be left out of such personal and political debates. The more we know about the world the better positioned we are to make the best possible choices. But when science is used to replace thinking instead of complement it, when we claim to see in its results the reduction of all the complexity that constitutes the emergence of a human life or the choices and responsibilities of the person it may develop into, we relinquish something that Kant showed more than two hundred years ago was essential to the very idea of a human being: our freedom.

OCTOBER 28, 2012

Depression and the Limits of Psychiatry

—Gary Gutting

I'VE RECENTLY BEEN FOLLOWING THE CONTROVERSIES ABOUT revisions to the psychiatric definition of depression. I've also been teaching a graduate seminar on Michel Foucault, beginning with a reading of his *History of Madness*. This massive volume tries to discover the origins of modern psychiatric practice and raises questions about its meaning and validity. The debate over depression is an excellent test case for Foucault's critique.

At the center of that critique is Foucault's claim that modern psychiatry, while purporting to be grounded in scientific truths, is primarily a system of moral judgments. "What we call psychiatric practice," he says, "is a certain moral tactic . . . covered over by the myths of positivism." Indeed, what psychiatry presents as the "liberation of the mad" (from mental illness) is in fact a "gigantic moral imprisonment."

Foucault may well be letting his rhetoric outstrip the truth, but his essential point requires serious consideration. Psychiatric practice does seem to be based on implicit moral assumptions in addition to explicit empirical considerations, and efforts to treat mental illness can be society's way of controlling what it views as immoral (or otherwise undesirable) behavior. Not long ago, homosexuals and women who rejected their stereotypical roles were judged "mentally ill," and there's no guarantee that even today psychiatry is free of similarly dubious judgments. Much later, in a more subdued tone, Foucault said that the point of his social critiques was "not that everything is bad but that everything is dangerous." We can best take his critique of psychiatry in this moderated sense.

Current psychiatric practice is guided by the *Diagnostic and Statistical Manual of Mental Disorders (DSM)*. Its new fifth edition makes controversial revisions in the definition of depression, eliminating a long-standing "bereavement exception" in the guidelines for diagnosing a "major depressive disorder." People grieving after the deaths of loved ones may exhibit the same sorts of symptoms (sadness, sleeplessness and loss of interest in daily activities among them) that characterize major depression. For many years, the *DSM* specified that, since grieving is a *normal* response to bereavement, such symptoms are not an adequate basis for diagnosing major depression. The new edition removes this exemption.

Disputes over the bereavement exemption center on the significance of "normal." Although the term sometimes signifies merely what is usual or average, in discussions of mental illness it most often has normative force. Proponents of the exemption need not claim that depressive symptoms are usual in the bereaved, merely that they are appropriate (fitting).

Opponents of the exemption have appealed to empirical studies that compare cases of normal bereavement to cases of major depression. They offer evidence that normal bereavement and major depression can present substantially the same symptoms, and conclude that there is no basis for treating them differently. But this logic is faulty. Even if the symptoms are exactly the same, proponents of the exemption can still argue that they are appropriate for someone mourning a loved one but not otherwise. The suffering may be the same, but suffering from the death of a loved one may still have a value that suffering from other causes does not. No amount of empirical information about the nature and degree of suffering can, by itself, tell us whether someone ought to endure it.

Foucault is, then, right: psychiatric practice makes essential use of moral (and other evaluative) judgments. Why is this dangerous? Because, first of all, psychiatrists as such have no special knowledge about how people should live. They can, from their clinical experience, give us crucial information about the likely psychological consequences of living in various ways (for sexual pleasure, for one's children, for a political cause). But they have no special insight into what sorts of consequences make for a good human life. It is, therefore, dangerous to make them privileged judges of what syndromes should be labeled "mental illnesses."

This is especially so because, like most professionals, psychiatrists are more than ready to think that just about everyone needs their services. (As the psychologist Abraham Maslow said, "If all you have is a hammer, everything looks like a nail.") Another factor is the pressure the pharmaceutical industry puts on psychiatrists to expand the use of psychotropic drugs. The result has been the often criticized "medicalization" of what had previously been accepted as normal behavior—for example, shyness, little boys unable to sit still in school, and milder forms of anxiety.

Of course, for a good number of mental conditions there is almost universal agreement that they are humanly devastating and should receive psychiatric treatment. For these, psychiatrists are good guides to the best methods of diagnosis and treatment. But when there is significant ethical disagreement about treating a given condition, psychiatrists, who are trained as physicians, may often have a purely medical viewpoint that is not especially suited to judging moral issues.

For cases like the bereavement exclusion, the *DSM* should give equal weight to the judgments of those who understand the medical view but who also have a broader perspective. For example, humanistic psychology (in the tradition of Maslow, Carl Rogers, and Rollo May) would view bereavement not so much as a set of symptoms as a way of living in the world, with its meaning varying for different personalities and social contexts. Specialists in medical ethics would complement the heavily empirical focus of psychiatry with the explicitly normative concerns of rigorously developed ethical systems such as utilitarianism, Kantianism and virtue ethics.

Another important part of the mix should come from a new

but rapidly developing field, philosophy of psychiatry, which analyzes the concepts and methodologies of psychiatric practice. Philosophers of psychiatry have raised fundamental objections to the *DSM*'s assumption that a diagnosis can be made solely from clinical descriptions of symptoms, with little or no attention to the underlying causes of the symptoms. Given these objections, dropping the bereavement exception—a rare appeal to the cause of symptoms—is especially problematic.

Finally, we should include those who have experienced severe bereavement, as well as relatives and friends who have lived with their pain. In particular, those who suffer (or have suffered) from bereavement offer an essential first-person perspective. As Foucault might have said, the psyche is too important to be left to the psychiatrists.

FEBRUARY 6, 2013

Why Are States So Red and Blue?

—*Steven Pinker*

REGARDLESS OF WHO WINS THE PRESIDENTIAL ELECTION, WE already know now how most of the electoral map will be colored, which will be close to the way it has been colored for decades. Broadly speaking, the southern and western desert and mountain states will vote for the candidate who endorses an aggressive military, a role for religion in public life, laissez-faire economic policies, private ownership of guns and relaxed conditions for using them, less regulation and taxation, and a valorization of the traditional family. Northeastern and most coastal states will vote for the candidate who is more closely aligned with international cooperation and engagement, secularism and science, gun control, individual freedom in culture and sexuality, and a greater role for the government in protecting the environment and ensuring economic equality.

But why do ideology and geography cluster so predictably? Why, if you know a person's position on gay marriage, can you predict that he or she will want to increase the military budget and decrease the tax rate and is more likely to hail from Wyoming or Georgia than from Minnesota or Vermont? To be sure, some of these affinities may spring from coalitions of convenience. Economic libertarians and Christian evangelicals, united by their common enemy, are strange bedfellows in today's Republican Party, just as the two Georges—the archconservative Wallace and the uberliberal McGovern—found themselves in the same Democratic Party in 1972.

But there may also be coherent mind-sets beneath the diverse opinions that hang together in right-wing and left-wing belief systems. Political philosophers have long known that the ideologies are rooted in different conceptions of human nature—a conflict of visions so fundamental as to align opinions on dozens of issues that would seem to have nothing in common.

Conservative thinkers like the economist Thomas Sowell and the *Times* columnist David Brooks have noted that the political right has a tragic vision of human nature, in which people are permanently limited in morality, knowledge and reason. Human beings are perennially tempted by aggression, which can be prevented only by the deterrence of a strong military, of citizens resolved to defend themselves, and of the prospect of harsh criminal punishment. No central planner is wise or knowledgeable enough to manage an entire economy, which is better left to the invisible hand of the market, in which intelligence is distributed across a network of hundreds of millions of individuals implicitly transmitting information about scarcity and abundance through the prices they negotiate. Humanity is always in danger of backsliding into barbarism, so we should respect customs in sexuality, religion and public propriety, even if no one can articulate their rationale, because they are time-tested work-arounds for our innate shortcomings. The left, in contrast, has a utopian vision, which emphasizes the malleability of human nature, puts customs under the microscope, articulates rational plans for a better society and seeks to implement them through public institutions.

Cognitive scientists have recently enriched this theory with details of how the right-left divide is implemented in people's cognitive and moral intuitions. The linguist George Lakoff suggests that the political right conceives of society as a family ruled by a strict father, whereas the left thinks of it as a family guided by a nurturant parent. The metaphors may be corollaries of the tragic and utopian visions, since different parenting practices are called for depending on whether you think of children as noble savages or as nasty, brutish and short. The psychologist Jonathan Haidt notes that right-ists and leftists invest their moral intuitions in different sets of concerns: conservatives place a premium on deference to authority, conformity to norms, and the purity and sanctity of the body; liberals restrict theirs to fairness, the provision of care and the avoidance of harm. Once again, the difference may flow from the clashing conceptions of human nature. If individuals are inherently flawed, their behavior must be restrained by custom, authority and sacred values. If they are capable of wisdom and reason, they can determine for themselves what is fair, harmful or hurtful.

But while these theories help explain why the seemingly diverse convictions within the right-wing and left-wing mind-sets hang together, they don't explain why they are tied to geography. The historian David Hackett Fischer traces the divide back to the British settlers of colonial America. The North was largely settled by English farmers, the inland South by Scots-Irish herders. Anthropologists have long noted that societies that herd livestock in rugged terrain tend to develop a "culture of honor." Since their wealth has feet and can be stolen in an eyeblink, they are forced to deter rustlers by cultivating a hair-trigger for violent retaliation against any trespass or insult that probes their resolve. Farmers can afford to be less belligerent because it is harder to steal their land out from under them, particularly in territories within the reach of law enforcement. As the settlers moved westward, they took their respective cultures with them. The psychologist Richard Nisbett has shown that Southerners today continue to manifest a culture of honor that legitimizes violent retaliation. It can be seen in their laws (like capital punishment and a stand-your-ground right to self-defense), in their customs (like paddling children in schools and volunteering for military service), even in their physiological reactions to trivial insults.

Admittedly, it's hard to believe that today's Southerners and Westerners carry a cultural memory of sheepherding ancestors. But it may not be the herding profession itself that nurtures a culture of honor so much as living in anarchy. All societies must deal with the dilemma famously pointed out by Hobbes: in the absence of government, people are tempted to attack one another out of greed, fear and vengeance. European societies, over the centuries, solved this problem as their kings imposed law and order on a medieval patchwork of fiefs ravaged by feuding knights. The happy result was a thirty-fivefold reduction in their homicide rate from the Middle Ages to the present. Once the monarchs pacified the people, the people then had to rein in the monarchs, who had been keeping the peace with arbitrary edicts and gruesome public torture-executions. Beginning in the age of reason and the Enlightenment, governments were forced to implement democratic procedures, humanitarian reforms and the protection of human rights.

When the first American settlers fanned out from the coasts and other settled areas, they found themselves in anarchy all over again. The historian David Courtwright has shown that there is considerable truth to the cinematic clichés of the Wild West and the mountainous South of Davy Crockett, Daniel Boone and the Hatfields and McCoys. The nearest sheriff might be ninety miles away, and a man had to defend himself with firearms and a reputation for toughness. In the all-male enclaves of cattle and mining towns, young men besotted with honor and alcohol constantly challenged one another's mettle and responded to these challenges, pushing rates of violence through the roof.

Another cliché of the cowboy movies also had an element of historical truth. As more women moved west, they worked to end the lifestyle of brawling, boozing and whoring they found there, joining forces with the officials in charge of the rowdy settlements. They found a natural ally in the church, with its coed membership, norms of temperance and Sunday morning discipline. By the time the government consolidated its control over the West (and recall that the "closing of the frontier," marking the end of American anarchy, took place just more than a century ago), the norms of self-defense through masculine honor, and the restraint of ruffianism by women and church, had taken root.

But then why, once stable government did arrive, did it not lay claim to the monopoly on violence that is the very definition of government? The historian Pieter Spierenburg has suggested that "democracy came too soon to America"—namely, before the government had disarmed its citizens. Since American governance was more or less democratic from the start, the people could choose not to cede to it the safeguarding of their personal safety but to keep it as their prerogative. The unhappy result of this vigilante justice is that American homicide rates are far higher than those of Europe, and those of the South higher than those of the North.

If this history is right, the American political divide may have arisen not so much from different conceptions of human nature as from differences in how best to tame it. The North and coasts are extensions of Europe and continued the government-driven civilizing process that had been gathering momentum since the Middle Ages. The South and West preserved the culture of honor that emerged in the anarchic territories of the growing country, tempered by their own civilizing forces of churches, families and temperance.

OCTOBER 24, 2012

The Enigma of Chinese Medicine

—Stephen T. Asma

A FEW YEARS AGO, WHILE VISITING BEIJING, I CAUGHT A COLD. My wife, who is Chinese and wanted me to feel better, took me to a local restaurant. After we sat down, she ordered a live turtle. The proprietors sent it over. I startled as the waiters unceremoniously cut the turtle's throat, then poured its blood into a glass. To this frightening prospect, they added a shot of baijiu, very strong grain alcohol. The proprietor and waiters, now tableside, gestured with obvious pride for me to drink the potent medicine. I winced, found the courage, and drank up.

I felt better later that night and in the days that followed, but I wasn't sure why. Was it the placebo effect? Perhaps my body was already on the mend that night, rendering the medicine superfluous. Or did the turtle blood–baijiu potion speed my recovery? Maybe in years to come we will discover some subtle chemical properties in turtle blood that ameliorate certain illnesses.

Many Westerners will scoff at the very idea that turtle blood could have medicinal effects. But at least some of those same people will quaff a tree-bark tincture or put on an eggplant compress recommended by Dr. Oz to treat skin cancer. We are all living in the vast gray area between leech-bleeding and antibiotics. Alternative medicine has exploded in recent years, reawakening a philosophical problem that epistemologists call the "demarcation problem."

The demarcation problem is primarily the challenge of distinguishing real science from pseudoscience. It often gets trotted out in the fight between evolutionists and creation scientists. In that tired debate, creationism is usually dismissed on the grounds that its claims cannot be falsified (evidence cannot prove or disprove its natural theology beliefs). This criterion of "falsifiability" was originally formulated by Karl Popper, perhaps the most influential philosopher of science of the twentieth century, and, at first blush, it seems like a good one—it nicely rules out the spooky claims of pseudoscientists and snake oil salesmen, Or does it?

The contemporary philosopher of science Larry Laudan claims that philosophers have failed to give credible criteria for demarcating science from pseudoscience. Even falsifiability, the benchmark for positivist science, rules *out* many of the legitimate theoretical claims of cutting-edge physics and rules *in* many wacky claims, like astrology—if the proponents are clever about which observations corroborate their predictions. Moreover, historians of science since Thomas Kuhn have pointed out that legitimate science rarely abandons a theory the moment falsifying observations come in, preferring instead (sometimes for decades) to chalk up counterevidence to experimental error. The Austrian philosopher Paul Feyerabend even gave up altogether on a so-called scientific method, arguing that science is not a special technique for producing truth but a flawed species of regular human reasoning (loaded with error, bias and rhetorical persuasion). And finally, increased rationality doesn't always decrease credulity.

We like to think that a rigorous application of logic will eliminate kooky ideas. But it doesn't. Even a person as well versed in induction and deduction as Arthur Conan Doyle believed that the death of Lord Carnarvon, the patron of the Tutankhamun expedition, may have been caused by a pharaoh's curse.

The issue of alternative medicine, especially traditional Chinese medicine (TCM), brings fresh passion to the demarcation problem. Americans are gravitating to acupuncture and herbal medicines (less so the zoological pharmacology, like my turtle blood), but we crave some scientific validation for these ancient practices. And the Chinese are themselves looking for ways to legitimize TCM to the Western world and distinguish it from the more superstitious aspects of traditional culture.

A couple years after the Beijing visit, while I was looking for a place to live in Shanghai, a realtor assured me that the apartment we were viewing was in a very auspicious location. Looking out the window ten floors up, I could see the bend of Suzhou Creek as it passed the building. He explained that this curve and flow was very good feng shui. It was a prosperous channel of "positive qi energy."

I took the apartment.

The general facts of feng shui (literally "wind and water") strike many of us as relatively indisputable. Simply put, if you arrange your furniture in certain patterns and directions, it feels to most people psychologically better than certain other patterns. But the metaphysical "causal theory" behind these facts is more controversial. Chinese medicine holds that energy meridians mark the flow of a force called "qi," and this force is streaming throughout nature and our bodies—causing harmony and health or disharmony and illness (depending on the degree to which it is blocked or unblocked).

I certainly don't need this theory to be true to explain why I feel less agitated when my office desk faces the doorway than I do when my back is to the door. And I don't think I need it to explain the sense of peace I get from looking out my window at Suzhou Creek. Perhaps the metaphysical qi theory of feng shui will eventually give way to one that aligns with our understanding of sensory perception or psychology. Growing clinical evidence showing the palliative effects of placebos has led many tough-minded doctors to conclude that beneficial physiological responses (like endorphin and dopamine release) can be triggered by subtle suggestions, sugar pills, prayer, music and other seemingly gratuitous mechanisms. So, why not furniture placement?

ARISTOTLE DISTINGUISHED SCIENCE from other kinds of knowledge on the grounds that it gave a causal explanation for observable experience, and its claims were systematic (logically coherent). By these

Aristotelian criteria, TCM at least looks fairly scientific—the system of qi provides the causal foundation for specific associations within acupuncture healing, kung fu skills, feng shui architecture, herbal remedies and so on.

Starting in the seventeenth century, however, the definition of science changed significantly. It wasn't enough to have a systematic causal story, since many competing stories could fit the same observable phenomenon. Retrograde planetary motion could be explained by Ptolemaic epicycle causation, for example, but that causal picture was eventually unseated by a shift to heliocentric astronomy. What's needed is the *correct* and *verifiable* causal explanation; and the scientific method (the "hypothetico-deductive model" in philosophy of science parlance) arose in order to put causal explanations through a gantlet of empirical tests.

Can qi theory be scientific in this more rigorous sense? Skepticism seems reasonable here because no one has seen qi directly. Even the meridians (or channels) of qi in the body remain undetectable to Western instruments, yet TCM practitioners spend years mastering the meridian anatomical charts.

Are they chasing an illusion that takes authority from tradition alone, or are we still only at the commencement stage of discovery? Qi energy looks unfalsifiable, but maybe the promissory note will soon be paid. After all, scientists theorized, hypothesized and assumed the reality of the gene (a unit of heredity) long before anyone actually observed one. And the Higgs boson was posited in the 1960s but only confirmed in 2013. Will qi energy be confirmed as the causal underpinning for the often-reported correspondence between acupuncture and healing?

In the nineteenth century, Darwin's scientific revolution didn't correspond to the experimental method of the falsifiability model. Galileo had been rolling balls down inclined planes and making direct observations to evaluate his gravitation theory, but Darwin's theory of natural selection was less observable. Instead, Darwin's natural selection attained increasing scientific acceptance because it explained so many diverse phenomena (like adaptive structures, anatomical homologies, the fossil record, and so on). The paradigm of qi is as explanatorily resourceful and deeply rooted in China as Darwinism is in Western science. But there's a major difference, too, and it needs articulation.

Darwinism only posits three major ingredients for evolution: offspring vary from their parents and siblings, offspring resemble their parents more than nonkin, and more offspring are born than can survive in their environment. Each of these facts is easily observable, and when you put them together, you get adaptive evolution of populations. No additional metaphysical force, like qi, is being posited.

WHILE LYING on the acupuncturist's table in China recently, I wondered if I was too skeptical or too gullible about qi. Dr. Shao Lei, at the Huashan Hospital, was nationally renowned as a skillful manager of this mysterious force. I explained to him that I had chronic lower back pain. Dr. Shao made a study of my tongue and informed me that my back pain was actually a qi problem with my kidney, but he could strengthen the weak qi area. He stuck me with ten needles in my lumbar region and a couple of pins behind my knees. He hooked these to an electrical voltage generator and zapped me gently for twenty minutes while warming my back with a heat lamp that looked like it could be keeping French fries hot at a fast-food joint. I did not engage in this mild torture once, but several times—just to make a thorough, albeit anecdotal, study of the matter. And I can honestly say that my back improved in the few days that followed each session.

It seems entirely reasonable to believe in the effectiveness of TCM and still have grave doubts about qi. In other words, it is possible for people to practice a kind of "accidental medicine"—in the sense that symptoms might be alleviated even when their causes are misdiagnosed (it happens all the time in Western medicine, too). Acupuncture, turtle blood, and many similar therapies are not superstitious but may be morsels of practical folk wisdom. The causal theory that's concocted to explain the practical successes of treatment is not terribly important or interesting to the poor schlub who's thrown out his back or taken ill.

Ultimately, one can be skeptical of both qi and a sacrosanct scientific method but still be a devotee of fallible pragmatic truth. In the end, most of us are gamblers about health treatments. We play as many options as we can; a little acupuncture, a little ibuprofen, a little turtle's blood. Throw enough cards (or remedies), and eventually some odds will go your way. Is that superstition or wisdom?

SEPTEMBER 28, 2013

The Dangers of Pseudoscience

—Massimo Pigliucci and Maarten Boudry

P HLOSOPHERS OF SCIENCE HAVE BEEN PREOCCUPIED FOR A WHILE with what they call the "demarcation problem," the issue of what separates good science from bad science and pseudoscience (and everything in between). The problem is relevant for at least three reasons.

The first is philosophical: demarcation is crucial to our pursuit of knowledge; its issues go to the core of debates on epistemology and of the nature of truth and discovery. The second reason is civic: our society spends billions of tax dollars on scientific research, so it is important that we also have a good grasp of what constitutes money well spent in this regard. Should the National Institutes of Health finance research on "alternative medicine"? Should the Department of Defense fund studies on telepathy? Third, as an ethical matter, pseudoscience is not—contrary to popular belief—merely a harmless pastime of the gullible; it often threatens people's welfare, sometimes fatally so. For instance, millions of people worldwide have died of AIDS because they (or, in some cases, their governments) refuse to accept basic scientific findings about the disease, entrusting their fates to folk remedies and "snake oil" therapies.

It is precisely in the area of medical treatments that the science-pseudoscience divide is most critical and where the role of philosophers in clarifying things may be most relevant. Our colleague Stephen T. Asma raised the issue in a recent Stone column ("The Enigma of Chinese Medicine"), pointing out that some traditional

Chinese remedies (like drinking fresh turtle blood to alleviate cold symptoms) may in fact work and therefore should not be dismissed as pseudoscience.

This, however, risks confusing the possible effectiveness of folk remedies with the arbitrary theoretical-metaphysical baggage attached to it. There is no question that some folk remedies do work. The active ingredient of aspirin, for example, is derived from willow bark, which had been known to have beneficial effects since the time of Hippocrates. There is also no mystery about how this happens: people have more or less randomly tried solutions to their health problems for millennia, sometimes stumbling upon something useful. What makes the use of aspirin "scientific," however, is that we have validated its effectiveness through properly controlled trials, isolated the active ingredient, and understood the biochemical pathways through which it has its effects (it suppresses the production of prostaglandins and thromboxanes by way of interference with the enzyme cyclooxygenase, just in case you were curious).

Asma's example of Chinese medicine's claims about the existence of "qi" energy, channeled through the human body by way of "meridians," though, is a different matter. This sounds scientific, because it uses arcane jargon that gives the impression of articulating explanatory principles. But there is no way to test the existence of qi and associated meridians, or to establish a viable research program based on those concepts, for the simple reason that talk of qi and meridians only looks substantive, but it isn't even in the ballpark of an empirically verifiable theory.

In terms of empirical results, there are strong indications that acupuncture is effective for reducing chronic pain and nausea, but sham therapy, where needles are applied at random places, or are not even pierced through the skin, turn out to be equally effective thus seriously undermining talk of meridians and qi lines. In other words, the notion of qi only mimics scientific notions such as enzyme actions on lipid compounds. This is a standard modus operandi of pseudoscience: it adopts the external trappings of science but without the substance.

Asma at one point compares the current inaccessibility of qi energy to the previous (until this year) inaccessibility of the famous Higgs boson, a subatomic particle postulated by physicists to play a crucial role in literally holding the universe together (it provides mass to all other particles). But the analogy does not hold. The existence of the Higgs had been predicted on the basis of a very successful physical theory known as the Standard Model. This theory is not only exceedingly mathematically sophisticated, but it has been verified experimentally over and over again. The notion of qi, again, is not really a theory in any meaningful sense of the word. It is just an evocative word to label a mysterious force of which we do not know and we are not told how to find out anything at all.

Philosophers of science have long recognized that there is nothing wrong with positing unobservable entities per se; it's a question of what work such entities actually do within a given theoretical-empirical framework. Qi and meridians don't seem to do any, and that doesn't seem to bother supporters and practitioners of Chinese medicine. But it ought to.

Still, one may reasonably object, what's the harm in believing in qi and related notions if in fact the proposed remedies seem to help? Well, setting aside the obvious objections that the slaughtering of turtles might raise on ethical grounds, there are several issues to consider. To begin with, we can incorporate whatever serendipitous discoveries from folk medicine into modern scientific practice, as in the case of the willow bark turned aspirin. In this sense, there is no such thing as "alternative" medicine—there's only stuff that works and stuff that doesn't.

Second, if we are positing qi and similar concepts, we are attempting to provide explanations for why some things work and others don't. If these explanations are wrong, or unfounded as in the case of vacuous concepts like qi, then we ought to correct or abandon them. Most importantly, pseudo medical treatments often do not work, or are even positively harmful. If you take folk herbal "remedies," for instance, while your body is fighting a serious infection, you may suffer severe, even fatal, consequences.

That is precisely what happens worldwide to people who deny the connection between HIV and AIDS, as superbly documented by the journalist Michael Specter. Indulging in a bit of pseudoscience in some instances may be relatively innocuous, but the problem is that doing so lowers your defenses against more dangerous delusions that are based on similar confusions and fallacies. For instance, you may expose yourself and your loved ones to harm because your pseudoscientific proclivities lead you to accept notions that have been scientifically disproved, like the increasingly (and worryingly) popular idea that vaccines cause autism.

Philosophers nowadays recognize that there is no sharp line dividing sense from nonsense and moreover that doctrines starting out in one camp may over time evolve into the other. For example, alchemy was a (somewhat) legitimate science in the times of Newton and Boyle, but it is now firmly pseudoscientific (movements in the opposite direction, from full-blown pseudoscience to genuine science, are notably rare). The verdict by philosopher Larry Laudan, echoed by Asma, that the demarcation problem is dead and buried, is not shared by most contemporary philosophers who have studied the subject.

Even the criterion of falsifiability, for example, is still a useful benchmark for distinguishing science and pseudoscience, as a first approximation. Asma's own counterexample inadvertently shows this: the "cleverness" of astrologers in cherry-picking what counts as a confirmation of their theory is hardly a problem for the criterion of a falsifiability, but rather a nice illustration of Popper's basic insight—the bad habit of creative fudging and finagling with empirical data ultimately makes a theory impervious to refutation. And all pseudoscientists do it, from parapsychologists to creationists and 9/11 truthers.

Asma's equating of qi energy with the "sacrosanct scientific method," as if both are on the same par, is especially worrisome. Aside from comparing a doctrine about how the world works (qi) with an *open-ended method for* obtaining knowledge, what exactly is "sacrosanct" about a method that readily allows for the integration of willow bark and turtle blood, provided that they hold up to scrutiny? The open-ended nature of science means that there is nothing sacrosanct in either its results or its methods.

The borderlines between genuine science and pseudoscience may be fuzzy, but this should be even more of a call for careful distinctions, based on systematic facts and sound reasoning. To try a modicum of turtle blood here and a little aspirin there is not the hallmark of wisdom and even-mindedness. It is a dangerous gateway to superstition and irrationality.

OCTOBER 10, 2013

CAN WE LIVE WITH UNCERTAINTY?

Nothing to See Here:
Demoting the Uncertainty Principle

—Craig Callender

"Y OU'VE OBSERVED THE ROBBERS. THEY KNOW IT. THAT WILL change their actions," says Charlie Eppes, the math savant who helps detectives on television's *Numb3rs*. Eppes claims that this insight follows from quantum physics, in particular, Werner Heisenberg's infamous "uncertainty principle." Not all mischaracterizations of Heisenberg's principle are as innocent as Eppes's. The film *What the Bleep Do We Know!?* uses it to justify many articles of faith in New Age philosophy. Asserting that observing water molecules changes their molecular structure, the film reasons that since we are 90 percent water, physics therefore tells us that we can fundamentally change our nature via mental energy. Fundamentally inaccurate uses of the principle are also common in the academy, especially among social theorists, who often argue that it undermines science's claims to objectivity and completeness. As Jim Holt has written, "No scientific idea from the last century is more fetishized, abused and misunderstood—by the vulgar and the learned alike—than Heisenberg's uncertainty principle."

Why exactly is the uncertainty principle so misused? No doubt our sensationalist and mystery-mongering culture is partly responsible. But much of the blame should be reserved for the founders of quantum physics themselves, Heisenberg and Niels Bohr. Though neither physicist would have sanctioned the aforementioned nonsense, it's easy to imagine how such misapprehensions arise, given the things they do say about the principle, and especially the central place they both give to the concept of measurement. Heisenberg vividly explained uncertainty with the example of taking a picture of an electron. To photograph an electron's position—its location in space—one needs to reflect light off the particle. But bouncing light off an electron imparts energy to it, causing it to move, thereby making uncertain its velocity. To know velocity with certainty would then require another measurement. And so on. While this "disturbance" picture of measurement is intuitive—A—and no doubt what inspires the common understanding exemplified in *Numb3rs*—it leaves the reason for uncertainty mysterious. Measurement always *disturbs, yet that didn't stop classical physicists from in principle knowing* position and velocity simultaneously.

For this reason Heisenberg supplemented this picture with a theory in which measurement figures prominently. It's not simply that we can't simultaneously measure definite values of position and momentum, he thought. It's that before measurement those values don't simultaneously exist. The act of observation brings into existence the properties of the world. Here we find the seeds of the claims made by some social theorists and found in *What the Bleep Do We Know!?* If reality depends on interaction with us, it's natural to suppose that objectivity is undermined and that we, from the outside, make reality, possibly with some kind of mental energy.

Bohr, for his part, explained uncertainty by pointing out that answering certain questions necessitates not answering others. To measure position, we need a stationary measuring object, like a fixed photographic plate. This plate defines a fixed frame of reference. To measure velocity, by contrast, we need an apparatus that allows for some recoil, and hence movable parts. This experiment requires a movable frame. Testing one therefore means not testing the other. Here we find inspiration for the idea that the principle shows that science can never answer everything.

But as interpretations of the principle, both views are baffling, most of all for the undue weight they give to the idea of measurement.

To understand what the uncertainty principle actually says, one needs to understand the broader physical theory in which it figures: quantum mechanics. It's a complex theory, but its basic structure is simple. It represents physical systems—particles, cats, planets—with abstract quantum states. These quantum states provide the chances for various things happening. Think of quantum mechanics as an oddsmaker. You consult the theory, and it provides the odds of something definite happening. You ask, "Oddsmaker, what are the chances of finding this particle's location in this interval?" and the equations of the theory answer, "twenty-five percent." Or "Oddsmaker, what are the chances of finding the particle's energy in this range?" and they answer, "fifty percent."

The quantum oddsmaker can answer these questions for every conceivable property of the system. Sometimes it really narrows down what might happen: for instance, "There is a 100 percent chance the particle is located here, and 0 percent chance elsewhere." Other times it spreads out its chances to varying degrees: "There is a 1 percent chance the particle is located here, a 2 percent change it is located there, a 1 percent chance over there, and so on."

The uncertainty principle simply says that for some pairs of questions to the oddsmaker, the answers may be interrelated. Famously, the answer to the question of a particle's position is constrained by the answer to the question of its velocity, and vice versa. In particular, if we have a huge ensemble of systems each prepared in the same quantum state, the more the position is narrowed down, the less the velocity is, and vice versa. In other words, the oddsmaker is stingy: it won't give us good odds on both position and velocity at once.

Note that nowhere in my explanation of the principle did I mention anything about measurement. The principle is about quantum states and what odds follow from these states. To add the notion of measurement is to import extra content. And as the great physicist John S. Bell has said, formulations of quantum mechanics invoking measurement as basic are "unprofessionally vague and ambiguous."

After all, why is a concept as fuzzy as measurement part of a fundamental theory? Interactions abound. What qualifies some as measurements? Inasmuch as disturbance is related to uncertainty, it's hardly surprising that observing something causes it to change, since one observes by interacting. But a clear and complete physical theory should describe the physical interaction in its own terms.

Today there are several interpretations of quantum mechanics that do just that. Each gives its own account of interactions, and hence gives different meaning to the principle.

Consider the theory invented by the physicists Louis de Broglie and David Bohm, commonly referred to as the de Broglie-Bohm view. It supplements the quantum state with particles that always have determinate positions, contra Heisenberg. Measurement interactions are simply a species of particle interaction. Uncertainty still exists. The laws of motion of this theory imply that one can't know everything, for example, that no perfectly accurate measurement of the particle's velocity exists.

This is still surprising and nonclassical, yes, but the limitation to our knowledge is only temporary. It's perfectly compatible with the uncertainty principle as it functions in this theory that I measure position exactly and then later calculate the system's velocity exactly. But the bigger point is that because of the underlying physical picture, we here know exactly why uncertainty exists.

Other interpretations exist. For example, there are the "collapse" theories associated with the physicist Giancarlo Ghirardi. In these theories the quantum state abruptly changes its development ("collapses") when big things interact with small things. Here fields of mass interact with one another. And in the "many worlds" picture of the physicist Hugh Everett III, all the possibilities given odds by the oddsmaker come to fruition, but in parallel worlds. Here the abstract quantum state is regarded as physical, and interactions are connections that develop between different bits of this strange reality.

All of these interpretations have their pros and cons, but in none do observers play a fundamental role. You and I are big clumps or aspects of the basic stuff. Measurement is simply a type of interaction among those types of stuff, no different than a basketball's redirection when bounced off a patch of uneven gym floor.

Once one removes the "unprofessional vagueness" surrounding the notion of measurement in quantum physics, the principle falls out as a clear corollary of quantum physics. Weirdness remains, of course. The stingy quantum oddsmaker is genuinely odd. But all the truly wild claims—that observers are metaphysically important, that objectivity is impossible, that we possess a special kind of mental energy—are the result of foggy interpretations made even less sharp by those wanting to validate their pet metaphysical claims with quantum physics.

To prevent future temptation to misuse, I urge that we demote the uncertainty principle. If Pluto can be reclassified as a dwarf planet, then surely we can do something similar here. Going forward, let's agree to call the uncertainty principle the "uncertainty relations" or even the less provocative "quantum standard deviation constraints." Not many people outside of a lab are likely to invoke a principle with a name like this.

And that's probably a good thing.

JULY 21, 2013

The Dangers of Certainty: A Lesson From Auschwitz

—Simon Critchley

A S A KID IN ENGLAND, I WATCHED A LOT OF TELEVISION. THERE weren't any books in our house, not even the Bible. TV was therefore pretty important, omnipresent actually. Of course, most of what it delivered was garbage. But in 1973, the BBC aired an extraordinary documentary series called *The Ascent of Man*, hosted by one Dr. Jacob Bronowski in thirteen hour-long episodes. Each episode was what he called an "essay" and involved some exotic and elaborate locations, but the presentation was never flashy and consisted mostly of Dr. Bronowski speaking directly and deliberately to the camera.

Dr. Bronowski (he was always referred to as "Dr." and I can't think of him with any other, more familiar moniker) died forty years ago this year, at the relatively young age of sixty-six. He was a Polish-born British mathematician who wrote a number of highly regarded books on science, but who was equally at home in the world of literature. He wrote his own poetry as well as a book on William Blake.

He was a slight, lively, lovely man. Because it was the early '70s, some of his fashion choices were bewilderingly pastel, especially his socks, though on some occasions he sported a racy leather box jacket. He often smiled as he spoke, not out of conceit or because he lived in California (which, incidentally, he did, working at the Salk Institute in San Diego), but out of a sheer, greedy joy at explaining what he thought was important. But there was a genuine humility in his demeanor that made him utterly likable.

The Ascent of Man (admittedly a little sexist now—great men abound, but there are apparently few great women) deliberately inverted the title of Darwin's 1871 book. It was not an account of human biological evolution, but cultural evolution—from the origins of human life in the Rift Valley to the shifts from hunter/gatherer societies to nomadism and then settlement and civilization, from agriculture and metallurgy to the rise and fall of empires: Assyria, Egypt, Rome.

Bronowski presented everything with great gusto, but with a depth that never sacrificed clarity and which was never condescending. The tone of the programs was rigorous yet permissive, playful yet precise, and always urgent, open and exploratory. I remember in particular the programs on the trial of Galileo, Darwin's hesitancy about publishing his theory of evolution, and the dizzying consequences of Einstein's theory of relativity. Some of it was difficult for a thirteen-year-old to understand, but I remember being absolutely riveted.

The ascent of man was secured through scientific creativity. But unlike many of his more glossy and glib contemporary epigones, Dr. Bronowski was never reductive in his commitment to science. Scientific activity was always linked to artistic creation. For Bronowski, science and art were two neighboring mighty rivers that flowed from a common source: the human imagination. Newton and Shakespeare, Darwin and Coleridge, Einstein and Braque: all were interdependent facets of the human mind and constituted what was best and most noble about the human adventure.

For most of the series, Dr. Bronowski's account of human development was a relentlessly optimistic one. Then, in the eleventh episode, called "Knowledge or Certainty," the mood changed to something more somber. Let me try and recount what has stuck in my memory for all these years.

He began the show with the words, "One aim of the physical sciences has been to give an actual picture of the material world. One achievement of physics in the twentieth century has been to show that such an aim is unattainable." For Dr. Bronowski, there was no absolute knowledge and anyone who claims it—whether a scientist, a politician or a religious believer—opens the door to tragedy. All scientific information is imperfect and we have to treat it with humility. Such, for him, was the human condition.

This is the condition for what we can know, but it is also, crucially, a moral lesson. It is the lesson of twentieth-century painting from cubism onward, but also that of quantum physics. All we can do is to push deeper and deeper into better approximations of an ever-evasive reality. The goal of complete understanding seems to recede as we approach it.

There is no God's-Eye view, Dr. Bronowski insisted, and the people who claim that there is and that they possess it are not just wrong, they are morally pernicious. Errors are inextricably bound up with pursuit of human knowledge, which requires not just mathematical calculation but insight, interpretation and a personal act of judgment for which we are *responsible*. The emphasis on the moral responsibility of knowledge was essential for all of Dr. Bronowski's work. The acquisition of knowledge entails a responsibility for the integrity of what we are as ethical creatures.

Dr. Bronowski's eleventh essay took him to the ancient university city of Göttingen in Germany, to explain the genesis of Werner Heisenberg's uncertainty principle in the hugely creative milieu that surrounded the physicist Max Born in the 1920s. Dr. Bronowski insisted that the principle of uncertainty was a misnomer, because it gives the impression that in science (and outside of it) we are always uncertain. But this is wrong. Knowledge is precise, but that precision is confined within a certain *toleration* of uncertainty. Heisenberg's insight is that the electron is a particle that yields only limited information; its speed and position are confined by the tolerance of Max Planck's quantum, the basic element of matter.

Dr. Bronowski thought that the uncertainty principle should therefore be called the principle of tolerance. Pursuing knowledge means accepting uncertainty. Heisenberg's principle has the consequence that no physical events can ultimately be described with absolute certainty or with "zero tolerance," as it were. The more we know, the less certain we are.

In the everyday world, we do not just accept a lack of ultimate exactitude with a melancholic shrug, but we constantly employ such inexactitude in our relations with other people. Our relations with others also require a principle of tolerance. We encounter other people across a gray area of negotiation and approximation. Such is the business of listening and the back and forth of conversation and social interaction.

For Dr. Bronowski, the moral consequence of knowledge is that we must never judge others on the basis of some absolute, godlike conception of certainty. All knowledge, all information that passes between human beings, can be exchanged only within what we might call "a play of tolerance," whether in science, literature, politics or religion. As he eloquently put it, "Human knowledge is personal and responsible, an unending adventure at the edge of uncertainty."

The relationship between humans and nature and humans and other humans can take place only within a certain play of tolerance. Insisting on certainty, by contrast, leads ineluctably to arrogance and dogma based on ignorance.

At this point, in the final minutes of the show, the scene suddenly shifts to Auschwitz, where many members of Bronowski's family were murdered. He then delivers this soliloqy:

> *It's said that science will dehumanize people and turn them into numbers. That is false, tragically false. Look for yourself. This is the concentration camp and crematorium at Auschwitz. This is where people were turned into numbers. Into this pond were flushed the ashes of some four million people. And that was not done by gas. It was done by arrogance. It was done by dogma. It was done by ignorance. When people believe that they have absolute knowledge, with no test in reality, this is how they behave. This is what men do when they aspire to the knowledge of gods.*
>
> *Science is a very human form of knowledge. We are always at the brink of the known, we always feel forward for what is to be*

hoped. Every judgment in science stands on the edge of error, and is personal. Science is a tribute to what we can know although we are fallible. In the end the words were said by Oliver Cromwell: "I beseech you, in the bowels of Christ, think it possible you may be mistaken."

I owe it as a scientist to my friend Leo Szilard, I owe it as a human being to the many members of my family who died at Auschwitz, to stand here by the pond as a survivor and a witness. We have to cure ourselves of the itch for absolute knowledge and power. We have to close the distance between the push-button order and the human act. We have to touch people.

It is an extraordinary and moving moment. Bronowski dips his hand into the muddy water of a pond which contained the remains of his family members and the members of countless other families. All victims of the same hatred: the hatred of the other human being. By contrast, he says—just before the camera hauntingly cuts to slow motion—"We have to touch people."

The play of tolerance opposes the principle of monstrous certainty that is endemic to fascism and, sadly, not just fascism but all the various faces of fundamentalism. When we think we have certainty, when we aspire to the knowledge of the gods, then Auschwitz can happen and can repeat itself. Arguably, it has repeated itself in the genocidal certainties of past decades.

The pursuit of scientific knowledge is as personal an act as lifting a paintbrush or writing a poem, and they are both profoundly human. If the human condition is defined by limitedness, then this is a glorious fact because it is a moral limitedness rooted in a faith in the power of the imagination, our sense of responsibility and our acceptance of our fallibility. We always have to acknowledge that we might be mistaken. When we forget that, then we forget ourselves and the worst can happen.

In 1945, nearly three decades before *The Ascent of Man*, Dr. Bronowski—who was a close friend of the Hungarian physicist Leo Szilard, the reluctant father of the atomic bomb—visited Nagasaki to help assess the damage there. It convinced him to discontinue his work for British military research with which he had been engaged extensively during the Second World War. From that time onward, he focused on the relations between science and human values. When someone said to Szilard in Bronowski's company that the bombing of Hiroshima and Nagasaki was science's tragedy, Szilard replied firmly that this was wrong: it was a human tragedy.

Such was Dr. Bronowski's lesson for a thirteen-year-old boy some forty years ago. Being slightly old school, I treated myself last Christmas to a DVD deluxe boxed set of *The Ascent of Man*. I am currently watching it with my ten-year-old son. Admittedly, it is not really much competition for *Candy Crush* and his sundry other video games, but he is showing an interest. Or at least he is tolerating my enthusiasm. And of course beginning to learn such toleration is the whole point.

FEBRUARY 2, 2014

The Riddle of the Human Species

—*Edward O. Wilson*

T HE TASK OF UNDERSTANDING HUMANITY IS TOO IMPORTANT AND too daunting to leave to the humanities. Their many branches, from philosophy to law to history and the creative arts, have described the particularities of human nature with genius and exquisite detail, back and forth in endless permutations. But they have not explained why we possess our special nature and not some other out of a vast number of conceivable possibilities. In that sense, the humanities have not accounted for a full understanding of our species' existence.

So, just what are we? The key to the great riddle lies in the circumstance and process that created our species. The human condition is a product of history, not just the six millenniums of civilization but very much further back, across hundreds of millenniums. The whole of it, biological and cultural evolution, in seamless unity, must be explored for an answer to the mystery. When thus viewed across its entire traverse, the history of humanity also becomes the key to learning how and why our species survived.

A majority of people prefer to interpret history as the unfolding of a supernatural design, to whose author we owe obedience. But that comforting interpretation has grown less supportable as knowledge of the real world has expanded. Scientific knowledge (measured by numbers of scientists and scientific journals) in particular has been doubling every ten to twenty years for over a century. In traditional explanations of the past, religious creation stories have been blended with the humanities to attribute meaning to our species's existence. It is time to consider what science might give to the humanities and the humanities to science in a common search for a more solidly grounded answer to the great riddle.

To begin, biologists have found that the biological origin of advanced social behavior in humans was similar to that occurring elsewhere in the animal kingdom. Using comparative studies of thousands of animal species, from insects to mammals, they have concluded that the most complex societies have arisen through eusociality—roughly, "true" social condition. The members of a eusocial group cooperatively rear the young across multiple generations. They also divide labor through the surrender by some members of at least some of their personal reproduction in a way that increases the "reproductive success" (lifetime reproduction) of other members.

Eusociality stands out as an oddity in a couple of ways. One is its extreme rarity. Out of hundreds of thousands of evolving lines of animals on the land during the past 400 million years, the condition, so far as we can determine, has arisen only about two dozen times. This is likely to be an underestimate, due to sampling error. Nevertheless, we can be certain that the number of originations was very small.

Furthermore, the known eusocial species arose very late in the history of life. It appears to have occurred not at all during the great Paleozoic diversification of insects, 350 to 250 million years before the present, during which the variety of insects approached that of today. Nor is there as yet any evidence of eusocial species during the Mesozoic Era until the appearance of the earliest termites and ants between 200 and 150 million years ago. Humans at the *Homo* level appeared only very recently, following tens of millions of years of evolution among the primates.

Once attained, advanced social behavior at the eusocial grade has proved a major ecological success. Of the two dozen independent lines, just two within the insects—ants and termites—globally dominate invertebrates on the land. Although they are represented by fewer than twenty thousand of the million known living insect species, ants and termites compose more than half of the world's insect body weight.

The history of eusociality raises a question: given the enormous advantage it confers, why was this advanced form of social behavior so rare and long delayed? The answer appears to be the special sequence of preliminary evolutionary changes that must occur before the final step to eusociality can be taken. In all of the eusocial species analyzed to date, the final step before eusociality is the construction of a protected nest, from which foraging trips begin and within which the young are raised to maturity. The original nest builders can be a lone female, a mated pair, or a small and weakly organized group. When this final preliminary step is attained, all that is needed to create a eusocial colony is for the parents and offspring to stay at the nest and cooperate in raising additional generations of young. Such primitive assemblages then divide easily into risk-prone foragers and risk-averse parents and nurses.

What brought one primate line to the rare level of eusociality? Paleontologists have found that the circumstances were humble. In Africa about two million years ago, one species of the primarily vegetarian australopithecine evidently shifted its diet to include a much higher reliance on meat. For a group to harvest such a high-energy, widely dispersed source of food, it did not pay to roam about as a loosely organized pack of adults and young like present-day chimpanzees and bonobos. It was more efficient to occupy a campsite (thus, the nest) and send out hunters who could bring home meat, either killed or scavenged, to share with others. In exchange, the hunters received protection of the campsite and their own young offspring kept there.

From studies of modern humans, including hunter-gatherers, whose lives tell us so much about human origins, social psychologists have deduced the mental growth that began with hunting and campsites. A premium was placed on personal relationships geared to both competition and cooperation among the members. The process was ceaselessly dynamic and demanding. It far exceeded in intensity anything similar experienced by the roaming, loosely organized bands of most animal societies. It required a memory good enough to assess the intentions of fellow members, to predict their responses, from one moment to the next; and it resulted in the ability to invent and inwardly rehearse competing scenarios of future interactions.

The social intelligence of the campsite-anchored prehumans evolved as a kind of nonstop game of chess. Today, at the terminus of this evolutionary process, our immense memory banks are smoothly activated across the past, present, and future. They allow us to evaluate the prospects and consequences variously of alliances, bonding, sexual contact, rivalries, domination, deception, loyalty and betrayal. We instinctively delight in the telling of countless stories about others as players upon the inner stage. The best of it is expressed in the creative arts, political theory, and other higher-level activities we have come to call the humanities.

The definitive part of the long creation story evidently began with the primitive *Homo habilis* (or a species closely related to it) two million years ago. Prior to the *habilines* the prehumans had been animals. Largely vegetarians, they had humanlike bodies, but their cranial capacity remained chimpanzee-size, at or below 500 cubic centimeters. Starting with the *habiline* period the capacity grew precipitously: to 680 cubic centimeters in *Homo habilis*, 900 in *Homo erectus*, and about 1,400 in *Homo sapiens*. The expansion of the human brain was one of the most rapid episodes of evolution of complex organs in the history of life.

STILL, TO RECOGNIZE THE RARE coming together of cooperating primates is not enough to account for the full potential of modern humans that brain capacity provides. Evolutionary biologists have searched for the grandmaster of advanced social evolution, the combination of forces and environmental circumstances that bestowed greater longevity and more successful reproduction on the possession of high social intelligence. At present there are two competing theories of the principal force. The first is kin selection: individuals favor collateral kin (relatives other than offspring) making it easier for altruism to evolve among members of the same group. Altruism in turn engenders complex social organization and, in the one case that involves big mammals, human-level intelligence.

The second, more recently argued theory (full disclosure: I am one of the modern version's authors), the grandmaster is multilevel selection. This formulation recognizes two levels at which natural selection operates: individual selection based on competition and cooperation among members of the same group, and group selection, which arises from competition and cooperation between groups. Multilevel selection is gaining in favor among evolutionary biologists because of a recent mathematical proof that kin selection can arise only under special conditions that demonstrably do not exist, and the better fit of multilevel selection to all of the two dozen known animal cases of eusocial evolution.

The roles of both individual and group selection are indelibly stamped (to borrow a phrase from Charles Darwin) upon our social behavior. As expected, we are intensely interested in the minutiae of behavior of those around us. Gossip is a prevailing subject of conversation, everywhere from hunter-gatherer campsites to royal courts. The mind is a kaleidoscopically shifting map of others, each of whom is drawn emotionally in shades of trust, love, hatred, suspicion, admiration, envy and sociability. We are compulsively driven to create and belong to groups, variously nested, overlapping or separate, and large or small. Almost all groups compete with those of similar kind in some manner or other. We tend to think of our own as superior, and we find our identity within them.

The existence of competition and conflict, the latter often violent, has been a hallmark of societies as far back as archaeological evidence is able to offer. These and other traits we call human nature are so deeply resident in our emotions and habits of thought as to seem just part of some greater nature, like the air we all breathe and the molecular machinery that drives all of life. But they are not. Instead, they are among the idiosyncratic hereditary traits that define our species.

The major features of the biological origins of our species are coming into focus, and with this clarification the potential of a more fruitful contact between science and the humanities. The convergence between these two great branches of learning will matter hugely when enough people have thought it through. On the science side, genetics, the brain sciences, evolutionary biology, and paleontology will be seen in a different light. Students will be taught prehistory as well as conventional history, the whole presented as the living world's greatest epic.

We will also, I believe, take a more serious look at our place in nature. Exalted we are indeed, risen to be the mind of the biosphere without a doubt, our spirits capable of awe and ever more breathtaking leaps of imagination. But we are still part of earth's fauna and flora. We are bound to it by emotion, physiology, and not least, deep history. It is dangerous to think of this planet as a way station to a better world, or continue to convert it into a literal, human-engineered spaceship. Contrary to general opinion, demons and gods do not vie for our allegiance. We are self-made, independent, alone and fragile. Self-understanding is what counts for long-term survival, both for individuals and for the species.

FEBRUARY 24, 2013

RELIGION AND MORALS

T HE UNITED STATES IS A RELIGION-OBSESSED COUNTRY. SINCE its founding by English Puritans in the early seventeenth century seeking a safe haven from persecution, the country has been the destination for wave after wave of immigrants trying to protect and cultivate their own distinctive varieties of religious practice and experience. The core value of the settlement and ever-Westering expansionism of America has been the claim to religious freedom, which has found expression in both extraordinarily imaginative religious poetry and bloody violence. Once here, settlers and immigrants didn't just adapt their existing faith to the new environment, but often created entirely new forms of religious life and enthusiasm, from the Shakers to the Mormons to the Scientologists.

It was perhaps to be expected that much of the writing and debate in The Stone should find its focus in religion, the experience of faith and in questions of the latter's legitimacy or illegitimacy. The appearance of The Stone coincided with both the high-water mark and receding of the tide of the so-called New Atheism, of figures like Richard Dawkins and Christopher Hitchens, whom Terry Eagleton playfully combined into the novel creature called "Ditchkins." Such "Ditchkinsianism" was particularly evident in many of the readers' comments over the years, as were any number of vigorous defenses of religious belief or claims to spirituality.

In the first two parts of this third section, "What Is Faith?" and "The Varieties of Religious Disagreement," the reader will find an array of defenses of the experience of faith, all the way to the argument that faith might not even require some metaphysical belief in the existence of God. Also on display in a powerful manner are discussions of the nature and limits of religious toleration, with particular relation to the question of blasphemy as it arises in Islam's troubled location in the Western, secular world. Also, a series of essays provides some welcome and possibly surprising insights on the nature of Judaism and its relation to Israel and the fraught question of Zionism.

In "Morality's God Problem," the reader will find a fascinating set of discussions of one of the most frequently debated questions in The Stone: Does the practice of morality require religious faith and the existence of God? Or, on the contrary, must morality be conducted independently of any foundational religious claims? Where exactly should one draw the line between the sacred domain of religion and the humane experience of moral reflection? Is God necessary for goodness? Or is belief in a deity an obstacle that stands in the way of the choices of our allegedly autonomous selves?

Many people have never had the good fortune to take a philosophy class in school or college. But if they have, then it is probable that the class was called Introduction to Ethics or Moral Philosophy or even Applied Ethics. Philosophy is often at its best, sharpest, and most disturbing when working through the difficulties provoked by competing moral theories in relation to real-life issues like abortion and euthanasia. In the final part of this section, the reader will find a series of hard moral cases, where philosophers rigorously and without sentimentality address familiar ethical dilemmas in an often unfamiliar light.

Does morality imply a claim to universality, or can we live with the relativism of our ethical practices? Given what we think we know about the nature of human behavior, does it make any sense to talk about altruism? Is there any way to defend the death penalty or to justify solitary confinement? Given the ecological disaster that is unfolding before our eyes, is it right to have children or to even want to have children? Should ours perhaps be the last generation? Is it morally plausible at once to respect animals and to eat them for pleasure? Should forgiveness be a universal moral requirement or is it a phenomenon mired within a particular religious tradition? Are free markets in any way consistent with morality or does the existence of the former entail the eradication of the latter? And finally, does love make sense? Should it really be a fundamental component of ethical life?

It will, I trust, not disappoint the reader to learn that these perennial questions are not decided once and for all in these pages, but simply debated in a manner that will allow one to think through the questions for oneself, and in conversation with our authors.

—Simon Critchley

WHAT IS FAITH?

Philosophy and Faith

—*Gary Gutting*

O NE OF MY JOBS AS A TEACHER OF BRIGHT, MOSTLY CATHOLIC undergraduates is to get them thinking about why they hold their religious beliefs. It's easy enough to spark discussion about the problem of evil ("Can you really read the newspaper every day and continue to believe in an all-perfect God?") or about the diversity of religious beliefs ("If you'd been born in Saudi Arabia, don't you think you'd be a Muslim?"). Inevitably, however, the discussion starts to fizzle when someone raises a hand and says (sometimes ardently, sometimes smugly), "But aren't you forgetting about faith?"

That seems to be enough for most students. The trump card has been played, and they—or at least the many who find religion more a comfort than a burden—happily remember that believing means never having to explain why.

I myself, the product of a dozen years of intellectually self-confident Jesuit education, have little sympathy with the "it's just faith" response. "How can you say that?" I reply. "You wouldn't buy a used car just because you had faith in what the salesperson told you. Why would you take on faith far more important claims about your eternal salvation?" And, in fact, most of my students do see their faith not as an intellectually blind leap but as grounded in evidence and argument.

"Well, if there's no God," they say, "how can you explain why anything at all exists or why the world is governed by such precise laws of nature?"

At this point, the class perks up again as I lay out versions of the famous arguments for the existence of God, and my students begin to think that they're about to get what their parents have paid for at a great Catholic university: some rigorous intellectual support for their faith.

Soon enough, however, things again fall apart, since our best efforts to construct arguments along the traditional lines face successive difficulties. The students realize that I'm not going to be able to give them a convincing proof, and I let them in on the dirty secret: philosophers have never been able to find arguments that settle the question of God's existence or any of the other "big questions" we've been discussing for 2,500 years.

This seems to bring us back to where we started: "It's all faith." I, with my Jesuit-inspired confidence in reason and evidence, have always resisted this. But I have also felt the tug of my students' conclusion that philosophy, although a good intellectual exercise and the source of tantalizing puzzles and paradoxes, has no real significance for religious faith.

Recently, however, I've realized a mistake in the way that I—and most of my professional colleagues—tend to think about philosophy and faith. (One of the great benefits of getting to teach philosophy to bright undergraduates is that it makes it easier to think outside the constraints of current professional assumptions.) The standard view is that philosophers' disagreements over arguments about God make their views irrelevant to the faith of ordinary believers and nonbelievers. The claim seems obvious: If we professionals can't agree among ourselves, what can we have to offer nonprofessionals? An appeal to experts requires consensus among those experts, which philosophers don't have.

This line of thought ignores the fact that when philosophers disagree, it is only about specific aspects of the most subtle and sophisticated versions of arguments for and against God's existence (for example, my colleague Alvin Plantinga's modal-logic formulation of St. Anselm's ontological argument or William Rowe's complex version of a probabilistic argument from evil). There is no disagreement among philosophers about the more popular arguments to which theists and atheists typically appeal: as formulated, they do not prove (that is, logically derive from uncontroversial premises) what they claim to prove. They are clearly inadequate in the judgment of qualified professionals. Further, there are no more sophisticated formulations that theists or atheists can accept—the way we do scientific claims—on the authority of expert consensus.

In these popular debates about God's existence, the winners are neither theists nor atheists, but agnostics—the neglected stepchildren of religious controversy, who rightly point out that neither side in the debate has made its case. This is the position supported by the consensus of expert philosophical opinion.

This conclusion should particularly discomfit popular proponents of atheism, such as Richard Dawkins, whose position is entirely based on demonstrably faulty arguments. Believers, of course, can fall back on the logically less rigorous support that they characterize as faith. But then they need to reflect on just what sort of support faith can give to religious belief. How are my students' warm feelings of certainty as they hug one another at Sunday Mass in their dorm really any different from the trust they might experience while under the spell of a really plausible salesperson?

An answer may lie in work by philosophers as different as David Hume, Ludwig Wittgenstein, and Alvin Plantinga. In various ways, they have shown that everyday life is based on "basic" beliefs for which we have no good arguments. There are, for example, no more basic truths from which we can prove that the past is often a good guide to the future, that our memories are reliable, or that other people have a conscious inner life. Such beliefs simply—and quite properly—arise from our experience in the world. Plantinga in particular has argued that core religious beliefs can have a status similar to these basic but unproven beliefs. His argument has clear plausibility for some sorts of religious beliefs. Through experiences of, for example, natural beauty, moral obligation, or loving and being loved, we may develop an abiding sense of the reality of an extraordinarily good and powerful being who cares about us. Who is to say that such experiences do not give reason for belief in God as much as parallel (though different) experiences give reason for belief in reliable knowledge of the past and future and of other human minds? There is still room for philosophical disputes about this line of thought, but it remains the most plausible starting point of a philosophical case for religious belief.

But this defense of faith faces a steep hurdle. Although it may support generic religious claims about a good and powerful being who cares for us, it is very hard to see it sustaining the specific and robust claims of Judaism, Christianity and Islam about how God is concretely and continually involved in our existence. God is said to be not just good and powerful but morally perfect and omnipotent, a sure ultimate safeguard against any evil that might threaten us. He not only cares about us but has set up precise moral norms and liturgical practices that we must follow to ensure our eternal salvation. Without such specificity, religion lacks the exhilarating and terrifying possibilities that have made it such a powerful force in human history.

But how can religious experience sustain faith in a specific salvation narrative, particularly given the stark differences among the accounts of the great religious traditions? What sort of religious experience could support the claim that Jesus Christ was God incarnate and not just a great moral teacher? Or that the Bible rather than the Koran is the revelation of God's own words? Believers may have strong feelings of certainty, but each religion rejects the certainty of all the others, which leaves us asking why they privilege their own faith.

I am not saying that religious believers are in principle incapable of finding satisfactory answers to such questions. I am saying that philosophy and religion can and must speak to each other, and that those who take their beliefs seriously need to reflect on these questions, and that contemporary philosophical discussions (following on Hume and Wittgenstein) about knowledge, belief, certainty and disagreement are highly relevant to such reflection—and potentially, to an individual's belief. This is what I will try to convey to my students the next time I teach introductory philosophy of religion.

AUGUST 1, 2010

Mystery and Evidence

—Tim Crane

T HERE IS A STORY ABOUT BERTRAND RUSSELL GIVING A PUBLIC lecture somewhere or other, defending his atheism. A furious woman stood up at the end of the lecture and asked, "And Lord Russell, what will you say when you stand in front of the throne of God on judgment day?" Russell replied, "I will say: 'I'm terribly sorry, but you didn't give us enough evidence.'"

This is a very natural way for atheists to react to religious claims: to ask for evidence, and reject these claims in the absence of it. Certainly this is the way that today's New Atheists tend to approach religion. According to their view, religions—by this they mean basically Christianity, Judaism and Islam, and I will follow them in this—are largely in the business of making claims about the universe that are a bit like scientific hypotheses. In other words, they are claims—like the claim that God created the world—that are supported by evidence, that are proved by arguments and tested against our experience of the world. And against the evidence, these hypotheses do not seem to fare well.

But is this the right way to think about religion? Here I want to suggest that it is not and to try and locate what seem to me some significant differences between science and religion.

To begin with, scientific explanation is a very specific and technical kind of knowledge. It requires patience, pedantry, a narrowing of focus and (in the case of the most profound scientific theories) con-

siderable mathematical knowledge and ability. No one can understand quantum theory—by any account, the most successful physical
theory there has ever been—unless they grasp the underlying mathematics. Anyone who says otherwise is fooling themselves.

Religious belief is a very different kind of thing. It is not restricted
only to those with a certain education or knowledge, it does not
require years of training, it is not specialized, and it is not technical. (I'm talking here about the content of what people who regularly
attend church, mosque or synagogue take themselves to be thinking;
I'm not talking about how theologians interpret this content.)

What is more, while religious belief is widespread, scientific
knowledge is not. I would guess that very few people in the world are
actually interested in the details of contemporary scientific theories.
Why? One obvious reason is that many lack access to this knowledge.
Another reason is that even when they have access, these theories
require sophisticated knowledge and abilities, which not everyone
is capable of getting.

Yet another reason—and the one I am interested in here—is that
most people aren't deeply interested in science, even when they have
the opportunity and the basic intellectual capacity to learn about it.
Of course, educated people who know about science know roughly
what Einstein, Newton and Darwin said. Many educated people
accept the modern scientific view of the world and understand its
main outlines. But this is not the same as being interested in the
details of science, or being immersed in scientific thinking.

This lack of interest in science contrasts sharply with the worldwide interest in religion. It's hard to say whether religion is in
decline or growing partly because it's hard to identify only one thing
as religion—not a question I can address here. But it's pretty obvious
that whatever it is, religion commands and absorbs the passions and
intellects of hundreds of millions of people, many more people than
science does. Why is this? Is it because—as the New Atheists might
argue—they want to explain the world in a scientific kind of way, but
since they have not been properly educated they haven't quite gotten
there yet? Or is it because so many people are incurably irrational

and are incapable of scientific thinking? Or is something else going on?

Some philosophers have said that religion is so unlike science that it has its own "grammar" or "logic" and should not be held accountable to the same standards as scientific or ordinary empirical belief. When Christians express their belief that "Christ has risen," for example, they should not be taken as making a factual claim but as expressing their commitment to what Wittgenstein called a certain "form of life," a way of seeing significance in the world, a moral and practical outlook that is worlds away from scientific explanation.

This view has some merits, as we shall see, but it grossly misrepresents some central phenomena of religion. It is absolutely essential to religions that they make certain factual or historical claims. When Saint Paul says, "If Christ is not risen, then our preaching is in vain and our faith is in vain," he is saying that the point of his faith depends on a certain historical occurrence.

Theologians will debate exactly what it means to claim that Christ has risen, what exactly the meaning and significance of this occurrence is, and will give more or less sophisticated accounts of it. But all I am saying is that whatever its specific nature, Christians must hold that there was such an occurrence. Christianity does make factual, historical claims. But this is not the same as being a kind of proto-science. This will become clear if we reflect a bit on what science involves.

The essence of science involves making hypotheses about the causes and natures of things, in order to explain the phenomena we observe around us and to predict their future behavior. Some sciences—medical science, for example—make hypotheses about the causes of diseases and test them by intervening. Others—cosmology, for example—make hypotheses that are more remote from everyday causes and involve a high level of mathematical abstraction and idealization. Scientific reasoning involves an obligation to hold a hypothesis only to the extent that the evidence requires it. Scientists should not accept hypotheses that are "ad hoc"—that is, just tailored for one specific situation but cannot be generalized to others. Most scientific theories involve some kind of generalization: they don't just make claims about one thing, but about things of a general kind. And their hypotheses are designed, on the whole, to make predictions; and if these predictions don't come out true, then this is something for the scientists to worry about.

Religions do not construct hypotheses in this sense. I mentioned that Christianity rests upon certain historical claims, like the claim of the resurrection. But this is not enough to make scientific hypotheses central to Christianity any more than it makes such hypotheses central to history. It is true, as I have just said, that Christianity does place certain historical events at the heart of their conception of the world, and to that extent, one cannot be a Christian unless one believes that these events happened. Speaking for myself, it is because I reject the factual basis of the central Christian doctrines that I consider myself an atheist. But I do not reject these claims because I think they are bad hypotheses in the scientific sense. Not all factual claims are scientific hypotheses. So I disagree with Richard Dawkins when he says, "Religions make existence claims, and this means scientific claims."

Taken as hypotheses, religious claims do very badly: they are ad hoc, they are arbitrary, they rarely make predictions and when they do, they almost never come true. Yet the striking fact is that it does not worry Christians when this happens. In the Gospels, Jesus predicts the end of the world and the coming of the kingdom of God. It does not worry believers that Jesus was wrong (even if it causes theologians to reinterpret what is meant by "the kingdom of God"). If Jesus was framing something like a scientific hypothesis, then it should worry them. Critics of religion might say that this just shows the manifest irrationality of religion. But what it suggests to me is that something else is going on, other than hypothesis formation.

Religious belief tolerates a high degree of mystery and ignorance in its understanding of the world. When the devout pray and their prayers are not answered, they do not take this as evidence that has to be weighed alongside all the other evidence that prayer is effective. They feel no obligation whatsoever to weigh the evidence. If God does not answer their prayers, well, there must be some explanation of this, even though we may never know it. Why do people suffer if an omnipotent God loves them? Many complex answers have been offered, but in the end they come down to this: it's a mystery.

Science, too, has its share of mysteries (or rather, things that must simply be accepted without further explanation). But one aim of science is to minimize such things, to reduce the number of primitive concepts or primitive explanations. The religious attitude is very different. It does not seek to minimize mystery. Mysteries are accepted as a consequence of what, for the religious, makes the world meaningful.

This point gets to the heart of the difference between science and religion. Religion is an attempt to make sense of the world, but it does not try and do this in the way science does. Science makes sense of the world by showing how things conform to its hypotheses. The characteristic mode of scientific explanation is showing how events fit into a general pattern.

Religion, on the other hand, attempts to make sense of the world by seeing a kind of meaning or significance in things. This kind of significance does not need laws or generalizations but just the sense that the everyday world we experience is not all there is, and that behind it all is the mystery of God's presence. The believer is already convinced that God is present in everything, even if they cannot explain this or support it with evidence. But it makes sense of their life by suffusing it with meaning. This is the attitude (seeing God in everything) expressed in George Herbert's poem, "The Elixir." Equipped with this attitude, even the most miserable tasks can come to have value: "Who sweeps a room as for Thy laws / Makes that and th' action fine."

None of these remarks are intended as being for or against religion. Rather, they are part of an attempt (by an atheist, from the outside) to understand what it is. Those who criticize religion should have an accurate understanding of what it is they are criticizing. But to understand a worldview, or a philosophy or system of thought, it is not enough just to understand the propositions it contains. You also have to understand what is central and what is peripheral to the view. Religions do make factual and historical claims, and if these claims are false, then the religions fail. But this dependence on fact does not make religious claims anything like hypotheses in the scientific sense. Hypotheses are not central. Rather, what is central is the commitment to the meaningfulness (and therefore the mystery) of the world.

I have suggested that while religious thinking is widespread in the world, scientific thinking is not. I don't think that this can be accounted for merely in terms of the ignorance or irrationality of human beings. Rather, it is because of the kind of intellectual, emotional and practical appeal that religion has for people, which is a very different appeal from the kind of appeal that science has.

Stephen Jay Gould once argued that religion and science are "nonoverlapping magisteria." If he meant by this that religion makes no factual claims that can be refuted by empirical investigations, then he was wrong. But if he meant that religion and science are very different kinds of attempts to understand the world, then he was certainly right.

SEPTEMBER 5, 2010

The Rigor of Love

—Simon Critchley

Can the experience of faith be shared by those unable to believe in the existence of a transcendent God? Might there be a faith of the faithless?

For a non-Christian, such as myself, but one out of sympathy with the triumphal evangelical atheism of the age, the core commandment of Christian faith has always been a source of both fascinated intrigue and perplexity. What is the status and force of that deceptively simple five-word command "you shall love your neighbor"? With Gary Gutting's wise counsel on the relation between philosophy and faith still ringing in our ears, I'd like to explore the possible meaning of these words through a reflection on a hugely important and influential philosopher not yet even mentioned so far in The Stone: Søren Kierkegaard (1813–55).

In the conclusion to *Works of Love* (1847)—which some consider the central work in Kierkegaard's extensive and often pseudonymous authorship—he ponders the nature of the commandment of love that he has been wrestling with throughout the book. He stresses the strenuousness and, in the word most repeated in these pages, the *rigor* of love. As such, Christian love is not, as many nonbelievers contend, some sort of "coddling love," which spares believers any particular effort. Such love can be characterized as "pleasant days or delightful days without self-made cares." This easy and fanciful idea of love reduces Christianity to "a second childhood" and renders faith infantile.

Kierkegaard then introduces the concept of "the Christian like-for-like," which is the central and decisive category of *Works of Love*. The latter is introduced by distinguishing it from what Kierkegaard calls "the Jewish like-for-like," by which he means "an eye for an eye, a tooth for a tooth": namely, a conception of obligation based on the equality and reciprocity of self and other. Although, as a cursory reading of Franz Rosenzweig's *The Star of Redemption*—one of the great works of German-Jewish thought—could easily show, this is a stereotypical and limited picture of Judaism, Kierkegaard's point is that Christian love cannot be reduced to what he calls the "worldly" conception of love where you do unto others what others do unto you and no more. The Christian like-for-like brackets out the question of what others may owe to me and instead "makes every relationship to other human beings into a God-relationship."

This move coincides with a shift from the external to the inward. Although the Christian, for Kierkegaard, "must remain in the world and the relationships of earthly life allotted to him," he or she views those relationships from the standpoint of inwardness—that is, mediated through the relationship to God. As Kierkegaard puts it emphatically in part 1 of *Works of Love*,

> *Worldly wisdom thinks that love is a relationship between man and man. Christianity teaches that love is a relationship between: man-God-man, that is, that God is the middle term.*

The rigor of Christianity is a conception of love based on radical inequality—namely, the absolute difference between the human and the divine. This is how Kierkegaard interprets Jesus's words from the Sermon on the Mount, "Why do you see the speck that is in your brother's eye, but do not notice the log that is in your own eye?" (Matthew 7:3). The log in my own eye does not permit me to *judge* the speck in the other's. Rather, I should abstain from any judgment of what others might or might not do. To judge others is to view matters from the standpoint of externality rather than inwardness. It is arrogance and impertinence. What others owe to me is none of my business.

This is why it is very hard to be Christian. And maybe there are not as many true Christians around as one might have thought. Kierkegaard writes, "Christianly understood you have absolutely nothing to do with what others do to you." "Essentially," he continues, "you have only to do with yourself before God." Once again, the move to inwardness does not turn human beings away from the world; it is rather "a new version of what other men call reality, this is reality."

The address of Kierkegaard's writing has a specific direction: the second person singular, *you*. He tells the story from the Gospels (versions appear in Matthew and Luke) of the Roman centurion in Capernaum who approached Jesus and asked him to cure his servant or boy, the sense is ambiguous, "sick with the palsy, grievously tormented" (Matthew 8:6). After Jesus said that he would visit the boy, the centurion confessed that, as a representative of the occupying imperial authority with soldiers under his command, he did not feel worthy that Jesus should enter his house. When Jesus heard this, he declared that he had not experienced a person of such great faith in the whole of Israel. He added, and this is the line that interests Kierkegaard, "Be it done for you, as you believed."

This story reveals the essential insecurity of faith. Kierkegaard writes that it does not belong to Christian doctrine to vouchsafe that you—"precisely *you*," as he emphasizes—have faith. If someone were to say, "It is absolutely certain that I have faith because I have been baptized in the church and follow its rituals and ordinances," then Kierkegaard would reply, "Be it done for you, as you believed." The point of the story is that the centurion, although he was not baptized as a Christian, nonetheless believed. As Kierkegaard writes, "In his faith, *the* Gospel is first *a* gospel." The New Testament Greek for *gospel* is *euaggelion*, which can mean good tidings but can also be thought of as the act of proclamation or pledging. On this view, faith is a proclamation or pledge that brings the inward subject of faith into being over against an external everydayness. Such a proclamation is as true for the non-Christian as for the Christian. Indeed, it is arguably *more* true for the non-Christian, because their faith is not supported by the supposed guarantee of baptism, creedal dogma, regular church attendance or some notion that virtue will be rewarded with happiness if not here on earth, then in the afterlife. Thus, paradoxically, non-Christian faith might be said to reveal the true nature of the faith that Christ sought to proclaim. Even—and indeed especially— those who are denominationally faithless can have an experience of faith. If faith needs to be underpinned by some sort of doctrinal security, then inwardness becomes externalized and the strenuous rigor of faith evaporates.

What sort of certainty, then, is the experience of faith? Kierkegaard writes, and again the second-person singular direction of address should be noted, "It is eternally certain that it will be done for you as you believe, but the certainty of faith, or the certainty that *you, you in particular*, believe, you must win at every moment with God's help, consequently not in some external way" (emphasis mine).

Kierkegaard insists—and one feels here the force of his polemic against the irreligious, essentially secular order of so-called Christendom, in his case what he saw as the pseudo-Christianity of the Danish National Church—that no pastor or priest has the right to say that one has faith or not according to doctrines like baptism and the like. To proclaim faith is to abandon such external or worldly guarantees. Faith has the character of a continuous "striving . . . in which you get occasion to be tried every day." This is why faith and the commandment of love that it seeks to sustain is not law. It has no coercive, external force. As Rosenzweig writes, "The commandment of love can only proceed from the mouth of the lover." He goes on to contrast this with law, "which reckons with times, with a future, with duration." By contrast, the commandment of love "knows only the moment; it awaits the result in the very moment of its promulgation." The commandment of love is mild and merciful, but, as Kierkegaard insists, "there is rigor in it." We might say love is that disciplined act of absolute spiritual daring that eviscerates the old self of externality so something new and inward can come into being.

As Kierkagaard puts it earlier in *Works of Love*, citing Paul, "Owe no one anything, except to love one another" (Romans 13:8). It sounds simple. But what is implicit in this minimal-sounding command is a conception of love as an experience of infinite debt—a debt that it is impossible to repay: "When a man is gripped by love, he feels that this is like being in infinite debt." To be is to be in debt—I owe, therefore I am.

If sin is the theological name for the essential ontological indebtedness of the self, then love is the experience of a countermovement to sin that is orientated around a demand that exceeds the capacity or ability of the self. Love is shaped in relation to what, in my parlance, can be called an infinite demand. Kierkegaard writes, and the double emphasis on the "moment" that finds an echo in Rosenzweig should be noted, "God's relationship to a human being is the infinitizing at every moment of that which at every moment is in a man." Withdrawn into inwardness and solitude ("If you have never been solitary, you have never discovered that God exists," Kierkegaard writes), each and every word and action of the self resounds through the infinite demand of God.

At this point, in the penultimate paragraph of *Works of Love* Kierkegaard shifts to auditory imagery. God is a vast echo chamber where each sound, "the slightest sound," is duplicated and resounds back loudly into the subject's ears. God is nothing more than the name for the *repetition* of each word that the subject utters. But it is a repetition that resounds with "the intensification of infinity." In what Kierkegaard calls "the urban confusion" of external life, it is nigh impossible to hear this repetitive echo of the infinite demand. This is why the bracketing out of externality is essential: "externality is too dense a body for resonance, and the sensual ear is too hard-of-hearing to catch the eternal's repetition." We need to cultivate the inner or inward ear that infinitizes the words and actions of the self. As Kierkegaard makes clear, what he is counseling is not "to sit in the anxiety of death, day in and day out, listening for the repetition of the eternal." What is rather being called for is a rigorous and activist conception of faith that proclaims itself into being at each instant without guarantee or security and that abides with the infinite demand of love.

Faith is not a like-for-like relationship of equals, but the asymmetry of the like-to-unlike. It is a subjective strength that only finds its power to act through an admission of weakness. Faith is an enactment of the self in relation to an infinite demand that both exceeds my power and yet requires all my power. Such an experience of faith is not only shared by those who are faithless from a creedal or denominational perspective, but can—in my view—be had by them in an exemplary manner. Like the Roman centurion of whom Kierkegaard writes, it is perhaps the faithless who can best sustain the rigor of faith without requiring security, guarantees and rewards: "Be it done for you, as you believed."

AUGUST 8, 2010

Does It Matter Whether God Exists?

—Gary Gutting

DISCUSSIONS OF RELIGION ARE TYPICALLY ABOUT GOD. ATHE-
ists reject religion because they don't believe in God; Jews, Christians
and Muslims take belief in God as fundamental to their religious
commitment. The philosopher John Gray, however, has recently
been arguing that belief in God should have little or nothing to do
with religion. He points out that in many cases—for instance, "polytheism, Hinduism and Buddhism, Daoism and Shinto, many strands
of Judaism and some Christian and Muslim traditions"—belief is of
little or no importance. Rather, "practice—ritual, meditation, a way
of life—is what counts." He goes on to say that "it's only religious
fundamentalists and ignorant rationalists who think the myths we
live by are literal truths" and that "what we believe doesn't in the end
matter very much. What matters is how we live."

The obvious response to Gray is that it all depends on what you hope
to find in a religion. If your hope is simply for guidance and assistance
in leading a fulfilling life here on earth, a "way of living" without firm
beliefs in any supernatural being may well be all you need. But many
religions, including mainline versions of Christianity and Islam,
promise much more. They promise ultimate salvation. If we are faithful to their teachings, they say, we will be safe from final annihilation
when we die and will be happy eternally in our life after death.

If our hope is for salvation in this sense—and for many that is the
main point of religion—then this hope depends on certain religious

beliefs being true. In particular, for the main theistic religions, it depends on there being a God who is good enough to desire our salvation and powerful enough to achieve it.

But here we come to a point that is generally overlooked in debates about theism, which center on whether there is reason to believe in God, understood as all-good and all-powerful. Suppose that the existence of such a God could be decisively established. Suppose, for example, we were to be entirely convinced that a version of the ontological argument, which claims to show that the very idea of an all-perfect being requires that such a being exist, is sound. We would then be entirely certain that there is a being of supreme power and goodness. But what would this imply about our chances for eternal salvation?

On reflection, very little. Granted, we would know that our salvation was possible: an all-powerful being could bring it about. But would we have any reason to think that God would in fact do this? Well, how could an all-good being not desire our salvation? The problem is that an all-good being needs to take account of the entire universe, not just us.

Here, discussions of the problem of evil become crucial. An all-good being, even with maximal power, may have to allow considerable local evils for the sake of the overall good of the universe; some evils may be necessary for the sake of avoiding even worse evils. We have no way of knowing whether we humans might be the victims of this necessity.

Of course, an all-good God would do everything possible to minimize the evil we suffer, but for all we know that minimum might have to include our annihilation or eternal suffering. We might hope that any evil we endure will at least be offset by an equal or greater amount of good for us, but there can be no guarantee. As defenders of theism often point out, the freedom of moral agents may be an immense good, worth God's tolerating horrendous wrongdoing. Perhaps God in his omniscience knows that the good of allowing some higher type of beings to destroy our eternal happiness outweighs the good of that happiness. Perhaps, for example, their destroying our happiness is an unavoidable step in the moral drama leading to their salvation and eternal happiness.

My point here reflects the two-edged character of religious responses to the problem of evil. The only plausible answer to the question, "How could an all-good and all-powerful God allow immense evils?" is that such a God may well have knowledge beyond our understanding. As David Hume suggested in his *Dialogues Concerning Natural Religion*, the problem of evil is solved only by an appeal to our own ignorance. (There are powerful formulations of this approach by philosophers called "skeptical theists.")

Such an appeal may save us from the apparent contradiction of evil in a world created by an all-good God. But it also severely limits our judgments about what an all-good God would do. It may seem to us that if we live as we should, God will ensure our salvation. But it also seems, from our limited viewpoint, that God would not permit things like the Holocaust or the death of innocent children from painful diseases. Once we appeal to the gap between our limited knowledge and God's omniscience, we cannot move from what we *think* God will do to what he *will* in fact do. So the fact that we think an all-good God would ensure our salvation does not support the conclusion that, all things considered, he will in fact do so.

It follows, then, that even a decisive proof that there is an all-good, all-powerful God cannot assure us that we are ultimately safe. Even if we insist on a religion that goes beyond John Gray's beliefless way of living, belief that there is a God leaves us far short of what we hope for from religion.

Many believers will agree. Their confidence in salvation, they say, comes not from philosophical arguments but from their personal contact with God, either through individual experience or a religious tradition. But what can such contact provide concretely? At best, certainty that there is a very powerful being who promises to save us. But there may well be—and many religions insist that there are—very powerful beings (demons or devils) intent on leading us away from salvation. How could we possibly know that the power we are in contact with is not deceiving us?

The inevitable response is that an all-good God would not permit such a thing. But that takes us back to the previous difficulty: there is no reason to think that we are good judges of what God is likely to permit. God may have to allow us to be deceived to prevent even greater evils.

We can, of course, simply will to believe that we are not being deceived. But that amounts to blind faith, not assured hope. If that doesn't satisfy us, we need to find a better response to the problem of evil than an appeal to our ignorance. Failing that, we may need to reconsider John Gray's idea of religion with little or no belief.

MARCH 22, 2012

The Importance of the Afterlife. Seriously.

—Samuel Scheffler

I BELIEVE IN LIFE AFTER DEATH.

No, I don't think that I will live on as a conscious being after my earthly demise. I'm firmly convinced that death marks the unqualified and irreversible end of our lives.

My belief in life after death is more mundane. What I believe is that other people will continue to live after I myself have died. You probably make the same assumption in your own case. Although we know that humanity won't exist forever, most of us take it for granted that the human race will survive, at least for a while, after we ourselves are gone.

Because we take this belief for granted, we don't think much about its significance. Yet I think that this belief plays an extremely important role in our lives, quietly but critically shaping our values, commitments and sense of what is worth doing. Astonishing though it may seem, there are ways in which the continuing existence of other people after our deaths—even that of complete strangers—matters more to us than does our own survival and that of our loved ones.

Consider a hypothetical scenario. Suppose you knew that although you yourself would live a long life and die peacefully in your sleep, the earth and all its inhabitants would be destroyed thirty days after your death in a collision with a giant asteroid. How would this knowledge affect you?

If you are like me, and like most people with whom I have discussed the question, you would find this doomsday knowledge profoundly disturbing. And it might greatly affect your decisions about how to live. If you were a cancer researcher, you might be less motivated to continue your work. (It would be unlikely, after all, that a cure would be found in your lifetime, and even if it were, how much good would it do in the time remaining?) Likewise if you were an engineer working to improve the seismic safety of bridges, or an activist trying to reform our political or social institutions or a carpenter who cared about building things to last, what difference would these endeavors make if the destruction of the human race was imminent?

If you were a novelist or playwright or composer, you might see little point in continuing to write or compose, since these creative activities are often undertaken with an imagined future audience or legacy in mind. And faced with the knowledge that humanity would cease to exist soon after your death, would you still be motivated to have children? Maybe not.

Notice that people do not typically react with such a loss of purpose to the prospect of their own deaths. Of course, many people are terrified of dying. But even people who fear death (and even those who do not believe in a personal afterlife) remain confident of the value of their activities despite knowing that they will die someday. Thus there is a way in which the survival of other people after our deaths matters more to us than our own survival.

The explanation for this may seem simple: if the earth will be destroyed thirty days after we die, then everyone we care about who is alive at that time will meet a sudden, violent end. Spouses and partners, children and grandchildren, friends and lovers: all would be doomed. Perhaps it is our concern for our loved ones that explains our horror at the prospect of a postmortem catastrophe.

But I don't think this is the full story. Consider another hypothetical scenario, drawn from P. D. James's novel *The Children of Men*. In Ms. James's novel, humanity has become infertile, with no recorded birth having occurred in over twenty-five years. Imagine that you found yourself living in such circumstances. Nobody now alive is younger than twenty-five and the disappearance of the human race is imminent as an aging population inexorably fades away. How would you react?

As in the case of the asteroidal collision, many activities would begin to seem pointless under these conditions: cancer research, seismic safety efforts, social and political activism, and so on. Beyond that, as Ms. James's novel vividly suggests, the onset of irreversible global infertility would be likely to produce widespread depression, anxiety and despair.

Some people would seek consolation in religious faith, and some would find it. Others would take what pleasure they could in activities that seemed intrinsically rewarding: listening to music, exploring the natural world, spending time with family and friends and enjoying the pleasures of food and drink. But even these activities might seem less fulfilling and be tinged with sadness and pain when set against the background of a dying humanity.

Notice that in this scenario, unlike that of the asteroidal collision, nobody would die prematurely. So what is dismaying about the prospect of living in an infertile world cannot be that we are horrified by the demise of our loved ones. (They would die eventually, of course, but that is no different from our actual situation.) What is dismaying is simply that no new people would come into existence.

This should give us pause. The knowledge that we and everyone we know and love will someday die does not cause most of us to lose confidence in the value of our daily activities. But the knowledge that no new people would come into existence would make many of those things seem pointless.

I think this shows that some widespread assumptions about human egoism are oversimplified at best. However self-interested or narcissistic we may be, our capacity to find purpose and value in our lives depends on what we expect to happen to others after our deaths. Even the egotistic tycoon who is devoted to his own glory might discover that his ambitions seemed pointless if humanity's disappearance was imminent. Although some people can afford not to depend on the kindness of strangers, virtually everyone depends on the future existence of strangers.

Similarly, I think that familiar assumptions about human individualism are oversimplified. Even though we as individuals have diverse values and goals, and even though it is up to each of us to judge what we consider to be a good or worthy life, most of us pursue our goals and seek to realize our values within a framework of belief that assumes an ongoing humanity. Remove that framework of belief, and our confidence in our values and purposes begins to erode.

There is also a lesson here for those who think that unless there is a personal afterlife, their lives lack any meaning or purpose. What is necessary to underwrite the perceived significance of what we do, it seems, is not a belief in the afterlife but rather a belief that humanity will survive, at least for a good long time.

But will humanity survive for a good long time? Although we normally assume that others will live on after we ourselves have died, we also know that there are serious threats to humanity's survival. Not all of these threats are human-made, but some of the most pressing certainly are, like those posed by climate change and nuclear proliferation. People who worry about these problems often urge us to remember our obligations to future generations, whose fate depends so heavily on what we do today. We are obligated, they stress, not to make the earth uninhabitable or to degrade the environment in which our descendants will live.

I agree. But there is also another side to the story. Yes, our descendants depend on us to make possible their existence and well-being. But we also depend on them and their existence if we are to lead flourishing lives ourselves. And so our reasons to overcome the threats to humanity's survival do not derive solely from our obligations to our descendants. We have another reason to try to ensure a flourishing future for those who come after us: it is simply that, to an extent that we rarely recognize or acknowledge, they already matter so much to us.

THE VARIETIES OF RELIGIOUS DISAGREEMENT

In Praise of the Clash of Cultures

—Carlos Fraenkel

ABOUT TWELVE YEARS AGO, WHILE STUDYING ARABIC IN CAIRO, I became friends with some Egyptian students. As we got to know each other better we also became concerned about each other's way of life. They wanted to save my soul from eternally burning in hell by converting me to Islam. I wanted to save them from wasting their real life for an illusory afterlife by converting them to the secular world-view I grew up with. In one of our discussions they asked me if I was sure that there is no proof for God's existence. The question took me by surprise. Where I had been intellectually socialized, it was taken for granted that there was none. I tried to remember Kant's critique of the ontological proof for God. "Fine," Muhammad said, "but what about this table? Does its existence depend on a cause?" "Of course," I answered. "And its cause depends on a further cause?" Muhammad was referring to the metaphysical proof for God's existence, first formulated by the Muslim philosopher Avicenna in the eleventh century: since an infinite regress of causes is impossible, Avicenna argues, things that depend on a cause for their existence must have something that exists through itself as their first cause. And this necessary existent is God. I had a counterargument to that to which they in turn had a rejoinder. The discussion ended inconclusively.

I did not convert to Islam, nor did my Egyptian friends become atheists. But I learned an important lesson from our discussions: that I hadn't properly thought through some of the most basic convictions underlying my way of life and worldview—from God's existence to the human good. The challenge of my Egyptian friends forced me to think hard about these issues and defend views that had never been questioned in the European student milieu where I came from.

The other thing I realized was how contested my views were. I completed high school in a West German town in 1990 in the middle of Germany's turbulent reunification (I ended my final exam in history describing the newest political developments I had heard on the radio that same morning). For a few years after the breakdown of the Soviet Bloc, many thought that everyone would be secular and live in a liberal democracy before long. The discussions with my Egyptian friends brought home that I better not hold my breath.

Since that time I have organized philosophy workshops at a Palestinian university in East Jerusalem, at an Islamic university in Indonesia, with members of a Hasidic community in New York, with high school students in Salvador da Bahia (the center of Afro-Brazilian culture), and in a First Nations community in Canada. These workshops gave me firsthand insight into how deeply divided we are on fundamental moral, religious, and philosophical questions. While many find these disagreements disheartening, I will argue that they can be a good thing—if we manage to make them fruitful for a culture debate.

Can we be sure that our beliefs about the world match how the world actually is and that our subjective preferences match what is objectively in our best interest? If the truth is important to us, these are pressing questions.

We might value the truth for different reasons: because we want to live a life that is good and doesn't just appear so; because we take knowing the truth to be an important component of the good life; because we consider living by the truth a moral obligation independent of any consequences; or because, like my Egyptian friends, we want to come closer to God who is the Truth (al-Haqq in Arabic, one of God's names in Islam). Of course we wouldn't hold our beliefs and values if we weren't *convinced* that they are true. But that's no evidence that they are. Weren't my Egyptian friends just as convinced of their views as I was of mine? More generally, don't we find a bewildering diversity of beliefs and values, all held with great conviction, across different times and cultures? If considerations such as these lead you to concede that your present convictions could be false, then you are a *fallibilist*. And if you are a fallibilist, you can see why valuing the truth and valuing a culture of debate are related: because you will want to critically examine your beliefs and values, for which a culture of debate offers an excellent setting.

Of course we don't need to travel all the way to Cairo to subject our beliefs and values to critical scrutiny; in theory we can also do so on our own. In practice, however, we seem to need some sort of unsettling experience that confronts us with our fallibility, or, as the great Muslim thinker al-Ghazâlî (d. 1111) puts it in his intellectual autobiography *The Deliverance from Error*, that breaks the "bonds of taqlîd"— the beliefs and values stemming from the contingent circumstances of our socialization rather than from rational deliberation.

In his own case, al-Ghazâlî writes, the bonds of taqlîd broke when he realized that he would have been just as fervent a Jew or Christian as he was a Muslim had he been brought up in a Jewish or Christian community. He explains taqlîd as the authority of "parents and teachers," which we can restate more generally as all things other than rational argument that influence what we think and do: from media, fashion and marketing to political rhetoric and religious ideology.

The problem of taqlîd (or what social psychologists today call "conformism") has a long history. Socrates explained the need for his gadfly mission by comparing Athenian citizens to a "sluggish" horse that "needed to be stirred up." Note that philosophers, too, fall prey to taqlîd. Galen, the second-century Alexandrian doctor and philosopher, complained that in his time Platonists, Aristotelians, Stoics and Epicureans simply "name themselves after the sect in which they were brought up" because they "form admirations" for the school founders, not because they choose the views supported by the best arguments.

If we take taqlîd to be a fact about human psychology and agree that it is an undesirable state to be in—at least when it comes to the core convictions that underlie our way of life and worldview—then we should particularly welcome debates across cultural boundaries. For if we engage someone who does not share the cultural narratives we were brought up in (historical, political, religious, etc.), we cannot rely on their authority, but are compelled to argue for our views—as I had to in my discussions with Egyptian students in Cairo. Consider a theological debate in the multicultural world of medieval Islam, described by the historian al-Humaydi (d. 1095):

> At the . . . meeting there were present not only people of various [Islamic] sects but also unbelievers, Magians, materialists, atheists, Jews and Christians, in short unbelievers of all kinds. Each group had its own leader, whose task it was to defend its views. . . . One of the unbelievers rose and said to the assembly: we are meeting here for a debate; its conditions are known to all. You, Muslims, are not allowed to argue from your books and prophetic traditions since we deny both. Everybody, therefore, has to limit himself to rational arguments [hujaj al-'aql]. The whole assembly applauded these words.

We can consider ourselves lucky to live at a time in which societies are becoming increasingly heterogeneous and multicultural and globalization forces us to interact across national, cultural, religious, and other boundaries; for all this is conducive to breaking the bonds of taqlîd.

Of course diversity and disagreement on their own are not sufficient to bring about a culture of debate (otherwise the Middle East, the Balkans and many other places would be philosophical debating clubs!). Instead they often generate frustration and resentment or, worse, erupt in violence. That's why we need a *culture* of debate. In my view, the last years of high school are the best place to lay the groundwork for such a culture.

The high school curriculum already includes subjects such as evolution, which are much more controversial than the skills

required for engaging difference and disagreement in a constructive way. To provide the foundation for a culture of debate, the classes
I have in mind would focus on two things: conveying techniques of
debate (logical and semantic tools that allow students to clarify their
views and to make and respond to arguments—a contemporary version of what Aristotelians called the organon, the "tool kit" of the
philosopher) and cultivating virtues of debate (loving the truth more
than winning an argument, and trying one's best to understand the
viewpoint of the opponent).

When we can transform the disagreements arising from diversity
into a culture of debate, they cease to be a threat to social peace. I now
live in Montréal, one of the world's most multicultural cities. When
a couple of years ago I had to see a doctor, the receptionist was from
China, in the waiting room I sat between a Hasidic Jew and a secular
Québécois couple, the doctor who attended me was from Iran, and
the nurse from Haiti. This was an impressive example of how Canadians, despite their deep moral, religious, and philosophical differences, can work together to provide the basic goods and services that
we all need irrespective of our way of life and worldview.

But while I certainly didn't want to get into a shouting match
about God's existence in the doctor's office, or wait for treatment
until everyone had agreed on how to live, I see no reason why we
should ignore our differences altogether. Some advocates of multi-
culturalism ask us to celebrate, rather than just tolerate, diversity,
as if our differences weren't a reason for disagreement in the first
place, but something good and beautiful—a multicultural "mosaic"!
Others argue that our moral, religious, and philosophical convictions shouldn't leave the private sphere. A good example is French
laïcité: you are a *citoyen* in public and a Jew, Christian, or Muslim at
home. Both models try to remove our reasons for objecting to beliefs
and values we don't share—one tries to remove them altogether, the
other tries at least to keep them out of sight. A culture of debate, on
the other hand, allows us to engage our differences in a way that is
serious, yet respectful and mutually beneficial.

Some object that a culture of debate is of no value to religious citizens. Don't they take God's wisdom to be infallible, claim to have access to it through revelation, and accept its contents on faith rather than arguments? Yet a brief look at the history of religions shows that plenty of arguing was going on about how to understand God's wisdom—within a religious tradition, with members of other religious traditions and more recently, with secular opponents. Al-Ghazâlî, for one, writes how, after the bonds of taqlîd were broken, he "scrutinized the creed of every sect" and "tried to lay bare the inmost doctrines of every community" in order to "distinguish between true and false."

The rich philosophical literatures we find in Judaism, Christianity and Islam as well as in the Eastern religious traditions offer plenty of resources for a culture of debate. The privatization of moral, religious, and philosophical views in liberal democracies and the cultural relativism that often underlies Western multicultural agendas are a much greater obstacle to a culture of debate than religion. My friends in Cairo, at any rate, and the participants in the workshops I subsequently organized all enjoyed arguing for their views and criticizing mine.

SEPTEMBER 2, 2012

What's Wrong With Blasphemy?

—Andrew F. March

Suppose there had not been a single riot in response to the now infamous video "The Innocence of Muslims." Not a single car burned, not a single embassy breached, not a single human being physically hurt. Would the makers of this risible little clip have done anything wrong? If so, to whom, and why?

These questions are now at the center of an international debate. President Obama himself touched on the issue in his speech to the United Nations General Assembly this month (September 2012), in which he directly addressed the violent reaction in the Muslim world to the "crude and disgusting video." But does philosophy have anything to say to the view that many people have that there is something about this kind of speech itself—not just its harm to public order or its adding of insult to the injury of imperialism and war—that should not be uttered or produced?

Obviously, we think this about many other kinds of speech. Most of us think that it is wrong for white people to use the "n-word." (Use it? I can't even bring myself to *mention* it.) Personally, I would feel a shiver of guilt and shame if that word crossed my mind as a thought about another person. And it's not hard to account for that feeling. It is a word that is intimately associated with a chain of some of humanity's greatest historical evils—the trans-Atlantic slave trade, the practice of chattel slavery and countless legal, social and psychological practices aiming at the effective dehumanization of persons of black African origin. To perpetuate it publicly is to harm other persons, and this matters objectively even if I don't personally, sub-jectively care about the persons in question. But my feelings about this word are even deeper than this: I don't even want to participate in the history that produced it and its meaning by letting it grow roots in my own mind.

This word is just an archetype to fix our thoughts. I feel that way about a lot of other words, even if nothing can quite rise to the level of emotion as that one. I can account in a very similar way for my disgust at similar epithets that seek to target for exclusion, suffer-ing and disrespect gays, Jews, Arabs, Muslims, women and others. The suffering and disadvantage of humans matters, and I am doing nothing important in the world when I use such an epithet without considering the well-being of other humans. Even when it should be legal to do so, I have good—often decisive—reasons for not using such speech.

Can the same be said not about epithets but about speech that mocks, insults or tells lies about things that others hold sacred, whether they be texts, human prophets or physical objects? What reasons do we have to censor ourselves (something we do all the time, and often for very good reasons) in how we speak about things other people hold sacred?

Most secular philosophical approaches to the morality of speech about the sacred are going to begin with three starting points:

- *Human beings have very strong interests in being free to express themselves.*

- *The "sacred" is an object of human construction and thus the fact that something is called "sacred" is insufficient itself to explain why all humans ought to respect it.*

- *Respect is owed to persons but not everything they value or vener-ate, even if other persons themselves do not uphold such a differ-ence between their selves and their attachments.*

These three premises make it hard for some common arguments about speech and the sacred to fully persuade. Here are six I find to be common.

1. Blasphemy transgresses a boundary and violates the sacred.

From the perspective of the religious, this is the greatest harm in blasphemy. In Islamic law, for example, both God and the Prophet Muhammad not only have value for the believers but also have interests and rights themselves. But what reason does this give others not to violate the sacred if they do not agree that x or y is sacred or has such awesome value? No reason at all.

2. We should respect whatever people regard as "sacred" or treat as religious.

I have no objection to this as one principle of the morality of speech. Certainly, the fact that x is called "sacred" by someone else should give me some reason to rethink what I am about to say. But there are two obvious problems here: (a) this gives other persons wide latitude to claim a veto over my speech by calling "sacred" things I find anything but—the American flag, David Miscavige, Mormon underpants—and (b) it is so easy to think of examples where I am doing valuable and important things in speaking that outweigh the otherwise regrettable fact that others are injured or pained as an unintended consequence of my speech.

3. People are deeply hurt and injured by violations of the sacred or objects of love.

This matters. The pain of others always matters. But pain alone cannot explain the totality of our moral relationships. People are pained by all kinds of things. People attach themselves to all kinds of histories, symbols and institutions. Pain is sometimes deserved.

At the very least, it is sometimes a reasonable cost to bear for other things we value. The religious know this better than most of us.

4. Blasphemy is dangerous.

The great Thomas Hobbes went so far as to declare insults to be a violation of natural law, even before we enter the social contract. He would not have been surprised at the reaction to the Danish cartoons, the "Innocence of Muslims" film or any bar fight: "Any sign of hatred and contempt is more provocative of quarrels and fighting than anything else, so that most men prefer to lose their peace and even lives rather than suffer insult." So, yes, the fact that an offensive word will contribute to an outbreak of violence is a very good reason not to utter it, often a decisive and sufficient reason. The problem is, what kind of reason? If we think that our words were reasonable and not meant to provoke and we still censor ourselves, we are acting out of prudence or fear, and in a way treating the other as irrational. Aren't humans capable of more inspiring terms of association than mutual fear?

5. Blasphemy is hate speech.

There is no question that many in the West today use speech about Muhammad and "Islam" as cover for expressing hatred toward Muslims. They know that if they are talking about "religion," they can deny they are talking about persons. Many people doing this—from Geert Wilders to those behind "Innocence of Muslims"—are indeed hatemongers. But we should avoid the all-too-common conclusion that because much speech about Muhammad is de facto barely coded hate speech about Muslims (and much of it is), *all* such speech is. Many believers will in good faith testify that no one who expresses hatred for Islam's doctrines and prophet can respect them as persons. I believe them. But from a secular moral perspective, there is no way to completely eliminate the gap between whatever qualities or value we imagine all humans to have and the many valuable attachments and beliefs actual humans are made of. After all, many religious thinkers will say that they despise secular materialism or atheism and yet still respect the misguided humans enslaved to those doctrines. I believe them then, too.

6. *Blasphemy disrupts social harmony.*

This is a different argument from the one that blasphemy is dangerous. Let us return to the "n-word." A plausible case can be made that the widespread public use of this word does more than offend, harm or intimidate African-Americans. It harms a certain kind of public good that many Americans are striving hard to attain—the public good of a society where people feel safe, valued and at home in their social home. There is a way in which *all* Americans are the victims of such speech; for I as a white American have an interest in an America where my sense of belonging is not achieved at the expense of others. In Europe and North America today, lots of public blasphemy about Islam (especially in visual form) performs this function. It serves to tell Muslims, "We don't trust you, we don't like you, and it's your job to change." All we have to do is remember speech about Catholicism in this country until quite recently. Cartoons of Catholic bishops as crocodiles coming to devour potentially Protestant children were much worse than an assault on the institution of the bishopric or a theological disputation about where Christ's ecclesia is embodied. It was Protestant nativism directed at Catholics as persons, not only as believers.

For all the instinctive talk about the need for "respect for religion" or "sensitivity toward the sacred," this I think is what most people find most troubling about everything from the "Innocence of Muslims" to the (much worse) "Muslim Rage" *Newsweek* cover of last week. And I agree. But there are at least two caveats: (a) it leaves us with the conclusion that there is absolutely nothing wrong with the blasphemous content of such speech per se (nothing about Catholic bishops or the Prophet Muhammad that should never be maligned), and (b) we have to explain what kinds of social relationships we are obligated to care for in this way. Yes, I have an obligation not to make my Scientologist neighbor feel unwelcome . . . but Tom Cruise? Bombs away.

WHAT I HAVE TRIED to argue is that none of these common arguments alone gives us sufficient reason to refrain from blasphemous speech merely because it is blasphemous, the way that I do feel I have more than sufficient reason to never use (and to try to never think) then n-word. But that doesn't mean that none of the aforementioned were reasons not to violate what others hold sacred. They were reasons, just ones that might be outweighed by the value of the things I want to say.

So are we left with some crude felicific arithmetic: (amount of emotional pain) - (value of blasphemous speech uttered) = net morality of this or that utterance? I think there is something more to be said here.

We all too often speak about the harms of speech either in abstract terms (the speech is wrong) or in attribute-sensitive terms (one should not be mocked for this). But what is missing here is the sense of *relational duties* that so many of us feel. The view that one just says whatever one wishes regardless of the company one is keeping is not virtuous honesty or moral heroism, but a kind of moral autism. The content of speech is just one element of its morality; the recipient is another.

While certain aspects of morality ought to apply without regard for the identity of other persons and any relationships I may have with them, many other aspects of morality are precisely relational. I care about specific persons and my relationship with them. This increases the costs to my own conscience, moral costs, in saying things that I otherwise think are worth saying. There are lots of things I would normally say that I do not say to or around specific people. This is sometimes because I am scared of them, or scared of experiencing social awkwardness. Other times it is because I care about them and our relationship. They matter to me, and our relationship is a good worth sacrificing for. This is why we don't tell lies, or do tell lies, to certain people.

Could the morality of blasphemy be something like this? No—there is no abstract, relation-independent wrong in mocking someone else's prophet, even to the extent that I think there is wrong in using speech like the n-word. Instead, given the awareness of the impact such speech on others whom you might care about might have (even if you think it is wrong or silly for such speech to impact them in this way), the value you place on these relationships alters your moral judgment about such speech. The emotional world of someone about whom you care, or with whom you have a social relationship about which you care, matters to you when you speak.

Now, this is not a shortcut to merely condemning blasphemy. I may continue to judge my friends to be oversensitive, or my speech to be so important as to outweigh their emotional pain. And, of course, fellow citizens do not usually matter as much to me as people in my day-to-day life. And distant strangers matter still less. But, nonetheless, I think there is something for philosophy to encourage us to think about beyond the recycled clichés that emerge on all sides each time some new utterance creates an international crisis. At the very least, it encourages us to see conflicts over such speech not only as a conflict between the value of free speech and the value of sensitivity, but also in terms of social and political relationships that we have some obligation to care for.

SEPTEMBER 25, 2012

Why I Love Mormonism

—Simon Critchley

I'VE SPENT WHAT IS RAPIDLY BECOMING NINE YEARS IN NEW YORK City. It's been a total blast. But as a transplanted Englishman one thing to which I've become rather sensitive in that time is which prejudices New Yorkers are permitted to express in public. Among my horribly overeducated and hugely liberal friends, expressions of racism are completely out of the question, Islamophobia is greeted with a slow shaking of the head, and anti-Semitism is a memory associated with distant places that one sometimes visits—like France.

But anti-Mormonism is another matter. It's really fine to say totally uninformed things about Mormonism in public, at dinner parties or wherever. "It's a cult," says one. "With thirteen million followers and counting?" I reply. "Polygamy is disgusting," says another. "It was made illegal in Utah and banned by the church in 1890, wasn't it?" I counter. And so on. This is a *casual* prejudice that is not like the visceral hatred that plagued the early decades of Mormonism—lest it be forgotten, Joseph Smith was shot to death on June 27, 1844, by an angry mob who broke into a jail where he was detained—but a symptom of a thoughtless incuriousness.

There is just something *weird* about Mormonism, and the very mention of the Book of Mormon invites smirks and giggles, which is why choosing it as the name for Broadway's most hard-to-get-into show was a smart move. As a scholar of Mormonism once remarked, one does not need to read the Book of Mormon in order to have an opinion about it.

But every now and then during one of those New York soirées, when anti-Mormon prejudice is persistently pressed and expressed, and I perhaps feel momentarily and un-Mormonly emboldened by wine, I begin to try and share my slim understanding of Joseph Smith and my fascination with the Latter-Day Saints. After about forty-five seconds, sometimes less, it becomes apparent that the prejudice is based on sheer ignorance of the peculiar splendors of Mormon theology. "They are all Republicans anyway," they add in conclusion. "I mean, just look at that Mitbot Romney. He's an alien." As an alien myself, I find this thoughtless anti-Mormon sentiment a little bewildering.

This is mainly because my experience with Mormonism was somewhat different. Very early on in my philosophical travels, near the Italian city of Perugia to be precise, I met Mormon philosophers—Heideggerians actually, but this was the 1980s when many such dinosaurs roamed the earth—and got to know them quite well. They were from Brigham Young University and they were some of the kindest, most self-effacing and honest people I have ever met. They were also funny, warm, genuine, completely open-minded, smart and terribly well read. We became friends.

There was still suspicion, of course, perhaps even more so back then. I remember being pulled aside late at night by an American friend and told, "You know that guy from BYU? They say he's a bishop and conducts secret services." "Does he eat babies, too?" I wondered out loud.

Thereby hangs a story. Because of my convivial contact with these philosophers from BYU, I was invited in 1994 to give a series of lectures. I stayed for more than a week in Provo, Utah. The absence of caffeine or any other stimulants was tough, but the hospitality was fulsome and I was welcomed into people's homes and treated with great civility and care. My topic was romanticism, and the argument kicked off from the idea that the extraordinary burst of creative energy that we associate with romantic poetry comes out of a disappointment with a religious, specifically Christian, worldview. Poetry becomes secular scripture. In other words, romantic art announces the death of God, an idea that catches fire in the later nineteenth century. It's a familiar story.

Things went pretty well. But right at the end of the final lecture, something peculiar happened. A member of the audience asked me a question. He said, "What you have been telling us this week about romanticism and the death of God where religion becomes art is premised on a certain understanding of God—namely, that God is unitary and infinite. Would you agree?" "Sure," I said. "At least two of the predicates of the divinity are that he/she/it is unitary and infinite." Gosh, I was smart back then. "But what if," he went on, "God were plural and finite?"

Concealing my slight shock, I simply said, "Pray, tell." Everyone in the room laughed, somewhat knowingly. And with that the chairman closed the session. I went straight up to my questioner and pleaded, "Tell me more." Thirty minutes later, over a caffeine-free Diet Coke in the university cafeteria, he explained what lay behind his question.

"You see," my questioner said, "in his late sermons, Joseph Smith developed some really radical ideas. For a start, God did not create space and time but is subject to them and therefore a finite being. The Mormon God is somewhat hedged in by the universe and not master of it. The text to look at here is an amazing sermon called 'King Follett,' which was named after an elder who had just died and was delivered in Nauvoo, IL, a few months before the prophet was murdered. He asks repeatedly, 'What kind of being is God?' And his reply is that God himself was once as we are now."

He leaned in closer to me and continued in a lower voice, "If you were to see God right now, Smith says, *right now*, you would see a being just like you, the very form of a man. The great secret is that, through heroic effort and striving, God was a man who became exalted and now sits enthroned in the heavens. You see, God was not God from all eternity, but *became* God. Now, the flip side of this claim is that if God is an exalted man, then we, too, can become exalted.

The prophet says to the company of the saints something like, 'You have to learn how to be gods. You have to inherit the same power and glory as God and become exalted like him.' Namely, you can arrive at the station of God. One of our early leaders summarized the King Follett sermon with the words, 'As man now is, God once was. As God now is, man may be.'"

"So, dear Simon," my new friend concluded, "we, too, can become Gods, American Gods, no less." He chuckled. I was astonished.

My host, Jim, arrived to pick me up for an early dinner at his home and then drove me back to Salt Lake City to make a late flight to Chicago. I kept looking at the vast night sky in the Utah desert and thinking about what my interlocutor had said. I read the King Follett sermon and anything else I could find, particularly a very late sermon by Smith on the plurality of Gods, given around ten days before the prophet's murder. They totally blew me away. I also stole a copy of the Book of Mormon from the Marriott hotel in Chicago and waded through as much of it as I could. To be honest, it's somewhat tedious.

Of course, I knew that what the audience member told me was heresy. Christianity is premised on the fact of the incarnation. There was a God-man rabbi in occupied Palestine a couple of millenniums ago. But that doesn't mean that *anyone* can go around claiming divinity, like Joachim of Fiore in the twelfth century or the recently deceased and much-missed Reverend Sun Myung Moon. There was only one incarnation. God became man, was crucified and resurrected and we're still waiting for him to come back. The New Testament, especially the book of Revelation, is very clear that he is coming soon. Admittedly, it's been a while.

In order to explain the consubstantiality of God and man in the person of Christ, third- and fourth-century Christian fathers, including Saint Augustine, built up the wonderful theological edifice of the Trinity. The three persons of the Trinity, the Father, Son and Holy Ghost, are distinct but participate in the same substance. Three in one is one in three. It is a heretical act of arrogance to arrogate divinity for oneself or to claim multiple incarnations. God is indeed unitary and infinite.

Joseph Smith believed none of that. He taught that God the Father and the Son were separate substances, both of them material. Speaking directly of the Trinity, Smith remarked, "I say that is a strange God," and goes on, in a line that must have gotten big laughs back in 1844, "It would make the biggest God in the world. He would be a wonderfully big God—he would be a giant or a monster." Not only is the Mormon God not as big as the Christian God, there are any number of Gods within Mormonism. In the late sermons, Smith repeatedly talks about a council of the Gods that was meant to take place sometime before the book of Genesis begins. This is based on a rather windy interpretation of various Hebrew words, which concludes with the claim, "The head God called together the Gods and sat in grand council to bring forth the world."

But wait, things get even weirder. Smith accepts that Jesus Christ had a father, namely God, but goes on, "You may suppose that He had a Father," adding, "Was there ever a son without a father?" Common sense would answer no, but Christians must answer "Yes, there was." Namely, that God created all creatures but was himself uncreated. God is *causa sui*, a self-caused cause. Smith explicitly rejects this idea, saying, "We say that God Himself is a self-existing being. Who told you so?" He goes on, "I might with boldness proclaim from the house-tops that God never had the power to create the spirit of man at all. God himself could not create himself." God is not an uncaused cause but himself part of the chain of causation.

This is a little like that amazing exchange said to have taken place following Bertrand Russell's lecture, "Why I Am Not a Christian," given at Battersea Town Hall in South London in 1927. After Russell had made his case for atheism, a female questioner asked him, "What Mr. Russell has said is well enough, but he has forgotten that the entire universe stands on the back of a turtle." Quite unfazed, Russell answered, "Madam, upon what does the turtle stand?" "Oh," she said, "it's turtles all the way down."

For Joseph Smith, it is turtles all the way down. There is an endless regress of Gods which beget one another but which do not beget the universe. That is, creation is not ex nihilo, as it is in Christianity, where God created heaven and earth, as it says at the beginning of the Bible. Rather, matter precedes creation. This makes the Mormon God like the Demiurge in Plato's pagan creation myth in the *Timaeus*. The Mormon God does not create matter. He simply organizes it. Admittedly, he organized it pretty impressively. Just look at the design of trees.

The great thing about Mormonism is that Mormons take very seriously the doctrine of incarnation. So seriously, indeed, that they have succeeded in partially democratizing it. For Christians, incarnation is a one-time, long-distance ski jump from the divine to the human. But for Joseph Smith, incarnation is more of a two-way street, and potentially a rather congested thoroughfare. If God becomes man, then man can become God. And the word *man* has to be understood literally here. Women cannot be priests or prophets or aspire to an exclusively masculine divinity, which seems petty, a pity, and rather silly to me. But there we are. And I don't even want to get into questions of race and the historical exclusion of blacks from the Mormon priesthood until 1978.

The point is that any number of Mormon men can become God—potentially even you-know-who. It's an intriguing thought.

There is a potential equality of the human and the divine within Mormonism, at least in the extraordinary theology that Joseph Smith speedily sketched in the King Follett sermon. Divinity is the object of that much-admired Mormon striving. Perhaps this is why Mormons are so hardworking.

Smith says, and one gets a clear sense of the persecution that he felt and that indeed engulfed and killed him, "They found fault with Jesus Christ because He said He was the Son of God, and made Himself equal with God. They say of me, like they did of the apostles of old, that I must be put down. What did Jesus say? 'Is it not written in your law, I said: Ye are Gods' . . . Why should it be blasphemy that I should say I am the son of God?"

Of course, for Christians, this is the highest blasphemy. But the Mormon vision is very distinctive. The idea is that within each of us is a spirit or what Smith calls an "intelligence" that is coequal with

God. Smith says in the King Follett sermon, "The first principles of man are self-existent with God." This intelligence is immortal. Smith goes on, "There never was a time when there were not spirits, for they are co-equal (co-eternal) with our father in heaven." If God could not create himself, then one might say that each of us has within us something uncreated, something that precedes God and that is itself divine.

Having accepted to be sent into the world, as Mormons sometimes put it, the task is to exalt ourselves such that we, too, can become Gods. God the Father was just a stronger, more intelligent God capable of guiding the weaker intelligences, like us. As Smith says in a marvelously sensuous, indeed gustatory, turn of phrase, "This is good doctrine. It tastes good. I can taste the principles of eternal life, and so can you." Who wouldn't want a taste of God or to taste what it might be like to be a God oneself?

THE HERETICAL VISTAS of Mormonism, particularly the idea of something uncreated within the human being, excited the self-described Gnostic Jew, Harold Bloom. I read his wonderful 1992 book *The American Religion* shortly after my trip to Utah and just reread it recently with great pleasure. Bloom sees Mormonism as the quintessential expression of an American religion and controversially links the idea of the plurality of Gods to plural marriage. The argument is very simple: If you are or have the potential to become divine, and divinity is corporeal, then plural marriage is the way to create as much potential saints, prophets and Gods as possible. Indeed, plural marriage has to be seen as a Mormon obligation: If divinity tastes so good, then why keep all the goodness to oneself? Spread the big love. It makes perfect sense (at least for heterosexual men).

In his quasi-prophetic manner, Bloom thought the future belonged to Mormonism, concluding, "I cheerfully prophesy that some day, not too far in the twenty-first century, the Mormons will have enough political and financial power to sanction polygamy again. Without it, in some form or other, the complete vision of Joseph Smith never can be fulfilled."

It makes little sense to say that Mormonism is *not* Christian. It's right there in the Mormon articles of faith that were adapted from Smith's famous Wentworth Letter from 1842. Article 1 reads, "We believe in God, the Eternal Father, and in his Son, Jesus Christ, and in the Holy Ghost." But, as Bloom makes compellingly clear, Mormonism is not *just* Christian. The new revelation given to Joseph Smith in his visions and the annual visits of the angel Moroni from 1820 onward is a new gospel for the new world. Mormonism is an American religion, which beautifully, if fallaciously, understands the native inhabitants of the New World as ancient descendants of inhabitants of the Old World, the scattered tribes of Israel. Article 10 reads, "We believe in the literal gathering of Israel and the restoration of the ten tribes; that Zion (the New Jerusalem) will be built upon the American continent." I don't know whether Prime Minister Benjamin Netanyahu has read this article of faith, but it might have some specific consequences for American foreign policy should his close friend and former colleague at the Boston Consulting Group, Mitt Romney, be elected.

Mormonism is properly and powerfully *post*-Christian, as Islam is post-Christian. Where Islam, which also has a prophet, claims the transcendence of God, Mormonism makes God radically immanent. Where Islam unifies all creatures under one mighty God to whom we must submit, Mormonism pluralizes divinity, making it an immanent, corporeal matter and making God a more fragile, hemmed-in and finite being. And obviously, both Islam and Mormonism have a complex relation to the practice of plural marriage.

Yet unlike Islam, for whom Muhammad is the last prophet, Mormonism allows for *continuing* revelation. In a way, it is very democratic, very American. Article 9 reads, "We believe all that God has revealed, all that He does now reveal, and we believe that He will yet reveal many great and important things pertaining to the Kingdom of God." In principle, any male saint can add to the stock and never-ending story of revelation and thereby become exalted. From the standpoint of Christianity, both Islam and Mormonism are heresies and—if one is genuine about one's theology, and religion is not reduced to a set of banal moral platitudes—should be treated as such.

Like Bloom, I see Joseph Smith's apostasy as strong poetry, a gloriously presumptive and delusional creation from the same climate as Whitman, if not enjoying quite the same air quality. Perhaps Mormonism is not so far from romanticism after all. To claim that it is simply Christian is to fail to grasp its theological, poetic and political audacity. It is much more than mere Christianity. Why are Mormons so keen to conceal their pearl of the greatest price? Why is no one really talking about this? In the context of you-know-who's presidential bid, people *appear* to be endlessly talking about Mormonism, but its true theological challenge is entirely absent from the discussion.

SEPTEMBER 16, 2012

An Imperfect God

—Yoram Hazony

Is God perfect? You often hear philosophers describe "theism" as the belief in a perfect being—a being whose attributes are said to include being all-powerful, all-knowing, immutable, perfectly good, perfectly simple, and necessarily existent (among others). And today, something like this view is common among lay-people as well.

There are two famous problems with this view of God. The first is that it appears to be impossible to make it coherent. For example, it seems unlikely that God can be both perfectly powerful and per-fectly good if the world is filled (as it obviously is) with instances of terrible injustice. Similarly, it's hard to see how God can wield his infinite power to instigate alteration and change in all things if he is flat-out immutable. And there are more such contradictions where these came from.

The second problem is that while this "theist" view of God is supposed to be a description of the God of the Bible, it's hard to find any evidence that the prophets and scholars who wrote the Hebrew Bible (or "Old Testament") thought of God in this way at all. The God of Hebrew scripture is not depicted as immuta-ble, but repeatedly changes his mind about things (for example, he regrets having made man). He is not all-knowing, since he's repeatedly surprised by things (like the Israelites abandoning him for a statue of a cow). He is not perfectly powerful either, in that he famously cannot control Israel and get its people to do what he wants. And so on.

Philosophers have spent many centuries trying to get God's supposed perfections to fit together in a coherent conception, and then trying to get that to fit with the Bible. By now it's reasonably clear that this can't be done. In fact, part of the reason God-bashers like Richard Dawkins and Sam Harris are so influential (apart from the fact that they write so well) is their insistence that the doctrine of God's perfections makes no sense and that the idealized "being" it tells us about doesn't resemble the biblical God at all.

So is that it, then? Have the atheists won? I don't think so. But it does look like the time has come for some rethinking in the theist camp.

I'd start with this: Is it really necessary to say that God is a "perfect being," or perfect at all, for that matter? As far as I can tell, the biblical authors avoid asserting any such thing. And with good reason. Normally, when we say that something is "perfect," we mean it has attained the best possible balance among the principles involved in making it the kind of thing it is. For example, if we say that a bottle is perfect, we mean it can contain a significant quantity of liquid in its body, that its neck is long enough to be grasped comfortably and firmly, that the bore is wide enough to permit a rapid flow of liquid, and so on. Of course, you can always manufacture a bottle that will hold more liquid, but only by making the body too broad (so the bottle doesn't handle well) or the neck too short (so it's hard to hold). There's an inevitable trade-off among the principles, and perfection lies in the balance among them. And this is so whether what's being judged is a bottle or a horse, a wine or a gymnastics routine or natural human beauty.

What would we say if some philosopher told us that a perfect bottle would be one that can contain a perfectly great amount of liquid while being perfectly easy to pour from at the same time? Or that a perfect horse would bear an infinitely heavy rider while at the same time being able to run with perfectly great speed? I should think we'd say he's made a fundamental mistake here: you can't perfect something by maximizing all its constituent principles simultane-ously. All this will get you is contradictions and absurdities. This is not less true of God than it is of anything else.

The attempt to think of God as a perfect being is misguided for another reason as well. We can speak of the perfection of a bottle or a horse because these are things that can be encompassed (at least in some sense) by our senses and understanding. Having the whole bottle before us, we feel we can judge how close it is to being a perfect instance of its type. But if asked to judge the perfection of a bottle poking out of a paper bag, or of a horse that's partly hidden in the stable, we'd surely protest, "How am I supposed to know? I can only see part of it."

Yet the biblical accounts of our encounters with God emphasize that all human views of God are partial and fragmentary in just this way. Even Moses, the greatest of the prophets, is told that he can't see God's face, but can only catch a glimpse of God's back as he passes by. At another point, God responds to Moses's request to know his name (that is, his nature) by telling him, "ehi'eh asher ehi'eh"—"I will be what I will be." In most English-language Bibles this is translated "I am that I am," following the Septuagint, which sought to bring the biblical text into line with the Greek tradition (descended from Xenophanes, Parmenides and Plato's *Timaeus*) of identifying God with a perfect being. But in the Hebrew original, the text says almost exactly the opposite of this: the Hebrew "I will be what I will be" is in the imperfect tense, suggesting to us a God who is incomplete and changing. In their run-ins with God, human beings can glimpse a corner or an edge of something too immense to be encompassed, a "coming-into-being" as God approaches, and no more. The belief that any human mind can grasp enough of God to begin recognizing perfections in him would have struck the bib-lical authors as a pagan conceit.

So if it's not a bundle of "perfections" that the prophets and schol-ars who wrote the Hebrew Bible referred to in speaking of God, what was it they were talking about? As Donald Harman Akenson writes, the God of Hebrew scripture is meant to be an "embodiment of what is, of reality" as we experience it. God's abrupt shifts from action to seeming indifference and back, his changing demands from the human beings standing before him, his at-times devastating responses to mankind's deeds and misdeeds—all these reflect the hardship so often present in the lives of most human beings. To be sure, the biblical God can appear with sudden and stunning generosity as well, as he did to Israel at the Red Sea. And he is portrayed, ultimately, as faithful and just. But these are not the "perfections" of a God known to be a perfect being. They don't exist in his character "necessarily," or anything remotely similar to this. On the contrary, it is the *hope* that God is faithful and just that is the subject of ancient Israel's faith: we hope that despite the frequently harsh reality of our daily experience, there is nonetheless a faithfulness and justice that rules in our world in the end.

The ancient Israelites, in other words, discovered a more *realistic* God than that descended from the tradition of Greek thought. But philosophers have tended to steer clear of such a view, no doubt out of fear that an imperfect God would not attract mankind's allegiance. Instead, they have preferred to speak to us of a God consisting of a series of sweeping idealizations—idealizations whose relation to the world in which we actually live is scarcely imaginable. Today, with theism rapidly losing ground across Europe and among Americans as well, we could stand to reconsider this point. Surely a more plausible conception of God couldn't hurt.

NOVEMBER 25, 2012

The Politics of the Binding of Isaac

—*Omri Boehm*

*Take your son, your only son Isaac, whom you love, and go to the land of
Moriah, and offer him there as a burnt offering on one of the mountains
of which I shall tell you.*

—Genesis 22:2

With these words, spoken to Abraham by his God, begins
one of the most enduring and ethically problematic narratives in the
Jewish religion, one that still resonates today in questions about faith
and obedience, religion and the state. Must Abraham obey his God?

It is common to understand the binding of Isaac as a symbol of blind religious obedience. If not for the intervention of an
angel, Abraham would have killed his son. Moreover, since Abraham in this story isn't just the father of Isaac—he is also the father
of monotheism—the narrative seems to teach that faith in general
is synonymous with obedience, that God's command overrides the
command of the ethical. It is interesting to notice that even the philosopher Yeshayahu Leibowitz, the father of Israeli "refusal movement," which supported Israeli Army resistors who refused to fight
in the occupied territories, accepted this interpretation of the binding and of religion. Leibowitz held that the essence of true faith,
according to both the Bible and the great medieval Jewish philosopher Maimonides, is obedience.

This theology has been deeply encrypted into the Jewish tradition and continues to hold sway, especially where the Jewish religion and the Jewish state intertwine. Rabbi Shlomo Riskin, the former leader of the Lincoln Square Synagogue in Manhattan and a founder of the West Bank settlement Efrat, spoke for many when he wrote, "The paradox of Jewish history is that, had we not been willing to sacrifice our children to God, we would never have survived as a God-inspired and God-committed nation." Rabbi Riskin has commented elsewhere that what Abraham was asked to do will be demanded from "all subsequent generations of Jews." The nod to current Israeli reality is evident, especially to those who, like myself, served long enough in Israel's military to confront its manifestly immoral demands.

Consciously or not, views like Riskin's draw on a theology that explicitly identifies the Zionist cause with God's will. The theology is pervasive in Israel, a country where a constitution could never be written because its authority would conflict with God's, where every young soldier receives a copy of the Bible to go along with his first gun, where even left-leaning liberals eulogize a figure such as Ariel Sharon. Contrary to appearances, the focus of this theology and of this politics has never been on sacrifice. The focus has always been on obedience. Substitute "God's will" with "the Jewish state" and you get the political theology of the binding of Isaac—of obedience to the state's decree, immoral though it may well be.

Sharon is worth a comment here, because he insisted on identifying himself as a Jew first and an Israeli second—a Jew for whom reviving biblical Judaism in the Promised Land was the principal value. Such fundamentalism is irregular among secular Israel-born Jews like Sharon and it may at least partly explain the ruthlessness with which he fought (one thinks of the brutal attack against the West Bank village of Qibya) or the zeal with which for so long he created settlements in the West Bank and Gaza. Sharon embodied better than most the political theology of the binding of Isaac: the Jewish state always first, morality second.

But there are reasons to think that this political theology is distorted, not just when viewed ethically but also when viewed from within the standpoint of faith—indeed, within the Jewish faith.

Consider Maimonides's conception of the binding of Isaac. The key to understanding Maimonides's interpretation lies not in his explicit comments on Genesis 22, but rather in his classification of the eleven degrees of prophecy in his masterwork, *The Guide for the Perplexed*. The eleventh and highest degree of prophecy discussed by Maimonides is one in which a prophet "sees an angel who addresses him in a vision"—and Maimonides immediately adds, "as Abraham in the time of the binding." According to Maimonides, "this is the highest of the degrees of the prophets whose states are attested by the prophetic books."

The binding of Isaac begins when God addresses Abraham, commanding him to sacrifice Isaac. We know that hearing this command doesn't stand for the highest manifestation of prophecy attested by the Bible: hearing God is, according to Maimonides's taxonomy, an inferior prophetic degree. Certainly it isn't what Maimonides had in mind when evoking the binding to exemplify the "highest of the degrees of the prophets," which consists in the appearance of an angel. Indeed, it is only later in Genesis that an angel appears to Abraham—when commanding him to stop the sacrifice.

You may legitimately ask, as the tradition repeatedly has, by what authority Abraham decides to follow the angel's command rather than God's. The question is especially appropriate because this angel is the "angel of Yahweh," while it was God who had given the initial decree. And you must in any case wonder why, according to Maimonides, it is in virtue of doing just that—obeying the angel of Yahweh rather than God—that Abraham exemplifies the highest prophetic degree.

The answer to these questions is found in Maimonides's account of the divine names. While, according to this view, Yahweh stands for the deity's proper name, Maimonides interprets "God"—"Elohim" in the Hebrew—as a merely equivocal term. Originally signifying rulers and judges of states, "Elohim" came only derivatively to signify the deity, whom the Bible at times depicts as a state's ruler or judge.

The theological implications of this view become clearer in Maimonides's interpretation of the story of the fall of Adam and Eve. The serpent in the story states that by eating from the forbidden fruit Adam and Eve will became "like God"—Elohim—"knowing good and evil." It is tempting to read this as "They will become divine-like by virtue of gaining ethical knowledge." But Maimonides reads this exactly the other way around. Gaining godlike knowledge of good and evil represents rather the *punishment* imposed on Adam and Eve. Gaining this knowledge consists in losing the absolute knowledge possessed in Eden, conforming instead to the mere norms of the land and the contingent laws of the state.

Apply this to Maimonides's account of the binding of Isaac—and thereby to his account of prophecy. You get a political theology very different from that commonly assumed by religious thinkers and critics of religion alike. Prophecy, as Spinoza argued more than anyone, is the chief political-theological institution. Yet supreme prophecy consists, as Maimonides's interpretation of the binding shows, in *disobedience* to contingent norms and degenerate state decrees.

God commands the sacrifice of the son. Maimonides reads this command metaphorically, as standing for the human, all-too-human temptation to follow the established law and the ethical-political norm as if they were absolute decrees. Indeed—and this is the critical point— the pagan ritual of child sacrifice *was* the established ethical-political norm in Abraham's world. This pagan ritual continues to reverberate in current politics and folk imagination. In Israel, it finds followers in those who teach absolute obedience to the state, the military and the myths that justify them. Maimonides would have disobeyed. For him, the highest prophetic degree consisted in obeying Yahweh's cancellation of God's decree. This is demanded not just by morality but by faith. This, then, is the true political theology of the binding of Isaac.

The Jewish state's citizens may have to take this into account if they look up to Abraham as their model of Judaism. Soldiers may have to consider it when receiving the Bible along with an M16. Following the Jewish prophets rather than the pagan ritual of child sacrifice consists in moral disobedience to the state's decree.

On Questioning the Jewish State

—*Joseph Levine*

I WAS RAISED IN A RELIGIOUS JEWISH ENVIRONMENT, AND THOUGH we were not strongly Zionist, I always took it to be self-evident that "Israel has a right to exist." Now anyone who has debated the Israeli-Palestinian conflict will have encountered this phrase often. Defenders of Israeli policies routinely accuse Israel's critics of denying her right to exist, while the critics (outside of a small group on the left, where I now find myself) bend over backward to insist that, despite their criticisms, of course they affirm it. The general mainstream consensus seems to be that to deny Israel's right to exist is a clear indication of anti-Semitism (a charge Jews like myself are not immune to), and therefore not an option for people of conscience.

Over the years I came to question this consensus and to see that the general fealty to it has seriously constrained open debate on the issue, one of vital importance not just to the people directly involved— Israelis and Palestinians—but to the conduct of our own foreign policy and, more important, to the safety of the world at large. My view is that one really *ought* to question Israel's right to exist and that doing so does not manifest anti-Semitism. The first step in questioning the principle, however, is to figure out what it means.

One problem with talking about this question calmly and rationally is that the phrase "right to exist" sounds awfully close to "right to life," so denying Israel its right to exist sounds awfully close to permitting the extermination of its people. In light of the history of Jewish persecution, and the fact that Israel was created immediately after and largely as a consequence of the Holocaust, it isn't surprising that the phrase "Israel's right to exist" should have this emotional impact. But as even those who insist on the principle will admit, they aren't claiming merely the impermissibility of exterminating Israelis. So what is this "right" that many uphold as so basic that to question it reflects anti-Semitism and yet is one that I claim ought to be questioned?

The key to the interpretation is found in the crucial four words that are often tacked onto the phrase "Israel's right to exist"— namely, ". . . as a Jewish state." As I understand it, the principle that Israel has a right to exist as a Jewish state has three parts: first, that Jews, as a collective, constitute a people in the sense that they possess a right to self-determination; second, that a people's right to self-determination entails the right to erect a state of their own, a state that is their particular people's state; and finally, that for the Jewish people the geographical area of the former Mandatory Palestine, their ancestral homeland, is the proper place for them to exercise this right to self-determination.

The claim then is that anyone who denies Israel's right to exist as a Jewish state is guilty of anti-Semitism because they are refusing to grant Jews the same rights as other peoples possess. If indeed this were true, if Jews were being singled out in the way many allege, I would agree that it manifests anti-Jewish bias. But the charge that denying Jews a right to a Jewish state amounts to treating the Jewish people differently from other peoples cannot be sustained.

To begin, since the principle has three parts, it follows that it can be challenged in (at least) three different ways: either deny that Jews constitute "a people" in the relevant sense, deny that the right to self-determination really involves what advocates of the principle claim it does, or deny that Jews have the requisite claim on the geographical area in question.

In fact, I think there is a basis to challenge all three, but for present purposes I will focus on the question of whether a people's right to self-determination entails their right to a state of their own, and set aside whether Jews count as a people and whether Jews have a claim on that particular land. I do so partly for reasons of space, but mainly because these questions have largely (though not completely) lost their importance.

The fact is that today millions of Jews live in Israel and, ancestral homeland or not, this is their home now. As for whether Jews constitute a people, this is a vexed question given the lack of consensus in general about what it takes for any particular group of people to count as "a people." The notion of "a people" can be interpreted in different ways, with different consequences for the rights that they possess. My point is that even if we grant Jews their peoplehood and their right to live in that land, there is still no consequent right to a Jewish state.

However, I do think that it's worth noting the historical irony in insisting that it is anti-Semitic to deny that Jews constitute a people. The eighteenth and nineteenth centuries were the period of Jewish "emancipation" in Western Europe, when the ghetto walls were torn down and Jews were granted the full rights of citizenship in the states within which they resided. The anti-Semitic forces in those days, those opposing emancipation, were associated not with denying Jewish peoplehood but with emphatically insisting on it! The idea was that since Jews constituted a nation of their own, they could not be loyal citizens of any European state. The liberals who strongly opposed anti-Semitism insisted that Jews could both practice their religion and uphold their cultural traditions while maintaining full citizenship in the various nation-states in which they resided.

But, as I said, let's grant that Jews are a people. Well, if they are, and if with the status of a people comes the right to self-determination, why wouldn't they have a right to live under a Jewish state in their homeland? The simple answer is because many non-Jews (rightfully) live there, too. But this needs unpacking.

First, it's important to note, as mentioned, that the term "a people" can be used in different ways, and sometimes they get confused. In particular, there is a distinction to be made between a people in the ethnic sense and a people in the civic sense. Though there is no general consensus on this, a group counts as a people in the ethnic sense by virtue of common language, common culture, common history and attachment to a common territory. One can easily see why Jews, scattered across the globe, speaking many different languages and defined largely by religion, present a difficult case. But, as I said, for my purposes it doesn't really matter, and I will just assume the Jewish people qualify.

The other sense is the civic one, which applies to a people by virtue of their common citizenship in a nation-state or, alternatively, by virtue of their common residence within relatively defined geographic borders. So whereas there is both an ethnic and a civic sense to be made of the term "French people," the term "Jewish people" has only an ethnic sense. This can easily be seen by noting that the Jewish people is not the same group as the Israeli people. About 20 percent of Israeli citizens are non-Jewish Palestinians, while the vast majority of the Jewish people are not citizens of Israel and do not live within any particular geographic area. "Israeli people," on the other hand, has only a civic sense. (Of course, often the term "Israelis" is used as if it applies only to Jewish Israelis, but this is part of the problem. More on this in what follows.)

So, when we consider whether or not a people has a right to a state of their own, are we speaking of a people in the ethnic sense or the civic one? I contend that insofar as the principle that all peoples have the right to self-determination entails the right to a state of their own, it can apply to peoples only in the civic sense.

After all, what is it for a people to have a state "of their own"? Here's a rough characterization: the formal institutions and legal framework of the state serves to express, encourage and favor that people's identity. The distinctive position of that people would be manifested in a number of ways, from the largely symbolic to the more substantive—for example, it would be reflected in the name of the state, the nature of its flag and other symbols, its national holidays, its education system, its immigration rules, the extent to which membership in the people in question is a factor in official planning, how resources are distributed, and so forth. If the people being favored in this way are just the state's citizens, it is not a problem. (Of course, those who are supercosmopolitan, denying any legitimacy to the borders of nation-states, will disagree. But they aren't a party to this debate.)

But if the people who "own" the state in question are an ethnic subgroup of the citizenry, even if the vast majority, it constitutes a serious problem indeed, and this is precisely the situation of Israel as the Jewish state. Far from being a natural expression of the Jewish people's right to self-determination, it is in fact a violation of the right to self-determination of its non-Jewish (mainly Palestinian) citizens. It is a violation of a people's right to self-determination to exclude them—whether by virtue of their ethnic membership, or for any other reason—from full political participation in the state under whose sovereignty they fall. Of course, Jews have a right to self-determination in this sense as well—this is what emancipation was all about. But so do non-Jewish peoples living in the same state.

Any state that "belongs" to one ethnic group within it violates the core democratic principle of equality, and the self-determination rights of the non-members of that group.

If the institutions of a state favor one ethnic group among its citizenry in this way, then only the members of that group will feel themselves fully a part of the life of the state. True equality, therefore, is only realizable in a state that is based on civic peoplehood. As formulated by both Jewish- and Palestinian-Israeli activists on this issue, a truly democratic state that fully respects the self-determination rights of everyone under its sovereignty must be a "state of all its citizens."

This fundamental point exposes the fallacy behind the common analogy, drawn by defenders of Israel's right to exist as a Jewish state, between Israel's right to be Jewish and France's right to be French. The appropriate analogy would instead be between France's right to be French (in the civic sense) and Israel's right to be Israeli.

I conclude, then, that the very idea of a Jewish state is undemocratic, a violation of the self-determination rights of its non-Jewish citizens, and therefore morally problematic. But the harm doesn't stop with the inherently undemocratic character of the state. For if an ethnic national state is established in a territory that contains a significant number of nonmembers of that ethnic group, it will inevitably face resistance from the land's other inhabitants. This will force the ethnic nation controlling the state to resort to further undemocratic means to maintain their hegemony. Three strategies to deal with resistance are common: expulsion, occupation and institutional marginalization. Interestingly, all three strategies have been employed by the Zionist movement: expulsion in 1948 (and, to a lesser extent, in 1967), occupation of the territories conquered in 1967, and institution of a complex web of laws that prevent Israel's Palestinian citizens from mounting an internal challenge to the Jewish character of the state. (The recent outrage in Israel over a proposed exclusion of ultra-Orthodox parties from the governing coalition, for example, failed to note that no Arab political party has ever been invited to join the government.) In other words, the wrong of ethnic hegemony within the state leads to the further wrong of repression against the Other within its midst.

There is an unavoidable conflict between being a Jewish state and a democratic state. I want to emphasize that there's nothing anti-Semitic in pointing this out, and it's time the question was discussed openly on its merits, without the charge of anti-Semitism hovering in the background.

MARCH 9, 2013

The Freedom of Faith: A Christmas Sermon

—*Simon Critchley*

I N A 2012 ESSAY IN THE *TIMES'* SUNDAY BOOK REVIEW THE writer Paul Elie asks the intriguing question, Has fiction lost its faith? As we are gathered here today, let us consider one of the most oddly faithful of all fiction writers, Fyodor Dostoevsky. More specifically, I'd like to focus pretty intensely on what some consider to be the key moment in his greatest novel—arguably one of the greatest of all time—*The Brothers Karamazov*. (Elie himself notes the 1880 masterpiece as an example of the truly faith-engaged fiction of yore.) I speak in particular of the "Grand Inquisitor" scene, a sort of fiction within a fiction that draws on something powerful from the New Testament—Jesus's refusal of Satan's three temptations—and in doing so digs at the meaning of faith, freedom, happiness and the diabolic satisfaction of our desires.

First a little biblical background.

SCENE I—IN WHICH CHRIST IS SORELY TEMPTED BY SATAN

After fasting for forty days and forty nights in the desert, Jesus is understandably a little hungry. Satan appears and tempts him. The temptation takes the form of three questions. The first involves food. The devil says, and I paraphrase, "If you are, as you say, the Son of God, then turn these stones in the parched and barren wilderness into loaves of bread. Do this, not so much to feed yourself, starved as you are, but in order to feed those that might follow you, oh Son of God. Turn these stones into loaves and people will follow you like sheep ever after. Perform this miracle and people will happily become your slaves."

Jesus replies, "Not on bread alone shall man live, but on every word proceeding through the mouth of God." In other words, "Eat the bread of heaven." Jesus refuses to perform the miracle that he could easily carry out—he is, after all, God—in the name of what? We will get to that.

Next Jesus is brought up to the roof of the temple in Jerusalem. Satan invites him to throw himself down. For if he is the Son of God, then the armies of angels at his command will save him from smashing his feet against the rocks below. Such a party trick, performed in the crowded hubbub of the holy city, would appear to all to be an awesome mystery that would incite the loyal to devotion. Mystery, by definition, cannot be understood. But Jesus flatly refuses the temptation, saying, "Thou shalt not tempt the God of thee."

The third temptation raises the stakes even higher. Satan takes Jesus to an exceedingly high mountain and shows him all the kingdoms of the inhabited earth. He says to him, "To thee I will give authority and the glory of them, for such is my power and in my power to give. But if you will worship me, then I will give all the power and the glory to you." Jesus's reply is just two words in the New Testament Greek: "Go, Satan!"

With these words, the devil evaporates like dew under a desert sun.

SCENE 2—IN WHICH CHRIST DENIES AUTHORITY
AND AFFIRMS THE FREEDOM OF FAITH

In refusing these three temptations and refuting these three questions, Jesus is denying three potent forces: *miracle, mystery* and *authority*. Of course, the three forces are interlinked: the simplest way to get people to follow a leader is by the miraculous guarantee of bread—namely, endless economic abundance and wealth. It is the mystery of authority that confirms our trust in it, the idea of an invisible hand or mysterious market forces, all of which tend benevolently toward human well-being.

What Satan promises Jesus in the last temptation is complete political authority, the dream of a universal state—namely, that one no longer has to render to God what is God's and to Caesar what is Caesar's. Temporal and eternal power can be unified under one catholic theological and political authority with the avowed aim of assuring universal happiness, harmony and unity.

It sounds great, doesn't it? So why does Jesus refuse Satan's temptations? In John 8, when Jesus is trying to persuade the scribes and Pharisees of his divinity—which proves somewhat difficult—he says that if they have faith in him, then this will be faith in the truth and this truth shall make them free or, better translated, the truth will free (eleutherosei). The first thing that leaps out of this passage is the proximity of faith and truth. Namely, that truth does not consist of the empirical truths of natural science or the propositional truths of logic. It is truth as a kind of *troth*, a loyalty or fidelity to that which one is betrothed, as in the act of love. The second is the idea that truth, understood as the truth of faith, will free.

The question arises: What is meant by freedom here and is it in the name of such freedom that Jesus refuses Satan's temptations? Such, of course, is the supremely tempting argument of the Grand Inquisitor at the heart of *The Brothers Karamazov*. Truth to tell, it appears to be a rather strange argument, placed as it is in the mouth of the avowed sensualist for whom everything is permitted: Ivan Karamazov. As his younger brother, Alyosha (the purported hero of the book), points out, the argument is apparently in praise of Jesus and not in blame of him.

SCENE 3—BE HAPPY! WHY JESUS MUST BURN

Ivan has written a prose poem, set in the sixteenth century, in Seville, Spain, during the most terrible time of the Inquisition, when heretics were being burnt alive willy-nilly like fireflies. In the poem, after a particularly magnificent auto-da-fé—when almost a hundred heretics were burnt by the Grand Inquisitor, the eminent cardinal, in the presence of the king, the court and its charming ladies—Christ suddenly appears and is recognized at once. People weep for joy, children throw flowers at his feet and a large crowd gathers outside the cathedral. At that moment, the Grand Inquisitor passes by the cathedral and grasps what is happening. His face darkens. Such is his power and the fear he inspires that the crowd suddenly falls silent and parts for him. He orders Jesus arrested and thrown into prison.

Later, the Grand Inquisitor enters the cell and silently watches Jesus from the doorway for a long time. Face-to-face, they retain eye contact throughout. Neither of them flinches. Eventually, the cardinal says, "Tomorrow, I shall condemn thee at the stake as the worst of heretics. And the people who today kissed Thy feet tomorrow at the faintest sign from me will rush to heap up the embers of Thy fire. Knowest Thou that? Yes, maybe Thou knowest it." He adds, "Why, then, art Thou come to hinder us?" Jesus says nothing.

The Grand Inquisitor's final question appears paradoxical: How might the reappearance of Jesus interfere with the functioning of the most holy Catholic Church? Does the church not bear Christ's name? The answer is fascinating. For the Grand Inquisitor, what Jesus brought into the world was freedom, specifically the freedom of faith: the truth that will free. And this is where we perhaps begin to sympathize with the Grand Inquisitor. He says that for 1,500 years, Christians have been wrestling with this freedom. The Grand Inquisitor too, when younger, also went into the desert, lived on roots and locusts, and tried to attain the perfect freedom espoused by Jesus. "But now it is ended and over for good." He adds, "After fifteen centuries of struggle, the Church has at last vanquished freedom, and has done so to make men happy."

SCENE 4—OBEDIENCE OR HAPPINESS?

What is it that makes human beings happy? In a word, bread. And here we return to Jesus's answers to Satan's desert temptations. In refusing to transform miraculously the stones into loaves, Jesus rejected bread for the sake of freedom, for the bread of heaven. Jesus refuses miracle, mystery and authority in the name of a radical freedom of conscience. The problem is that this freedom places an excessive burden on human beings. It is too demanding—infinitely demanding, one might say. As Father Mapple, the preacher in the whaleboat pulpit early in Melville's *Moby-Dick*, says, "God's command is a hard command. In order to obey it, we must disobey ourselves." If the truth shall set you free, then it is a difficult freedom.

The hardness of God's command, its infinitely demanding character, is the reason why, for the Grand Inquisitor, "Man is tormented by no greater anxiety than to find someone quickly to whom he can hand over that gift of freedom with which the miserable creature is born." Give people the miracle of bread, and they will worship you. Remove their freedom with submission to a mystery that passeth all understanding, and they will obey your authority. They will be happy. Lord knows, they may even believe themselves to be free in such happiness.

Freedom as expressed here is not the rigorous freedom of faith, but the multiplication of desires whose rapid satisfaction equals happiness. Freedom is debased and governed by a completely instrumental, means-end rationality. Yet, to what does it lead? In the rich, it leads to the isolation of hard hedonism and spiritual suicide. In the poor, it leads to a grotesque and murderous envy to be like the rich. And—as the hypocritical pièce de résistance—both rich and poor are in the grip of an ideology that claims that human beings are becoming more and more globalized and interconnected, and thereby united into a virtual world community that overcomes distance. But we are not.

SCENE 5—OH LORD: THE CHURCH IS IN LEAGUE WITH THE DEVIL

Back in the prison cell with the ever-silent Jesus, the Grand Inquisitor acknowledges that because of the excessive burden of freedom of conscience, "We have corrected Thy work and founded it on miracle, mystery and authority." This is why the Grand Inquisitor says, "Why has Thou come to hinder us?"

Then comes the truly revelatory moment in the Grand Inquisitor's monologue, which Jesus knows already (obviously, because he is God). Knowing that he knows, the cardinal says, "Perhaps it is Thy will to hear it from my lips. Listen, then. We are not working with Thee, but with him—that is our mystery." The church is in league with the devil. It sits astride the Beast and raises aloft the cup marked "Mystery." The Grand Inquisitor is diabolical. This explains why he is so fascinated with the temptations that Jesus faced in the desert. The church has been seduced by those temptations in Jesus's name.

The paradox is that the church accepted those temptations in the hope of finding—as the Grand Inquisitor elegantly puts it—"some means of uniting all in one unanimous and harmonious ant-heap." The dream of a universal church, or a universal state, or the unity of all nations, or a cosmopolitan world order founded on perpetual peace, or whatever, is Satan's most persuasive and dangerous temptation. The freedom proclaimed by Jesus is too demanding and makes people unhappy. We prefer a demonic happiness to an unendurable freedom. All that human beings want is to be saved from the great anxiety and terrible agony they endure at present in making a free decision for themselves.

SCENE 6—THE KISS AND THE CURSE

And so, all will be happy, except those, like the Grand Inquisitor, who guard the mystery and know the secret. They will be unhappy. But it is a price worth paying. The true Christians, by contrast, see themselves as the elect, the twelve thousand from each of the twelve tribes who will be the company of saints in the millennium that follows Christ's Second Coming. This is why the Grand Inquisitor says, "I turned back and joined the ranks of those who have corrected Thy work. I left the proud and went back to the humble, for the happiness

THE FREEDOM OF FAITH: A CHRISTMAS SERMON

of the humble." This is why Christ hinders the work of the church and why he must burn like a heretic.

At this point, the Grand Inquisitor stops speaking. Silence descends. The prisoner Jesus continues to look gently into the old cardinal's face, who longs for him to say something, no matter how terrible. Jesus rises, approaches the old man and softly kisses his bloodless lips. The Grand Inquisitor shudders, but the kiss still glows in his heart. He stands and heads for the door, saying to Jesus, "Go, and come no more . . . come not at all . . . never, never!"

SCENE 7—DEMONIC HAPPINESS OR UNBEARABLE FREEDOM?

Back with the two brothers: Ivan immediately disavows the poem as senseless and naive. But Alyosha upbraids Ivan, claiming he is an atheist and saying, "How will you live and how will you love with such a hell in your heart?" As Father Zossima—whose recollections and exhortations are intended as a refutation of Ivan in the following chapters of the book—says, "What is hell? I maintain that it is the incapacity to love." The scene ends with Alyosha softly kissing Ivan on the lips, an act that the latter objects to as plagiarism.

Dostoevsky in no way wants to defend the position that Ivan Karamazov outlines in his poem. But Dostoevsky's great virtue as a writer is to be so utterly convincing in outlining what he doesn't believe and so deeply unconvincing in defending what he wants to believe. As Blake said of *Paradise Lost*, Satan gets all the best lines. The story of the Grand Inquisitor places a stark choice in front of us: demonic happiness or unbearable freedom?

And this choice conceals another deeper one: truth or falsehood? The truth that sets free is not, as we saw, the freedom of inclination and passing desire. It is the freedom of faith. It is the acceptance— submission to, even—a demand that both places a perhaps intolerable burden on the self, but which also energizes a movement of subjective conversion, to begin again. In disobeying ourselves and obeying this hard command, we may put on new selves. Faith hopes for grace.

SCENE 8—IN WHICH DOUBT AND FAITH UNITE

To be clear, such an experience of faith is not certainty, but is only gained by going into the proverbial desert and undergoing diabolical temptation and radical doubt. On this view, doubt is not the enemy of faith. On the contrary, it is certainty. If faith becomes certainty, then we have become seduced by the temptations of miracle, mystery and authority. We have become diabolical. There are no guarantees in faith. It is defined by an essential insecurity, tempered by doubt and defined by a radical experience of freedom.

This is a noble and, indeed, godlike position. It is also what Jesus demands of us elsewhere in his teaching, in the Sermon on the Mount, when he says, "Love your enemies, bless them that curse you, do good to them that hate you, and pray for them which despitefully use you, and persecute you." If that wasn't tough enough, Jesus adds, "Be ye therefore perfect, even as your Father which is in heaven is perfect." This is a sublime demand. It is a glorious demand. But it is, finally, a ridiculous demand. Inhuman, even. It is the demand to become perfect, godlike. Easy for Jesus to say, as he was God. But somewhat more difficult for us.

SCENE 9—IN WHICH THE GRAND INQUISITOR IS, FINALLY, DEFENDED

So what about us human beings, feeble, imperfect, self-deceived— the weakest reeds in nature? Does not Jesus's insistence on the rigor and purity of faith seem like, if not pride, then at least haughtiness? The Grand Inquisitor, and the institution of the church that he represents, accepted Satan's temptations not out of malice but out of a genuine love for humanity. This was based on the recognition of our flawed imperfection and need to be happy, which we perhaps deserve.

If the cost of the pure rigor of true faith is the salvation of the happy few, then this condemns the rest of us, in our millions and billions, to a life that is a kind of mockery. The seemingly perverse outcome of Dostoevsky's parable is that perhaps the Grand Inquisitor is morally justified in choosing a lie over the truth.

The Grand Inquisitor's dilemma is, finally, tragic: he knows that the truth which sets us free is too demanding for us and that the lie that grants happiness permits the greatest good of the greatest number. But he also knows that happiness is a deception that leads ineluctably to our damnation. Is the Grand Inquisitor's lie not a noble one?

SCENE 10—IN WHICH THE AUTHOR EXPRESSES DOUBT

To be perfectly (or imperfectly) honest, I don't know the answer to this question. Which should we choose: diabolical happiness or unendurable freedom? Perhaps we should spend some days and nights fasting in the desert and see what we might do. Admittedly, this is quite a difficult thing to sustain during the holiday period.

Happy Holidays!

DECEMBER 23, 2012

MORALITY'S GOD PROBLEM

Good Minus God

—*Louise M. Antony*

I WAS HEARTENED TO LEARN RECENTLY THAT ATHEISTS ARE NO longer the most reviled group in the United States: according to the political scientists Robert Putnam and David Campbell, we've been overtaken by the Tea Party. But even as I was high-fiving my fellow apostates ("We're number two! We're number two!"), I was wondering anew: Why do so many people dislike atheists?

I gather that many people believe that atheism implies nihilism—that rejecting God means rejecting morality. A person who denies God, they reason, must be, if not actively evil, at least indifferent to considerations of right and wrong. After all, doesn't the dictionary list *wicked* as a synonym for *godless*? And isn't it true, as Dostoevsky said, that "if God is dead, everything is permitted"?

Well, actually—no, it's not. (And for the record, Dostoevsky never said it was.) Atheism does not entail that anything goes.

Admittedly, some atheists *are* nihilists. (Unfortunately, they're the ones who get the most press.) But such atheists' repudiation of morality stems more from an antecedent cynicism about ethics than from any philosophical view about the divine. According to these nihilistic atheists, "morality" is just part of a fairy tale we tell each other in order to keep our innate, bestial selfishness (mostly) under control. Belief in objective "oughts" and "ought nots," they say, must fall away once we realize that there is no universal enforcer to dish out rewards and punishments in the afterlife. We're left with pure self-interest, more or less enlightened.

This is a Hobbesian view: in the state of nature "the notions of right and wrong, justice and injustice have no place. Where there is no common power, there is no law: where no law, no injustice." But no atheist has to agree with this account of morality, and lots of us do not. We "moralistic atheists" do not see right and wrong as artifacts of a divine protection racket. Rather, we find moral value to be immanent in the natural world, arising from the vulnerabilities of sentient beings and from the capacities of rational beings to recognize and to respond to those vulnerabilities and capacities in others.

This view of the basis of morality is hardly incompatible with religious belief. Indeed, anyone who believes that God made human beings in his image believes something like this—that there is a moral dimension of things, and that it is in our ability to apprehend it that we resemble the divine. Accordingly, many theists, like many atheists, believe that moral value is inherent in morally valuable things. Things don't become morally valuable because God prefers them; God prefers them because they are morally valuable. At least this is what I was taught as a girl, growing up Catholic: that we could see that God was good because of the things he commands us to do. If helping the poor were not a good thing on its own, it wouldn't be much to God's credit that he makes charity a duty.

It may surprise some people to learn that theists ever take this position, but it shouldn't. This position is not only consistent with belief in God, it is, I contend, a *more* pious position than its opposite. It is only if morality is independent of God that we can make moral sense out of religious worship. It is only if morality is independent of God that any person can have a *moral* basis for adhering to God's commands.

Let me explain why. First let's take a cold, hard look at the consequences of pinning morality to the existence of God. Consider the following moral judgments—judgments that seem to me to be obviously true:

- *It is wrong to drive people from their homes or to kill them because you want their land.*

- *It is wrong to enslave people.*

- *It is wrong to torture prisoners of war.*

- *Anyone who witnesses genocide, or enslavement, or torture is morally required to try to stop it.*

To say that morality depends on the existence of God is to say that none of these specific moral judgments is true unless God exists. That seems to me to be a remarkable claim. If God turned out not to exist, then slavery would be OK? There'd be nothing wrong with torture? The pain of another human being would mean nothing?

Think now about our personal relations—how we love our parents, our children, our life partners, our friends. To say that the moral worth of these individuals depends on the existence of God is to say that these people are, in themselves, worth nothing—that the concern we feel for their well-being has no more ethical significance than the concern some people feel for their boats or their cars. It is to say that the historical connections we value—the traits of character and personality that we love—all count for nothing in themselves. Other people warrant our concern only because they are valued by someone else—in this case, God. (Imagine telling a child, "You are not inherently lovable. I love you only because I love your father, and it is my duty to love anything he loves.")

What could make anyone think such things? Ironically, I think the answer is the same picture of morality that lies behind atheistic nihilism. It's the view that the only kind of "obligation" there could possibly be is the kind that is disciplined by promise of reward or threat of punishment. Such a view cannot find or comprehend any value inherent in the nature of things, value that could warrant particular attitudes and behavior on the part of anyone who can apprehend it. For someone who thinks that another being's pain is not in itself a reason to give aid, or that the welfare of a loved one is not on its own enough to justify sacrifice, it is only the Divine Sovereign that stands between us and—as Hobbes put it—the war of "all against all."

This will seem a harsh judgment on the many theists who subscribe to what is called divine command theory—the view that what is morally good is constituted by what God commands. Defenders of DCT will say that their theory explains a variety of things about morality that nontheistic accounts of moral value cannot, and that it should be preferred for that reason. For example, they will say that atheists cannot explain the objectivity of morality—how there could be moral truths that are independent of any human being's attitudes, will, or knowledge and how moral truths could hold universally. It is true that DCT would explain these things. If God exists, then he exists independently of human beings and their attitudes, and so his commands do, too. If we didn't invent God, then we didn't invent his commands, and hence didn't invent morality. We can be ignorant of God's will, and hence mistaken about what is morally good. Because God is omnipresent, his commands apply to all people at all times and in all places.

That's all fine. It would follow from DCT that moral facts are objective. The problem is that it wouldn't follow that they are *moral*. Commands issued by a tyrant would have all the same features. For DCT to explain morality, it must also explain what makes God good.

The problem I'm pointing to is an ancient one, discussed by Plato. In his dialogue *Euthyphro*, the eponymous character tries to explain his conception of piety to Socrates: "The pious acts," Euthyphro says, "are those which are loved by the gods." But Socrates finds this definition ambiguous and asks Euthyphro, "Are the pious acts pious because they are loved by the gods, or are the pious acts loved by the gods because they are pious?"

What's the difference? Well, if the first reading is correct, then it's the god's loving those particular acts that *makes* them count as pious acts, that *grounds* their piousness. "Pious," on this alternative, is just shorthand for "something the gods love." *Whatever* the gods happen to love, bingo—that's pious. If the gods change their preferences on a whim—and they did, if Homer knew his stuff—then the things that are pious change right along with them. In contrast, on the second reading, pious acts are presumed to have a distinctive, substantive property in common, a property in virtue of which the gods love them, a property that *explains why* the gods love them.

Translated into contemporary terms, the question Socrates is asking is this: Are morally good actions morally good simply *in virtue* of God's favoring them? Or does God favor them because they are—independently of his favoring them—morally good? DCT picks the first option; it says that it's the mere fact that God favors them that makes morally good things morally good.

Theories that endorse the second option—let's call any such theory a "divine independence theory" (DIT)—contend, on the contrary, that the goodness of an action is a feature that is independent of, and antecedent to, God's willing it. God could have commanded either this action or its opposite, but in fact, he commands only the good one.

Both DCT and DIT entail a perfect correspondence between the class of actions God commands and the class of actions that are good (or rather, they do so on the assumption that God is perfectly benevolent). The two theories differ, however, on what accounts for this congruence. DCT says that it is God's command that explains why the good acts are "good"—it becomes true *merely by definition* that God commands "good" actions. "Goodness," on this view, becomes an empty honorific, with no independent content. To say that God chooses the good is like saying that the prime meridian is at zero degrees longitude, or that in baseball, three strikes make an out. DIT, on the other hand, says that it is a substantive property of the acts—their goodness—that explains why God commanded them. Indeed, it says that God's goodness consists in his choosing all and only the good. DIT presumes that we have an independent grasp of moral goodness, and that it is because of that that we can properly appreciate the goodness of God.

DCT is arguably even more radical and bizarre than the Hobbesian nihilism I discussed earlier. On the nihilistic view, there is no pretense that a sovereign's power would generate moral obligation—the view is rather that "morality" is an illusion. But DCT insists both that there is such a thing as moral goodness and that it is defined by what God commands. This makes for really appalling consequences from an intuitive, moral point of view. DCT entails that anything at all could be "good" or "right" or "wrong." If God were to command you to eat your children, then it would be "right" to eat your children. The consequences are also appalling from a religious point of view. If all "moral" means is "commanded by God," then we cannot have what we would otherwise have thought of as moral reasons for obeying him. We might have prudential reasons for doing so, self-interested reasons for doing so. God is extremely powerful and so can make us suffer if we disobey him, but the same can be said of tyrants, and we have no moral obligation (speaking now in ordinary terms) to obey tyrants. (We might even have a moral obligation to disobey tyrants.) The same goes for worshipping God. We might find it in our interest to flatter or placate such a powerful person, but there could be no way in which God was deserving of praise or tribute.

This is the sense in which I think that it is a more pious position to hold that morality is independent of the existence of God. If the term *good* is not just an empty epithet that we attach to the Creator, whoever or whatever that turns out to be, then it must be that the facts about what is good are independent of the other facts about God. If "good" is to have normative force, it must be something that we can understand independently of what is commanded by a powerful omnipresent being.

So what about atheism? What I think all this means is that the capacity to be moved by the moral dimension of things has nothing to do with one's theological beliefs. The most reliable allies in any moral struggle will be those who respond to the ethically significant aspects of life, whether or not they conceive these things in religious terms. You do not lose morality by giving up God; neither do you necessarily find it by finding him.

I want to close by conceding that there are things one loses in giving up God, and they are not insignificant. Most importantly, you lose the guarantee of redemption. Suppose that you do something morally terrible, something for which you cannot make amends, something, perhaps, for which no human being could ever be expected to forgive you. I imagine that the promise made by many religions, that God will forgive you if you are truly sorry, is a thought that would bring enormous comfort and relief. You cannot have that if you are an atheist. In consequence, you must live your life and make your choices with the knowledge that every choice you make contributes, in one way or another, to the only value your life can have.

Some people think that if atheism were true, human choices would be insignificant. I think just the opposite—they would become surpassingly important.

DECEMBER 18, 2011

Morals Without God?

—*Frans de Waal*

I WAS BORN IN DEN BOSCH, THE CITY AFTER WHICH HIERONYMUS Bosch named himself. This obviously does not make me an expert on the Dutch painter, but having grown up with his statue on the market square, I have always been fond of his imagery, his symbolism and how it relates to humanity's place in the universe. This remains relevant today since Bosch depicts a society under a waning influence of God.

His famous triptych with naked figures frolicking around—*The Garden of Earthly Delights*—seems a tribute to paradisaical innocence. The tableau is far too happy and relaxed to fit the interpretation of depravity and sin advanced by puritan experts. It represents humanity free from guilt and shame either before the Fall or without any Fall at all. For a primatologist, like myself, the nudity, references to sex and fertility, the plentiful birds and fruits and the moving about in groups are thoroughly familiar and hardly require a religious or moral interpretation. Bosch seems to have depicted humanity in its natural state, while reserving his moralistic outlook for the right-hand panel of the triptych in which he punishes *not* the frolickers from the middle panel but monks, nuns, gluttons, gamblers, warriors and drunkards.

Five centuries later, we remain embroiled in debates about the role of religion in society. As in Bosch's days, the central theme is morality. Can we envision a world without God? Would this world be good? Don't think for one moment that the current battle lines between biology and fundamentalist Christianity turn around evidence. One has to be pretty immune to data to doubt evolution, which is why books and documentaries aimed at convincing the skeptics are a waste of effort. They are helpful for those prepared to listen but fail to reach their target audience. The debate is less about the truth than about how to handle it. For those who believe that morality comes straight from God the creator, acceptance of evolution would open a moral abyss.

OUR VAUNTED FRONTAL LOBE

Echoing this view, Reverend Al Sharpton opined in a recent videotaped debate, "If there is no order to the universe, and therefore some being, some force that ordered it, then who determines what is right or wrong? There is nothing immoral if there's nothing in charge." Similarly, I have heard people echo Dostoevsky's Ivan Karamazov, exclaiming that "if there is no God, I am free to rape my neighbor!"

Perhaps it is just me, but I am wary of anyone whose belief system is the only thing standing between them and repulsive behavior. Why not assume that our humanity, including the self-control needed for livable societies, is built into us? Does anyone truly believe that our ancestors lacked social norms before they had religion? Did they never assist others in need or complain about an unfair deal? Humans must have worried about the functioning of their communities well before the current religions arose, which is only a few thousand years ago. Not that religion is irrelevant—I will get to this—but it is an add-on rather than the wellspring of morality.

Deep down, creationists realize they will never win factual arguments with science. This is why they have construed their own science-like universe, known as Intelligent Design, and eagerly jump on every tidbit of information that seems to go their way. The most recent opportunity arose with the Hauser affair. A Harvard colleague, Marc Hauser, has been accused of eight counts of scientific misconduct, including making up his own data. Since Hauser studied primate behavior and wrote about morality, Christian websites were eager to claim that "all that people like Hauser are left with are unsubstantiated propositions that are contradicted by millennia of human experience" (Chuck Colson, September 8, 2010). A major newspaper asked, "Would it be such a bad thing if Hausergate resulted in some intellectual humility among the new scientists of morality?" (Eric Felten, August 27, 2010). Even a linguist could not resist this occasion to reaffirm the gap between human and animal by warning against "naive evolutionary presuppositions."

These are rearguard battles, however. Whether creationists jump on this scientific scandal or linguists and psychologists keep selling human exceptionalism does not really matter. Fraud has occurred in many fields of science, from epidemiology to physics, all of which are still around. In the field of cognition, the march toward continuity between human and animal has been inexorable—one misconduct case won't make a difference. True, humanity never runs out of claims of what sets it apart, but it is a rare uniqueness claim that holds up for over a decade. This is why we don't hear anymore that only humans make tools, imitate, think ahead, have culture, are self-aware or adopt another's point of view.

If we consider our species without letting ourselves be blinded by the technical advances of the last few millennia, we see a creature of flesh and blood with a brain that, albeit three times larger than a chimpanzee's, doesn't contain any new parts. Even our vaunted prefrontal cortex turns out to be of typical size: recent neuron-counting techniques classify the human brain as a linearly scaled-up monkey brain. No one doubts the superiority of our intellect, but we have no basic wants or needs that are not also present in our close relatives. I interact on a daily basis with monkeys and apes, which just like us strive for power, enjoy sex, want security and affection, kill over territory and value trust and cooperation. Yes, we use cell phones and fly airplanes, but our psychological makeup remains that of a social primate. Even the posturing and deal-making among the alpha males in Washington is nothing out of the ordinary.

THE PLEASURE OF GIVING

Charles Darwin was interested in how morality fits the human-animal continuum, proposing in *The Descent of Man*, "Any animal whatever, endowed with well-marked social instincts . . . would inevitably acquire a moral sense or conscience, as soon as its intellectual powers had become as well developed . . . as in man."

Unfortunately, modern popularizers have strayed from these insights. Like Robert Wright in *The Moral Animal*, they argue that true moral tendencies cannot exist—not in humans and even less in other animals—since nature is 100 percent selfish. Morality is just a thin veneer over a cauldron of nasty tendencies. Dubbing this position "veneer theory" (similar to Peter Railton's "moral camouflage"), I have fought it ever since my 1996 book *Good Natured*. Instead of blaming atrocious behavior on our biology ("We're acting like animals!"), while claiming our noble traits for ourselves, why not view the entire package as a product of evolution? Fortunately, there has been a resurgence of the Darwinian view that morality grew out of the social instincts. Psychologists stress the intuitive way we arrive at moral judgments while activating emotional brain areas, and economists and anthropologists have shown humanity to be far more cooperative, altruistic, and fair than predicted by self-interest models. Similarly, the latest experiments in primatology reveal that our close relatives will do each other favors even if there's nothing in it for themselves.

Chimpanzees and bonobos will voluntarily open a door to offer a companion access to food, even if they lose part of it in the process. And capuchin monkeys are prepared to seek rewards for others, such as when we place two of them side by side, while one of them barters with us with differently colored tokens. One token is "selfish," and the other "prosocial." If the bartering monkey selects the selfish token, it receives a small piece of apple for returning it, but its partner gets nothing. The prosocial token, on the other hand, rewards both monkeys. Most monkeys develop an overwhelming preference for the prosocial token, which preference is not due to fear of repercussions, because dominant monkeys (who have least to fear) are the most generous.

Even though altruistic behavior evolved for the advantages it confers, this does not make it selfishly motivated. Future benefits rarely figure in the minds of animals. For example, animals engage in sex without knowing its reproductive consequences, and even humans had to develop the morning-after pill. This is because sexual motivation is unconcerned with the reason why sex exists. The same is true for the altruistic impulse, which is unconcerned with evolutionary consequences. It is this disconnect between evolution and motivation that befuddled the veneer theorists and made them reduce everything to selfishness. The most quoted line of their bleak literature says it all: "Scratch an 'altruist,' and watch a 'hypocrite' bleed."

It is not only humans who are capable of genuine altruism; other animals are, too. I see it every day. An old female, Peony, spends her days outdoors with other chimpanzees at the Yerkes Primate Center's field station. On bad days, when her arthritis is flaring up, she has trouble walking and climbing, but other females help her out. For example, Peony is huffing and puffing to get up into the climbing frame in which several apes have gathered for a grooming session. An unrelated younger female moves behind her, placing both hands on her ample behind, and pushes her up with quite a bit of effort until Peony has joined the rest.

We have also seen Peony getting up and slowly moving toward the water spigot, which is at quite a distance. Younger females sometimes run ahead of her, take in some water, then return to Peony and give it to her. At first, we had no idea what was going on, since all we saw was one female placing her mouth close to Peony's, but after a while the pattern became clear: Peony would open her mouth wide, and the younger female would spit a jet of water into it.

Such observations fit the emerging field of animal empathy, which deals not only with primates, but also with canines, elephants, even rodents. A typical example is how chimpanzees console distressed parties, hugging and kissing them, which behavior is so predictable that scientists have analyzed thousands of cases. Mammals are sensitive to each other's emotions and react to others in need. The whole reason people fill their homes with furry carnivores and not with, say, iguanas and turtles, is because mammals offer something no reptile ever will. They give affection, they want affection, and they respond to our emotions the way we do to theirs.

Mammals may derive pleasure from helping others in the same way that humans feel good doing good. Nature often equips life's essentials—sex, eating, nursing—with built-in gratification. One study found that pleasure centers in the human brain light up when we give to charity. This is of course no reason to call such behavior "selfish" as it would make the word totally meaningless. A selfish individual has no trouble walking away from another in need. Someone is drowning: let him drown. Someone cries: let her cry. These are truly selfish reactions, which are quite different from empathic ones. Yes, we experience a "warm glow," and perhaps some other animals do as well, but since this glow reaches us *via* the other, and *only* via the other, the helping is genuinely other-oriented.

BOTTOM-UP MORALITY

A few years ago Sarah Brosnan and I demonstrated that primates will happily perform a task for cucumber slices until they see others getting grapes, which taste so much better. The cucumber eaters become agitated, throw down their measly veggies and go on strike. A perfectly fine food has become unpalatable as a result of seeing a companion with something better.

We called it *inequity aversion*, a topic since investigated in other animals, including dogs. A dog will repeatedly perform a trick without rewards but refuse as soon as another dog gets pieces of sausage for the same trick. Recently, Sarah reported an unexpected twist to the inequity issue, however. While testing pairs of chimps, she found that also the one who gets the *better* deal occasionally refuses. It is as if they are satisfied only if both get the same. We seem to be getting close to a sense of fairness.

Such findings have implications for human morality. According to most philosophers, we reason ourselves toward a moral position. Even if we do not invoke God, it is still a top-down process of us formulating the principles and then imposing those on human conduct. But would it be realistic to ask people to be considerate of others if we had not already a natural inclination to be so? Would it make sense to appeal to fairness and justice in the absence of powerful reactions to their absence? Imagine the cognitive burden if every decision we took needed to be vetted against handed-down principles. Instead, I am a firm believer in the Humean position that reason is the slave of the passions. We started out with moral sentiments and intuitions, which is also where we find the greatest continuity with other primates. Rather than having developed morality from scratch, we received a huge helping hand from our background as social animals.

At the same time, however, I am reluctant to call a chimpanzee a "moral being." This is because sentiments do not suffice. We strive for a logically coherent system and have debates about how the death penalty fits arguments for the sanctity of life, or whether an unchosen sexual orientation can be wrong. These debates are uniquely human. We have no evidence that other animals judge the appropriateness of actions that do not affect themselves. The great pioneer of morality research, the Finn Edward Westermarck, explained what makes the moral emotions special: "Moral emotions are disconnected from one's immediate situation: they deal with good and bad at a more abstract, disinterested level." This is what sets human morality apart: a move toward universal standards combined with an elaborate system of justification, monitoring and punishment.

At this point, religion comes in. Think of the narrative support for compassion, such as the Parable of the Good Samaritan, or the challenge to fairness, such as the Parable of the Workers in the Vineyard, with its famous conclusion "The last will be first, and the first will be last." Add to this an almost Skinnerian fondness of reward and punishment—from the virgins to be met in heaven to the hellfire that awaits sinners—and the exploitation of our desire to be "praiseworthy," as Adam Smith called it. Humans are so sensitive to public opinion that we only need to see a picture of two eyes glued to the wall to respond with good behavior, which explains the image in some religions of an all-seeing eye to symbolize an omniscient God.

THE ATHEIST DILEMMA

Over the past few years, we have gotten used to a strident atheism arguing that God is not great (Christopher Hitchens) or a delusion (Richard Dawkins). The New Atheists call themselves "brights," thus hinting that believers are not so bright. They urge trust in science and want to root ethics in a naturalistic worldview.

While I do consider religious institutions and their representatives—popes, bishops, megapreachers, ayatollahs and rabbis—fair game for criticism, what good could come from insulting individuals who find value in religion? And more pertinently, what alternative does science have to offer? Science is not in the business of spelling out the meaning of life and even less in telling us how to live our lives. We scientists are good at finding out why things are the way they are, or how things work, and I do believe that biology can help us understand what kind of animals we are and why our morality looks the way it does. But to go from there to offering moral guidance seems a stretch.

Even the staunchest atheist growing up in Western society cannot avoid having absorbed the basic tenets of Christian morality. Our societies are steeped in it: everything we have accomplished over the centuries, even science, developed either hand in hand with or in opposition to religion, but never separately. It is impossible to know what morality would look like without religion. It would require a visit to a human culture that is not now and never was religious. That such cultures do not exist should give us pause.

Bosch struggled with the same issue—not with being an atheist, which was not an option, but science's place in society. The little figures in his paintings with inverted funnels on their heads or the buildings in the form of flasks, distillation bottles, and furnaces reference chemical equipment. Alchemy was gaining ground yet mixed with the occult and full of charlatans and quacks, which Bosch depicted with great humor in front of gullible audiences. Alchemy turned into science when it liberated itself from these influences and developed self-correcting procedures to deal with flawed or fabricated data. But science's contribution to a moral society, if any, remains a question mark.

Other primates have of course none of these problems, but even they strive for a certain kind of society. For example, female chimpanzees have been seen to drag reluctant males toward each other to make up after a fight, removing weapons from their hands, and high-ranking males regularly act as impartial arbiters to settle disputes in the community. I take these hints of *community concern* as yet another sign that the building blocks of morality are older than humanity, and that we do not need God to explain how we got where we are today. On the other hand, what would happen if we were able to excise religion from society? I doubt that science and the naturalistic worldview could fill the void and become an inspiration for the good. Any framework we develop to advocate a certain moral outlook is bound to produce its own list of principles, its own prophets, and attract its own devoted followers so that it will soon look like any old religion.

OCTOBER 17, 2010

The Sacred and the Humane

—*Anat Biletzki*

UMAN RIGHTS ARE ALL THE RAGE. THEY HAVE BECOME, CUR-
rently, a very popular arena for both political activism and rampant
discourse. Human rights, as we all know, are the rights humans
are due simply by virtue of being human. But there is nothing simple here, since both "human" and "rights" are concepts in need of
investigation.

One deep philosophical issue that invigorates debates in human
rights is the question of their foundation and justification, the question Where do human rights come from, and what grounds them?
There are two essentially different approaches to answering that
question—the religious way and the secular, or philosophical, way.
Writing in *The New York Times Magazine* in 1993 ("Life Is Sacred:
That's the Easy Part"), Ronald Dworkin put this very succinctly: "We
almost all accept . . . that human life in all its forms is *sacred*—that it
has intrinsic and objective value quite apart from any value it might
have to the person whose life it is. For some of us, this is a matter of
religious faith; for others, of secular but deep philosophical belief."
A good representative of the first camp is the religious historian and
educator R. H. Tawney: "The essence of all morality is this: to believe
that every human being is of infinite importance, and therefore that
no consideration of expediency can justify the oppression of one by
another. But to believe this it is necessary to believe in God."

The second, nonreligious grounding of human rights is harder to give voice to by a single representative since there is a multiplicity of distinct, nonreligious groundings of human rights. But think again of Dworkin's words. We all accept, he says, that human life is *sacred*. By using that word—sacred—he seems to have already put the ball in the religious field. And that field, the field of the sacred as opposed to the mundane, plays a straightforward game, claiming that the only possible answer to the question of the foundations of human rights is the religious answer. Only by positing a divine creator of everything (including human beings) can we give a satisfactory account of the sacredness of human beings, of why we "deserve" or "are entitled" to something that derives from our being just that— sacred human beings.

On this view, any highfalutin philosophical concept that is called upon to be a comparable base for human rights is no more than a religious foundation clothed in secular garb; it is really just God by any other name. Thus, in a recent book, *The Idea of Human Rights*, Michael Perry is unequivocal about the worthlessness of the secular bunch: "There is, finally, no intelligible (much less persuasive) secular version of the conviction that every human being is sacred; the only intelligible versions are religious." Think of conspicuous elements in the vocabulary of human rights, the notions of "dignity," "inviolable," "end in himself," and the like. Although we try to give them meaning and standing without a turn to religious essence, these terms hold no secular water according to thinkers like Perry. There can be no human dignity, no inviolable person, no end in herself without the supposition of the human as sacred, and therefore as a godly creation.

There is, however, no philosophically robust reason to accept this claim. True, the religious answer is straightforward and clear-cut. True, philosophical theorizing on the foundations of human rights in particular, and morality in general, may be complex, or nuanced, or even convoluted. True, the word *sacred* carries religious connotations. But that could just be a manner of speaking—and dignity and inviolability certainly do not need to be tied down to the sacred.

Aristotelian virtue and natural justice or the Kantian categorical imperative (arising from reason, of course) offer philosophical bases for morality at large. Theories of human needs, human interests and human agency provide analytical foundations for the idea of human rights. And then there is Hart's one natural right (the equal right to be free), Gewirth's turn to human action and logic, Sen and Nussbaum's talk of basic human capabilities, and oh-so-many others, all affording *humanistic* starting points for the human dignity at the base of human rights that need nary a wink at religion. There is also a legitimate and, to my mind, strong critique of the individualism guiding the *liberal* idea of human rights that enjoins us to rethink our mantras regarding the autonomous self who is the "human." That these are intricate and sometimes problematic, that they might be in tension with, even contradict, each other, that we must do considerable analytic and philosophical work in their explication does not cancel out their equal profundity—equal to religion, that is—in justifying human rights.

What difference does it make? Beyond the theoretical discussions on human rights—What grounds them *theoretically*? What justifies them *theoretically*? What legal implications do they carry *theoretically*?—there is the "so what?" question. Why do we care, or why should we care, if the practice of human rights is born of religious or secular motivation?

Take a look at how we work on the ground, so to speak; look at how we do human rights, for example, in Israel-Palestine. When Rabbi Arik Ascherman, the leader of Rabbis for Human Rights in Israel, squats in the mud trying to stop soldiers who have come to set a blockade around a village or fights settlers who have come to uproot olive trees (as he has done so often, in villages like Yanoun and Jamain and Biddu, in the last decade) along with me (from B'Tselem—the Information Center for Human Rights in the Occupied Territories), or a group of secular kids from Anarchists against the Wall, or people from the Israeli Committee against House Demolitions—and he does this on a Friday afternoon, knowing full well that he might be courting religious transgression should the Sabbath arrive—does it matter that his reasons for doing so spring from his faith while the anarchists' derive from their secular political worldview and B'Tselem's and ICAHD's from secular international human rights law? The end product, the human rights *activity*, is similar, even identical; but the reason, the intention, the motivation for it are distinctly different. Does that matter?

I think it does. I dare say that religion, even when indirectly in the service of human rights, is not really working for human rights. Although there is recognition of the human as sacred, it is not the concept of *rights* that propels the religious person. For him, the human status of sacredness draws from divine creation and directive, from man (and woman) having been created in God's image, and therefore has nothing to do with a human right. As Jack Donnelly says in *Universal Human Rights in Theory and Practice*, "'Traditional' societies . . . typically have had elaborate systems of duties . . . conceptions of justice, political legitimacy, and human flourishing that sought to realize human dignity, flourishing, or well-being entirely independent of human rights. These institutions and practices are alternative to, rather than different formulations of, human rights."

The question, we have seen, is what functions as the source of moral authority, assuming that "human rights" are morally based. Hilary Putnam, in *Jewish Philosophy as a Guide to Life*, says it beautifully: "Every human being should experience him/herself as commanded to be available to the neediness, the suffering, the vulnerability of the other person." But notice Putnam's terminology: "commanded." Who commands us? The question boils down to who or what is the source of moral authority—God or the human being, religion or ethics? I want to say that that makes a great difference. And I want to ask, If we—the religious person and the secular person—end up engaging in the same activity and also, more so, do it by thinking of ourselves as available to another's neediness, why does it make a difference?

The problem arises not when we act together, but rather when we don't. Or put differently, when we act together, the problem stays in the realm of theory, providing fodder for the philosophical game of human rights. It is when we disagree—about abortion, about capital punishment, about settling occupied lands—that the religious authority must vacate the arena of human rights. This is not to say that all religious people hold the same views on these issues or that secular persons are always in agreement (although opinion polls, for whatever they are worth, point to far more unity of thought on the religious side). It is rather that an internal, secular debate on issues that pertain to human rights is structurally and essentially different from the debate between the two camps. In the latter, the authority that is conscripted to "command" us on the religious side is God, while on the secular side it is the human, with her claim to reason, her proclivity to emotion, and her capacity for compassion. In a sense, that is no commandment at all. It is a turn to the human, and a (perhaps axiomatic, perhaps even dogmatic) posit of human dignity, that turns the engine of human rights, leaving us open to discussion, disagreement, and questioning without ever deserting that first posit. The parallel turn to God puts our actions under his command; if he commands a violation of human rights, then so be it. There is no meaning to human *rights* under divine commandment. A deep acceptance of divine authority—and that is what true religion demands—entails a renunciation of human rights if God so wills. Had God's angel failed to call out, "Abraham! Abraham!" Abraham would have slain Isaac.

THERE MIGHT SEEM to be a dogmatic antireligiosity arising from my reluctance to admit religion as a legitimate player in the human rights game. I have been using *religion* all along in, you might say, a very conservative, traditional way. Philosophers of religion and anthropologists have opened up the study of religion to recognize a variety of religious *experience*, religion as a *form of life*, religion as a *cultural* framework, religion as a system of *symbols*, a religious *phenomenology*, etc. Adopting a certain view on religion or a specific definition of religion is hugely pertinent to how one sees human rights functioning in a religious context. Let me, then, make explicit the definition of religion at the root of my unrest: religion is a system of myth and ritual; it is a communal system of propositional attitudes—beliefs, hopes, fears, desires—that are related to super-human agents. This very common definition (recently recognized in academic circles as that of the "Dartmouth School"), along with several essential terms (*myth*, *ritual*, *communal*, *propositional*), asserts the unconditional "superhuman agents,"—that is, God(s)—that are necessary for the divorce I espouse between religion and human rights. Other perceptions of religion that are "God-less" would not, perhaps, suffer the same fate.

And, you may say, what about the wonder of religion, the majestic awe that encompasses the religious person when confronted by a spiritual revelation that motivates and "regulates for in all his life"? (This was Ludwig Wittgenstein's "definition" of religion.) Can secular morals live up to that type of enchantment? Is there not something about secular rationalism that conduces rather to skepticism, fallibility and indifference than to the kind of awesome respect for the sacred human being that comes with religion? Here I have no choice than to turn to dogmatism—call it Kantian dogmatism: "Two things fill the mind with ever new and increasing admiration and awe, the more often and steadily we reflect upon them: the starry heavens above me and the moral law within me." For some, the physics that runs the natural world and the ethics that provide for our moral sense are seen to be more ordinary than religious experience. I, on the other hand, can think of nothing more awe inspiring than humanity and its fragility and its resilience.

JULY 17, 2011

Confessions of an Ex-Moralist

—Joel Marks

T HE DAY I BECAME AN ATHEIST WAS THE DAY I REALIZED I HAD been a believer.

Up until then I had numbered myself among the "secular ethicists." Plato's *Euthyphro* had convinced me, as it had so many other philosophers, that religion is not needed for morality. Socrates puts the point characteristically in the form of a question: "Do the gods love something because it is pious, or is something pious because the gods love it?" To believe the latter would be to allow that any act whatever might turn out to be the "pious" or right thing to do, provided only that one of the gods (of Olympus), or the God of Genesis and Job in one of his moods, "loved" or willed it. Yet if God commanded that we kill our innocent child in cold blood, would we not resist the rightness of this act?

This would seem to be the modern, sane view of the matter. We have an intuitive sense of right and wrong that trumps even the commands of God. We have the ability to judge that God is good or bad. Therefore, even if God did not exist, we could fend for ourselves in matters of conscience. Ethics, not divine revelation, is the guide to life. That is indeed the clarion call of the New Atheists. As the philosopher Louise Antony puts it in the introduction to a recent collection of philosophers' essays, *Philosophers without Gods: Meditations on Atheism and the Secular Life*, "Another charge routinely leveled at atheists is that we have no moral values. The essays in this volume should serve to roundly refute this. Every writer in this volume adamantly affirms the objectivity of right and wrong."

But I don't. Not any longer. Yet I once devoted my professional life to studying ethics in the spirit of Anthony's book. The task seemed squarely on our human shoulders to figure out how to act on particular occasions and how to live in general. Yes, there were deep problems to unravel, but they were subject to rational resolution. Most of my thinking concerned the dispute between the moral doctrine known as consequentialism and so-called deontological ethics: Is it the outcome of our actions that determines their moral value, or, alternatively, the quality of the act itself? For example, is a lie that leads to something good thereby permissible, perhaps even obligatory, or would it be forbidden simply in virtue of being a lie? This kind of inquiry is known as normative ethics.

Then there is another kind of motive for doing ethics, more practical in nature. So-called applied ethics seeks to find answers for the pressing moral problems of the day. Can abortion ever be justified? Capital punishment? Euthanasia? War? In my case the plight of nonhuman animals at human hands became the great preoccupation. I could think of no greater atrocity than the confinement and slaughter of untold billions of innocent creatures for sustenance that can be provided through other, more humane diets.

In my most recent published book, I defended a particular moral theory—my own version of deontological ethics—and then "applied" that theory to defend a particular moral claim: that other animals have an inherent right not to be eaten or otherwise used by humans. Oddly enough, it was as I crossed the final t and dotted the final i of that monograph that I underwent what I call my anti-epiphany.

A friend had been explaining to me the nature of her belief in God. At one point she likened divinity to the beauty of a sunset: the quality lay not in the sunset but in her relation to the sunset. I thought to myself, "Ah, if that is what she means, then I could believe in *that* kind of God. For when I think about the universe, I am filled with awe and wonder; if that feeling is God, then I am a believer."

But then it hit me: Is not morality like this God? In other words, could I believe that, say, the wrongness of a lie was any more intrinsic to an intentionally deceptive utterance than beauty was to a sunset or wonderfulness to the universe? Does it not make far more sense to suppose that all of these phenomena arise in my breast, that they are the responses of a particular sensibility to otherwise valueless events and entities?

So someone else might respond completely differently from me, such that for him or her, the lie was permissible, the sunset banal, the universe nothing but atoms and the void. Yet that prospect was so alien to my conception of morality that it was tantamount to there being no morality at all. For essential to morality is that its norms apply with equal legitimacy to everyone; moral relativism, it has always seemed to me, is an oxymoron. Hence I saw no escape from moral nihilism.

The dominoes continued to fall. I had thought I was a secularist because I conceived of right and wrong as standing on their own two feet, without prop or crutch from God. We should do the right thing because it is the right thing to do, period. *But this was a God, too.* It was the Godless God of secular morality, which commanded without commander—whose ways were thus even more mysterious than the God I did not believe in, who at least had the intelligible motive of rewarding us for doing what he wanted.

And what is more, I had known this. At some level of my being there had been the awareness, but I had brushed it aside. I had therefore lived in a semiconscious state of self-delusion—what Sartre might have called bad faith. But in my case this was also a pun, for my bad faith was precisely *the belief that I lacked faith in a divinity.*

In the three years since my anti-epiphany I have attempted to assess these surprising revelations and their implications for my life and work. I found myself in the thick of metaethics, which looks at the nature of morality, including whether there even is such a thing as right and wrong. I myself had ignored the latter issue for most of my career, since, if there was one thing I knew in this entire universe, it was that some things are morally wrong. It is wrong to toss male chicks, alive and conscious, into a meat grinder, as happens in the egg industry. It is wrong to scorn homosexuals and deny them civil rights. It is wrong to massacre people in death camps. All of these things have met with general approval in one society or another. And yet I knew in my soul, with all of my conviction, with a passion, that they were wrong, wrong, wrong. I knew this with more certainty than I knew that the earth is round.

But suddenly I knew it no more. I was not merely skeptical or agnostic about it; I had come to believe, and do still, that these things are not wrong. But neither are they right; nor are they permissible. The entire set of moral attributions is out the window. Think of this analogy: A tribe of people lives on an isolated island. They have no formal governmental institutions of any kind. In particular they have no legislature. Therefore in that society it would make no sense to say that someone had done something "illegal." But neither would anything be "legal." The entire set of legal categories would be inapplicable. In just this way I now view moral categories.

Certainly I am not the first to have had thoughts like these, and today the philosopher Richard Garner in particular is a soul mate. Nor has there been a shortage of alternative conceptions of morality to the one I held. But the personal experiment of excluding all moral concepts and language from my thinking, feeling and actions has proved so workable and attractive, I am convinced that anyone who gives it a fair shot would likely find it to his liking.

One interesting discovery has been that there are fewer practical differences between moralism and amoralism than might have been expected. It seems to me that what could broadly be called desire has been the moving force of humanity, no matter how we might have window-dressed it with moral talk. By desire I do not mean sexual craving, or even only selfish wanting. I use the term generally to refer to whatever motivates us, which ranges from selfishness to altruism and everything in between and at right angles. Mother Teresa was acting as much from desire as was the Marquis de Sade. But the sort of desire that now concerns me most is what we would want if we were absolutely convinced that there is no such thing as moral right and wrong. I think the most likely answer is this: pretty much the same as what we want now.

For instance, I used to think that animal agriculture was wrong. Now I will call a spade a spade and declare simply that I very much dislike it and want it to stop. Has this lessened my commitment to ending it? I do not find that to be the case at all. Does this lessen my ability to bring others around to sharing my desires, and hence diminish the prospects of ending animal agriculture? On the contrary, I find myself in a far better position than before to change minds—and, what is more important, hearts. For to argue that people who use animals for food and other purposes are doing something terribly wrong is hardly the way to win them over. That is more likely to elicit their defensive resistance.

Instead I now focus on conveying information: about the state of affairs on factory farms and elsewhere, the environmental devastation that results and, especially, the sentient, intelligent, gentle and noble natures of the animals who are being brutalized and slaughtered. It is also important to spread knowledge of alternatives, like how to adopt a healthy and appetizing vegan diet. If such efforts will not cause people to alter their eating and buying habits, support the passage of various laws and so forth, I don't know what will.

So nothing has changed, and everything has changed. For while my desires are the same, my manner of trying to implement them has altered radically. I now acknowledge that I cannot count on either God or morality to back up my personal preferences or clinch the case in any argument. I am simply no longer in the business of trying to derive an *ought* from an *is*. I must accept that other people sometimes have opposed preferences, even when we are agreed on all the relevant facts and are reasoning correctly.

My outlook has therefore become more practical: I desire to influence the world in such a way that my desires have a greater likelihood of being realized. This implies being an active citizen. But there is still plenty of room for the sorts of activities and engagements that characterize the life of a philosophical ethicist. For one thing, I retain my strong preference for honest dialectical dealings in a context of mutual respect. It's just that I am no longer giving premises in moral arguments; rather, I am offering considerations to help us figure out what to do. I am not attempting to justify anything; I am trying to motivate informed and reflective choices.

In the process my own desires are likely to undergo further change as well, in the direction of greater compassion and respect, I would anticipate—and not only for the victims of the attitudes, behaviors and policies I don't like, but also for their perpetrators. But this won't be because a god, a supernatural law or even my conscience told me I must, I ought, I have an obligation. Instead I will be moved by my head and my heart. Morality has nothing to do with it.

AUGUST 21, 2011

Are We Ready for a "Morality Pill"?

—Peter Singer and Agata Sagan

Ⅰɴ Oᴄᴛᴏʙᴇʀ 2011, ɪɴ Fᴏsʜᴀɴ, Cʜɪɴᴀ, ᴀ ᴛᴡᴏ-ʏᴇᴀʀ-ᴏʟᴅ ɢɪʀʟ ᴡᴀs run over by a van. The driver did not stop. Over the next seven minutes, more than a dozen people walked or bicycled past the injured child. A second truck ran over her. Eventually, a woman pulled her to the side, and her mother arrived. The child died in a hospital. The entire scene was captured on video and caused an uproar when it was shown by a television station and posted online. A similar event occurred in London in 2004, as have others, far from the lens of a video camera.

Yet people can, and often do, behave in very different ways.

A news search for the words *hero saves* will routinely turn up stories of bystanders braving oncoming trains, swift currents and raging fires to save strangers from harm. Acts of extreme kindness, responsibility and compassion are, like their opposites, nearly universal.

Why are some people prepared to risk their lives to help a stranger when others won't even stop to dial an emergency number?

Scientists have been exploring questions like this for decades. In the 1960s and early '70s, famous experiments by Stanley Milgram and Philip Zimbardo suggested that most of us would, under specific circumstances, voluntarily do great harm to innocent people. During the same period, John Darley and C. Daniel Batson showed that even some seminary students on their way to give a lecture about the parable of the Good Samaritan would, if told that they were running late, walk past a stranger lying moaning beside the path. More recent research has told us a lot about what happens in the brain when people make moral decisions. But are we getting any closer to understanding what drives our moral behavior?

Here's what much of the discussion of all these experiments missed: some people did the right thing. A recent experiment (about which we have some ethical reservations) at the University of Chicago seems to shed new light on why.

Researchers there took two rats who shared a cage and trapped one of them in a tube that could be opened only from the outside. The free rat usually tried to open the door, eventually succeeding. Even when the free rats could eat up all of a quantity of chocolate before freeing the trapped rat, they mostly preferred to free their cage mate. The experimenters interpret their findings as demonstrating empathy in rats. But if that is the case, they have also demonstrated that individual rats vary, for only twenty-three of thirty rats freed their trapped companions.

The causes of the difference in their behavior must lie in the rats themselves. It seems plausible that humans, like rats, are spread along a continuum of readiness to help others. There has been considerable research on abnormal people, like psychopaths, but we need to know more about relatively stable differences (perhaps rooted in our genes) in the great majority of people as well.

Undoubtedly, situational factors can make a huge difference, and perhaps moral beliefs do as well, but if humans are just different in their predispositions to act morally, we also need to know more about these differences. Only then will we gain a proper understanding of our moral behavior, including why it varies so much from person to person and whether there is anything we can do about it.

If continuing brain research does in fact show biochemical differences between the brains of those who help others and the brains of those who do not, could this lead to a "morality pill"—a drug that makes us more likely to help? Given the many other studies linking biochemical conditions to mood and behavior, and the proliferation of drugs to modify them that have followed, the idea is not far-fetched. If so, would people choose to take it? Could criminals be given the option, as an alternative to prison, of a drug-releasing implant that would make them less likely to harm others? Might governments begin screening people to discover those most likely to commit crimes? Those who are at much greater risk of committing a crime might be offered the morality pill; if they refused, they might be required to wear a tracking device that would show where they had been at any given time, so that they would know that if they did commit a crime, they would be detected.

Fifty years ago, Anthony Burgess wrote *A Clockwork Orange*, a futuristic novel about a vicious gang leader who undergoes a procedure that makes him incapable of violence. Stanley Kubrick's 1971 movie version sparked a discussion in which many argued that we could never be justified in depriving someone of his free will, no matter how gruesome the violence that would thereby be prevented. No doubt any proposal to develop a morality pill would encounter the same objection.

But if our brain's chemistry does affect our moral behavior, the question of whether that balance is set in a natural way or by medical intervention will make no difference in how freely we act. If there are already biochemical differences between us that can be used to predict how ethically we will act, then either such differences are compatible with free will or they are evidence that at least as far as some of our ethical actions are concerned, none of us have ever had free will anyway. In any case, whether or not we have free will, we may soon face new choices about the ways in which we are willing to influence behavior for the better.

JANUARY 28, 2012

The Light at the End of Suffering

—Peg O'Connor

HOW MUCH MORE CAN I TAKE?

This question has been at the root of the human experience for as long as we have been able to record it, if not longer. It was the lament of Job—or at least one of them—and is asked with no less frequency today in response to circumstances ranging from devastating loss and grief to the typical hardships of a trying job or a long winter.

But where is that actual point at which a person "breaks" or comes to believe not only that her life is devoid of value or meaning, but that the world is, too? The truth is that most people really do not want to ascertain just how much more they can suffer. A vast majority of people would look askance at someone who really wanted to experiment with her limits for suffering. But what if we are to treat it as a genuine question? In some of my recent work in the area of addiction and philosophy, I've found that many active addicts of all sorts confront that limit every day in ways that those fortunate enough to be free of addiction may never know. For some of them, the process of reaching that limit becomes an opportunity to effect radical transformation of their lives.

A broader understanding of this concept can be found in the work of William James, whose famous work, *The Varieties of Religious Experience*, provides significant insight about the limits of misery and its transformative potential. *Varieties* is a product of lectures James delivered at the University of Edinburgh in 1901 and 1902. His focus is the experience of individuals "for whom religion exists not as a dull habit, but as an acute fever." By "religion," James does not mean religious institutions and their long entrenched theological debates, but rather something more akin to an individual spiritual state, which may or may not include belief in a god.

James was uniquely suited to deliver these lectures. He was a physician, philosopher and a psychologist before the field of psychology was part of academe, and someone with a deep, abiding interest in psychic events. He was, in all senses, a student of human nature. He explored this question of what we may call the "misery threshold" because he wanted to know if some people were more capable or more prone to experience "the acute fever" of religious belief. His answer: it is those who suffer most who are inclined to experience that fever. These are the people who fascinated him: those who toed right up to and sometimes over the line of despair and meaninglessness.

James claims in *Varieties* that there are two kinds of people, differentiated from where they live in relation to their misery threshold. Each person, he argued, has a threshold for emotional pain akin to a threshold for physical pain. While some people at the slightest physical pain tend to run to the ibuprofen or painkillers, others seem able to tolerate excruciating physical pain. The same holds for misery.

James calls those who live on the sunnier side of their misery threshold "healthy-minded." Optimism fills their lives, though there are degrees of optimism. Some of the healthy-minded see the glass half full while others see it as half full with something really delicious. These are the sort of people who always look for the bright side and have a soul with "a sky-blue tint, whose affinities are rather with the flowers and birds and all enchanting innocencies than with dark human passions." Though the sunny-side people can be miserable at times, they have a low tolerance for misery. It would take something catastrophic for them to stay on the dark side of their misery lines.

The sunny-siders are somewhat interesting to James, if only because they constitute a type that is almost completely foreign to him. James knew himself and many of his family members to belong to the second category—"sick souls" and "divided selves," who live on the dark side of their misery threshold. Sick souls tend to say no to life, according to James, and are governed by fear. Sick souls tend to become anxious and melancholic, with apprehension that opportunistically spreads.

The person with a divided self suffers from what James calls "world sickness." This sickness is progressive, and James charts its development keenly and compassionately. Those with divided self experience a war within; their lives are "little more than a series of zig zags," their "spirit wars with their flesh, they wish for incompatibles," and "their lives are one long drama of repentance and of effort to repair misdemeanors and mistakes."

Perhaps not coincidentally, this is an accurate description of addiction. James knew a great deal about drunkenness or inebriety, to use the language of his time. For years, his brother Robertson (Bob) was in and out of asylums for the inebriate and spent his final years with James and his wife. This may explain why some of the most compelling first-person accounts in James's work of divided selves and sick souls who were later transformed come from people who were drunkards. (This may also explain why Bill Wilson, one of the founders of Alcoholics Anonymous, was so taken with William James. He was able to see himself in these stories and as a consequence, make sense of his own conversion experience when he sobered up for good in 1934.)

James's description tracks our knowledge of addiction accordingly. The first stage of world sickness is what I would call "pleasure diminished." What had previously brought joy or pleasure before now brings it less often and to lesser degrees. For an addict, the buzz just isn't as much fun. It just isn't the same, yet she will continue to seek it.

"Pleasure destroyed" is the second stage. More and more things are seen as or end in disappointments; pessimism becomes the most frequent response. The pessimism grows, though at this point it still attaches to particular situations in life rather than to the whole of life. An addict will take any disappointment as a reason to use. As more things become disappointing, the more a person will understand herself to have reasons to use.

The final stage in this world sickness is best described as "pathological melancholy." The progression in this final stage is significant. First a person is no longer able to recognize joy and happiness. She experiences a melancholy and dreariness about life that makes her incapable of generating any joy for herself. The next phase is a melancholy in which a person generates an acute anguish about herself and the world. In this stage, a person feels self-loathing and acute anxiety. Her entire being, James would say, is choked with these feelings. Quite significantly, not only does the person see herself as having no meaning or significance, but nothing in the world has meaning. This melancholy leads to a kind of utter hopelessness about the particular conditions in which one lives and the meaning of life in general. With this hopelessness, the drama of repentance and effort to repair will end. It would take too much energy and it just isn't worth it. Nothing is worth anything.

The person in the grips of the worst melancholy experiences a frightening anxiety about the universe and everything in it. At this point, panic and fright completely govern a person. James describes a man who admitted that a "horrible fear of my own existence" came upon him one night. The man suddenly remembered an epileptic patient he had seen in an asylum who had greenish skin and sat "like some sort of Egyptian cat or Peruvian mummy, moving nothing but his black eyes and looking absolutely nonhuman. This image and my fear entered a combination with each other. *That shape am I*, I felt potentially . . . I awoke morning after morning with a horrible dread at the pit of my stomach, and with a sense of the insecurity of life that I never knew before, and that I have never felt since." In a letter to a friend after the publication of *Varieties*, James admitted this was his very own experience as a young man. He himself had walked right up to the edge of a yawning abyss. James scholars debate the exact date of this crisis, but most locate it sometime when James was in his late twenties.

Nietzsche recognized that "when you gaze long into an abyss the abyss also gazes into you." Kierkegaard realized that some people were more afraid of jumping into that abyss than falling. James understood this fear and saw the potential for transformation "through a passion of renunciation of the self and surrender to the higher power." It is after this renunciation that one can experience "the acute fever" of a spiritual life.

The terms *surrender* and *higher power* and *powerlessness* are apt to leave some people uneasy (they are key phrases and concepts in twelve-step programs everywhere). To surrender, in more Jamesian terms, is to make oneself open to new possibilities. To surrender is to stop clutching core beliefs or parts of one's identity so tightly. When one loosens her grip, she makes it possible to hold something— perhaps very tentatively—in her hands. In the case of a person whose self-worth or humanity has been decimated, it is a matter of being open to the possibility that just *maybe* she is worthy of a little dignity and respect. Surrendering can be simultaneously liberating and terrifying.

The when, where and how of surrender depends on a person's misery threshold. Someone with a low threshold cannot suffer long and so is willing to make changes. Others will be able to suffer enormously and not surrender until there is nothing left to lose. Each person's "rock bottom" is the point where misery can no longer be tolerated.

"Higher power" may leave even more people uneasy. James, however, uses the term in an elastic way. He does admit that "we Christians" call this higher power "God." But to illustrate what he calls a "higher and friendly power," James uses Henry David Thoreau's description of walking in the gentle mist at Walden Pond. Thoreau wrote, "Every little pine-needle expanded and swelled with sympathy and befriended me." Higher power can be nature, moral principles, patriotism, or a sense of fellowship or good will to others. For some, higher power is "enthusiasm for humanity." Each of these, James might say, takes a person outside or beyond herself and connects her to others and thus can be a higher power.

It is easy to identify the ways that "the acute fever" burned in the Christian saints who engaged in all sorts of acts of self-mortification. But it is not easily spotted in someone who has surrendered to and embraced a higher power about their addictive behaviors; there is no equivalent of sackcloth. There is, however, a unification of a previously divided self. People who know addicts in recovery often see this before the addict herself. A person with the acute fever of sobriety or recovery comes to have a firmness of mind and character. She has clear beliefs and principles and acts from them. She also has stability that is achieved and maintained by keeping various relationships with relatives, friends congruent with personal history, commitments, goals and beliefs. Each of these helps to hold the others steady. Finally, a person who burns with the acute fever of sobriety has equilibrium. She is able to strike the balance between opposing forces, some of which are in her control and others not.

No one person will be immune from all suffering. However, the acute fever transforms a person's life so that the drama, chaos and despair are, as James says, "severed like cobwebs, broken like bubbles." And this, James would proclaim, shows that hope and redemption are just as much part of the human condition.

APRIL 7, 2013

SOME HARD MORAL CASES

The Maze of Moral Relativism

—Paul Boghossian

RELATIVISM ABOUT MORALITY HAS COME TO PLAY AN INCREAS-
ingly important role in contemporary culture. To many thoughtful
people, and especially to those who are unwilling to derive their
morality from a religion, it appears unavoidable. Where would absolute facts about right and wrong come from, they reason, if there is
no supreme being to decree them? We should reject moral absolutes,
even as we keep our moral convictions, allowing that there can be
right and wrong relative to this or that moral code, but no right and
wrong per se. (See, for example, Stanley Fish's 2001 op-ed, "Condemnation Without Absolutes.")[1]

Is it plausible to respond to the rejection of absolute moral facts
with a relativistic view of morality? Why should our response not
be a more extreme, nihilistic one, according to which we stop using
normative terms like *right* and *wrong* altogether, be it in their absolutist or relativist guises?

Relativism is not always a coherent way of responding to the rejection of a certain class of facts. When we decided that there were no such
things as witches, we didn't become relativists about witches. Rather,
we just gave up witch talk altogether, except by way of characterizing the attitudes of people (such as those in Salem) who mistakenly
believed that the world contained witches, or by way of characterizing
what it is that children find it fun to pretend to be on Halloween. We
became what we may call "eliminativists" about witches.

On the other hand, when Einstein taught us, in his special theory of relativity, that there was no such thing as the absolute simultaneity of two events, the recommended outcome was that we become relativists about simultaneity, allowing that there is such a thing as "simultaneity relative to a (spatio-temporal) frame of reference," but not simultaneity as such.

What's the difference between the witch case and the simultaneity case? Why did the latter rejection lead to relativism, but the former to eliminativism?

In the simultaneity case, Einstein showed that while the world does not contain simultaneity as such, it does contain its relativistic cousin—simultaneity relative to a frame of reference—a property that plays something like the same sort of role as classical simultaneity did in our theory of the world.

By contrast, in the witch case, once we give up on witches, there is no relativistic cousin that plays anything like the role that witches were supposed to play. The property, that two events may have, of "being simultaneous relative to frame of reference F" is recognizably a kind of simultaneity. But the property of "being a witch according to a belief system T" is not a kind of witch, but a kind of content (the content of belief system T): it's a way of characterizing what belief system T says, not a way of characterizing the world.

Now, the question is whether the moral case is more like that of simultaneity or more like that of witches? When we reject absolute moral facts, is moral relativism the correct outcome or is it moral eliminativism (nihilism)?

The answer, as we have seen, depends on whether there are relativistic cousins of "right" and "wrong" that can play something like the same role that absolute "right" and "wrong" play.

It is hard to see what those could be.

What's essential to "right" and "wrong" is that they are *normative* terms, terms that are used to say how things ought to be, in contrast with how things actually are. But what relativistic cousin of "right" and "wrong" could play anything like such a normative role?

Most moral relativists say that moral right and wrong are to be relativized to a community's "moral code." According to some such codes, eating beef is permissible; according to others, it is an abomination and must never be allowed. The relativist proposal is that we must never talk simply about what's right or wrong, but only about what's "right or wrong relative to a particular moral code."

The trouble is that while "Eating beef is wrong" is clearly a normative statement, "Eating beef is wrong relative to the moral code of the Hindus" is just a descriptive remark that carries no normative import whatsoever. It's just a way of characterizing what is claimed by a particular moral code, that of the Hindus. We can see this from the fact that anyone, regardless of their views about eating beef, can agree that eating beef is wrong relative to the moral code of the Hindus.

So, it looks as though the moral case is more like the witch case than the simultaneity case: there are no relativistic cousins of "right" and "wrong." Denial of moral absolutism leads not to relativism, but to nihilism.[2]

There is no halfway house called "moral relativism" in which we continue to use normative vocabulary with the stipulation that it is to be understood as relativized to particular moral codes. If there are no absolute facts about morality, "right" and "wrong" would have to join "witch" in the dustbin of failed concepts.

The argument is significant because it shows that we should not rush to give up on absolute moral facts, mysterious as they can sometimes seem, for the world might seem even more mysterious without any normative vocabulary whatsoever.

One might be suspicious of my argument against moral relativism. Aren't we familiar with some normative domains—such as that of etiquette—about which we are all relativists? Surely, no one in their right minds would think that there is some absolute fact of the matter about whether we ought to slurp our noodles while eating.

If we are dining at Buckingham Palace, we ought not to slurp, since our hosts would consider it offensive, and we ought not, other things being equal, offend our hosts. On the other hand, if we are dining in Xian, China, we ought to slurp, since in Xian slurping is considered to be a sign that we are enjoying our meal, and our hosts would consider it offensive if we didn't slurp, and we ought not, other things being equal, offend our hosts.

But if relativism is coherent in the case of etiquette, why couldn't we claim that morality is relative in the same way?

The reason is that our relativism about etiquette does not actually dispense with all absolute moral facts. Rather, we are relativists about etiquette in the sense that, with respect to a restricted range of issues (such as table manners and greetings), we take the correct absolute norm to be "we ought not, other things being equal, offend our hosts."

This norm is absolute and applies to everyone and at all times. Its relativistic flavor comes from the fact that, with respect to that limited range of behaviors (table manners and greetings, but not, say, the abuse of children for fun), it advocates varying one's behavior with local convention.

In other words, the relativism of etiquette depends on the existence of absolute moral norms. Since etiquette does not dispense with absolute moral facts, one cannot hope to use it as a model for moral relativism.

Suppose we take this point on board, though, and admit that there have to be some absolute moral facts. Why couldn't they all be like the facts involved in etiquette? Why couldn't they all say that, with respect to any morally relevant question, what we ought to do depends on what the local conventions are?

The trouble with this approach is that once we have admitted that there are some absolute moral facts, it is hard to see why we shouldn't think that there are many—as many as common sense and ordinary reasoning appear to warrant. Having given up on the purity of a thoroughgoing antiabsolutism, we would now be in the business of trying to figure out what absolute moral facts there are. To do that, we would need to employ our usual mix of argument, intuition and experience. And what argument, intuition and experience tell us is that whether we should slurp our noodles depends on what the local conventions are, but whether we should abuse children for fun does not.

A would-be relativist about morality needs to decide whether his view grants the existence of some absolute moral facts, or whether it is to be a pure relativism, free of any commitment to absolutes. The latter position, I have argued, is mere nihilism, whereas the former leads us straight out of relativism and back into the quest for the moral absolutes.

None of this is to deny that there are hard cases where it is not easy to see what the correct answer to a moral question is. It is merely to emphasize that there appears to be no good alternative to thinking that, when we are in a muddle about what the answer to a hard moral question is, we are in a muddle about what the absolutely correct answer is.

JULY 24, 2011

1.Pinning a precise philosophical position on someone, especially a nonphilosopher, is always tricky, because people tend to give nonequivalent formulations of what they take to be the same view. Fish, for example, after saying that his view is that "there can be no independent standards for determining which of many rival interpretations of an event is the true one," which sounds appropriately relativistic, ends up claiming that all he means to defend is "the practice of putting yourself in your adversary's shoes, not in order to wear them as your own but in order to have some understanding (far short of approval) of why someone else might want to wear them." The latter, though, is just the recommendation of empathetic understanding and is, of course, both good counsel and perfectly consistent with the endorsement of moral absolutes.

Another view with which moral relativism is sometimes conflated is the view that the right thing to do can depend on the circumstances. There is no question that the right thing to do can depend on the circumstances, even on an absolutist view. Whether you should help someone in need can depend on what your circumstances are, what their circumstances are, and so forth. What makes a view relativistic is its holding that the right thing to do depends not just on the circumstances, but on what the person (or his community) takes to be the right thing to do, on their moral code.

In this column, I am only concerned with those who wish to deny that there are any absolute moral truths in this sense. If that is not your view, then you are not the target of this particular discussion.

2.Some philosophers may think that they can evade this problem by casting the relativism in terms of a relativized truth predicate rather than a relativized moral predicate. But as I have explained elsewhere, the problem of the loss of normative content recurs in that setting.

Is Pure Altruism Possible?

—*Judith Lichtenberg*

W<small>HO COULD DOUBT THE EXISTENCE OF ALTRUISM?</small>
True, news stories of malice and greed abound. But all around us
we see evidence of human beings sacrificing themselves and doing
good for others. Remember Wesley Autrey? On January 2, 2007, Mr.
Autrey jumped down onto the tracks of a New York City subway platform as a train was approaching to save a man who had suffered a
seizure and fallen. A few months later the Virginia Tech professor
Liviu Librescu blocked the door to his classroom so his students
could escape the bullets of Seung-Hui Cho, who was on a rampage
that would leave thirty-two students and faculty members dead. In
so doing, Mr. Librescu gave his life.

Still, doubting altruism is easy, even when it seems at first glance
to be apparent. It's undeniable that people sometimes act in a way
that benefits others, but it may seem that they always get something
in return—at the very least, the satisfaction of having their desire
to help fulfilled. Students in introductory philosophy courses torture their professors with this reasoning. And its logic can seem
inexorable.

Contemporary discussions of altruism quickly turn to evolutionary explanations. Reciprocal altruism and kin selection are the two
main theories. According to reciprocal altruism, evolution favors
organisms that sacrifice their good for others in order to gain a favor
in return. Kin selection—the famous "selfish gene" theory popu-

larized by Richard Dawkins—says that an individual who behaves altruistically toward others who share its genes will tend to reproduce those genes. Organisms may be altruistic; genes are selfish. The feeling that loving your children more than yourself is hardwired lends plausibility to the theory of kin selection.

These evolutionary theories explain a puzzle: how organisms that sacrifice their own "reproductive fitness"—their ability to survive and reproduce—could possibly have evolved. But neither theory fully accounts for our ordinary understanding of altruism.

The defect of reciprocal altruism is clear. If a person acts to benefit another in the expectation that the favor will be returned, the natural response is, "That's not altruism!" Pure altruism, we think, requires a person to sacrifice for another without consideration of personal gain. Doing good for another person because something's in it for the doer is the very opposite of what we have in mind. Kin selection does better by allowing that organisms may genuinely sacrifice their interests for another, but it fails to explain why they sometimes do so for those with whom they share no genes, as Professor Librescu and Mr. Autrey did.

When we ask whether human beings are altruistic, we want to know about their motives or intentions. Biological altruism explains how unselfish behavior might have evolved, but as Frans de Waal suggested in his column in The Stone on Sunday, it implies nothing about the motives or intentions of the agent: after all, birds and bats and bees can act altruistically. This fact helps to explain why, despite these evolutionary theories, the view that people never intentionally act to benefit others except to obtain some good for themselves still possesses a powerful lure over our thinking.

The lure of this view—egoism—has two sources, one psychological, the other logical. Consider first the psychological. One reason people deny that altruism exists is that, looking inward, they doubt the purity of their own motives. We know that even when we appear to act unselfishly, other reasons for our behavior often rear their heads: the prospect of a future favor, the boost to reputation, or simply the good feeling that comes from appearing to act unselfishly. As

Kant and Freud observed, people's true motives may be hidden, even (or perhaps especially) from themselves. Even if we think we're acting solely to further another person's good, that might not be the real reason. (There might be no single "real reason"—actions can have multiple motives.)

So the psychological lure of egoism as a theory of human action is partly explained by a certain humility or skepticism people have about their own or others' motives. There's also a less flattering reason: denying the possibility of pure altruism provides a convenient excuse for selfish behavior. If "everybody is like that"—if everybody *must* be like that—we need not feel guilty about our own self-interested behavior or try to change it.

The logical lure of egoism is different: the view seems impossible to disprove. No matter how altruistic a person appears to be, it's possible to conceive of her motive in egoistic terms. On this way of looking at it, the guilt Mr. Autrey would have suffered had he ignored the man on the tracks made risking his life worth the gamble. The doctor who gives up a comfortable life to care for AIDS patients in a remote place does what she wants to do and therefore gets satisfaction from what only appears to be self-sacrifice. So, it seems, altruism is simply self-interest of a subtle kind.

The impossibility of disproving egoism may sound like a virtue of the theory, but, as philosophers of science know, it's really a fatal drawback. A theory that purports to tell us something about the world, as egoism does, should be falsifiable. Not false, of course, but capable of being tested and thus proved false. If every state of affairs is compatible with egoism, then egoism doesn't tell us anything distinctive about how things are.

A related reason for the lure of egoism, noted by Bishop Joseph Butler in the eighteenth century, concerns ambiguity in the concepts of desire and the satisfaction of desire. If people possess altruistic motives, then they sometimes act to benefit others without the prospect of gain to themselves. In other words, they desire the good of others for its own sake, not simply as a means to their own satisfaction. It's obvious that Professor Librescu desired that his students not die and acted accordingly to save their lives. He succeeded, so his desire was satisfied. But *he* was not satisfied—since he died in the attempt to save the students. From the fact that a person's desire is satisfied we can draw no conclusions about effects on his mental state or well-being.

Still, when our desires are satisfied, we normally experience satisfaction; we feel good when we do good. But that doesn't mean we do good only in order to get that "warm glow"—that our true incentives are self-interested (as economists tend to claim). Indeed, as de Waal argues, if we didn't desire the good of others for its own sake, then attaining it wouldn't produce the warm glow.

Common sense tells us that some people are more altruistic than others. Egoism's claim that these differences are illusory—that deep down, everybody acts only to further their own interests—contradicts our observations and deep-seated human practices of moral evaluation.

At the same time, we may notice that generous people don't necessarily suffer more or flourish less than those who are more self-interested. Altruists may be more content or fulfilled than selfish people. Nice guys don't always finish last.

But nor do they always finish first. The point is rather that the kind of altruism we ought to encourage, and probably the only kind with staying power, is satisfying to those who practice it. Studies of rescuers show that they don't believe their behavior is extraordinary; they feel they must do what they do, because it's just part of who they are. The same holds for more common, less newsworthy acts—working in soup kitchens, taking pets to people in nursing homes, helping strangers find their way, being neighborly. People who act in these ways believe that they ought to help others, but they also want to help because doing so affirms who they are and want to be and the kind of world they want to exist. As Professor Neera Badhwar has argued, their identity is tied up with their values, thus tying self-interest and altruism together. The correlation between doing good and feeling good is not inevitable—inevitability lands us again with that empty, unfalsifiable egoism—but it is more than incidental.

Altruists should not be confused with people who automatically sacrifice their own interests for others. We admire Paul Rusesabagina, the hotel manager who saved over one thousand Tutsis and Hutus during the 1994 Rwandan genocide; we admire health workers who give up comfortable lives to treat sick people in hard places. But we don't admire people who let others walk all over them; that amounts to lack of self-respect, not altruism.

Altruism is possible and altruism is real, although in healthy people it intertwines subtly with the well-being of the agent who does good. And this is crucial for seeing how to increase the amount of altruism in the world. Aristotle had it right in his *Nicomachean Ethics*: we have to raise people from their "very youth" and educate them "so as both to delight in and to be pained by the things that we ought."

OCTOBER 19, 2010

The Living Death of Solitary Confinement

—*Lisa Guenther*

T HERE ARE MANY WAYS TO DESTROY A PERSON, BUT THE SIMPLEST and most devastating might be solitary confinement. Deprived of meaningful human contact, otherwise healthy prisoners often come unhinged. They experience intense anxiety, paranoia, depression, memory loss, hallucinations, and other perceptual distortions. Psychiatrists call this cluster of symptoms SHU syndrome, named after the security housing units of many supermax prisons. Prisoners have more direct ways of naming their experience. They call it "living death," the "gray box," or "living in a black hole."

In June the Judiciary Subcommittee on the Constitution, Civil Rights, and Human Rights, headed by Senator Richard J. Durbin, Democrat, of Illinois, held the first Congressional hearing on solitary confinement. Advocates and experts in the field were invited to submit testimony on the psychological, ethical, social and economic issues raised by punitive isolation. Among the many contributors was Anthony Graves, who spent over eighteen years on death row in Texas, most of them in solitary confinement, for a crime he did not commit. Graves describes his isolation as a form of "emotional torture." Two years after his exoneration and release, he still feels trapped in isolation: "I am living amongst millions of people in the world today, but most of the time I feel alone. I cry at night because of this feeling. I just want to stop feeling this way, but I haven't been able to."

We tend to assume that solitary confinement is reserved for "the worst of the worst": violent inmates who have proved themselves unwilling or unable to live in the general population. But the truth is that an inmate can be sent to the hole for failing to return a meal tray, or for possession of contraband (which can include anything from weapons to spicy tortilla chips). According to the Bureau of Justice, there were 81,622 prisoners in some form of "restricted housing" (code for solitary confinement) in 2005. If anything, these numbers have increased as isolation units continue to be built in prisons, jails and juvenile detention centers across the country. Given that 95 percent of all inmates are eventually released into the public, and that many of these will be released without any form of transition or therapy, solitary confinement is a problem that potentially affects every one of us.

In my own statement for the Senate subcommittee, I made a philosophical argument against solitary confinement, drawing on my research in phenomenology. Phenomenology is a philosophical method for uncovering the structure of lived experience by describing *what it is like* from a first-person perspective. Rather than attempting to prove a set of objective facts, phenomenology tracks the way that a *meaningful* experience of the world emerges for someone in the total situation of their being-in-the-world. It's not that facts are unimportant, but rather that they are not meaningful in themselves; they become meaningful when they are experienced *by* someone in relation to a wider context or horizon. What happens when that horizon shrinks to the space of a six-by-nine cell?

Consider the following testimony from prisoners interviewed by the psychiatrist Stuart Grassian in Block 10 of Walpole Penitentiary in 1982:

> *I went to a standstill psychologically once—lapse of memory. I didn't talk for 15 days. I couldn't hear clearly. You can't see—you're blind—block everything out—disoriented, awareness is very bad. Did someone say he's coming out of it? I think what I'm saying is true—not sure. I think I was drooling—a complete standstill.*

I seem to see movements—real fast motions in front of me. Then seems like they're doing things behind your back—can't quite see them. Did someone just hit me? I dwell on it for hours.

Melting, everything in the cell starts moving; everything gets darker, you feel you are losing your vision.

I can't concentrate, can't read . . . Your mind's narcotized . . . sometimes can't grasp words in my mind that I know. Get stuck, have to think of another word. Memory is going. You feel you are losing something you might not get back.

Deprived of everyday encounters with other people, and cut off from an open-ended experience of the world as a place of difference and change, many inmates lose touch with reality. What is the prisoner in solitary confinement at risk of losing, to the point of not getting it back?

The prisoner in a control unit may have adequate food and drink, and the conditions of his confinement may meet or exceed court-tested thresholds for humane treatment. But there is something about the exclusion of other living beings from the space that they inhabit, and the absence of even the *possibility* of touching or being touched by another, that threatens to undermine the identity of the subject. The problem with solitary confinement is not just that it deprives the inmate of her freedom. This harm is already inflicted by our prison system, and depending on how you feel about justice and punishment, depriving people of freedom may be justifiable. But prolonged isolation inflicts another kind of harm, one that can never be justified. This harm is ontological; it violates the very structure of our relational being.

Think about it: Every time I hear a sound and see another person look toward the origin of that sound, I receive an implicit confirmation that what I heard was something real, that it was not just my imagination playing tricks on me. Every time someone walks around the table rather than through it, I receive an unspoken, usually unremarkable, confirmation that the table exists, and that my own way of relating to tables is shared by others. When I don't receive these implicit confirmations, I can usually ask someone—but for the most part, we don't need to ask because our experience is already interwoven with the experience of many other living, thinking, perceiving beings who relate to the same world from their own unique perspective. This multiplicity of perspectives is like an invisible net that supports the coherence of my own experience, even (or especially) when others challenge my interpretation of "the facts." These facts are up for discussion in the first place because we inhabit a shared world with others who agree, at the very least, that there is something to disagree about.

When we isolate a prisoner in solitary confinement, we deprive them of both the *support* of others, which is crucial for a coherent experience of the world, and also the *critical challenge* that others pose to our own interpretation of the world. Both of these are essential for a meaningful experience of things, but they are especially important for those who have broken the law, and so violated the trust of others in the community. If we truly want our prisons to rehabilitate and transform criminal offenders, then we must put them in a situation where they have a chance *and an obligation* to explain themselves to others, to repair damaged networks of mutual support, and to lend their own unique perspective to creating meaning in the world.

We ask *too little* of prisoners when we isolate them in units where they are neither allowed nor obliged to create and sustain meaningful, supportive relations with others. For the sake of justice, not only for them but for ourselves, we must put an end to the overuse of solitary confinement in this country, and we must begin the difficult but mutually rewarding work of bringing the tens of thousands of currently isolated prisoners back into the world.

AUGUST 26, 2012

Should This Be the Last Generation?

—Peter Singer

Have you ever thought about whether to have a child? If so, what factors entered into your decision? Was it whether having children would be good for you, your partner and others close to the possible child, such as children you may already have, or perhaps your parents? For most people contemplating reproduction, those are the dominant questions. Some may also think about the desirability of adding to the strain that the nearly seven billion people already here are putting on our planet's environment. But very few ask whether coming into existence is a good thing for the child itself. Most of those who consider that question probably do so because they have some reason to fear that the child's life would be especially difficult—for example, if they have a family history of a devastating illness, physical or mental, that cannot yet be detected prenatally.

All this suggests that we think it is wrong to bring into the world a child whose prospects for a happy, healthy life are poor, but we don't usually think the fact that a child is likely to have a happy, healthy life is a reason for bringing the child into existence. This has come to be known among philosophers as "the asymmetry," and it is not easy to justify. But rather than go into the explanations usually proffered—and why they fail—I want to raise a related problem. How good does life have to be to make it reasonable to bring a child into the world? Is the standard of life experienced by most people in developed nations today good enough to make this decision unproblematic in the absence of specific knowledge that the child will have a severe genetic disease or other problem?

The nineteenth-century German philosopher Arthur Schopenhauer held that even the best life possible for humans is one in which we strive for ends that, once achieved, bring only fleeting satisfaction. New desires then lead us on to further futile struggle and the cycle repeats itself.

Schopenhauer's pessimism has had few defenders over the past two centuries, but one has recently emerged in the South African philosopher David Benatar, author of a fine book with an arresting title: *Better Never to Have Been: The Harm of Coming into Existence*. One of Benatar's arguments trades on something like the asymmetry noted earlier. To bring into existence someone who will suffer is, Benatar argues, to harm that person, but to bring into existence someone who will have a good life is not to benefit him or her. Few of us would think it right to inflict severe suffering on an innocent child, even if that were the only way in which we could bring many other children into the world. Yet everyone will suffer to some extent, and if our species continues to reproduce, we can be sure that some future children will suffer severely. Hence continued reproduction will harm some children severely, and benefit none.

Benatar also argues that human lives are, in general, much less good than we think they are. We spend most of our lives with unfulfilled desires, and the occasional satisfactions that are all most of us can achieve are insufficient to outweigh these prolonged negative states. If we think that this is a tolerable state of affairs it is because we are, in Benatar's view, victims of the illusion of Pollyannaism. This illusion may have evolved because it helped our ancestors survive, but it is an illusion nonetheless. If we could see our lives objectively, we would see that they are not something we should inflict on anyone.

Here is a thought experiment to test our attitudes to this view. Most thoughtful people are extremely concerned about climate change. Some stop eating meat or flying abroad on vacation in order to reduce their carbon footprint. But the people who will be most severely harmed by climate change have not yet been conceived. If there were to be no future generations, there would be much less for us to feel guilty about.

So why don't we make ourselves the last generation on earth? If we would all agree to have ourselves sterilized, then no sacrifices would be required—we could party our way into extinction!

Of course, it would be impossible to get agreement on universal sterilization, but just imagine that we could. Then is there anything wrong with this scenario? Even if we take a less pessimistic view of human existence than Benatar, we could still defend it, because it makes us better off—for one thing, we can get rid of all that guilt about what we are doing to future generations—and it doesn't make anyone worse off, because there won't be anyone else to be worse off.

Is a world with people in it better than one without? Put aside what we do to other species—that's a different issue. Let's assume that the choice is between a world like ours and one with no sentient beings in it at all. And assume, too—here we have to get fictitious, as philosophers often do—that if we choose to bring about the world with no sentient beings at all, everyone will agree to do that. No one's rights will be violated—at least, not the rights of any existing people. Can nonexistent people have a right to come into existence?

I do think it would be wrong to choose the nonsentient universe. In my judgment, for most people, life is worth living. Even if that is not yet the case, I am enough of an optimist to believe that, should humans survive for another century or two, we will learn from our past mistakes and bring about a world in which there is far less suffering than there is now. But justifying that choice forces us to reconsider the deep issues with which I began. Is life worth living? Are the interest of a future child a reason for bringing that child into existence? And is the continuance of our species justifiable in the face of our knowledge that it will certainly bring suffering to innocent future human beings?

JUNE 6, 2010

The Meat Eaters

—Jeff McMahan

VIEWED FROM A DISTANCE, THE NATURAL WORLD OFTEN PRES-ents a vista of sublime, majestic placidity. Yet beneath the foliage and hidden from the distant eye, a vast, unceasing slaughter rages. Wherever there is animal life, predators are stalking, chasing, capturing, killing, and devouring their prey. Agonized suffering and violent death are ubiquitous and continuous. This hidden carnage provided one ground for the philosophical pessimism of Schopenhauer, who contended that "one simple test of the claim that the pleasure in the world outweighs the pain . . . is to compare the feelings of an animal that is devouring another with those of the animal being devoured."

The continuous, incalculable suffering of animals is also an important though largely neglected element in the traditional theological "problem of evil"—the problem of reconciling the existence of evil with the existence of a benevolent, omnipotent God. The suffering of animals is particularly challenging because it is not amenable to the familiar palliative explanations of human suffering. Animals are assumed not to have free will and thus to be unable either to choose evil or deserve to suffer it. Neither are they assumed to have immortal souls; hence, there can be no expectation that they will be compensated for their suffering in a celestial afterlife. Nor do they appear to be conspicuously elevated or ennobled by the final suffering they endure in a predator's jaws. Theologians have had enough trouble explaining to their human flocks why a loving God permits them to suffer; but their labors will not be over even if they are finally able to justify the ways of God to man. For God must answer to animals as well.

If I had been in a position to design and create a world, I would have tried to arrange for all conscious individuals to be able to survive without tormenting and killing other conscious individuals. I hope most other people would have done the same. Certainly this and related ideas have been entertained since human beings began to reflect on the fearful nature of their world—for example, when the prophet Isaiah, writing in the eighth century BCE, sketched a few of the elements of his utopian vision. He began with people's abandonment of war: "They shall beat their swords into plowshares, and their spears into pruning hooks: nation shall not lift up sword against nation." But human beings would not be the only ones to change; animals would join us in universal veganism: "The wolf also shall dwell with the lamb, and the leopard shall lie down with the kid; and the calf and the young lion and the fatling together; and a little child shall lead them. And the cow and the bear shall feed; their young ones shall lie down together: and the lion shall eat straw like the ox" (Isaiah 2:4 and 11:6—7).

Isaiah was, of course, looking to the future rather than indulging in whimsical fantasies of doing a better job of Creation, and we should do the same. We should start by withdrawing our own participation in the mass orgy of preying and feeding upon the weak.

Our own form of predation is of course more refined than those of other meat eaters, who must capture their prey and tear it apart as it struggles to escape. We instead employ professionals to breed our prey in captivity and prepare their bodies for us behind a veil of propriety, so that our sensibilities are spared the recognition that we, too, are predators, red in tooth if not in claw (though some of us, for reasons I have never understood, do go to the trouble to paint their vestigial claws a sanguinary hue). The reality behind the veil is, however, far worse than that in the natural world. Our factory farms, which supply most of the meat and eggs consumed in developed societies, inflict a lifetime of misery and torment on our prey, in contrast to the relatively brief agonies endured by the victims of predators in the wild. From the moral perspective, there is nothing that can plausibly be said in defense of this practice. To be entitled to regard ourselves as civilized, we must, like Isaiah's morally reformed lion, eat straw like the ox, or at least the moral equivalent of straw.

But ought we to go further? Suppose that we could arrange the gradual extinction of carnivorous species, replacing them with new herbivorous ones. Or suppose that we could intervene genetically, so that currently carnivorous species would gradually evolve into herbivorous ones, thereby fulfilling Isaiah's prophecy. If we could bring about the end of predation by one or the other of these means at little cost to ourselves, ought we to do it?

I concede, of course, that it would be unwise to attempt any such change given the current state of our scientific understanding. Our ignorance of the potential ramifications of our interventions in the natural world remains profound. Efforts to eliminate certain species and create new ones would have many unforeseeable and potentially catastrophic effects.

Perhaps one of the more benign scenarios is that action to reduce predation would create a Malthusian dystopia in the animal world, with higher birth rates among herbivores, overcrowding, and insufficient resources to sustain the larger populations. Instead of being killed quickly by predators, the members of species that once were prey would die slowly, painfully, and in greater numbers from starvation and disease.

Yet our relentless efforts to increase individual wealth and power are already causing massive, precipitate changes in the natural world. Many thousands of animal species either have been or are being driven to extinction as a side effect of our activities. Knowing this, we have thus far been largely unwilling even to moderate our rapacity to mitigate these effects. If, however, we were to become more amenable to exercising restraint, it is conceivable that we could do so in a selective manner, favoring the survival of some species over others. The question might then arise whether to modify our activities in ways that would favor the survival of herbivorous rather than carnivorous species.

At a minimum, we ought to be clear in advance about the values that should guide such choices if they ever arise, or if our scientific knowledge ever advances to a point at which we could seek to eliminate, alter, or replace certain species with a high degree of confidence in our predictions about the short- and long-term effects of our action. Rather than continuing to collide with the natural world with reckless indifference, we should prepare ourselves now to be able to act wisely and deliberately when the range of our choices eventually expands.

The suggestion that we consider whether and how we might exercise control over the prospects of different animal species, perhaps eventually selecting some for extinction and others for survival in accordance with our moral values, will undoubtedly strike most people as an instance of potentially tragic hubris, presumptuousness on a cosmic scale. The accusation most likely to be heard is that we would be "playing God," impiously usurping prerogatives that belong to the deity alone. This has been a familiar refrain in the many instances in which devotees of one religion or another have sought to obstruct attempts to mitigate human suffering by, for example, introducing new medicines or medical practices, permitting and even facilitating suicide, legalizing a constrained practice of euthanasia, and so on. So it would be surprising if this same claim were not brought into service in opposition to the reduction of suffering among animals as well. Yet there are at least two good replies to it.

One is that it singles out deliberate, morally motivated action for special condemnation, while implicitly sanctioning morally neutral action that foreseeably has the same effects as long as those effects are not intended. One plays God, for example, if one administers a lethal injection to a patient at her own request in order to end her agony, but not if one gives her a largely ineffective analgesic only to mitigate the agony, though knowing that it will kill her as a side effect. But it is hard to believe that any self-respecting deity would be impressed by the distinction. If the first act encroaches on divine prerogatives, the second does as well.

The second response to the accusation of playing God is simple and decisive. It is that there is no deity whose prerogatives we might usurp. To the extent that these matters are up to anyone, they are up to us alone. Since it is too late to prevent human action from affecting the prospects for survival of many animal species, we ought to guide and control the effects of our action to the greatest extent we can in order to bring about the morally best, or least bad, outcomes that remain possible.

Another equally unpersuasive objection to the suggestion that we ought to eliminate carnivorism if we could do so without major ecological disruption is that this would be "against Nature." This slogan also has a long history of deployment in crusades to ensure that human cultures remain primitive. And like the appeal to the sovereignty of a deity, it, too, presupposes an indefensible metaphysics. Nature is not a purposive agent, much less a wise one. There is no reason to suppose that a species has special sanctity simply because it arose in the natural process of evolution.

Many people believe that what happens among animals in the wild is not our responsibility, and indeed that what they do among themselves is none of our business. They have their own forms of life, quite different from our own, and we have no right to intrude upon them or to impose our anthropocentric values on them.

There is an element of truth in this view, which is that our moral reason to prevent harm for which we would not be responsible is weaker than our reason not to cause harm. Our primary duty with respect to animals is therefore to stop tormenting and killing them as a means of satisfying our desire to taste certain flavors or to decorate our bodies in certain ways. But if suffering is bad for animals when we cause it, it is also bad for them when other animals cause it. That suffering is bad for those who experience it is not a human prejudice; nor is an effort to prevent wild animals from suffering a moralistic attempt to police the behavior of other animals. Even if we are not morally *required* to prevent suffering among animals in the wild for which we are not responsible, we do have a moral *reason* to prevent it, just as we have a general moral reason to prevent suffering among human beings that is independent both of the cause of the suffering and of our relation to the victims. The main constraint on the permissibility of acting on our reason to prevent suffering is that our action should not cause bad effects that would be worse than those we could prevent.

That is the central issue raised by whether we ought to try to eliminate carnivorism. Because the elimination of carnivorism would require the extinction of carnivorous species, or at least their radical genetic alteration, which might be equivalent or tantamount to extinction, it might well be that the losses in value would outweigh any putative gains. Not only are most or all animal species of some instrumental value, but it is also arguable that all species have intrinsic value. As Ronald Dworkin has observed, "We tend to treat distinct animal species (though not individual animals) as sacred. We think it very important, and worth a considerable economic expense, to protect endangered species from destruction." When Dworkin says that animal species are sacred, he means that their existence is good in a way that need not be good *for* anyone; nor is it good in the sense that it would be better if there were more species, so that we would have reason to create new ones if we could. "Few people," he notes, "believe the world would be worse if there had always been fewer species of birds, and few would think it important to engineer new bird species if that were possible. What we believe important is not that there be any particular number of species but that a species that now exists not be extinguished by us."

The intrinsic value of individual species is thus quite distinct from the value of species diversity. It also seems to follow from Dworkin's claims that the loss involved in the extinction of an existing species cannot be compensated for, either fully or perhaps even partially, by the coming-into-existence of a new species.

The basic issue, then, seems to be a conflict between values: prevention of suffering and preservation of animal species. It is relatively uncontroversial that suffering is intrinsically *bad for* those who experience it, even if occasionally it is also instrumentally good for them, as when it has the purifying, redemptive effects that Dostoyevsky's characters so often crave. Nor is it controversial that the extinction of an animal species is normally instrumentally bad. It is bad for the individual members who die and bad for other individuals and species that depended on the existence of the species for their own well-being or survival. Yet the extinction of an animal species is not necessarily bad for its individual members. (To indulge in science fiction, suppose that a chemical might be introduced into their food supply that would induce sterility but also extend their longevity.) And the extinction of a carnivorous species could be instrumentally good for all those animals that would otherwise have been its prey. That simple fact is precisely what prompts the question whether it would be good if carnivorous species were to become extinct.

The conflict, therefore, must be between preventing suffering and respecting the alleged sacredness—or, as I would phrase it, the *impersonal* value—of carnivorous species. Again, the claim that suffering is bad for those who experience it and thus ought in general to be prevented when possible cannot be seriously doubted. Yet the idea that individual animal species have value in themselves is less obvious. What, after all, *are* species? According to Darwin, they "are merely artificial combinations made for convenience." They are collections of individuals distinguished by biologists that shade into one another over time and sometimes blur together even among contemporaneous individuals, as in the case of ring species. There are no universally agreed criteria for their individuation. In practice, the most commonly invoked criterion is the capacity for interbreeding, yet this is well known to be imperfect and to entail intransitivities of classification when applied to ring species. Nor has it ever been satisfactorily explained why a special sort of value should inhere in a collection of individuals simply by virtue of their ability to produce fertile offspring. If it is good, as I think it is, that animal life should continue, then it is instrumentally good that some animals can breed with one another. But I can see no reason to suppose that donkeys, as a group, have a special impersonal value that mules lack.

Even if animal species did have impersonal value, it would not follow that they were irreplaceable. Since animals first appeared on earth, an indefinite number of species have become extinct while an indefinite number of new species have arisen. If the appearance of new species cannot make up for the extinction of others, and if the earth could not simultaneously sustain all the species that have ever existed, it seems that it would have been better if the earliest species had never become extinct, with the consequence that the later ones would never have existed. But few of us, with our high regard for our own species, are likely to embrace that implication.

Here, then, is where matters stand thus far. It would be good to prevent the vast suffering and countless violent deaths caused by predation. There is therefore one reason to think that it would be instrumentally good if predatory animal species were to become extinct and be replaced by new herbivorous species, provided that this could occur without ecological upheaval involving more harm than would be prevented by the end of predation. The claim that existing animal species are sacred or irreplaceable is subverted by the moral irrelevance of the criteria for individuating animal species. I am therefore inclined to embrace the heretical conclusion that we have reason to desire the extinction of all carnivorous species, and I await the usual fate of heretics when this article is opened to comment.

SEPTEMBER 19, 2010

Think Before You Breed

—Christine Overall

As a young woman in my twenties I pondered whether or not to have children. Is there a way, I wondered, to decide thoughtfully rather than carelessly about this most momentous of human choices?

It's a tough decision because you can't know ahead of time what sort of child you will have or what it will be like to be a parent. You can't understand what is good or what is hard about the process of creating and rearing until after you have the child. And the choice to have a child is a decision to change your life forever. It's irreversible, and therefore, compared to reversible life choices about education, work, geographical location or romance, it has much greater ethical importance.

Choosing whether or not to procreate may not seem like the sort of decision that is deserving or even capable of analysis. The Canadian novelist Margaret Laurence wrote, "I don't really feel I have to analyze my own motives in wanting children. For my own reassurance? For fun? For ego-satisfaction? No matter. It's like (to me) asking why you want to write. Who cares? You have to, and that's that."

In fact, people are still expected to provide reasons *not* to have children, but no reasons are required to have them. It's assumed that if individuals do not have children it is because they are infertile, too selfish or have just not yet gotten around to it. In any case, they owe their interlocutor an explanation. On the other hand, no one says to the proud parents of a newborn, Why did you choose to have that child? What are your reasons? The choice to procreate is not regarded as needing any thought or justification.

Nonetheless, I think Laurence's "Who cares?" attitude is mistaken.

We are fortunate that procreation is more and more a matter of choice. Not always, of course—not everyone has access to effective contraception and accessible abortion, and some women are subjected to enforced pregnancy. But the growing availability of reproductive choice makes it clear that procreation cannot be merely an expression of personal taste.

The question whether to have children is of course prudential in part; it's concerned about what is or is not in one's own interests. But it is *also* an ethical question, for it is about whether to bring a person (in some cases more than one person) into existence—and that person cannot, by the very nature of the situation, give consent to being brought into existence. Such a question also profoundly affects the well-being of existing people (the potential parents, siblings if any, and grandparents). And it has effects beyond the family on the broader society, which is inevitably changed by the cumulative impact—on things like education, health care, employment, agriculture, community growth and design, and the availability and distribution of resources—of individual decisions about whether to procreate.

There are self-help books on the market that purport to assist would-be parents in making a practical choice about whether or not to have children. There are also informal discussions on websites, in newspapers and magazines, and in blogs. Yet the ethical nature of this choice is seldom recognized, even—or especially—by philosophers.

Perhaps people fail to see childbearing as an ethical choice because they think of it as the expression of an instinct or biological drive, like sexual attraction or "falling in love," that is not amenable to ethical evaluation. But whatever our biological inclinations may be, many human beings do take control over their fertility, thanks to contemporary means of contraception and abortion. The rapidly declining birthrate in most parts of the world is evidence of that fact.

While choosing whether or not to have children may involve feelings, motives, impulses, memories and emotions, it can and should
also be a subject for careful reflection.

If we fail to acknowledge that the decision of whether to parent or
not is a real choice that has ethical import, then we are treating childbearing as a mere expression of biological destiny. Instead of seeing
having children as something that women *do*, we will continue to see
it as something that simply *happens* to women, or as something that
is merely "natural" and animal-like.

The decision to have children surely deserves at least as much
thought as people devote to leasing a car or buying a house. Procreation decisions are about whether or not to assume complete responsibility, over a period of at least eighteen years, for a new life or new
lives. Because deciding whether to procreate has ethical dimensions,
the reasons people give for their procreative choices deserve examination. Some reasons may be better—or worse—than others.

My aim, I hasten to add, is not to argue for policing people's procreative motives. I am simply arguing for the need to think systematically and deeply about a fundamental aspect of human life.

The burden of proof—or at least the burden of justification—should
therefore rest primarily on those who choose to have children, not
on those who choose to be childless. The choice to have children calls
for more careful justification and thought than the choice not to have
children, because procreation creates a dependent, needy, and vulnerable human being whose future may be at risk. The individual
who chooses childlessness takes the ethically less risky path. After
all, nonexistent people can't suffer from not being created. They do
not have an entitlement to come into existence, and we do not owe it
to them to bring them into existence. But once children do exist, we
incur serious responsibilities to them.

Because children are dependent, needy and vulnerable, prospective parents should consider how well they can love and care for the
offspring they create, and the kind of relationship they can have with
them. The genuinely unselfish life plan may at least sometimes be
the choice not to have children, especially in the case of individu-

als who would otherwise procreate merely to adhere to tradition, to please others, to conform to gender conventions, or to benefit themselves out of the inappropriate expectation that children will fix their problems. Children are neither human pets nor little therapists.

Some people claim that the mere fact that our offspring will probably be happy gives us ample reason to procreate. The problem with this argument is, first, that there are no guarantees. The sheer unpredictability of children, the limits on our capacities as parents, and the instability of social conditions make it unwise to take for granted that our progeny will have good lives. But just as important, justifying having kids by claiming that our offspring will be happy provides no stopping point for procreative behavior. If two children are happy, perhaps four will be, or seven, or ten.

The unwillingness to stop is dramatized by the so-called Octomom, Nadya Suleman, who first had six children via in vitro fertilization, then ended up with eight more from just one pregnancy, aided by her reprehensible doctor, Michael Kamrava. Higher-order multiple pregnancies often create long-term health problems for the children born of them. It's also unlikely that Suleman can provide adequate care for and attention to her fourteen children under the age of twelve, especially in light of her recent bankruptcy, her very public attempts to raise money, and the impending loss of their home. Was Suleman's desire for a big family fair to her helpless offspring?

Consider also reality television "stars" Michelle and Jim Bob Duggar, the parents of nineteen children. The Duggars claim to have religious motives for creating their large family. But it's not at all clear that God places such a high value on the Duggar genetic heritage. Unlike Suleman, the Duggars don't struggle to support their brood, but mere financial solvency is not a sufficient reason to birth more than a dozen and a half offspring, even if the kids seem reasonably content.

People like the Duggars and Suleman might respond that they have a right to reproduce. Certainly they are entitled to be free from state interference in their procreative behavior; compulsory contraception and abortion, or penalties for having babies, are abhorrent.

But a right to non-interference does not, by itself, justify every decision to have a baby.

We should not regret the existence of the children in these very public families, now that they are here. My point is just that their parents' models of procreative decision making deserve skepticism. The parents appear to overlook what is ethically central: the possibility of forming a supportive, life-enhancing and close relationship with each of their offspring.

After struggling with our own decision about whether to procreate, in the end my spouse and I chose to have two children, whom we adore. The many rewards and challenges of raising kids have gradually revealed the far-reaching implications of procreative decision making. In choosing to become a parent, one seeks to create a relationship, and, uniquely, one also seeks to create the person with whom one has the relationship. Choosing whether or not to have children is therefore the most significant ethical debate of most people's lives.

JUNE 17, 2012

On Forgiveness

—Charles L. Griswold

AT EACH YEAR'S END, WE FIND OURSELVES IN A SEASON TRADI-
tionally devoted to good will among people and to the renewal of
hope in the face of hard times. As we seek to realize these lofty ideals, one of our greatest challenges is overcoming bitterness and divi-
siveness. We all struggle with the wrongs others have done to us as
well as those we have done to others, and we recoil at the vast extent
of injury humankind seems determined to inflict on itself. How to
keep hope alive? Without a constructive answer to toxic anger, addictive cycles of revenge, and immobilizing guilt, we seem doomed to
despair about chances for renewal. One answer to this despair lies
in forgiveness.

What is forgiveness? When is it appropriate? Why is it considered
to be commendable? Some claim that forgiveness is merely about rid-
ding oneself of vengeful anger; do that, and you have forgiven. But
if you were able to banish anger from your soul simply by taking a
pill, would the result really be *forgiveness*? The timing of forgiveness
is also disputed. Some say that it should wait for the offender to take
responsibility and suffer due punishment, others hold that the victim
must first overcome anger altogether, and still others that forgiveness
should be unilaterally bestowed at the earliest possible moment. But
what if you have every good reason to be angry and even to take your
sweet revenge as well? Is forgiveness then really to be commended?
Some object that it lets the offender off the hook, confesses to one's

own weakness and vulnerability, and papers over the legitimate demands of vengeful anger. And yet, legions praise forgiveness and think of it as an indispensable virtue. Recall the title of Archbishop Desmond Tutu's book on the subject: *No Future without Forgiveness*.

These questions about the what, when, and why of forgiveness have led to a massive outpouring of books, pamphlets, documentaries, television shows, and radio interviews. The list grows by the hour. It includes hefty representation of religious and self-help perspectives, historical analysis (much of which was sparked by South Africa's famed Truth and Reconciliation Commission), and increasingly, philosophical reflection as well. Yet there is little consensus about the answers. Indeed, the list of disputed questions is still longer. Consider: May forgiveness be demanded, or must it be a sort of freely bestowed gift? Does the concept of "the unforgivable" make sense? And what about the cultural context of forgiveness: Does it matter? Has the concept of "forgiveness" evolved, even within religious traditions such as Christianity? Is it a fundamentally religious concept?

On almost all accounts, interpersonal forgiveness is closely tied to vengeful anger and revenge. This linkage was brought to the fore by Bishop Joseph Butler (1692–1752) in his insightful sermons on resentment (his word for what is often now called vengeful anger) and forgiveness. These sermons are the touchstone of modern philosophical discussions of the topic. Butler is often interpreted as saying that forgiveness requires forswearing resentment, but what he actually says is that it requires tempering resentment and forswearing revenge. He is surely right that it requires at least that much. If you claim you've forgiven someone and then proceed to take revenge, then you are either dishonest or ignorant of the meaning of the term. Forgiveness comes with conditions, such as the giving up of revenge. What are other conditions?

If you seethe with vengeful thoughts and anger, or even simmer with them, can you be said to have forgiven fully? I would answer in the negative. That establishes another condition that successful forgiveness must meet. In the contemporary literature on forgiveness, the link between forgiveness and giving up vengefulness is so heavily emphasized that it is very often offered as *the* reason to forgive: forgive, so that you may live without toxic anger.

However, if giving up revenge and resentment were sufficient to yield forgiveness, then one could forgive simply by forgetting, or through counseling, or by taking the latest version of the nepenthe pill. But none of those really seems to qualify as forgiveness properly speaking, however valuable they may be in their own right as a means of getting over anger. The reason is that forgiveness is neither just a therapeutic technique nor simply self-regarding in its motivation; it is fundamentally a *moral* relation between self and other.

Consider its genesis in the interpersonal context: one person wrongs another. Forgiveness is a response to that wrong, and hence to the other person as author of that action. Forgiveness retains the bilateral or social character of the situation to which it seeks to respond. The anger you feel in response to having been treated unjustly is warranted only if, in its intensity and its target, it is fitting. After all, if you misidentified who did you wrong, then forgiving that person would be inappropriate, indeed, insulting. Or if the wrongdoer is rightly identified but is not culpable, perhaps by virtue of ignorance or youth, then once again it is not forgiveness that is called for but something else—say, excuse or pardon. (One consequence: as philosopher Jeffrie Murphy points out in his exchange with Jean Hampton in their book *Forgiveness and Mercy*, "They know not what they do" makes Christ's plea on the cross an appeal for excuse rather than forgiveness.) Moreover, it is not so much the action that is forgiven, but its author. So forgiveness assumes as its target, so to speak, an agent who knowingly does wrong and is held responsible. The moral anger one feels in this case is a reaction that is answerable to reason; and this would hold, too, with respect to giving up one's anger. In the best case, the offender would offer you reasons for forswearing resentment, most obviously by taking a series of steps that include admission of responsibility, contrition, a resolve to mend his or her ways and recognition of what the wrongdoing felt like from your perspective.

Of course, as the wronged party you don't always get anything close to that and are often left to struggle with anger in the face of the offender's unwillingness or inability to give you reason to forswear anger. But if the offender offered to take the steps just mentioned, you would very likely accept, as that would make it not only psychologically easier to forgive, but would much more perfectly accomplish one moral purpose of forgiveness—namely, restoration of mutual respect and reaffirmation that one is not to be treated wrongly. A similar logic holds on the flip side: if as the offender you take every step that could reasonably be asked of you, and your victim is unable or unwilling to forgive, you are left to struggle with your sense of being unforgiven, guilty, beholden. Offered the chance that your victim would set aside revenge and vengefulness, forgive you, and move on to the next chapter of his or her life, you would very probably accept.

The paradigm case of interpersonal forgiveness is the one in which all of the conditions we would wish to see fulfilled are in fact met by both offender and victim. When they are met, forgiveness will not collapse into either excuse or condonation—and on any account it is essential to avoid conflating these concepts. One of the several subparadigmatic or imperfect forms of forgiveness will consist in what is often called unconditional, or more accurately, unilateral forgiveness—as when one forgives the wrongdoer independently of any steps he or she takes. Some hold that unilateral forgiveness is the model, pointing to the much discussed case of the Amish unilaterally forgiving the murderer of their children (for an account of this case, see *Amish Grace: How Forgiveness Transcended Tragedy*, by D. B. Kraybill, S. M. Nolt, and D. L. Weaver-Zercher). I contend, by contrast, that the ideal is bilateral, one in which both sides take steps. I also hold that whether forgiveness is or is not possible will depend on the circumstances and reasons at play; not just *anything* is going to count as forgiveness. Establishing the minimal threshold for an exchange to count as "forgiveness" is a matter of some debate, but it must include the giving up of revenge by the victim, and an assumption of responsibility by the offender.

Other familiar cases of imperfect forgiveness present their own challenges, as when one seeks to forgive a wrong done to someone else (to forgive on behalf of another, or what is commonly called third-party forgiveness, as for example when the victim is deceased). Another case concerns self-forgiveness. The latter is particularly complicated, as one may seek to forgive oneself for wrongs one has done to others, or for a wrong one has done to oneself (say, degrading oneself) by wronging another, or simply for a wrong one has done only to oneself. Self-forgiveness is notoriously apt to lapse into easy self-exculpation; here too, conditions must be set to safeguard the integrity of the notion.

Excuse, mercy, reconciliation, pardon, political apology, and forgiveness of financial debt are not imperfect versions of inter-personal forgiveness; rather, they are related but distinct concepts. Take political apology, for example. As its name indicates, its context is political, meaning that it is transacted in a context that involves groups, corporate entities, institutions, and corresponding notions of moral responsibility and agency. Many of the complexities are discussed by philosopher Nick Smith in *I Was Wrong: The Meanings of Apologies*. Apology figures into interpersonal forgiveness, too. But in the case of political apology, the transaction may in one sense be quite impersonal: picture a spokesperson apologizing for a govern-ment's misdeeds, performed before the spokesperson was born, to a group representing the actual victims. A lot of the moral work is done by representation (as when a spokesperson represents the state). Further, the criteria for successful apology in such a context will overlap with but nevertheless differ from those pertinent to the interpersonal context. For example, financial restitution as negoti-ated through a legal process will probably form an essential part of political apology, but not of forgiveness.

But, one may object, if the wrongdoer is *unforgivable*, then both interpersonal forgiveness and political apology are impossible (one can pronounce the words, but the moral deed cannot be done). Are any wrongdoers unforgivable? People who have committed heinous acts such as torture or child molestation are often cited as examples. The question is not primarily about the psychological ability of the victim to forswear anger, but whether a wrongdoer can rightly be judged not-to-be-forgiven *no matter what* offender and victim say or do. I do not see that a persuasive argument for *that* thesis can be made; there is no such thing as the unconditionally unforgivable. For else we would be faced with the bizarre situation of declaring illegitimate the forgiveness reached by victim and perpetrator after each has taken every step one could possibly wish for. The implication may distress you: Osama bin Laden, for example, is not unconditionally unforgivable for his role in the attacks of 9/11. That being said, given the extent of the injury done by grave wrongs, their author may be rightly unforgiven for an appropriate period even if he or she has taken all reasonable steps. There is no mathematically precise formula for determining when it is appropriate to forgive.

Why forgive? What makes it the commendable thing to do at the appropriate time? It's not simply a matter of lifting the burden of toxic resentment or of immobilizing guilt, however beneficial that may be ethically and psychologically. It is not a merely therapeutic matter, as though this were just about you. Rather, when the requisite conditions are met, forgiveness is what a good person would seek because it expresses fundamental moral ideals. These include ideals of spiritual growth and renewal, truth telling, mutual respectful address, responsibility and respect, reconciliation and peace.

My sketch of the territory of forgiveness, including its underlying moral ideals, has barely mentioned religion. Many people assume that the notion of forgiveness is Christian in origin, at least in the West, and that the contemporary understanding of interpersonal forgiveness has always been the core Christian teaching on the subject. These contestable assumptions are explored by David Konstan in *Before Forgiveness: The Origins of a Moral Idea*. Religious origins of the notion would not invalidate a secular philosophical approach to the topic, any more than a secular origin of some idea precludes a religious appropriation of it. While religious and secular perspectives on forgiveness are not necessarily consistent with each other, however, they agree in their attempt to address the painful fact of the pervasiveness of moral wrong in human life. They also agree on this: few of us are altogether innocent of the need for forgiveness.

Questions for Free-Market Moralists

—Amia Srinivasan

IN 1971 JOHN RAWLS PUBLISHED *A THEORY OF JUSTICE*, THE MOST significant articulation and defense of political liberalism of the twentieth century. Rawls proposed that the structure of a just society was the one that a group of rational actors would come up with if they were operating behind a "veil of ignorance"—that is, provided they had no prior knowledge what their gender, age, wealth, talents, ethnicity and education would be in the imagined society. Since no one would know in advance where in society they would end up, rational agents would select a society in which everyone was guaranteed basic rights, including equality of opportunity. Since genuine (rather than "on paper") equality of opportunity requires substantial access to resources—shelter, medical care, education—Rawls's rational actors would also make their society a redistributive one, ensuring a decent standard of life for everyone.

In 1974, Robert Nozick countered with *Anarchy, State, and Utopia*. He argued that a just society was simply one that resulted from an unfettered free market—and that the only legitimate function of the state was to ensure the workings of the free market by enforcing contracts and protecting citizens against violence, theft and fraud. (The seemingly redistributive policy of making people pay for such a "night watchman" state, Nozick argued, was in fact nonredistributive, since such a state would arise naturally through free bargaining.) If one person—Nozick uses the example of Wilt Chamberlain, the great basketball player—is able to produce a good or service that is in high demand and others freely pay him for that good or service, then he is entitled to his riches. Any attempt to "redistribute" his wealth, so long as it is earned through free market exchange, is, Nozick says, "forced labor."

Rawls and Nozick represent the two poles of mainstream Western political discourse: welfare liberalism and laissez-faire liberalism, respectively. (It's hardly a wide ideological spectrum, but that's the mainstream for you.) On the whole, Western societies are still more Rawlsian than Nozickian: they tend to have social welfare systems and redistribute wealth through taxation. But since the 1970s, they have become steadily more Nozickian. Such creeping changes as the erosion of the welfare state, the privatization of the public sphere and increased protections for corporations go along with a moral worldview according to which the free market is the embodiment of justice. This rise in Nozickian thinking coincides with a dramatic increase in economic inequality in the United States over the past five decades—the top 1 percent of Americans saw their income multiply by 275 percent in the period from 1979 to 2007, while the middle 60 percent of Americans saw only a 40 percent increase. If the operations of the free market are always moral—the concrete realization of the principle that you get no more and no less than what you deserve—then there's nothing in principle wrong with tremendous inequality.

The current economic crisis is no exception to the trend toward Nozickian market moralizing. In the recent debates in the Senate and House of Representatives about food stamps—received by one out of six Americans, about two-thirds of them children, disabled or elderly—Republicans made their case for slashing food subsidies largely about fairness. As Senator Jeff Sessions, Republican, of Alabama, said in his speech, "This is more than just a financial issue. It is a moral issue as well."

The Harvard economist N. Gregory Mankiw recently published a draft of a paper titled "Defending the One Percent." In it he rehearses (but, oddly, does not cite) Nozick's argument for the right of the wealthy to keep their money, referring to the moral principle of "just deserts" as what makes distribution by the market essentially ethical. And in a recent issue of *Forbes*, the Ayn Rand apostle Harry Binswanger proposed that those earning over one million dollars should be exempt from paying taxes, and the highest earner each year should be awarded a medal of honor—as a reward (and incentive) for producing so much market value. Again, Binswanger explained that "the real issue is not financial, but moral."

The Nozickian outlook is often represented as moral common sense. But is it? Here I pose four questions for anyone inclined to accept Nozick's argument that a just society is simply one in which the free market operates unfettered. Each question targets one of the premises or implications of Nozick's argument. If you're going to buy Nozick's argument, you must say yes to all four. But doing so isn't as easy as it might first appear.

1. Is any exchange between two people in the absence of direct physical compulsion by one party against the other (or the threat thereof) necessarily free?

If you say yes, then you think that people can never be coerced into action by circumstances that do not involve the direct physical compulsion of another person. Suppose a woman and her children are starving, and the only way she can feed her family, apart from theft, is to prostitute herself or to sell her organs. Since she undertakes these acts of exchange not because of direct physical coercion by another, but only because she is compelled by hunger and a lack of alternatives, they are free.

2. Is any free (not physically compelled) exchange morally permissible?

If you say yes, then you think that any free exchange can't be exploitative and thus immoral. Suppose that I inherited from my rich parents a large plot of vacant land, and that you are my poor, landless neighbor. I offer you the following deal. You can work the land, doing all the hard labor of tilling, sowing, irrigating, and harvesting. I'll pay you $1 a day for a year. After that, I'll sell the crop for $50,000. You decide this is your best available option and so take the deal. Since you consent to this exchange, it is morally permissible.

3. Are people entitled to all they are able, and only what they are able, to get through free exchange?

If you say yes, you think that what people are entitled to is largely a matter of luck. Why? First, because only a tiny minority of the population is lucky enough to inherit wealth from their parents. (A fact lost on Mitt Romney, who famously advised America's youth to "take a shot, go for it, take a risk . . . borrow money if you have to from your parents, start a business.") Since giving money to your kids is just another example of free exchange, the accumulation of wealth and privilege in the hands of the few is morally permissible. Second, people's capacities to produce goods and services in demand on the market is largely a function of the lottery of their birth: their genetic predispositions, their parents' education, the amount of race- and sex-based discrimination to which they're subjected, their access to health care and good education.

It's also a function of what the market happens to value at a particular time. Van Gogh, William Blake, Edgar Allan Poe, Vermeer, Melville, and Schubert all died broke. If you're a good Nozickian, you think they weren't entitled to anything more.

4. Are people under no obligation to do anything they don't freely want to do or freely commit themselves to doing?

If you say yes, then you think the only moral requirements are the ones we freely bring on ourselves—say, by making promises or contracts. Suppose I'm walking to the library and see a man drowning in the river. I decide that the pleasure I would get from saving his life wouldn't exceed the cost of getting wet and the delay. So I walk on by.

Since I made no contract with the man, I am under no obligation to save him.

MOST OF US, I suspect, will find it difficult to say yes to all four of these questions. (Even Nozick, in *Anarchy, State, and Utopia*, found it hard to say yes to question 3.) In philosophical terms, we have a *reductio ad absurdum*. The Nozickian view implies what, from the perspective of common sense morality, is absurd: that a desperate person who sells her organs or body does so freely, that it's permissible to pay someone a paltry sum while profiting hugely off their labor, that people are entitled to get rich because of accidents of birth, that you're within your rights to walk by a drowning man. Thus Nozick's view must be wrong: justice is not simply the unfettered exercise of the free market. Free market "morality" isn't anything of the sort.

Some might object that these are extreme cases, and that all they show is that the market, to be fully moral, needs some tweaking. But to concede that there is more to freedom than consent, that there is such a thing as nonviolent exploitation, that people shouldn't be rewarded and punished for accidents of birth, that we have moral obligations that extend beyond those we contractually incur—this is to concede that the entire Nozickian edifice is structurally unsound. The proponent of free market morality has lost his foundations.

Why worry about the morally pernicious implications of Nozickianism? After all, I said that most Western societies remain Rawlsian in their organization, even if they are growing more Nozickian in their ideology. In the United States for example, there are legal prohibitions on what people can sell, a safety net to help those who suffer from really bad luck, and a civic ethos that prevents us from letting people drown. The first answer is, of course, that the material reality is being rapidly shaped by the ideology, as recent debates about welfare in the United States demonstrate.

The second is that most Western societies hardly constitute a Rawlsian utopia. People might be legally prohibited from selling their organs, but that doesn't remedy the desperate circumstances that might compel them to do so. The law does not stop people from falling into poverty traps of borrowing and debt, from being exploited by debt settlement companies promising to help them escape those traps, or losing their homes after buying mortgages they can't afford to pay back. And there is certainly no prohibition against the mind-numbing and often humiliating menial work that poor people do in exchange for paltry wages from hugely rich companies. A swiftly eroding welfare state might offer the thinnest of safety nets to those who fall on hard times, but it does nothing to address the lack of social mobility caused by the dramatic rise in inequality. And while it might be thought poor form to walk by a drowning man, letting children go hungry is considered not only permissible, but as Senator Sessions said, "a moral issue." These facts might be not quite as ethically outraging as walking past a drowning man, but they, too, grate against our commonsense notions of fairness.

Rejecting the Nozickian worldview requires us to reflect on what justice really demands, rather than accepting the conventional wisdom that the market can take care of morality for us. If you remain a steadfast Nozickian, you have the option of biting the bullet (as philosophers like to say) and embracing the counterintuitive implications of your view. This would be at least more consistent than what we have today: an ideology that parades as moral common sense.

OCTOBER 20, 2013

The Myth of Universal Love

—Stephen T. Asma

Now that the year-end holidays have passed, so have the barrage of entreaties to nurture a sense of "good will to all mankind," to extend our love and care to others beyond our usual circle of friends and family. Certainly, this is a message we are meant to take to heart not just in December but all year long. It is a central ideal of several religious and ethical systems.

In the light of the new year, it's worth considering how far we actually can, or should, extend this good will.

To some, the answer might seem obvious. One of the more deeply ingrained assumptions of Western liberalism is that we humans can indefinitely increase our capacity to care for others, that we can, with the right effort and dedication, extend our care to wider and wider circles until we envelop the whole species within our ethical regard. It is an inspiring thought. But I'm rather doubtful. My incredulity, though, is not because people are hypocritical about their ideals or because they succumb to selfishness. The problem lies, instead, in a radical misunderstanding about the true wellsprings of ethical care—namely, the emotions.

Two of the leading liberal social theorists, Jeremy Rifkin and Peter Singer, think we can overcome factional bias and eventually become one giant tribe. They have different prescriptions for arriving at ethical utopia.

Singer, who is perhaps the world's best known utilitarian philosopher, argues in his book *The Expanding Circle* that the relative neo-cortical sophistication of humans allows us to rationally broaden our ethical duty beyond the "tribe"—to an equal and impartial concern for all human beings. "If I have seen," Singer writes, "that from an ethical point of view I am just one person among the many in my society, and my interests are no more important, from the point of view of the whole, than the similar interests of others within my society, I am ready to see that, from a still larger point of view, my society is just one among other societies, and the interests of members of my society are no more important, from that larger perspective, than the similar interests of members of other societies."

Like mathematics, which can continue its recursive operations infinitely upward, ethical reasoning can spiral out (*should* spiral out, according to Singer) to larger and larger sets of equal moral subjects. "Taking the impartial element in ethical reasoning to its logical conclusion means, first, accepting that we ought to have equal concern for all human beings."

All this sounds nice at first—indeed, I would like it to be true—but let me throw a little cold water on the idea. Singer seems to be suggesting that I arrive at perfect egalitarian ethics by first accepting perfect egalitarian metaphysics. But I, for one, do not accept it. Nor, I venture to guess, do many others. All people are not equally entitled to my time, affection, resources or moral duties—and only conjectural assumption can make them appear so. (For many of us, family members are more entitled than friends, and friends more entitled than acquaintances, and acquaintances more than strangers, and so on.) It seems dubious to say that we should transcend tribe and be utilitarian because all people are equal, when the equal status of strangers and kin is an unproven and counterintuitive assumption.

Singer's abstract "ethical point of view" is not wrong so much as irrelevant. Our actual lives are punctuated by moral gravity, which makes some people (kith and kin) much more central and forceful in our daily orbit of values. (Gravity is actually an apt metaphor. Some people in our lives take on great "affection mass" and bend our continuum of values into a solar system of biases. Family members usually have more moral gravity—what Robert Nozick calls "ethical pull.")

One of the architects of utilitarian ethics, and a forerunner of Singer's logic, was William Godwin (1756–1836), who formulated a famous thought experiment. He asked us to imagine if you could save only one person from a burning building. One of those persons is Archbishop Fénelon and the other is a common chambermaid. Furthermore, the archbishop is just about to compose his famous work *The Adventures of Telemachus* (an influential defense of human rights). Now here's the rub. The chambermaid is your mother.

Godwin argues that the utilitarian principle (the greatest good for the greatest number) requires you to save the archbishop rather than your mother. He asks, "What magic is there in the pronoun 'my' that should justify us in overturning the decisions of impartial truth?"

Singer has famously pushed the logic further, arguing that we should do everything within our power to help strangers meet their basic needs, even if it severely compromises our kin's happiness. In the utilitarian calculus, needs always trump enjoyments. If I am to be utterly impartial to all human beings, then I should reduce my own family's life to a subsistence level, just above the poverty line, and distribute the surplus wealth to needy strangers.

Besides the impracticalities of such redistribution, the problems here are also conceptual. Say I bought a fancy pair of shoes for my son. In light of the one-tribe calculus of interests, I should probably give these shoes to someone who doesn't have any. I do research and find a child in a poor part of Chicago who needs shoes to walk to school every day. So, I take them off my son (replacing them with Walmart tennis shoes) and head off to the impoverished West Side. On the way, I see a newspaper story about five children who are malnourished in Cambodia. Now I can't give the shoeless Chicago child the shoes, because I should sell the shoes for money and use the money to get food for the five malnourished kids. On my way to sell the shoes, I remember that my son has an important job interview for a clean-water nonprofit organization and if he gets the job, he'll be able to help save whole villages from contaminated water. But he won't get the job if he shows up in Walmart tennis shoes. As I head back home, it dawns on me that for many people in the developing world, Walmart tennis shoes are truly luxurious when compared with burlap-sack shoes, and since needs always trump luxuries I'll need to sell the tennis shoes, too, and on, and on, and on.

THIS BRINGS US to the other recent argument for transcending tribe, and it's the idea that we can infinitely stretch our domain of care. Jeremy Rifkin voices a popular view in his recent book *The Empathic Civilization* that we can feel care and empathy for the whole human species if we just try hard enough. This view has the advantage over Singer's metric view, in that it locates moral conviction in the heart rather than the rational head. But it fails for another reason.

I submit that care or empathy is a very limited resource. But it is Rifkin's quixotic view that empathy is an almost limitless reserve. He sketches a progressive, ever-widening evolution of empathy. First, we had blood-based tribalism (in what Rifkin calls the time of "forager/hunter societies"), then religion-based tribalism (after the invention of agriculture and writing), then nation-state tribalism (circa the nineteenth century), but now we are poised for an empathic embrace of all humanity—and even beyond species-centric bias to Buddha-like compassion for all creatures. He argues that empathy is the real "invisible hand" that will guide us out of our local and global crises.

Using a secular version of Gandhi's nonattachment mixed with some old-fashioned apocalyptic fearmongering, Rifkin warns us that we must reach "biosphere consciousness and global empathy in time to avert planetary collapse." The way to do this, he argues, is to start feeling as if the entire human race is our extended family.

I have to concede that I want cosmic love to work. I want Rifkin to be right. And in some abstract sense, I agree with the idea of an evolutionary shared descent that makes us all "family." But feelings of care and empathy are very different from evolutionary taxonomy. Empathy is actually a biological emotion (centered in the limbic brain) that comes in degrees, because it has a specific physiological chemical progression. Empathy is not a concept, but a natural biological event—an activity, a process. (Affective neuroscience, including research by Jaak Panksepp, Richard Davidson, and others, has converged on the idea that care is actually a mammal emotion, part chemical, part psychological.)

The feeling of care is triggered by a perception or internal awareness and soon swells, flooding the brain and body with subjective feelings and behaviors (and oxytocin and opioids). Care is like sprint racing. It takes time—duration, energy, systemic warm-up and cooldown, practice and a strange mixture of pleasure and pain (attraction and repulsion). Like sprinting, it's not the kind of thing you can do all the time. You will literally break the system in short order if you ramp up the care system every time you see someone in need. The nightly news would render you literally exhausted. The limbic system can't handle the kind of constant stimulation that Rifkin and the cosmic love proponents expect of it. And that's because they don't take into account the biology of empathy, and imagine instead that care is more like a thought.

If care is indeed a limited resource, then it cannot stretch indefinitely to cover the massive domain of strangers and nonhuman animals. Of course, when we see the suffering of strangers in the street or on television, our heartstrings vibrate naturally. We can have contagion-like feelings of sympathy when we see other beings suffering, and that's a good thing—but that is a long way from the kinds of active preferential devotions that we marshal for members of our respective tribes. Real tribe members donate organs to you, bring soup when you're sick, watch your kids in an emergency, open professional doors for you, rearrange their schedules and lives for you, protect you, and fight for you—and you return all this hard work. Our tribes of kith and kin are "affective communities," and this unique emotional connection with our favorites entails great generosity and selfless loyalty. There's an upper limit to our tribal emotional expansion, and that limit is a good deal lower than the "biosphere."

For my purposes, I'll stick with Cicero, who said, "Society and human fellowship will be best served if we confer the most kindness on those with whom we are most closely associated."

WHY SHOULD OUR CARE be concentrated in small circles of kith and kin? I've tried to suggest that it can't be otherwise, given the bio-emotional origin of care, but more needs to be said if I'm making a normative claim.

If we embraced our filial biases, we could better exercise some disappearing virtues, like loyalty, generosity and gratitude.

Cultivating loyalty is no small thing. George Orwell, for example, considered preferential loyalty to be the "essence of being human." Critiquing Gandhi's recommendation—that we must have no close friendships or exclusive loves because these will introduce loyalty and favoritism, preventing us from loving *everyone* equally—Orwell retorted that "the essence of being human is that one does not seek perfection, that one is sometimes willing to commit sins for the sake of loyalty and that one is prepared in the end to be defeated and broken up by life, which is the inevitable price of fastening one's love upon other human individuals."

In general we have circles of favorites (family, friends, allies) and we mutually protect one another, even when such devotion disadvantages us personally. But the interesting thing about loyalty is that it ignores both merit-based fairness and equality-based fairness. It's not premised on *optimal* conditions. You need to have my back, even when I'm sometimes wrong. You need to have my back, even when I sometimes screw up the job. And I have to extend the same loyalty to you. That kind of pro-social risky virtue happens more among favorites.

I also think generosity can better flourish under the umbrella of favoritism. Generosity is a virtue that characterizes the kind of affection-based giving that we see in positive nepotism. So often, nepotism is confused with corruption, when it really just means family preference. And favoritists (if I can invent a word here) are very good at selflessly giving to members of their inner circle.

Gratitude is another virtue that thrives more in a favoritism context. The world of Singer's utilitarianism and Rifkin's one-tribism is a world of bare minimums, with care spread thinly to cover per capita needs. But in favoritism (like a love relation) people can get way more than they deserve. It's an abundance of affection and benefits. In a real circle of favorites, one needs to accept help gracefully. We must accept, without cynicism, the fact that some of our family and friends give to us *for our own sake* (our own flourishing) and not for their eventual selfish gain. However animalistic were the evolutionary origins of giving (and however vigorous the furtive selfish genes), the human heart, neocortex and culture have all united to eventually create true altruism. Gratitude is a necessary response in a sincere circle of favorites.

Finally, my case for small-circle care dovetails nicely with the commonly agreed upon crucial ingredient in human happiness—namely, strong social bonds. A recent Niagara of longitudinal happiness studies all confirm that the most important element in a good life (eudaimonia) is close family and friendship ties—ties that bind. These are not digital Facebook friends nor are they needy faraway strangers, but robust proximate relationships that you can count on one or two hands—and these bonds are created and sustained by the very finite resource of emotional care that I've outlined. As Graham Greene reminds us, "One can't love humanity, one can only love people."

JANUARY 5, 2013

SOCIETY

I WAS ONCE TOLD A STORY ABOUT A PHILOSOPHER (WHO SHALL remain nameless) who had just received the offer of a prestigious professorship at a major university (which shall also remain nameless) on the basis of a series of rather technical articles that had been accepted for publication by a number of leading professional philosophy journals. However, once being sure of the elevation to his new position, the philosopher withdrew the articles from the journals, one by one, prior to their publication. When asked why he had done this, he replied, "One must make oneself as small a target as possible."

This story describes well one version of philosophy, dominated by the cultivation of a restricted sense of professional propriety. One must avoid public exposure at all costs and tirelessly plow one's narrow philosophical furrow. However, there is another version of philosophy that is best captured by Hegel's remark that philosophy is its own time comprehended in thought. On this view, the task of the philosopher is to try to talk, teach and write about as much as possible and to let his or her critical eye fall on any and all objects. For Hegel, nothing should be alien to the philosopher, which means that the activity of philosophy should be closely concerned with all features of the society in which one finds oneself.

It hopefully goes without saying that The Stone, being a project of one of the world's great news organizations, is committed to this second version of philosophy. Since its inception in 2010, we have sought out and encouraged philosophers who were willing and able to engage closely, critically and analytically with the affairs of the society in which they live, which in this case largely means the United States. The closing of this final section of *The Stone Reader* gives a compelling overview of their insights.

Going back to Hegel's remark, the time that our philosophers were trying to grasp in thought was the period that followed the Great Recession that burst into view in the fall of 2008 and whose effects still dominate the lives of most ordinary Americans. In the first part of this section, "Economics and Politics," the reader will find a compelling series of critiques of the various shibboleths that contributed to the economic troubles of recent years: social Darwinism, possessive individualism, rational choice, the toleration of economic inequality and the belief in the autonomy of free markets. Each of these views is dissected with a philosophical scalpel.

One place that the effects of systemic economic problems and the myopia of much social and political policy are felt most acutely is at the level of family life. The articles gathered in "The Modern Family" consider the nature of fatherhood, motherhood and marriage in our time and the gender inequities that continue to shape social relations.

All across the wide world, but particularly in the United States, questions of race, racial inequality and racially motivated injustice continue to shape the political climate of our times. "Black, White or Other" features a compelling set of articles on and around race and immigration. The focus here is sometimes quite local and specific—for example, the killing of Trayvon Martin in February 2012—but it is often more global, as for example in the articles on the debates on race and immigration in Cuba and France.

What is so exciting about working on The Stone is our ability to respond very quickly to significant events. This is enabled by both the editorial assiduousness of Peter Catapano and his colleagues, but also by the flexibility that the online medium of *The New York Times* grants us. On December 14, 2012, Adam Lanza killed his mother, Nancy Lanza, with four gunshots to the head with her own rifle before using another rifle she owned to break into Sandy Hook Elementary School in Newtown, Connecticut, and murder twenty children and six adults before turning the gun on himself. All the children were between six and seven years old.

This truly shocking incident provoked both profound grief and a vigorous debate on the effectiveness of current gun control legislation in the United States. In "Freedom from the Barrel of a Gun," the reader will find a series of articles that begin from the gruesome fact of the Newtown massacre before moving into a series of reflections on the plausibility of an ethic of nonviolence, the morality (or otherwise) of drone warfare, the often traumatic ethical consequences of war on soldiers, and a detailed and compelling philosophical examination of "just war" theory.

Yet the reader should not be deceived into believing that all the philosophical reflections on society are defined by a weighty seriousness of tone. In "This American Life," we offer a series of essays that deploy the sundry phenomena of pop culture to make a philosophical case. One can find critiques of happiness-obsessed individualism, patriotism, the contemporary culture of irony and myth of "Just do it." In addition, our authors engage with "hacktivism," the Tea Party, the morality of revenge and whether a great American writer such as Melville can offer us resources for moving beyond the nihilism of our times.

—Simon Critchley

ECONOMICS AND POLITICS

Hegel on Wall Street

—J. M. Bernstein

As of today, the Troubled Asset Relief Program, known as TARP, the emergency bailouts born in the financial panic of 2008, is no more. Done. Finished. Kaput.

Last month the Congressional Oversight Panel issued a report assessing the program. It makes for grim reading. Once it is conceded that government intervention was necessary and generally successful in heading off an economic disaster, the narrative heads downhill quickly: TARP was badly mismanaged, the report says, it created significant moral hazard, and failed miserably in providing mortgage foreclosure relief.

That may not seem like a shocking revelation. Everyone left, right, center, red state, blue state, even Martians, hated the bailout of Wall Street, apart, of course, from the bankers and dealers themselves, who could not even manage a grace moment of red-faced shame before they eagerly restocked their far-from-empty vaults. A perhaps bare majority, or more likely just a significant minority, nonetheless thought the bailouts were necessary. But even those who thought them necessary were grieved and repulsed. There was, I am suggesting, no moral disagreement about TARP and the bailouts—they stank. The only significant disagreement was practical and causal: Would the impact of not bailing out the banks be catastrophic for the economy as a whole or not? No one truly knew the answer to this question, but that being so the government decided that it could not and should not play roulette with the future of the nation and did the dirty deed.

That we all agreed about the moral ugliness of the bailouts should have led us to implementing new and powerful regulatory mechanisms. The financial overhaul bill that passed Congress in July certainly fell well short of what would be necessary to head off the next crisis. Clearly, political deal making and the influence of Wall Street over our politicians are part of the explanation for this failure; but the failure also expressed continuing disagreement about the nature of the free market. In pondering this issue I want to, again, draw on the resources of Georg W. F. Hegel. He is not, by a long shot, the only philosopher who could provide a glimmer of philosophical illumination in this area. But the primary topic of his practical philosophy was analyzing the exact point where modern individualism and the essential institutions of modern life meet. And right now, this is also where many of the hot-button topics of the day reside.

Hegel, of course, never directly wrote about Wall Street, but he was philosophically invested in the logic of market relations. Near the middle of *The Phenomenology of Spirit* (1807), he presents an argument that says, in effect, if Wall Street brokers and bankers understood themselves and their institutional world aright, they would not only accede to firm regulatory controls to govern their actions, but would enthusiastically welcome regulation. Hegel's emphatic but paradoxical way of stating this is to say that if the free market individualist acts "in [his] own self-interest, [he] simply does not know what [he] is doing, and if [he] affirms that all men act in their own self-interest, [he] merely asserts that all men are not really aware of what acting really amounts to." For Hegel, the idea of unconditioned rational self-interest—of, say, acting solely on the motive of making a maximal profit—simply mistakes what human action is or could be, and is thus rationally unintelligible. Self-interested action, in the sense used by contemporary brokers and bankers, is impossible. If Hegel is right, there may be deeper and more basic reasons for strong market regulation than we have imagined.

The Phenomenology is a philosophical portrait gallery that presents depictions, one after another, of different, fundamental ways in which individuals and societies have understood themselves. Each self-understanding has two parts: an account of how a particular kind of self understands itself and, then, an account of the world that the self considers its natural counterpart. Hegel narrates how each formation of self and world collapses because of a mismatch between self-conception and how that self conceives of the larger world. Hegel thinks we can see how history has been driven by misshapen forms of life in which the self-understanding of agents and the worldly practices they participate in fail to correspond. With great drama, he claims that his narrative is a "highway of despair."

The discussion of market rationality occurs in a section of *The Phenomenology* called "Virtue and the Way of the World." Believing in the natural goodness of man, the virtuous self strives after moral self-perfection in opposition to the wicked self-interested practices of the marketplace, the so-called way of the world. Most of this section is dedicated to demonstrating how hollow and absurd is the idea of a "knight of virtue"—a fuzzy, liberal Don Quixote tramping around a modern world in which the free market is the central institution. Against the virtuous self's "pompous talk about what is best for humanity and about the oppression of humanity, this incessant chatting about the sacrifice of the good," the "way of the world" is easily victorious.

However, what Hegel's probing account means to show is that the defender of holier-than-thou virtue and the self-interested Wall Street banker are making the same error from opposing points of view. Each supposes he has a true understanding of what naturally moves individuals to action. The knight of virtue thinks we are intrinsically good and that acting in the nasty, individualist market world requires the sacrifice of natural goodness; the banker believes that only raw self-interest, the profit motive, ever leads to successful actions.

Both are wrong because, finally, it is not motives but actions that matter and how those actions hang together to make a practical world. What makes the propounding of virtue illusory—just so much rhetoric—is that there is no world, no interlocking set of practices into which its actions could fit and have traction: propounding peace and love without practical or institutional engagement is delusion, not virtue. Conversely, what makes self-interested individuality effective is not its self-interested motives, but that there is an elaborate system of practices that supports, empowers, and gives enduring significance to the banker's actions. Actions only succeed as parts of practices that can reproduce themselves over time. To will an action is to will a practical world in which actions of that kind can be satisfied—no corresponding world, no satisfaction. Hence the banker must have a world-interest as the counterpart to his self-interest or his actions would become as illusory as those of the knight of virtue. What bankers do, Hegel is urging, is satisfy a function within a complex system that gives their actions functional significance.

Actions are elements of practices, and practices give individual actions their meaning. Without the game of basketball, there are just balls flying around with no purpose. The rules of the game give the action of putting the ball through the net the meaning of scoring, where scoring is something one does for the sake of the team. A star player can forget all this and pursue personal glory, his private self-interest. But if that star—say, Kobe Bryant—forgets his team in the process, he may, in the short term, get rich, but the team will lose. Only by playing his role on the team, by having a Los Angeles Lakers interest as well as a Kobe Bryant interest, can he succeed. I guess in this analogy, Phil Jackson has the role of "the regulator."

The series of events leading up to near economic collapse have shown Wall Street traders and bankers to be essentially knights of self-interest—bad Kobe Bryants. The function of Wall Street is the allocation of capital; as Adam Smith instructed, Wall Street's task is to get capital to wherever it will do the most good in the production of goods and services. When the financial sector is fulfilling its function well, an individual banker succeeds only if he is routinely successful in placing investors' capital in business that over time are profitable. Time matters here because what must be promoted is the practice's capacity to reproduce itself. In this simplified scenario,

Wall Street profits are tightly bound to the extra wealth produced by successful industries.

Every account of the financial crisis points to a terrifying series of structures that all have the same character: the profit-driven actions of the financial sector became increasingly detached from their function of supporting and advancing the growth of capital. What thus emerged were patterns of action that may have seemed to reflect the "ways of the world" but in financial terms were as empty as those of a knight of virtue, leading to the near collapse of the system as a whole. A system of compensation that provides huge bonuses based on short-term profits necessarily ignores the long-term interests of investors. As does a system that ignores the creditworthiness of borrowers, allows credit-rating agencies to be paid by those they rate and encourages the creation of highly complex and deceptive financial instruments. In each case, the actions—and profits—of the financial agents became insulated from both the interests of investors and the wealth-creating needs of industry.

Despite the fact that we have seen how current practices are practically self-defeating for the system as a whole, the bill that emerged from the Congress comes nowhere near putting an end to the practices that necessitated the bailouts. Every one of those practices will remain in place with just a veneer of regulation giving them the look of legitimacy.

What market regulations should prohibit are practices in which profit-taking can routinely occur without wealth creation; wealth creation is the world-interest that makes bankers' self-interest possible. Arguments that market discipline, the discipline of self-interest, should allow Wall Street to remain self-regulating only reveal that Wall Street, as Hegel would say, "simply does not know what it is doing."

We know that nearly all the financial conditions that led to the economic crisis were the same in Canada as they were in the United States with a single, glaring exception: Canada did not deregulate its banks and financial sector, and, as a consequence, Canada avoided the worst of the economic crisis that continues to warp the infrastructure of American life. Nothing but fierce and smart government regulation can head off another American economic crisis in the future. This is not a matter of "balancing" the interests of free-market inventiveness against the need for stability; nor is it a matter of a clash between the ideology of the free market versus the ideology of government control. Nor is it, even, a matter of a choice between neoliberal economic theory and neo-Keynesian theory. Rather, as Hegel would have insisted, regulation is the force of reason needed to undo the concoctions of fantasy.

OCTOBER 3, 2010

What Is Economics Good For?

—Alex Rosenberg and Tyler Curtain

R ECENT DEBATES OVER WHO IS MOST QUALIFIED TO SERVE AS
the next chairman of the Federal Reserve have focused on more than
just the candidates' theory-driven economic expertise. They have
touched on matters of personality and character as well. This is as it
should be. Given the nature of economies, and our ability to understand them, the task of the Fed's next leader will be more a matter of
craft and wisdom than of science.

When we put a satellite in orbit around Mars, we have the scientific knowledge that guarantees accuracy and precision in the prediction of its orbit. Achieving a comparable level of certainty about
the outcomes of an economy is far dicier.

The fact that the discipline of economics hasn't helped us improve
our predictive abilities suggests it is still far from being a science
and may never be. Still, the misperceptions persist. A student who
graduates with a degree in economics leaves college with a bachelor
of *science* but possesses nothing so firm as the student of the real
world processes of chemistry or even agriculture.

Before the 1970s, the discussion of how to make economics a science was left mostly to economists. But like war, which is too important to be left to the generals, economics was too important to be left
to the Nobel-winning members of the University of Chicago faculty.
Over time, the question of why economics has not (yet) qualified as

a science has become an obsession among theorists, including philosophers of science like us.

It's easy to understand why economics might be mistaken for science. It uses quantitative expression in mathematics and the succinct statement of its theories in axioms and derived "theorems," so economics looks a lot like the models of science we are familiar with from physics. Its approach to economic outcomes—determined from the choices of a large number of "atomic" individuals—recalls the way atomic theory explains chemical reactions. Economics employs partial differential equations like those in a Black-Scholes account of derivatives markets, equations that look remarkably like ones familiar from physics. The trouble with economics is that it lacks the most important of science's characteristics—a record of improvement in predictive range and accuracy.

This is what makes economics a subject of special interest among philosophers of science. None of our models of science really fit economics at all.

The irony is that for a long time economists announced a semiofficial allegiance to Karl Popper's demand for falsifiability as the litmus test for science, and adopted Milton Friedman's thesis that the only thing that mattered in science was predictive power. Mr. Friedman was reacting to a criticism made by Marxist economists and historical economists that mathematical economics was useless because it made so many idealized assumptions about economic processes: perfect rationality, infinite divisibility of commodities, constant returns to scale, complete information, no price setting.

Mr. Friedman argued that false assumptions didn't matter any more in economics than they did in physics. Like the "ideal gas," "frictionless plane" and "center of gravity" in physics, idealizations in economics are both harmless and necessary. They are indispensable calculating devices and approximations that enable the economist to make predictions about markets, industries and economies the way they enable physicists to predict eclipses and tides or prevent bridge collapses and power failures.

But economics has never been able to show the record of improvement in predictive successes that physical science has shown through its use of harmless idealizations. In fact, when it comes to economic theory's track record, there isn't much predictive success to speak of at all.

Moreover, many economists don't seem troubled when they make predictions that go wrong. Readers of Paul Krugman and other like-minded commentators are familiar with their repeated complaints about the refusal of economists to revise their theories in the face of recalcitrant facts. Philosophers of science are puzzled by the same question. What is economics up to if it isn't interested enough in predictive success to adjust its theories the way a science does when its predictions go wrong?

Unlike the physical world, the domain of economics includes a wide range of social "constructions"—institutions like markets and objects like currency and stock shares—that even when idealized don't behave uniformly. They are made up of unrecognized but artificial conventions that people persistently change and even destroy in ways that no social scientist can really anticipate. We can exploit gravity, but we can't change it or destroy it. No one can say the same for the socially constructed causes and effects of our choices that economics deals with.

Another factor economics has never been able to tame is science itself. These are the drivers of economic growth, the "creative destruction" of capitalism. But no one can predict the direction of scientific discovery and its technological application. That was Popper's key insight. Philosophers and historians of science like Thomas S. Kuhn have helped us see why scientific paradigm shifts seem to come almost out of nowhere. As the rate of acceleration of innovation increases, the prospects of an economic theory that tames the economy's most powerful forces must diminish—and with it, any hope of improvements in prediction declines as well.

So if predictive power is not in the cards for economics, what is it good for?

Social and political philosophers have helped us answer this question and so understand what economics is really all about.

Since Hobbes, philosophers have been concerned about the design and management of institutions that will protect us from "the knave" within us all, those parts of ourselves tempted to opportunism, free riding and generally avoiding the costs of civil life while securing its benefits. Hobbes and, later, Hume—along with modern philosophers like John Rawls and Robert Nozick—recognized that an economic approach had much to contribute to the design and creative management of such institutions. Fixing bad economic and political institutions (concentrations of power, collusions and monopolies), improving good ones (like the Fed's open-market operations), designing new ones (like electromagnetic bandwidth auctions), in the private and public sectors, are all attainable tasks of economic theory.

Which brings us back to the Fed. An effective chair of the central bank will be one who understands that economics is not yet a science and may never be. At this point it is a craft, to be executed with wisdom, not algorithms, in the design and management of institutions. What made Ben S. Bernanke, the current chairman, successful was his willingness to use methods—like "quantitative easing," buying bonds to lower long-term interest rates—that demanded a feeling for the economy, one that mere rational-expectations macroeconomics would have denied him.

For the foreseeable future economic theory should be understood more on the model of music theory than Newtonian theory. The Fed chairman must, like a first violinist tuning the orchestra, have the rare ear to fine-tune complexity (probably a Keynesian ability to fine-tune at that). Like musicians', economists' expertise is still a matter of craft. They must avoid the hubris of thinking their theory is perfectly suited to the task, while employing it wisely enough to produce some harmony amid the cacophony.

AUGUST 24, 2013

The Taint of "Social Darwinism"

—Philip Kitcher

GIVEN THE WELL-KNOWN REPUBLICAN ANTIPATHY TO EVOLU-
tion, President Obama's recent description of the Republican budget
as an example of "social Darwinism" may be a canny piece of political
labeling. In the interests of historical accuracy, however, it should be
clearly recognized that social Darwinism has very little to do with
the ideas developed by Charles Darwin in *On the Origin of Species*.
Social Darwinism emerged as a movement in the late nineteenth
century and has had waves of popularity ever since, but its central
ideas owe more to the thought of a luminary of that time, Herbert
Spencer, whose writings are (to understate) no longer widely read.

Spencer, who coined the phrase "survival of the fittest," thought
about natural selection on a grand scale. Conceiving selection in pre-
Darwinian terms—as a ruthless process, "red in tooth and claw"—he
viewed human culture and human societies as progressing through
fierce competition. Provided that policy makers do not take foolish
steps to protect the weak, those people and those human achievements that are fittest—most beautiful, noble, wise, creative, virtuous, and so forth—will succeed in a fierce competition, so that, over
time, humanity and its accomplishments will continually improve.
Late nineteenth-century dynastic capitalists, especially the American "robber barons," found this vision profoundly congenial. Their
contemporary successors like it for much the same reasons, just as

some adolescents discover an inspiring reinforcement of their self-image in the writings of Ayn Rand.

Although social Darwinism has often been closely connected with ideas in eugenics (pampering the weak will lead to the "decline of the race") and with theories of racial superiority (the economic and political dominance of people of North European extraction is a sign that some racial groups are intrinsically better than others), these are not central to the position.

The heart of social Darwinism is a pair of theses: first, people have intrinsic abilities and talents (and, correspondingly, intrinsic weaknesses), which will be expressed in their actions and achievements, independently of the social, economic and cultural environments in which they develop; second, intensifying competition enables the most talented to develop their potential to the full and thereby to provide resources for a society that make life better for all. It is not entirely implausible to think that doctrines like these stand behind a vast swath of Republican proposals, including the recent budget, with its emphasis on providing greater economic benefits to the rich, transferring the burden to the middle classes and poor, and especially in its proposals for reducing public services. Fuzzier versions of the theses have pervaded Republican rhetoric for the past decade (and even longer).

There are very good reasons to think both theses are false. Especially in the case of the Republican dynasties of our day, the Bushes and the Romneys, success has been facilitated by all kinds of social structures, by educational opportunities and legal restrictions, that were in place prior to and independently of their personal efforts or achievements. For those born into environments in which silver spoons rarely appear—Barack Obama, for instance—the contributions of the social environment are even more apparent. Without enormous support, access to inspiring teachers and skillful doctors, the backing of self-sacrificing relatives and a broader community, and without a fair bit of luck, the vast majority of people, not only in the United States but throughout the world, would never achieve the things of which they are, in principle, capable. In short, Horatio

Alger needs lots of help, and a large thrust of contemporary Republican policy is dedicated to making sure he doesn't get it.

Second, even if rigorous competition enables the talented—or, better, the lucky—to realize their goals, it is completely unwarranted to suppose that their accomplishments will translate into any increased benefit for the overwhelming majority of those who are less fortunate. The strenuous struggle social Darwinism envisages might select for something, but the most likely traits are a tendency to take whatever steps are necessary to achieve a foreseeable end, a sharp focus on narrowly individual goals and a corresponding disregard for others. We might reasonably expect that a world run on social Darwinist lines would generate a cadre of plutocrats, each resolutely concerned to establish a dynasty and to secure his favored branch of industry against future competition. In practical terms it would almost certainly yield a world in which the gap between rich and poor was even larger than it is now.

Rather than the beauty, wisdom, virtue and nobility Spencer envisioned arising from fierce competition, the likely products would be laws repealing inheritance taxes and deregulating profitable activities, and a vast population of people whose lives were even further diminished.

Yet, even if stimulating competition would achieve greater economic productivity, and even if this would, by some miraculous mechanism, yield a more egalitarian distribution of economic resources (presumably through the provision of more remunerative jobs), these welcome material benefits are not all that is needed. To quote a much-cited book, we do not "live by bread alone." If the vast majority of citizens (or, globally, of people) are to enjoy any opportunities to develop the talents they have, they need the social structures social Darwinism perceives as pampering and counterproductive. Human well-being is profoundly affected by public goods, a concept that is entirely antithetical to social Darwinism or to contemporary Republican ideology, with their mythical citizens who can fulfill their potential without rich systems of social support. It is a callous fiction to suppose that what is needed is less investment in education, health care, public transportation and affordable public housing.

So long as social Darwinism is disentangled from the ancillary eugenic and racist ideas, so long as it is viewed in its core form of the two theses about the glories of competition, the label President Obama pinned on the Republican budget is completely deserved. Because the central ideas of social Darwinism are equally false and noxious, a commitment to truth in advertising should welcome the label. And all of us, including President Obama and the many people whose less spectacular successes have been enabled by social structures and public goods, should hope that the name leads Darwin-hating conservatives to worry about the Republican budget.

APRIL 8, 2012

The Veil of Opulence

—Benjamin Hale

ORE THAN FORTY YEARS AGO THE PHILOSOPHER JOHN RAWLS, in his influential political work *A Theory of Justice*, implored the people of the world to shed themselves of their selfish predispositions and to assume, for the sake of argument, that they were ignorant. He imposed this unwelcome constraint not so that his readers—mostly intellectuals, but also students, politicians and policy makers—would find themselves in a position of moribund stupidity but rather so they could get a grip on fairness.

Rawls charged his readers to design a society from the ground up, from an original position, and he imposed the ignorance constraint so that readers would abandon any foreknowledge of their particular social status—their wealth, their health, their natural talents, their opportunities or any other goodies that the cosmos may have thrown their way. In doing so, he hoped to identify principles of justice that would best help individuals maximize their potential, fulfill their objectives (whatever they may happen to be) and live a good life. He called this presumption the "veil of ignorance."

The idea behind the veil of ignorance is relatively simple: to force us to think outside of our parochial personal concerns in order that we consider others. What Rawls saw clearly is that it is not easy for us to put ourselves in the position of others. We tend to think about others always from our own personal vantage; we tend to equate another person's predicament with our own. Imagining what it must be like to be poor, for instance, we import presumptions about available resources, talents and opportunities—encouraging, say, the homeless to pull themselves up by their bootstraps and to just get a job, any job, as if getting a job is as simple as filling out an application. Meanwhile, we give little thought to how challenging this can be for those who suffer from chronic illnesses or disabling conditions. What Rawls also saw clearly was that other classic principles of justice, like the golden rule or mutual benevolence, are subject to distortion precisely because we tend to do this.

Nowadays, the veil of ignorance is challenged by a powerful but ancient contender: the veil of opulence. While no serious political philosopher actually defends such a device—the term is my own—the veil of opulence runs thick in our political discourse. Where the veil of ignorance offers a test for fairness from an impersonal, universal point of view—"What system would I want if I had no idea who I was going to be, or what talents and resources I was going to have?"—the veil of opulence offers a test for fairness from the first-person, partial point of view: "What system would I want if I were so-and-so?" These two doctrines of fairness—the universal view and the first-person view—are both compelling in their own way, but only one of them offers moral clarity impartial enough to guide our policy decisions.

Those who don the veil of opulence may imagine themselves to be fantastically wealthy movie stars or extremely successful business entrepreneurs. They vote and set policies according to this fantasy. "If I were such and such a wealthy person," they ask, "how would I feel about giving x percentage of my income, or y real dollars per year, to pay for services that I will never see nor use?" We see this repeatedly in our tax policy discussions, and we have just seen the latest instance of it in the Tax Policy Center's comparison of President Obama's tax plan versus Mitt Romney's tax plan. "He's asking you to pay more so that people like him can pay less," Obama said last week, "so that people like me pay less." Last Monday he drove the point even harder, saying that Romney's plan is like "Robin Hood in reverse." And certainly, Romney's selection on Saturday of Paul

Ryan as his running mate will keep this issue in the forefront of our political discourse.

Of course, the veil of opulence is not limited to tax policy. Supreme Court Justices Samuel Alito and Antonin Scalia advanced related logic in their oral arguments on the Affordable Care Act in March. "The mandate is forcing these [young] people," Justice Alito said, "to provide a huge subsidy to the insurance companies . . . to subsidize services that will be received by somebody else." By suggesting in this way that the policy was unfair, Alito encouraged the court to assess the injustice themselves. "If you were healthy and young," Justice Alito implied, "why should you be made to bear the burden of the sick and old?"

The answer to these questions, when posed in this way, is clear. It seems unfair, unjust, to be forced to pay so much more than someone of lesser means. We should all be free to use our money and our resources however we see fit. And so, the opulence argument for fairness gets off the ground.

It is one thing for the very well off to make these arguments. What is curious is that frequently the same people who pose these questions are not themselves wealthy, nor even particularly healthy. Instead, they ask these questions under the supposition that they are insisting upon fairness. But the veil of opulence operates only under the *guise* of fairness. It is rather a distortion of fairness, by virtue of the partiality that it smuggles in. It asks not whether a policy is fair given the huge range of advantages or hardships the universe might throw at a person but rather whether it is fair that a very fortunate person should shoulder the burdens of others. That is, the veil of opulence insists that people imagine that resources and opportunities and talents are freely available to all, that such goods are widely abundant, that there is no element of randomness or chance that may negatively impact those who struggle to succeed but sadly fail through no fault of their own. It blankets off the obstacles that impede the road to success. It turns a blind eye to the adversity that some people, let's face it, are born into. By insisting that we consider public policy from the perspective of the most advantaged, the veil of opulence obscures the vagaries of brute luck.

But wait, you may be thinking, what of merit? What of all those who have labored and toiled and pulled themselves up by their bootstraps to make their lives better for themselves and their families? This is an important question indeed. Many people work hard for their money and deserve to keep what they earn. An answer is offered by both doctrines of fairness.

The veil of opulence assumes that the playing field is level, that all gains are fairly gotten, that there is no cosmic adversity. In doing so, it is partial to the fortunate—for fortune here is entirely earned or deserved. The veil of ignorance, on the other hand, introduces the possibility that one might fall on hard luck or that one is not born into luck. It never once closes out the possibility that that same person might take steps to overcome that bad luck. In this respect, it is not partial to the fortunate but impartial to all. Some will win by merit, some will win by lottery. Others will lose by laziness, while still others will lose because the world has thrown them some unfathomably awful disease or some catastrophically terrible car accident. It is an illusion of prosperity to believe that each of us deserves everything we get.

If there's one thing about fairness, it is fundamentally an *impartial* notion, an idea that restricts us from privileging one group over another. When asking about fairness, we cannot ask whether x policy is fair *for me*, or whether y policy is fair for someone with a yacht and two vacation homes. We must ask whether z policy is fair, full stop. What we must ask here is whether the policy could be applied to all, whether it is the sort of system with which we could live, if we were to end up in one of the many socioeconomic groupings that make up our diverse community, whether most advantaged or least advantaged, fortunate or unfortunate. This is why the veil of ignorance is a superior test for fairness over the veil of opulence. It tackles the universality of fairness without getting wrapped up in the particularities of personal interest. If you were to start this world anew, unaware of who you would turn out to be, what sort of die would you be willing to cast?

We already employ this veil of ignorance logic in a wide range of areas, many of which are not limited to politics. An obvious case is in the game of football. During draft season, the NFL gives the losingest team the opportunity to take first pick at their player of choice. Just recently, the Indianapolis Colts, the worst team last year, selected as their new quarterback the aptly named Andrew Luck, arguably the most promising player in recent memory. In the interest of firming up the game, in the interest of being fair, the NFL decided long ago to give the worst teams in football the best shot at improving their game. At the beginning of the season, nobody knows who is going to be the worst off, but they all agree to the draft rules.

As a result, football is better for it. It is both more exciting, because the teams are better matched, and it is fairer, because there is no tyranny of one or two successful franchises over others. It's a game that even die-hard fans recognize as fair. It doesn't inspire the same sort of grumbling that has so many baseball fans thumbing their noses at the New York Yankees. It is true that in some instances, such a policy may encourage some to game the system, but on the whole it is an important policy, and most teams continue to play to win.

As this election season wears on, we will likely be hearing a lot about fairness. Romney recently signaled as much. Obama has been doing so for months. Far from a mere rhetorical concern, our two presidential candidates are each representatives of one of these views.

The question of fairness has widespread application throughout our political discourse. It affects taxation, health care, education, social safety nets, and so on. The veil of opulence would have us screen for fairness by asking what the most fortunate among us are willing to bear. The veil of ignorance would have us screen for fairness by asking what any of us would be willing to bear, if it were the case that we, or the ones we love, might be born into difficult circumstances or, despite our hard work, blindsided by misfortune. Society is in place to correct for the injustices of the universe, to ensure that our lives can run smoothly despite the stuff that is far out of our control: not to hand us what we need but to give us the opportunity to pursue life, liberty and happiness. The veil of ignorance helps us see that. The veil of opulence keeps us in the dark.

Dependents of the State

—Amia Srinivasan

OF ALL THE SINS TO WHICH AN AMERICAN CAN SUCCUMB, THE worst may be dependence on the state.

Think back for a moment to the two biggest missteps in the 2012 presidential election: Mitt Romney's dismissal of the "47 percent" of people "dependent on the government," and President Obama's "you didn't build that," intended to remind American business owners that their success wasn't all due to smarts and hard work, but also to the roads and bridges built by others, the government-sponsored research that produced the Internet and the "unbelievable American system we have that allowed you to thrive." Both statements came off as stinging insults directed at large groups of voters, and both were seen as tactical disasters.

Conservatives champion an ethos of hard work and self-reliance, and insist—heroically ignoring the evidence—that people's life chances are determined by the exercise of those virtues. Liberals, meanwhile, counter the accusation that their policies encourage dependence by calling the social welfare system a "safety net," there only to provide a "leg up" to people who have "fallen on hard times." Unlike gay marriage or abortion, issues that divide left from right, everyone, no matter where they lie on the American political spectrum, loathes and fears state dependence. If dependence isn't a moral failing to be punished, it's an addictive substance off which people must be weaned.

Like so many politically important notions, the concept of "state dependence" purports to do no more than describe the way things are but contains within it a powerful and suspect moral judgment. What is it for one thing to depend on another? Put most simply, x depends on y when it's the case that x wouldn't exist if y didn't exist. More subtly, x depends on y when it's the case that x wouldn't be in the state it is in without y's being in the state it is in. Americans who collect food stamps, Medicaid, unemployment insurance or welfare checks are said to be dependent on the state because the lives they lead would be different (indeed, worse) if the state did not provide these services—at least without their working harder and longer. Despite the symbolic resonance of Ronald Reagan's fictitious "welfare queen," most of the people who rely on means-tested social services either cannot work, have been recently laid off thanks to the economic downturn, or are already working in poorly paid, immiserating jobs. Of the 32 million American children currently being raised in low-income families—families who cannot afford to meet their basic needs—nearly half have parents who are in full-time, year-round jobs.

But if the poor are dependent on the state, so, too, are America's rich. The extraordinary accumulation of wealth enjoyed by the socioeconomic elite—in 2007, the richest 1 percent of Americans accounted for about 24 percent of all income—simply wouldn't be possible if the United States wasn't organized as it is. Just about every aspect of America's economic and legal infrastructure—the laissez-faire governance of the markets; a convoluted tax structure that has hedge fund managers paying less than their office cleaners; the promise of state intervention when banks go belly-up; the legal protections afforded to corporations as if they were people; the enormous subsidies given to corporations (in total, about 50 percent more than social services spending); electoral funding practices that allow the wealthy to buy influence in government—allows the rich to stay rich and get richer. In primitive societies, people can accumulate only as much stuff as they can physically gather and hold on to. It's only in "advanced" societies that the state provides the means to socioeconomic domination by a tiny minority. "The poverty of our century is unlike that of any other," the writer John Berger said about the twentieth century, though he might equally have said it of this one: "It is not, as poverty was before, the result of natural scarcity, but of a set of priorities imposed upon the rest of the world by the rich."

The irony isn't only that the poor are condemned for being dependent on the state while the rich are not. It's also that the rich get so much more out of their dependence on the state than the poor. Without the support of the state, poor people's quality of life would certainly drop, but only by degrees: their lives would go from bad to worse. Take the state's assistance away from the rich, however, and their lives would take a serious plunge in comfort. No wonder rich people are on the whole conservative: the most ferocious defenders of the status quo are usually those who are most dependent on the system.

So, the question should not be why Americans loathe and fear dependence on the state, but rather, why do Americans loathe and fear some forms of state dependence but not others? Why is state dependence condemned when evinced by the poor, but tolerated, even unrecognized, when enjoyed by the rich? What justifies this double standard?

Here's one possible answer. While the rich are dependent on the state, the state is in turn dependent on them. The elite might enjoy levels of comfort and prosperity that the majority can scarcely imagine, but it's no more than they deserve: they are, after all, the "job creators," the engines of economic growth. The poor, by contrast, are just a drag on the system.

Even if it were granted that some sort of market-driven economy is in the public interest (or, to adapt Churchill's quip about democracy, that it is the worst option except for all the rest), the case would remain to be made that the sort of market-driven economy we have in the United States serves that interest. Indeed, this case would be especially difficult to argue at a time when we are living with the effects of an economic recession caused by the wealthiest among us, the cost of which is being paid largely by the poor and middle classes—in the loss of their homes and jobs, but also in the form of tax-dollar-driven bank bailouts. The orthodoxy is that inequality is the necessary price of economic growth, but research strongly suggests that inequality of income causes economic instability and slows overall growth, and that the rapid rise in inequality in the last few decades is to blame for the current economic recession.

The case for our current arrangements is still harder to make once one acknowledges the argument, put forward by Richard G. Wilkinson and Kate Pickett in their book *The Spirit Level*, that economic inequality has a negative multiplier effect, making poor people in very unequal societies like the United States' worse off—in terms of mortality, education, imprisonment rates, social mobility and so on—than they would be in more equal societies, even if they were just as poor. In other words, when the rich get richer, it doesn't just make them better off: it makes everyone else worse off.

Neither will it help anyone trying to make the case for the American way to compare the United States with other developed nations, where the average citizen is healthier, happier, better educated and enjoys more social mobility. Here we have a real-life chance to apply the political philosopher John Rawls's test for a just society, what he called the "veil of ignorance." If you didn't know what kind of person you were going to be—your gender, family circumstances, ethnicity—which of the developed nations would you choose to be born into? Would you be hoping to have a home, a job and good medical care? Would you like to be able to clothe, feed and educate your children someday? In that case you'd be foolish to pick the United States. You'd be better off choosing Norway, or any one of a number of countries that have better evened the balance between rich and poor state dependence with higher taxes and greater investment in social services.

Here's another answer one might give when asked why we should tolerate state dependence on the part of the rich but not of the poor: the rich earn the benefits they accrue from the state, while the poor get something for nothing. Sure, the rich might have needed the state's help to get rich, but they have also had to work for their success; the poor can just sit back and wait for the welfare check to arrive. But this is to ignore the fact that most rich Americans didn't earn their wealth: they were given it, either directly through inheritance from their parents, or only slightly less directly through their access to elite secondary and higher education.

Despite the sustaining myth of American meritocracy, one of the most significant determinants of where a child will end up on the socioeconomic ladder is which rung his or her parents occupied. (This reminds me of a story I heard from a fellow philosopher, Jason Stanley, about a guy he met in a bar, who explained that he had lost his job in the economic downturn but that he had pulled himself up by his own bootstraps and relaunched his career as an entrepreneur. If he could do it, he said, anyone could. It turned out that he got his start-up capital from his father, a venture capitalist.) While middle-class and rich children no doubt have to burn the midnight oil to get into Harvard and Yale, they mostly end up at those places because of the huge advantages that wealth confers in the context of a failing public education system. Liberals and conservatives alike pin their hopes on education as the "great leveler," but the data tells us that the American education system magnifies the advantages of wealth and the disadvantages of poverty. The unearned advantages enjoyed by the children of rich parents dwarf the sums given to welfare recipients.

To claim that the rich earn what they have also ignores the fact that most of the people who depend on social services do work—only they work for their poverty rather than their wealth. Many of them depend on the state because the jobs available to them—the ones produced by the much-vaunted job creators—don't pay enough to allow them to live. Thus welfare payments to the poor effectively operate as yet another kind of corporate subsidy, making up for the difference between the increasing cost of living and declining real wages. California taxpayers alone pay $86 million annually to subsidize Walmart via state assistance to its employees and their children.

America's socioeconomic elite has been successful in part because it has been allowed to get away with the argument that its success has nothing to do with the state: with a little elbow grease, the rich seem to say, the poor can be just like them. And the poor may all be too ready to agree. "Socialism never took root in America," John Steinbeck said, "because the poor see themselves not as an exploited proletariat but as temporarily embarrassed millionaires." It's a myth dear to the American psyche, the myth that Obama tried to pierce when he insisted that "you didn't build that." And while Obama might have retained the presidency, Romney and his ideological comrades have won, it seems, the long fight against "state dependence."

The tax bill passed by Congress just in time to avert the "fiscal cliff," making the Bush tax cuts permanent for households under the $450,000 threshold, will cost the government $3.6 trillion over the next decade, as compared with the $4.5 trillion it would have cost if the Bush tax cuts had stayed in place. That isn't a lot in savings— and isn't enough to allow the government to continue funding social services at current levels. In the short term, America's rich, those earning above $450,000, will see their tax bills increase. But in the long term, it's America's poor who will be paying. Under the terms of the latest deal, the poor will enjoy a temporary extension on refundable tax credits; at the same time, the Bush-era estate tax cut, which will cost about $375 billion over the next decade as compared with the Clinton-era estate tax policy and will benefit only millionaires and their children, was made permanent. Now the once unthinkable sequester will almost surely go into effect on March 1, bringing $85 billion in budget cuts. The Democrats are scrambling to replace some of the most drastic of those spending cuts—to primary and secondary education, vaccination programs, medical research and environmental protection—with increased taxes on the rich, but the Republicans aren't budging. The sequester will almost certainly come into force by the end of this week and is estimated to cost 700,000 jobs. Meanwhile, of the 47 percent that Romney lambasted for not paying taxes and scrounging off the state, 7,000 are millionaires.

We are all dependents of the state, not just the poor, and it's certainly not the poor who benefit most from their dependence. The question isn't who is dependent on the state but whether the current political settlement treats everyone with fairness and dignity: whether the odds are stacked in particular people's favor, whether some are able to prosper only at the expense of others, whether everyone has an equal opportunity to make a decent human life. That we may not like the answers to these questions is the very reason we should ask them.

FEBRUARY 26, 2013

The Failure of Rational Choice Philosophy

—John McCumber

ACCORDING TO HEGEL, HISTORY IS IDEA DRIVEN. ACCORDING TO almost everyone else, this is foolish. What can "idea driven" even mean when measured against the passion and anguish of a place like Libya?

But Hegel had his reasons. Ideas for him are public, rather than in our heads, and serve to coordinate behavior. They are, in short, pragmatically meaningful words. To say that history is "idea driven" is to say that, like all cooperation, nation building requires a common basic vocabulary.

One prominent component of America's basic vocabulary is "individualism." Our society accords unique rights and freedoms to individuals, and we are so proud of these that we recurrently seek to install them in other countries. But individualism, the desire to control one's own life, has many variants. Tocqueville viewed it as selfishness and suspected it, while Emerson and Whitman viewed it as the moment-by-moment expression of one's unique self and loved it.

After World War II, a third variant gained momentum in America. It defined individualism as the making of choices so as to maximize one's preferences. This differed from "selfish individualism" in that the preferences were not specified: they could be altruistic as well as selfish. It differed from "expressive individualism" in having general algorithms by which choices were made. These made it rational.

This form of individualism did not arise by chance. Alex Abella's

Soldiers of Reason (2008) and S. M. Amadae's *Rationalizing Capitalist Democracy* (2003) trace it to the RAND Corporation, the hyperinfluential Santa Monica, CA, think tank, where it was born in 1951 as "rational choice theory." Rational choice theory's mathematical account of individual choice, originally formulated in terms of voting behavior, made it a point-for-point antidote to the collectivist dialectics of Marxism; and since, in the view of many cold warriors, Marxism was philosophically ascendant worldwide, such an antidote was sorely needed. Functionaries at RAND quickly expanded the theory from a tool of social analysis into a set of universal doctrines that we may call "rational choice philosophy." Governmental seminars and fellowships spread it to universities across the country, aided by the fact that any alternative to it would by definition be collectivist. During the early Cold War, that was not exactly a good thing to be.

The overall operation was wildly successful. Once established in universities, rational choice philosophy moved smoothly on the backs of their pupils into the "real world" of business and government (aided in the crossing, to be sure, by the novels of another Rand—Ayn). Today, governments and businesses across the globe simply assume that social reality is merely a set of individuals freely making rational choices. Wars have been and are still being fought to bring such freedom to Koreans, Vietnamese, Iraqis, Grenadans and now Libyans, with more nations surely to come.

At home, antiregulation policies are crafted to appeal to the view that government must in no way interfere with Americans' freedom of choice. Even religions compete in the marketplace of salvation, eager to be chosen by those who, understandably, prefer heaven to hell. Today's most zealous advocates of individualism, be they on Wall Street or at Tea Parties, invariably forget their origins in a long-ago program of government propaganda.

Rational choice philosophy, to its credit, made clear and distinct claims in philosophy's three main areas. Ontologically, its emphasis on individual choice required that reality present a set of discrete alternatives among which one could choose: linear "causal chains," which intersected either minimally, trivially, or not at all. Epistemologically, that same emphasis on choice required that at least the early stages of such chains be knowable with something akin to certainty, for if our choice is to be rational, we need to know what we are choosing. Knowledge thus became foundationalistic and incremental.

But the real significance of rational choice philosophy lay in ethics. Rational choice *theory*, being a branch of economics, does not question people's preferences; it simply studies how they seek to maximize them. Rational choice *philosophy* seems to maintain this ethical neutrality (see Hans Reichenbach's 1951 *The Rise of Scientific Philosophy*, an unwitting masterpiece of the genre), but it does not. Whatever my preferences are, I have a better chance of realizing them if I possess wealth and power. Rational choice philosophy thus promulgates a clear and compelling moral imperative: increase your wealth and power!

Today, institutions which help individuals do that (corporations, lobbyists) are flourishing; the others (public hospitals, schools) are basically left to rot. Business and law schools prosper; philosophy departments are threatened with closure.

Rational choice theory came under fire after the economic crisis of 2008 but remains central to economic analysis. Rational choice philosophy, by contrast, was always implausible. Hegel, for one, had denied all three of its central claims in his *Encyclopedia of the Philosophical Sciences* over a century before. In that work, as elsewhere in his writings, nature is not neatly causal, but shot through with randomness. Because of this chaos, we cannot know the significance of what we have done until our community tells us; and ethical life correspondingly consists, not in pursuing wealth and power, but in integrating ourselves into the right kinds of community.

Critical views soon arrived in postwar America as well. By 1953, W. V. O. Quine was exposing the flaws in rational choice epistemology. John Rawls, somewhat later, took on its sham ethical neutrality, arguing that rationality in choice includes moral constraints. The neat causality of rational choice ontology, always at odds with quantum physics, was further jumbled by the environmental crisis, exposed by Rachel Carson's 1962 book *Silent Spring*, which revealed that the causal effects of human actions were much more complex, and so less predictable, than previously thought.

These efforts, however, have not so far confronted rational choice individualism as Hegel did: on its home ground, in philosophy itself. Quine's "ontological relativity" means that at a sufficient level of generality, more than one theory fits the facts; we choose among the alternatives. Rawls's social philosophy relies on a free choice among possible social structures. Even Richard Rorty, the most iconoclastic of recent American philosophers, phrased his proposals, as Robert Scharff has written, in the "self-confident, post-traditional language of *choice*."

If philosophers cannot refrain from absolutizing choice within philosophy itself, they cannot critique it elsewhere. If they did, they could begin formulating a comprehensive alternative to rational choice philosophy—and to the blank collectivism of Cold War Stalinism—as opposed to the specific criticisms advanced so far. The result might look quite a bit like Hegel in its view that individual freedom is of value only when communally guided. Though it would be couched, one must hope, in clearer prose.

JUNE 19, 2011

Mandela's Socialist Failure

—Slavoj Žižek

IN THE LAST TWO DECADES OF HIS LIFE, NELSON MANDELA WAS celebrated as a model of how to liberate a country from the colonial yoke without succumbing to the temptation of dictatorial power and anticapitalist posturing. In short, Mandela was not Mugabe: South Africa remained a multiparty democracy with free press and a vibrant economy well-integrated into the global market and immune to hasty socialist experiments. Now, with his death, his stature as a saintly wise man seems confirmed for eternity: there are Hollywood movies about him—he was impersonated by Morgan Freeman, who also, by the way, played the role of God in another film—and rock stars and religious leaders, sportsmen, and politicians from Bill Clinton to Fidel Castro are all united in his beatification.

Is this, however, the whole story? Two key facts remain obliterated by this celebratory vision. In South Africa, the miserable life of the poor majority broadly remains the same as under apartheid, and the rise of political and civil rights is counterbalanced by the growing insecurity, violence, and crime. The main change is that the old white ruling class is joined by the new black elite. Secondly, people remember the old African National Congress, which promised not only the end of apartheid, but also more social justice, even a kind of socialism. This much more radical ANC past is gradually obliterated from our memory. No wonder that anger is growing among poor, black South Africans.

South Africa in this respect is just one version of the recurrent story of the contemporary left. A leader or party is elected with universal enthusiasm, promising a "new world"—but, then, sooner or later, they stumble upon the key dilemma: Does one dare to touch the capitalist mechanisms, or does one decide to "play the game"? If one disturbs these mechanisms, one is very swiftly "punished" by market perturbations, economic chaos, and the rest. This is why it is all too simple to criticize Mandela for abandoning the socialist perspective after the end of apartheid: Did he really have a choice? Was the move toward socialism a real option?

It is easy to ridicule Ayn Rand, but there is a grain of truth in the famous "hymn to money" from her novel *Atlas Shrugged*: "Until and unless you discover that money is the root of all good, you ask for your own destruction. When money ceases to become the means by which men deal with one another, then men become the tools of other men. Blood, whips and guns or dollars. Take your choice—there is no other." Did Marx not say something similar in his well-known formula of how, in the universe of commodities, "relations between people assume the guise of relations among things"?

In the market economy, relations between people can appear as relations of mutually recognized freedom and equality: domination is no longer directly enacted and visible as such. What is problematic is Rand's underlying premise: that the only choice is between direct and indirect relations of domination and exploitation, with any alternative dismissed as utopian. However, one should nonetheless bear in mind the moment of truth in Rand's otherwise ridiculously ideological claim: the great lesson of state socialism was effectively that a direct abolishment of private property and market-regulated exchange, lacking concrete forms of social regulation of the process of production, necessarily resuscitates direct relations of servitude and domination. If we merely abolish the market economy (inclusive of market exploitation) without replacing it with a proper form of the Communist organization of production and exchange, domination returns with a vengeance, and with it direct exploitation.

The general rule is that, when a revolt begins against an oppressive half-democratic regime, as was the case in the Middle East in 2011, it is easy to mobilize large crowds with slogans that one cannot but characterize as crowd pleasers—for democracy, against corruption, for instance. But then we gradually approach more difficult choices: when our revolt succeeds in its direct goal, we come to realize that what really bothered us (our unfreedom, humiliation, social corruption, lack of prospect of a decent life) goes on in a new guise. The ruling ideology mobilizes here its entire arsenal to prevent us from reaching this radical conclusion. They start to tell us that democratic freedom brings its own responsibility, that it comes at a price, that we are not yet mature if we expect too much from democracy. In this way, they blame us for our failure: in a free society, so we are told, we are all capitalists investing in our lives, deciding to put more into our education than into having fun if we want to succeed.

At a more directly political level, the United States foreign policy elaborated a detailed strategy of how to exert damage control by way of rechanneling a popular uprising into acceptable parliamentary-capitalist constraints—as was done successfully in South Africa after the fall of apartheid regime, in the Philippines after the fall of Marcos, in Indonesia after the fall of Suharto, and elsewhere. At this precise conjuncture, radical emancipatory politics faces its greatest challenge: how to push things further after the first enthusiastic stage is over, how to take the next step without succumbing to the catastrophe of the "totalitarian" temptation—in short, how to move further from Mandela without becoming Mugabe.

If we want to remain faithful to Mandela's legacy, we should thus forget about celebratory crocodile tears and focus on the unfulfilled promises his leadership gave rise to. We can safely surmise that, on account of his doubtless moral and political greatness, he was at the end of his life also a bitter, old man, well aware of how his very political triumph and his elevation into a universal hero were the mask of a bitter defeat. His universal glory is also a sign that he really didn't disturb the global order of power.

DECEMBER 6, 2013

When Hope Tramples Truth

—Roger Scruton

APOLLO GRANTED TO HIS TROJAN PRIESTESS CASSANDRA THE gift of prophecy. But because she resisted his advances he punished her by ensuring that nobody would ever believe what she said. Such has been the fate of pessimists down the ages. Those who interrupt the good cheer of their fellows with the thought that the things about which they are all agreed might go badly wrong are either dismissed as madmen or condemned as fools.

Consider only what we know from the twentieth century—the collective enthusiasm that launched the First World War, the belief in a new order of social justice that fired the Bolsheviks, the craze for national unity that brought Hitler to power and the simultaneous triumph of the Peace Pledge Union in Britain, which impeded the efforts to arm against him—these are just a few of the myriad examples which show us that, in any emergency, it is optimism that triumphs and the prophets of doom who are pushed aside.

We have witnessed something similar in the so-called Arab Spring. "Unscrupulous optimism," as Schopenhauer called it, led both the United States and the nations of Europe to embrace changes that have led, so far, to Islamist governments in Tunisia and Egypt, to the heightened persecution of Christians across the region, to the total destruction of Syria, to the murder of the American ambassador in Benghazi, to the destabilization of Mali and to a constant tally of death and destruction with no end in sight.

A small amount of thought about the forces that would inevitably be unleashed by the collapse of the Arab autocracies would have caused the Western powers to be a little more cautious in endorsing the changes. But in sudden emergencies optimism takes over. Political leaders choose their advisers from among those who already agree with them, and this is the primary reason for the irrationality of so much democratic politics. Dissenting voices appear, but only as "the other side," to be vanquished, or else in columns like this one, which our media have, to their credit, retained through all the mass movements of insanity that created the modern world. Just as Apollo protected Cassandra within his temple, at least until the fall of Troy, so do our newspapers protect scrupulous pessimists, who warn us, fruitlessly of course, against the passions of the day.

Consider one of our own day: gay marriage. What could be more sensible than to extend marriage to homosexuals, granting them the security of an institution devoted to lifelong partnership? The result will be improvements all around—not just improved toleration of homosexuals, but improvement in the lives of gay couples, as they adapt to established norms. Optimists have therefore united to promote this cause and, as is so often the case, have turned persecuting stares on those who dissent from it, dismissing them as intolerant, "homophobic," "bigoted," offenders against the principles of liberal democracy. Of course the optimist may be right. The important fact, however, is that hope is more important to them than truth.

People interested in truth seek out those who disagree with them. They look for rival opinions, awkward facts and the grounds that might engender hesitation. Such people have a far more complicated life than the optimists, who rush forward with a sense of purpose that is not to be deflected by what they regard as the cavilings of mean-minded bigots. Here in Britain, discussions on gay marriage have been conducted as though it were entirely a matter of extending rights and not of fundamentally altering the institution. Difficult issues, like the role of sexual difference in social reproduction, the nature of the family, the emotional needs of children and the meaning of rites of passage, have been ignored or brushed aside.

It is easy to trace disasters, in retrospect, to the burst of unfounded optimism that gave rise to them. We can trace the subprime mortgage crisis to President Carter's Community Reinvestment Act of 1977, which required lenders to override all considerations of prudence and fiscal rectitude in the pursuit of an impossible goal. We can trace the current crisis of the Euro to the belief that countries can share a single legal currency without also sharing loyalty, culture and habits of honest accounting. We can trace the disastrous attempt to introduce responsible government into Afghanistan to the idea that democracy and the rule of law are the default conditions of mankind, rather than precious achievements resulting from centuries of discipline and conflict. And we can trace the major disasters of twentieth-century politics to the impeccably optimistic doctrines of Marx, Lenin, Mao, and the many others for whom progress was the inevitable tendency of history. Pessimism, so obviously vindicated in retrospect, is almost always ineffective at the time. Why is this?

Our approaches to questions of that kind have been strongly influenced in recent years by evolutionary psychology, which tells us that we are endowed with traits of character and patterns of feeling that were "adaptive" in the conditions from which human societies first emerged. And what was adaptive then might be profoundly maladaptive today, in the mass societies that we ourselves have created. It was adaptive in those small bands of hunter-gatherers to join the crowd, to persecute the doubter, to go cheerfully forward against the foe. And from these traits have sprung certain patterns of thinking that serve the vital purpose of preventing people from perceiving the truth, when the truth will discourage them.

I don't go along entirely with the evolutionary psychologists, who in my view pay insufficient attention to the change that civilization has wrought in our ways of dealing with each other. But I agree with them about one thing, which is that when truth threatens hope, it is truth we usually sacrifice, often along with those who search for it.

MARCH 24, 2013

THE MODERN FAMILY

Is Forced Fatherhood Fair?

—Laurie Shrage

THIS WEEKEND MILLIONS OF AMERICANS WILL HAPPILY CELE-brate the role that fathers play in their families. For some families, though—specifically those in which dad's role was not freely assumed, but legally mandated—Father's Day can be an emotionally compli-cated occasion. And that somewhat messy reality raises a question that is worth examining today as the very definition of parents and families continues to undergo legal and social transformation.

Women's rights advocates have long struggled for motherhood to be a voluntary condition, and not one imposed by nature or culture. In places where women and girls have access to affordable and safe contraception and abortion services, and where there are programs to assist mothers in distress to find foster or adoptive parents, vol-untary motherhood is basically a reality. In many states, infant safe haven laws allow a birth mother to walk away from her newborn baby if she leaves it unharmed at a designated facility.

If a man accidentally conceives a child with a woman and does not want to raise the child with her, what are his choices? Surprisingly, he has few options in the United States. He can urge her to seek an abortion, but ultimately that decision is hers to make. Should she decide to continue the pregnancy and raise the child, and should she or our government attempt to establish him as the legal father, he can be stuck with years of child support payments.

Do men now have less reproductive autonomy than women?

Should men have more control over when and how they become parents, as many women now do?

The political philosopher Elizabeth Brake has argued that our policies should give men who accidentally impregnate a woman more options, and that feminists should oppose policies that make fatherhood compulsory. In a 2005 article in the *Journal of Applied Philosophy* she wrote, "If women's partial responsibility for pregnancy does not obligate them to support a fetus, then men's partial responsibility for pregnancy does not obligate them to support a resulting child." At most, according to Brake, men should be responsible for helping with the medical expenses and other costs of a pregnancy for which they are partly responsible.

Few feminists, including Brake, would grant men the right to coerce a woman to have (or not to have) an abortion, because they recognize a woman's right to control her own body. However, if a woman decides to give birth to a child without securing the biological father's consent to raise a child with her, some scholars and policy makers question whether he should be assigned legal paternity.

Historically, it was important for women to have husbands who acknowledged paternity for their children, as children born to unmarried parents were deemed "illegitimate" and had fewer rights than children born to married parents. Today, the marital status of a child's parents affects that child's future much less. Nevertheless, having two legal parents is a significant advantage for a child, and establishing legal paternity for both married and unmarried fathers is a complicated but necessary part of our public policies.

As more children are born to unmarried parents, the social and legal preference for awarding paternity to the mother's husband becomes more outdated. When there is a dispute about fatherhood rights and obligations, the courts can use different criteria for assigning legal paternity. These include a man's marital or marriage-like relationship with the child's mother, his caregiving and support role in the child's life, and his biological relationship to the child.

The legal scholar Jane Murphy has argued that a new definition of fatherhood is emerging in our laws and court decisions that privileges a man's biological tie to a child over other criteria. In a 2005 article in the *Notre Dame Law Review*, Murphy wrote about paternity "disestablishment" cases in which men who have assumed the father role in a child's life seek genetic testing to avoid the obligations of legal fatherhood, typically when they break up with the child's mother. Her research shows that replacing the limited "mother's husband" conception of fatherhood with a narrow biologically based one still leaves many children legally fatherless.

Furthermore, Murphy explains how the new definition of "fatherhood" is driven by the government's goal of collecting child support from men whose biological offspring are in the welfare system, as well as lawsuits from men aiming to avoid financial responsibility for their dependents. Murphy, then, reasonably proposes that judges and legislators "recognize multiple bases for legal fatherhood" and be guided by "the traditional goals of family law—protecting children and preserving family stability." Murphy argues for revising paternity establishment policies so that fewer men become legal fathers involuntarily or without understanding the legal responsibilities they are assuming.

Murphy's proposed reforms would apply to men who have different kinds of ties to a child. They would protect a naive man who, in a moment of exuberance with a girlfriend, allows his name to be put on a birth certificate, and a man whose only tie to a child is biological. Coercing legal paternity in such cases leads to painful "disestablishment" battles that are unlikely to be in the best interest of the child or promote stable family relationships. Murphy discusses cases in which legal fathers resort to violence or threats of violence against a mother and her children when child support orders are enforced against them.

I happen to be familiar with the social consequences of forced paternity because my mother worked in the district attorney's office in Santa Clara County, CA, in the 1970s and '80s. I remember the stories that she told about mothers on public assistance who lived in fear that a former abuser would return to harm them or their children because of the DA's enforcement of a child support settlement. Coerced paternity in such cases—where there has been little informed consent at the moment of assigning legal paternity—is typically costly to enforce and does not protect children or preserve family stability.

Feminists have long held that women should not be penalized for being sexually active by taking away their options when an accidental pregnancy occurs. Do our policies now aim to punish and shame men for their sexual promiscuity? Many of my male students (in Miami where I teach), who come from low-income immigrant communities, believe that our punitive paternity policies are aimed at controlling their sexual behavior. Moreover, the asymmetrical options that men and women now have when dealing with an unplanned pregnancy set up power imbalances in their sexual relationships that my male students find hugely unfair to them. Rather than punish men (or women) for their apparent reproductive irresponsibility by coercing legal paternity (or maternity), the government has other options, such as mandatory sex education, family planning counseling, or community service.

Court-ordered child support does make sense, say, in the case of a divorce, when a man who is already raising a child separates from the child's mother and when the child's mother retains custody of the child. In such cases, expectations of continued financial support recognize and stabilize a parent's continued caregiving role in a child's life. However, just as court-ordered child support does not make sense when a woman goes to a sperm bank and obtains sperm from a donor who has not agreed to father the resulting child, it does not make sense when a woman is impregnated (accidentally or possibly by her choice) from sex with a partner who has not agreed to father a child with her. In consenting to sex, neither a man nor a woman gives consent to become a parent, just as in consenting to any activity, one does not consent to yield to all the accidental outcomes that might flow from that activity.

Policies that punish men for accidental pregnancies also punish those children who must manage a lifelong relationship with an absent but legal father. These "fathers" are not "deadbeat dads" failing to live up to responsibilities they once took on—they are men who never voluntarily took on the responsibilities of fatherhood with respect to a particular child. We need to respect men's reproductive autonomy, as Brake suggests, by providing them more options in the case of an accidental pregnancy. And we need to protect children and stabilize family relationships, as Murphy suggests, by broadening our definition of "father" to include men who willingly perform fatherlike roles in a child's life and who, with informed consent, have accepted the responsibilities of fatherhood.

JUNE 12, 2013

"Mommy Wars" Redux: A False Conflict

—Amy Allen

THE "MOMMY WARS" HAVE FLARED UP ONCE AGAIN, SPARKED most recently by the publication of the English translation of Elisabeth Badinter's book, *The Conflict: How Modern Motherhood Undermines the Status of Women.* In it, Badinter argues that a certain contemporary style of mothering—a style that requires total devotion of mother to child, starting with natural childbirth and extending through exclusive and on-demand breastfeeding, baby wearing and cosleeping—undermines women's equality. Badinter claims that it does this in several ways: by squeezing fathers out of any meaningful role in parenting; by placing such high demands on mothers that it becomes nearly impossible to balance paid work with motherhood (especially once fathers have been sidelined); and by sending the message that day care, bottle feeding, sleep training and the other things that allow women to combine motherhood with paid work are harmful to children, and that the women who use them are selfish.

A post in the *Times*' Room for Debate forum earlier this month described the conflict staked out in Badinter's book as one of "motherhood vs. feminism." But what this discussion failed to capture is something that Badinter actually discusses in her book at some length—namely, that the debate over mothering is not just a conflict between feminists and women in general but rather a conflict *internal* to feminism itself.

Despite the fact that Badinter is frequently described in press coverage as "a leading French philosopher," the book could hardly be called a sophisticated philosophical analysis, especially not when compared with the kind of scholarship that is produced by feminist philosophers these days. The argument of the book is rather thin and much of the empirical evidence marshaled in support of that argument is unsystematic and anecdotal. Moreover, serious questions have been raised about Badinter's objectivity, particularly having to do with her arguments against breastfeeding, in light of her financial ties to corporations that produce infant formula, including Nestle and the makers of Similac and Enfamil.

Nevertheless, Badinter's book—and the discussion it has provoked—does manage to shed light on some profound challenges for feminist theory and practice.

Much work in second-wave feminist theory of the 1970s and 1980s converged around a diagnosis of the cultural value system that underpins patriarchal societies. Feminists argued that the fundamental value structure of such societies rests on a series of conceptual dichotomies: reason vs. emotion, culture vs. nature, mind vs. body and public vs. private. In patriarchal societies, they argued, these oppositions are not merely distinctions—they are implicit hierarchies, with reason valued over emotion, culture over nature, and so on. And in all cases, the valorized terms of these hierarchies are associated with masculinity and the devalued terms with femininity. Men are stereotypically thought to be more rational and logical, less emotional, more civilized and thus more fit for public life, while women are thought to be more emotional and irrational, closer to nature, more tied to their bodies, and thus less fit for public life.

Where second-wave feminists diverged was in their proposed solutions to this situation. Some feminists argued that the best solution was for women to claim the values traditionally associated with masculinity for themselves. From this point of view, the goal of feminism was more or less to allow or to encourage women to be more like men. In practical terms, this meant becoming more educated, more active in public life and less tied to the private sphere of the family, and more career focused.

Other feminists, by contrast, argued that this liberal assimilationist approach failed to challenge the deeply problematic value structure that associated femininity with inferiority. From this point of view, the practical goal of feminism was to revalue those qualities that have traditionally been associated with femininity and those activities that have traditionally been assigned to women, with childbirth, mothering and caregiving at the top of the list.

While both of these strategies have their merits, they also share a common flaw, which is that they leave the basic conceptual dichotomies intact. Hence, the liberal assimilationist approach runs the risk of seeming a bit too willing to agree with misogynists throughout history that femininity isn't worth very much, and the second cultural feminist approach, even as it challenges the prevailing devaluation of femininity, runs the risk of tacitly legitimating women's marginalization by underscoring how different they are from men.

This is why the predominant approach in so-called third-wave feminist theory (which is not necessarily the same thing as feminist philosophy) is deconstructive in the sense that it tries to call into question binary distinctions such as reason vs. emotion, mind vs. body, and male vs. female. Among other things, this means challenging the very assumptions by means of which people are split up into two and only two sexes and two and only two genders.

This short detour through the history of second-wave feminism suggests that the choice that has emerged in the debate over Badinter's book—that we either view attachment parenting as a backlash against feminism or embrace attachment parenting as feminism—is a false one. Neither vision of feminism challenges the fundamental conceptual oppositions that serve to rationalize and legitimate women's subordination.

Even if one accepts the diagnosis that I just sketched—and no doubt there are many feminist theorists who would find it controversial—one might think this is all well and good as far as theory goes, but what does it mean for practice, specifically for the practice of mothering? A dilemma that theorists delight in deconstructing must nevertheless still be negotiated in practice in the here and now, within our existing social and cultural world. And women who have to negotiate that dilemma by choosing whether to become mothers and, if they do become mothers, whether (if they are so economically secure as to even have such a choice) and (for most women) how to combine mothering and paid employment have a right to expect some practical insights on such questions from feminism.

This brings me to the question of the conflict to which Badinter refers in her title. Many discussions of the book have focused on the internal psychological conflict suffered by mothers who work outside of the home—either by choice or by necessity—and feel guilty for not living up to the unrealistic demands of the contemporary ideology of motherhood. As a working mother of four children who has juggled motherhood with an academic career for the last sixteen years, I am all too familiar with this particular conflict, and I agree that it is pernicious and harmful to women. But Badinter's book also points to another kind of conflict, one that isn't primarily internal and psychological but is rather structural. This is the conflict between economic policies and social institutions that set up systematic obstacles to women working outside of the home—in the United States, the lack of affordable, high-quality day care, paid parental leave, flex time and so on—and the ideologies that support those policies and institutions, on the one hand, and equality for women, on the other hand.

This is the conflict that we should be talking about. Unfortunately this is also a conversation that is difficult for us to have in the United States where discussions of feminism always seem to boil down to questions of choice. The problem with framing the mommy wars in terms of choice is not just that only highly educated, affluent, mostly white women have a genuine choice about whether to become über moms (though the ways in which educational, economic and racial privilege structure women's choices is a serious problem that must not be overlooked). The problem is also that under current social, economic, and cultural conditions, no matter what one chooses, there will be costs: for stay-at-home mothers, increased economic vulnerability and dependence on their spouses, which can decrease their exit options and thus their power in their marriages; for work-

ing mothers, the high costs of quality child care and difficulty keeping up at work with those who either have no children or have spouses
at home taking care of them, which exacerbates the wage gap and
keeps the glass ceiling in place. (Families with working mothers and
fathers who are primary caregivers avoid some of these problems but
have to pay the costs associated with transgressing traditional gender norms and expectations.)

If "the conflict" continues to be framed as one between women—
between liberal and cultural feminists, or between stay-at-home
mothers and working women, or between affluent professionals and
working-class women, or between mothers and childless women—it
will continue to distract us from what we should really be doing:
working together (women *and* men together) to change the cultural,
social and economic conditions within which these crucial choices
are made.

MAY 27, 2012

When Culture, Power and Sex Collide

—Linda Martín Alcoff

THE RECENT EVENTS SWIRLING ABOUT THE EX-NEXT-PRESIDENT of France, Dominique Strauss-Kahn, have revived old tropes about how culture affects sex, including sexual violence. Before this scandal, many continued to believe that Americans are still infected by their Puritan past in matters *sexuel*, while the French are just *chauds lapins*: hot rabbits. The supposed difference consisted of not only a heightened sexual activity but an altered set of conventions about where to draw the line between benign sexual interaction and harassment. The French, many believed, drew that line differently.

The number of women speaking out in France postscandal calls into question this easy embrace of relativism. French women, it appears, don't appreciate groping any more than anyone else, at least not unwanted groping. A French journalist, Tristane Banon, who alleged that she was assaulted by Strauss-Kahn in 2002, described him as a "chimpanzee in rut," which draws a much less sympathetic picture than anything to do with rabbits. Still, some continue to hold that the French have a higher level of tolerance for extramarital affairs and a greater respect for a politician's right to privacy. But neither of these factors provide an excuse for harassment and rape.

Conventions of workplace interaction do vary by culture. In Latin America and parts of Europe, kissing is the normal mode of greeting, and to refuse a kiss may well appear cold. Kissing coworkers in New York, however, can elicit mixed signals, at least outside of the fashion district. One does need to know the relevant cultural conventions to be able to communicate with effective ease. In other words, one needs to be a cultural relativist to know when one is being hit upon.

The more thorny question is whether relativism is relevant to those domains we generally want to put in the nonbenign category: harassment, sexual coercion, even sexual violence. Could it be that *offensiveness* is relative to the perspective of the recipient, based on her own cultural sensibilities? More troubling, could it be that our very experience of an encounter might be significantly affected by our background, upbringing, culture, ethnicity, in short, by what Michel Foucault called our discourse?

Violent and brutal encounters, even for sadomasochists, are unlikely candidates as culturally relative experiences. But much harassment and even rape is cloudier than this: date rapes, statutory rapes, and many instances of harassment can be subject to multiple interpretations, which has given rise to the new term popular on college campuses—"gray" rape. The writer Mary Gaitskill famously argued some years back that the binary categories of rape/not-rape were simply insufficient to classify the thick complexity of her own experience. In this netherworld of ambiguous experiences, can understanding cultural relativism be useful?

Feminist theory, some might be surprised to learn, has been exploring this possibility for some years. There is a great deal of work on the realm of fantasy, and desires approached through fantasy, as a means to understand the different ways women can experience varied sexual practices. Women's sexual responsiveness varies, and feminism has endeavored to honor the variation rather than move too quickly toward moral and political hierarchies of legitimate practice.

Fantasies can vary by culture and context, and they operate to create an overlay of meaningfulness on top of actual experience. The result is that fantasies provide projections of meanings that seem to control the determination of events, affecting the way we narrate and name our experience, and even the sensations we feel. This suggests a picture of an idea-body encountering another idea-body, with the fantasy projections rather than any physical characteristics of the encounter, controlling the production of experience.

Such an approach, however, can lead one to discount experience altogether. Whether workplace pornography is experienced as threatening or a reminder of the sexual power of women is simply relative to one's expectations and prior predilections, some might say. Those who take offense are simply operating with the "wrong paradigm." This has the danger of returning us to pre-feminist days when women's own first-person reports and interpretations of their experiences were routinely set aside in favor of more "objective" analyses given by doctors, psychiatrists, and social scientists, inevitably male.

The slide toward a complete relativism on these matters can be halted on two counts. First, there is the question of the physical body. Sex, as Lenin correctly argued, is not akin to having a glass of water. It involves uniquely sensitive parts of the body around which every culture has devised elaborate meanings, from adulation to abomination. The genitals are simply unique in the role they play for reproduction and physical ecstasy, and no discourse can operate as if this is not true. A light touch on the shoulder and a light touch on the genitals elicit distinct sensations. The body is not infinitely alterable by discourse.

Second, there is the question of power. Differences in status and the capacity for economic self-sufficiency—not to mention the capacity for self-regard—compromise the integrity of consent, no matter the culture. Status differences can occur along the lines of age, class, race, nationality, citizenship, and gender (all of which apply to the alleged attempted rape by Strauss-Kahn of an immigrant housekeeper). Power differences alone cannot determine whether something is benign or harmful, but they do signal danger. It cannot be the case that cultural context can render power differences completely meaningless. Obvious power differences in sexual relations should raise a red flag, no matter which color one's culture uses to signal danger.

While cultural conventions on power and sex may vary, the impact of sexual violence does not. Sexual violations should be universally defined and universally enforced.

JUNE 8, 2011

Lady Power

—*Nancy Bauer*

IF YOU WANT TO GET A BEAD ON THE STATE OF FEMINISM THESE days, look no further than the ubiquitous pop star Lady Gaga. Last summer, after identifying herself as a representative for "sexual, strong women who speak their mind," the twenty-three-year-old Gaga seemed to embrace the old canard that a feminist is by definition a man hater when she told a Norwegian journalist, "I'm not a feminist. I hail men! I love men!" But by December she was praising the journalist Ann Powers, in a profile in the *Los Angeles Times*, for being "a little bit of a feminist, like I am." She continued, "When I say to you, there is nobody like me, and there never was, that is a statement I want every woman to feel and make about themselves." Apparently, even though she loves men—she hails them!—she is a little bit of a feminist because she exemplifies what it looks like for a woman to say, and to believe, that there's nobody like her.

There is nobody like Lady Gaga in part because she keeps us guessing about who she, as a woman, really is. She has been praised for using her music and videos to raise this question and to confound the usual exploitative answers provided by "the media." Powers compares Gaga to the artist Cindy Sherman: both draw our attention to the extent to which being a woman is a matter of artifice, of artful self-presentation. Gaga's gonzo wigs, her outrageous costumes, and her fondness for dousing herself in what looks like blood, are supposed to complicate what are otherwise conventionally sexualized performances.

In her "Telephone" video, which has in its various forms received upward of 60 million YouTube hits since it was first posted in March, Gaga plays a model-skinny and often skimpily dressed inmate of a highly sexualized women's prison who, a few minutes into the film, is bailed out by Beyoncé. The two take off in the same truck Uma Thurman drove in *Kill Bill*—à la Thelma and Louise by way of Quentin Tarantino—and stop at a diner, where they poison, first, a man who stares lewdly at women and, then, all the other patrons (plus—go figure—a dog). Throughout, Gaga sings to her lover about how she's too busy dancing in a club and drinking champagne with her girlfriends to talk to or text him on her telephone.

Is this an expression of Lady Gaga's strength as a woman or an exercise in self-objectification? It's hard to decide. The man who drools at women's body parts is punished, but then again so is everyone else in the place. And if this man can be said to drool, then we need a new word for what the camera is doing to Gaga's and Beyoncé's bodies for upward of ten minutes. Twenty years ago, Thelma and Louise set out on their road trip to have fun and found out, as they steadily turned in lipstick and earrings for bandannas and cowboy hats, that the men in their world were hopelessly unable to distinguish between what a woman finds fun and what she finds hateful, literally death dealing. The rejection by Gaga and Beyoncé of the world in which they are—to use a favorite word of Gaga's—"freaks" takes the form of their exploiting their hyperbolic feminization to mow down everyone in their way, or even not in their way.

The tension in Gaga's self-presentation, far from being idiosyncratic or self-contradictory, epitomizes the situation of a certain class of comfortably affluent young women today. There's a reason they love Gaga. On the one hand, they have been raised to understand themselves according to the old American dream, one that used to be beyond women's grasp: the world is basically your oyster, and if you just believe in yourself, stay faithful to who you are, and work hard and cannily enough, you'll get the pearl. On the other hand, there is more pressure on them than ever to care about being sexually attractive according to the reigning norms. The genius of Gaga is to make it seem obvious—more so than even Madonna once did—that feminine sexuality is the perfect shucking knife. And Gaga is explicit in her insistence that, since feminine sexuality is a social construct, anyone, even a man who's willing to buck gender norms, can wield it.

Gaga wants us to understand her self-presentation as a kind of deconstruction of femininity, not to mention celebrity. As she told Ann Powers, "Me embodying the position that I'm analyzing is the very thing that makes it so powerful." Of course, the more successful the embodiment, the less obvious the analytic part is. And since Gaga herself literally embodies the norms that she claims to be putting pressure on (she's pretty, she's thin, she's well-proportioned), the message, even when it comes through, is not exactly stable. It's easy to construe Gaga as suggesting that frank self-objectification is a form of real power.

If there's anything that feminism has bequeathed to young women of means, it's that power is their birthright. Visit an American college campus on a Monday morning and you'll find any number of amazingly ambitious and talented young women wielding their brain power, determined not to let anything—including a relationship with some needy, dependent man—get in their way. Come back on a party night, and you'll find many of these same girls (they stopped calling themselves "women" years ago) wielding their sexual power, dressed as provocatively as they dare, matching the guys drink for drink—and then hookup for hookup.

Lady Gaga idealizes this way of being in the world. But real young women, who, as has been well documented, are pressured to make themselves into boy toys at younger and younger ages, feel torn. They tell themselves a Gaga-esque story about what they're doing. When they're on their knees in front of a worked-up guy they just met at a party, they genuinely do feel powerful—sadistic, even. After all, though they don't stand up and walk away, they in principle could. But the morning after, students routinely tell me, they are vulnerable to what I've come to call the "hookup hangover." They'll see the guy in the quad and cringe. Or they'll find themselves wishing in vain for more—if not for a prince (or a vampire, maybe) to sweep them off their feet, at least for the guy actually to have programmed their number into his cell phone the night before. When the text doesn't come, it's off to the next party.

What's going on here? Women of my generation—I have a Gaga-savvy daughter home for the summer from her first year of college—have been scratching our heads. When we hear our daughters tell us that in between taking AP Statistics and fronting your own band you may be expected to perform a few oral sexual feats, we can't believe it. Some critics of "hookup culture" have suggested, more or less moralistically, that the problem is that all this casual sex is going to mess with girls' heads. But whatever you think of casual sex, it's not new. What's mind-boggling is how girls are able to understand engaging in it, especially when it's unidirectional, as a form of power.

Jean-Paul Sartre, taking a cue from Hegel's master-slave dialectic, proposed in *Being and Nothingness* that what moves human beings to do things that don't quite square with one another is that we are metaphysical amalgams. Like everything else in the world, we have a nature: we're bodily, we can't control what happens around us, and we are constantly the objects of other people's judgments. Sartre called this part of ourselves "being-in-itself." But at the same time we're subjects, or what he, following Hegel, called "being-for-itself": we make choices about what we do with our bodies and appetites, experience ourselves as the center of our worlds, and judge the passing show and other people's roles in it. For Sartre, the rub is that it's impossible for us to put these two halves of ourselves together. At any given moment, a person is either an object or a subject.

The Cartesian dualism that drives Sartre's understanding of human beings as metaphysically divided from themselves is decidedly out of fashion these days. Most contemporary philosophers of all stripes reject the idea that we possess selves that are made of more than one type of metaphysical stuff. But we shouldn't forget that the claim at the heart of Sartre's picture is thoroughly phenomenological: it's not so much that people *are* split as that they *experience them-selves* as such. Notoriously, Sartre was convinced that we are inclined to deal with the schism by acting in "bad faith." On occasion we find ourselves pretending that we're pure subjects, with no fixed nature, no past, no constraints, no limits. And at other times we fool our-selves into believing that we're pure objects, the helpless victims of others' assessments, our own questionable proclivities, our material circumstances, our biology. Sartre's view gives us a way to under-stand how a girl might construe her sexually servicing a random guy or shaking her thong-clad booty at a video camera as an act of unadul-terated self-expression and personal power. But this interpretation comes at the cost of an epistemic superiority complex, according to which young women are hiding from themselves the ugly truth about what they're "really" doing.

Leave it to Simone de Beauvoir to take her lifelong partner Sar-tre to task on this very point. If you have it in your head that *The Second Sex* is just warmed-over Sartre, look again. When it comes to her incredibly detailed descriptions of women's lives, Beauvoir repeatedly stresses that our chances for happiness often turn on our capacity for canny self-objectification. Women are—still—heavily rewarded for pleasing men. When we make ourselves into what men want, we are more likely to get what we want, or at least thought we wanted. Unlike Sartre, Beauvoir believed in the possibility of human beings' encountering each other simultaneously as subjects and as objects. In fact, she thought that truly successful erotic encounters positively demand that we be "in-itself-for-itself" with one another, mutually recognizing ourselves and our partners as both subjects and objects. The problem is that we are inclined to deal with the dis-comfort of our metaphysical ambiguity by splitting the difference: men, we imagine, will relentlessly play the role of subjects; women, of objects. Thus our age-old investment in norms of femininity and masculinity. The few times that Beauvoir uses the term "bad faith" she's almost always lamenting our cleaving to gender roles as a way of dealing with what metaphysically ails us, rather than, à la Sartre, scolding women for doing the best they can in an unjust world.

The goal of *The Second Sex* is to get women, and men, to crave freedom—social, political and psychological—more than the precarious kind of happiness that an unjust world intermittently begrudges to the people who play by its rules. Beauvoir warned that you can't just will yourself to be free—that is, to abjure relentlessly the temptations to want only what the world wants you to want. For her the job of the philosopher, at least as much as the fiction writer, is to redescribe how things are in a way that competes with the status quo story and leaves us craving social justice and the truly wide berth for self-expression that only it can provide.

Lady Gaga and her shotgun companions should not be seen as barreling down the road of bad faith. But neither are they living in a world in which their acts of self-expression or self-empowerment are distinguishable, even in theory, from acts of self-objectification. It remains to be seen whether philosophers will be able to pick up the gauntlet that's still lying on the ground more than half a century after Beauvoir tossed it down: whether we can sketch a vision of a just world seductive enough to compete with the allures of the present one.

JUNE 20, 2010

The End of "Marriage"

—Laurie Shrage

THE INSTITUTION OF MARRIAGE HAS BECOME THE FOCUS OF PUB-
lic debate and reform, not just in the state-by-state political battles
familiar to us in the United States, but across the world. Some of the
long-standing practices currently being scrutinized both here and in
other countries include parental approval in the choice of a spouse,
permission for a husband to take more than one wife (polygyny),
temporary marriage, close relative (incestuous) marriage, strict or
permissive divorce terms, mandatory bride virginity, child marriage or betrothal and gender-structured marriage in which wives
and husbands have different duties and privileges and therefore
must be gender "opposites."

Marriage reform is typically part of a larger agenda for social
change. In earlier eras, challenges to bans on interfaith and interra-
cial marriage were tied to political movements promoting religious,
ethnic and racial equality and social integration. In the Middle East,
Africa, and Asia today, marriage reformers often aim to expand the
rights and liberty of girls and women, while in the Americas and
Europe, their primary aim is to advance social equality and respect
for lesbians and gay men.

While marriage reform is moving forward in many countries
(for example, to extend access to same-sex couples), many prominent legal and political theorists—such as Cass Sunstein, Richard Thaler, Martha Fineman, Tamara Metz, Lisa Duggan, Andrew

March and Brook Sadler (to name only some of those who have put their views in writing)—are proposing that the institution of marriage be privatized. More specifically, they propose that we eliminate the term *marriage* from our civil laws and policies, and replace it with a more neutral term, such as *civil union* or *domestic partnership*. The state would then recognize and regulate civil unions rather than civil marriage, and people would exchange marriage-like rights and duties by becoming "civilly united." Some private organizations, such as religious institutions, might still perform and solemnize marriages among their congregants, but these marriages would have no official state recognition.

The primary argument for this change of policy is that the state allegedly has no business regulating marriage, which is a complex cultural and religious practice. However, the state does have an interest in promoting private caregiving within families—the care of children, elderly parents and sick or disabled relatives. According to advocates for marriage privatization, the state can better pursue its interest in promoting nongovernmental forms of caregiving by establishing and regulating civil unions for all who qualify, and steering clear of defining, interfering with or regulating "marriage."

Of course, private lives are complicated. Many different kinds of families and households exist and are capable of providing care and nurturance to their members. This includes single-parent families, unmarried partners who care for each other and/or children, and nonspousal relatives—for example, siblings—who together care for parents and children. Those who advocate for replacing civil marriage with civil union maintain that the many tangible benefits of civil marriage (such as tax relief, benefit sharing and inheritance rights) should be available, not only to families headed by heterosexual couples, but to all families that relieve taxpayers of much of the cost of the care and nurturance of their members.

The aforementioned political theorists argue that the best way for the state to begin treating all families equally is for governments to avoid the highly contested terrain of licensing marriage and granting a package of rights only to citizens who achieve this status. Instead, they contend, governments should license civil unions for a wide range of caregiving units and extend the benefits that promote private caregiving to those units that gain this status. Caregiving units are defined in terms of the commitments of ongoing support that adults make to each other and their dependents, rather than in terms of the sexual/ romantic attachments that happen to exist between a pair of adults.

This is an ingenious proposal that has many advantages. First, by eliminating "marriage" and revising state policies to focus on caregiving activities rather than sexual/romantic relationships, the state advances its legitimate interest in insuring that vulnerable citizens receive care and nurturing without illegitimately interfering in the private sphere of marriage. Our sexual, romantic or marital relationships are governed by values and beliefs that may not be shared by all citizens, and so noninterference in this sphere is generally a good policy. Keeping the government out of our bedrooms is especially important for democracies that value religious diversity and personal freedom.

Second, by licensing a wide range of caregiving units, the state treats families that are differently structured equally. Some families may be headed by a heterosexual married couple, but others may be organized around one or more nonromantically attached adults and there is no good reason for the state to prefer one caregiving arrangement over others. State support for diverse families is especially good for democracies that value social equality among citizens and equality of opportunity for all, no matter how one starts out in life.

So why not advocate for the end of civil "marriage"?

Unfortunately, this proposal has some serious problems. First, "privatizing" marriage will not cause it to disappear—it will just leave it to be regulated by private institutions, especially religious and ethnic ones. For many centuries, marriage has been the primary mechanism by which people who are not related "by blood" become relatives, and it is unclear that civil unions will acquire this social power. Many families will then be structured and governed primarily by private marriage customs and practices now freed of state regulation. Because of the deep and rich cultural significance of marriage, in many cases marriage arrangements will take precedence over the terms of civil unions. When these arrangements exist in tension with widely shared public values—like those that subordinate wives and daughters and limit their opportunities—privatizing and deregulating marriage will curtail the government's ability to promote gender equality within families structured by marriage. In other words, privatizing marriage will give private organizations, including inegalitarian ones, more influence over the institution of marriage without giving individuals negatively affected much protection by having access to civil union status.

Second, because civil unions are designed to include many kinds of households, their terms will need to be flexible and individually negotiated. Importantly, adults who are not in marriage-like relationships may not want to exchange the same set of rights as those who are, such as debt and income sharing. An inclusive institution of civil union, then, is likely to become equivalent to a system of privately negotiated domestic contracts that the state merely enforces and also protects from outside interference. The problem with this is that, when the terms of civil unions are individually rather than publicly negotiated, they will be less responsive to widely shared public values and beliefs. Moreover private negotiations will require hiring legal professionals to protect the interests of all parties, which will put civil unions outside the reach of many.

In short, the arguments against privatizing marriage are similar to those against privatizing formal schooling or all forms of public assistance. Private institutions may do socially valuable work, but because they are governed by their own rules, they may also engage in forms of discrimination that conflict with public values.

Those advocating for privatizing and deregulating marriage are operating with too narrow a vision of the state's (and society's) interest in recognizing families. I agree with marriage privatizers that the state should not promote marriage among adults as a way to establish parent responsibility or to avoid poverty. The state can pursue these aims less intrusively—by formalizing agreements of child support and custody between both unmarried and married parents (that is, independently of marriage). Indeed the terms of marriage are not comprehensive enough to cover this, though they traditionally assigned the bulk of childcare to wives. But not promoting marriage is different from deregulating or privatizing it. In countries or states where women have achieved formally equal rights, such as the United States, there is no need to support heterosexual marriage as a way to insure the well-being and security of women.

Sadly, for many women today, marriage rarely is a means to economic and social security and often puts these goals at risk. Wives who perform unpaid caregiving and place their economic security in the hands of husbands, who may or may not be good breadwinners, often find their options for financial support severely constrained the longer they remain financially dependent. Decades of research on the feminization of poverty show that women who have children, whether married or not, are systematically disadvantaged when competing for good jobs. Marriage is neither a recipe for economic security nor responsible parenting.

To help move the state away from promoting marriage as a way to advance its interest in protecting children, we need to design policies that support caregivers of all kinds and cooperative caregiving schemes among parents, whether they are married or unmarried, or civilly united or not. Flexible civil unions may work for some, marriage for others, but the state should offer a mechanism for formalizing coparenting agreements independently of the commitments that adults make to each other.

While many marriage privatizers are anxious to limit state control over sexual intimacy between adults, they seem to forget the importance of state regulation in protecting the fundamental rights of those whose intimate social relationships become abusive, coercive and exploitative. Public regulation of marriage is critical for protecting vulnerable citizens in such situations. Public reform of marriage is also critical for improving the general social condition of women and children in many countries today, as well as the social standing of lesbians and gay men. Having the state regulate only civil unions is much less certain to accomplish profound social change.

Imagine that the states had not repealed "head and master" laws (which gave a husband in a marriage ultimate control of the family's property) or made other changes that rendered spouses formally equal and profoundly changed the status of married women in American society. These changes include the right of married women to own property in their name and greater protections against domestic violence. They also include laws prohibiting credit and employment discrimination against married women. Suppose instead the states had simply privatized marriage and accomplished these reforms for people who become civilly united.

Under a system in which the state only recognizes and supports civil unions, shouldn't it still prohibit discrimination against women who are married and protect them against domestic violence, whether they are also civilly united or not? Shouldn't the state also restrict child marriage and nonconsensual marriage? And shouldn't the state also prohibit terms of marriage that require involuntary servitude from a spouse? Without these restrictions, the condition of married women and girls would be unlikely to improve much. But if the state has to regulate marriage to protect married women or minors in some ways, then it has not fully privatized marriage or eliminated "marriage" from our laws.

The state need not (and should not) use its power to coerce domestic and sexual intimacy (civil marriage or union) between coparents in order to advance its legitimate goal in protecting the welfare of children. Instead the state can pursue the latter goal less intrusively by formalizing schemes of cooperation among parents in different kinds of relationships. Moreover, the state should recognize the marriages of same-sex couples that desire to participate in this institution and make the commitments thought appropriate to it. Even if marriage becomes more inclusive in ways that protect equality and freedom for all, some caregivers will prefer more flexible civil union agreements, or only to formalize their child support and custody arrangement. Public regulation and recognition of all of these options is an important step toward achieving social justice for women, lesbians and gay men, ethnic and religious minorities and children.

BLACK, WHITE OR OTHER

Fugitive Slave Mentality

—Robert Gooding-Williams

Before he temporarily stepped down from his position last week as chief of the Sanford, FL, police department, Bill Lee Jr. gave an explanation of his decision not to arrest George Zimmerman for killing Trayvon Martin. Lee said he had no reason to doubt Zimmerman's claim of self-defense. Though Lee is no longer in the spotlight, his words linger for at least one compelling reason: his explanation bears an eerie resemblance to cases brought under the Fugitive Slave Law during the antebellum period. Today, a legal standard that allowed the police chief to take Zimmerman *at his word* recalls the dark past of slave owners claiming their property. The writings of Martin Delany, the African-American political philosopher and activist, shed light on the uncanny resemblance.

During his trip through the free states west of New York to solicit subscriptions for the *North Star*, the newspaper that he and Frederick Douglass published, Martin Delany regularly corresponded with Douglass. One of his letters to Douglass, dated July 14, 1848 (Bastille Day), details the events of the so-called Crosswhite affair, which involved a court case brought under the Fugitive Slave Law of 1793. The presiding judge for the case was John McLean, associate justice of the US Supreme Court. Delany's philosophical analysis of McLean's charge to the jury is enlightening. A little background may be helpful.

In 1843 Adam Crosswhite, his wife, Sarah, and their four children, after learning that their master Frank Giltner intended to break up the family, fled Carroll County, KY, where they lived as slaves. After traveling through Indiana and southwest Michigan, the family settled in Marshall, MI, where a fifth child was born, and where close to fifty blacks, many of them escaped slaves from Kentucky, already resided. Only a few years had passed when in 1847 Frank Giltner's son, David Giltner, and his nephew, Francis Troutman, came to Marshall with two other Kentuckians to arrest the Crosswhites and reclaim them as Frank Giltner's property under the Fugitive Slave Law. That law authorized slave owners residing in one state to enter another state to recapture their property.

Soon a crowd of more than two hundred people gathered at the Crosswhite home, some of whom strongly supported Michigan's status as a free state. One man, Charles Gorham, a local banker, protested Troutman's attempt to seize the Crosswhites, after which Troutman was arrested, tried, and fined $100 for trespassing. In the meantime, the Crosswhites were spirited out of Marshall and escaped to Canada.

Delany's discussion of the Crosswhite affair came more than a year later when he arrived in Detroit during a trial (*Giltner v. Gorham*) in which suit was brought against Gorham and other members of the Marshall crowd concerning their role in hindering the arrest and abetting the rescue of the Crosswhites. Ultimately the jury was hung and the case discharged, yet Delany dwells on it due to what he considers to be the implications of McLean's charge to the jury. In particular, Delany responds to the judge's elaboration of his charge in his reply "to an interrogatory by one of the counsel for defense":

> *It is not necessary that the persons interfering should know that the persons claimed are slaves. If the claimant has made the declaration that they are such, though he should only assert it to the fugitives themselves—indeed, it could not be expected that the claimant would be required the trouble of repeating this to persons who might be disposed to interfere—should any one inter-*

fere at all, after the declaration of the claimant, he is liable and
responsible to the provisions of the law in such cases.

Delany's main point against McLean is that the fact that the judge holds interfering persons to be criminally accountable shows that he takes the 1793 Fugitive Slave Law to carry the presumption that any individual, having declared that one or another "colored" person is an escaped slave (whom he is entitled to arrest), is simply to be *taken at his word*, and so cannot legally be interfered with in his effort to arrest that colored person. In conclusion, then, Delany reasons that the Fugitive Slave Law reduces "each and all of us [that is, each and all colored persons] to the mercy and discretion of any white man in the country," and that under its jurisdiction, "every colored man in the nominally free states . . . is reduced to abject slavery; because all slavery is but the arbitrary will of one person over another."

On Delany's account, the effect of the Fugitive Slave Law, at least as Judge McLean interprets it, is to subject all unowned black persons to the domination of all white persons. For by requiring that the self-proclaimed slave catcher be taken at his word, the law leaves unconstrained the ability of any white person to arrest and seize any black person. In effect, it renders all titulary free blacks vulnerable to the power available to all whites in exactly the way that, according to Frederick Douglass, a black slave is vulnerable to the power exercised by his or her white master.

The affinity to the Trayvon Martin incident is perhaps obvious. Chief Lee's statement that Zimmerman was not arrested for lack of evidence sufficient to challenge his claim that he had not acted in self-defense ("We don't have anything to dispute his claim of self-defense") appears to imply that, absent such evidence, a white or otherwise nonblack man (there is some controversy as to whether Zimmerman should be identified as white, or Hispanic, or both, although no one seems to be claiming he is black) claiming self-defense after killing a black man is simply to be taken at his word. It is hard to resist the thought that race matters here, for who believes that, had an adult African-American male killed a white teenager under similar circumstances, the police would have taken him at his word and so declined to arrest him?

In contrast to Judge McLean, Lee does not propose that, if a certain sort of declaration has been issued, interference with a white man's attempt to seize a black man would be illegal. Rather he argues that, if a certain sort of declaration has been issued—"I acted from self-defense"—a white or other nonblack person who has admitted to killing a black person cannot legally be arrested if the police have no reason to dispute the truth of his declaration; or more technically, if in keeping with sections 776.032 and 776.013 of the Florida Statutes the police have no "probable cause" to believe that Zimmerman did not "reasonably believe" that killing Martin was necessary "to prevent death or great bodily harm to himself." Though the two cases are different, we should notice that Lee, like McLean, intends to highlight considerations that legally constrain action (interference in one case, arrest in the other) in the face of an assault on an African-American. This should give us pause to worry that Florida's stand-your-ground legislation, in its application to cases where whites (or other nonblacks) kill blacks and then claim self-defense, could prove to be the functional equivalent of a fugitive slave law.

In short, it appears that whites (or other nonblacks) may hunt down blacks with immunity from arrest so long as they leave behind no clue that they were not acting to defend themselves; or, to echo Martin Delany, that Florida's stand-your-ground law threatens to render some citizens subject to the arbitrary wills of others.

If it seems a stretch, finally, to paint Zimmerman in the image of the slave catchers of yesteryear, recall that he himself invited the comparison when, while stalking the African-American teenager against the advice of a 911 dispatcher, he complained, using an expletive to refer to Trayvon, that they "always get away."

MARCH 27, 2012

Walking While Black in the "White Gaze"

—George Yancy

I.

"Man, I almost blew you away!"

Those were the terrifying words of a white police officer—one of those who policed black bodies in low-income areas in North Philadelphia in the late 1970s—who caught sight of me carrying the new telescope my mother had just purchased for me.

"I thought you had a weapon," he said.

The words made me tremble and pause; I felt the sort of bodily stress and deep existential anguish that no teenager should have to endure.

This officer had already inherited those poisonous assumptions and bodily perceptual practices that make up what I call the "white gaze." He had already come to "see" the black male body as different, deviant, ersatz. He failed to conceive, or perhaps could not conceive, that a black teenage boy living in the Richard Allen Project Homes for very low-income families would own a telescope and enjoyed looking at the moons of Jupiter and the rings of Saturn.

A black boy carrying a telescope wasn't conceivable—unless he had stolen it—given the white racist horizons within which my black body was policed as dangerous. To the officer, I was something (not some*one*) patently foolish, perhaps monstrous or even fictional. My telescope, for him, *was* a weapon.

In retrospect, I can see the headlines: "Black Boy Shot and Killed while Searching the Cosmos."

That was more than thirty years ago. Only last week, our actual headlines were full of reflections on the fiftieth anniversary of the 1963 March on Washington, Rev. Dr. Martin Luther King's "I Have a Dream" speech, and President Obama's own speech at the steps of the Lincoln Memorial to commemorate it fifty years on. As the many accounts from that long-ago day will tell you, much has changed for the better. But some things—those perhaps more deeply embedded in the American psyche—haven't. In fact, we should recall a speech given by Malcolm X in 1964 in which he said, "For the 20 million of us in America who are of African descent, it is not an American dream; it's an American nightmare."

II.

Despite the ringing tones of Obama's Lincoln Memorial speech, I find myself still often thinking of a more informal and somber talk he gave. And despite the inspirational and ethical force of Dr. King and his work, I'm still thinking about someone who might be considered old news already: Trayvon Martin.

In his now much-quoted White House briefing several weeks ago, not long after the verdict in the trial of George Zimmerman, the president expressed his awareness of the ever-present danger of death for those who inhabit black bodies. "You know, when Trayvon Martin was first shot, I said that this could have been my son," he said. "Another way of saying that is Trayvon Martin could have been me 35 years ago." I wait for the day when a white president will say, "There is no way that I could have experienced what Trayvon Martin did (and other black people do) because I'm white and through white privilege I am immune to systematic racial profiling."

Obama also talked about how black men in this country know

what it is like to be followed while shopping and how black men have had the experience of "walking across the street and hearing the locks click on the doors of cars." I have had this experience on many occasions as whites catch sight of me walking past their cars: *Click, click, click, click*. Those clicks can be deafening. There are times when I want to become their boogeyman. I want to pull open the car door and shout, "Surprise! You've just been carjacked by a fantasy of your own creation. Now get out of the car."

The president's words, perhaps consigned to a long-ago news cycle now, remain powerful: they validate experiences that blacks have undergone in their everyday lives. Obama's voice resonates with those philosophical voices (Frantz Fanon, for example) that have long attempted to describe the lived interiority of racial experiences. He has also deployed the power of narrative autobiography, which is a significant conceptual tool used insightfully by critical race theorists to discern the clarity and existential and social gravity of what it means to experience white racism. As a black president, he has given voice to the epistemic violence that blacks often face as they are stereotyped and profiled within the context of quotidian social spaces.

III.

David Hume claimed that to be black was to be "like a parrot who speaks a few words plainly." And Immanuel Kant maintained that to be "black from head to foot" was "clear proof" that what *any* black person says is stupid. In his *Notes on the State of Virginia*, Thomas Jefferson wrote, "In imagination they [Negroes] are dull, tasteless and anomalous," and inferior. In the first American edition of the *Encyclopædia Britannica* (1798), the term Negro was defined as someone who is cruel, impudent, revengeful, treacherous, nasty, idle, dishonest, a liar and given to stealing.

My point here is to say that the white gaze is global and historically mobile. And its origins, while from Europe, are deeply seated in the making of America.

Black bodies in America continue to be reduced to their surfaces and to stereotypes that are constricting and false, that often force those black bodies to move through social spaces in ways that put white people at ease. We fear that our black bodies incite an accusation. We move in ways that help us to survive the procrustean gazes of white people. We dread that those who see us might feel the irrational fear to stand their ground rather than "finding common ground," a reference that was made by Bernice King as she spoke about the legacy of her father at the steps of the Lincoln Memorial.

The white gaze is also hegemonic, historically grounded in material relations of white power: it was deemed disrespectful for a black person to violate the white gaze by looking directly into the eyes of someone white. The white gaze is also ethically solipsistic: within it only whites have the capacity of making valid moral judgments.

Even with the unprecedented White House briefing, our national discourse regarding Trayvon Martin and questions of race have failed to produce a critical and historically conscious discourse that sheds light on what it means to be black in an antiblack America. If historical precedent says anything, this failure will only continue. Trayvon Martin, like so many black boys and men, was under surveillance (etymologically, "to keep watch"). Little did he know that on February 26, 2012, he would enter a space of social control and bodily policing, a kind of Benthamian panoptic nightmare that would truncate his being as suspicious—a space where he was, paradoxically, both invisible and yet hypervisible.

"I am invisible, understand, simply because people [in this case white people] refuse to see me." Trayvon was invisible to Zimmerman; he was not seen as the black child that he was, trying to make it back home with Skittles and an iced tea. He was not seen as having done nothing wrong, as one who dreams and hopes.

As black, Trayvon was already known and rendered invisible. His childhood and humanity were already criminalized as part of a white racist narrative about black male bodies. Trayvon needed no introduction: "Look, the black; the criminal!"

IV.

Many have argued that the site of violence occurred upon the confrontation between Trayvon and Zimmerman. Yet, the violence began with Zimmerman's nonemergency dispatch call, a call that was racially assaultive in its discourse, one that used the tropes of anti-black racism. Note, Zimmerman said, "There's a real suspicious guy." He also said, "This guy looks like he's up to no good or he's on drugs or something." When asked by the dispatcher, he said, within seconds, that "he looks black." Asked what he is wearing, Zimmerman says, "A dark hoodie, like a gray hoodie." Later, Zimmerman said that "now he's coming toward me. He's got his hands in his waistband." And then, "And he's a black male." But what does it mean to be "a real suspicious guy"? What does it mean to look like one is "up to no good"? Zimmerman does not give any details, nothing to buttress the validity of his narration. Keep in mind that Zimmerman is in his vehicle as he provides his narration to the dispatcher. As "the looker," it is *not* Zimmerman who is in danger; rather, it is Trayvon Martin, "the looked at," who is the target of suspicion and possible violence.

After all, it is Trayvon Martin who is wearing the hoodie, a piece of "racialized" attire that apparently signifies black criminality. Zimmerman later said, "Something's wrong with him. Yep, he's coming to check me out," and, "He's got something in his hands." Zimmerman also said, "I don't know what his deal is." A black young male with "something" in his hands, wearing a hoodie, looking suspicious, and perhaps on drugs, and there being "something wrong with him" is a racist narrative of fear and frenzy. The history of white supremacy underwrites this interpretation. Within this context of *discursive violence*, Zimmerman was guilty of an act of aggression against Trayvon Martin, even before the trigger was pulled. Before his physical death, Trayvon Martin was rendered "socially dead" under the weight of Zimmerman's racist stereotypes. Zimmerman's aggression was enacted through his gaze, through the act of profiling, through his discourse and through his warped reconstruction of an innocent black boy that instigates white fear.

V.

What does it say about America when to be black is the ontological crime, a crime of simply being?

Perhaps the religious studies scholar Bill Hart is correct: "To be a black man is to be marked for death." Or as the political philosopher Joy James argues, "Blackness as evil [is] destined for eradication." Perhaps this is why when writing about the death of his young black son, the social theorist W. E. B. Du Bois said, "All that day and all that night there sat an awful gladness in my heart—nay, blame me not if I see the world thus darkly through the Veil—and my soul whispers ever to me saying, 'Not dead, not dead, but escaped; not bond, but free.'"

Trayvon Martin was killed walking while black. As the protector of all things "gated," of all things standing on the precipice of being endangered by black male bodies, Zimmerman created the conditions upon which he *had no grounds to stand on*. Indeed, through his racist stereotypes and his pursuit of Trayvon, he created the conditions that belied the applicability of the stand-your-ground law and created a situation where Trayvon was killed. This is the narrative that ought to have been told by the attorneys for the family of Trayvon Martin. It is part of the narrative that Obama brilliantly told, one of black bodies being racially policed and having suffered a unique history of racist vitriol in this country.

Yet it is one that is perhaps too late, one already rendered mute and inconsequential by the verdict of "not guilty."

SEPTEMBER 1, 2013

Getting Past the Outrage on Race

—Gary Gutting

GEORGE YANCY'S RECENT PASSIONATE RESPONSE IN THE STONE to Trayvon Martin's killing—and the equally passionate comments on his response—vividly present the seemingly intractable conflict such cases always evoke. There seems to be a sense in which each side is right but no way to find common ground on which to move discussion forward. This is because, quite apart from the facts of the case, Trayvon Martin immediately became a symbol for two apparently opposing moral judgments. I will suggest, however, that both these judgments derive from the same underlying injustice—one at the heart of the historic March on Washington fifty years ago and highlighted in Rev. Dr. Martin Luther King Jr.'s speech on that occasion.

Trayvon Martin was, for the black community, a symbol of every young black male, each with vivid memories of averted faces, abrupt street crossings, clicking car locks and insulting police searches. As we move up the socioeconomic scale, the memories extend to attractive job openings that suddenly disappear when a black man applies, to blacks interviewed just to prove that a company tried, and even to a president some still hate for his color. It's understandable that Trayvon Martin serves as a concrete emblem of the utterly unacceptable abuse, even today, of young black men.

But for others this young black man became a symbol of other disturbing realities—that, for example, those most likely to drop out of school, belong to gangs and commit violent crimes are those who "look like" Trayvon Martin. For them—however mistakenly—his case evokes the disturbing amount of antisocial behavior among young black males.

Trayvon Martin's killing focused our national discussion because Americans made him a concrete model of opposing moral judgments about the plight of young black men. Is it because of their own lack of values and self-discipline, or the vicious prejudice against them? Given either of these judgments, many conclude that we need more laws—against discrimination if you are in one camp, and against violent crime if you are in the other—and stronger penalties to solve our racial problems.

There may be some sense to more legislation, but after many years of both "getting tough on crime" and passing civil rights acts, we may be scraping the bottom of the legal barrel. In any case, underlying the partial truths of the two moral pictures, there is a deeper issue. We need to recognize that our continuing problems about race are essentially rooted in a fundamental injustice of our economic system.

This is a point that Martin Luther King Jr. made in his "I Have a Dream" speech, one rightly emphasized by a number of commentators on the anniversary of that speech, including President Obama and Joseph Stiglitz. Dr. King made the point in a striking image at the beginning of his speech. "The Negro is not free," he said, because he "lives on a lonely island of poverty in the midst of a vast sea of material prosperity." In 2011, for 28 percent of African-Americans, the island was still there, the source of both images of Trayvon Martin.

The poverty is not an accident. Our free-enterprise system generates enough wealth to eliminate Dr. King's island. But we primarily direct the system toward individuals' freedom to amass personal wealth. Big winners beget big losers, and a result is a socioeconomic underclass deprived of the basic goods necessary for a fulfilling human life: adequate food, housing, health care and education, as well as meaningful and secure employment. (Another Opinionator series, The Great Divide, examines such inequalities in detail each week.)

People should be allowed to pursue their happiness in the competitive market. But it makes no sense to require people to compete in the market for basic goods. Those who lack such goods have little chance of winning them in competition with those who already have them. This is what leads to an underclass exhibiting the antisocial behavior condemned by one picture of young black men and the object of the prejudice condemned by the other picture.

We need to move from outrage over the existence of an underclass to serious policy discussions about economic justice, with the first issue being whether our current capitalist system is inevitably unjust. If it is, is there a feasible way of reforming or even replacing it? If it is not, what methods does it offer for eliminating the injustice?

It is easy—and true—to say that a society as wealthy as ours should be able to keep people from being unhappy because they do not have enough to eat, have no safe place to live, have no access to good education and medical care, or cannot find a job. But this doesn't tell us how—if at all—to do what needs to be done. My point here is just that saying it can't be done expresses not realism but despair. Unless we work for this fundamental justice, then we must reconcile ourselves to a society with a permanent underclass, a class that, given our history, will almost surely be racially defined. Then the bitter conflict between the two pictures of this class will never end, because the injustice that creates it will last forever. Dr. King's island will never disappear, and there will always be another Trayvon Martin.

SEPTEMBER 11, 2013

A Lesson From Cuba on Race

—Alejandro de la Fuente

I
N A RECENT ARTICLE FOR THE STONE, GARY GUTTING POSED A
challenge. He urged readers to look "past the outrage on race" provoked by the Trayvon Martin case and to focus on what he aptly
described as the "deeper issue" that sustains the edifice of racial
inequality—our unjust economic system. Under this system, people
compete for basic goods and services in what seems to be a fair and
nondiscriminating market. But since they enter this market from
vastly different social circumstances, competition is anything but
fair. Those who already possess goods have a much better chance of
renewing their access to them, whereas those who don't have little
chance of ever getting them.

Gutting asks the right questions. If issues of economic justice are
at the root of racial problems, what are the policy implications of this
realization? Are such policies compatible with or even possible in a
capitalist system? Is capitalism inexorably unjust?

It is tempting for people of any country—and perhaps especially
the United States—to view the conditions of their political and public
life as unique. But of course, other multiracial societies have grappled with similar problems. It is frequently overlooked that the race
problems in the United States are, in fact, not just ours, but part of a
much larger story of racial differentiation and discrimination in the
Americas. Less than 10 percent of the Africans forcibly transported
to the New World came to what is now the United States. Most people

of African descent in the hemisphere do not live here, but in Latin America and the Caribbean. Have any of these societies had the sort of debate that Gutting suggests? Have they tried to answer his questions concerning economic justice?

Few in the United States would think to turn to a socialist state for wisdom on the matter, but an examination of the recent history of Cuba does in fact provide valuable lessons about the complex links between economic justice, access to basic goods and services, racial inequality, and what Gutting refers to as "continuing problems about race."

The Cuban answer to the deep issue of social justice is well known. After the revolution of 1959, Cuban authorities believed that capitalism was unable to correct social injustices like racism. Beginning in the early 1960s, the Cuban government nationalized vast sectors of the economy, dismantled market-driven mechanisms of resource allocation, introduced central economic planning, and guaranteed the egalitarian distribution of basic goods through a rationing system. At the same time, the socialization of educational, health-care and recreational facilities democratized access to social and cultural services. If by economic justice we mean egalitarian access to basic goods and services such as food, health, housing, employment and education, then Cuba came closer than any other country in our hemisphere to fulfilling this ideal.

The enthusiasm generated by these changes was perhaps captured best by the African-American writer and activist Julian Mayfield, author of an article about the impact of the Cuban revolution on race, published in October of 1960 in the newspaper *The Afro-American*. Its title was graphic enough: "Cuba Has Solution to Race Problem."

According to research that I conducted in the 1990s for my book *A Nation for All: Race, Inequality, and Politics in Twentieth-Century Cuba*, the economic and social programs promoted by the Cuban government produced dramatic results. By the early 1980s, when reliable data to measure the impact of such programs became available, inequality according to race had declined noticeably in a number of key indicators. The life expectancy of nonwhite Cubans was only one year lower than that of whites; life expectancy was basically identical for all racial groups. A powerful indicator of social well-being, linked to access to health services (as reflected, particularly, in infant mortality), nutrition and education, the Cuban race gap in life expectancy was significantly lower than those found in more affluent multiracial societies such as Brazil (about 6.7 years) and the United States (about 6.3 years) during the same period.

Racial differences in education and employment had also diminished or, in some cases, even disappeared. The proportion of high school graduates was actually higher among blacks than among whites in Cuba, whereas the opposite was true in both Brazil and the United States. Whites continued to enjoy an advantage at the college level, but it was minuscule. About 4.4 percent of white adults (twenty-five or older) had a college degree, compared to 3.5 for those counted as black in the census or 3.2 for those counted as mestizos or mixed race. Meanwhile, in the United States the proportion of white college degree holders (20.5 percent) was twice as large as among blacks (10.7 percent); in Brazil it was nine times larger among whites (9.2 percent) than among blacks (1 percent).

Advances in education translated into impressive gains in the occupational structure. The proportion of nonwhites employed in professional services was similar to the proportion of whites. The same was true about retail, a sector that prior to 1959 had been basically out of reach for most Afro-Cubans. A national survey of people in managerial positions conducted in 1986 found that, although whites were overrepresented, the racial gap was very small. The proportion of blacks in manual labor activities in construction and manufacturing continued to be larger than whites', and blacks were also poorly represented in some of the upper echelons of government. But, particularly in comparison to other multiracial societies in the Americas, the Cuban occupational structure was significantly less unequal according to race. On top of that, salaries in the massive public sector (over 90 percent of employment at the time) were regulated by law, so income differences were also extremely low.

I do not mean to claim that the Cuban revolution had created a socialist paradise in the tropics. Cuban society had numerous and profound problems. My point is that, in terms of what Gutting calls the "deeper issue" behind racial problems and divisions, Cuba had advanced a great deal, dismantling key pillars of inequality and providing more or less egalitarian access to education, health, employment and recreation.

Yet the Cubans were not able to go past their own "outrage on race." Despite the massive changes discussed here, blackness continued to be associated with negative social and cultural features. Black was still ugly. Black still meant deficit of culture and refinement, rates of schooling notwithstanding. Black was still associated with violence, rape, robbery, crime. Black continued to be black. The justice system kept criminalizing black youths, sending a scandalous number of them to prison. In this regard, Cuba looked very much like the United States. We do not have good empirical data on this issue, but every available report and testimony confirms that in the 1980s blacks represented the vast majority of the inmate population in Cuba.

A study I conducted in 1987 (I lived in Cuba at the time) illustrates how racist perceptions could have devastating consequences for Afro-Cubans. This study dealt with "social dangerousness," a legal figure that the Cuban Criminal Code defined as conducts that, although not constitutive of a crime per se, suggested "a special proclivity" to break the law and were "manifestly against the norms of socialist morality." Those found to be "dangerous" could be deprived of freedom even without committing acts defined as crimes by the law. In other words, this was a legal institution particularly vulnerable to the influence of preconceptions and stereotypes. The conclusions of this study, which was never made public, were devastating: whereas nonwhites represented 34 percent of the adult population as a whole, their proportion among the socially "dangerous" was a staggering 78 percent. For each white person facing charges of social dangerousness, there were 5,430 white adults living in the city. Among blacks (excluding mestizos) the ratio was one in just 713.

In other words, despite Cuba's success in reducing racial inequality, young black males continued to be seen as potential criminals. Perceptions of people of African descent as racially differentiated and inferior continued to permeate Cuban society and institutions. The point is not that issues of economic justice and access to resources are irrelevant. Eliminating massive inequality is a necessary step if we are ever going to dismantle racial differences. There is, as Gutting argues, a deeper issue of access to basic resources that does need a solution. But the Cuban experience suggests that there are other equally deep issues that need to be addressed as well.

Those issues relate to what another writer here, George Yancy, in writing about the Trayvon Martin case, referred to as a "white gaze" that renders all black bodies dangerous and deviant. Unless we dismantle this gaze and its centuries-strong cultural pillars, it will be difficult to go past the outrage on race.

NOVEMBER 17, 2013

Is the United States a "Racial Democracy"?

—Jason Stanley and Vesla Weaver

I.

Plato's *Republic* is the wellspring from which all subsequent Western philosophy flows, and political philosophy is no exception. According to Plato, liberty is democracy's greatest good; it is that which "in a democratic city you will hear . . . is the most precious of all possessions." Subsequently, two notions of liberty emerged in the writings of democratic political philosophers. The dispute about which of these two notions of liberty is most central to human dignity is at the heart of Western philosophy. Both are central to American democracy. Indeed, it is best to think of these as two different aspects of the conception of liberty at the heart of American democracy, rather than distinct concepts.

The standard source of the distinction between two senses of "liberty" is a speech in 1819 by the great political theorist Benjamin Constant. The first, "the liberty of the ancients," consists in having a voice into the policies and representatives that govern us. The second, "the liberty of the moderns," is the right to pursue our private interests free from state oversight or control. Though the liberty of moderns is more familiar to Americans, it is in fact the liberty of the ancients that provides the fundamental justification for the central political ideals of the American democratic tradition. For example, we have the freedom of speech so that we can express our interests and political views in deliberations about policies and choice of representatives.

Given the centrality of liberty to democracy, one way to assess the democratic health of a state is by the fairness of the laws governing its removal. The fairness of a system of justice is measured by the degree to which its laws are fairly and consistently applied across all citizens. In a fair system, a group is singled out for punishment only insofar as its propensity for unjustified violations of the laws demands. What we call a *racial democracy* is one that unfairly applies the laws governing the removal of liberty primarily to citizens of one race, thereby singling out its members as especially unworthy of liberty, the coin of human dignity.

There is a vast chasm between democratic political ideals and a state that is a racial democracy. The philosopher Elizabeth Anderson argues that when political ideals diverge so widely from reality, the ideals themselves may prevent us from seeing the gap. Officially, the laws in the United States that govern when citizens can be sent to prison or questioned by the police are color-blind. But when the official story differs greatly from the reality of practice, the official story becomes a kind of mask that prevents us from perceiving it. And it seems clear that the practical reality of the criminal justice system in the United States is far from color-blind. The evidence suggests that the criminal justice system applies in a radically unbalanced way, placing disproportionate attention on our fellow black citizens. The United States has a legacy of enslavement followed by forced servitude of its black population. The threat that the political ideals of our country veil an underlying reality of racial democracy is therefore particularly disturbing.

II.

Starting in the 1970s, the United States has witnessed a drastic increase in the rate of black imprisonment, both absolutely and relative to whites. Just from 1980 to 2006, the black rate of incarceration (jail and prison) increased four times as much as the increase in the white rate. The increase in black prison admissions from 1960 to 1997 is 517 percent. In 1968, 15 percent of black adult males had been convicted of a felony and 7 percent had been to prison; by 2004, the numbers had risen to 33 percent and 17 percent, respectively.

About 9 percent of the world's prison population is black American (combining these two studies). If the system of justice in the United States were fair, and if the 38 million black Americans were as prone to crime as the average ethnic group in the world (where an ethnic group is, for example, the 61 million Italians, or the 45 million Hindu Gujarati), you would expect that black Americans would also be about 9 percent of the 2013 estimated world population of 7.135 billion people. There would then be well over 600 million black Americans in the world. If you think that black Americans are like anybody else, then the nation of black America should be the third largest nation on earth, twice as large as the United States. You can of course still think, in the face of these facts, that the United States prison laws are fairly applied and color-blind. But if you do, you almost certainly must accept that black Americans are among the most dangerous groups in the multithousand-year history of human civilization.

The Columbia professor Herbert Schneider told the following story about John Dewey. One day, in an ethics course, Dewey was trying to develop a theme about the criteria by which you should judge a culture. After having some trouble saying what he was trying to say, he stopped, looked out the window, paused for a long time and then said, "What I mean to say is that the best way to judge a culture is to see what kind of people are in the jails." Suppose you were a citizen of another country, looking from the outside at the composition of the United States prison population. Would you think that the formerly enslaved population of the United States was one of the most dangerous groups in history? Or would you rather suspect that tendrils of past mind-sets still remain?

Our view is that the system that has emerged in the United States over the past few decades is a racial democracy. It is widely thought that the civil rights movement in the 1960s at last realized the remarkable political ideals of the United States Constitution. If political ideals have the tendency to mask the reality of their violation, it will be especially difficult for our fellow American citizens to acknowledge that we are correct. More argument is required, which we supply in making the case for the following two claims.

First, encountering the police or the courts causes people to lose their status as participants in the political process, either officially, by incarceration and its consequences, or unofficially, via the strong correlation that exists between such encounters and withdrawal from political life. Secondly, blacks are unfairly and disproportionately the targets of the police and the courts. We briefly summarize part of the case for these claims here; they are substantiated at length elsewhere.

In the United States, 5.85 million people cannot vote because they are in prison or jail, currently under supervision (probation, for example), or live in one of the two states, Virginia and Kentucky, with lifetime bans on voting for those with felony convictions (nonviolent first-time drug offenders are no longer disenfranchised for life in the former). Yet the effects also extend to the large and growing ranks of the nation's citizens who experience involuntary contact with police regardless of whether their right to vote is formally eliminated.

As one of us has helped document in a forthcoming book, punishment and surveillance by itself causes people to withdraw from political participation—acts of engagement like voting or political activism. In fact, the effect on political participation of having been in jail or prison dwarfs other known factors affecting political participation, such as the impact of having a college-educated parent, being in the military or being in poverty.

In a large survey of mostly marginal men in American cities, the probability of voting declined by 8 percent for those who had been stopped and questioned by the police; by 16 percent for those who had experienced arrest; by 18 percent for those with a conviction; by 22 percent for those serving time in jail or prison; and, if this prison sentence was a year or more in duration, the probability of voting declined by an overwhelming 26 percent, even after accounting for race, socioeconomic position, self-reported engagement in criminal behavior and other factors. Citizens who have been subject to prison, jail or merely police surveillance not only withdrew but actively avoided dealings with government, preferring instead to "stay below the radar." As *subjects*, they learned that government was something to be avoided, not participated in. Fearful avoidance is not the mark of a democratic citizen.

"Man is by nature a political animal," declares Aristotle in the first book of his *Politics*. "Nature, as we often say, makes nothing in vain, and man is the only animal whom she has endowed with the gift of speech . . . the power of speech is intended to set forth the expedient and the inexpedient, and therefore likewise the just and the unjust." Aristotle here means that humans fully realize their nature in political participation, in the form of discussions and decision making with their fellow citizens about the affairs of state. To be barred from political participation is, for Aristotle, the most grievous possible affront to human dignity.

III.

In the United States, blacks are by far the most likely to experience punishment and surveillance and thus are most likely to be prevented from realizing human dignity. One in nine young black American men experienced the historic 2008 election from their prison and jail cells; 13 percent of black adult men could not cast a vote in the election because of a felony conviction. And among blacks lacking a high school degree, only one-fifth voted in that election because of incarceration, according to research conducted by Becky Pettit, a professor of sociology at the University of Washington. We do not know how many others did not get involved because they were trying to keep a low profile where matters of government are concerned.

If the American criminal justice system were color-blind, we would expect a tight link between committing crime and encountering the police. Yet most people stopped by police are not arrested, and most of those who are arrested are not found guilty; of those who are convicted, felons are the smallest group; and of those, many are non-serious offenders. Thus a large proportion of those who involuntarily encounter criminal justice—indeed, the majority of this group—have never been found guilty of a serious crime (or any crime) in a court of law. An involuntary encounter with the police by itself leads to withdrawal from political participation. If one group has an unjustifiably large rate of involuntary encounters, that group can be fairly regarded as being targeted for removal from the political process.

Evidence suggests that minorities experience contact with the police at rates that far outstrip their share of crime. One study found that the probability that a black male eighteen or nineteen years of age will be stopped by police in New York City at least once during 2006 is 92 percent. The probability for a Latino male of the same age group is 50 percent. For a young white man, it is 20 percent. In 90 percent of the stops of young minorities in 2011, there wasn't evidence of wrongdoing, and no arrest or citation occurred. In over half of the stops of minorities, the reason given for the stop was that the person made "furtive movements." In 60 percent of the stops, an additional reason listed for the stop was that the person was in a "high crime area."

Blacks are not necessarily having these encounters at greater rates than their white counterparts because they are more criminal. National surveys show that, with the exception of crack cocaine, blacks consistently report using drugs at *lower* levels than whites. Some studies also suggest that blacks are engaged in drug trafficking at lower levels. Yet once we account for their share of the population, blacks are ten times as likely to spend time in prison for offenses related to drugs.

Fairness would also lead to the expectation that once arrested, blacks would be equally likely to be convicted and sentenced as whites. But again, the evidence shows that black incarceration is out of step with black offending. Most of the large racial differences in sentencing for drugs and assault remain unexplained even once we take into account the black arrest rates for those crimes.

The founding political ideals of our country are, as ideals, some of the most admirable in history. They set a high moral standard, one that in the past we have failed even to approximate. We must not let their majestic glow blind us to the possibility that now is not so different from then. The gap between American ideals and American reality may remain just as cavernous as our nation's troubled history suggests.

JANUARY 12, 2014

What If We Occupied Language?

—H. Samy Alim

WHEN I FLEW OUT FROM THE SAN FRANCISCO AIRPORT LAST October, we crossed above the ports that Occupy Oakland helped shut down, and arrived in Germany to be met by traffic caused by Occupy Berlin protestors. But the movement has not only transformed public space; it has transformed the public discourse as well.

Occupy.

It is now nearly impossible to hear the word and not think of the Occupy movement.

Even as distinguished an expert as the lexicographer and columnist Ben Zimmer admitted as much this week: "Occupy," he said, is the odds-on favorite to be chosen as the American Dialect Society's word of the year.

It has already succeeded in shifting the terms of the debate, taking phrases like "debt ceiling" and "budget crisis" out of the limelight and putting terms like "inequality" and "greed" squarely in the center. This discursive shift has made it more difficult for Washington to continue to promote the spurious reasons for the financial meltdown and the unequal outcomes it has exposed and further produced.

To most, the irony of a progressive social movement using the term "occupy" to reshape how Americans think about issues of democracy and equality has been clear. After all, it is generally nations, armies and police who occupy, usually by force. And in this, the United States has been a leader. The American government is just now after nine years ending its overt occupation of Iraq, is still entrenched in Afghanistan, and is maintaining troops on the ground in dozens of countries worldwide. All this is not to obscure the fact that the United States as we know it came into being by way of an occupation—a gradual and devastatingly violent one that all but extinguished entire Native American populations across thousands of miles of land.

Yet in a very short time, this movement has dramatically changed how we think about occupation. In early September, "occupy" signaled ongoing military incursions. Now it signifies progressive political protest. It's no longer primarily about force of military power; instead, it signifies standing up to injustice, inequality and abuse of power. It's no longer about simply occupying a space; it's about transforming that space.

In this sense, Occupy Wall Street has occupied language, has made "occupy" its own. And, importantly, people from diverse ethnicities, cultures and languages have participated in this linguistic occupation—it is distinct from the history of forcible occupation in that it is built to accommodate all, not just the most powerful or violent.

As Geoff Nunberg, the longtime chair of the usage panel for *The American Heritage Dictionary*, and others have explained, the earliest usage of "occupy" in English that was linked to protest can be traced to English media descriptions of Italian demonstrations in the 1920s, in which workers "occupied" factories until their demands were met. This is a far cry from some of its earlier meanings. In fact, *The Oxford English Dictionary* tells us that "occupy" once meant "to have sexual intercourse with." One could imagine what a phrase like "Occupy Wall Street" might have meant back then.

In October, Zimmer, who is also the chair of the American Dialect Society's New Words Committee, noted on NPR's *On the Media* that the meaning of "occupy" has changed dramatically since its arrival into the English language in the fourteenth century. "It's almost always been used as a transitive verb," Zimmer said. "That's a verb that takes an object, so you occupy a place or a space. But then it became used as a rallying cry, without an object, just to mean to take part in what are now called the Occupy protests. It's being used as a modifier—Occupy protest, Occupy movement. So it's this very flexible word now that's filling many grammatical slots in the language."

What if we transformed the meaning of "occupy" yet again? Specifically, what if we thought of Occupy Language as more than the language of the Occupy movement, and began to think about it as a movement in and of itself? What kinds of issues would Occupy Language address? What would taking language back from its self-appointed "masters" look like? We might start by looking at these questions from the perspective of race and discrimination, and answer with how to foster fairness and equality in that realm.

Occupy Language might draw inspiration from both the way that the Occupy movement has reshaped definitions of "occupy," which teaches us that we give words meaning and that discourses are not immutable, *and* the way indigenous movements have contested its use, which teaches us to be ever mindful about how language both empowers and oppresses, unifies and isolates.

For starters, Occupy Language might first look inward. In a recent interview, Julian Padilla of the People of Color Working Group pushed the Occupy movement to examine its linguistic choices:

> To occupy means to hold space, and I think a group of anti-capitalists holding space on Wall Street is powerful, but I do wish the NYC movement would change its name to "decolonise Wall Street" to take into account history, indigenous critiques, people of colour and imperialism. . . . Occupying space is not inherently bad, it's all about who and how and why. When white colonizers occupy land, they don't just sleep there over night, they steal and destroy. When indigenous people occupied Alcatraz Island it was (an act of) protest.

This linguistic change can remind Americans that a majority of the 99 percent has benefited from the occupation of native territories. Occupy Language might also support the campaign to stop the media from using the word "illegal" to refer to "undocumented" immigrants. From the campaign's perspective, only inanimate objects and actions are labeled illegal in English; therefore the use of "illegals" to refer to human beings is dehumanizing. *The New York Times* style book currently asks writers to avoid terms like "illegal alien" and "undocumented," but says nothing about "illegals." Yet the *Times'* standards editor, Philip B. Corbett, did recently weigh in on this, saying that the term "illegals" has an "unnecessarily pejorative tone" and that "it's wise to steer clear."

Pejorative, discriminatory language can have real-life consequences. In this case, activists worry about the coincidence of the rise in the use of the term "illegals" and the spike in hate crimes against all Latinos. As difficult as it might be to prove causation here, the National Institute for Latino Policy reports that the FBI's annual Hate Crime Statistics show that Latinos comprised *two-thirds* of the victims of ethnically motivated hate crimes in 2010. When some*one* is repeatedly described as some*thing*, language has quietly paved the way for violent action.

But Occupy Language should concern itself with more than just the words we use; it should also work toward eliminating language-based racism and discrimination. In the legal system, CNN recently reported that the US Justice Department alleges that Arizona's infamous Sheriff Joe Arpaio, among other offenses, has discriminated against "Latino inmates with limited English by punishing them and denying critical services." In education, as linguistic anthropologist Ana Celia Zentella notes, hostility toward those who speak "English with an accent" (Asians, Latinos and African-Americans) continues to be a problem. In housing, the National Fair Housing Alliance has long recognized "accents" as playing a significant role in housing discrimination. On the job market, language-based discrimination intersects with issues of race, ethnicity, class and national origin to make it more difficult for well-qualified applicants with an "accent" to receive equal opportunities.

In the face of such widespread language-based discrimination, Occupy Language can be a critical, progressive linguistic movement that exposes how language is used as a means of social, political and economic control. By occupying language, we can expose how educational, political, and social institutions use language to further marginalize oppressed groups; resist colonizing language practices that elevate certain languages over others; resist attempts to define people with terms rooted in negative stereotypes; and begin to reshape the public discourse about our communities, and about the central role of language in racism and discrimination.

As the global Occupy movement has shown, words can move entire nations of people—even the world—to action. Occupy Language, as a movement, should speak to the power of language to transform how we think about the past, how we act in the present, and how we envision the future.

DECEMBER 21, 2011

Does Immigration Mean "France Is Over"?

—Justin E. H. Smith

I.

PARIS—It is difficult to go more than a day in France without hearing someone express the conviction that the greatest problem in the country is its ethnic minorities, that the presence of immigrants compromises the identity of France itself. This conviction is typically expressed without any acknowledgment of the country's historical responsibility as a colonial power for the presence of former colonial subjects in metropolitan France, nor with any willingness to recognize that France will be ethnically diverse from here on out, and that it's the responsibility of the French as much as of the immigrants to make this work.

In the past year I have witnessed incessant stop-and-frisks of young black men in the Gare du Nord; in contrast with New York, here in Paris this practice is scarcely debated. I was told by a taxi driver as we passed through a black neighborhood, "I hope you got your shots. You don't need to go to Africa anymore to get a tropical disease." On numerous occasions, French strangers have offered up the observation to me, in reference to ethnic minorities going about their lives in the capital, "This is no longer France. France is over." There is a constant, droning presupposition in virtually all social interactions that a clear and meaningful division can be made between the people who make up the real France and the impostors.

I arrived here in 2012—an American recently teaching in a Canadian university—to take a position at a French university in Paris. I had long been a moderately interested observer of French history, culture, and politics, but had never lived here for any length of time, and had on previous stays never grown attuned to the deep rifts that mark so much of daily life here.

When I am addressed by strangers anxious about the fate of their country, I try to reply patiently. They hear my American accent, but this in itself does not dissuade them, for I belong to a different category of foreigner. I am not read as an "immigrant," but rather as an "expatriate," here for voluntary and probably frivolous reasons, rather than out of economic necessity or fear for my own survival or freedom. This division is not just a street-level prejudice: it is also written into the procedure at French immigration offices, where all foreigners must go to obtain their residence permits, but where the Malians and Congolese are taken into one room, and Americans and Swedes into another. For the former, the procedure has an air of quarantine, and the attitude of the officials is something resembling that of prison guards; for the latter, the visit to the immigration office feels rather more like a welcome ceremony, and everything about our interaction with the officials bespeaks a presumption of equality.

Equality is, of course, one of the virtues on which the French Republic was founded, yet critics of the Enlightenment philosophy behind the revolution have long noticed a double standard: when equality is invoked, these critics note, it is understood that this is equality *among equals*. Political and social inequality is allowed to go on as before, as long as it is presumed that this is rooted in a natural inequality. In the late eighteenth century, such a presumption informed the reactions of many in the French to the revolution led by François-Dominique Toussaint Louverture in Haiti, who was himself inspired by the events of 1789 and who took the idea of equality to be one with universal scope.

For most of the history of the French Republic, the boundary between the equal and the unequal was determined by the dynamics of empire: equality within continental France was in principle absolute, while in the colonies it was something that had to be cultivated—only if a colonial subject could demonstrate full embodiment in his manners and tastes of the French identity was he to be considered truly equal.

With the contraction of the empire and the reorientation of French nationalism from an imperial to a cultural focus, the distinction between equal and unequal contracted from a global to a local scale. Francophones from around the world began to move to metropolitan France in large numbers, but now their status was transformed from that of colonial subjects to that, simply, of foreigners. But of course the fact that these unequal subjects have settled in France has very much to do with the historical legacy of French imperialism; Francophone Africans do not choose to come to France on a whim, but because of a long history of imposed Frenchness at home.

II.

I became a philosopher, like many others, in large part because I imagined that doing so would enable me to rise above the murky swamp of local attachment, of ethnic and provincial loyalty, and to embrace the world as a whole, to be a true cosmopolitan. Yet history shows that many philosophers only grow more attached to their national or ethnic identity as a result of their philosophical education.

This second tendency seems particularly widespread in Europe today, and most of all in France. Many Americans imagine that French philosophy is dominated by mysterians like the late Jacques Derrida, who famously beguiled innocent followers with koan-like proclamations. But a far more dangerous subspecies of French philosopher is the "public intellectual," whose proclamations, via the French mass media, are perfectly comprehensible, indeed not just simple but downright simplistic, and often completely irresponsible.

Take, for example, the self-styled philosopher Alain Finkielkraut, who in his recent popular book, *L'identité malheureuse* (The unhappy identity), proclaims, in effect, that immigration is destroying French cultural identity. He bemoans the "métissage" of France, a term one often sees in the slogans of the far right, which translates roughly as "mongrelization." The author, whose father was a Polish immigrant and a survivor of Auschwitz, and who has made much throughout his career of what he calls "the duty of memory," claims to be defending the values of the "français de souche"—the real French. In this way, he is stoking the rising xenophobia in France, a trend that has been exacerbated here, as elsewhere in Europe, by recent economic uncertainty.

Is there any justification for the two-tiered distinction between expatriates and immigrants, or for the extra impediments members of the latter group face when they try to settle in a new country? Nativist Europeans such as Finkielkraut will often express a concern about being "overrun" by members of ethnic groups from economically disadvantaged states or regions. Most of us can agree that even if there is not an absolute right to preserve one's culture's purity, it is at least a genuine good to be able to spend one's life surrounded by others who share many of the same values and traditions. Something would be lost if, say, massive immigration led to a sudden shift in the demographics of Iceland, so that native Icelanders were now a minority in that once homogeneous island nation—and this would be a loss both for the country itself, as well as for those of us on the outside who value something akin to the cultural equivalent of biodiversity.

But there is nowhere in Europe where anything remotely like a shift on such a scale is taking place, even in the countries that have seen the most immigration, like France and Britain. Alongside the genuine good of a life spent among others who share one's values and traditions, there is also what the philosopher Michael Dummett describes in his influential work *On Immigration and Refugees* as the right to live one's life as a first-class citizen. This right, he notes, depends in part on the conduct of a state, and in part on the behavior of its people. Whether or not the right of immigrants to first-class citizenship is set up in conflict with the right of earlier inhabitants to cultural preservation has very much to do with both state policy and with popular opinion.

III.

Even if the numbers of immigrants in Europe were much higher, it would be an illusion to suppose that the immigrants are mounting a concerted effort to change the character of the place to which they have come. Talk of "overrunning" and "invasion" is analogical, and in fact describes much more accurately the earlier motion of European states into their former colonies, a motion that, again, is a crucial part of the account of patterns of migration toward Europe today. Immigration in Europe, as in, say, the Southwestern United States or within the former Soviet Union, is determined by deep historical links and patterns of circulation between the immigrants' countries of origin—in France's case, particularly North Africa and sub-Saharan Françafrique—and the places of destination.

Europe has enjoyed constant traffic—human, financial, material, and cultural—with the extra-European world since the end of the Renaissance, yet within a few centuries of the great global expansion at the end of the fifteenth century a myth would set in throughout Europe that European nations are entirely constituted from within, that their cultures grow up from the soil and belong to a fixed parcel of land as if from time immemorial. It is this conception of the constitution of a nation that has led to the fundamental split that still distinguishes European immigration policies from those of the United States.

The American approach to immigration is plainly rooted in historical exigencies connected to the appropriation of a continent, and it is this same history of appropriation that continues to induce shame in most Euro-Americans who might otherwise be tempted to describe themselves as natives. America has to recognize its hybrid and constructed identity, since the only people who can plausibly lay claim to native status are the very ones this new identity was conjured to displace. But in Europe no similar displacement plays a role in historical memory: Europeans can more easily imagine themselves to be their own natives and so can imagine any demographic impact on the continent from the extra-European world as the harbinger of an eventual total displacement.

There are values that are not easy to mock or dismiss informing European nativist anxiety. These values are not completely unconnected to the various movements to defend local traditions: the celebration of terroir and of "slow food," the suspicion of multinational corporations. But like the celebrated tomato and so many other staples of various European cuisines, European cultural identity, too, is a product of long-standing networks of global exchange. These networks have tended to function for the enrichment of Europe and to the detriment of the rest of the world for the past several centuries, and it is this imbalance that in large part explains current patterns of immigration. Europe has never been self-contained, and its role in the world has both made it rich and left it with a unique legacy of responsibility to the great bulk of the world from which this wealth came.

I witness the present situation from a position of privilege, as a special kind of foreigner: not the kind who is thought to be here to take up resources and to threaten tradition, but rather, it is supposed, to celebrate these traditions and to passively assent to native sentiments. The privilege, for me, is not just that I am not the target of discrimination, but also that I am able to learn quite a bit that would be kept from me if I had a different kind of accent or darker skin. And while it is disheartening, what I hear in the streets is really only an echo of the rhetoric of politicians and purported intellectuals, who have found it convenient to blame the most powerless members of French society for the instability of the present and the uncertainty of the future.

JANUARY 5, 2014

FREEDOM FROM THE BARREL OF A GUN

Who Needs a Gun?

—*Gary Gutting*

Ⅰɴ Sᴇᴘᴛᴇᴍʙᴇʀ, ᴛʜᴇ Nᴀᴠʏ Yᴀʀᴅ; ɪɴ Nᴏᴠᴇᴍʙᴇʀ, ᴀ ʀᴀᴄɪᴀʟʟʏ fraught shooting in Michigan and a proposed stand-your-ground law in Ohio; now the first anniversary of the Newtown massacre—there's no avoiding the brutal reality of guns in America. Once again, we feel the need to say something, but we know the old arguments will get us nowhere. What's the point of another impassioned plea or a new subtlety of constitutional law or further complex analyses of statistical data?

Our discussions typically start from the right to own a gun, go on to ask how, if at all, that right should be limited, and wind up with intractable disputes about the balance between the right and the harm that can come from exercising it. I suggest that we could make more progress if each of us asked a more direct and personal question: Should I own a gun?

A gun is a tool, and we choose tools based on their function. The primary function of a gun is to kill or injure people or animals. In the case of people, the only reason I might have to shoot them—or threaten to do so—is that they are immediately threatening serious harm. So a first question about owning a gun is whether I'm likely to be in a position to need one to protect human life. A closely related question is whether, if I were in such a position, the gun would be available and I would be able to use it effectively.

Unless you live in (or frequent) dangerous neighborhoods or have family or friends likely to threaten you, it's very unlikely that you'll need a gun for self-defense. Further, counterbalancing any such need is the fact that guns are dangerous. If I have one loaded and readily accessible in an emergency (and what good is it if I don't?), then there's a nonnegligible chance that it will lead to great harm. A gun at hand can easily push a family quarrel, a wave of depression or a child's curiosity in a fatal direction.

Even when a gun makes sense in principle as a means of self-defense, it may do more harm than good if I'm not trained to use it well. I may panic and shoot a family member coming home late, fumble around and allow an unarmed burglar to take my gun, have a cleaning or loading accident. The NRA rightly sets high standards for gun safety. If those unable or unwilling to meet these standards gave up their guns, there might well be a lot fewer gun owners.

Guns do have uses other than defense against attackers. There may, for example, still be a few people who actually need to hunt to feed their families. But most hunting now is recreational and does not require keeping weapons at home. Hunters and their families would be much safer if the guns and ammunition were securely stored away from their homes and available only to those with licenses during the appropriate season. Target shooting, likewise, does not require keeping guns at home.

Finally, there's the idea that citizens need guns so they can, if need be, oppose the force of a repressive government. Those who think there are current (or likely future) government actions in this country that would require armed resistance are living a paranoid fantasy. The idea that armed American citizens could stand up to our military is beyond fantasy.

Once we balance the potential harms and goods, most of us—including many current gun owners—don't have a good reason to keep guns in their homes. This conclusion follows quite apart from whether we have a right to own guns or what restrictions should be put on this right. Also, the conclusion derives from what makes sense for each of us as individuals and so doesn't require support from contested interpretations of statistical data.

I entirely realize that this line of thought will not convince the most impassioned gun supporters, who see owning guns as fundamental to their way of life. But about 70 million Americans own guns and only about 4 million belong to the NRA, which must include a large number of the most impassioned. So there's reason to think that many gun owners would be open to reconsidering the dangers their weapons pose. Also, almost 30 percent of gun owners don't think that guns make a household safer, and only 48 percent cite protection (rather than hunting, target shooting, etc.) as their main reason for having a gun.

It's one thing to be horrified at gun violence. It's something else to see it as a meaningful threat to your own existence. Our periodic shock at mass shootings and gang wars has little effect on our gun culture because most people don't see guns as a particular threat to them. This is why opposition to gun violence has lacked the intense personal commitment of those who see guns as essential to their safety—or even their self-identity.

I'm not suggesting that opponents of gun violence abandon political action. We need to make it harder to buy guns (through background checks, waiting periods, etc.) both for those with criminal intentions and for law-abiding citizens who have no real need. But on the most basic level, much of our deadly violence occurs because we so often have guns readily available. Their mere presence makes suicide, domestic violence and accidents more likely. The fewer people with guns at hand, the less gun violence.

It's easier to get people to see that they don't want something than that they don't have a right to it. Focusing on the need rather than the right to own a gun, many may well conclude that for them a gun is more a danger than a protection. Those fewer guns will make for a safer country.

DECEMBER 10, 2013

The Weapons Continuum

—Michael Boylan

HOW DO PEOPLE JUSTIFY THEIR OWNERSHIP OF GUNS?

In the outcry that follows nearly every case of mass gun violence in the United States, there is nearly always a fixation on "the right to bear arms" clause in the Bill of Rights. There is, however, a specific human rights claim that justifies gun ownership that should instead be the focus of this debate: self-defense.

"Protection from unwarranted bodily harm" is a basic right that we all can claim. It makes sense that people should be able to possess a weapon appropriate to that end. But what sort of weapon? There are two important concepts that can help us make this determination: (a) weapon damage coefficient (basically, the extent of damage that the use of a particular weapon is designed to cause) and (b) minimum force necessary to produce a result (that result being protection against bodily harm).

Trauma surgeons I've spoken with on this matter report to me that those admitted to intensive care, for the most part, are *not* those who have suffered from weapons with a low damage coefficient: fists and small percussive objects (like sticks, books, china plates and thin drinking glasses). These patients have a very high recovery rate. Those who are treated for knife wounds are next—they have a lower recovery rate. Then come those admitted for injuries caused by larger percussive objects (like thick bottles, bats, and chairs). Then there are the firearms injuries.

With firearms, the weapon damage coefficient makes a jump in kind. Death and permanent injury rates are significantly higher. When the firearms are rapid-fire automatic weapons (like assault weapons), not only does the rate get even higher but so does the collateral damage (more people killed or injured aside from the intended victim). This trend continues with rocket-propelled grenade launchers. No longer is one able to contain the target to a single person, but the target will almost by necessity include a score or more of victims (and considerably more property damage). Next are antiaircraft handheld devices, and finally, if one continues on the weapons continuum, there is the nuclear bomb. Depending upon where it is detonated, it could kill as many as six million people in one of the world's most populous cities.

Weapons exist on a continuum. Some weapons advocates seem intent on moving along the continuum in order to possess weapons of higher and higher damage coefficient. Their rationale is that *the bad guys will have more powerful weapons and so must I in order to defend myself.* The logical end of such a scenario is the destruction of humankind. Since no rational person wants that, everyone must, upon pain of logical contradiction of what it means to be human (an agent seeking purposeful action to achieve what he thinks is good), agree that there must be weapons control somewhere on the continuum.

Weapons control is a given. No one can logically claim that everyone should be able to possess nuclear weapons. Thus everyone must agree to the concept of weapons control somewhere on the continuum. This point is logically necessary. The only question is where on the continuum of weapons do we begin banning weapons? And as we see in the case of state nuclear proliferation, the fact that rogue countries may develop nuclear weapons does not deter us from trying to stop each new potential member in the ultimate annihilation club. Among citizens of any country, the fact that weapons bans are hard to enforce is not an argument against trying to enforce them. Moral "oughts" (in a deontological sense) are not determined by what is easy but by what is *right*.

Second, we have the "minimal force dictum," which says that

instead of the aforementioned escalating scenario, individuals should always employ the minimum force necessary to deter a threat, and that they should first depend upon law enforcement (in developed societies) to protect them.

The first condition refers to stopping an attack with words or fleeing the scene if no weapon is necessary. If a fight is going to occur and you can stop it with your fists, then they should be used. If a stick is needed, then use it only so long as one is in jeopardy. The problem occurs when one cannot thwart an attack with these natural means. Should people resort to knives or even guns? For the sake of clarity, let us call these situations *extreme*. There might be some personal prudential advantages to using weapons like guns for personal protection, but there are alternatively some severe dangers to public health.

This leads to the second condition: people should first depend upon law enforcement to protect themselves. What stands behind this provision is very important: the real good of having a social structure in which individuals give up certain individual liberties in order to become citizens of a society. When one leaves the state of nature, then one relinquishes the right personally to inflict punishment upon wrongdoers. This right is given over to the society (the sovereign—which in a democracy is the people; see John Locke).

One condition for a citizen entering a society is the trust that societal institutions will protect her and run the society fairly. If one is unhappy with the current state of affairs, the legitimate venue is the ballot box and not a rifle or some other weapon. The rule of law dictates that within a society we rely upon our police and legal system to make us secure. The inclination to resort to gun ownership to do this is really a form of vigilantism. This worldview arises when people seek to exercise state-of-nature authority when they have left the state of nature. This is really a form of the free-rider mentality and works contrary to the rule of law. This vigilante worldview ends up making us all less secure.

I agree that the world *is* a dangerous place, but the greatest threats occur because of viruses and bacteria. There is a greater cause to be afraid of drug-resistant tuberculosis than there is being shot while on the way to work. There is also statistically more cause to be afraid of driving on the freeways of the United States than there is of being a potential victim of a criminal wielding a weapon. The reason for this failure in accurate risk assessment is that people have false conceptions of individual dangers and what is and what is not in their power.

This inability to adequately assess risk and socially responsible avoidance strategies causes irrational response reactions. This is the acceleration on the continuum of the aforementioned weapon damage coefficients. There must be a limit. The question is how to draw it and how to interpret the minimum force dictum.

I have argued elsewhere that the imagined safety of owning a gun is illusionary for most ordinary people. Part of this illusion concerns the dual concepts of (a) ease of use, balanced by (b) apparent ease of effective use. These are not the same; and because of this much confusion results. Under the ease-of-use criterion, most low caliber handguns are easy to use. You point and pull the trigger. Low caliber handguns have virtually no kickback. This ease of use makes them the weapon of choice for teenage gangs and the nonorganized-crime-drug subculture—when was the last time you heard of a *drive-by knifing*?

But the ease of use is not the same as ease of effective use. Those drive-by shootings often miss the real target and kill bystanders. This is because it is not easy to be an effective pistol shooter. Unless one regularly puts in practice time at a firing range and engages in emergency drills, the risk of being ineffective with one's firearm and causing injury to innocents is significant.

A colleague of mine in our criminal justice program, Michael Bolton (who was an Arlington County police officer for more than twenty years), told me that even experienced police officers need constant practice or they will not be allowed to carry guns. He told me that often experienced officers thought that such checkups were not necessary, but Bolton assured me that the regulations were there for a fact-based reason: guns carry such a high damage coefficient, and are so difficult to use effectively—particularly in emergency situations—that they should only be in the hands of people competent to carry them. This reality of the difficulty of *effective use* is often dismissed by the general public because of the simple *ease of use*. Most ordinary citizens do not credit the need for constant training and practice in order to be responsible gun owners.

How many civilians who wish to carry guns would submit to semiannual range reviews and emergency drills in order to keep their licenses? Without such continuing education and documented competency, a gun owner is very likely to falsely believe that he is safe and protected (because of ease of use and the high damage coefficient) when he really is not (because guns require a high level of skill in order to be used effectively). Those who fall short of such accountability standards are a public health threat that is more dangerous than their constructed worldview of fear.

DECEMBER 18, 2012

The Freedom of an Armed Society

—Firmin DeBrabander

THE NIGHT OF THE SHOOTINGS AT SANDY HOOK ELEMENTARY School in Newtown, CT, I was in the car with my wife and children, working out details for our eldest son's twelfth birthday the following Sunday—convening a group of friends at a showing of the film *The Hobbit*. The memory of the Aurora movie theater massacre was fresh in his mind, so he was concerned that it not be a late-night showing. At that moment, like so many families, my wife and I were weighing whether to turn on the radio and expose our children to coverage of the school shootings in Connecticut. We did. The car was silent in the face of the flood of gory details. When the story was over, there was a long, thoughtful pause in the back of the car. Then my eldest son asked if he could be homeschooled.

That incident brought home to me what I have always suspected but found difficult to articulate: an armed society—especially as we prosecute it at the moment in this country—is the opposite of a civil society.

The Newtown shootings occurred at a peculiar time in gun rights history in this nation. On one hand, since the mid-1970s, fewer households each year on average have had a gun. Gun control advocates should be cheered by that news, but it is eclipsed by a flurry of contrary developments. As has been well publicized, gun sales have steadily risen over the past few years and spiked with each of Obama's election victories.

Furthermore, of the weapons that proliferate among the armed public, an increasing number are high caliber weapons (the weapon of choice in the goriest shootings in recent years). Then there is the legal landscape, which looks bleak for the gun control crowd.

Every state except for Illinois has a law allowing the carrying of concealed weapons—and just last week, a federal court struck down Illinois's ban. States are now lining up to allow guns on college campuses. In September, Colorado joined four other states in such a move, and statehouses across the country are preparing similar legislation. And of course, there was Oklahoma's ominous open carry law approved by voters this election day—the fifteenth of its kind, in fact—which, as the name suggests, allows those with a special permit to carry weapons in the open, with a holster on their hip.

Individual gun ownership—and gun violence—has long been a distinctive feature of American society, setting us apart from the other industrialized democracies of the world. Recent legislative developments, however, are progressively bringing guns out of the private domain, with the ultimate aim of enshrining them in public life. Indeed, the NRA strives for a day when the open carry of powerful weapons might be normal, a fixture even, of any visit to the coffee shop or grocery store—or classroom.

As NRA president Wayne LaPierre expressed in a recent statement on the organization's website, more guns equal more safety, by their account. A favorite gun rights saying is "An armed society is a polite society." If we allow ever more people to be armed, at any time, in any place, this will provide a powerful deterrent to potential criminals. Or if more citizens were armed—like principals and teachers in the classroom, for example—they could halt senseless shootings ahead of time, or at least early on, and save society a lot of heartache and bloodshed.

As ever more people are armed in public, however—even brandishing weapons on the street—this is no longer recognizable as a civil society. Freedom is vanished at that point.

And yet, gun rights advocates famously maintain that individual gun ownership, even of high caliber weapons, is the defining mark of our freedom as such, and the ultimate guarantee of our enduring liberty. Deeper reflection on their argument exposes basic fallacies.

In her book *The Human Condition*, the philosopher Hannah Arendt states that "violence is mute." According to Arendt, speech dominates and distinguishes the polis, the highest form of human association, which is devoted to the freedom and equality of its component members. Violence—and the threat of it—is a prepolitical manner of communication and control, characteristic of undemocratic organizations and hierarchical relationships. For the ancient Athenians who practiced an incipient, albeit limited form of democracy (one that we surely aim to surpass), violence was characteristic of the master-slave relationship, not that of free citizens.

Arendt offers two points that are salient to our thinking about guns: For one, they insert a hierarchy of some kind, but fundamental nonetheless, and thereby undermine equality. But furthermore, guns pose a monumental challenge to freedom, and in particular, the liberty that is the hallmark of any democracy worthy of the name—that is, freedom of speech. Guns do communicate, after all, but in a way that is contrary to free speech aspirations: for, guns chasten speech.

This becomes clear if only you pry a little more deeply into the NRA's logic behind an armed society. An armed society is polite, by their thinking, precisely because guns would compel everyone to tamp down eccentric behavior and refrain from actions that might seem threatening. The suggestion is that guns liberally interspersed throughout society would cause us all to walk gingerly—not make any sudden, unexpected moves—and watch what we say, how we act, whom we might offend.

As our Constitution provides, however, liberty entails precisely the freedom to be reckless, within limits, also the freedom to insult and offend as the case may be. The Supreme Court has repeatedly upheld our right to experiment in offensive language and ideas, and in some cases, offensive action and speech. Such experimentation is inherent to our freedom as such. But guns by their nature do not mix with this experiment—they don't mix with taking offense. They are combustible ingredients in assembly and speech.

I often think of the armed protestor who showed up to one of the famously raucous town hall hearings on Obamacare in the summer of 2009. The media was very worked up over this man, who bore a sign that invoked a famous quote of Thomas Jefferson, accusing the president of tyranny. But no one engaged him at the protest; no one dared approach him even, for discussion or debate—though this was a town hall meeting, intended for just such purposes. Such is the effect of guns on speech—and assembly. Like it or not, they transform the bearer and end the conversation in some fundamental way. They announce that the conversation is not completely unbounded, unfettered and free; there is or can be a limit to negotiation and debate—definitively.

The very power and possibility of free speech and assembly rests on their nonviolence. The power of the Occupy Wall Street movement, as well as the Arab Spring protests, stemmed precisely from their nonviolent nature. This power was made evident by the ferocity of government response to the Occupy movement. Occupy protestors across the country were increasingly confronted by police in military-style garb and affect.

Imagine what this would have looked like had the protestors been armed: in the face of the New York Police Department assault on Zuccotti Park, there might have been armed insurrection in the streets. The nonviolent nature of protest in this country ensures that it can occur.

Gun rights advocates also argue that guns provide the ultimate insurance of our freedom, insofar as they are the final deterrent against encroaching centralized government, and an executive branch run amok with power. Any suggestion of limiting guns rights is greeted by ominous warnings that this is a move of expansive, would-be despotic government. It has been the means by which gun rights advocates withstand even the most seemingly rational gun control measures. An assault weapons ban, smaller ammunition clips for guns, longer background checks on gun purchases— these are all measures centralized government wants, they claim, in order to exert control over us and ultimately impose its arbitrary will. I have often suspected, however, that contrary to holding centralized authority in check, broad individual gun ownership gives the powers-that-be exactly what they want.

After all, a population of privately armed citizens is one that is increasingly fragmented, and vulnerable as a result. Private gun ownership invites retreat into extreme individualism—I heard numerous calls for homeschooling in the wake of the Newtown shootings—and nourishes the illusion that I can be my own police, or military, as the case may be. The NRA would have each of us steeled for impending government aggression, but it goes without saying that individually armed citizens are no match for government force. The NRA argues against that interpretation of the Second Amendment that privileges armed militias over individuals, and yet it seems clear that armed militias, at least in theory, would provide a superior check on autocratic government.

As Michel Foucault pointed out in his detailed study of the mechanisms of power, nothing suits power so well as extreme individualism. In fact, he explains, political and corporate interests aim at nothing less than "individualization," since it is far easier to manipulate a collection of discrete and increasingly independent individuals than a community. Guns undermine just that—community. Their pervasive, open presence would sow apprehension, suspicion, mistrust and fear—all emotions that are corrosive of community and civic cooperation. To that extent, then, guns give license to autocratic government.

Our gun culture promotes a fatal slide into extreme individualism. It fosters a society of atomistic individuals, isolated before power—and one another—and in the aftermath of shootings such as at Newtown, paralyzed with fear. That is not freedom, but quite its opposite. And as the Occupy movement makes clear, also the demonstrators that precipitated regime change in Egypt and Myanmar last year, assembled masses don't require guns to exercise and secure their freedom and wield world-changing political force. Arendt and Foucault reveal that power does not lie in armed individuals, but in assembly—and everything conducive to that.

DECEMBER 16, 2012

Is American Nonviolence Possible?

—*Todd May*

*The choice is not between violence and nonviolence but between nonvio-
lence and nonexistence.*

—MARTIN LUTHER KING JR.

W̶E ARE STEEPED IN VIOLENCE.

This past week was, of course, a searing reminder: Monday's bombing at the Boston Marathon and the ensuing manhunt that ended on
Friday with the death of one suspect and the capture of another, his
brother, dominated the news. But there were other troubling, if less
traumatic, reminders, too. On Tuesday, a 577-page report by the Constitution Project concluded that the United States had engaged in torture after the September 11 attacks. On Wednesday, a turning point in
the heated national debate on gun control was reached when the United
States Senate dropped consideration of some minimal restrictions on
the sale and distribution of guns. Looming above all this is the painful
memory of the mass killing at Sandy Hook Elementary School.

Now is as good a time as any to reflect on our responses to the
many recent horrors that seem to have engulfed us, and to consider
whether we can hope to move from an ethos of violence to one of nonviolence. Facing ourselves squarely at this difficult moment might
provide a better lesson for the future than allowing ourselves to once
again give in to blind fury.

We might begin by asking the question, *Who are we now?*

Clearly, we are a violent country. Our murder rate is three to five times that of most other industrialized countries. The massacres that regularly take place here are predictable in their occurrence, if not in their time and place. Moreover, and more telling, our response to violence is typically more violence. We display our might—or what is left of it—abroad in order to address perceived injustices or a threat to our interests. We still have not rid ourselves of the death penalty, a fact that fills those in other countries with disbelief. Many of us, in response to the mindless gun violence around us, prescribe more guns as the solution, as the Republicans sought to do during the gun debate. And we torture people. It is as though, in thinking that the world responds only to violence, we reveal ourselves rather than the world.

Why is this? How has the United States become so saturated in slaughter?

There are, of course, many reasons, but three stand out, one of which is deep and long-standing and the others are of more recent vintage. The deep reason lies in our competitive individualism. Americans are proud of our individualism, and indeed it is not entirely a curse. To believe that one has a responsibility to create oneself rather than relying on others for sustenance has its virtues. No doubt many of the advances—scientific, technological and artistic—that have emerged from the United States have their roots in the striving of individuals whose belief in themselves bolstered their commitment to their work. However, the dark side of this individualism is a wariness of others and a rejection of the social solidarity characteristic of countries like Denmark, Sweden, New Zealand and, at least to some extent, France. We make it, if we do make it, but we do so alone. Our neighboring citizens are not so much our fellows as our competitors.

The second reason is the decline of our ability to control events in the world. We might date this decline from our military failure in Vietnam, or, if we prefer, more recently to the debacle in Iraq. In any event, it is clear that the United States cannot impose its will as it did during much of the twentieth century. We live in a different world now, and this makes many of us insecure. We long for a world more cooperative with our wishes than the one we now live in. Our insecurity, in turn, reinforces our desire to control, which reinforces violence. If we cannot control events in the world, this must be a result not of our impotence or the complexity of the world's problems but of our unwillingness to "man up." And so we tell ourselves fairy tales about what would have happened if we had committed to victory in Vietnam or bombed one or another country back to the Stone Age.

The third reason is economic. The welfare state has been in decline for more than thirty years now. The embrace of classical liberalism or neoliberalism erodes social solidarity. Each of us is an investor, seeking the best return on our money, our energies, our relationships, indeed our lives. We no longer count on government, which is often perceived as the enemy. And we no longer have obligations to those with whom we share the country, or the planet. It is up to each of us to take our freedom and use it wisely. Those who do not are not unlucky or impoverished. They are simply imprudent.

Competitive individualism, insecurity, neoliberalism: the triad undergirding our penchant for violence. This, as much as anything else, is the current exceptionalism of America. Others are not our partners, nor even our colleagues. They are our competitors or our enemies. They are hardly to be recognized, much less embraced. They are to be vanquished.

What would the alternative, nonviolence, look like? And what does it require of us?

We must understand first that nonviolence is not passivity. It is instead creative activity. That activity takes place within particular limits. To put the point a bit simply, those limits are the recognition of others as fellow human beings, even when they are our adversaries. That recognition does not require that we acquiesce to the demands of others when we disagree. Rather, it requires that our action, even when it coerces the other (as boycotts, strikes, sit-ins and human blockades often do), does not aim to destroy that other in his or her humanity. It requires that we recognize others as fellow human beings, even when they are on the other side of the barricades.

This recognition limits what we can do, but at the same time it forces us to be inventive. No longer is it a matter of bringing superior firepower to bear. Now we must think more rigorously about how to respond, how to make our voices heard and our aims prevail. In a way it is like writing a Shakespearean sonnet, where the fourteen-line structure and iambic pentameter require thoughtful and creative work rather than immediate and overwhelming response.

To recognize someone's humanity is, in perhaps the most important way, to recognize him or her as an equal. Each of us, nonviolence teaches, carries our humanity within us. That humanity cannot always be appealed to. In some cases, as with the tragedy at Sandy Hook, it can even become nearly irrelevant. However, in all but the most extreme cases nonviolence summons us to recognize that humanity even when it cannot serve as the basis for negotiation or resolution. It demands that we who act do so with a firm gaze upon the face of the other. It demands the acknowledgment that we are all fragile beings, nexuses of hope and fear, children of some mother, and perhaps parents to others: that is, no more and no less than fellow human beings in a world fraught with imponderables.

Can we do this? Are we capable at this moment of taking on the mantle of nonviolence?

The lessons are already there in our history. The civil rights movement is perhaps the most shining example of nonviolence in our human legacy. After 9/11, after Hurricane Katrina and Hurricane Sandy, and now, in the immediate on-the-ground responses to the Boston bombing, Americans pulled together with those they did not know in order to restore the web of our common existence. We are indeed violent, but we have shown flashes of nonviolence—that is to say moments where our competitive individualism, our insecurity, our desire for the highest return on our investment of time and money has been trumped by the vividness of the likeness of others. Granted, these are only moments. They have not lasted. But they teach us that when it comes to nonviolent relations with others, we are not entirely bereft.

What would it require for these lessons to become sedimented in our collective soul? There is much work to be done. We must begin to see our fellow human beings as precisely that: fellows. They need not be friends, but they must be counted as worthy of our respect, bearers of dignity in their own right. Those who struggle must no longer be seen as failures but more often as unlucky, and perhaps worthy of our extending a hand. Those who come to our shores, whatever our policy toward them, must be seen as human beings seeking to stitch together a decent life rather than as mere parasites upon our riches. Those who are unhealthy must be seen as more than drains upon our taxes but instead as peers that, but for good fortune, might have been us.

None of this requires that we allow others to abdicate responsibility for their lives. Nor does it require that we refuse, when no other means are available, to defend ourselves with force. Instead it calls upon us to recognize that we, too, have a responsibility to more than our own security and contentment. It commands us to look *to* ourselves and *at* others before we start casting stones.

Would this end all senseless killing? No, it would not. Would it substitute for the limits on guns that are so urgently needed? Of course not. While the recently rejected limits on guns, however timid, might have provided a first public step toward the recognition of the requirements of our situation, our task would remain: to create a culture where violence is seen not as the first option but as the last, one that would allow us to gaze upon the breadth of space that lies between an unjust act and a violent response.

The philosopher Immanuel Kant said that the core of morality lay in treating others not simply as means but also as ends in themselves. Nonviolence teaches us nothing more than this. It is a simple lesson, if difficult to practice—especially so at a moment like this when our rage and grief are still raw. But it is a lesson that has become buried under our ideology and our circumstances. We need to learn it anew.

Learning this lesson will not bring back the life of Martin Richard, Krystle Campbell or the other murdered victims in Boston. It will not return to health those who were injured on that day. It won't bring back Trayvon Martin or the children of Sandy Hook. But it will, perhaps, point the way toward a future where, instead of recalling yet more victims of violence in anger and with vows of retribution, we find ourselves with fewer victims to recall.

APRIL 21, 2013

The Moral Hazard of Drones

—John Kaag and Sarah Kreps

As the debate on the morality of the United States' use of unmanned aerial vehicles (UAVs, also known as drones) has intensified in recent weeks, several news and opinion articles have appeared in the media. Two, in particular, both published this month, reflect the current ethical divide on the issue. A feature article in *Esquire* by Tom Junod censured the "Lethal Presidency of Barack Obama" for the administration's policy of targeted killings of suspected militants; another, "The Moral Case for Drones," a news analysis by the *Times*' Scott Shane, gathered opinions from experts that implicitly commended the administration for replacing Dresden-style strategic bombing with highly precise attacks that minimize collateral damage.

Amid this discussion, we suggest that an allegory might be helpful to illustrate some of the many moral perils of drone use that have been overlooked. It shows that our attempts to avoid obvious ethical pitfalls of actions like firebombing may leave us vulnerable to other, more subtle, moral dangers.

While drones have become the weapons of our age, the moral dilemma that drone warfare presents is not new. In fact, it is very, very old:

Once upon a time, in a quiet corner of the Middle East, there lived a shepherd named Gyges. Despite the hardships in his life, Gyges was relatively satisfied with his meager existence. Then, one day, he found a ring buried in a nearby cave.

This was no ordinary ring; it rendered its wearer invisible. With this new power, Gyges became increasingly dissatisfied with his simple life. Before long, he seduced the queen of the land and began to plot the overthrow of her husband. One evening, Gyges placed the ring on his finger, sneaked into the royal palace, and murdered the king.

In his *Republic*, Plato recounts this tale but does not tell us the details of the murder. Still, we can rest assured that, like any violent death, it was not a pleasant affair. However, the story ends well, at least for Gyges. He marries the queen and assumes the position of king.

This story, which is as old as Western ethics itself, is meant to elicit a particular moral response from us: disgust. So why do we find Plato's story so appalling?

Maybe it's the way that the story replaces moral justification with practical efficiency: Gyges's being able to commit murder without getting caught, without any real difficulty, does not mean he is justified in doing so. (Expediency is not necessarily a virtue.)

Maybe it's the way that Gyges's ring obscures his moral culpability: it's difficult to blame a person you can't see and even harder to bring them to justice.

Maybe it's that Gyges is successful in his plot: a wicked act not only goes unpunished but is rewarded.

Maybe it's the nagging sense that any kingdom based on such deception could not be a just one: What else might happen in such a kingdom under the cover of darkness?

Our disgust with Gyges could be traced to any one of these concerns, or to all of them.

One might argue that the myth of Gyges is a suitable allegory to describe the combatants who have attacked and killed American civilians and troops in the last ten years. A shepherd from the Middle East discovers that he has the power of invisibility, the power to strike a fatal blow against a more powerful adversary, the power to do so without getting caught, the power to benefit from his deception. These, after all, are the tactics of terrorism.

But the myth of Gyges is really a story about modern counterterrorism, not terrorism.

We believe a stronger comparison can be made between the myth and the moral dangers of employing precision-guided munitions and drone technologies to target suspected terrorists. What is distinctive about the tale of Gyges is the ease with which he can commit murder and get away scot-free. The technological advantage provided by the ring ends up serving as the justification of its use.

Terrorists, whatever the moral value of their deeds, may be found and punished; as humans they are subject to retribution, whether it be corporal or legal. They may lose or sacrifice their lives. They may, in fact, be killed in the middle of the night by a drone. Because remote-controlled machines cannot suffer these consequences, and the humans who operate them do so at a great distance, the myth of Gyges is more a parable of modern counterterrorism than it is about terrorism.

Only recently has the use of drones begun to touch on questions of morality. Perhaps it's because the answers to these questions appear self-evident. What could be wrong with the use of unmanned aerial vehicles? After all, they limit the cost of war, in terms of both blood and treasure. The US troops who operate them can maintain safer standoff positions in Eastern Europe or at home. And armed with precision-guided munitions, these drones are said to limit collateral damage. In 2009, Leon Panetta, who was then the director of the Central Intelligence Agency, said UAVs are "very precise and very limited in terms of collateral damage . . . the only game in town in terms of confronting or trying to disrupt the al Qaeda leadership." What could be wrong with all this?

Quite a bit, it turns out.

Return, for a minute, to the moral disgust that Gyges evokes in us. Gyges also risked very little in attacking the king. The success of his mission was almost assured, thanks to the technological advantage of his ring. Gyges could sneak past the king's guards unscathed, so he did not need to kill anyone he did not intend on killing. These are the facts of the matter.

What we find unsettling here is the idea that these facts could be confused for moral justification. Philosophers find this confusion particularly abhorrent and guard against it with the only weapon they have: a distinction. The "fact-value distinction" holds that statements of fact should never be confused with statements of value. More strongly put, this distinction means that statements of fact do not even *imply* statements of value. "Can" does not imply "ought." To say that we *can* target individuals without incurring troop casualties does not imply that we *ought* to.

This seems so obvious. But, as Peter W. Singer noted earlier this year in the *Times*, when the Obama administration was asked why continued US military strikes in the Middle East did not constitute a violation of the 1973 War Powers Resolution, it responded that such activities did not "involve the presence of U.S. ground troops, U.S. casualties or a serious threat thereof." The justification of these strikes rested solely on their ease. The Ring of Gyges has the power to obscure the obvious.

This issue has all the hallmarks of what economists and philosophers call a "moral hazard"—a situation in which greater risks are taken by individuals who are able to avoid shouldering the cost associated with these risks. It thus seems wise, if not convenient, to underscore several ethical points if we are to avoid our own "Gyges moment."

First, we might remember Marx's comment that "the windmill gives you a society with the feudal lord; the steam engine gives you one with the industrial capitalist." And precision-guided munitions and drones give you a society with perpetual asymmetric wars.

The creation of technology is a value-laden enterprise. It creates the material conditions of culture and society and therefore its creation should be regarded as always already moral and political in nature. However, technology itself (the physical stuff of robotic warfare) is neither smart nor dumb, moral nor immoral. It can be used more or less precisely, but precision and efficiency are not inherently morally good. Imagine a very skilled dentist who painlessly removes the wrong tooth. Imagine a drone equipped with a precision-guided munition that kills a completely innocent person but spares the people who live in his or her neighborhood. The use of impressive technologies does not grant one impressive moral insight. Indeed, as Gyges demonstrates, the opposite can be the case.

Second, assassination and targeted killings have always been in the repertoires of military planners, but never in the history of warfare have they been so cheap and easy. The relatively low number of troop casualties for a military that has turned to drones means that there is relatively little domestic blowback against these wars. The United States and its allies have created the material conditions whereby these wars can carry on indefinitely. The noncombatant casualty rates in populations that are attacked by drones are slow and steady, but they add up. That the casualty rates are relatively low by historical standards—this is no Dresden—is undoubtedly a good thing, but it may allow the international media to overlook pesky little facts like the slow accretion of foreign casualties.

Third, the impressive expediency and accuracy in drone targeting may also allow policy makers and strategists to become lax in their moral decision making about who exactly should be targeted. Consider the stark contrast between the ambiguous language used to define legitimate targets and the specific technical means a military uses to neutralize these targets. The terms *terrorist, enemy combatant* and *contingent threat* are extremely vague and do very little to articulate the legitimacy of military targets. In contrast, the technical capabilities of weapon systems define and "paint" these targets with ever-greater definition. As weaponry becomes more precise, the language of warfare has become more ambiguous.

This ambiguity has, for example, altered the discourse surrounding the issue of collateral damage. There are two very different definitions of collateral damage, and these definitions affect the truth of the following statement: "Drone warfare and precision-guided munitions limit collateral damage." One definition views collateral damage as the inadvertent destruction of property and persons in a given attack. In other words, collateral damage refers to "stuff we don't mean to blow up." Another definition characterizes collateral damage as objects or individuals "that would not be lawful military targets in the circumstances ruling at the time." In other words, collateral damage refers to "the good guys." Since 1998, this is the definition that has been used. What is the difference between these definitions?

The first is a description of technical capabilities (being able to hit x while not hitting y); the second is a normative and indeed legal judgment about who is and is not innocent (and therefore who is a legitimate target and who is not). The first is a matter of fact, the second a matter of value. There is an important difference between these statements, and they should not be confused.

Fourth, questions of combatant status should be the subject of judicial review and moral scrutiny. Instead, if these questions are asked at all, they are answered as if they were mere matters of fact, unilaterally, behind closed doors, rather than through transparent due process. That moral reasoning has become even more slippery of late, as the American government has implied that all military-aged males in a strike area are legitimate targets: a "guilt by association" designation.

Finally, as the strategic repertoires of modern militaries expand to include drones and precision-guided munitions, it is not at all clear that having more choices leads strategists to make better and more-informed ones. In asking, "Is More Choice Better than Less?" the philosopher Gerald Dworkin once argued that the answer is "not always." In the words of Kierkegaard, "In possibility everything is possible. Hence in possibility one can go astray in all possible ways."

Some might object that these guidelines set unrealistically high expectations on military strategists and policy makers. They would probably be right. But no one—except Gyges—said that being ethical was easy.

JULY 22, 2012

A Crack in the Stoic's Armor

—*Nancy Sherman*

IN A REMARKABLY PRESCIENT MOMENT IN SEPTEMBER 1965, JAMES B. Stockdale, then a senior navy pilot shot down over Vietnam, muttered to himself as he parachuted into enemy hands, "Five years down there at least. I'm leaving behind the world of technology and entering the world of Epictetus." As a departing graduate student at Stanford, Stockdale received a gift of Epictetus's famous *Enchiridion*, a first-century Stoic handbook. The text looked esoteric, but in his long nights aboard the USS *Ticonderoga*, he found himself memorizing its content. Little did he know then that Stoic tonics would become his salvation for seven and a half years as the senior prisoner of war, held under brutal conditions by the North Vietnamese at Hoa Lo prison, the Hanoi Hilton.

Epictetus, who was a slave around the time of Nero, wrote, "Our thoughts are up to us, and our impulses, desires, and aversions—in short, whatever is our doing. . . . Of things that are outside your control, say they are nothing to you."

With these words, Stockdale drew a stripe between what he could and could not control. But he never lost the sense that what he could control was what mattered most and that his survival, even when tortured and in solitary confinement for four years, required constant refortification of his will.

Stockdale's resilience is legendary in the military. And it remains a living example, too, for philosophers, of how you might put into practice ancient Stoic consolations. But for many in the military, taking up Stoic armor comes at a heavy cost.

The Stoic doctrine is essentially about reducing vulnerability. And it starts off where Aristotle leaves off. Aristotle insists that happiness depends to some degree on chance and prosperity. Though the primary component of happiness is virtue—and that, a matter of one's own discipline and effort—realizing virtue in the world goes beyond one's effort. Actions that succeed and relationships that endure and are reciprocal depend upon more than one's own goodness. For the Stoics, this makes happiness far too dicey a matter. And so in their revision, virtue, and virtue alone, is sufficient for happiness. Virtue itself becomes purified, based on reason only, and shorn of ordinary emotions, like fear and grief, that cling to objects beyond our control.

In the military, even those who have never laid eyes on a page of Epictetus, still live as if they have. To suck it up is to move beyond grieving and keep fighting; it is to stare death down in a death-saturated place; it is to face one more deployment after two or three or four already. It is hard to imagine a popular philosophy better suited to deprivation and constant subjection to stressors.

And yet in the more than thirty interviews I conducted with soldiers who have returned from the long current wars, what I heard was the wish to let go of the Stoic armor. They wanted to feel and process the loss. They wanted to register the complex inner moral landscape of war by finding some measure of empathy with their own emotions. One retired army major put it flatly to me, "I've been sucking it up for twenty-five years, and I'm tired of it." For some, like this officer, the war after the war is unrelenting. It is about psychological trauma and multiple suicide attempts, exacerbated by his own sense of shame in not being the Stoic warrior that he thought he could and should be. He went to war to prove himself but came home emasculated.

Still we oversimplify grossly if we view all returning warriors through the lens of pathology and post-traumatic stress. Many soldiers wrestle with what they have seen and done in uniform, even when their conflicts don't rise to the level of acute or chronic psychological trauma. And they feel guilt and shame even when they do no wrong by war's best standards. Some anguish about having interrogated detainees not by torture, but the proper way, by slowly and deliberately building intimacy only in order to exploit it. Others feel shame for going to war with a sense of revenge and for then feeling its venom well up when a sniper guns down their buddy and their own survival depends on the raw desire for payback. They worry that their triumph in coming home alive is a betrayal of battle buddies who didn't make it. And then once home, they worry that their real family is back on the battlefield, and they feel guilt for what feels like a misplaced intimacy.

These feelings of guilt and shame are ubiquitous in war. They are not just responses to committing atrocities or war crimes. They are the feelings good soldiers bear, in part as testament to their moral humanity. And they are feelings critical to shaping soldiers' future lives as civilians. Yet these are feelings blocked off by idealized notions of Stoic purity and strength that leave little room for moral conflict and its painful residue.

One of the more compelling stories I heard was from a former army interrogator, Will Quinn, who had been at Abu Ghraib as part of the "clean-up" act a year after the torture scandal. This young interrogator had not engaged in torture or "enhanced" interrogation techniques: he did not subject detainees to waterboarding, or prolonged stress positions, or extreme sleep or sensory deprivation. Still, what he did do did not sit well with his civilian sensibilities. In one incident that especially bothered him, he showed a detainee a picture of a friend killed by American soldiers in order to get identification of the body. The detainee broke down. Will told me, "When I was going in, I was excited by the prospect of seeing his reaction, because it would make me feel good to know that the bad guy got killed. It was a sense of victory, a bit like Osama Bin Laden being killed. But when you encounter others for whom the death of a friend is a deeply personal loss, you have to humanize the experience."

He offered a striking analogy for what it felt like to be the interrogator he once was: Entering the interrogation cell was a bit like going into a mass with Gregorian chants sung in Latin. It takes place, he said, "in a different universe. . . . War, too, takes place in a different time and space." In essence, he was describing dissociation, or for the Stoics, what amounts to detachment from certain objects so they cannot affect you. Yet for this young interrogator detachment was not ultimately a viable solution: "I know I am the same person who was doing those things. And that's what tears at your soul."

Cicero, a great translator and transmitter of the earliest Greek Stoic texts, records a similar inner struggle. After the loss of his daughter Tullia in childbirth, he turned to Stoicism to assuage his grief. But ultimately he could not accept its terms: "It is not within our power to forget or gloss over circumstances which we believe to be evil. . . . They tear at us, buffet us, goad us, scorch us, stifle us—and you tell us to forget about them?"

Put in the context of today's wars, this could just as easily be a soldier's narrative about the need to put on Stoic armor and the need to take it off.

MAY 30, 2010

Rethinking the "Just War"

—*Jeff McMahan*

HERE IS VERY LITTLE IN THE REALM OF MORALITY THAT NEARLY everyone agrees on. Surprising divergences—as moral relativists delight in pointing out—occur among the moral beliefs in different societies. And there are, of course, fundamental moral disagreements within individual societies as well. Within the United States people hold radically opposing views on abortion, sexual relations, the fair distribution of wealth and many other such issues. The disagreements extend from the particular to the general, for in most areas of morality there are no commonly recognized principles to which people can appeal in trying to resolve their disputes. But there is at least one contentious moral issue for which there is a widely accepted moral theory, one that has been embraced for many centuries by both religious and secular thinkers, not just in the United States, but in many societies. The issue is war and the theory is *just war theory*.

"Just war theory" refers both to a tradition of thought and to a doctrine that has emerged from that tradition. There is no one canonical statement of the doctrine, but there is a core set of principles that appears, with minor variations, in countless books and articles that discuss the ethics of war in general or the morality of certain wars in particular. In recent decades, the most influential defense of the philosophical assumptions of the traditional theory has been Michael Walzer's classic book, *Just and Unjust Wars*, which also presents his understanding of the theory's implications for a range of issues, such as preemptive war, humanitarian intervention, terrorism, and nuclear deterrence.

The traditional just war theory, allied as it has been with the international law of armed conflict, has sustained a remarkable consensus for at least several centuries. But that consensus—for reasons I will describe shortly—has finally begun to erode. In the following two-part post, I will briefly summarize the evolution of the traditional just war theory, then make a case for why that theory can no longer stand.

THE EVOLUTION OF THE THEORY

The origin of just war theory is usually traced to the writings of Augustine, though many of the theory's elements became well established only much later, during its "classical" period between the early sixteenth and mid-seventeenth centuries. The principles of just war theory were then understood to be part of a unified set of objective moral principles governing all areas of life. Like the principles concerned with truth telling, commerce, sexual relations, and so on, just war principles were to be used in guiding and judging the acts of individuals. Later, however, as individuals became more firmly sorted into sovereign states and the regulation of warfare through treaties between states became increasingly effective, the theory began to conceive of war as an activity of states, in which individual soldiers were merely the instruments through which states acted.

Beginning in earnest in the seventeenth century and continuing through the twentieth, the theory of the just war evolved in conjunction with international law. While the theory initially guided the development of the law, by the nineteenth century and especially over the course of the twentieth, the law had acquired such great practical importance that the most significant developments in normative thought about war were pioneered by legal theorists, with just war theorists trailing humbly along behind.

During the aftermath of World War II, a consensus began to

emerge that a set of just war principles, which coincided closely with the law as codified in the United Nations Charter and the Geneva Conventions, provided the correct account of the morality of war.

Both just war theory and the law distinguished between the justification for the resort to war (*jus ad bellum*) and justified conduct in war (*jus in bello*). In most presentations of the theory of the just war, there are six principles of *jus ad bellum*, each with its own label: just cause, legitimate authority, right intention, necessity or last resort, proportionality and reasonable hope of success. *Jus in bello* comprises three principles: discrimination, necessity or minimal force, and, again, proportionality. These principles articulate in a compressed form an understanding of the morality of war that is, in its fundamental structure, much the same as it was three hundred years ago. Mainly as a result of its evolution in tandem with a body of law that has states rather than individual persons as its subjects, the theory in its present form is quite different from the classical theory from which it is descended. To distinguish it from its classical predecessor, some just war theorists refer to it as the *traditional* theory of the just war, though for brevity I will generally refer to it simply as "the Theory."

THE THEORY'S IMPORTANCE

The Theory is routinely invoked in public debates about particular wars and military policies. When both the Episcopal Church and the United States Catholic Bishops released documents in the early 1980s on the morality of nuclear deterrence, they judged the practice by reference to just war principles, which the Catholic Bishops expounded and analyzed in detail. Several years later the United Methodist Bishops published a book in which they stated that "while the Roman Catholic and Episcopal documents finally appeal to just-war arguments to support nuclear deterrence, we are persuaded that the logic of this tradition ultimately discredits nuclear deterrence as a morally tenable position," and went on to criticize deterrence by appeal to roughly the same principles to which the Catholics and Episcopalians had appealed.

Some military professionals also take the Theory quite seriously. It is taught in the United States' principal military academies, often by officers who themselves publish scholarly work that seeks to elucidate or apply it. (Occasionally some element of the Theory is cynically deployed, as when General Colin Powell remarked that he was pleased that the American invasion of Panama was named "Operation Just Cause," because "even our severest critics would have to utter 'Just Cause' while denouncing us.")

Even political leaders sometimes appeal to the Theory for guidance or justification. Ten days before the United States invaded Iraq in 2003, Jimmy Carter argued in *The New York Times* that an invasion would be wrong because it would violate the just war requirements of last resort, discrimination, proportionality and legitimate authority—though he regrettably managed to misinterpret all four. When Barack Obama delivered his Nobel Peace Prize acceptance speech, he, too, made reference to the concept of a just war, citing the Theory's principles of last resort, proportionality, and discrimination. More recently, one of Obama's aides sought to explain the president's close involvement in acts of targeted killing by suggesting that his study of the writings on just war by Augustine and Aquinas had convinced him that he had to take personal responsibility for these acts.

THE TRADITIONAL THEORY UNDER ATTACK

As I mentioned, the consensus on the Theory has recently begun to break down. The cracks first became visible when a few philosophers challenged some of the assumptions of Walzer's *Just and Unjust Wars* shortly after its publication in 1977. But over the last fifteen years, the cracks have widened into gaping crevices. There are two reasons for this.

One is the changing character of war. Most recent wars have not been of the sort to which the Theory most readily applies—namely, wars between regular armies deployed by states. Many have instead been between the regular army of a state and "rogue" forces not under the control of any state. This description fits the major segments of the United States' wars in Vietnam, Afghanistan, and Iraq, as well as the recent smaller-scale civil conflicts in Libya and Syria. And there is also, of course, the continuing conflict between states and decentralized terrorist organizations such as Al Qaeda. These types of conflict, especially those with terrorists, are resistant to moral evaluation within the state-centric framework of the traditional theory.

The second reason for the decline in allegiance to the Theory is largely independent of changes in the practice of war. It does, however, derive from the fact that the wars in Vietnam, the Persian Gulf, Yugoslavia, and the Middle East provoked a resurgence of work in just war theory by philosophers trained in the analytic tradition. When these philosophers consulted the traditional theory to evaluate these wars, they discovered problems that had somehow eluded earlier thinkers. They have subsequently sought to develop a more plausible theory of the just war. As it turns out, this "revisionist" account, though not as yet fully worked out, is in certain respects a reversion to the classical theory that was superseded by the traditional theory several centuries ago. It returns, for example, to the idea that it is individual persons, not states, who kill and are killed in war, and that they, rather than their state, bear primary responsibility for their participation and action in war.

The revisionist approach has gained considerable support among contemporary just war theorists, but news of this shift has scarcely reached beyond the small community of academic philosophers and scholars who work on these issues. As a proponent of the revisionist approach, I believe it is important for those outside academia to be aware of the challenges to the set of beliefs that has dominated moral thought about war for many centuries and that still frames public discourse about the morality of war.

Revisionist just war theory is a school of thought, not a body of doctrine. There are many disagreements among revisionists, but they have the benefit of a long tradition of thought about the morality of war on which to build as well as a more recent tradition of rigorous, meticulous analytical thinking about moral issues that has, among other things, given them a richer range of distinctions and other analytical tools than their predecessors had access to. The result of their efforts promises to be an understanding of the just war that is not only quite different from the traditional Theory but substantially more plausible.

Before presenting a critique of traditional just war theory I should make two points of clarification. Although the Theory is largely congruent with the international law of war, the subject of just war theory is *not law but morality*. If the inconsistencies and absurdities I will describe were confined to the law, they would be less troubling. Because the law is an artifact and does not purport to state truths about a reality that is independent of human invention, it can tolerate considerable disunity. But just war theory is usually understood as a set of principles that have been discovered rather than designed, and that provide an objective account of the morality of war. If just war theory is more than just a set of conventions, and if the objections I will advance here are correct, the traditional version of just war theory must be rejected.

Second, the term *war* is ambiguous. There is one sense in which a war is composed of all the acts of war by all the parties to a conflict. World War II was a war in this sense. But *war* can also refer to the belligerent action of only one side—for example, the *war* that Britain fought against Germany, which was a part of World War II. My remarks will generally be concerned with wars in the second sense, for only such wars can be just or unjust. Thus, while Britain's war against Germany was just, World War II was neither just nor unjust.

PERMISSIBLE ACTS, UNJUST WAR?

I turn now to the critique of the Theory. As I noted earlier, just war theory distinguishes between the principles of *jus ad bellum* (resort to war) and those of *jus in bello* (conduct in war). According to the Theory, the latter are independent of the former, in the sense that what it is permissible for a combatant to do in war is unaffected by whether his war is just or unjust. Whatever acts are permissible for those who fight in a just war ("just combatants") are also permissible for those ("unjust combatants") who fight for aims that are unjust. Combatants on both sides have the same rights, permissions and liabilities—a view commonly known as the "moral equality of combatants." According to this view, if we accept that it is permissible for just combatants to participate in warfare, we must also accept that the same is true of unjust combatants. Both just combatants and unjust combatants act impermissibly only if they violate the rules of *jus in bello*—that is, only if they fight in an impermissible manner.

This has one immediately paradoxical implication: namely, that if unjust combatants fight without violating the rules governing the conduct of war, all their individual acts of war are permissible; yet these individual acts together constitute a war that is unjust and therefore impermissible. But how can a series of individually permissible acts be collectively impermissible?

To resolve this paradox, the Theory has to claim that the principles of *jus ad bellum* apply only to the state, or the government that represents it. Hence only the members of the government responsible for decisions about the resort to war act impermissibly when a state fights an unjust war. Suppose, for example, that the armies of Aggressia have unjustly invaded and conquered neighboring Benignia. Aggressian soldiers never once violated the principles of *jus in bello*. But to defeat the Benignian army, it was necessary for them to kill more than a million Benignian soldiers, most of whom were civilians when the invasion began and enlisted in the military only to defend their country from Aggressia. According to the Theory, the *only* people who have done anything wrong in bringing about this vast slaughter are a handful of Aggressian political leaders who spent the war in their offices and never killed anyone.

This is incompatible with what we believe about killing in other contexts. Normally, the perpetrator of an act of killing is responsible for the victim's death to *at least* as high a degree as an accessory who may have paid or pressured him to do it. Yet the Theory holds that in an unjust war fought in accordance with the principles of *jus in bello*, only the accessories who have instigated the killing (the political leaders) are responsible for it and have therefore done wrong, while the perpetrators (the unjust combatants) bear no responsibility and have done no wrong. But how can unjust combatants act permissibly when, as the Theory concedes, their ends are unjust, their means include the intentional killing of people who have done no wrong, and their action also kills innocent bystanders as a side effect? They may, of course, be *excused*—that is, they may not be culpable—if they mistakenly though blamelessly believe that their war is just, or if they fight under irresistible duress. But that is quite different from acting permissibly in the objective sense, which is what the Theory claims they do.

The Theory's assurance that unjust combatants do no wrong provided they follow the rules makes it easier for governments to initiate unjust wars. The Theory cannot offer any moral reason why a person ought not to fight in an unjust war, no matter how criminal. If a young German in 1939 had consulted the Theory for guidance about whether to join the Wehrmacht, it would have told him that it was permissible to participate in Nazi aggression provided that he obeyed the principles of *jus in bello* (for example, by refraining from intentionally attacking civilians). To the extent that the theory has shaped our ways of thinking about the morality of war, it has enabled soldiers to believe that it is permissible to kill people who are merely trying to defend themselves and others from unjust aggression, provided the victims are wearing uniforms and the killing is done under orders from appropriate authorities.

THE MORALITY OF SELF-DEFENSE

Traditional theorists seek to justify their extraordinary claim—that those who fight and kill in an unjust war never do wrong provided they kill in accordance with the rules—by appealing to the familiar idea that, while it is not permissible to attack people who are *innocent*, it can be permissible to attack and kill those who are *noninnocent*. But the Theory uses these words in a special way. Innocent means "unthreatening," so that in war noncombatants are innocent while all combatants are noninnocent. Thus, in Walzer's words, the right not to be attacked "is lost by those who bear arms . . . because they pose a danger to other people." This is true of the just and the unjust alike. "Simply by fighting," Walzer claims, they lose "their title to life . . . even though, unlike aggressor states, they have committed no crime." According to this view, all violent action that is defensive is self-justifying, assuming it is also necessary and proportionate.

This account of defensive rights accords no significance to the distinction between wrongful aggressors and their victims, or between unjust and just combatants. Each has a right of defense against the other. Such a view has no plausibility outside the context of war. If a police officer, for example, is about to shoot a murderer on a rampage, the murderer has no right to kill the officer in self-defense, even if that is the only way to save himself. In this and other situations outside of war, the morality of defense is asymmetrical between wrongful aggressors and innocent victims (and third parties who attempt to defend them). While the victim has both a right against attack and a right of defense, the aggressor has neither. This asymmetrical understanding of the morality of defense is found even in the traditional doctrine of *jus ad bellum*, for the Theory accepts that the morality of defense among *states* is asymmetrical. It is only in the doctrine of *jus in bello*, which applies to combatants, that the morality of defense is symmetrical. The Theory thus comprises two distinct accounts of the morality of defense—an asymmetrical account for states and a symmetrical account for combatants.

SELF-DEFENSE BY CIVILIANS

According to the second, symmetrical account, all combatants are liable to defensive attack simply because they pose a threat to others. Curiously, however, they are in general liable to attack only by other combatants, not by civilians. Why? Traditional theorists might claim that civilians can attack *defensively* only when they are being intentionally attacked, in which case the attacking combatants are indeed liable to defensive attack by the civilians. Yet there are actually three other ways in which attacks by civilians against combatants can be defensive:

- *Civilians might attack combatants to defend themselves against being harmed as an unintended effect of the combatants' military action—that is, to prevent themselves from becoming "collateral damage."*

- *Civilians might attack enemy combatants in defense of combatants on their own side. Not all defense is* self-*defense.*

- *Civilians might attack combatants to prevent themselves from being harmed by the achievement of the adversary's war aims— for example, to defend their property or liberty, just as soldiers do when they fight in defense of territory or political independence.*

The issue of self-defense by civilians against combatants has received only scant attention in the just war tradition. But since it would be highly implausible to suppose that civilians have no right of self-defense against an intentional and wrongful attack by combatants, I will assume that the Theory permits this form of defense.

It is also generally assumed that it prohibits the last of these types of defense, primarily on the ground that self-defense in these circumstances is tantamount to participation in the war without identifying oneself as a combatant, and tends to undermine respect for the distinction between combatants and noncombatants. (The second and third types have been so little discussed in the tradition that I will not consider them here.) Yet if the Theory recognizes that civilians have a right to defend themselves against soldiers who will otherwise intentionally physically harm them, consistency demands that it also recognize that they are permitted to defend themselves against soldiers who will otherwise expose them to the harms involved in defeat, such as rule by an alien regime that may steal their land and other possessions, dismantle their political institutions, and imprison or kill them if they later resist. In part because these latter harms can be long-lasting, they can be more serious than those that civilians might suffer from an intentional physical attack, provided the attack is not lethal. How could the civilians have a right of defense against a lesser harm but not against a greater harm inflicted by the same people?

Although the Theory permits civilians to defend themselves against intentional attack by combatants, it also reduces their moral status if they do so. For if civilians attempt to defend themselves, they then pose a threat and hence satisfy the Theory's criterion of liability to attack. Thus, by engaging in self-defense, they cease to be innocent and become legitimate targets. It does not matter that the only reason they pose a threat is that the unjust attack to which they have been subjected has forced them to try to defend themselves. If that exempted them from liability for posing a threat, it would also exempt just combatants who fight in defense only because they and their innocent compatriots have been unjustifiably attacked.

Defenders of the Theory will doubtless recoil from the conclusion that by intentionally attacking civilians, combatants can create conditions in which they may then permissibly kill those same civilians in self-defense. But that is what their view implies.

IMPLICATIONS OF THE CLAIM THAT ALL COMBATANTS ARE LIABLE TO ATTACK

The forgoing criticisms involve an element of speculation because the Theory has never had a fully explicit and determinate view about the permissibility of defense by civilians against combatants. But it has never been vague about the claim that all combatants are liable to attack by other combatants at any time during a state of war (assuming that soldiers who are wounded, have surrendered, or are attempting to surrender have ceased to pose a threat and are thus no longer combatants). It is worth noting two implications of this claim, one repugnant, the other doubtfully coherent.

Suppose that unjust combatants are engaged in a continuing atrocity, such as a massacre of civilians. Just combatants arrive and attack them as a means of stopping the slaughter. According to the Theory, even though the unjust combatants are acting impermissibly in killing the civilians, they nevertheless act permissibly if they kill those who are trying to rescue the civilians. It is hard to believe that morality could permit *that*.

A further and perhaps even more damaging objection is that the Theory's claim that all combatants are liable because they pose a threat to others seems incompatible with its further claim that combatants do no wrong when they initiate a war with a surprise attack on the unmobilized forces of another state. If the aggressing combatants act permissibly, that must be because those they attack are legitimate targets—that is, because they are liable to attack. Yet at the time they are attacked they pose no threat.

A defender of the Theory might respond that all combatants pose a threat in a state of war and that a state of war exists when the first act of war occurs. To test the plausibility of this claim, consider the position of an American sailor at Pearl Harbor immediately prior to the Japanese surprise attack. He has done nothing to lose his right not to be attacked by the Japanese. There is no state of war between the United States and Japan, so this sailor poses no threat to any Japanese. He is, of course, likely to try to defend himself if he is attacked, but that does not mean that he poses a threat to anyone now. If it did, that would mean that most people pose a threat to others most of the time, since most people would defend themselves if attacked. So the sailor seems not to pose a threat and thus to retain his right against attack. Yet when the Japanese crews conduct their surprise attack, they act permissibly according to the Theory, even though their attack violates the principles of *jus ad bellum*. For those principles apply only to their government, not to the crews.

But how can it be that the crews act permissibly if they attack this American sailor, along with many others like him, who pose no threat to them? The answer I suggested on behalf of the Theory is that the Japanese attack itself creates a state of war in which the morality of *jus in bello* comes into effect. A surprise attack that initiates a war thus activates the morality by which it is governed. Prior to the attack, there was no state of war, so the American sailor had a right not to be attacked. But when the attack occurs, a state of war exists and he has lost his right not to be attacked by enemy combatants. How did he lose it? The only answer the Theory can give is *by being attacked*.

But this cannot be right, for two obvious reasons.

First, as I noted, it is incompatible with the Theory's criterion of liability, for the sailor posed no threat at the time when he was attacked. Second, it assumes that unjust combatants who initiate a war through a surprise attack deprive their victims of their right not to be attacked merely by attacking them. Yet a right not to be attacked that disappears when its bearer is attacked is no right at all.

IS WAR GOVERNED BY A DIFFERENT MORALITY?

I remarked earlier that symmetrical accounts of the morality of defense have no plausibility outside the context of war. Defenders of the Theory seem to recognize this, for they often claim that war is so different from conditions of ordinary life that it must be governed by principles different from those that operate in other contexts. Traditional just war theorists are thus in partial agreement with political realists, who also claim that ordinary moral principles do not apply in war. The difference is that realists make the radical claim that *no* alternative moral principles fill the space vacated by ordinary morality, so that war is outside the scope of morality altogether, while traditional just war theorists make only the more modest claim that when war begins, the familiar asymmetrical account of defensive rights ceases to apply to combatants and is replaced by the symmetrical account found in the doctrine of *jus in bello*.

The idea that conditions of war summon a different set of moral principles into effect is common but highly implausible. If it were true, the concept of war would be of the utmost practical significance. For whether a particular conflict is a war would determine which set of moral principles applies to the acts of those involved in it. A particular act of killing might be wholly permissible if the conflict in which it occurs is a war yet be an instance of murder if the conflict falls short of war. The difference between wars and conflicts that are not wars would therefore have to be sufficiently significant to explain how the same act could be permissible in the one context but murder in the other.

By what criteria, then, are wars distinguished from other conflicts? A recent op-ed piece in *The New York Times* by Joshua Goldstein and Steven Pinker noted that "a common definition [of war] picks out armed conflicts that cause at least 1,000 battle deaths a year." This criterion is, however, merely a matter of scale. Combining it with the idea that different, symmetrical moral principles come into effect in a state of war yields absurd conclusions. The combined claims imply, for example, that all killings committed in a conflict that continues over many years are permissible in those years in which more than one thousand participants are killed but not during those years when fewer than one thousand are killed. Or suppose that in one year of such a conflict, only the aggressors manage to do any killing. Their first one thousand killings are all murders, but any killings they do after that are permissible acts of war.

As a matter of law, a war exists whenever one state uses armed force against another, regardless of the scale or duration of the conflict. When this happens, something of considerable legal significance does occur: the law of armed conflict begins to govern belligerent relations between the states. But this is a wholly conventional phenomenon, and there is no reason to suppose that what is sufficient to activate a certain body of law automatically activates a different set of moral principles as well.

The truth is that there is no univocal concept of war. There are various different criteria for distinguishing between wars and other forms of armed conflict that are invoked in different contexts and for different reasons. What is notable here is that traditional just war theorists have not advanced any criterion of their own that would make it plausible to suppose that the commencement of war suspends the moral principles that govern other forms of violent conflict and brings quite different principles into effect instead.

THE REVISIONIST ALTERNATIVE

There are many incoherencies and inconsistencies in the traditional theory of the just war of which those noted in this article are merely a sampling. But the implausibility of the traditional theory should not lead us to conclude that no plausible account of the just war can be given. Revisionist theorists have been working not just to expose the problems with the Theory but also to develop an alternative. The revisionist approach treats war as morally continuous with other forms of violent conflict and therefore rejects the idea that a different morality comes into effect in conditions of war. It asserts that the principles of *jus ad bellum* apply not only to governments but also to individual soldiers, who in general ought not to fight in wars that are unjust. It denies that *jus in bello* can be independent of *jus ad bellum* and therefore concludes that in general it is not possible to fight in a way that is objectively permissible in an unjust war.

As these claims imply, the revisionist account of *jus in bello* is based on an asymmetrical understanding of the morality of defense. While just combatants are usually justified in attacking unjust combatants, unjust combatants are seldom justified in attacking just combatants. The main exception is when just combatants are acting impermissibly—for example, by pursuing their just goals by impermissible means. But the fact that most acts of war by unjust combatants are objectively impermissible does not entail that unjust combatants are blameworthy or deserving of punishment. Revisionists recognize that combatants act under duress and in conditions of factual and moral uncertainty. These mitigating conditions usually diminish their responsibility for the wrongs they do, sometimes making their action wholly excusable (though not objectively justified). Many revisionists, myself included, argue that in current conditions, it would be both unfair and counterproductive to subject soldiers to legal punishment for mere participation in an unjust war.

These revisionists therefore accept that it is necessary, at least at present, for the *law* of war to retain a code of *jus in bello* that is symmetrical between just and unjust combatants. They accept, in other words, that the law of war as it applies to combatants must at present diverge not only from morality but also from domestic criminal law, which assigns asymmetrical defensive rights to wrongful aggressors and their potential victims. The principal reasons for this are the absence of a publicly accessible and morally and legally authoritative means of distinguishing between just and unjust wars, and the absence of an impartial, supranational mechanism for enforcing an asymmetrical code. What revisionists hope is that their work can be a source of guidance in establishing new international institutions that will eventually make it possible to reform the law of armed conflict in ways that will bring it into closer congruence with the morality of war.

NOVEMBER II, 2012

THIS AMERICAN LIFE

The Gospel According to "Me"

—*Simon Critchley and Jamieson Webster*

THE BOOMING SELF-HELP INDUSTRY, NOT TO MENTION THE CASH cow of New Age spirituality, has one message: be authentic! Charming as American optimism may be, its twenty-first-century incarnation as the search for authenticity deserves pause. The power of this new version of the American dream can be felt through the stridency of its imperatives: Live fully! Realize yourself! Be connected! Achieve well-being!

Despite the frequent claim that we are living in a secular age defined by the death of God, many citizens in rich Western democracies have merely switched one notion of God for another—abandoning their singular, omnipotent (Christian or Judaic or whatever) deity reigning over all humankind and replacing it with a weak but all-pervasive idea of spirituality tied to a personal ethic of authenticity and a liturgy of inwardness. The latter does not make the exorbitant moral demands of traditional religions, which impose bad conscience, guilt, sin, sexual inhibition and the rest.

Unlike the conversions that transfigure the born-again's experience of the world in a lightning strike, this one occurred in stages: a postwar existentialist philosophy of personal liberation and "becoming who you are" fed into a 1960s counterculture that mutated into the most selfish conformism, disguising acquisitiveness under a patina of personal growth, mindfulness and compassion. Traditional forms of morality that required extensive social cooperation in relation to a hard reality defined by scarcity have largely collapsed and been replaced with this New Age therapeutic culture of well-being that does not require obedience or even faith—and certainly not feelings of guilt. Guilt must be shed; alienation, both of body and mind, must be eliminated, most notably through yoga practice after a long day of mind-numbing work.

In the gospel of authenticity, well-being has become the primary goal of human life. Rather than being the by-product of some collective project, some upbuilding of the New Jerusalem, well-being is an end in itself. The stroke of genius in the ideology of authenticity is that it doesn't really require a belief in anything, and certainly not a belief in anything that might transcend the serene and contented living of one's authentic life and baseline well-being. In this, one can claim to be beyond dogma.

Whereas the American dream used to be tied to external reality—say, America as the place where one can openly practice any religion, America as a safe haven from political oppression, or America as the land of opportunity where one need not struggle as hard as one's parents—now, the dream is one of pure psychological transformation.

This is the phenomenon that one might call, with an appreciative nod to Nietzsche, passive nihilism. Authenticity is its dominant contemporary expression. In a seemingly meaningless, inauthentic world awash in nonstop media reports of war, violence and inequality, we close our eyes and turn ourselves into islands. We may even say a little prayer to an obscure but benign Eastern goddess and feel some weak spiritual energy connecting everything as we listen to some tastefully selected ambient music. Authenticity, needing no reference to anything outside itself, is an evacuation of history. The power of now.

This ideology functions prominently in the contemporary workplace, where the classical distinction between work and nonwork has broken down. Work was traditionally seen as a curse or an obligation for which we received payment. Nonwork was viewed as an experience of freedom for which we pay but that gives us pleasure.

But the past thirty years or so has ushered in an informalization of the workplace where the distinction between work and nonwork is harder and harder to draw. With the rise of corporations like Google, the workplace has increasingly been colonized by nonwork experiences to the extent that we are not even allowed to feel alienation or discontent at the office because we can play Ping-Pong, ride a Segway, and eat organic lunches from a menu designed by celebrity chefs. If we do feel discontent, it must mean that something is wrong with us rather than with the corporation.

With the workplace dominated by the maxim of personal authenticity—Be different! Wear your favorite T-shirt to work and listen to Radiohead on your iPhone while at your desk! Isn't it nifty?—there is no room for worker malaise. And contrary to popular belief, none of this has assuaged the workplace dynamics of guilt, bad conscience and anxiety, which are more rampant than ever. In fact, the blurring of the boundary between work and nonwork in the name of flexibility has led to an enormous increase in anxiety—a trend well-documented in the work of Peter Fleming, a professor of work, organization and society at the University of London. Women in particular feel totally inadequate for not being able to have it all—climb the ladder at work, make the same wages as men, have a family, have a voluminous sex life, still look attractive and act as if they are having a great time through all of it.

Work is no longer a series of obligations to be fulfilled for the sake of sustenance: it is the expression of one's authentic self. With the extraordinary rise of internships—not just filled by college students anymore, but more and more by working-age adults—people from sufficiently privileged backgrounds are even prepared to work without pay because it allows them to "grow" as persons. Every aspect of one's existence is meant to water some fantasy of growth.

But here's the rub: if one believes that there is an intimate connection between one's authentic self and glittering success at work, then the experience of failure and forced unemployment is accepted as one's own fault. I feel shame for losing my job. I am morally culpable for the corporation's decision that I am excess to requirements.

To take this one step further, the failure of others is explained by their merely partial enlightenment for which they, and they alone, are to be held responsible. At the heart of the ethic of authenticity is a profound selfishness and callous disregard of others. As New Age interpreters of Buddha say, "You yourself, as much as anybody in the entire universe, deserve your love and affection."

A naive belief in authenticity eventually gives way to a deep cynicism. A conviction in personal success that must always hold failure at bay becomes a corrupt stubbornness that insists on success at any cost. Cynicism, in this mode, is not the expression of a critical stance toward authenticity but is rather the runoff of this failure of belief. The self-help industry itself runs the gamut in both directions—from *The Power of Now*, which teaches you the power of meditative self-sufficiency, to *The Rules*, which teaches a woman how to land a man by pretending to be self-sufficient. Profit rules the day, inside and out.

Nothing seems more American than this forced choice between cynicism and naive belief. Or rather, as Herman Melville put it in his 1857 novel *The Confidence-Man*, it seems the choice is between being a fool (having to believe what one says) or being a knave (saying things one does not believe). For Melville, who was writing on the cusp of modern capitalism, the search for authenticity is a white whale.

This search is an obsession that is futile at best and destructive at worst. The lingering question for Melville, on the brink of poverty as he wrote *The Confidence-Man*, is, what happens to charity? When the values of Judeo-Christian morality have been given a monetary and psychological incarnation—as in credit, debt, trust, faith and fidelity—can they exist as values? Is the prosperous self the only God in which we believe in a radically inauthentic world?

As usual, the Bard of Avon got there first. In *Hamlet*, Shakespeare puts the mantra of authenticity into the mouth of the ever-idiotic windbag Polonius in his advice to his son, Laertes: "To thine own self be true." This is just before Polonius sends a spy to follow Laertes to Paris and tell any number of lies in order to catch him out.

And who, finally, is more inauthentic than Hamlet? Ask yourself: Is Hamlet true to himself, doubting everything, unable to avenge his father's murder, incapable of uttering the secret that he has learned from the ghost's lips, and unwilling to declare his love for Ophelia whose father he kills? Hamlet dies wearing the colors of his enemy, Claudius. We dare say that we love *Hamlet* not for its representation of our purportedly sublime authenticity, but as a depiction of the drama of our radical inauthenticity that, in the best of words and worlds, shatters our moral complacency.

JUNE 29, 2013

Deluded Individualism

—*Firmin DeBrabander*

THERE IS A CURIOUS PASSAGE EARLY IN FREUD'S *EGO AND THE ID* where he remarks that the id behaves "as if" it were unconscious. The phrase is puzzling, but the meaning is clear: the id is the secret driver of our desires, the desires that animate our conscious life, but the ego does not recognize it as such. The ego—what we take to be our conscious, autonomous self—is ignorant to the agency of the id and sees itself in the driver seat instead. Freud offers the following metaphor: the ego is like a man on horseback, struggling to contain the powerful beast beneath; to the extent that the ego succeeds in guiding this beast, it's only by "transforming the id's will into action *as if* it were its own."

By Freud's account, conscious autonomy is a charade. "We are lived," as he puts it, and yet we don't see it as such. Indeed, Freud suggests that to be human is to rebel against that vision—the truth. We tend to see ourselves as self—determining, self-conscious agents in all that we decide and do, and we cling to that image. But why? Why do we resist the truth? Why do we wish—strain, strive against the grain of reality—to be autonomous individuals, and see ourselves as such?

Perhaps Freud is too cynical regarding conscious autonomy, but he is right to question our presumption to it. He is right to suggest that we typically—wrongly—ignore the extent to which we are determined by unknown forces and overestimate our self-control. The path to happiness for Freud, or some semblance of it in his stormy account of the psyche, involves accepting our basic condition. But why do we presume individual agency in the first place? Why do we insist on it stubbornly, irrationally, often recklessly?

I was reminded of Freud's paradox by a poignant article in the *Times* a few months back, which described a Republican-leaning district in Minnesota and its constituents' conflicted desire to be self-reliant ("Even Critics of Safety Net Increasingly Depend on It," February 11). The article cited a study from Dartmouth political science professor Dean Lacy, which revealed that, though Republicans call for deep cuts to the safety net, their districts rely more on government support than their Democratic counterparts.

In Chisago County, MN, the *Times*' reporters spoke with residents who supported the Tea Party and its proposed cuts to federal spending, even while they admitted they could not get by without government support. Tea Party aficionados, and many on the extreme right of the Republican Party for that matter, are typically characterized as self-sufficient middle-class folk, angry about sustaining the idle poor with their tax dollars. Chisago County revealed a different aspect of this anger: economically struggling Americans professing a robust individualism and self-determination, frustrated with their failures to achieve that ideal.

Why the stubborn insistence on self-determination, in spite of the facts? One might say there is something profoundly American in this. It's our fierce individualism shining through. Residents of Chisago County are clinging to notions of past self-reliance before the recession, before the welfare state. It's admirable in a way. Alternately, it evokes the delusional autonomy of Freud's poor ego.

These people, like many across the nation, rely on government assistance but pretend they don't. They even resent the government for their reliance. If they looked closely, though, they'd see that we are all thoroughly saturated with government assistance in this country: farm subsidies that lower food prices for us all, mortgage interest deductions that disproportionately favor the rich, federal mortgage guarantees that keep interest rates low, a bloated Department of Defense that sustains entire sectors of the economy and puts hundreds of thousands of people to work. We can hardly fathom the depth of our dependence on government and pretend we are bold individualists instead.

As we are in an election year, the persistence of this delusion has manifested itself politically, particularly as a foundation in the Republican Party ideology—from Ron Paul's insistence during the primaries that the government shouldn't intervene to help the uninsured even when they are deathly ill to Rick Santorum's maligning of public schools to Mitt Romney's selection of Paul Ryan as a running mate. There is no doubt that radical individualism will remain a central selling point of their campaign. Ryan's signature work, his proposal for the federal budget, calls for drastic cuts to Medicaid, Medicare, Pell grants and job-training programs, among others. To no surprise, as *The New Yorker* revealed in a recent profile of Ryan, the home district that supports him is boosted by considerable government largesse.

Of course the professed individualists have an easy time cutting services for the poor. But this is misguided. There are many counties across the nation that, like Chisago County, might feel insulated from the trials of the destitute. Perhaps this is because they are able to ignore the poverty in their midst, or because they are rather homogeneous and geographically removed from concentrations of poverty, like urban ghettos. But the fate of the middle-class counties and urban ghettos is entwined. When the poor are left to rot in their misery, the misery does not stay contained. It harms us all. The crime radiates, the misery offends, it debases the whole. Individuals, much less communities, cannot be insulated from it.

Thanks to a decades-long safety net, we have forgotten the trials of living without it. This is why, the historian Tony Judt argued, it's easy for some to speak fondly of a world without government: we can't fully imagine or recall what it's like. We can't really appreciate the horrors Upton Sinclair witnessed in the Chicago slaughterhouses before regulation, or the burden of living without Social Security and Medicare to look forward to. Thus, we can entertain nostalgia for a time when everyone pulled his own weight, bore his own risk, and was the master of his destiny. That time was a myth. But the notion of self-reliance is also a fallacy.

Spinoza greatly influenced Freud, and he adds a compelling insight we would do well to reckon with. Spinoza also questioned the human pretense to autonomy. Men believe themselves free, he said, merely because they are conscious of their volitions and appetites, but they are wholly determined. In fact, Spinoza claimed—to the horror of his contemporaries—that we are all just modes of one substance, "God or Nature" he called it, which is really the same thing. Individual actions are no such thing at all; they are expressions of another entity altogether, which acts through us unwittingly. To be human, according to Spinoza, is to be party to a confounding existential illusion—that human individuals are independent agents—which exacts a heavy emotional and political toll on us. It is the source of anxiety, envy, anger—all the passions that torment our psyche—and the violence that ensues. If we should come to see our nature as it truly is, if we should see that no "individuals" properly speaking exist at all, Spinoza maintained, it would greatly benefit humankind.

There is no such thing as a discrete individual, Spinoza points out. This is a fiction. The boundaries of "me" are fluid and blurred. We are all profoundly linked in countless ways we can hardly perceive. My decisions, choices, actions are inspired and motivated by others to no small extent. The passions, Spinoza argued, derive from seeing people as autonomous individuals responsible for all the objectionable actions that issue from them. Understanding the interrelated nature of everyone and everything is the key to diminishing the passions and the havoc they wreak.

In this, Spinoza and President Obama seem to concur: we're all in this together. We are not the sole authors of our destiny, each of us; our destinies are entangled—messily, unpredictably. Our cultural demands of individualism are too extreme. They are constitutionally irrational, Spinoza and Freud tell us, and their potential consequences are disastrous. Thanks to our safety net, we live in a society that affirms the dependence and interdependence of all. To that extent, it affirms a basic truth of our nature. We forsake it at our own peril.

AUGUST 18, 2012

The Very Angry Tea Party

—J. M. Bernstein

SOMETIMES IT IS HARD TO KNOW WHERE POLITICS ENDS AND metaphysics begins: when, that is, the stakes of a political dispute concern not simply a clash of competing ideas and values but a clash about what is real and what is not, what can be said to exist on its own and what owes its existence to an other.

The seething anger that seems to be an indigenous aspect of the Tea Party movement arises, I think, at the very place where politics and metaphysics meet, where metaphysical sentiment becomes political belief. More than their political ideas, it is the anger of Tea Party members that is already reshaping our political landscape. As Jeff Zeleny reported last Monday in the *Times*, the vast majority of House Democrats are now avoiding holding town-hall-style forums—just as you might sidestep an enraged, jilted lover on a subway platform—out of fear of confronting the incubus of Tea Party rage that routed last summer's meetings. This fear-driven avoidance is, Zeleny stated, bringing the time-honored tradition of the political meeting to the brink of extinction.

It would be comforting if a clear political diagnosis of the Tea Party movement were available—if we knew precisely what political events had inspired the fierce anger that pervades its meetings and rallies, what policy proposals its backers advocate, and, most obviously, what political ideals and values are orienting its members.

Of course, some things can be said, and have been said by commentators, under each of these headings. The bailout of Wall Street, the provision of government assistance to homeowners who cannot afford to pay their mortgages, the pursuit of health-care reform and, as a cumulative sign of untoward government expansion, the mounting budget deficit are all routinely cited as precipitating events. I leave aside the election of a—"foreign-born"—African-American to the presidency.

When it comes to the Tea Party's concrete policy proposals, things get fuzzier and more contradictory: keep the government out of health care, but leave Medicare alone; balance the budget, but don't raise taxes; let individuals take care of themselves, but leave Social Security alone; and, of course, the paradoxical demand not to support Wall Street, to let the hardworking producers of wealth get on with it without regulation and government stimulus, but also to make sure the banks can lend to small businesses and responsible homeowners in a stable but growing economy.

There is a fierce logic to these views, as I will explain. But first, a word about political ideals.

In a bracing and astringent essay in the *New York Review of Books*, pointedly titled "The Tea Party Jacobins," Mark Lilla argued that the hodgepodge list of animosities Tea Party supporters mention fail to cohere into a body of political grievances in the conventional sense: they lack the connecting thread of achieving political power. It is not for the sake of acquiring political power that Tea Party activists demonstrate, rally and organize; rather, Lilla argues, the appeal is to "individual opinion, individual autonomy, and individual choice, all in the service of neutralizing, not using, political power." He calls Tea Party activists a "libertarian mob" since they proclaim the belief "that they can do everything themselves if they are only left alone." Lilla cites as examples the growth in home schooling and, amid a mounting distrust in doctors and conventional medicine, growing numbers of parents refusing to have their children vaccinated, not to mention our resurgent passion for self-diagnosis, self-medication and home therapies.

What Lilla cannot account for, and what no other commentator I have read can explain, is the passionate anger of the Tea Party movement, or, the flip side of that anger, the ease with which it succumbs to the most egregious of fearmongering falsehoods. What has gripped everyone's attention is the exorbitant character of the anger Tea Party members express. Where do such anger and such passionate attachment to wildly fantastic beliefs come from?

My hypothesis is that what all the events precipitating the Tea Party movement share is that they demonstrated, emphatically and unconditionally, the depths of the absolute *dependence* of us all on government action, and in so doing they undermined the deeply held fiction of individual autonomy and self-sufficiency that are intrinsic parts of Americans' collective self-understanding.

The implicit bargain that many Americans struck with the state institutions supporting modern life is that they would be politically acceptable only to the degree to which they remained invisible, and that for all intents and purposes each citizen could continue to believe that she was sovereign over her life; she would, of course, pay taxes, use the roads and schools, receive Medicare and Social Security, but only so long as these could be perceived not as radical dependencies, but simply as the conditions for leading an autonomous and self-sufficient life. Recent events have left that bargain in tatters.

But even this way of expressing the issue of dependence is too weak, too merely political; after all, although recent events have revealed the breadth and depths of our dependencies on institutions and practices over which we have little or no control, not all of us have responded with such galvanizing anger and rage. Tea Party anger is, at bottom, metaphysical, not political: what has been undone by the economic crisis is the belief that each individual is metaphysically self-sufficient, that one's very standing and being as a rational agent *owes* nothing to other individuals or institutions. The opposing metaphysical claim, the one I take to be true, is that the very idea of the autonomous subject is an *institution*, an artifact created by the practices of modern life: the intimate family, the market economy, the liberal state. Each of these social arrangements articulate and express the value and the authority of the individual; they *give* to the individual a standing she would not have without them.

Rather than participating in arranged marriages, as modern subjects we follow our hearts, choose our beloved, decide for ourselves who may or may not have access to our bodies, and freely take vows promising fidelity and loyalty until death (or divorce) do us part. There are lots of ways property can be held and distributed—as hysterical Tea Party incriminations of creeping socialism and communism remind us, we moderns have opted for a system of private ownership in which we can acquire, use, and dispose of property as we see fit, and even workers are presumed to be self-owning, selling their labor time and labor power to whom they wish (when they can). And as modern citizens we presume the government is answerable to us; governs only with our consent, our dependence on it a matter of detached, reflective endorsement; and further, that we intrinsically possess a battery of moral rights that say we can be bound to no institution unless we possess the rights of "voice and exit."

If stated in enough detail, all these institutions and practices should be seen as together *manufacturing*, and even inventing, the idea of a sovereign individual who becomes, through them and by virtue of them, the ultimate source of authority. The American version of these practices has, from the earliest days of the republic, made individuality autochthonous while suppressing to the point of disappearance the manifold ways that individuality is beholden to a complex and uniquely modern form of life.

Of course, if you are a libertarian or even a certain kind of liberal, you will object that these practices do not manufacture anything; they simply give individuality its due. The issue here is a central one in modern philosophy: Is individual autonomy an irreducible metaphysical given or a social creation? Descartes famously argued that self or subject, the "I think," was metaphysically basic, while Hegel argued that we only become self-determining agents through *being recognized* as such by others who we recognize in turn. It is by recognizing one another as autonomous subjects through the institutions of family, civil society and the state that we become such subjects;

those practices are how we recognize and so bestow on one another the title and powers of being free individuals.

All the heavy lifting in Hegel's account turns on revealing how human subjectivity only emerges through intersubjective relations, and hence how practices of independence, of freedom and autonomy, are held in place and made possible by complementary structures of dependence. At one point in his *Philosophy of Right*, Hegel suggests love or friendship as models of freedom through recognition. In love I regard you as of such value and importance that I spontaneously set aside my egoistic desires and interests and align them with yours: your ends are my desires, I desire that you flourish, and when you flourish, I do, too. In love, I experience you not as a limit or restriction on my freedom but as what makes it possible: I can only be truly free and so truly independent in being harmoniously joined with you; we each recognize the other as endowing our life with meaning and value, with living freedom. Hegel's phrase for this felicitous state is "to be with oneself in the other."

Hegel's thesis is that *all* social life is structurally akin to the conditions of love and friendship; we are all bound to one another as firmly as lovers are, with the terrible reminder that the ways of love are harsh, unpredictable and changeable. And here is the source of the great anger: because you are the source of my being, when our love goes bad, I am suddenly, absolutely dependent on someone for whom I no longer count and who I no longer know how to count; I am exposed, vulnerable, needy, unanchored and without resource. In fury, I lash out. I deny that you are my end and my satisfaction; in rage I claim that I can manage without you, that I can be a full person, free and self-moving, without you. I am everything and you are nothing.

This is the rage and anger I hear in the Tea Party movement; it is the sound of jilted lovers furious that the other—the anonymous blob called simply "government"—has suddenly let them down, suddenly made clear that they are dependent and limited beings, suddenly revealed them as vulnerable. And just as in love, the one-sided reminder of dependence is experienced as an injury. All the rhetoric of self-sufficiency, all the grand talk of wanting to be left alone is just the hollow insistence of the bereft lover that she can and will survive without her beloved. However, in political life, unlike love, there are no second marriages; we have only the one partner, and although we can rework our relationship, nothing can remove the actuality of dependence. That is permanent.

In politics, the idea of divorce is the idea of revolution. The Tea Party rhetoric of taking back the country is no accident: since they repudiate the conditions of dependency that have made their and our lives possible, they can only imagine freedom as a new beginning, starting from scratch. About this imaginary, Mark Lilla was right: it corresponds to no political vision, no political reality. The great and inspiring metaphysical fantasy of independence and freedom is simply a fantasy of destruction.

In truth, there is nothing that the Tea Party movement wants; terrifyingly, it wants *nothing*. Lilla calls the Tea Party "Jacobins"; I would urge that they are nihilists. To date, the Tea Party has committed only the minor, almost atmospheric violences of propagating falsehoods, calumny and the disruption of the occasions for political speech—the last already to great and distorting effect. But if their nihilistic rage is deprived of interrupting political meetings as an outlet, where might it now go? With such rage driving the Tea Party, might we anticipate this atmospheric violence becoming actual violence, becoming what Hegel called, referring to the original Jacobins' fantasy of total freedom, "a fury of destruction"? There is indeed something not just disturbing but frightening in the anger of the Tea Party.

JUNE 13, 2010

Is Our Patriotism Moral?

—*Gary Gutting*

To my mind, the Fourth of July has a lot going for it compared with other holidays: great food without a lot of work, warm weather, no presents, and fireworks. And in our house, at least, there's the special moment when we read out loud the Declaration of Independence and follow with a toast (American sparkling wine, of course), "To the United States of America!" And I have to force back tears of pride at being an American.

This is my own distinctive experience of what we call "patriotism," and I suspect that many Americans experience something similar and acknowledge it in their own ways. Amid the frequent confusion, frustration and anger of our political disagreements, patriotism—a deep-seated love of our country—remains something that has the potential to bring us together, particularly at times of national crisis or triumph.

But within my own particular intellectual tribe of philosophers, patriotism is often regarded as a "problem," an emotion that many find hard to defend as morally appropriate. Of course, many Americans are uneasy with, even repelled by, certain expressions of patriotism—perhaps the obligatory flag pins of politicians, the inanity of "freedom fries," the suggestion in the revised Pledge of Allegiance that atheists aren't patriotic, or even readings of the Declaration of Independence. But the philosophical problem of patriotism is not about whether or not certain expressions of patriotism are appropriate; it is about the moral defensibility of the attitude as such.

At the beginning of Plato's *Republic*, Socrates asks what justice (doing the morally right thing) is, and Polemarchus replies that it's helping your friends and harming your enemies. That was the answer among the ancient Greeks as well as many other traditional societies. Moral behavior was the way you treated those in your "in-group," as opposed to outsiders.

Socrates questioned this ethical exclusivism, thus beginning a centuries-long argument that, by modern times, led most major moral philosophers (for example, Mill and Kant) to conclude that morality required an impartial, universal viewpoint that treated all human beings as equals. In other words, the "in-group" for morality is not any particular social group (family, city, nation) but humankind as a whole. This universal moral viewpoint seems to reject patriotism for "cosmopolitanism"—the view perhaps first formulated by Diogenes, who, when asked where he came from, replied that he was a citizen of the world.

Certainly, patriotism can take an explicitly amoral form: "My country, right or wrong." But even strong traditional patriots can accept moral limits on the means we use to advance the cause of our country. They may agree, for example, that it's wrong to threaten Canada with nuclear annihilation to obtain a more favorable trade agreement.

But the moral problem for patriotism arises at a deeper level. Suppose the question is not about blatantly immoral means but simply about whether our country should flourish at the expense of another. Suppose, for example, that at some point Saudi Arabia, now allied with China, threatened to curtail our access to its oil, thereby significantly reducing our productivity and tipping the balance of world economic power to China. Imagine an American president who declined to oppose this action because he had concluded that, from a disinterested moral viewpoint, it was better for mankind as a whole. Even if we admired such a response, it's hard to think that it would express patriotic regard for the United States.

Should we therefore conclude that patriotism is ultimately at odds with a moral viewpoint? There remains the option of denying that morality has the universal, all-inclusive nature modern philosophers think it has. Alasdair MacIntyre, for example, argues that morality is rooted in the life of a specific real community—a village, a city, a nation, with its idiosyncratic customs and history—and that, therefore, adherence to morality requires loyalty to such a community. Patriotism, on this view, is essential for living a morally good life. MacIntyre's argument (in his Lindley Lecture, "Is Patriotism a Virtue?") has provided the most powerful contemporary defense of a full-blooded patriotism.

It may seem, then, that we must either accept modern universalist ethics and reject patriotism as a basic moral virtue or accept patriotism along with MacIntyre's traditional localist morality. But perhaps, at least in the American context, there is a way of avoiding the dilemma.

For what is the animating ideal of American patriotism if not the freedom of all persons, not just its own citizens? This is apparent in our Declaration, which bases its case for independence on the principle that government exist to "secure the rights" of "life, liberty and the pursuit of happiness" to which all persons are equally entitled. This principle is the avowed purpose of all our actions as a nation, and we may read our history as the story of our successes and failures in carrying out this principle. America, then, is the paradox of a local historical project that aims at universal liberation. Through this project, we have a way of combining traditional patriotism with universal morality.

This project has had many failures, most often when we forget that the freedom of a nation must always grow from its own historical roots. We cannot simply wage a war that rips up those roots and then transplant shoots from our own stock (American-style capitalism, political parties, our popular culture). We have also often forgotten that the liberation of our own citizens is by no means complete. But none of this alters the fact that our governments have often worked and our soldiers died not just for our own freedom but for the freedom of all nations.

We are a MacIntyrean community that is still trying to live out a modern morality that seeks the freedom of everyone. I love America because I still believe that this sublime project is possible.

JULY 3, 2012

The Cycle of Revenge

—*Simon Critchley*

I'VE NEVER UNDERSTOOD THE PROVERBIAL WISDOM THAT REVENGE is a dish best served cold. Some seem to like it hot. Better is the Chinese proverb, attributed to Confucius, "Before you embark on a journey of revenge, dig two graves." Osama bin Laden's grave was watery, but the other still appears empty. Is it intended for us?

Revenge is the desire to repay an injury or a wrong by inflicting harm, often the violent sort. If you hit me, I will hit you back. Furthermore, by the logic of revenge, I am right to hit you back. The initial wrong justifies the act of revenge. But does that wrong really make it right for me to hit back? Once we act out of revenge, don't we become mired in a cycle of violence and counterviolence with no apparent end? Such is arguably our current predicament.

Of course, moving from ends to beginnings, the other peculiarity of revenge is that it is often unclear who committed the first wrong or threw the first stone. If someone, George W. Bush say, asserts that the United States is justified in revenging itself on Al Qaeda by invading Afghanistan, then Iraq and the rest of the brutal saga of the last ten years, what would Bin Laden have said? Well, the opposite of course.

In a scarily fascinating 2004 video, called "The Towers of Lebanon," in which Bin Laden claimed direct responsibility for 9/11 for the first time, he says that the September 11 attacks were justified as an act of revenge. If the United States violates the security of the

Muslim world—especially by using his homeland of Saudi Arabia as a base during the first Gulf War—then Al Qaeda is justified in violating American security. If there had been no initial violation, he claims, there would be no need for revenge. Bin Laden contrasts the United States with Sweden: as the Swedes have never been aggressors in the Muslim world, he says, they have nothing to fear from Al Qaeda.

Bin Laden then reveals the extraordinary fact that the idea for 9/11 originated in his visual memory of the 1982 Israeli bombardments of West Beirut's high-rise apartment blocks. He recalls his intense reaction to seeing images of the destroyed towers there and formed the following notion: "It occurred to me to punish the oppressor in kind by destroying towers in America." ("Missile into towers," he might have whispered; the idea stuck.) The September 11 attacks, which most of us remember as a series of visual images repeatedly televised and published, originate with an earlier series of images. For Bin Laden, there was a strange kind of visual justice in 9/11, the retributive paying back of an image for an image, an eye for an eye.

Opposites attract—the awful violence of 9/11 is justified by Al Qaeda as an act of revenge that in turn justifies the violence of America's and Bush's revenge. My point is that revenge is an inevitably destructive motive for action. When we act out of revenge, revenge is what we will receive in return. The wheel of violence and counterviolence spins without end and leads inevitably to destruction.

This is exactly what Bin Laden hoped to bring about. He admits that Al Qaeda spent $500,000 on the 9/11 attacks, while estimating that the United States lost, at the lowest estimate, $500 billion in the event and the aftermath. He even does the math. "That makes a million American dollars for every Al Qaeda dollar, by the grace of God Almighty." He concludes, ominously, "This shows the success of our plan to bleed America to the point of bankruptcy, with God's will."

Like it or not (I don't like it at all), Bin Laden had a point. The last ten years of unending war on terror has also led, at least partly, to the utter financial precariousness that we see at every level of life in the

United States: federal, state, city and individuals laden with debt. We are bankrupt.

But why grant Bin Laden some sick posthumous victory? Consider an alternative scenario.

In a 1999 Republican debate George W. Bush, then a candidate, responded—to the accompaniment of complacent guffaws from liberals—to a question about which political philosopher he most identified with: "Christ, because he changed my heart," Bush said. In that case, it was fair to wonder what might Jesus have recommended in response to 9/11. The answer, of course, is clear: turn the other cheek.

In the New Testament, Peter asks Jesus about the quantity of forgiveness: How many times should we forgive someone who has sinned against us? Is seven times enough? He wonders out loud, to which Jesus replies, from his full messianic height, "No, not seven times, but seventy times seven," meaning, there is no quantity to forgiveness, just an infinite quality.

Think back ten years, if you will. In the days and weeks that followed 9/11, the people of New York City, Washington, and indeed the entire United States were the recipients of an unquantifiable wave of empathy from across the world. The initial effect of 9/11 (I was still living in England at the time) was the confirmation in the minds of many millions of people that New York was an extraordinary place that rightly engendered huge affection, indeed love.

Ask yourself: What if nothing had happened after 9/11? No revenge, no retribution, no failed surgical strikes on the Afghanistan-Pakistan border, no poorly planned bloody fiasco in Iraq, no surges and no insurgencies to surge against—nothing.

What if the government had simply decided to turn the other cheek and forgive those who sought to attack it, not seven times, but seventy times seven? What if the grief and mourning that followed 9/11 were allowed to foster a nonviolent ethics of compassion rather than a violent politics of revenge and retribution? What if the crime of the September 11 attacks had led not to an unending war on terror but the cultivation of a practice of peace—a difficult, fraught and ever-compromised endeavor, but perhaps worth the attempt?

As we know all too well, this didn't happen. Instead, all of that glorious global fellow feeling was wasted and allowed to dissipate in acts of revenge that have bankrupted this country, both financially and spiritually.

Perhaps the second grave is ours. We dug it ourselves. The question now is, do we have to lie in it?

SEPTEMBER 8, 2011

What Is a "Hacktivist"?

—Peter Ludlow

THE UNTIMELY DEATH OF THE YOUNG INTERNET ACTIVIST AARON Swartz, apparently by suicide, has prompted an outpouring of reaction in the digital world. Foremost among the debates being reheated—one which had already grown in the wake of larger and more daring data breaches in the past few years—is whether Swartz's activities as a "hacktivist" were being unfairly defined as malicious or criminal. In particular, critics (as well as Swartz's family in a formal statement) have focused on the federal government's indictment of Swartz for downloading millions of documents from the scholarly database JSTOR, an action which JSTOR itself had declined to prosecute.

I believe the debate itself is far broader than the specifics of this unhappy case, for if there was prosecutorial overreach, it raises the question of whether we as a society created the enabling condition for this sort of overreach by letting the demonization of hacktivists go unanswered. Prosecutors do not work in a vacuum, after all; they are more apt to pursue cases where public discourse supports their actions. The debate thus raises an issue that, as a philosopher of language, I have spent time considering: the impact of how words and terms are defined in the public sphere.

"Lexical warfare" is a phrase that I like to use for battles over how a term is to be understood. Our political discourse is full of such battles; it is pretty routine to find discussions of who gets to be called

"Republican" (as opposed to RINO—Republican in Name Only), what "freedom" should mean, what legitimately gets to be called "rape"— and the list goes on.

Lexical warfare is important because it can be a device to marginalize individuals within their self-identified political affiliation (for example, branding RINOs defines them as something other than true Republicans), or it can beguile us into ignoring true threats to freedom (focusing on threats from government while being blind to threats from corporations, religion, and custom), and in cases in which the word in question is "rape," the definition can have far-reaching consequences for the rights of women and social policy.

Lexical warfare is not exclusively concerned with changing the definitions of words and terms—it can also work to attach either a negative or positive affect to a term. Ronald Reagan and other conservatives successfully loaded the word "liberal" with negative connotations, while enhancing the positive aura of terms like "patriot" (few today would reject the label "patriotic" but rather argue for why they are entitled to it).

Over the past few years we've watched a lexical warfare battle slowly unfold in the treatment of the term "hacktivism." There has been an effort to redefine what the word means and what kinds of activities it describes; at the same time there has been an effort to tarnish the hacktivist label so that anyone who chooses to label themselves as such does so at their peril.

In the simplest and broadest sense, a hacktivist is someone who uses technology hacking to effect social change. The conflict now is between those who want to change the meaning of the word to denote immoral, sinister activities and those who want to defend the broader, more inclusive understanding of hacktivist. Let's start with those who are trying to change the meaning so that it denotes sinister activities.

Over the past year several newspapers and blogs have cited Verizon's 2012 *Data Breach Investigations Report*, which claimed that 58 percent of all data leaked in 2011 was owing to the actions of "ideologically motivated hacktivists." An example of the concern was an article in *Infosecurity Magazine*:

> *The year 2011 is renowned for being the year that hacktivists out-stole cybercriminals to take top honors according to the Verizon data breach report. Of the 174 million stolen records it tracked in 2011, 100 million were taken by hacktivist groups.*
>
> *Suddenly, things are looking black and white again. Regardless of political motivation or intent, if there are victims of the attacks they perpetrate, then hacktivism has crossed the line. Not OK.*

Meanwhile an article in *Threatpost* proclaimed "Anonymous: Hacktivists Steal Most Data in 2011."

The first thing to note is that both of these media sources are written by and for members of the information security business—it is in their interest to manufacture a threat, for the simple reason that threats mean business for these groups. But is it fair to say that the threat is being "manufactured"? What of the Verizon report that they cite?

The problem is that the headlines and articles, designed to tar hacktivists and make us fear them, did not reflect what the Verizon report actually said. According to page 19 of the report, only 3 percent of the data breaches in the survey were by hacktivists—the bulk of them were by routine cybercriminals, disgruntled employees and nation-states (83 percent were by organized criminals).

The "most data" claim, while accurate, gives a skewed picture. According to Chris Novak, the managing principal of investigative response on Verizon's RISK Team, interviewed in *Threatpost*, 2 percent of the ninety actions analyzed in the report accounted for 58 percent of the data released. The interview with Novak suggests that this data loss came from precisely two hacktivist actions—both by spin-offs of the well-known hacktivist group Anonymous—and that these large data dumps stemmed from the actions against the security firm HBGary Federal, which had publicly announced their efforts to expose Anonymous, and a computer security firm called

Stratfor. That means that in 2011 if you were worried about an intrusion into your system, it was thirty-three times more likely that the perpetrator would be a criminal, nation-state or disgruntled employee than a hacktivist. If you weren't picking fights with Anonymous, the chances would have dropped to zero—at least according to the cases analyzed in the report.

In effect, these infosecurity media outlets cited two actions by Anonymous spin-offs, implicated that actions like this were a principle project of hacktivism, and thereby implicated a larger, imminent threat of hacktivism. Meanwhile, the meaning of hacktivist was being narrowed from people who use technology in support of social causes to meaning individuals principally concerned with infiltrating and releasing the data of almost anyone.

Now let's turn to an attempt to maintain the broader understanding of hacktivism. Several months ago I attended a birthday party in Germany for Daniel Domscheit-Berg, who was turning thirty-four. As it happened, Domscheit-Berg had also been the spokesperson for WikiLeaks and, after Julian Assange, the group's most visible person. He had left the organization in 2010, and now he had a new venture, OpenLeaks. The party was also meant to be a coming-out party for OpenLeaks.

The party was to be held in the new headquarters and training center for OpenLeaks—a large house in a small town about an hour outside of Berlin. I was half-expecting to find a bunker full of hackers probing websites with SQL injections and sifting through State Department cables, but what I found was something else altogether.

When I arrived at the house, the first thing I noticed was a large vegetable garden outside. The second thing I noticed was that a tree out front had been fitted out with a colorful knit wool sweater. This was the effort of Daniel's wife Anke—"knit hacking," she called it. And around the small town I saw evidence of her guerilla knit hacking. The steel poles of nearby street signs had also been fitted with woolen sweaters. Most impressively, though, a World War II tank, sitting outside a nearby former Nazi concentration camp for women, had also been knit-hacked; the entire barrel of the tank's gun had been fit with a tight, colorful wool sweater and adorned with some woolen flowers for good measure. I interpreted these knit hackings as counteractions to the attempts to define hacktivist as something sinister; they serve as ostensive definitions of what hacktivism is and what hacktivists do.

Of course the birthday party had elements of hackerdom understood more narrowly. There were some members of the Chaos Computer Club (a legendary hacker group), and there was a healthy supply of Club-Mate (the energy drink of choice of European hackers), but the main message being delivered was something else: a do-it-yourself aesthetic—planting your own garden, knitting your own sweaters, foraging for mushrooms and counting on a local friend to bag you some venison. What part of this lifestyle was the hacktivism part? Daniel and his friends would like to say that all of it is.

The intention here was clear: an attempt to defend the traditional, less sinister understanding of hacktivism and perhaps broaden it a bit, adding some positive affect to boot; more specifically, that hacking is fundamentally about refusing to be intimidated or cowed into submission by any technology, about understanding the technology and acquiring the power to repurpose it to our individual needs and for the good of the many. Moreover, they were saying that a true hacktivist doesn't favor new technology over old—what is critical is that the technologies be in our hands rather than out of our control. This ideal, theoretically, should extend beyond computer use to technologies for food production, shelter and clothing, and of course, to all the means we use to communicate with one another. It would also, of course, extend to access to knowledge more generally—a value that was inherent in Aaron Swartz's hacking of the JSTOR database.

Our responsibility in this particular episode of lexical warfare is to be critical and aware of the public uses of language and to be alert to what is at stake—whether the claims made by the infosecurity industry or the government, or the gestures by the hacktivists, are genuine, misleading or correct. We are not passive observers in this dispute. The meaning of words is determined by those of us who use language, and it has consequences. Whether or not Aaron Swartz suffered because of the manipulation of the public discourse surrounding hacking, his case is a reminder that it is important that we be attuned to attempts to change the meanings of words in consequential ways. It is important because we are the ones who will decide who will win.

JANUARY 13, 2013

The Myth of "Just Do It"

—Barbara Gail Montero

YOGI BERRA, THE FORMER MAJOR LEAGUE BASEBALL CATCHER and coach, once remarked that you can't hit and think at the same time. Of course, since he also reportedly said, "I really didn't say everything I said," it is not clear we should take his statements at face value. Nonetheless, a widespread view—in both academic journals and the popular press—is that thinking about what you are doing, as you are doing it, interferes with performance. The idea is that once you have developed the ability to play an arpeggio on the piano, putt a golf ball or parallel park, attention to what you are doing leads to inaccuracies, blunders and sometimes even utter paralysis. As the great choreographer George Balanchine would say to his dancers, "Don't think, dear; just do."

Perhaps you have experienced this destructive force yourself. Start thinking about just how to carry a full glass of water without spilling, and you'll end up drenched. How, exactly, do you initiate a telephone conversation? Begin wondering, and before long, the recipient of your call will notice the heavy breathing and hang up. Our actions, the French philosopher Maurice Merleau-Ponty tells us, exhibit a "magical" efficacy; yet when we focus on them, they degenerate into the absurd. A thirteen-time winner on the Professional Golfers' Association Tour, Dave Hill, put it like this: "Golf is like sex. You can't be thinking about the mechanics of the act while you are performing."

But why not?

A classic study by Timothy Wilson and Jonathan Schooler is frequently cited in support of the notion that experts, when performing at their best, act intuitively and automatically and don't think about what they are doing as they are doing it, but just do it. The study divided subjects, who were college students, into two groups. In both groups, participants were asked to rank five brands of jam from best to worst. In one group they were asked to also explain their reasons for their rankings. The group whose sole task was to rank the jams ended up with fairly consistent judgments both among themselves and in comparison with the judgments of expert food tasters, as recorded in *Consumer Reports.* The rankings of the other group, however, went haywire, with subjects' preferences neither in line with one another's nor in line with the preferences of the experts. Why should this be? The researchers posit that when subjects explained their choices, they thought more about them. Thinking, it is therefore suggested, interferes with doing. Malcolm Gladwell sums it more colorfully: "By making people think about jam, Wilson and Schooler turned them into jam idiots."

But the take-home message from Wilson and Schooler's experiment ought to be quite the opposite. The expert food tasters were able to both provide reasons for their choices and, arguably, make the best choices. Thus, we should conclude that poor choices come not from thinking but from not being trained how to think.

Although novice athletes need to think about what they are doing, experts in normal situations, we are told by the University of Chicago psychologist Sian Beilock in her recent book *Choke*, ought not to since, as she puts it, "careful consideration can get them in trouble." Based on experiments she and her colleagues have performed, she concludes that high-pressure situations lead experts to think in action and that such thinking tends to cause choking, or "paralysis by analysis." To prevent this, she advises, you need to "play outside your head."

Yet contrary to Beilock's findings, rather than keeping their minds out of the picture, experts at least sometimes seem to avoid the type of performance detriments associated with high-pressure situations precisely by concentrating intensely and focusing on the details of their movements. When one's mind is consumed by the angular momentum of one's golf swing, there is no room for the type of nerves that lead to a choke.

That experts increase their focus on the task at hand in order to cope with pressure is suggested by studies, like those carried out by the University of Hull sports and exercise psychologist Adam Nicholls, which ask professional or elite athletes to keep a diary of stressors that occur and coping strategies that they employ during games. Though small scale, these studies do indicate that a common method of dealing with stress involves redoubling both effort and attention. As Nicholls told me when I asked him about it, "Increasing effort was an effective strategy and really helped the players."

Of course, one may wonder whether athletes, or anyone for that matter, have accurate insight into what goes on in their minds. Beilock's work, for the most part, avoids this worry since her methods are comparatively objective. For example, in one study she and her research team measured the accuracy of golf putts when players were distracted from what they were doing compared with when they were asked to focus on what they were doing. Such a procedure does not rely on subjective reports.

Yet there is a trade-off between greater objectivity and what researchers call "ecological validity." Nicholls's work, while perhaps less objective, is more ecologically valid because it looks at experts in real-life settings, asking them to do nothing other than what they would normally do. In contrast, Beilock—in a study suggesting that "well-learned performance may actually be compromised by attending to skill execution"—asks subjects who are putting golf balls to say, "Stop," out loud at the exact moment they finish the follow-through of their swing. True enough, this interfered with performance. Yet expert golfers do not normally focus on the exact moment they complete their follow-through; expert golfers, when thinking about their actions, focus on something that matters. In fact, such a task would seem to be more distracting than any of the study's explicit distractions.

Moreover, in contrast to Beilock's studies, which typically use college students as subjects, Nicholls works with professional-level experts. This is relevant since, as with Wilson and Schooler's experiment, it is the expert and not necessarily the college student with a couple of years, or sometimes a couple of hours, of experience who has the ability to hit and think at the same time.

Though the University of California at Berkeley philosopher Hubert Dreyfus takes his inspiration more from Merleau-Ponty and Martin Heidegger than from empirical studies, the conclusions he arrives at resonate with Beilock's. Dreyfus has long argued that "the enemy of expertise is thought" and that the apogee of human performance is exemplified in seamless, unreflective actions in which the self disappears. In a debate with the University of Pittsburgh philosopher John McDowell, published in the journal *Inquiry*, Dreyfus tells us that whenever Homer describes his heroes at a feast, instead of having them deliberately reach for bread in baskets or bowls brimful of drink, "their arms shot out to the food lying ready before them." Similarly, says Dreyfus, the grandmaster chess player might find "his arm going out and making a move before he can take in the board position." As with the master archer in Eugen Herrigel's perennially popular *Zen in the Art of Archery*, neither Odysseus feasting at a banquet nor the grandmaster playing chess moves his arm; rather, "it shoots."

It may very well be that our ordinary actions, like eating—especially when famished after a battle—do in some sense just happen to us. Yet what are we to say about the grandmaster as he closes the mating net? According to Dreyfus, Merleau-Ponty and Heidegger teach us that "what we are directly open to is not rational or even conceptual . . . [rather,] it is the affordance's solicitation—such as the attraction of an apple when I'm hungry." The problem with this picture for chess, however, is that the attractive apple is often poisoned. In such cases, leaving reason behind leads you right into your opponent's trap.

In *All Things Shining: Reading the Western Classics to Find Meaning in a Secular Age*, which can be seen as a paean to the idea that exemplary performance happens to, rather than is done by, an individual, Dreyfus and his coauthor, the Harvard philosopher Sean Kelly, argue that letting the self get washed away in action is the key to living a meaningful life: it is when we are "taken over by the situation" that life "really shines and matters most." But is this right? The question "What is the meaning of life?" is, of course, a big one; however, if it includes developing one's potential, what Immanuel Kant spoke of in the *Groundwork for the Metaphysics of Morals* as our duty to cultivate our "predispositions to greater perfection," a duty he saw as often involving a struggle, then the idea that the expert should stand back and effortlessly let it happen just isn't going to do it.

I remember how difficult philosophy seemed when I was an undergraduate at Berkeley. I was taking epistemology with Barry Stroud at the time and, feeling a bit disheartened, went to his office and asked, "Does it ever get easier?" No, it doesn't, he told me, since as you grow as a philosopher you work on increasingly more difficult problems. Although this was not the response I was hoping for, it made sense immediately, for I was entering college directly from a career as a professional ballet dancer. Ballet, I knew, never gets easier; if anything, it gets harder, because as you develop as a dancer you develop both stricter standards for what counts as good dancing and your ability to evaluate your dancing, finding flaws that previously went unnoticed. Just as in Plato's dialogue, *The Apology*, Socrates is wise because he knows that he is ignorant, it is, among other things, the ability to recognize where there is room for improvement that allows expert dancers to reach great heights.

The ability to see room for improvement, however, is not of much use unless one also has a strong and continuing desire to improve. And it may be that, more so than talent, it is this desire to improve, an attitude the Japanese call "kaizen," that turns a novice into an expert. I certainly had kaizen in abundance, as did most every professional dancer I knew. It was ingrained in my body and mind to the extent that every class, rehearsal and performance was in part aimed at self-improvement. And improving, especially after you have acquired a high level of skill, typically requires an enormous amount of effort. Sometimes this effort is physical—and it certainly involves more physical effort than philosophy—yet it also involves concentration, thought, deliberation and will power.

The philosophers and psychologists who advocate a just-do-it mentality all admit that during those rare occasions when something goes wrong, performers or athletes need to direct their attention to their actions. Yet although from an audience's point of view, things rarely go wrong, from the expert's point of view, things are going wrong all the time. Lynn Seymour, who was a principal dancer with the Royal Ballet, commented that when she danced with Rudolph Nureyev in the film *I Am a Dancer*, she was too cowardly to ever watch it: "Whenever I see myself dancing I practically die."

When we make the morning coffee, tie our shoes, or drive to work, we are satisfied with performance that is good enough. And it is easy to see how an evolutionary advantage could accrue to those who could think about more important things during routine activities like grooming. Yet there are significant differences between everyday actions and the actions of experts, since for a golfer at the US Open or a dancer on stage at the Royal Opera House, there is nothing more important than the task at hand.

Perhaps golf is like sex, not because, as Dave Hill claimed, attention to performance interferes with expert action, but rather because both the sex drive and the expert's drive to excel can be all-encompassing. And excelling in such highly competitive arenas as professional-level golf requires not just doing what has normally worked but doing better than ever. Yet doing better than ever cannot be automatic.

In its "just do it" advertising campaign, Nike presumably used the phrase to mean something like, "Stop procrastinating, get off your posterior and get the job done." Interpreted as such, I'm in favor of "just do it." However, when interpreted as "Experts perform best when not thinking about what they are doing," the idea of just-do-it is a myth.

If so, the enormous popularity of books that tell us how to achieve mastery in chess, cinch a business deal or become a better parent with neither effort nor thought nor attention may turn on our preference for "magical" efficiency over honest toil. They reach the status of best sellers for the same reason as do diet books that advocate eating as much as you want as long as you abstain from some arbitrary category of food: not because they work, but because they are easy to follow.

As for Balanchine's claim that his dancers shouldn't think, I asked Violette Verdy about this. Verdy was a principal dancer with the New York City Ballet for eighteen years under Balanchine's direction. But she brushed off the question. "Oh, that," she replied. "He only said that when a dancer was stuck; like an elevator between floors."

JUNE 9, 2013

How to Live Without Irony

—*Christy Wampole*

I F IRONY IS THE ETHOS OF OUR AGE—AND IT IS—THEN THE HIP-
ster is our archetype of ironic living.

The hipster haunts every city street and university town. Man-
ifesting a nostalgia for times he never lived himself, this contemporary urban harlequin appropriates outmoded fashions (the
mustache, the tiny shorts), mechanisms (fixed-gear bicycles, porta-
ble record players) and hobbies (home brewing, playing trombone).
He harvests awkwardness and self-consciousness. Before he makes
any choice, he has proceeded through several stages of self-scrutiny.
The hipster is a scholar of social forms, a student of cool. He studies
relentlessly, foraging for what has yet to be found by the mainstream.
He is a walking citation; his clothes refer to much more than themselves. He tries to negotiate the age-old problem of individuality, not
with concepts, but with material things.

He is an easy target for mockery. However, scoffing at the hipster
is only a diluted form of his own affliction. He is merely a symptom and the most extreme manifestation of ironic living. For many
Americans born in the 1980s and 1990s—members of Generation Y,
or Millennials—particularly middle-class Caucasians, irony is the
primary mode with which daily life is dealt. One need only dwell in
public space, virtual or concrete, to see how pervasive this phenomenon has become. Advertising, politics, fashion, television: almost
every category of contemporary reality exhibits this will to irony.

Take, for example, an ad that calls itself an ad, makes fun of its own format, and attempts to lure its target market to laugh at and with it. It preemptively acknowledges its own failure to accomplish anything meaningful. No attack can be set against it, as it has already conquered itself. The ironic frame functions as a shield against criticism. The same goes for ironic living. Irony is the most self-defensive mode, as it allows a person to dodge responsibility for his or her choices, aesthetic and otherwise. To live ironically is to hide in public. It is flagrantly indirect, a form of subterfuge, which means etymologically to "secretly flee" (subter + fuge). Somehow, directness has become unbearable to us.

How did this happen? It stems in part from the belief that this generation has little to offer in terms of culture, that everything has already been done, or that serious commitment to any belief will eventually be subsumed by an opposing belief, rendering the first laughable at best and contemptible at worst. This kind of defensive living works as a preemptive surrender and takes the form of reaction rather than action.

Life in the Internet age has undoubtedly helped a certain ironic sensibility to flourish. An ethos can be disseminated quickly and widely through this medium. Our incapacity to deal with the things at hand is evident in our use of, and increasing reliance on, digital technology. Prioritizing what is remote over what is immediate, the virtual over the actual, we are absorbed in the public and private sphere by the little devices that take us elsewhere.

Furthermore, the nostalgia cycles have become so short that we even try to inject the present moment with sentimentality, for example, by using certain digital filters to "prewash" photos with an aura of historicity. Nostalgia needs time. One cannot accelerate meaningful remembrance.

While we have gained some skill sets (multitasking, technological savvy), other skills have suffered: the art of conversation, the art of looking at people, the art of being seen, the art of being present. Our conduct is no longer governed by subtlety, finesse, grace and attention, all qualities more esteemed in earlier decades. Inwardness and narcissism now hold sway.

Born in 1977, at the tail end of Generation X, I came of age in the 1990s, a decade that, bracketed neatly by two architectural crumblings—of the Berlin Wall in 1989 and the Twin Towers in 2001—now seems relatively irony-free. The grunge movement was serious in its aesthetics and its attitude, with a combative stance against authority, which the punk movement had also embraced. In my perhaps overnostalgic memory, feminism reached an unprecedented peak, environmentalist concerns gained widespread attention, questions of race were more openly addressed: all of these stirrings contained within them the same electricity and euphoria touching generations that witness a centennial or millennial changeover.

But Y2K came and went without disaster. We were hopeful throughout the '90s, but hope is such a vulnerable emotion; we needed a self-defense mechanism, for every generation has one. For Gen Xers, it was a kind of diligent apathy. We actively did not care. Our archetype was the slacker who slouched through life in plaid flannel, alone in his room, misunderstood. And when we were bored with not caring, we were vaguely angry and melancholic, eating antidepressants like they were candy.

From this vantage, the ironic clique appears simply too comfortable, too brainlessly compliant. Ironic living is a first-world problem. For the relatively well educated and financially secure, irony functions as a kind of credit card you never have to pay back. In other words, the hipster can frivolously invest in sham social capital without ever paying back one sincere dime. He doesn't own anything he possesses.

Obviously, hipsters (male or female) produce a distinct irritation in me, one that until recently I could not explain. They provoke me, I realized, because they are, despite the distance from which I observe them, an amplified version of me.

I, too, exhibit ironic tendencies. For example, I find it difficult to give sincere gifts. Instead, I often give what in the past would have been accepted only at a white elephant gift exchange: a kitschy painting from a thrift store, a coffee mug with flashy images of "Texas, the Lone Star State," plastic Mexican wrestler figures. Good for a chuckle in the moment, but worth little in the long term. Something about the responsibility of choosing a personal, meaningful gift for a friend feels too intimate, too momentous. I somehow cannot bear the thought of a friend disliking a gift I'd chosen with sincerity. The simple act of noticing my self-defensive behavior has made me think deeply about how potentially toxic ironic posturing could be.

First, it signals a deep aversion to risk. As a function of fear and preemptive shame, ironic living bespeaks cultural numbness, resignation and defeat. If life has become merely a clutter of kitsch objects, an endless series of sarcastic jokes and pop references, a competition to see who can care the least (or, at minimum, a performance of such a competition), it seems we've made a collective misstep. Could this be the cause of our emptiness and existential malaise? Or a symptom?

Throughout history, irony has served useful purposes, like providing a rhetorical outlet for unspoken societal tensions. But our contemporary ironic mode is somehow deeper; it has leaked from the realm of rhetoric into life itself. This ironic ethos can lead to a vacuity and vapidity of the individual and collective psyche. Historically, vacuums eventually have been filled by something—more often than not, a hazardous something. Fundamentalists are never ironists; dictators are never ironists; people who move things in the political landscape, regardless of the sides they choose, are never ironists.

Where can we find other examples of nonironic living? What does it look like? Nonironic models include very young children, elderly people, deeply religious people, people with severe mental or physical disabilities, people who have suffered, and those from economically or politically challenged places where seriousness is the governing state of mind. My friend Robert Pogue Harrison put it this way in a recent conversation: "Wherever the real imposes itself, it tends to dissipate the fogs of irony."

Observe a four-year-old child going through her daily life. You will not find the slightest bit of irony in her behavior. She has not, so to speak, taken on the veil of irony. She likes what she likes and declares it without dissimulation. She is not particularly conscious of the scrutiny of others. She does not hide behind indirect language. The most pure nonironic models in life, however, are to be found in nature: animals and plants are exempt from irony, which exists only where the human dwells.

What would it take to overcome the cultural pull of irony? Moving away from the ironic involves saying what you mean, meaning what you say, and considering seriousness and forthrightness as expressive possibilities, despite the inherent risks. It means undertaking the cultivation of sincerity, humility and self-effacement, and demoting the frivolous and the kitschy on our collective scale of values. It might also consist of an honest self-inventory.

Here is a start: Look around your living space. Do you surround yourself with things you really like or things you like only because they are absurd? Listen to your own speech. Ask yourself, Do I communicate primarily through inside jokes and pop culture references? What percentage of my speech is meaningful? How much hyperbolic language do I use? Do I feign indifference? Look at your clothes. What parts of your wardrobe could be described as costume-like, derivative or reminiscent of some specific style archetype (the secretary, the hobo, the flapper, yourself as a child)? In other words, do your clothes refer to something else or only to themselves? Do you attempt to look intentionally nerdy, awkward or ugly? In other words, is your style an antistyle? The most important question is, How would it feel to change yourself quietly, offline, without public display, from within?

Attempts to banish irony have come and gone in past decades. The loosely defined New Sincerity movements in the arts that have sprouted since the 1980s positioned themselves as responses to postmodern cynicism, detachment, and metareferentiality. (New Sincerity has recently been associated with the writing of David Foster Wallace, the films of Wes Anderson and the music of Cat Power.) But these attempts failed to stick, as evidenced by the new age of Deep Irony.

What will future generations make of this rampant sarcasm and unapologetic cultivation of silliness? Will we be satisfied to leave an archive filled with video clips of people doing stupid things? Is an ironic legacy even a legacy at all?

The ironic life is certainly a provisional answer to the problems of too much comfort, too much history and too many choices, but it is my firm conviction that this mode of living is not viable and conceals within it many social and political risks. For such a large segment of the population to forfeit its civic voice through the pattern of negation I've described is to siphon energy from the cultural reserves of the community at large. People may choose to continue hiding behind the ironic mantle, but this choice equals a surrender to commercial and political entities more than happy to act as parents for a self-infantilizing citizenry. So rather than scoffing at the hipster—a favorite hobby, especially of hipsters—determine whether the ashes of irony have settled on you as well. It takes little effort to dust them away.

NOVEMBER 17, 2012

Navigating Past Nihilism

—Sean D. Kelly

"NIHILISM STANDS AT THE DOOR," WROTE NIETZSCHE. "WHENCE comes this uncanniest of all guests?" The year was 1885 or 1886, and Nietzsche was writing in a notebook whose contents were not intended for publication. The discussion of nihilism—the sense that it is no longer obvious what our most fundamental commitments are, or what matters in a life of distinction and worth, the sense that the world is an abyss of meaning rather than its God-given preserve—finds no sustained treatment in the works that Nietzsche prepared for publication during his lifetime. But a few years earlier, in 1882, the German philosopher had already published a possible answer to the question of nihilism's ultimate source. "God is dead," Nietzsche wrote in a famous passage from *The Gay Science*. "God remains dead. And we have killed him."

There is much debate about the meaning of Nietzsche's famous claim, and I will not attempt to settle that scholarly dispute here. But at least one of the things that Nietzsche could have meant is that the social role that the Judeo-Christian God plays in our culture is radically different from the one he has traditionally played in prior epochs of the West. For it used to be the case in the European Middle Ages, for example, that the mainstream of society was grounded so firmly in its Christian beliefs that someone who did not share those beliefs could therefore not be taken seriously as living an even potentially admirable life. Indeed, a life outside the church was not only execrable but condemnable, and in certain periods of European history it invited a close encounter with a burning pyre.

Whatever role religion plays in our society today, it is not this one. For today's religious believers feel strong social pressure to admit that someone who doesn't share their religious belief might nevertheless be living a life worthy of their admiration. That is not to say that every religious believer accepts this constraint. But to the extent that they do not, then society now rightly condemns them as dangerous religious fanatics rather than sanctioning them as scions of the church or mosque. God is dead, therefore, in a very particular sense. He no longer plays his traditional social role of organizing us around a commitment to a single right way to live. Nihilism is one state a culture may reach when it no longer has a unique and agreed-upon social ground.

The twentieth century saw an onslaught of literary depictions of the nihilistic state. The story had both positive and negative sides. On the positive end, when it is no longer clear in a culture what its most basic commitments are, when the structure of a worthwhile and well-lived life is no longer agreed upon and taken for granted, then a new sense of freedom may open up. Ways of living life that had earlier been marginalized or demonized may now achieve recognition or even be held up and celebrated. Social mobility—for African-Americans, gays, women, workers, people with disabilities or others who had been held down by the traditional culture—may finally become a possibility. The exploration and articulation of these new possibilities for living a life was found in such great twentieth-century figures as Martin Luther King Jr., Simone de Beauvoir, Studs Terkel and many others.

But there is a downside to the freedom of nihilism as well, and the people living in the culture may experience this in a variety of ways. Without any clear and agreed-upon sense for what to be aiming at in a life, people may experience the paralyzing type of indecision depicted by T. S. Eliot in his famously vacillating character Prufrock; or they may feel, like the characters in a Samuel Beckett play, as though they are continuously waiting for something to become clear in their lives before they can get on with living them; or they may feel the kind of "stomach level sadness" that David Foster Wallace described, a sadness that drives them to distract themselves by any number of entertainments, addictions, competitions or arbitrary goals, each of which leaves them feeling emptier than the last. The threat of nihilism is the threat that freedom from the constraint of agreed-upon norms opens up new possibilities in the culture only through its fundamentally destabilizing force.

There may be parts of the culture where this destabilizing force is not felt. The *Times*' David Brooks argued recently, for example, in a column discussing Jonathan Franzen's novel *Freedom*, that Franzen's depiction of America as a society of lost and fumbling souls tells us "more about America's literary culture than about America itself." The suburban life full of "quiet desperation," according to Brooks, is a literary trope that has taken on a life of its own. It fails to recognize the happiness, and even fulfillment, that is found in the everyday engagements with religion, work, ethnic heritage, military service and any of the other pursuits in life that are "potentially lofty and ennobling."

There is something right about Brooks's observation, but he leaves the crucial question unasked. Has Brooks's happy, suburban life revealed a new kind of contentment, a happiness that is possible even after the death of God? Or is the happy suburban world Brooks describes simply self-deceived in its happiness, failing to face up to the effects of the destabilizing force that Franzen and his literary compatriots feel? I won't pretend to claim which of these options actually prevails in the suburbs today, but let me try at least to lay them out.

Consider the options in reverse order. To begin with, perhaps the writers and poets whom Brooks questions have actually noticed something that the rest of us are ignoring or covering up. This is what Nietzsche himself thought. "I have come too early," he wrote. "God is dead; but given the way of men, there may still be caves for thousands of years in which his shadow will be shown." On this account there really is no agreement in the culture about what constitutes a well-lived life; God is dead in this particular sense. But many people carry on in God's shadow nevertheless; they take the life at which they are aiming to be one that is justifiable universally. In this case the happiness that Brooks identifies in the suburbs is not genuine happiness but self-deceit.

What would such a self-deceiving life look like? It would be a matter not only of finding meaning in one's everyday engagements, but of clinging to the meanings those engagements offer as if they were universal and absolute. Take the case of religion, for example. One can imagine a happy suburban member of a religious congregation who, in addition to finding fulfillment for herself in her lofty and ennobling religious pursuits, experiences the aspiration to this kind of fulfillment as one demanded of all other human beings as well. Indeed, one can imagine that the kind of fulfillment she experiences through her own religious commitments *depends upon* her experiencing those commitments as universal and therefore depends upon her experiencing those people not living in the fold of her church as somehow living depleted or unfulfilled lives. I suppose this is not an impossible case. But if this is the kind of fulfillment one achieves through one's happy suburban religious pursuit, then in our culture today it is self-deception at best and fanaticism at worst. For it stands in constant tension with the demand in the culture to recognize that those who don't share your religious commitments might nevertheless be living admirable lives. There is therefore a kind of happiness in a suburban life like this. But its continuation depends upon deceiving oneself about the role that any kind of religious commitment can now play in grounding the meanings for a life.

But there is another option available. Perhaps Nietzsche was wrong about how long it would take for the news of God's death to reach the ears of men. Perhaps he was wrong, in other words, about how long it would take before the happiness to which we can imagine aspiring would no longer need to aim at universal validity in order for us to feel satisfied by it. In this case the happiness of the suburbs would be consistent with the death of God, but it would be a radically different kind of happiness from that which the Judeo-Christian epoch of Western history sustained.

Herman Melville seems to have articulated and hoped for this kind of possibility. Writing thirty years before Nietzsche, in his great novel *Moby-Dick*, the canonical American author encourages us to "lower the conceit of attainable felicity"; to find happiness and meaning, in other words, not in some universal religious account of the order of the universe that holds for everyone at all times, but rather in the local and small-scale commitments that animate a life well-lived. The meaning that one finds in a life dedicated to "the wife, the heart, the bed, the table, the saddle, the fire-side, the country"—these are genuine meanings. They are, in other words, completely sufficient to hold off the threat of nihilism, the threat that life will dissolve into a sequence of meaningless events. But they are nothing like the kind of universal meanings for which the monotheistic tradition of Christianity had hoped. Indeed, when taken up in the appropriate way, the commitments that animate the meanings in one person's life—to family, say, or work, or country, or even local religious community—become completely consistent with the possibility that someone else with radically different commitments might nevertheless be living in a way that deserves one's admiration.

The new possibility that Melville hoped for, therefore, is a life that steers happily between two dangers: the monotheistic aspiration to universal validity, which leads to a culture of fanaticism and self-deceit, and the atheistic descent into nihilism, which leads to a culture of purposelessness and angst. To give a name to Melville's new possibility—a name with an appropriately rich range of historical resonances—we could call it polytheism. Not every life is worth living from the polytheistic point of view—there are lots of lives that don't inspire one's admiration. But there are nevertheless many different lives of worth, and there is no single principle or source or meaning in virtue of which one properly admires them all.

Melville himself seems to have recognized that the presence of many gods—many distinct and incommensurate good ways of life— was a possibility our own American culture could and should be aiming at. The death of God therefore, in Melville's inspiring picture, leads not to a culture overtaken by meaninglessness but to a culture directed by a rich sense for many new possible and incommensurate meanings. Such a nation would have to be "highly cultured and poetical," according to Melville. It would have to take seriously, in other words, its sense of itself as having grown out of a rich history that needs to be preserved and celebrated, but also a history that needs to be reappropriated for an even richer future. Indeed, Melville's own novel could be the founding text for such a culture. Though the details of that story will have to wait for another day, I can at least leave you with Melville's own cryptic, but inspirational comment on this possibility. "If hereafter any highly cultured, poetical nation," he writes, "shall lure back to their birthright, the merry May-day gods of old; and livingly enthrone them again in the now egotistical sky; on the now unhaunted hill; then be sure, exalted to Jove's high seat, the great Sperm Whale shall lord it."

DECEMBER 5, 2010

ACKNOWLEDGMENTS

Over the years, readers have often asked us whether material from The Stone would ever appear in the form of a book. We hoped it would but did not have the time or means to bring it to realization. Both were provided by the generosity of the Mellon Foundation, who supported a civic arts and humanities seminar in spring 2014. The work of the seminar was very simple: together with a group of undergraduate students from Eugene Lang College, at the New School for Liberal Arts, who functioned as a kind of ad hoc editorial committee, we read systematically through the entire archive of Stone articles (some 350 pieces at the time) in order to see which might still be of interest to readers and how they might be organized thematically. It was a fascinating, if arduous, task. And the book, as it exists now, is largely a result of that effort.

Although a good deal of interesting material had to be omitted because of lack of space, we are convinced that this book represents the best of what The Stone has been doing since its beginning: providing a large, brightly lit and open window into contemporary philosophy that is not intimidating, but enticing and exciting. We hope readers will be encouraged and emboldened to think for themselves, which of course is the aim of philosophy as both an intellectual pursuit and, most importantly, a way of life.

We have amassed many debts in editing *The Stone Reader*. We would like to thank Stefania de Kenessey for inviting us to teach the civic arts and humanities seminar in 2014. We would like to thank the students for their hard work, especially Kyle Trevett and Brianna Lyle, and another young scholar, Rivky Mondal, for her assistance in putting an early version of the essays into readable form.

The number of people at *The New York Times* we should rightly thank is very long, and this list will no doubt be incomplete. The fact that The Stone could exist and thrive in a branch of a news organization is a testament to the open-mindedness, depth and flexibility of the entire opinion section. But in particular: Andy Rosenthal, the editorial page editor, and Trish Hall, the editor of the op-ed page and Sunday Review, who guide the entire section and consistently support our work; the former editorial page editor and now columnist Gail Collins for her loyal friendship and wise counsel; David Shipley, the *Times* op-ed editor in 2010, who, along with Andy, approved the project for takeoff; a surprisingly merry band of philosophically inclined current and former colleagues—James Ryerson, Mark de Silva, A. C. Lee and Taylor Adams, who freely shared their time, wisdom and help; editors Snigdha Koirala and Whitney Dangerfield, who help produce the series and give it digital life; art directors Aviva Michealov and Alexandra Zsigmond, who curated illustrations for many of the essays in our first three years; and photo editor Sara Barrett, who gives The Stone a visual dimension now.

We also owe special gratitude to Gary Gutting, the indefatigable philosopher, gentleman, scholar and professor at the University of Notre Dame, who helped anchor The Stone early on with regular contributions and who has provided much editorial guidance along the way.

We are also grateful to our many friends and family members, especially Joanna Sit and Eva Catapano, philosophers in their own right.

Finally, we'd like to thank Norton/Liveright for publishing this book and Philip Marino, Bob Weil and the rest of the staff for their faith in this project and for their continued enthusiasm and support.

—Peter Catapano and Simon Critchley

CONTRIBUTORS

LINDA MARTÍN ALCOFF is a professor of philosophy at Hunter College and the City University of New York Graduate Center, and a former president of the American Philosophical Association, Eastern Division. She is the author of *Visible Identities: Race, Gender, and the Self.*

H. SAMY ALIM directs the Center for Race, Ethnicity, and Language (CREAL) at Stanford University. His latest book, *Articulate While Black: Barack Obama, Language, and Race in the U.S.* (Oxford University Press, 2012), written with Geneva Smitherman, examines the racial politics of the Obama presidency through a linguistic lens.

AMY ALLEN is Liberal Arts Professor of Philosophy and head of the Philosophy Department at Penn State University.

COLIN ALLEN is Provost Professor of Cognitive Science and History and Philosophy of Science at Indiana University, Bloomington. He works on animal cognition, philosophical foundations of cognitive science and computing applications for philosophy.

LOUISE M. ANTONY is a professor of philosophy at the University of Massachusetts Amherst and currently the president of the Eastern Division of the American Philosophical Association. She has edited or coedited several books, including *Philosophers without Gods: Meditations on Atheism and the Secular Life*, *Chomsky and His Critics* and *A Mind of One's Own: Feminist Essays on Reason and Objectivity.* She is cofounder and codirector (with Ann Cudd) of the Mentoring Program for Early-Career Women in Philosophy.

STEPHEN T. ASMA is a professor of philosophy at Columbia College Chicago, with research interests in the relationship between biology and culture. He has written several books, including *Against Fairness* and *On Monsters.* He was a Fulbright Scholar in Beijing in 2014.

NANCY BAUER is a professor of philosophy and dean of Academic Affairs for Arts and Sciences at Tufts University. She is the author of *How to Do Things with Pornography* and *Simone de Beauvoir, Philosophy, and Feminism.*

J. M. BERNSTEIN is University Distinguished Professor of Philosophy at the New School for Social Research and the author of five books. His *Torture and Dignity* is forthcoming from University of Chicago Press.

ANAT BILETZKI is Albert Schweitzer Professor of Philosophy at Quinnipiac University and a professor of philosophy at Tel Aviv University. She has written and edited several books, including *Talking Wolves: Thomas Hobbes on the Language of Politics and the Politics of Language* and *(Over)Interpreting Wittgenstein.* From 2001 to 2006 she was chairperson of B'Tselem—the Israeli Information Center for Human Rights in the Occupied Territories.

SIMON BLACKBURN is a distinguished research professor at the University of North Carolina at Chapel Hill and Fellow of Trinity College, Cambridge, and taught for twenty years at Pembroke College, Oxford. He is the author of many books, including *Think, Truth: A Guide for the Perplexed* and, most recently, *Mirror, Mirror: The Uses and Abuses of Self-Love.*

OMRI BOEHM is an assistant professor of philosophy at the New School for Social Research, working on Kant, early modern philosophy and the philosophy of religion. He is the author of *The Binding of Isaac: A Religious Model of Disobedience* and, most recently, *Kant's Critique of Spinoza*.

PAUL BOGHOSSIAN is Silver Professor of Philosophy at New York University. He works primarily in epistemology but has also written about many other topics, including the aesthetics of music and the concept of genocide. He is the author of several books, including *Fear of Knowledge: Against Relativism and Constructivism*, *Content and Justification: Philosophical Papers* and *Debating the A Priori and the Analytic* (with Timothy Williamson, forthcoming from Oxford University Press).

MAARTEN BOUDRY is a postdoctoral fellow at Ghent University (FWO—Research Foundation Flanders). He is a coeditor, with Missimo Pigliucci, of *Philosophy of Pseudoscience: Reconsidering the Demarcation Problem*.

MICHAEL BOYLAN is a professor of philosophy and chair at Marymount University. He has given invited lectures in fifteen countries on five continents and is the author of twenty-six books—most recently, *Natural Human Rights: A Theory* (Cambridge University Press, 2014) and his human rights novel, *Rainbow Curve* (Booktrope, 2015).

COSTICA BRADATAN is an associate professor of humanities in the Honors College at Texas Tech University and honorary research associate professor of philosophy at the University of Queensland, Australia. He also serves as religion and comparative studies editor for the *Los Angeles Review of Books*. His latest book is *Dying for Ideas: The Dangerous Lives of the Philosophers* (Bloomsbury, 2015).

TYLER BURGE is Distinguished Professor of Philosophy at UCLA. He is the author of many papers on philosophy of mind and four books with Oxford University Press: *Truth, Thought, Reason: Essays on Frege*, *Foundations of Mind*, *Origins of Objectivity*, which discusses the origins of mind in perception and the success of perceptual psychology as a science, and, most recently, *Understanding Through Cognition*.

CRAIG CALLENDER is a professor of philosophy at the University of California, San Diego. He recently edited *The Oxford Handbook for the Philosophy of Time*, and he is finishing a book on time and physics entitled *What Makes Time Special*.

ULRIKA CARLSSON completed a doctorate in philosophy at Yale University in 2013.

ANDY CLARK is a professor of logic and metaphysics in the School of Philosophy, Psychology and Language Sciences at Edinburgh University, Scotland. He is the author of several books, including *Supersizing the Mind: Embodiment, Action, and Cognitive Extension* (Oxford University Press, 2008) and *Surfing Uncertainty: Prediction, Action, and the Embodied Mind* (Oxford University Press, 2015).

TIM CRANE is Knightbridge Professor of Philosophy at the University of Cambridge. He is the author of two books, *The Mechanical Mind* (1995) and *Elements of Mind* (2001), and several other publications. He is currently working on two books: one on the representation of the nonexistent and another on atheism and humanism.

SIMON CRITCHLEY is Hans Jonas Professor of Philosophy at the New School for Social Research in New York and the author of many books. He is the moderator of The Stone and coeditor of this book.

GREGORY CURRIE is a professor of philosophy at the University of York.

TYLER CURTAIN is a philosopher of science and an associate professor of English and comparative literature at the University of North Carolina at Chapel Hill. He is the 2013 Robert Frost Distinguished

Chair of Literature and associate director of the Bread Loaf School of English, Middlebury College, Vermon.

Hamid Dabashi is the Hagop Kevorkian Professor of Iranian Studies and Comparative Literature at Columbia University in New York. He is the author of numerous books on the social and intellectual history of Iran and Islam, including *The World of Persian Literary Humanism* and, most recently, *Persophilia: Persian Culture on the Global Scene.*

Firmin DeBrabander is a professor of philosophy at the Maryland Institute College of Art in Baltimore and is the author of *Spinoza and the Stoics* and *Do Guns Make Us Free?*

Alejandro de la Fuente is the director of the Afro-Latin American Research Institute at Harvard University's Hutchins Center for African and African American Research. He is the author of *A Nation for All: Race, Inequality, and Politics in Twentieth-Century Cuba.*

Frans de Waal is a biologist interested in primate behavior. He is C. H. Candler Professor in Psychology, director of the Living Links Center at the Yerkes National Primate Research Center at Emory University, in Atlanta, and a member of the National Academy of Sciences and the Royal Dutch Academy of Sciences. His latest book is *The Bonobo and The Atheist* (Norton, 2013).

William Egginton is Andrew W. Mellon Professor in the Humanities at the Johns Hopkins University. He is the author of *In Defense of Religious Moderation* and *The Man Who Invented Fiction: How Cervantes Ushered in the Modern World.*

Adam Etinson is a lecturer in human rights at the Pozen Family Center for Human Rights at the University of Chicago, where he is also a visiting assistant professor in the Department of Philosophy. His work has appeared in *Utilitas,* the *Journal of Social Philosophy,* the

Journal of Moral Philosophy, Human Rights Quarterly, Res Publica and *Dissent.*

BENJAMIN Y. FONG is a Harper Fellow at the University of Chicago and is at work on a book on psychoanalysis and critical theory.

CARLOS FRAENKEL teaches philosophy and religion at the University of Oxford and McGill University in Montreal. His most recent book is *Teaching Plato in Palestine: Philosophy in a Divided World* (Princeton University Press, 2015).

ALEXANDER GEORGE is Rachel and Michael Deutch Professor of Philosophy at Amherst College. His most recent book is *The Everlasting Check: Hume on Miracles* (Harvard University Press, 2015). He is the founder of AskPhilosophers.org.

ROBERT GOODING-WILLIAMS is M. Moran Weston/Black Alumni Council Professor of African-American Studies and a professor of philosophy at Columbia University, where he directs the Center for Race, Philosophy and Social Justice. He is the author of *Zarathustra's Dionysian Modernism* (Stanford University Press, 2001), *Look, A Negro!: Philosophical Essays on Race, Culture, and Politics* (Routledge, 2005) and *In The Shadow of Du Bois: Afro-Modern Political Thought in America* (Harvard University Press, 2009).

CHARLES L. GRISWOLD is Borden Parker Bowne Professor of Philosophy at Boston University. His books include *Forgiveness: a Philosophical Exploration* (2007) and, most recently, a volume coedited with David Konstan, *Ancient Forgiveness: Classical, Judaic, and Christian* (2012). An exchange between Griswold and Father William Meninger about forgiveness was published in *Tikkun* in its March/April 2008 issue.

LISA GUENTHER is an associate professor of philosophy at Vanderbilt University with an interest in feminism, race and the carceral state.

She is the author of *Solitary Confinement: Social Death and Its Afterlives* (2013) and coeditor of *Death and Other Penalties: Philosophy in a Time of Mass Incarceration* (2015).

GARY GUTTING is a professor of philosophy at the University of Notre Dame and an editor of *Notre Dame Philosophical Reviews*. He is the author, most recently, of *What Philosophy Can Do* (Norton, 2015) and writes regularly for The Stone.

BENJAMIN HALE is an associate professor of philosophy and environmental studies at the University of Colorado Boulder and coeditor of the journal *Ethics, Policy & Environment*.

ESPEN HAMMER is a professor of philosophy at Temple University. His most recent book is *Philosophy and Temporality from Kant to Critical Theory*, published by Cambridge University Press.

SALLY HASLANGER is Ford Professor of Philosophy and Women's and Gender Studies at the Massachusetts Institute of Technology. She specializes in metaphysics, epistemology, feminist theory and critical race theory. Her book *Resisting Reality: Social Construction and Social Critique* (Oxford University Press, 2012) won the Joseph B. Gittler Award for work in philosophy of the social sciences.

CAROL HAY is an assistant professor of philosophy and the director of Gender Studies at the University of Massachusetts Lowell and the author of *Kantianism, Liberalism, and Feminism: Resisting Oppression*.

YORAM HAZONY is an Israeli philosopher and political theorist. He is president of the Herzl Institute in Jerusalem and is the author, most recently, of *The Philosophy of Hebrew Scripture*.

JIM HOLT is the author of *Why Does the World Exist? An Existential Detective Story* (Norton, 2012).

PAUL HORWICH is a professor of philosophy at New York University. He is the author of several books, including *Reflections on Meaning, Truth-Meaning-Reality* and, most recently, *Wittgenstein's Metaphilosophy*.

JOHN KAAG is an associate professor of philosophy at the University of Massachusetts Lowell and the author of *American Philosophy, A Love Story* (forthcoming with Farrar, Straus and Giroux in 2016).

SEAN D. KELLY is Teresa G. and Ferdinand F. Martignetti Professor of Philosophy and chair of the Department of Philosophy at Harvard University. He is the author of numerous scholarly articles and the coauthor, with Hubert Dreyfus, of *All Things Shining: Reading the Western Classics to Find Meaning in a Secular Age*.

PHILIP KITCHER is John Dewey Professor of Philosophy at Columbia University. He is the author of many books, including *The Ethical Project, Preludes to Pragmatism, Deaths in Venice* and, most recently, *Life After Faith: The Case for Secular Humanism*.

FRIEDA KLOTZ is a journalist and editor. She holds a doctorate in ancient Greek literature, and her coedited book of essays about Plutarch, *The Philosopher's Banquet: Plutarch's Table Talk in the Intellectual Culture of the Roman Empire*, was published by Oxford University Press in 2011.

JOSHUA KNOBE is a professor at Yale University, where he is appointed in both cognitive science and philosophy. He is a coeditor, with Shaun Nichols, of *Experimental Philosophy*.

JOHN W. KRAKAUER is a professor of neurology and neuroscience at the Johns Hopkins University School of Medicine. He is director of the Brain, Learning, Animation and Movement Lab.

SARAH KREPS is an associate professor of government at Cornell University.

RAE LANGTON is a professor of philosophy at the University of Cambridge and a fellow of Newnham College. She taught at the Massachusetts Institute of Technology from 2004 to 2012. Her most recent book, *Sexual Solipsism: Philosophical Essays on Pornography and Objectification*, was published by Oxford University Press in 2009.

ERNIE LEPORE is a Board of Governors professor of philosophy and codirector of the Center for Cognitive Science at Rutgers University. He is the author of many books, including *Imagination and Convention* (with Matthew Stone), *Insensitive Semantics* (with Herman Cappelen), *Holism: A Shopper's Guide* (with Jerry Fodor) and *The Compositionality Papers*.

JOSEPH LEVINE is a professor of philosophy at the University of Massachusetts Amherst, where he teaches and writes on philosophy of mind, metaphysics and political philosophy. He is the author of *Purple Haze: The Puzzle of Consciousness*.

JUDITH LICHTENBERG is a professor of philosophy at Georgetown University with a focus in ethics and political theory. She is the author of *Distant Strangers: Ethics, Psychology, and Global Poverty* (2014).

PETER LUDLOW is a professor of philosophy at Northwestern University and writes frequently on digital culture, hacktivism and the surveillance state.

MICHAEL P. LYNCH is director of the Humanities Institute and a professor of philosophy at the University of Connecticut. He is the author of *The Knowledge Machine*, *In Praise of Reason* and *Truth as One and Many*.

ANDREW F. MARCH is an associate professor of political science at Yale University with an interest in contemporary political philosophy and Islamic ethics and political thought. He is the author of *Islam and Liberal Citizenship: The Search for an Overlapping Consensus* and won the 2006 Aaron Wildavsky Award for Best Dissertation in Religion and Politics from the American Political Science Association.

Michael Marder is Ikerbasque Research Professor at the University of the Basque Country (UPV/EHU), Vitoria-Gasteiz. His most recent book is *Pyropolitics: When the World Is Ablaze.*

Gordon Marino is a boxing trainer, director of the Hong Kierkegaard Library and a professor of philosophy at St. Olaf College. He covers boxing for the *Wall Street Journal* and is the editor of *Ethics: The Essential Writings* (Modern Library Classics, 2010).

Joel Marks is a professor emeritus of philosophy at the University of New Haven and a scholar at the Interdisciplinary Center for Bioethics at Yale University. He has written a trilogy of books: *Ethics without Morals: In Defense of Amorality, It's Just a Feeling: The Philosophy of Desirism* and *Bad Faith: A Philosophical Memoir.*

Andy Martin is a lecturer at Cambridge University and the author of *Sartre and Camus: The Boxer and the Goalkeeper* and, most recently, *Reacher Said Nothing: Lee Child and the Making of* Make Me.

Todd May is Class of 1941 Memorial Professor of the Humanities at Clemson University and the author of, most recently, *A Significant Life: Human Meaning in a Silent Universe* and *Nonviolent Resistance: A Philosophical Introduction.*

John McCumber is the author of *Time in the Ditch: American Philosophy and the McCarthy Era* (2001) and, most recently, *On Philosophy: Notes from a Crisis* (2013) and *Time and Philosophy: A History of Continental Thought* (2011), as well as the forthcoming *Philosophical Excavations: Reason, Truth, and Politics in the Early Cold War.*

Jeff McMahan is White's Professor of Moral Philosophy and a fellow of Corpus Christi College at the University of Oxford. Previously a

Rhodes Scholar, he is the author of many works on ethics and political philosophy, including *The Ethics of Killing: Problems at the Margins of Life* (2002) and *Killing in War* (2009).

BARBARA GAIL MONTERO is an associate professor of philosophy at the City University of New York and is the author of a forthcoming Oxford University Press book on thought and effort in expert action.

STEVEN NADLER is the William H. Hay II Professor of Philosophy and the Evjue-Bascom Professor in Humanities at the University of Wisconsin–Madison. His book *A Book Forged in Hell: Spinoza's Scandalous Treatise and the Birth of the Secular Age* was published by Princeton University Press in 2011. His most recent book is *The Philosopher, the Priest, and the Painter: A Portrait of Descartes* (Princeton University Press, 2013).

THOMAS NAGEL is University Professor Emeritus in the Department of Philosophy and the School of Law at New York University. He is the author of *Mortal Questions*, *The View from Nowhere*, *The Last Word*, *Mind and Cosmos*, and other books.

EDDY NAHMIAS is Professor of Philosophy and Neuroscience at Georgia State University. He is the author of many articles on free will. He is the coeditor of the book *Moral Psychology: Historical and Contemporary Readings* and is currently writing a book on free will.

PEIMIN NI is a professor of philosophy at Grand Valley State University. He served as the president of the Association of Chinese Philosophers in America and the Society for Asian and Comparative Philosophy and is editor-in-chief of a book series on Chinese and comparative philosophy. His most recent book is *Confucius: Making the Way Great*.

PEG O'CONNOR is a professor of philosophy and gender, women, and sexuality studies at Gustavus Adolphus College in St. Peter, Minnesota. Her interests include Wittgenstein's approach to ethics and the philosophy of addiction. Her book *Life on the Rocks: Finding Meaning in Addiction in Recovery* is forthcoming with Central Recovery Press.

CHRISTINE OVERALL is a professor of philosophy and holds a university research chair at Queen's University, Kingston, Ontario. Her publications are in bioethics and feminist philosophy. She is the editor or coeditor of four books and the author of six, including *Why Have Children? The Ethical Debate* (MIT Press, 2012) and *Aging, Death, and Human Longevity: A Philosophical Inquiry* (University of California Press, 2003).

MASSIMO PIGLIUCCI is the K.D. Irani Professor of Philosophy at the City College of New York. He edits the Scientia Salon webzine and produces the Rationally Speaking podcast. His latest book, coedited with Maarten Boudry, is *Philosophy of Pseudoscience: Reconsidering the Demarcation Problem*.

STEVEN PINKER is Johnstone Professor of Psychology at Harvard University and the author, most recently, of *The Sense of Style: The Thinking Person's Guide to Writing in the 21st Century*.

HUW PRICE is Bertrand Russell Professor of Philosophy at the University of Cambridge. He is also academic director of the Centre for the Study of Existential Risk (CSER), which he cofounded with Martin Rees and Jaan Tallinn.

GRAHAM PRIEST is a Distinguished Professor of Philosophy at the Graduate Center, City University of New York, and Boyce Gibson Professor Emeritus at the University of Melbourne (Australia). His books include *In Contradiction*, *Beyond the Limits of Thought*, *Towards Non-Being*, *Introduction to Non-Classical Logic* and *One*.

PETER RAILTON is a professor of philosophy at the University of Michigan, Ann Arbor, where he has taught since 1979. A collection of some of his papers in ethics and meta-ethics, *Facts, Values, and Norms*, was published by Cambridge University Press in 2003.

Avital Ronell is University Professor of the Humanities at New York University and the Jacques Derrida Professor of Philosophy and Media at the European Graduate School in Switzerland. She is the author of several books, including *The Telephone Book: Technology, Schizophrenia, Electric Speech* and most recently, *Loser Sons: Politics and Authority*.

Alex Rosenberg is the R. Taylor Cole Professor and Philosophy Department chair at Duke University. He is the author of twelve books in the philosophy of biology and economics. W. W. Norton published his book *The Atheist's Guide to Reality* in 2011 and Lake Union published his novel, *The Girl from Krakow*, in 2015.

Agata Sagan is an independent researcher.

Samuel Scheffler is a professor of philosophy and law at New York University with an interest in moral and political philosophy. He has written five books, including, most recently, *Death and the Afterlife* (2013).

Roy Scranton is the author of *Learning to Die in the Anthropocene* (City Lights, 2015) and coeditor of *Fire and Forget: Short Stories from the Long War* (Da Capo, 2013). He has written for *Rolling Stone*, *The New York Times*, *The Appendix*, *Contemporary Literature* and *Theory & Event*.

Roger Scruton is the author of *The Uses of Pessimism*, *Green Philosophy*, *The Soul of the World* and *Notes from Underground*.

Nancy Sherman is University Professor of Philosophy at Georgetown University, a Guggenheim Fellow (2013–2014) and has served as the inaugural Distinguished Chair in Ethics at the United States Naval Academy. She is the author, most recently, of *Afterwar: Healing the Moral Wounds of Our Soldiers*. Her other books on related themes are *The Untold War: Inside the Hearts, Minds, and Souls of Our Soldiers* and *Stoic Warriors: The Ancient Philosophy Behind the Military Mind*.

LAURIE SHRAGE is a professor of philosophy and women's and gender studies at Florida International University.

PETER SINGER is currently the Ira W. DeCamp Professor of Bioethics at Princeton University and a laureate professor at the University of Melbourne. He is well known for his text *Animal Liberation* (1975) and, most recently, is the author of *The Most Good You Can Do*.

JUSTIN E. H. SMITH is University Professor of Philosophy at the Université Paris Diderot—Paris 7. He is the author, most recently, of *Nature, Human Nature, and Human Difference: Race in Early Modern Philosophy*.

DAVID SOSA is Louann and Larry Temple Centennial Professor in the Humanities at the University of Texas at Austin, where he is chair of the Department of Philosophy. He is editor of the journal *Analytic Philosophy* and author of numerous articles. He is now completing a book, *A Table of Contents*, about how we get the world in mind.

AMIA SRINIVASAN is a fellow at All Souls College, University of Oxford, where she works mainly on epistemology and ethics. She is a contributor to the *London Review of Books* and BBC Radio 4.

JASON STANLEY is a professor of philosophy at Yale. He is the author of three books for Oxford University Press, *Knowledge and Practical Interests*, *Language in Context* and *Know How*, and one book for Princeton University Press, *How Propaganda Works*.

GALEN STRAWSON holds the President's Chair in Philosophy at the University of Texas at Austin. He is the author of several books, including *Freedom and Belief* (2nd edition, 2010), *The Secret Connexion* (2nd edition, 2014) and *Selves* (2009), from Oxford University Press.

CHRISTY WAMPOLE is an assistant professor of French at Princeton University. Her research focuses primarily on twentieth- and twenty-first-century French and Italian literature and thought. She is the author of *The Other Serious: Essays for the New American Generation.*

VESLA WEAVER, an assistant professor of political science and African-American studies at Yale University, is the coauthor of *Creating a New Racial Order: How Immigration, Multiracialism, Genomics, and the Young Can Remake Race in America* and the coauthor of *Arresting Citizenship: The Democratic Consequences of American Crime Control.*

JAMIESON WEBSTER, a psychoanalyst in New York, is the author of *The Life and Death of Psychoanalysis* and the coauthor of *Stay, Illusion!: The Hamlet Doctrine*, with Simon Critchley.

TIMOTHY WILLIAMSON is the Wykeham Professor of Logic at Oxford University, a fellow of the British Academy and a Foreign Honorary Member of the American Academy of Arts and Sciences. He has been a visiting professor at the Massachusetts Institute of Technology and at Princeton University. His books include *Vagueness* (1994), *Knowledge and Its Limits* (2000), *The Philosophy of Philosophy* (2007) and *Tetralogue: I'm Right, You're Wrong* (2015).

EDWARD O. WILSON is Honorary Curator in Entomology and University Research Professor Emeritus, Harvard University. He has received more than one hundred awards for his research and writing, including the U. S. National Medal of Science, the Crafoord Prize and two Pulitzer Prizes. His most recent book is *The Meaning of Human Existence* (Norton, 2014).

GEORGE YANCY is a professor of philosophy at Emory University. He has written, edited and coedited numerous books, including *Black*

Bodies, White Gazes, Look, a White! and *Pursuing Trayvon Martin*, coedited with Janine Jones.

SLAVOJ ŽIŽEK is a Slovenian philosopher, psychoanalyst and social theorist at the Birkbeck School of Law, University of London. He is the author of many books, including the forthcoming *Absolute Recoil*.